Composer	Title	Text Page	Study Guide CD-ROM	6-CD Set	3-CD Set
Mozart	*Don Giovanni*, Act I, "Alfin siam liberati"	211		2:40	
Mozart	*Don Giovanni*, Act I, "Là ci darem la mano"	211		2:41	
Global Perspectives 4	Japanese gagaku, *Etenraku*	213		3:26	
Global Perspectives 4	Balinese gamelan, *Bopong* (I Lotring)	216		3:27	
Global Perspectives 4	North Indian rag, *Mauj-Khammaj* (Shankar)	219		3:28–29	
Beethoven	Symphony No. 5 in C Minor, I	227		3:6–14	2:1–9
Beethoven	Symphony No. 5, II	231		3:15–16	2:10–11
Beethoven	Symphony No. 5, III	231		3:17–18	2:12–13
Beethoven	Symphony No. 5, IV	231		3:19–20	2:14–15
Beethoven	String Quartet in F, II	232		3:21	
Schubert	"Erlkonig" ("The Erlking")	250		3:22	1:34
R. Schumann	*Dichterliebe*, "Im wunderschonen Monat Mai"	254		3:23	1:35
R. Schumann	*Dichterliebe*, "Die alten, bösen Lieder"	255		3:24	
C. Schumann	"Der Mond kommt still gegangen"	256		3:25	1:36
Schubert	Moment Musical No. 2 in A-flat	259		4:1	
R. Schumann	*Carnaval*, "Eusebius"	260		4:2	1:38
R. Schumann	*Carnaval*, "Florestan"	260		4:3	1:39
Chopin	Nocturne in F-sharp, Op. 15, No. 2	261		4:4	1:37
Berlioz	*Fantastic* Symphony, V	267		4:5–11	2:16–22
Verdi	*Aida*, Tomb Scene	275		4:12–15	2:23–26
Wagner	*Tristan und Isolde*, Prelude	283		4:16–20	
Wagner	*Tristan und Isolde*, Act I, Philter Scene	285		4:21–23	
Chaikovsky	*Romeo and Juliet*, Overture-Fantasy	290		4:24–35	2:27–38
Musorgsky	*Pictures at an Exhibition*	295		5:1–4	3:1–4
Brahms	Violin Concerto in D, III	300		5:5–10	
Mahler	Symphony No. 1, III (Funeral March)	304		5:11–18	3:5–12
Global Perspectives 5	Japanese kabuki: *Dojoji*	309		5:44	
Global Perspectives 5	Beijing opera: *The Prince Who Changed into a Cat*	311		5:45	
Debussy	*Clouds* (from Three Nocturnes)	331		5:19–24	2:39–44
Stravinsky	*The Rite of Spring*, Part I (excerpt)	334		5:25–31	3:13–19
Schoenberg	*Pierrot lunaire*, No. 8: "Night"	341		5:32	
Schoenberg	*Pierrot lunaire*, No. 18: "The Moonfleck"	341		5:33	
Berg	*Wozzeck*, Act III, scenes iii and iv	343		5:34–38	
Ives	Second Orchestral Set, II, "The Rockstrewn Hills Join in the People's Outdoor Meeting"	349		4:36–37	3:20–21
Ravel	Piano Concerto in G, I	355		5:39–43	
Bartók	Music for Strings, Percussion, and Celesta, II	359		6:1–7	3:22–28
Copland	*Appalachian Spring* (excerpts)	364		6:8–11	3:29–31
Webern	Five Orchestral Pieces, IV	370		6:12	3:32
Ligeti	*Lux aeterna*	373		6:13–16	
Varèse	*Poème électronique* (excerpt)	374		6:17	
Crumb	*Black Angels*, No. 1: "Night of the Electric Insects"	378		6:18	
Crumb	*Black Angels*, No. 2: "Sounds of Bones and Flutes"	378		6:19	
Crumb	*Black Angels*, No. 3: "Lost Bells"	378		6:20	
Crumb	*Black Angels*, No. 4: "Devil-music"	378		6:21	
Crumb	*Black Angels*, No. 5: "Danse Macabre"	378		6:22	
Saariaho	*From the Grammar of Dreams* (excerpts)	379		6:23–25	3:33–35
Reich	*Tehillim*, Section 4	381		6:26–30	
Thomas	"If You Ever Been Down" Blues	391		6:31	3:36
Ellington	*Conga Brava*	395		6:32	3:37
Global Perspectives 6	Yoruba drumming, "Ako"	398		6:38	3:41
Parker	*Out of Nowhere*	400		6:33	3:38
Davis	*Bitches Brew* (excerpt)	402		6:34	3:39
Gershwin	Prelude No. 1	404		6:35	3:40
Bernstein	*West Side Story*, Meeting Scene	408		6:36	
Bernstein	*West Side Story*, "Cool"	408		6:37	
Global Perspectives 7	South African popular song, "Anoku Gonda" (Solomon Linda)	420		6:39	

LISTEN BRIEF FIFTH EDITION

LISTEN

BRIEF FIFTH EDITION

JOSEPH KERMAN
University of California, Berkeley

GARY TOMLINSON
University of Pennsylvania

with

VIVIAN KERMAN

BEDFORD/ST. MARTIN'S
Boston ◆ New York

For Bedford/St. Martin's

Developmental Editor: Maura Shea
Senior Production Editor: Karen S. Baart
Senior Production Supervisor: Dennis Conroy
Marketing Manager: Jenna Bookin Barry
Editorial Assistant: Anne Noyes
Production Assistants: Michaela Dodd, Kristen Merrill
Copyeditor: Clia M. Goodwin
Text Design: Malcolm Grear Designers; revised by Wanda Kossak
Cover Design: Donna Lee Dennison
Cover Art: Dominique Guillemard, *La Phalange.* Courtesy of Galerie Arpé, Cannes, France
Composition and Layout: DeNee Reiton Skipper
Music Composition: A-R Editions, Inc.
Printing and Binding: R.R. Donnelley & Sons Company

President: Joan E. Feinberg
Editorial Director: Denise B. Wydra
Editor in Chief: Karen S. Henry
Director of Marketing: Karen Melton
Director of Editing, Design, and Production: Marcia Cohen
Managing Editor: Elizabeth M. Schaaf

Library of Congress Control Number: 2003101702

For information, write: Bedford/St. Martin's, 75 Arlington Street, Boston, MA 02116
(617-399-4000)

ISBN: 0–312–40115–9 (paperback)
        0–312–41123–5 (hardcover)

Acknowledgments

Preface
To the Instructor

Times have changed in the nearly thirty years since *Listen* first appeared, and with them the book has changed substantially. Instructors familiar with previous editions of this textbook will observe three main changes in *Listen*, Brief Fifth Edition. The first is a return, in a simpler version, of the "Overture" idea used in earlier editions. Heard on the CD-ROM packaged with the book, our Study Guide, the March to the Scaffold from Berlioz's *Fantastic* Symphony can give students an immediate listening experience, which is also a learning experience, to light up day one in any music course. We talk about this a little more below.

Next, the short listening exercises in Unit I (Fundamentals) have been much expanded, and music provided for them on the CD-ROM. There are a dozen short excerpts illustrating rhythm, melody, texture, and so on, plus the redoubtable *Young Person's Guide to the Orchestra* by Benjamin Britten. We show students how to listen to this work as an informal summary of fundamentals at the end of Unit I.

A third change is in the sections on non-Western music. Some have been dropped and others grouped together after the book's main units, under the name *Global Perspectives*. This grouping has been done programmatically, yielding more substantial teaching elements, we believe, as well as fewer interruptions to the basic text.

In addition, responding to many thoughtful suggestions from readers, we have once again worked to improve the selection of music for the CD sets, our basic teaching materials. Some of the changes are significant: See plainchant, the symphony, and music of the late twentieth century. The coverage of popular music has been expanded, though to do it full justice here with recorded examples was not feasible.

What has not changed is our basic coverage, organization, treatment, and style, which have proved so solid over many editions. For new users, we draw attention to the following strong features that we believe set *Listen* apart:

¶ *Overture* Most instructors work out a special introductory session to break the ice and interest students in the subject matter of their course. The Overture to this book is a specific suggestion for such an ice-breaker—students listen to a short, rousing piece, the March to the Scaffold from Berlioz's *Fantastic* Symphony, with a short commentary that will give them a taste of what the semester will be like. (The Overture also provides an easy introduction to the Listening Charts that are so important to the book.) At this stage the emphasis is on direct impressions rather than on terminology, but some technical terms are introduced in passing, terms that will be presented formally in Unit I.

❡   *Overall organization*   The book's coverage is simple and clear, and evident at once from the listing of "Contents in Brief," on page xix. (This may seem like an elementary, obvious thing, but in our judgment not a few texts give first impressions that are muddled and forbidding.) After "Fundamentals," the historical scheme goes from "Early Music"—in effect, everything before Bach and Handel, when the standard repertory begins—to the three great periods of Western classical music: the eighteenth, nineteenth, and twentieth centuries. Each century is treated as a unit—Unit III, Unit IV, and Unit V—containing several chapters.

❡   *Flexible coverage*   Coverage—that perpetual (and probably insoluble) problem for instructors, and for textbook writers also! How much time or space does one devote to music of the so-called common-practice period, and how much to Early Music and music of the twentieth century? How much to popular music? Music from beyond Europe and America?

The main emphasis of *Listen* is on the common-practice repertory, basically for reasons of time. Only so much can be accomplished in a semester course, and most instructors will agree that students learn more from exposure to a limited amount of material in some depth than from overambitious surveys. Probably all agree that beginning courses in music should introduce students to the good music they will most likely hear in later life.

By the end of many a semester, the final pages of books like this one tend be sacrificed on account of time constraints. For those who would rather save time at the beginning, Unit II, "Early Music: An Overview," has been made *strictly optional* in the book's sequence. Nothing later in the book depends on having studied it, so if your course plan begins with Unit III, "The Eighteenth Century," no one will need to skip back for explanations of continuo texture, recitative, fugue, and so on.

And for those who prefer to use some selections of early music without teaching the entire unit, the fairly modest amount of prose in Unit II should prove manageable as a general orientation for the music chosen.

❡   *Non-Western music*   The Global Perspectives segments are positioned so as to elaborate the European and American topics discussed around them. Three of them come at the ends of the Early Music chapters; they take up sacred chant (at the end of the Middle Ages chapter), European colonialism (Renaissance), and ostinato techniques (early Baroque). Two more, on African drumming and on global pop, come in the last chapter, "Jazz and Beyond." The remaining two segments come at the ends of the eighteenth- and nineteenth-century units of the book and treat, respectively, complexities of form in instrumental music and musical drama. We believe we have tailored these materials so that they can broaden in a meaningful way the coverage of *Listen*, but we certainly do not offer them as a token survey of world musics. If they are a token of anything, it is the authors' belief that music-making worldwide shows certain common, deep tendencies in which the European classical tradition has shared.

❡   *Cultural background*   The Baroque and Classical eras and the nineteenth and twentieth centuries are introduced by what we call "Prelude" chapters. These summarize some features of the culture of the times, in particular those that can be seen to affect music. (Generously captioned color illustrations for these chapters, and others, are an original *Listen* specialty that has now become a standard textbook feature.) The Prelude chapters also contain concise accounts of the musical styles of the eras, so that these chapters furnish background of two kinds—cultural and stylistic—for listening to specific pieces of music in the chapters that follow.

¶ *Recordings* The main compositions studied in *Listen* are available in multiple recordings, and much time and effort has gone into searching for what seem to us the best ones. (The search becomes increasingly difficult as licensing rights are denied by more and more record companies.) It is gratifying to learn from market research that many users consider our choices superior. We hope that instructors and students will get the same charge out of our selections that we do, and it's our further fond hope that students may keep these recordings and keep listening to them in future years.

Seventy-seven of the selections discussed in the text appear on the accompanying 6-CD set. The 3-CD set contains thirty-three selections. (To allow for the maximum use of disc space, a few selections in the CD sets appear out of order: that is, not in the sequence of their appearance in the book. The Global Perspectives tracks have all been put at the ends of the CDs.) An icon tells the listener *which number* CD to select from the sets (this is the numeral inside the circle) and then *which track* to play (the numeral below it). The Study Guide CD-ROM has its own icon with track numbers marked below it.

¶ *Design* Obviously this book is attractive to look at (an early version of it won a design award). But the real point of a good design is to make it easy to find your way around in a book and make the book inviting to use. If the temptation to cram more and more into a text is not resisted, the text will be cluttered and confused and will itself be resisted by its targeted readership.

In particular, we think the *Listen* format for Listening Charts is superior. The charts all fit onto one page, visible at a glance, with concise descriptions and identifications. Off at the side, brief music tags can easily be consulted by those who read music—and just as easily ignored by those who don't. As to the timings, in selections divided into several CD tracks, the timings to the *left* of the vertical rule give the time elapsed from the start of the previous track, while those to the *right* of the rule give the total time from the start of the piece.

Standardized biography boxes segregate material on the lives of the major composers from discussions of their music—again, making the book easier to read and easier to work from. The boxes all include portraits, concise lists of works that can serve for study or reference, and, under the heading "Encore," suggestions for further listening.

And we think we have introduced some new elements in an uncluttered way: a certain number of maps throughout the text, and quick references to resources on the Web site. (See under "Supplements Package" for a complete description of the Web site.) We have expanded the time lines to show historical events and movements as well as individuals.

¶ *Appendix* "Further Listening, Suggested Readings, and Recommended Web Sites" provides students with recommendations for audio, print, and online materials for further study and (we hope, once again) reference for a lifetime of engagement with music. Suggestions for further listening go beyond the Encore recommendations given in the composer biographies and extend to world music and jazz. The readings are mostly standard reference works, with a few of the authors' personal favorites included. Finally, "Recommended Web Sites" gives URLs of useful sites related to the composers and non-Western cultures covered in the text as well as some excellent general music sites containing a broad range of relevant topical information. Brief annotations make it easy to scan the list and quickly find the Web resource needed. These Web addresses also appear in the "Links" section of the companion Web site (bedfordstmartins.com/listen) where students and instructors alike can find valuable learning and teaching aids.

Supplements Package

Recognizing how much the teaching and learning experience of this course may be enhanced through a mixture of media, we have updated and expanded the supplements for the Brief Fifth Edition as follows:

✻ The **Study Guide CD-ROM** is entirely new and bound into each copy of the book. It provides two valuable, essential resources. First, it contains the thirteen audio recordings (listed below) that correspond to the new listening exercises in Unit I, including Benjamin Britten's *Young Person's Guide to the Orchestra*. Second, it presents all of the book's Listening Charts in a newly enhanced interactive format. These multimedia charts encourage the listener to delve more deeply into major works through guided multiple listenings.

    1–3   Berlioz, *Fantastic* Symphony, IV, March to the Scaffold
      4   Schubert, from Symphony No. 8 ("Unfinished"), I
      5   Joplin, "Maple Leaf Rag"
      6   Rachmaninov, from *Rhapsody on a Theme by Paganini*
      7   Gershwin, "Who Cares?"
      8   Beethoven, "Joy Theme" from Symphony No. 9, IV
      9   Stravinsky, from *Symphony of Psalms*, II
     10   Schubert, Moment Musical No. 3
     11   Beethoven, from Piano Concerto No. 5 ("Emperor")
     12   Mahler, from Symphony No. 1, III
     13   Chaikovsky, from *The Nutcracker Suite*: Dance of the Sugar-Plum Fairy
   14–16 Beethoven, Symphony No. 5, III
   17–22 Britten, *The Young Person's Guide to the Orchestra*

✻ The **companion Web site** *Listen Online* at bedfordstmartins.com/listen is now integrated with the book (references throughout the text direct students to related content on the Web site) and newly expanded to include listening and content quizzes for every chapter, demos (real, not synthesized) and photographs of instruments of the orchestra, interactive Listening Charts, annotated research links organized by chapter, vocabulary flashcards, a hyperlinked glossary, and other instructor and student resources. (See illustration on facing page.)

✻ The *Instructor's Resource Manual* (prepared by Mark Harbold) offers Chapter Outlines, Important Terms, Teaching Objectives, and Lecture Suggestions for each chapter, as well as Class Discussion Ideas, Lecture-Demonstration Ideas, Listening Ideas, and hundreds of Further Listening Examples going beyond the textbook chapters. A Multimedia Resources section gives many suggestions for video, DVD, and software enhancements, additional Listening Charts, and much more.

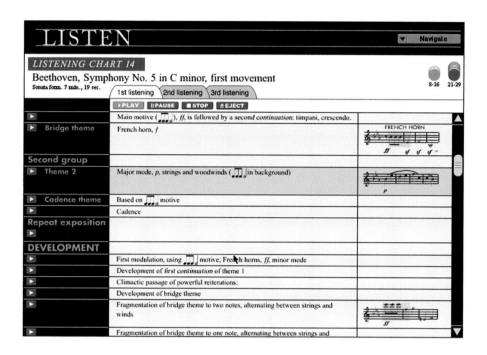

 The **Test Bank** (by Jane Viemeister) has 1,290 multiple-choice and 560 essay questions. It serves as a database for a Computerized Test-Generation System, available in a cross-platform CD-ROM, which makes it easy to tailor exams on your IBM-compatible or Macintosh computer. It is also available in a print version.

 The **Overhead Transparencies** set includes acetates of each of the Listening Charts in this edition, with several other diagrams and texts and translations from the book.

 Videos and DVDs of live performances of works discussed in this edition are available to qualified adopters. Contact your local Bedford/St. Martin's sales representative for more information.

 E-content for Online Learning includes special content from *Listen* that helps instructors using the book develop custom Web sites with Web CT and Blackboard.

Ultimately, though, this text owes its success less to "features" than to two basic attributes, which we have been grateful to hear about many times from many instructors over the history of *Listen*. *Listen* is distinctive in its writing style and, related to that, in the sense it conveys of personal involvement with the music that is treated. The tone is lively and alert, authoritative but not stiff and not without humor. We sound (because we are) engaged with music and we work to engage the student. One should never condescend to students, any more than one should begrudge them careful explanation of matters that we as musicians find elementary.

The excitement and joy that the experience of music can provide—this, more than historical or analytical data about music—is what most of us want to pass on to our students. This is what teaching is about (which is why CD-ROMs will never replace live instructors), and this is what we have always tried to do in *Listen*.

Acknowledgments

It remains to express the authors' gratitude to the numerous battle-scarred "music apprec" instructors who have reviewed sections of the book in draft and given us the benefit of their advice for this revision. Their criticisms and suggestions have significantly improved the text, as have the market surveys in which an even larger number of instructors have generously participated. In addition to the users of previous editions who over the years have given us suggestions, we wish to thank:

Mary Catherine Adams, James Madison University
James Arnwine, Pasadena City College
Joseph Baldassare, Boise State University
Mary Kay Bauer, Western Carolina University
Hubert Beckwith, George Mason University
Ian Bent, Columbia University
Steven Bresnen, Bucks County Community College
Geoffrey Burgess, SUNY Stony Brook
Angela Carlson, Oregon State University
Keith Clifton, University of Central Arkansas
Richard Cole, Virginia Polytechnic Institute and State College
Steven Cornelius, Bowling Green State University
Robert Culbertson, Lamar University
Vicki Curry, University of Utah
Andrew Dell'Antonio, University of Texas–Austin
Jeffrey Donovick, St. Petersburg College
Stuart Alan Duke, Truckee Meadows Community College
JanClaire Elliott, Pt. Loma Nazarene University
David Feingold, Western Washington University
Lawrence Ferrara, City College of San Francisco
Karen Garrison, Auburn University
Laura Greenberg, John Jay College–CUNY
Rolf Groesbeck, University of Arkansas–Little Rock
Michael Grose, University of Oregon
David Haas, University of Georgia
Kimberly Harris, Collin County Community College
Hillary Hight, Kenesaw State University
Jaren Hinckley, Brigham Young University
David Johansen, Southeastern Louisiana University
Randall Johnson, University of Guam
Folkert H. Kadyk, Pennsylvania State University–Delaware City
Jeffrey Kallberg, University of Pennsylvania
Maiko Kawabata, SUNY Stony Brook
Ken Keaton, Florida Atlantic University
Thomas Kittinger, Harrisburg Area Community College
Nancy Kudlawiec, University of West Alabama

Beth Anne Lee-De Amici, University of Virginia
Andrew Levin, Clemson University
Kay Lipton, Pasadena City College
Peggy Lupton, Cape Fear Community College
Melissa Mann, University of Connecticut–Storrs
Robert Mann, Stephen F. Austin State University
Ross Mann, Bucks County Community College
Karen Marston, San Jacinto College
David Maves, College of Charleston
Kevin McCarthy, University of Colorado–Boulder
Michael McGowan, Panola College
Herbert Midgley, Stephen F. Austin State University
Simon Morrison, Princeton University
Rena Mueller, New York University
Lynn Raley, Emory & Henry College
Jennifer Roth-Burnette, Birmingham-Southern College
George Ruckert, Massachusetts Institute of Technology
Kevin Salfen, University of North Texas
Michael Samball, Boise State University
Carolyn Sanders, University of Alabama–Huntsville
Jack Sheinbaum, University of Denver
William Shepherd, University of Northern Iowa
Marc Siegel, Cape Fear Community College
Glenn Stanley, University of Connecticut–Storrs
Michael Strasser, Baldwin-Wallace College
Helen Stringham, Salt Lake Community College
Jonathan Sturm, Iowa State University
Katherine Syer, University of Illinois–Urbana
Dane Teter, El Camino College
Richard Thorell, Indiana University of Pennsylvania
Christopher Ulffers, East Carolina University
Roger Walworth, Judson College
Scott Warfield, Centre College
Mary Joanna White, Cape Fear Community College
Noel Wilkins, San Jacinto College Central
Cathryn Wilkinson, Concordia University
Charles Youmans, Pennsylvania State University
Steve Zohn, Temple University

Professor Mark Harbold of Elmhurst College agreed to prepare the instructors' manual for *Listen*, Brief Fifth Edition, as he has done so successfully for previous editions. We are very grateful to him, to Dr. Jane Viemeister for writing hundreds of questions for the testbank and online listening and content quizzes, to Dr. Kristi Brown, who has done a fantastic job of searching and appraising hundreds of music Web sites for the Appendix and companion Web site, and to Tom Millioto, who reviewed every CD track timing in the text, and to Fletcher Moore and Professor Andrew Dell'Antonio for creating our newly enhanced electronic Listening Charts. Thanks are also due to the cartographers at Mapping Specialists Ltd.

The production of a major textbook is a complex, arduous process drawing on professionals from very many areas. This time around we had a terrific team consisting of some old friends, some new. We are indebted to Joan Feinberg of Bedford/St. Martin's for her enthusiastic support, Editor in Chief (Boston) Karen Henry for her wise and deft guidance, our superb text editor Maura Shea, equally superb production editor Karen Baart, and compositor and layout wizard DeNee Reiton Skipper, as well as art director Donna Dennison, new media editor David Mogolov, permissions editor Sandy Schechter, editorial assistant Anne Noyes, and production assistants Kristen Merrill and Michaela Dodd. Our oldest good friends are still with us: picture consultant Elaine Bernstein and Tom Laskey of Sony Special Products. (Tom is voted MVP, having made spectacular saves on the distinctly unlevel playing field known as the recording industry.) The high quality of *Listen* is a tribute to the expertise, dedication, and artistry of all these people, and we are indebted to them all.

Finally, warm thanks to Davitt Moroney for recording the Frescobaldi Suite for Unit II, on the seventeenth-century Spanish organ (in meantone tuning) by Greg Harrold at the University of California at Berkeley.

J. K.

G. T.

Berkeley and Philadelphia, 2003

Introduction
To the Student

The Virgin Megastore in San Francisco is a grand space with walls nearly as high as the floor is wide. A dozen monitors promoting videos of the newest singles look down on bins of CDs divided up between the many kinds of popular music. Near a tall window looking out onto the street, handsome escalators lead up to the second floor, the place for World Music, Jazz, and—behind soundproof glass doors—Classical. On the third floor, DVDs, Software, and Customer Service.

A Rip van Winkle waking up after a fifty-year sleep in the redwood groves would be amazed at the variety of music available, and even more amazed that all the different kinds could be played, one right after another, on an apparatus called a CD player costing the equivalent of a 1950s ten-spot. Multiplicity and instant availability are twin attributes of today's culture. Music megastores exist to feed that culture. Bookstores are an older example of the same phenomenon, with their multiple shelves for Fiction, Business, Cooking—and even Music. A newer example is the Internet.

And in the spirit of multiplicity, our idea in this book is to bring classical music out from behind those soundproof glass doors so that it can live harmoniously in your ear along with world music, jazz, country music, rock in all its varieties, rap, pop, techno, post-rock, and more.

Classical Music

Classical music: just what is meant by that? The ordinary meaning of "classical" or "classic" is something old and established and valued on that account. The term is applied to many kinds of music, as we know: Classic Jazz, Classic Rock, even Classic Rap. "Classical music" itself can be very old indeed; it covers more than a thousand years of music as practiced and heard in Europe and America. You may also hear this music called "art music," or "Western music," or music of the Western tradition.

Classical music continues today; musical composition in the classical tradition is probably being taught this semester at your own college or university. The coverage in this book extends to music composed fifteen years ago by a composer who was then in her thirties. But nobody doubts that the great age of classical music is in the past. (Some would say the same for poetry, and even painting. Some would say the same for jazz . . .) Listening to classical music is listening to history. Why do that?

Ultimately, because classical music has stayed the course. Over history, it has provided generations (dozens of generations, to push the point) with pleasure, joy, inspiration, and solace. So they have said, repeatedly. It can do the same for us today.

It's important to acknowledge the "otherness" of people in history, the differences between them and people today. Nonetheless, we relate to them; they are unquestionably *us,* as we can tell from their diaries and their poems, their portraits, their political aspirations and indeed also from their philosophical reflections, if we are prepared to give them the time it takes to really grasp them. We treasure our Declaration of Independence, written more than two hundred years ago, and it will be a bad day when we lose touch with the Constitution. There is a case to be made for also staying in touch with the poetry, art, and music of what one historian has called the "usable past."

On one level, music serves as entertainment, of course, and is none the worse for that. On another level, it provides a kind of knowledge or, at least, insight into human experience and feeling and time. How music manages to do this is a famous philosophical puzzle. The best short hypothesis is that music, which on a basic level is a strange and wonderful way of filling up time, vividly represents the way time feels as we actually live through it.

Music and History

The era of Classical music extends over more than a thousand years. Naturally, music changed vastly over that time—not only in its sound but also in its function and its institutions in society, its basic support system. Classical music is not monolithic. Another trip to the Virgin Megastore will reveal that many categories exist within the Classical sanctum. In addition to one big untitled section organized by composer, the store has smaller sections labeled Early Music and Contemporary. In this book, indeed, Early Music is set apart as an optional topic of study. We should try to explain why.

In sociological terms (very quickly, now!), Western musical history can be said to fall into three great phases. The later phases overlap, as forces underlying the earlier phases decay over long periods of time and others take their place.

❧ In the first millennium C.E., European culture was the culture of Christianity. All musicians (or at least all musicians that we know about) were churchmen, and all their music was sung in churches, abbeys, and cathedrals. The function of church music was to stimulate and enhance worship, to make prayer more fervent, and to make services more solemn and impressive.

❧ Around 1100, music composed for princely courts begins to appear in richly illuminated manuscripts. Slowly the church was yielding power to kings and nobles. Courts furnished the locale for instrumental and vocal music for many centuries. Music was now entertainment for court society, and indeed there were some famous monarchs who were keen musicians: Henry VIII of England and Frederick the Great of Prussia are two examples. But also, and increasingly with time, the function of court music was to glorify kings and princes.

Music at court, 1550: King Henry VIII of England playing the harp, posing as a modern King David. Only his court jester Will Sommers was allowed to pull long faces about this.

Music at court, 1750: Frederick II of Prussia, an accomplished flutist. His court composer
J. J. Quantz composed over three hundred flute concertos.

Court music also included music for the court chapels, which not only
praised the Almighty in lavish terms, but also celebrated the mighty rulers who
could put on such lavish services.

As aristocratic power declined and the middle classes (the bourgeoisie)
gained control, public opera houses and concert halls were invented and became the new social spaces for music. The first opera house opened around
1650, the first concert hall around 1750. From then on concert music was in
principle available to all who cared to buy tickets and could afford them.

Meanwhile European music took a big leap to South America and then
to North America—first in the California missions and then in the English
colonies. In the twentieth century it also became a major presence in Japan and
other non-European countries.

Today classical music has entered a new phase. Now a worldwide phenomenon,
it is played and heard more and more via digitally encoded, and sometimes
downloaded, aluminum-and-plastic discs. However, the concert still counts as
classical music's main site and paradigm, so for this reason it seems right to
concentrate on music of the concert hall in a book of this kind, rather than
music of the church and music at court. Concert music all dates from within
the span of U. S. history, plus about seventy-five years at the beginning—from
around 1700 to the present.

Music earlier than that had mostly died out until the twentieth century.
Many old scores slumbered in libraries, but they were often hard to decipher
and nobody was much interested in singing or playing the music. But Early
Music experienced a significant revival in the last half of the twentieth century,
thanks to enthusiastic efforts by imaginative musicologists and performers—
and thanks also to recordings, which (as never before) spread the word with
instant efficiency. People now listen to Early Music widely, and we include this
topic as a concise optional unit at the beginning of this book.

Global Perspectives   The main concern of this book is European classical music and its offshoots in the United States, which remained a cultural colony of Europe for many years after our declaration of political independence.

But on our trips to visit the Classical department on the second floor of the Megastore, it is impossible to ignore World Music: We walk right through it. And all through this text, too, we will take stock of the multiplicity of musical traditions ("musics") around the world, by engaging a number of traditions outside the European classical heritage. Though our glimpses of these other musics will be brief, they will not be arbitrary or superficial, because the Global Perspectives inserts are connected to the European issues in the chapters around them. Our inserts point out broad similarities between European and non-European music, similarities sometimes of musical technique, sometimes of social uses of music, and sometimes of both together.

By making such sweeping *comparisons,* we mean at the same time to highlight the real *differences* between European and other traditions. This is, basically, the kind of approach anthropologists take. Our almost instinctive sense of common aims and interests attracts us and draws us near to foreign cultures. Then a finer sense of precise differences—of a crucial strangeness, in fact—deepens our understanding of them. It can also deepen our understanding of ourselves.

Listening

A potent resource for music instruction is the easy availability of so much music on recordings—the Megastore phenomenon that started up this whole discussion. The recordings accompanying this book can hardly be thought of as supplements. The recorded sound of music from many different eras and many different cultures is an integral feature of the text.

But of course, total recall has only been achieved at a price. No one should forget that recordings are abstractions, at some distance from the experience of actual live music. Music is human communication, and human presence is leached out of a recorded performance. Missing is the immediacy, the empathy that springs up between listener and performer; missing, too, is the special push that performers deliver when they feel that an audience is with them.

People probably tend to supply these feelings imaginatively when listening to records, by extrapolating them from their own experience of live performance occasions. Be that as it may, a classroom is not a concert site, and if the abstractness of recordings encourages us to really *listen* to music, and not treat it as a background to some other activity, some good will have come of it.

Often you just *hear* music—out of the corner of the ear, as it were. The center of your attention is elsewhere—on the chemistry equation you are balancing, or the car ahead of you cutting in from the other lane, or your date at a restaurant. Instead it's necessary to make a listening commitment to music, comparable to the dedication on the part of composers and performers that goes into its making. Background listening won't do. Real listening means recognizing specific events in the music as it goes by in time, holding them in the memory, and relating them to one another in the mind. Classical music requires full attention if it is to yield its full rewards.

Listening to individual pieces again and again is the basic activity that leads to the understanding and love of music; that is why this book is called *Listen.* Focused listening, whether "live" or through earphones, is the one essential thing.

Listening Charts   Listening Charts that focus listening are another integral feature of this text. Look at the portion of Listening Chart 5 below to see how they work (the complete chart is found on page 136). After choosing the appropriate musical selection, begin by finding the logo for your recording set at the top right corner of the chart. The numeral inside the logo tells you *which number CD* to choose from the set. The numeral below the logo tells you *which track* to play. For long selections with multiple CD tracks, small boxes running down the left side show where each new track begins. In these boxes, track numbers from discs in the 6-CD set are printed in green, those from the 3-CD set in black.

In essence this Listening Chart is a table of the main musical events in Bach's *Brandenburg* Concerto ("Ritornello," "Solo," and so on) with brief explanatory notes where needed. As you listen, follow down this list with the timing figures. To the *left* of the vertical line are the CD timings that you will see on your display, starting anew with each track. The timings to the *right* of the line give the total time from the beginning of the composition.

Refer to the logo that corresponds to your recordings package. The number in the center tells you which CD to play. The numbers beneath the logo are track numbers.

Track number reminders. The upper number is the track number for this piece in the 6-CD set; the lower number is the track number for the 3-CD set.

6-CD set

3-CD set

2
1-5

1
5-9

LISTENING CHART 5

Bach, *Brandenburg* Concerto No. 5, first movement

Ritornello form. 9 min., 56 sec.

1 / 5	0:00	**Ritornello**	Complete ritornello is played by the orchestra, **forte**: bright and emphatic.
	0:21	**Solo**	Harpsichord, flute, and violin in a contrapuntal texture (often in trio style). Includes faster rhythms; the soloists play new themes and also play some of the motives from the ritornello.
	0:46	**Ritornello** (**first phrase**)	Orchestra, *f*
	0:51	**Solo**	Similar material to that of the first solo.
	1:12	**Ritornello** (**middle phrase**)	Orchestra, *f*
	1:18	**Solo**	Similar solo material
	1:40	**Ritornello** (**middle phrase**)	Orchestra, *f*; minor mode
	1:45	**Solo**	Similar solo material at first, then fast harpsichord runs are introduced.
2 / 6	2:28	**Ritornello** (**middle phrase**)	Orchestra, *f*
0:06	2:34	**Solo**	This solo leads directly into the central solo.

This left-hand column of timings gives you the time elapsed since the start of the current CD track.

The right-hand column of timings gives you the total time elapsed since the start of the piece.

For the benefit of those who are able to read music, the charts include a few brief notations of the main themes, directly across from the timing indications and the reference to the musical event. They are an extra; it is not necessary to read musical notation or even follow it in a general way to use these charts. Even people who think they are tone deaf (there's no such condition) can follow the music with the help of the timings.

Study Guide CD-ROM   The Listening Charts are also available in an interactive format on the Study Guide CD-ROM in the back of this book and on the companion Web site at <bedfordstmartins.com/listen>. The interactive charts work in conjunction with the recordings, indicating when each new section of a piece begins and allowing you to play back specific themes or motives with a single mouse click.

The user guide for the CD-ROM can be found on the page facing the CD-ROM envelope. In addition to all the Listening Charts in an interactive format, the disk contains recordings of the listening examples in Unit I, "Fundamentals." This is the place you will go for live examples of the concepts introduced in this unit and to test your hearing of them. A logo and track numbers indicate specific recordings on the Study Guide CD-ROM.

1-3

J. K.

G. T.

About the Authors

J oseph Kerman and Gary Tomlinson are leading musicologists and music educators. Kerman, who with his wife, Vivian Kerman, was *Listen*'s original author, served for two terms as chair of the Music Department at the University of California at Berkeley, and Tomlinson has done the same at the University of Pennsylvania. Both are known as inspirational and wide-ranging teachers; between them, their course offerings encompass harmony and ear training, opera, world music, interdisciplinary studies, seminars in music history and criticism, and—many times—Introduction to Music for nonmajor students.

Kerman's books include *Opera as Drama* (second edition, 1988), *Contemplating Music* (1985), and studies of Beethoven and William Byrd. His lectures as Charles Eliot Norton Professor of Poetry at Harvard in 1997–1998 have been published as *Concerto Conversations* (1999). Tomlinson, a former MacArthur Fellow, is the author of *Monteverdi and the End of the Renaissance* (1987), *Music in Renaissance Magic* (1993), and *Metaphysical Song: An Essay on Opera* (1999). He has also published on jazz and native music of Latin America.

Contents in Brief

Global Perspectives

Maps

Listening Charts

Contents

Fundamentals

U nit I, the introductory unit in this book, covers music fundamentals and
their standard terminology. We start right away with a piece of music,
the Fantastic Symphony by the nineteenth-century French composer Hector
Berlioz. Chapter 1 presents the basic concepts of sound and time—pitch, dynamics, tone color, and duration—and introduces the terms used by musicians
for these phenomena. Chapter 2 explains how, in music, time is organized
into rhythm and meter, and how pitch is deployed in scales. Then Chapter 3
deals with melody and harmony in Western music, and other combinations of
the basic elements that have already been treated. Chapter 4 carries the discussion one stage further, to a consideration of musical form and style. Our
"Interludes" treat musical instruments and musical notation.

Listening

The basic activity that leads to the love of music and to its understanding—
to what is sometimes called "music appreciation"—is listening to particular
pieces of music again and again. Such, at least, is the premise of this book. Its
pages are filled mostly with discussions of musical compositions—symphonies,
concertos, operas, and the like—that people have found more and more rewarding as they have listened to them repeatedly. These discussions are meant
to introduce you to the contents of these works and their aesthetic qualities:
what goes on in the music, and how it affects us.

The kind of hands-on knowledge of music that is necessary for a music
professional—for a composer or a performer—is of no special use to you as
a nonprofessional listener. But an acquaintance with musical concepts and
musical terms can be useful, by helping you grasp more clearly what you
already hear in music. Analyzing things, pinpointing things, even simply using
the right names for things all make us more actively aware of them. Sometimes, too, this process of analyzing, pinpointing, and naming can actually
assist listening. We become more alert, as it were, to aspects of music when
they have been pointed out. And sharper awareness contributes to greater
appreciation of music, and of the other arts as well.

Since our emphasis is on music, this is where we start—with an actual
listening experience, our "overture" to this book. It will exemplify in a general way some of the concepts introduced in the following chapters, and
make understanding the terminology of music, when we come to explain it,
seem less abstract and mysterious, more immediate and alive.

OVERTURE

A March by
Hector Berlioz

L isten, then, to what we are calling our overture, which is the fourth movement, a march, from one of the most famous of all symphonies, the
Fantastic Symphony by the French composer Hector Berlioz. An overture is
the orchestral music played prior to a play, ballet, or opera, or (stretching the
point a little) a book. A movement is a section of a multisectional work such
as a symphony, sonata, or concerto.

We study the whole of the *Fantastic* Symphony in Chapter 16, which also
provides a short biography of the composer with a work list. For now we need
only say that Berlioz was one of a galaxy of great composers born in the early
1800s, and one of the first Romantics in music. He was a near-contemporary
of the American Edgar Allan Poe, a poet-storyteller with a mindset not so far
from that of Berlioz, at least as manifested in the *Fantastic* Symphony. The
symphony was Berlioz's first major composition, a wild success at its premiere
in Paris in 1830 and a turning point in the history of music. And it is still popular today. When last tallied, the *Fantastic* Symphony was available in more
than fifty CD recordings.

Listen to the movement in one or, preferably, all of three ways: (1) cold,
(2) while at the same time following the prose discussion below, and (3) while following the Listening Chart on page 4. (For directions on working with Listening
Charts, see page xvi.) In the discussion, we mention and cross-reference a few
of the terms that will be introduced officially later and employed throughout
this book. The idea is not to learn these terms at the present stage, just to get
a feel for their use in the context of an actual piece of music, movement 4 of
the Berlioz *Fantastic* Symphony.

Preliminaries   A great deal of music of all kinds begins not with the main
"song," or tune, or other main material, but with preliminaries to establish a
background, usually some kind of pulse, in preparation for the material to
come. (For an example from Africa, see page 108.) In our symphony, drums
and low instruments set up a pulse consisting of a *beat,* an arrangement of
beats (called the *meter:* duple meter in this case, ONE *two*|ONE *two*|ONE *two*),
and a *tempo* or speed of the beats—a solid march tempo.

After a short time the music surges up into the first *theme.*

beat, page 10
meter, page 11
tempo, page 14
theme, page 26

The sheer loudness of Berlioz's music (though not all of it is as loud as the March to the Scaffold) shocked the Parisian public and inspired many cartoons.

Scale Theme   Think of a theme in music as analogous to the theme of a political speech: the main subject matter that is going to be laid out and developed. A theme can be a tune, or merely a rhythm, or, as in this case, a downward scale. (Those with musical background will recognize it as a *minor* scale, changing in some of its repetitions to the *major*.) What makes an abstract entity like a scale into a theme is the distinctive *rhythm* given to it: DA-**DA**-DA da da-DA-DA-**DA**-DA da da DA-**DA** . . . Looks simple on paper, but the rhythm really invigorates that simple scale.

major and minor, page 32

rhythm, page 10

To be sure nobody fails to recognize the scale as something significant, something that will function as a theme, Berlioz plays it five times in succession. The second time a different melody is played simultaneously—in *counterpoint* with the Scale Theme, to use the technical term—by a lively low wind instrument. (Lively and somewhat grotesque; this is one characteristic sound of a *bassoon*). The combination of two melodies in counterpoint—or for that matter, the same melody in more than one instrument or voice, as in a round like "Row, row, row your boat"—is a musical resource of great importance. At the third appearance of the Scale Theme, the counterpoint shifts to low *stringed instruments,* or *strings.* Later the bassoon returns.

counterpoint, page 29

instruments:
  bassoon, page 39

strings, page 36

In between playings of the theme there are excited flare-ups in various instruments of the orchestra. This music sits on a powder keg. It soon explodes.

LISTENING CHART 1

Berlioz, *Fantastic* Symphony, fourth movement, March to the Scaffold

4 min., 45 sec.

1	0:00	Preliminaries: Drums and low instruments establish the beat, meter, and tempo
	0:27 **A**	Scale Theme (theme 1)—five times
	0:38	+ Counterpoint in the bassoon
	0:51	+ Counterpoint in low string instruments Abrupt flare-up
	1:04	+ Counterpoint in low string instruments
	1:16	+ Counterpoint in the bassoon Bassoon tapers off
2	1:36 **B**	March Theme (theme 2) Band instruments
0:31	2:07	Theme 1 in "broken" orchestration
		Repetition, but with extra instruments added:
0:42	2:18	March Theme (theme 2)
1:12	2:48	Theme 1 in "broken" orchestration
1:20	2:56	Build-up to a climax: *crescendo*
	3:10 **A'**	Scale Theme *fortissimo*
3	3:21	Modulation
0:02	3:23	Inversion of the Scale Theme
0:14	3:35	Cadential section (the music sounds as though it is ending)
0:48	4:09 **C**	

March   The Scale Theme counts as the first theme in this piece; the second theme, a positively manic March, contrasts with it strongly. Here the composer uses wind instruments alone, with *trumpets* and *trombones* prominent, like a marching band. But into the very noisy, blatant music of theme 2 a bizarre version of theme 1 intrudes, broken up almost note by note among different instruments. Berlioz is famous for his innovations in *orchestration*, the art of combining and juxtaposing the sounds of orchestral instruments in effective and imaginative ways. Here is an arresting example.

instruments:
   trombone, page 39
   trumpet, page 39

(Perhaps this intricately "broken" version of theme 1 serves as compensation for the extreme simplicity of the original scale. Berlioz lets us hear it twice.)

Crescendo   We have not said much up to now about the volume of sound in this movement, its loudness, or *dynamics*. After the March the music swells up in volume, getting louder and louder in expectation of some major event. This effect is called a *crescendo*. (*Crescendo* means "growing," in Italian. The opposite is *diminuendo*, diminishing.)

dynamics, page 7

crescendo and **diminuendo**, page 8

Scale Theme   The Scale Theme returns in a mighty climax. Dynamics reach a peak; all the instruments are going at full tilt. Berlioz writes *ff* on the score, short for *fortissimo*, the musicians' conventional term for "very loud."

fortissimo, page 7

At track 3 all the instruments play a sudden new note forcibly, in unison: that is, all playing the same note. The new note seems almost to strike the music and knock it off base. This is a change of *key*, or *modulation*, a powerful and important effect in music of Berlioz's time. Modulation is hard to explain but (often) easy to hear. Typically it gives music a special spurt of energy, over and above what increased dynamics, different instrumentation, and other factors can do.

key, page 32
modulation, page 32

And then Berlioz gets a magnificent lift by *inverting* the Scale Theme, going up the scale instead of down. He trumps the immediately preceding climax.

inversion, page 140

The music has worked up to an almost superhuman level and needs to wind down—a long process as Berlioz does it, and exuberant as ever, but from now on, after the inversion of theme 1, he gives us the distinct feeling that things are coming to a close. *Cadence* is the term for a moment or passage that concludes and settles a piece of music or a section. It takes half a minute here to make a cadence and achieve closure.

cadence, page 25

Surprise   But we should say "comes to the point of making a cadence," for after all the buildup the whole thing suddenly collapses. And what is *this*—the fragment of a hitherto unheard slow, quiet, even plaintive melody without any accompaniment whatsoever? It too collapses, crushed by a military drum roll and a final great blare.

Go to page 266 for the answer. We'll only tell you two things at this point. First, this final section was not part of the original music. It was added when Berlioz revisited an earlier piece and changed it to fit into his *Fantastic* Symphony as one of the movements. And second, he now gave this movement a title. It is not just a march, it is a "March to the Scaffold."

In retrospect, the main elements we have heard in this thrilling movement (there's no other word) are the Scale Theme, five times, followed by the contrasting March, leading to the Scale Theme again—not as many times as before, but now reconstituted as a formidable climax. Then comes the utterly surprising ending section. Putting together the whole experience, we can represent those main elements as **A B A′ C**. This is a letter diagram of a kind conventionally used for the *form* of music; *musical form* is a subject treated at some length in this book.

musical form, page 46

CHAPTER 1

Music, Sound, and Time

usic is the art of sound in time. We start with an outline of the basic properties of sound when it is produced, each of which corresponds to an effect that we experience when sound is heard. The scientific terms for sound all have their analogues in the terminology of music.

1 Sound Vibrations

As everyone who has taken a course in elementary physics knows, sound is produced by vibrations that occur when objects are struck, plucked, stroked, or agitated in some other way. The vibrations are transmitted through the air, or another medium, and picked up by our ears.

For the production of sound in general, almost anything will do—the single rusted hinge on a creaky door as well as the great air masses of a thunderstorm. For the production of musical sounds, the usual objects are taut strings and membranes, columns of air enclosed in pipes of various kinds, and silicon chips. These produce relatively simple vibrations, which translate into clearly focused or, as we say, "musical" sounds. Often the membranes are alive: They are called vocal cords.

Sound-producing vibrations are very fast; the range of sound that can be heard extends from around 20 to 20,000 cycles (that is, our vocal cords warble close to that many times every second). The vibrations are also very small. Look inside a piano while it is being played: You will not detect any movement in the strings, except possibly for some blurring of the very longest ones. To be heard, sound vibrations often need to be *amplified*, either electronically or with the aid of something physical that echoes or *resonates* along with the vibrating body. In a piano, this is the whole big wooden soundboard. The resonator in a guitar is the hollow box that the strings are stretched across.

Pitch (Frequency)

The term for the rate of sound vibration is **frequency**. Frequency is measured in cycles (per second). On the level of perception, our ears respond differently to sounds of high and low frequencies, and to very fine gradations in between.

It has always seemed to me more important for the listener to be sensitive to the musical tone than to know the number of vibrations that produce the tone. . . . What the composer desires above all is to encourage you to become as completely conscious and wide-awake a listener as possible.

From what is still one of the best books on "music appreciation," *What to Listen For in Music* by composer Aaron Copland, 1939 (see page 363)

Early musical instruments often have resonators found in nature: *above*, gourds in a pair of Mexican maracas; *on page 7*, a tortoise shell in the ancient Greek lyre, a small harplike instrument.

Indeed, people speak about "high" and "low" sounds quite unselfconsciously, as though they know that the latter actually have a low frequency—relatively few cycles—and the former a high frequency.

The musical term for this quality of sound, which is recognized so instinctively, is **pitch.** Low pitches (low frequencies) result from *long* vibrating elements, high pitches from *short* ones—a trombone sounds lower than a flute. Tap on a (tall) glass of water as you fill it up, and the pitch gets higher as the column of vibrating air gets shorter.

Noises, with their complex, unfocused vibrations, do not have pitch. And the totality of musical sounds, as distinct from noises, serves as a kind of quarry from which musicians of every age and every culture carve the exact building blocks they want for their music. We hear this totality in the sliding scale of a siren, starting low and going higher and higher until it is out of earshot.

But musicians never (or virtually never) use the full range of pitches. Instead a limited number of fixed pitches is selected from the sound continuum. These pitches are calibrated scientifically (European-style orchestras these days tune to a pitch with a frequency of 440 cycles), given names (that pitch is labeled A), and collected in *scales*. Scales are discussed in Chapter 2.

The experience of pitch is gained very early; babies only a few hours old respond to human voices, and they soon distinguish between high and low ones. They seem to prefer higher pitches, naturally—those in their mothers' pitch range. At the other end of life, it is the highest frequencies that older people find they are losing. The range of pitches that strike us as "normal," those that can be sung by most men and women, is shown to the right. (If you are not familiar with the notation for pitch, consult pages 20–22.)

NORMAL
VOICE RANGES
as in a chorus

2 Dynamics (Amplitude)

In scientific terminology, *amplitude* is the level of strength of sound vibrations—more precisely, the amount of energy they contain and convey. As anyone who has been near a big guitar amplifier knows, very small string vibrations can be amplified until the energy in the air transmitting them rattles the eardrums. Amplitude is measured in *decibels*.

In musical terminology, the level of sound is called its **dynamics.** Musicians use very subtle dynamic gradations from very soft to very loud, but they have never worked out a calibrated scale of dynamics, as they have for pitch. The terms used are only approximate. Because all European music looked to Italy when this terminology first came into use, the terms used for dynamics are in Italian.

The main categories are simply loud and soft, **forte** (pronounced fórteh) and **piano,** which may be qualified by expanding to "very loud" or "very soft" and by adding the Italian word for "medium," **mezzo** (medzo):

pianissimo	piano	mezzo piano	mezzo forte	forte	fortissimo
pp	*p*	*mp*	*mf*	*f*	*ff*
very soft	soft	medium soft	medium loud	loud	very loud

Other terms are **più forte** and **meno forte,** "more loud" and "less loud" (pyōo, méhno). Changes in dynamics can be sudden (*subito*), or they can be

*LISTEN
for pitch and
dynamics*

4

*For explanation of
this icon, see page xvii.*

In Unit I of this book, we will illustrate the concepts that are introduced with listening examples drawn from the enclosed CD-ROM. Follow the timings on these LISTEN charts, which are simplified versions of the Listening Charts provided for complete compositions. The charts are explained on page xvi.

High and low *pitch* and loud and soft *dynamics* are heard so instinctively that they hardly need illustration. Listen, however, to the vivid way they are deployed in one of the most famous of classical compositions, the "Unfinished" Symphony by Franz Schubert. Symphonies consist of four separate big segments, called movements; musicologists are still baffled as to why Schubert wrote two superb movements for this work and started but never finished the rest.

		PITCH	DYNAMIC
0:00	Quiet and mysterious	Low range	*pp*
0:15	Rustling sounds	Middle range	
0:22	Wind instruments	High	
0:35	Single sharp accent		*sf*
0:47	Gets louder	Higher instruments added	Long *crescendo,* leading to *f,* then *ff,* more accents
1:07	Sudden collapse		*piano* followed by *diminuendo*
1:15	New tune	First low, then high	(Marked *pp* by Schubert, but usually played *p* or *mp*.)
1:52	Cuts off sharply; big sound		*ff,* more accents
	(Similar pitch and dynamic effects for the rest of the excerpt)		
3:07	Sinking passage	Individual pitches, lower and lower	
3:45	Ominous	Lowest pitch of all	*pp*

gradual—a soft passage swells into a loud one, or a powerful blare fades into quietness. Below are the terms for changing dynamics and their notational signs (sometimes called "hairpins"):

crescendo (**cresc.**)

decrescendo (**decresc.**), or *diminuendo* (**dim.**)

gradually getting louder

gradually getting softer

3 Tone Color: Overtones

At whatever pitch, and whether loud or soft, musical sounds differ in their general *quality,* depending on the instruments or voices that produce them. **Tone color** and **timbre** are the terms for this quality.

Tone color is produced in a more complex way (and a more astonishing way, it must seem, the first time you learn about it) than pitch and dynamics. Piano strings and other sound-producing bodies vibrate not only along their total length, but also simultaneously in half-lengths, quarters, eighths, and so on.

STRING VIBRATIONS

FULL-LENGTH: HALF-LENGTH: BOTH
                                                                      SIMULTANEOUSLY:
¼ cycle   ¾ cycle   ¼ cycle   ¾ cycle   ¼ cycle   ¾ cycle
       ½ cycle   ½ cycle   ½ cycle

The diagrams above attempt to illustrate this. The amplitudes of these fractional vibrations, called **partials** by scientists, **overtones** by musicians, are much lower than the amplitude of the main vibration. Indeed, overtones are not heard as distinct pitches, but as part of the string's basic or fundamental pitch. The amount and proportion of overtones are what give a sound its characteristic tone color. A flute has few overtones. Luciano Pavarotti has many.

Musicians make no attempt to tally or describe tone colors; about the best one can do is apply imprecise adjectives such as *bright, warm, ringing, hollow,* or *brassy.* Yet tone color is surely the most easily recognized of all musical elements. Even people who cannot identify instruments by name can distinguish between the smooth, rich sound of violins playing together, the bright sound of trumpets, and the thump of drums.

Listen to orchestral tone colors with the Listening Chart on page 52, after following the discussion of European musical instruments in Interlude B (pages 36–45). Look forward to hearing many more non-European instruments in connection with the Global Perspectives sections of this text. The variety of devices invented for the different tone colors that people have desired for their music, in all societies, is almost unbelievable.

The most distinctive tone color of all, however, belongs to the first, most beautiful, and most universal of all the sources of music—the human voice.

4 Duration

Sound exists in time, and any sound we hear has its **duration**—the length of time we hear it in minutes, seconds, or microseconds. Though duration is not an actual property of sound, like frequency, amplitude, and other of sound's attributes that are taught in physics courses, it is obviously of central importance for music, which is the art of sounds in time. The broad term for the time aspect of music is **rhythm.**

The primacy of rhythm in the experience of music is practically an act of faith in our culture—and in most other cultures as well. However, there is some music in which rhythm counts for less than, say, tone color; such a piece will be studied in Chapter 22, *Lux aeterna* by the contemporary composer György Ligeti. Think also of New Age music. But rhythm is the main driving force in music both popular and classical, music of all ages and all cultures, and rhythm is where we will begin our discussion of the elements of music in Chapter 2.

Web: *To test your understanding of music, sound, and time, take an online quiz at* <bedfordstmartins.com/listen>.

The singing voice, "the first, most beautiful, and most universal of all the sources of music": Renée Fleming, a star in the opera world of the 2000s.

Rhythm and Pitch

We start this chapter by discussing *rhythm*, the way musical time is organized by the use of durations of various magnitudes. We then go on to the organization of pitch into *scales* and *intervals*.

Music has four essential elements: rhythm, melody, harmony, and tone color. These four ingredients are the composer's materials. He works with them in the same way that any other artisan works with his materials.

Aaron Copland, *What to Listen For in Music*

1 Rhythm

As we have seen, the term **rhythm** in its broadest sense refers to the time aspect of music. In a more specific sense, "*a* rhythm" refers to the actual arrangement of durations—long and short notes—in a particular melody or some other musical passage. Of course, the term is also used in other contexts, about golfers, quarterbacks, poems, and even paintings. But no sport and no other art handles rhythm with such precision and refinement as does music.

The term *rhythmic* is often used to describe music that features simple patterns, such as ONE *two*|ONE *two*, repeating over and over again, but that is not really correct (think about what a golfer or tennis player means by rhythm). Such patterns should be described as *metrical*, or strongly metrical, not rhythmic. See the section "Rhythm and Meter" on page 12.

Beat

The basic unit for measuring time in music is the **beat**. When listening to a marching band, to take a clear example, we surely sense a regular recurrence of short durational units. These units serve as a steady, vigorous background for other, more complicated durational patterns that we discern at the same time. We can't help beating time to the music, waving a hand or tapping a foot, following the motion of the drum major's baton and the big-drum players' drumsticks. The simple durational pattern that is being signaled by waving, tapping, or thumping is the music's beat.

Accent

Beats provide the basic unit of measurement for time; if ordinary clock time is measured in seconds, musical time is measured in beats. There is, however, an all-important difference between a clock ticking and a drum beating time. Mechan-

The beat: There are times when the drummers in a band do little more than bang it out.

ically produced ticks all sound exactly the same, but it is virtually impossible to beat time without making some beats more emphatic than others. This is called giving certain beats an **accent.**

And accents are really what enable us to beat time, since the simplest way to do this is to alternate accented ("strong") and unaccented ("weak") beats in patterns such as ONE *two*|ONE *two*|ONE *two* . . . or ONE *two three*|ONE *two three*|ONE *two three*. . . . To beat time, then, is not only to measure time but also to organize it, at least into these simple two- and three-beat patterns. That is why a drum is a musical instrument and a clock is not.

Accents are not usually indicated in musical notation, since in most types of music they are simply taken for granted. When composers want a particularly strong accent—something out of the ordinary—they put the sign > above or below a note. Thus a pattern of alternating very strong and weak beats is indicated as shown to the right. An even stronger accent is indicated by the mark *sfz* or *sf,* short for *sforzando,* the Italian word for "forcing."

Meter

Any recurring pattern of strong and weak beats, such as the ONE *two* and ONE *two three* we have referred to and illustrated above, is called a **meter.** Meter is a strong/weak pattern repeated again and again.

Each occurrence of this repeated pattern, consisting of a principal strong beat and one or more weaker beats, is called a **measure,** or **bar.** In musical notation, measures are indicated by vertical lines called **bar lines.** The meter indicated schematically in the margin above is notated as shown to the right.

In Western music there are only two basic kinds of meter, called **simple meters:** duple meter and triple meter, plus a third, **compound meter,** which involves a subdivision of one of the simple meters.

In duple meter the beats are grouped in twos (ONE *two*|ONE *two*). Duple meter is instantly familiar from marches—such as "Yankee Doodle"—which tend always to use it in deference to the human anatomy (LEFT *right*, LEFT *right*, LEFT *right*).

In triple meter the beats are grouped in threes (ONE *two three*|ONE *two three*). As it happens, our national songs "The Star-Spangled Banner" and "My Country, 'Tis of Thee" are in triple meter. "My Country, 'Tis of Thee" starts on the strong beat ONE of the triple meter; "The Star-Spangled Banner" starts on the weak beat *three*.

Not infrequently, there is a clearly marked subdivision of the main beats into threes, resulting in *compound meters* with six or nine beats:

ONE		two			ONE		two		three	
ONE *two three*		FOUR *five six*			ONE *two three*		FOUR *five six*		SEVEN *eight nine*	

Compound meters are really best thought of as subtypes of duple and triple meter. The round "Row, row, row your boat" is in compound meter, **6/8**, but while the first voice is moving at a fast six-beat clip at the words "Merrily, merrily," the second voice comes in pounding out the basic duple meter, "Row, *row,* row":

first voice:

Row,	row,	row your	boat	gently	down the	stream,		Merrily,	merrily,	merrily,	merrily,
1 2 3	4 5 6	1 2 3	4 5 6	1 2 3	4 5 6	1 2 3	4 5 6	1 2 3	4 5 6	1 2 3	4 5 6
ONE	*two*	ONE	*two*	ONE	*two*	ONE	*two*	ONE	*two*	ONE	*two*

						second voice:		Row,	row,	row . . .	
								ONE	*two*	ONE	*two*

Meters with five beats, seven beats, and so on have never been used widely in Western music, though they are found frequently enough in some other musical cultures. It was an unusual tour de force for Chaikovsky to have provided his popular Sixth Symphony with a very convincing waltzlike movement in *quintuple* meter (five beats to a bar).

Chaikovsky, Symphony No. 6

Rhythm and Meter

We have already seen that *rhythm* in the most general sense refers to the entire time aspect of music and, more specifically, that *a* rhythm refers to the particular arrangements of long and short notes in a musical passage. In most Western music, duple or triple *meter* serves as the regular background against which we perceive music's actual rhythms.

As the rhythm now coincides with the meter, then cuts across it independently, then even contradicts it, all kinds of variety, tension, and excitement can result. Meter is background; rhythm is foreground.

Musical notation has developed a conventional system of signs (see pages 20–21) to indicate relative durations; combining various signs is the way of indicating rhythms. Following are examples of well-known tunes in duple and triple meters. Notice from the shading (even better, sing the tunes to yourself and *hear*) how the rhythm sometimes corresponds with the meter and sometimes departs from it. The shading indicates passages of rhythm-meter correspondence:

The most exciting rhythms seem unexpected and complex, the most beautiful melodies simple and inevitable.

Poet W. H. Auden, 1962

The above diagrams should not be taken to imply that meter is always emphasized behind music's rhythms. Often the meter is not explicitly beaten out at all. It does not need to be, for the listener can almost always sense it under the surface. People will even imagine they hear a duple or triple meter behind the steady dripping of a faucet or the ticking of a clock.

Naturally, meter is strongly stressed in music designed to stimulate regular body movements, such as marches, dances, and much popular music. The connection between strongly metrical music and sex is acknowledged by the uninhibited gesturing of rock stars and the explicit imagery of MTV.

At the other extreme, there is *nonmetrical* music. The meandering, nonmetrical rhythms of Gregorian chant contribute to the cool, unworldly, and spiritual quality that devotees of this music cherish. Sometimes these two different kinds of rhythmic organization are joined together. In the classical music of India, for example, most performances begin with a long section of nonmetrical music, and then proceed to music with a clearly defined meter. See page 219.

Rhythm might be described as, to the world of sound, what light is to the world of sight. It shapes and gives new meaning.

Edith Sitwell, poet and critic, 1965

Syncopation

One way of obtaining interesting, striking effects in music is to displace the accents in a foreground *rhythm* away from their normal position on the beats of the background *meter*. This is called **syncopation**. In duple meter, accents can be displaced so they go *one* TWO|*one* TWO instead of ONE *two*|ONE *two*. Or the syncopation can occur in between beats ONE and *two,* as in this Christmas ballad:

Ru*dolf* __ the   red - nosed rein - deer _____

ONE   *two* | ONE   *two* | ONE   *two* | ONE   *two*

If you know the George M. Cohan classic "Give my regards to Broadway," you know that it starts with the same syncopation as in "Rudolf," and has another syncopation in its second line:

Give *my* __ re- gards   to   Broad - - - way,   Re - member me to   Her*ald* ____   Square

ONE   *two* | ONE   *two* | ONE   *two* | ONE   *two* | ONE   *two* | ONE   *two*   ONE

The consistent use of syncopation is the hallmark of African American–derived popular music, from jazz to world beat. See Chapter 23.

Tempo

Our discussion so far has referred to the *relative* duration of sounds—all beats are equal; some notes are twice as long as others, and so on—but nothing has been said yet about their *absolute* duration in fractions of a second. The term for the speed of music is **tempo;** in metrical music, the tempo is the rate at which the basic, regular beats of the meter follow one another.

Tempo can be expressed quantitatively by such indications as ♩ = 60, meaning 60 quarter-note beats per minute. These indications are called **metronome marks,** after the metronome, a mechanical or electrical device that ticks out beats at any desired tempo.

When composers give directions for tempo, however, they usually prefer general terms. Rather than freezing the music's speed by means of a metronome mark, they prefer to leave some latitude for different performers, different acoustical conditions in concert halls, and other factors. Like the indications for dynamics, the conventional terms for tempo are Italian:

An early metronome owned by Beethoven, who was a friend of the inventor, Johannes Maelzel. A clockwork mechanism made the bar swing back and forth, ticking, at a rate determined by a little movable weight on the bar.

COMMON TEMPO INDICATIONS		LESS COMMON TEMPO INDICATIONS	
adagio:	slow	*largo, lento, grave:*	slow, very slow
andante:	on the slow side, but not too slow	*larghetto:*	somewhat faster than *largo*
moderato:	moderate tempo	*andantino:*	somewhat faster than *andante*
allegretto:	on the fast side, but not too fast	*vivace, vivo:*	lively
allegro:	fast	*molto allegro:*	faster than *allegro*
presto:	very fast	*prestissimo:*	very fast indeed

In their original meaning, many of these Italian words refer not to speed itself but rather to a mood, action, or quality that can be associated with tempo only in a general way. Thus, *vivace* is close to our "vivacious," *allegro* means "cheerful," and *andante,* derived from the Italian word for "go," might be translated as "moving along steadily."

Other terms indicate irregularities of tempo and tempo changes:

accelerando (acheleráhndo) (accel.)	gradually getting faster
ritardando (rit.) or *rallentando (rall.)*	gradually getting slower
più lento, più allegro	slower, faster
⌢ (fermata symbol)	a hold of indefinite length on a certain note or rest, which in effect suspends the tempo
a tempo	back to the main tempo

The most important terms to remember are those listed under "common tempo indications" above. When they appear at the top of a symphony movement or the like, they usually constitute its only heading. People refer to the "Andante" of Beethoven's Fifth Symphony, meaning a certain movement of the symphony (the second), which is played at an *andante* tempo.

2 Pitch

Music, as we noted in Chapter 1, generally does not use the total continuous range of musical sounds. Instead, it draws on only a limited number of fixed pitches. These pitches can be assembled in a collection called a **scale.** In effect, a scale is the pool of pitches available for making music.

Which exact pitches constitute a scale differ from culture to culture. Twelve basic pitches have been fixed for most of the music we know—and so people tend to think of the Western scale as "natural." This is a mistake. Five pitches were once used in Japan, as many as twenty-four have been used in Near Eastern countries, and Western Europe itself originally used seven.

LISTEN
for rhythm,
meter, and
tempo

1, 4-14, 17

For samples of *duple, triple,* and *compound meters,* listen to tracks on the Study Guide CD-ROM that we are also using in Unit 1 to illustrate more complex concepts. (With duple meter, it is often hard to hear whether the music is in **2/4** or **4/4.** If the performer doesn't distinguish the beats clearly enough, ONE *two* THREE *four* in **4/4** is going to sound very much like ONE *two*|ONE *two* in **2/4.**)

1,5, 7, 9, 10	Duple meter **2/4** or **2/2**	Count ONE *two*	ONE *two* . . . etc., for about half a minute.
12, 13	Duple meter **4/4** or **4/8**	Count ONE *two* THREE *four*	ONE *two* THREE *four* . . . etc.
4, 14, 17	Triple meter **3/4**	Count ONE *two three*	ONE *two* three . . . etc. In track 4, count nine beats (three bars) in the tenth note from the beginning. In track 14, note several *fermatas.*
11	Compound meter **6/8**	Count ONE *two three* FOUR *five six* . . . etc.

6, 7 *Tempo* is best illustrated when tempo changes, as at 0:48 in track 7 (and, for a more extended example, several times in track 6).

5 *Syncopation* is at its most insistent and most delightful in rags, such as Scott Joplin's signature "Maple Leaf Rag." See page 391. Listen to the piano left hand, with its steady ONE *two*|ONE *two* beat in duple meter; the right hand cuts across it with syncopations in almost every measure.

For a more leisurely experience of different meters (and tempos), and syncopation effects of different kinds, listen to the *Rhapsody on a Theme by Paganini* for piano and orchestra, by the great twentieth-century pianist-composer Sergei Rachmaninov (1873–1943). The example on our CD-ROM is only a segment of this lengthy work.

The example contains several subunits, around a minute or two each, in different meters and tempos. If you note a family likeness between the subunits, that is because they are all variations on a single theme. (See page 187.)

6 0:00 Piano starts in *duple meter.* The loud orchestral interruptions are *syncopated.* (After the interruptions the meter is somewhat obscured, but it gets clearer.)

0:33 Clear duple meter by this time; then the music comes to a stop.

0:49 No meter. The piano seems to be engaged in a meditative improvisation, as though dreaming up the music to come.

1:45 Orchestral instruments suggest a slow *duple meter?* Not for long.

2:24 Slow *triple meter*

3:40 *Ritardando* (getting slower)

3:56 Fast *triple meter,* marchlike (note one or two syncopated notes)

4:26 Faster *triple meter*

Intervals (I): The Octave

The difference, or distance, between any two pitches is called an **interval.** Of the many different intervals used in music, one has a special character that makes it particularly important. This is the **octave.**

If a series of successive pitches is sounded, one after another—say, running up the white keys on a keyboard—there comes a point at which the pitch seems in some sense to "duplicate" an earlier pitch, but at a higher level. This

Choral singing, the route by which millions of people come to know and love music.

new pitch does not sound identical to the old one, but somehow the two sounds are very similar. They blend extremely well; they almost seem to melt into each other.

What causes the phenomenon of octaves? Recall from Chapter 1 that when strings vibrate to produce sound they vibrate in partials, that is, not only along their full length but also in halves and other fractions (page 9). A vibrating string that is exactly half as long as another will *reinforce* the longer one's strongest partial. This reinforcement causes the duplication effect of octaves.

As strings go, so go vocal cords: When men and women sing along together, they automatically sing in octaves, duplicating each other's singing an octave or two apart. If you ask them, they will say they are singing "the same tune"—not many will think of adding "at different octave levels."

As a result of the phenomenon of octaves, the full continuous range of pitches that exists in nature (and that is covered, for example, by a siren starting low and going up higher and higher) falls into a series of "duplicating" segments. Human ears are able to detect about ten of these octave segments. Two or three octaves is a normal range for most voices and instruments. A large pipe organ covers all ten and a piano covers about seven. Two octaves are shown on our next diagram.

The Diatonic Scale

The set of seven pitches originally used in Western music is called the **diatonic scale.** Dating from ancient Greek times, it is still in use today. When the first of the seven pitches is repeated at a higher duplicating pitch, the total is eight—hence the name *octave*, meaning "eight span."

Anyone who knows the series *do re mi fa sol la ti do* is at home with the diatonic scale. You can count out the octave for yourself starting with the first *do* as *one* and ending with the second *do* as *eight*. The set of white keys on the piano (or other) keyboard constitutes this scale. Shown below is a keyboard and diatonic scale notes running through two octaves, marked with their conventional letter names (see page 21).

The Chromatic Scale

The diatonic scale was the original, basic scale of Western music. At a later period, five more pitches were added between certain of the seven pitches of the diatonic scale, making a total of twelve. This is the **chromatic scale,** represented by the complete set of white and black keys on a keyboard.

However, the chromatic scale did not make the diatonic scale obsolete. For centuries Western composers used the chromatic scale freely while favoring the diatonic scale that is embedded in it; in fact, most composers still do this today. Our keyboards reflect this practice, with their chromatic notes colored differently from the diatonic ones, set back and thinner. (On medieval church organs, designed to accommodate the diatonic scale only, the keyboards had no "black notes," or at most just one.)

These extra pitches caused a problem for musical notation. The pitches of the diatonic scale are indicated on the lines and spaces of the staff; there are no positions in between, so symbols such as those shown to the right were introduced. B♭ stands for B **flat,** the pitch inserted between A and B; C♯ stands for C **sharp,** the pitch between C and D, and so on.

Intervals (II): Half Steps and Whole Steps

As previously noted, the difference, or distance, between any two pitches is called the interval between them. Look at the chromatic scale in the diagram above. Besides the C-to-C octave interval marked with a bracket, eleven other kinds of intervals exist between C and the other notes of the scale.

For our purposes, only two additional interval types need be considered:

❧   The smallest interval is the **half step**, or semitone, which is the distance be-tween any two successive notes of the chromatic scale. ("Step" is a name for small intervals.) On a keyboard, a half step is the interval between the closest adjacent notes, white or black. The distance from E to F is a half step; so is the distance from F to F sharp (F♯), G to A flat (A♭), and so on.

As the smallest interval in regular use, the half step is also the smallest that most people can "hear" easily and identify. Many tunes, such as "The Battle Hymn of the Republic," end with two half steps, one half step going down and then the same one going up again ("His truth is *march-ing on*").

❧   The **whole step**, or whole tone, is equivalent to two half steps: D to E, E to F♯, F♯ to G♯, and so on. "Three Blind Mice" starts with two whole steps, going down.

The chromatic scale consists exclusively of half steps. Therefore, this scale can be described as "symmetrical," in the sense that one can start on any of its pitches and sing up or down the scale by half steps with exactly the same effect as if one started anywhere else. The diatonic scale is *not* symmetrical in this sense. It includes both half steps and whole steps. Between B and C and be-tween E and F, the interval is a half step, but between the other pairs of adjacent notes the interval is twice as big—a whole step.

Music is made out of these scales, and the diatonic and chromatic scales differ in the intervals between their constituent pitches—hence the importance of intervals. In the diagram below, the two scales are lined up in order to show the differences in their interval structure.

Scales and Instruments

Until fairly recently, Western music used the twelve pitches of the chromatic scale, duplicated through all the octaves, and in principle no other pitches. Features of many instruments are designed to produce these particular pitches exactly: frets on guitars, carefully measured holes in flutes, and the tuned sets of strings of harps and pianos.

Other instruments, such as the violin and the slide trombone, have a more continuous range of pitches available to them (as does a police siren or the human voice). In mastering these instruments, one of the first tasks is learning

A pioneer of modern design, the German-American painter Josef Albers (1888–1976) produced twenty-seven of these wonderful treble clefs, all in different color combinations.

to pick out exactly the right pitches. This is called *playing in tune*; singing in tune is a big concern for vocalists, too.

It is true that many instrumentalists and all singers regularly perform certain notes slightly out of tune for important and legitimate artistic effects. "Blue" notes in jazz are an example. However, these "off" pitches are only small, temporary deviations from the main pitches of the scale—the same twelve pitches that, on instruments such as the piano, are absolutely fixed.

Web: *To test your understanding of rhythm and pitch, take an online quiz at* <bedfordstmartins.com/listen>.

INTERLUDE A: Musical Notation

Many cultures around the world employ different notations for writing their music down. It is never necessary, obviously, to read these notations in order to understand the music or to love it; indeed, many cultures have no notation at all. However, written music examples can help clarify many points about musical style—even ones not written down by their creators—and it will help if you learn to follow the music examples in this book in an approximate way. The following brief survey of Western musical notation can be used for study or review or reference.

As we have seen in our discussion of musical elements, *time* and *pitch* are really the only ones that can be specified (and therefore notated) with any precision. Think of pitch and time as coordinates of a graph on which music is going to be plotted. The resulting pitch/time grid is quite close to actual musical notation, as shown in the diagrams below.

Notes and Rests

The longest note in common use is the *whole note:* o (we are dealing here with proportional lengths; how long a whole note lasts in absolute time depends on the tempo: see page 14). A half note (♩) lasts for half the time of a whole note, a quarter note (♩) lasts for a quarter of the time, an eighth note (♪) for an eighth, a sixteenth (♪) for a sixteenth, and so on.

When the shorter notes come in groups, they can also be notated as shown at the top of the next column.

The "flags"—they look more like pennants—at the sides of the note "stems" have been "starched" up into horizontal "beams," for easier reading:

Rests To make rhythms, composers use not only sounds but also short silences called **rests**. The diagram below shows the relation between rests, which are equivalent in duration to their corresponding notes. (Compare the whole- and half-note rests, which are slugs beneath or atop one of the lines of the staff.)

The shorter rests have their own sort of flags. As with notes, more flags can be added to rests, with each flag cutting the time value in half. Thus, three flags on a rest (𝄿) make it a thirty-second rest.

Rhythmic Notation

Beyond the notation of basic notes and rests, a number of other conventions are necessary to indicate the combining of notes and rests into actual rhythms.

Dotted Notes and Dotted Rhythms A dot placed after a note or rest lengthens its duration by 50 percent. Thus a dotted half note lasts as long as a half plus a quarter note: ♩. = ♩ + ♩ And a dotted quarter-note rest equals a quarter plus an eighth: 𝄽. = 𝄽 + 𝄾 Even simple tunes, such as "America," make use of the dot convention.

A *dotted rhythm* is one consisting of dotted (long) notes alternating with short ones:

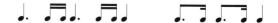

Ties Two notes of the same pitch can be connected by means of a curved line called a *tie.* This means they are played continuously, as though they were one note of the combined duration. Any number of notes of the same pitch can be tied together, so that this notational device can serve to indicate a pitch of very long duration.

Ties

Beware: The same sort of curved line is also used to connect notes that are *not* of the same pitch. In this case it means that they are to be played smoothly, one following the next without the slightest break (*legato* or "bound" playing). These curved lines are called *slurs*.

Slurs: legato

To indicate that notes are to be played in a detached fashion (*staccato*), dots are placed above or below them.

Staccato dots

Triplets Three notes bracketed together and marked with a 3 (♩ ♩ ♩) are called a *triplet*. This indicates that the three notes take exactly the same time that would normally be taken by two. A quarter-note triplet has the same duration as two ordinary quarter notes: ♩ ♩ ♩ = ♩ ♩.

The convention is occasionally extended to groups of five notes, seven notes, etc. For an example, see page 260.

Meter: Measures and Bar Lines A *measure* (or *bar*) is the basic time unit chosen for a piece of music, corresponding to the meter of the piece (see page 11). Measures are marked in musical notation by vertical *bar lines*. Each measure covers the same time span. In the following example, the time span covered by each measure is one whole note, equivalent to two half notes (measure 1), or four quarter notes (measure 2), or eight eighth notes (measures 3, 4).

Time Signatures In the example above, the meter is indicated by means of a *time signature*. Time signatures are printed on the staffs at the beginning of all pieces of music; they are not repeated on later staffs.

In spite of appearances, time signatures are not fractions. The top digit shows *how many beats* are in each

measure, and the bottom digit shows *what kind of note* represents a beat. If the bottom digit is 2, the beat is represented by a half note; if 4, by a quarter note, and so on.

In our example, the 2 at the top indicates there are two beats in each measure (duple meter), and the 2 at the bottom indicates that the beats are half-note beats. This time signature is often indicated by the sign ¢.

Pitch Notation

The letter names A B C D E F G are assigned to the original seven pitches of the diatonic scale. Then the letters are used over and over again for pitches in the duplicating octaves. Octaves are distinguished by numbers (c^1, c^2) or prime marks (A', A''); so-called "middle C" (c^1) is the comfortable note that virtually any man, woman, or child can sing and that can be played by the great majority of instruments. On a keyboard, middle C sits in the middle, right under the maker's name—Casio, Yamaha, Steinway.

The Staff: Ledger Lines For the notation of pitch, notes are placed on a set of five parallel lines called a staff. The notes can be put on the lines of the staff, in the spaces between them, or right at the top or bottom of the staff:

Above and below the regular five lines of the staff, short extra lines can be added to accommodate a few higher and lower notes. These are called *ledger lines*.

Clefs Nothing has been said so far about which pitch each position on the staff represents. To clue us in to precise pitches, signs called *clefs* (French for "key" or "clue") are placed at the beginning of each staff. Clefs calibrate the staff: that is, they connect one of the five lines of the staff to a specific pitch.

Thus in the treble clef or G clef (𝄞), the spiral in the middle of this antique capital G curves around line 2, counting up from the bottom of the staff. Line 2, then, is the line for the pitch G—the first G above middle C. In the bass clef or F clef (𝄢), the two dots straddle the fourth line up. The pitch F goes on this line—the first F below middle C.

Adjacent lines and spaces on the staff have adjacent letter names, so we can place all the other pitches on the staff in relation to the fixed points marked by the clefs:

There are other clefs, but these two are the most common. Used in conjunction, they accommodate the maximum span of pitches without overlapping. The treble and bass clef staffs fit together as shown in Figure 1 below.

The notation of six A's, covering five octaves, requires two staffs and seven ledger lines (see Figure 2).

Sharps and Flats; Naturals The pitches produced by the black keys on the piano are not given letter names of their own. (This is a consequence of the way they arose in history; see page 17.) Nor do they get their own individual lines or spaces on the staffs. The pitch in between A and B is called A sharp (or A♯, using the conventional sign for a sharp), meaning "higher than A." It can also be called B flat (B♭), meaning "lower than B." In musical notation, the signs ♯ and ♭ are placed on the staff just *before* the note that is to be sharped or flatted.

Which of these two terms is used depends partly on convenience, partly on convention, and partly on theoretical considerations that do not concern us here. In the example below, the third note, A♯, sounds just like the B♭ later in the measure, but for technical reasons the composer (Béla Bartók) notated it differently.

The original pitches of the diatonic scale, played on the white keys of the piano, are called "natural." If it is necessary to cancel a sharp or a flat within a measure and to indicate that the natural note should be played instead, the natural sign is placed before a note (♮♩) or after a letter (A♮) to show this. The following example shows A sharp and G sharp being canceled by natural signs:

Key Signatures In musical notation, it is a convention that a sharp or flat placed before a note will also affect any later appearance of that same note *in the same measure*—but not in the next measure.

There is also a way of specifying that certain sharps or flats are to be applied throughout an entire piece, in every measure, and in every octave. Such sharps and flats appear on the staffs at the very beginning of the piece, even prior to the time signature, and at the beginning of each staff thereafter. They constitute the *key signature:*

is equivalent to:

Scores

Music for a melody instrument such as a violin or a trumpet is written on one staff; keyboard instruments require two—one staff for the right hand, another staff for the left hand. Music for two or more voices or instruments, choirs, bands, and orchestras is written in *scores*. In scores, each instrument and voice that has its own independent music gets one staff. Simultaneously sounding notes and measure lines are aligned vertically. In general, high-sounding instruments go on top, the low ones on the bottom.

Shown on page 23 is a page from Mozart's "Jupiter" Symphony, with arrows pointing to the various details of notation that have been explained above.

Figure 1

Figure 2

CHAPTER 3

The Structures of Music

I n this chapter we take up musical concepts that combine the basic elements discussed in Chapters 1 and 2. Listening to an actual piece of music, it's obvious that we do not experience its rhythm, pitch, tone color, and dynamics in isolation from one another. Indeed, rhythms, pitches, and the rest are seldom experienced one at a time. Rather, music consists of simple and complex "structures" built from these elements.

1 Melody

A **melody** is an organized series of pitches. Think for a moment, if you can, of pitch and time as the two coordinates of a graph on which music is going to be plotted. A series of single pitches played in a certain rhythm will appear as dots, high or low, on the pitch/time grid, and the dots can be connected by a line (see the marginal diagram). Musicians commonly speak of "melodic line" (or simply "line") in this connection.

Just as an actual line in a painting or a drawing can possess character— can strike the viewer as forceful, graceful, or tentative—so can a melodic line. A melody in which each note is higher than the last can seem to soar; a low note can feel like a setback; a long series of repeated notes on the same pitch can seem to wait ominously. The listener develops a real interest in how the line of a satisfactory melody is going to come out.

In such a melody, the succession of notes seems to hold together in a meaningful, interesting way—interesting, and also emotional. Of all music's structures, melody is the one that moves people the most, that seems to evoke human sentiment most directly. Familiar melodies "register" simple qualities of feeling instantly and strongly. These qualities vary widely: romantic in "Yesterday," martial in "Dixie," mournful in "St. Louis Blues," extroverted and cheerful in "Happy Birthday to You."

Tunes

These are the most familiar of melodies in Western music. A simple, easily singable, catchy melody such as a folk song, or a dance, or a Christmas carol is a **tune**. A tune is a special kind of melody. *Melody* is a term that includes tunes, but also much else.

"The Star-Spangled Banner," which everyone knows, can be used to illustrate the general characteristics of tunes. See the box on the next page.

Always remember that in listening to a piece of music you must hang on to the melodic line. It may disappear momentarily, withdrawn by the composer, in order to make its presence more powerfully felt when it reappears. But reappear it surely will . . .

Aaron Copland, *What to Listen For in Music*

PITCH

Melody
(melodic line)

TIME

Characteristics of Tunes

The best way to grasp the characteristics of tunes is by singing one you know, either out loud or "in your head."

❧ *Division into Phrases* Tunes fall naturally into smaller sections, called **phrases.** This is, in fact, true of all melodies, but with tunes the division into phrases is particularly clear and sharp.

In tunes with words (that is, songs), phrases tend to coincide with poetic lines. Most lines in a song lyric end with a rhyming word and a punctuation mark such as a comma. These features clarify the musical phrase divisions:

> And the rockets' red ***glare,***
> The bombs bursting in ***air***

Singing a song, one has to breathe—and one tends to breathe at the end of phrases. You may not need to breathe after phrase 1 of our national anthem, but you'd better not wait any longer than phrase 2:

❧ *Balance between Phrases* In many tunes, all the phrases are 2, 4, or 8 measures long. (The *measure* or bar is the basic time unit of music; see page 11.) Blues tunes, for example, usually consist of three four-measure phrases; hence the term *twelve-bar blues.*

Most phrases of "The Star-Spangled Banner" are two measures long (see phrase 1 and phrase 2, above). But one phrase broadens out to four measures, with a fine effect: "Oh say, does that star-spangled banner yet wave." Try not to breathe in the middle of this long phrase.

Other phrase lengths—three measures, five, and others—can certainly occur in a tune and make for welcome contrast. For a good tune, the main requirement is that we sense a balance between the phrases, in terms of phrase lengths and in other terms, too, so that taken together the phrases add up to a well-proportioned whole.

❧ *Parallelism and Contrast* Balance between phrases can be strengthened by means of *parallelism.* For example, phrases can be exactly parallel except for the words ("Oh, say can you see," "Whose broad stripes and bright stars"). Others have the same rhythm but different pitches ("Oh say can you see," "By the dawn's early light").

Sometimes phrases have the same general *pattern of pitches,* but one phrase is slightly higher or lower than the other ("And the rockets' red glare," "The bombs bursting in air"). Such duplication of a phrase at two or more different pitch levels, called **sequence,** occurs frequently in music, and is a hallmark of certain musical styles.

Composers also take care to make certain phrases *contrast* with their neighbors—one phrase short, another long, or one phrase low, another high (perhaps even *too*

high, at "O'er the land of the *free*"). A tune with some parallel and some contrasting phrases will seem to have logic, or coherence, and yet will avoid monotony.

❧ *Climax and Cadence* A good tune has *form:* a clear, purposeful beginning, a feeling of action in the middle, and a firm sense of winding down at the end.

Many tunes have a distinct high point, or **climax,** which their earlier portions seem to be heading toward. A melodic climax is always an emotional climax; feelings rise as voices soar. The climax of our national anthem highlights what was felt to be the really crucial word in it—"free." Patriot Francis Scott Key put that word in that place (Key wrote the words of "The Star-Spangled Banner"—the words only, adapted to an old melody).

Then the later part of the tune relaxes from this climax, until it reaches a solid stopping place at the end. Emotionally, this is a point of relaxation and satisfaction. In a less definite way, the music also stops at earlier points in the tune—or, if it does not fully stop, at least seems to pause. The term for these interim stopping or pausing places is **cadence.**

Composers can write cadences with all possible shades of finality. "And the home of the brave" is a very final-sounding cadence; "That our flag was still there" has an interim feeling. The art of making cadences is one of the most subtle and basic processes in musical composition.

LISTEN
for melody
and tune

7

Division into phrases, parallelism and *contrast* between phrases, *sequence, climax, cadence:* These are some characteristics of tunes that we have observed in "The Star-Spangled Banner." They are not just inert characteristics—they are what make the tune work. They are at work in tunes of all kinds.

Our example is a depression-era song, "Who Cares?" by George Gershwin, a show tune from the musical comedy *Of Thee I Sing* (1932). In "The Star-Spangled Banner" the *climax* matches the text perfectly at "free." Here "jubilee" makes a good match for the climax, and a melodic *sequence* fits the words "I care for you/you care for me" neatly.

Show tunes usually have an introduction, called the *verse,* in effect another, less striking tune with more words. On our recording, by the great jazz singer Ella Fitzgerald, the band begins "Who Cares?" when she sings it a second time (with slightly different words).

7	0:12	**Verse**	
		Let it rain and thunder . . . (eight more lines)	Includes a long (six-fold) *sequence*
	0:48		Tempo changes
	0:57	**Tune**	
		Who cares if the sky cares to fall in the sea?	
		Who cares what banks fail in Yonkers?	*Contrasting* phrase
		Long as you've got a kiss that conquers.	*Parallel* phrase—starts like the preceding, ends higher
		Why should I care? Life is one long jubilee,	Three-fold *sequence* ("should I care/life is one/jubilee") *Climax* on "jubilee"
		So long as I care for you and you care for me.	Free *sequence* ("I care for you"/ "You care for me")—*cadence*
	1:55	**Tune**	Begun by the band

Motives and Themes

Tunes are relatively short; longer pieces, such as symphonies, may have tunes embedded in them, but they also contain other musical material. Two terms are frequently encountered in connection with melody in longer pieces of music.

The first is **motive.** A motive is a distinctive fragment of melody, distinctive enough so that it will be easily recognized when it returns again and again within a long composition. Motives are shorter than tunes, shorter even than phrases of tunes; they can be as short as two notes. Probably the most famous motive in all music is the four-note *da da da DA* motive in Beethoven's Fifth Symphony.

da da da DA

The second term, **theme,** is the most general term for the basic subject matter of longer pieces of music. *Theme* is another name for "topic": The themes or topics of a political speech are the main points that the politician announces, repeats, develops, and hammers home. The composer of a symphony or a fugue treats musical themes in much the same way.

Since the term *theme* refers to the *function,* not the *nature,* of musical material, in principle almost anything can serve as a theme. A melody can perform this function, or a phrase, a motive, even a distinctive tone color. It depends on the kind of music. The theme of the last movement of Beethoven's Ninth Symphony is the tune we will hear several times on the CD-ROM, track 8 (see page 30).

The theme of Beethoven's Fifth Symphony consists of the *da da da DA* motive played twice in sequence. Many of the themes of Richard Wagner's operas are closely identified with a particular tone color and instrument (the trombone, in the excerpt discussed on page 286).

2 Harmony

Melody and harmony: a folk-singer playing the Appalachian dulcimer.

A single melodic "line" in time is enough to qualify as music: sometimes, indeed, as great music. When people sing in the shower and when parents sing to their babies they are producing melody, and that is all, to everyone's full satisfaction. The same was true of the early Christian Church, whose music, Gregorian chant, consisted of over two thousand subtly differentiated melodies, sung without instruments or any kind of "harmonizing."

Today, however—and this is the outcome of a long and complicated historical development—it seems very natural to us to hear melodies together with other sounds, which we call "accompaniments." A folk singer singing and playing a guitar is performing a song and its accompaniment. The congregation sings hymns in church; the organist plays the accompaniment.

The folk singer uses a number of standard groupings of simultaneous pitches, or **chords,** that practice has shown are sure to work well in combination. Imaginative players will also discover nonstandard chords and unexpected successions of chords in order to enrich their accompaniments. The song is said to be **harmonized;** the continuous matrix of changing chords provides a sort of constantly shifting sound-background for the song.

Any melody can be harmonized in different ways using different chords, and the overall effect of the music depends to a great extent on the nature of these chords, or the **harmony** in general. We can instinctively sense the difference in harmony between Mozart and Wagner or Debussy, or between New Orleans jazz and rock. However, to characterize the differences requires technical language, and we shall not make the attempt in this book.

Consonance and Dissonance

A pair of terms used in discussions of harmony is **consonance** and **dissonance,** meaning (roughly speaking) chords that sound at rest and those that sound tense, respectively. *Discord* is another term for dissonance. These qualities depend on the kinds of intervals (see pages 15–18) that are sounding simultaneously to make up these chords. Octaves are the most consonant of intervals. Half steps are among the most dissonant.

In everyday language, "discord" implies something unpleasant; discordant human relationships are to be avoided. But music does not avoid dissonance in its technical meaning, for a little discord supplies the subtle tensions that are essential to make music flow along. A dissonant chord leaves the listener with a feeling of expectation; it requires a consonant chord following it to complete the gesture and to make the music come to a point of stability. This is called *resolution;* the dissonance is said to be **resolved.** Without dissonance, music would be like food without salt or spices.

Important cadences—say, at the ends of pieces of music—are almost always helped by the use of dissonance. Movement from tension (dissonance) to rest (consonance) contributes centrally to a sense of finality and satisfaction.

Medicine, to produce health, must know disease; music, to produce harmony, must know discord.

Plutarch, c. 46–120 C.E.

3 Texture

Texture is the term used to refer to the blend of the various sounds and melodic lines occurring simultaneously in music. The word is adopted from textiles, where it refers to the weave of the various threads—loose or tight, even or mixed. A cloth such as tweed, for instance, leaves the different threads clearly visible. In fine silk or percale, the weave is so tight and smooth that the constituent threads can be impossible to detect.

Thinking again of the pitch/time graph on page 24, we can see that it is possible to plot more than one pitch for every time slot. Melody exists in the "horizontal" dimension, texture in the "vertical" dimension. For the moment, we leave the lower dots (below the melody) unconnected.

Monophony

This is the term for the simplest texture, a single unaccompanied melody: Gregorian chant; singing in the shower; "Row, Row, Row Your Boat" before the second person comes in:

Simple as this texture is, some very beautiful and sophisticated **monophonic** music has been composed, just as artists have done wonderful things with line drawings: See page 334.

Heterophony

A special kind of monophonic texture, not much used in the European classical tradition but more prominent elsewhere, is called **heterophony.** This is a texture in which subtly different versions of a single melody are presented simultaneously. We will hear several examples of heterophony in the non-European musics discussed throughout this book.

Homophony

When there is only one melody of real interest and it is combined with other sounds, the texture is called **homophonic.** A harmonized melody is an example of homophonic texture: for instance, one person singing the tune of "Row, Row, Row Your Boat" while playing chords on a guitar:

We might indicate a chord on the pitch/time graph by a vertical box enclosing the dots. The sum of these boxes represents the harmony. Homophony can be thought of as a tight, smooth texture—like silk, among the textiles.

Polyphony

When two or more melodies are played or sung simultaneously, the texture is described as **polyphonic.** In polyphony, the melodies are felt to be independent and of approximately equal interest. The whole is more than the sum of the parts, however: the way the melodies play off against one another makes for the possibility of greater richness and interest than if they were played singly. In the textile analogy, polyphony would be compared to a rough texture where the strands are all perceptible, such as tweed.

It is also important to recognize that polyphonic music automatically has harmony. For at every moment in time, on every beat, the multiple horizontal melodies create vertical chords; those chords make harmony.

A word often used for polyphonic texture is *contrapuntal,* which comes from the word **counterpoint,** the technique of writing two or more melodies that fit together. Strictly speaking, polyphony refers to the texture and counterpoint to the technique of producing that texture—one *writes* counterpoint to *produce* polyphony—but in practice the two terms are used interchangeably.

Imitation

In fact polyphonic texture, like so many other musical elements, cannot be categorized with any precision. It is impossible to distinguish all the kinds of polyphony found in Western music, to say nothing of the enormously intricate kinds in non-Western musics.

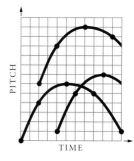

One useful and important distinction, however, is between *imitative polyphony* and *non-imitative polyphony.* **Imitative polyphony** results when the various lines sounding together use the same or fairly similar melodies, with one coming in shortly after another. The simplest example of imitative polyphony is a round, such as "Row, Row, Row Your Boat" or "Frère Jacques"; the richest kind is a fugue (see Chapter 8). When people sing a round, by singing the same tune at staggered time intervals, the result is imitative polyphony:

Non-imitative polyphony occurs when the melodies are essentially different from one another. An example that many will know is the typical texture of a New Orleans jazz band, with the trumpet playing the main tune flanked top and bottom by the clarinet and the trombone playing exhilarating melodies of their own. Here is a made-up example of non-imitative polyphony, with a new melody added to the tune of "Row, Row, Row Your Boat":

LISTEN
for texture

8, 9

A famous passage from Beethoven furnishes a clear example of *monophonic, polyphonic,* and *homophonic textures*—the initial presentation of the so-called Joy Theme in Symphony No. 9, the "Choral" Symphony. The theme, a tune known around the world, takes its name from the words it is set to, an enthusiastic ode to the joy that comes from human freedom, companionship, and reverence for the Deity. The words are sung by soloists and a chorus.

But before anyone sings, the theme is played several times by the orchestra, in a way that suggests that joy is emerging out of nothingness into its full realization. Beginning with utterly simple *monophony,* and growing successively higher and louder, it is enriched by *polyphony* and then reaches its grand climax in *homophony.*

8	0:00	Joy Theme	Low register	*Monophony:* a single melodic line; cellos and double basses playing together, with no accompaniment whatsoever
	0:49	Theme	An octave higher	*Polyphony, non-imitative:* the theme with two lines of *counterpoint,* in low strings (cello) and a mellow wind instrument (bassoon)
	1:36	Theme	Two octaves higher	
	2:21	Theme	Three octaves higher	*Homophony:* full orchestra with trumpets prominent

Our example of *imitative polyphony* comes from the *Symphony of Psalms,* another symphony with chorus, a major work by the twentieth-century composer Igor Stravinsky. For brief characterizations of the instruments that play the contrapuntal lines, see Interlude B on pages 38–39.

9	0:00	A slow, winding melody, unaccompanied, played by a wind instrument (oboe)
	0:25	The same melody enters in another instrument (flute), as the oboe continues with new material; this produces two-part *imitative counterpoint.*
	0:58	Third entry, second flute plays in a lower register —three-part counterpoint
	1:19	Fourth entry, second oboe —four-part counterpoint

This imaginative portrayal of imitative counterpoint is like our first pitch/time graph on page 24, at least in principle. Paul Klee (1879–1940) titled this painting *Fugue in Red*; a fugue is the supreme example of imitative texture, as we shall see.

4 Tonality and Modality

Tonality and modality are aspects of harmony, and as such they could logically have been taken up at an earlier point in this chapter. We have deferred them till last because, more than the other basic structures of music, these require careful explanation.

Tonality

We start with a basic fact about melodies and tunes: Melodies nearly always give a sense of focusing around a single "home" pitch that feels more important than do all the other members of the scale. Usually this is *do* in the *do re mi fa sol la ti do* scale. This pitch feels fundamental, and on it the melody seems to come to rest most naturally. The other notes in the melody all sound close or remote, dissonant or consonant, in reference to the fundamental note, and some of them may actually seem to "lean" or "lead" toward it.

This homing instinct that we sense in melodies can be referred to in the broadest terms as the feeling of **tonality**. The music in question is described as **tonal**. The "home" pitch (*do*) is called the *tonic pitch*, or simply the **tonic**.

The easy way to identify the tonic is to sing the whole melody through, because the last note is almost invariably *it*. Thus "The Star-Spangled Banner" ends on its tonic, *do*. (It also includes the tonic pitch in two different octaves as its first two accented notes: "Oh, *say* can you *see*.") An entire piece of music, as well as just a short melody, can give this feeling of focusing on a home pitch and wanting to end there.

The difficulty of describing the facts of tonality is not the difficulty of describing red to the color-blind. It is the difficulty of describing red to anybody; you can only point to red things and hope that other people see them as you do. It is even more like trying to describe the taste of a peach. . . .

Sir Donald Tovey, pianist, conductor, and educator, 1935

Modality: Major and Minor

Turn back to page 17 and the diagram of the diatonic scale, the basic scale of Western music. We have been speaking of melodies in the *do re mi fa sol la ti do* segment of this scale focusing on *do* as their tonic. But there is another important class of melodies that focus on *la* as tonic. The term for these different ways of centering or organizing the diatonic scale is **modality**; the different "home" pitches are said to determine different **modes** of music.

We will get to the actual listening experience of the modes in a moment. Music with the *do* center is in the **major mode**. Music with the *la* orientation is in the **minor mode**.

Keys

Mode and key are concepts that are often confused. Let us see if we can clarify them.

We have just seen how the two modes, the major with its "tonic" or home note on C and the minor on A, are derived from the diatonic scale (and this was the way it happened in history). At the piano, if you try to play a scale starting with any other note of the diatonic scale—D, E, F, or B—you will find that in each case, if you stick to the white notes, the arrangement of intervals is different from that of either the major or the minor mode. The scales you play will sound wrong.

However, if you avail yourself of all the twelve notes of the *chromatic* scale, the black notes as well as the white, you can construct both the major and the minor modes starting from any note at all. Whichever note you choose as tonic, starting from there you can pick out the correct sequence of half steps and whole steps. (This is because the chromatic scale is "symmetrical"—it includes all possible half steps and whole steps.) If C is the starting point, the major mode comes out all on the white notes; if the same mode is started from D, two black notes are required, and so on.

Thanks to the chromatic scale, then, many positions are possible for the major and minor modes. These different positions are called **keys.** If the major mode is positioned on C, the music is said to be in the key of C major, or just "in C"; positioned on D, the key is D major. Likewise we have the keys of C minor, D minor, and—since there are twelve pitches in the chromatic scale—a grand total of twenty-four different major and minor keys.

This already hints at an important resource available to composers: the possibility of changing (or moving) from one key to another. Changing keys in the course of a composition is called **modulation**.

Hearing the Major and Minor Modes

On paper, it is easiest to show the difference between major and minor if we compare a major and minor key that has the same tonic: C major and C minor. We therefore *modulate* (see above!) from the A-minor scale shown in the previous diagram to C minor:

Is it fair to represent the major and minor modes by comedy and tragedy masks? Yes, but only in a very general sense—there are many "delicate nuances," as Schumann put it.

The difference between the modes is easy to see: Three of the scale degrees are lower in the minor (hence the term "minor," of course). This means that the arrangement of intervals is not the same when you sing up the scale, and this in turn makes a great difference in the "feel" of the modes.

Easy to see—but *hearing* the difference is another matter. This comes easily to some listeners, less easily to others. As a result of the three lower scale degrees, music in the minor mode tends to sound more subdued, more clouded than music in the major. It is often said that major sounds cheerful and minor sounds sad, and this is true enough in a general way; but there are many exceptions, and in any case people can have different ideas about what constitutes "sadness" and "cheerfulness" in music.

Learning to distinguish the major and minor modes requires comparative listening. Listen especially for the third scale degree up from the tonic. "Joshua Fit the Battle of Jericho," "Summertime," and "We Three Kings of Orient Are" are all in the minor mode. Singing them through, we come to recognize the characteristic minor-mode sound involving the third scale degree at the final cadence.

Joshua Fit the Battle of Jericho

walls came tum-blin' down.

Summertime

don't ___ you   cry. ___

We Three Kings

fol-low-ing yon - der star.

Compare this with the third note up from the tonic at the end of major-mode songs such as "Happy Birthday to You," "Row, Row, Row Your Boat," "The Star-Spangled Banner," and many others. It sounds brighter, more positive.

Happy Birthday to You

Hap-py birth-day to you!

Row, Row, Row Your Boat

life   is but   a dream.

The Star-Spangled Banner

home   of   the   brave.

And here is the whole of "Row, Row, Row Your Boat" one more time—but this time in an altered version, with the mode switched from major to minor. Can you sing it?

Row, row, row your boat   gently down the   stream,   Merrily,   merrily, merrily,   merrily, life is but a   dream.

Hearing Keys and Modulation

The major and minor modes can be said to differ from one another "intrinsically," for in each mode the pitches form their own special set of intervals and interval relationships. As we have seen, C major and C minor, while sharing the same central or tonic note, have their own individual arrangements of half- and whole-step intervals.

Different keys, however, merely entail the same set of intervals moved to a new position within the pitch continuum. This is a significant difference, but not an "intrinsic" one. First base is different from second base, but only because the same sort of bag, intrinsically, has been put in a significant new place.

As for actually *hearing* keys—that is, recognizing the different keys and the modulations between them—for some listeners this presents an even greater problem than hearing modality, though to others it comes more easily. The latter are the fortunate ones born with perfect pitch, the innate faculty of identifying pitches the way most people can identify colors.

However, this is not the great boon of nature it is sometimes believed to be. The important thing is not to be able to identify keys in themselves, but rather to be able to hear when keys change. For modulating or changing the key of music changes its mood or the way it feels; generations of composers have used this resource for some of their most powerful effects, as we shall see. And in large compositions we can hear *changes* of tonality, that is, changes of the tonic or "home" note, whether or not we were born with perfect pitch.

Indeed, we hear such changes instinctively in shorter compositions. If you know "The Twelve Days of Christmas," you will remember the modulation at the words "Five gold rings." (Try singing this cumulative carol all the way through leaving out the fifth gift with its modulation—the result is utter monotony.) In another Christmas carol, "Deck the Halls," modulation causes an agreeable little lift at the end of the third line, "Don we now our gay apparel, *Fa-la la, la-la la, la la la.*"

At hard-fought baseball and basketball games the organist plays a little musical figure over and over, higher and higher, louder and louder. This is brute-force modulation, and like all modulations, it changes the mood and the way you feel—it makes you feel *excited*.

The "Structures of Music" we have discussed in this chapter apply particularly to Western classical music. Two points need to be made regarding other musical traditions, outside of the European orbit.

First, questions of melody, texture, harmony, and tonality are fully as important in understanding most of these other musics as they are in understanding music closer to home. This will be clear from our discussions in the Global Perspectives sections throughout the book. But second, each musical tradition tends to have its own characteristic ways of approaching the structures of music. What counts as a tune, which textures are preferred above others, how tonality is asserted, even which combinations of pitches are considered conso-

LISTEN
for mode and key

10, 11, 12

The difference between the *major* and *minor modes* is most obvious, perhaps, when a distinctive musical fragment in one mode is repeated in the other mode—soon enough so that both can be kept clearly in mind. This happens at the end of a very short piano piece by Schubert, Moment Musical in F Minor ("Musical Moment"—not Schubert's title, but his publisher's).

The phrases in this Moment Musical are in two different *keys:* the first in a minor key (the F minor of the title), the second in a major key, with the third starting in minor and ending in major.

10	0:00	*p:* Introduction
	0:02 **Phrase 1 (played twice)**	Begins and ends in *minor* mode
	0:26 **Phrase 2 (twice)**	New key: begins and ends in the *major*
	0:49 **Phrase 3 (twice)**	*f:* Begins in the key of phrase 1 (*minor*) and ends in the key of phrase 2 (*major*)
	1:14 **Phrase 1 returns, once**	*pp:* (original minor key) New continuation—repeated cadences, using fragments of phrase 1
	1:36	Turns to the *major* mode

For a series of fast *modulations,* turn to a passage from Beethoven's Piano Concerto No. 5, the "Emperor" Concerto. Here key changes are easy to hear because the modulations are carried out so brusquely—a Beethoven specialty—and also because the music in between them is harmonically very simple.

11	0:00	Lively music for the piano, *f,* followed by a *f* response from the orchestra
	0:28	Modulation (French horns)
		New key: here similar music for piano is heard, *pp,* and the same orchestral response, *f*
	1:03	Similar modulation
		New key: piano, *p,* and orchestra, *f,* as before
	1:36	The piano bursts in, *f,* in the same key but in the *minor mode;* begins modulating to further new keys in a more complicated way than before

The example that follows won't mean much to you unless you know the venerable round "Frère Jacques" ("Are you sleeping"). Gustav Mahler, in his Symphony No. 1, writes a bizarre, slow version of "Frère Jacques" *in the minor mode.* This is vivid evidence of how music's mood changes when the mode changes.

12	0:00	Drum beat
	0:07	"Frère Jacques" melody enters in the minor
	0:27	Melody repeated by various instruments, as in a round: This is low-lying *imitative polyphony.*

nant or dissonant—all these differ widely from tradition to tradition. They may even differ from style to style within a single tradition.

As a result, the vocabulary we develop here for Western music cannot, in its most specific form, encompass all this variety. But the general issues raised in this vocabulary are issues you will meet also in musics from around the world.

Web: *To test your understanding of the structures of music, take an online quiz at* <bedfordstmartins.com/listen>.

INTERLUDE B: Musical Instruments

17-22

Different voices and different instruments produce different tone colors, or timbres. Over the course of history and over the entire world, an enormous number of devices have been invented for making music, and the range of tone colors they can produce is almost endless.

This interlude will discuss and illustrate the instruments of Western music that make up the orchestra, and a few others. Later, in our Global Perspectives sections, we will meet many instruments from other musical traditions.

Musical instruments can be categorized into four groups: *stringed instruments* or *strings, woodwinds, brass,* and *percussion.* Musical sound, as we know, is caused by rapid vibrations. Each of the four groups of instruments produces sound vibrations in its own distinct way.

Stringed Instruments

These are instruments that have their sound produced by taut strings. The strings are always attached to a "sound box," a hollow box containing a body of air that resonates (that is, vibrates along with the strings) to amplify the string sound.

The strings themselves can be played with a bow, as with the violin and other orchestral strings; the *bow* is strung tightly with horsehair, which is coated with a substance called rosin, so that the bow grips the strings. Or else the strings can be plucked or strummed, as on the guitar or the harp, using the fingers or a small pick.

Strings can be plucked on bowed instruments, too, for special effects. This is called **pizzicato.**

Listen to The Young Person's Guide to the Orchestra, *by Benjamin Britten: See page 53.*

The Violin and Its Family The **violin** is often called the most beautiful instrument used in Western music. Also one of the most versatile of instruments, its large range covers alto and soprano registers and many much higher pitches. As a solo instrument, it can play forcefully or delicately, and it excels in both brilliant and songlike music. Violinists also play chords by bowing two or more of the four strings at once, or nearly so.

As in a guitar, the (four) violin strings are stopped with a finger—that is, pressed down on the "neck" of the violin under the strings—to shorten the string length and get different pitches (see the illustrations below). Unlike a guitar, a violin has no frets, so the player has to feel for the exact places to press.

The violin is an excellent ensemble instrument, and it blends especially well with other violins. An orchestra violin section, made up of ten or more instruments playing together, can produce a strong, yet sensitive, flexible tone. Hence the orchestra has traditionally relied on strings as a solid foundation for its composite sound.

Like most instruments, violins come in *families,* that is, in several sizes with different pitch ranges. Three members of the violin family are basic to the orchestra.

The **viola** is the tenor-range instrument, larger than a violin by several inches. It has a throaty quality in its lowest range, from middle C down an octave; yet it fits especially smoothly into accompaniment textures. The viola's highest register is powerful and intense.

The violin family: violin, viola, and cello

Violin ➤

⁷   The **cello,** short for *violoncello,* is the bass of the violin family. This large instrument is played between the legs. Unlike the viola, the cello has a rich, gorgeous sound in its low register. It is a favorite solo instrument, as well as an indispensable member of the orchestra.

Bass Viol   Also called **string bass, double bass,** or just **bass,** this deep instrument is used to back up the violin family in the orchestra. (However, in various details of construction the bass viol differs from members of the violin family; the bass viol actually belongs to another, older stringed instrument family, the *viol* family.)

Played with a bow, the bass viol provides a splendid deep support for orchestral sound. The bass viol is often (in jazz, nearly always) plucked to give an especially vibrant kind of accent and to emphasize the meter.

Harp   **Harps** are plucked stringed instruments with one string for each pitch available. The modern orchestral harp is a large instrument with forty-seven strings covering a range of six and a half octaves. A pedal mechanism allows the playing of chromatic (black-key) as well as diatonic (white-key) pitches.

In most orchestral music, the swishing, watery quality of the harp is treated as a striking occasional effect rather than as a regular timbre.

Woodwind Instruments

As the name indicates, woodwind instruments were formerly made of wood, and some still are; but today certain woodwinds are made of metal. Sound in these instru-

Cellist Yo-Yo Ma—perhaps this country's preeminent instrumentalist, certainly the most versatile and most honored.

◄ Orchestral harp   Orchestras usually have two or three *oboes:* See page 39.

Flutist James Galway

Clarinetist Sabine Meyer

ments is created by setting up vibrations in the column of air in a tube. A series of precisely spaced holes are bored in the tube, which the player opens or closes with his fingers or with a lever device. (This channels the air into columns of different lengths, producing all the different pitches of the scale.)

Of the main woodwind instruments, *flutes, clarinets,* and *oboes* have approximately the same range. All three are used in the orchestra because each has a quite distinct tone quality, and composers can obtain a variety of effects from them. It is not hard to learn to recognize and appreciate the different sounds of these woodwinds.

The Flute and Its Family   The **flute** is a long cylinder, held horizontally; the player sets the air vibrating by blowing through a side hole. The flute is the most agile of the woodwind instruments and also the gentlest. It nonetheless stands out clearly in the orchestra when played in its high register.

⁊   The **piccolo,** the small, highest member of the flute family, adds special sparkle to band and orchestral music.

⁊   The **alto flute** and **bass flute**—larger flutes—are less frequently employed.

⁊   The **recorder,** a different variety of flute, is blown not at the side of the tube but through a mouthpiece at the end. Used in older orchestral music, the recorder was superseded by the horizontal, or "transverse," flute because the latter was more agile and stronger.

In the late twentieth century recorders made a comeback for modern performances of old music using reconstructed period instruments. The instrument is also popular (in various family sizes) among musical amateurs today. It is easy to learn and fun to play.

Clarinet   The **clarinet** is a slightly conical tube made, usually, of ebony (a dark wood). The air column is not made to vibrate directly by blowing into the tube, as with the flute. The way the player gets sound is by blowing on a reed—a small piece of cane fixed at one end—in much the same way as one can blow on a blade of grass held taut between the fingers. The vibrating reed vibrates the air within the clarinet tube itself.

Compared to the flute, clarinet sound is richer and more flexible, more like the human voice. The clarinet is capable of warm, mellow tones and strident, shrill ones; it has an especially intriguing quality in its low register, below middle C.

The small **E-flat clarinet** and the large **bass clarinet** are family members with a place in the modern orchestra. The tube of the bass clarinet is so long that it has to be bent back, like a thin black saxophone.

Oboe The **oboe,** pictured on page 37, also uses a reed, like the clarinet, but it is a double reed—two reeds lashed together so that the air must be forced between them. This kind of reed gives the oboe its clearly focused, crisply clean, and sometimes plaintive sound.

The **English horn** is a larger, lower oboe, descending into the viola range. (Scores often give the French equivalent, *cor anglais;* in either language, the name is wildly deceptive, since the instrument is not a horn but an oboe, and it has nothing to do with England.)

Bassoon The **bassoon** is a low (cello-range) instrument with a double reed and other characteristics similar to the oboe's. It looks somewhat bizarre: The long tube is bent double, and the reed has to be linked to the instrument by a long, narrow pipe made of metal. Of all the double-reed

Bassoon (with a clarinet in the background)

woodwinds, the bassoon is the most varied in expression, ranging from the mournful to the comical.

The **contrabassoon** or **double bassoon** is a very large member of the bassoon family, in the bass viol range.

Saxophone The **saxophone** is the outstanding case in the history of music of the successful invention of a new instrument family. Its inventor, the Belgian instrument maker Adolphe Sax, also developed saxhorns and other instruments. First used around 1840 in military bands, the saxophone (or "sax") is sometimes included in the modern orchestra, but it really came into its own in jazz.

Saxophones are close to clarinets in the way they produce sound. Both use single reeds. Since the saxophone tube is wider and made of brass, its tone is even mellower than that of the clarinet, yet at the same time more forceful. The long saxophone tube has a characteristic bent shape and a flaring "bell," as its opening is called.

Most common are the **alto saxophone** and the **tenor saxophone.** But the big family also includes *bass, baritone, soprano,* and even *contrabass* (very low) and *sopranino* (very high) members. An alto saxophone is illustrated across from page 1.

Brass Instruments

The brass instruments are the loudest of all the wind instruments because of the rather remarkable way their sound is produced. The player blows into a small cup-shaped mouthpiece of metal, and this actually sets the player's lips vibrating. The lip vibration activates vibration of the air within the brass tube.

All brass instruments have long tubes, and these are almost always coiled in one way or another—something that is easy to do with the soft metal they are made from.

Trumpet The **trumpet,** highest of the main brass instruments, has a bright, strong, piercing tone that provides the ultimate excitement in band and orchestral music alike. Pitch is controlled by three pistons or valves that connect auxiliary tubes with the main tube or disconnect them, so as to lengthen or shorten the vibrating air column.

French Horn The **French horn** has a lower, mellower, "thicker" tone than the trumpet. It is capable of mysterious, romantic sounds when played softly; played loudly, it can sound like a trombone. Chords played by several French horns in harmony have a rich, sumptuous tone.

Trombone The **tenor trombone** and the **bass trombone** are also pitched lower than the trumpet. The pitch is controlled by a sliding mechanism (thus the term "slide trombone") rather than a valve or piston, as in the trumpet and French horn.

French horn and timpani

Less bright and martial in tone than the trumpet, the trombone can produce a surprising variety of sounds, ranging from an almost vocal quality in its high register to a hard, powerful blare in the low register.

Tuba The **bass tuba** is typically used as a foundation for the trombone group in an orchestra. It is less flexible than other brass instruments. And like most other deep bass instruments, it is not favored for solo work.

Other Brass Instruments All the brass instruments described so far are staples of both the orchestra and the band. Many other brass instruments (and even whole families of instruments) have been invented for use in marching bands and have then sometimes found their way into the orchestra.

Among these are the *cornet* and the *flügelhorn,* which resemble the trumpet, the *euphonium, baritone horn,* and *saxhorn,* which are somewhere between the French horn and the tuba, and the *sousaphone,* a handsome type of bass tuba named after the great American bandmaster and march composer, John Philip Sousa.

Finally there is the *bugle.* This simple trumpetlike instrument is very limited in the pitches it can play because it has no piston or valve mechanism. Buglers play "Taps" and military fanfares and not much else.

The way buglers get different pitches is by "overblowing," that is, by blowing harder into the mouthpiece so as to get strong partials (see page 9). Overblowing is, indeed, a basic, important resource of all wind instruments.

Percussion Instruments

Instruments in this category produce sound by being struck (or sometimes rattled, as with the South American maraca). Some percussion instruments, such as drums and gongs, have no fixed pitch, just a striking tone color. Other percussion instruments, such as the vibraphone, have whole sets of wooden or metal elements tuned to regular scales.

Timpani The **timpani** (or *kettledrums*) are large hemispherical drums that can be tuned precisely to certain low pitches. They are used in groups of two or more. As with most drums, players can obtain different sounds by using different kinds of drumsticks, tapping at different places on the drumhead, and so on.

Timpani are tuned by tightening the drumhead by means of screws set around the rim. During a concert, one can often see the timpani player, when there are rests in the music, leaning over the drums, tapping them quietly to hear whether the tuning is just right. Also available is a pedal mechanism to retune the timpani instantaneously.

Since they are tuned to precise pitches, timpani are the most widely used percussion instruments in the orchestra. They have the effect of "cementing" loud sounds when the whole orchestra plays.

Pitched Percussion Instruments These are all "scale" instruments, capable of playing melodies and consisting of whole sets of metal or wooden bars or plates struck with sticks or hammers. While they add unforgettable special sound effects to many compositions, they are not usually

The trombones with their horizontal slides, sousaphones with their dramatic bells: a striking Navy Band picture.

heard consistently throughout a piece, as the timpani are. They differ in their materials:

ª   The **glockenspiel** has small steel bars. It is a high instrument with a bright, penetrating sound.

ª   The **xylophone** has hardwood plates or slats. It plays as high as the glockenspiel but also lower, and it has a drier, sharper tone.

ª   The **marimba,** an instrument of African and South American origins, is a xylophone with tubular resonators under each wooden slat, making the tone much mellower.

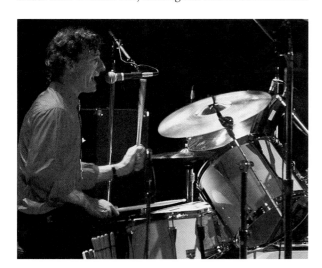

Drum kit with cymbals

ª   The **vibraphone** has metal plates, like a glockenspiel with a large range, and is furnished with a controllable electric resonating device. This gives the "vibes" a flexible, funky quality unlike that of any other instrument.

ª   Like the glockenspiel, the **celesta** has steel bars, but its sound is more delicate and silvery. This instrument, unlike the others in this section, is not played directly by a percussionist wielding hammers or sticks. The hammers are activated from a keyboard; a celesta looks like a miniature upright piano.

ª   **Tubular bells** or **chimes** are hanging tubes that are struck with a big mallet. They sound like church bells.

Unpitched Percussion Instruments In the category of percussion instruments without a fixed pitch, the following are the most frequently found in the orchestra:

ª   **Cymbals** are concave metal plates, from a few inches to several feet in diameter. In orchestral music, pairs of large cymbals are clapped together to support climactic moments in the music with a grand clashing sound.

ª   The **triangle**—a simple metal triangle—gives out a bright tinkle when struck.

ª   The **tam-tam** is a large unpitched gong with a low, often sinister quality.

ª   The **snare drum, tenor drum,** and **bass drum** are among the unpitched drums used in the orchestra.

ORCHESTRAL SEATING PLAN

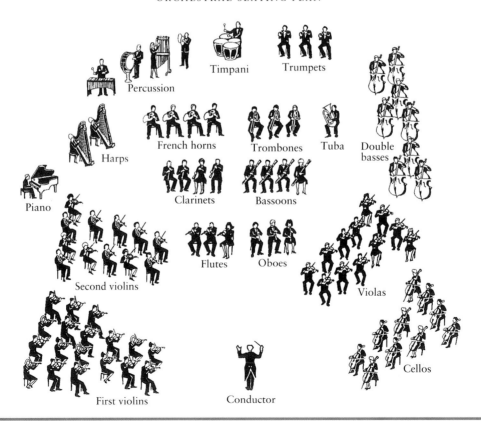

The Orchestra

The orchestra has changed over the centuries just as greatly as orchestral music has. Bach's orchestra in the early 1700s was about a fifth of the size of the orchestra required by ambitious composers today. (See pages 123, 173, and 244 for charts showing the makeup of the orchestra at various historical periods.)

So today's symphony orchestra is a fluid group. Eighty musicians or more will be on the regular roster, but some of them sit out some of the pieces on almost every program. And freelancers have to be engaged for many special compositions in which composers have imaginatively expanded the orchestra for their own expressive purposes. A typical large orchestra today includes the following sections or *choirs:*

❧ *Strings:* about thirty to thirty-six violinists, twelve violists, ten to twelve cellists, and eight double basses.

❧ *Woodwinds:* two flutes and a piccolo, two clarinets and a bass clarinet, two oboes and an English horn, two bassoons and a contrabassoon.

❧ *Brass:* at least two trumpets, four French horns, two trombones, and one tuba.

❧ *Percussion:* one to four players, who between them manage the timpani and all the other percussion instruments, moving from one to the other. For unlike the violins, for example, the percussion instruments seldom have to be played continuously throughout a piece. If a composition uses a great deal of percussion—and many modern compositions do—more players will be needed.

There are several seating plans for orchestras; which is chosen depends on at least two factors. The conductor judges which arrangement makes the best sound in the particular hall. And some conductors feel they can control the orchestra better with one arrangement, some with another. One such seating plan is shown opposite.

Keyboard Instruments

Though most orchestras today include a pianist, the piano is a relatively new addition to the symphony orchestra. In earlier times, the orchestra regularly included another keyboard instrument, the harpsichord.

The great advantage of keyboard instruments, of course, is that they can play chords and full harmony as well as melodies. One can play a whole piece on a keyboard instrument without requiring any other musicians at all. Consequently the solo music that has been written for piano, harpsichord, and organ is much more extensive than (accompanied) solo music for other instruments—more extensive, and ultimately more important.

Piano The tuned strings of a **piano** are struck by felt-covered hammers, activated from a keyboard. Much technological ingenuity has been devoted to the activating mechanism, or *action*.

A fantastically ornamented Victorian square piano

An elaborately painted eighteenth-century harpsichord

The hammers must strike the string and then fall back at once, while a damping device made of felt touches the string to stop the sound instantly. All this must be done so fast that the pianist can play repeated notes as fast as the hand can move. Also, all possible shades of loudness and softness must lie ready under the player's fingers. This dynamic capability is what gave the piano its name: "piano" is short for *pianoforte*, meaning "soft-loud."

In the nineteenth century, the piano became *the* solo instrument. The list of great virtuoso pianists who were also major composers extends from Frédéric Chopin to Sergei Rachmaninov. At the same time, every middle-class household had a piano. Obligatory piano lessons served and still serve for millions of young people as a magical introduction to the world of music (we hope).

Harpsichord The **harpsichord** is an ancient keyboard instrument that has enjoyed a healthy revival in recent years for the playing of Baroque music, in particular.

Like the piano, the harpsichord has a set of tuned strings activated from a keyboard. The action is much simpler, however. There is no damping, and instead of hammers striking the strings, little bars flip up with quills that pluck them. This means, first, that the tone is brittle and ping-y. Second, it means that the player cannot vary dynamics; when a string is plucked in this way, it always sounds the same.

Harpsichord makers had to compensate for this limitation in dynamics by adding one or two extra full sets of strings, controlled by an extra keyboard. One keyboard could be soft, the other loud. A mechanism allowed the keyboards to be coupled together for the loudest sound of all.

In spite of its brittle tone and its lack of flexibility in dynamics, the harpsichord can be a wonderfully expressive instrument. Good harpsichord playing requires, first and foremost, great rhythmic subtlety.

Clavichord Another ancient keyboard instrument, the **clavichord**, was strictly for private use. Small and relatively inexpensive, its strings (only one set) are struck by simple metal levers. The clavichord has a very sensitive but also very quiet sound—it cannot be heard across a large room, let alone a concert hall.

A five-manual organ. The player pulls out *stops* (or *stop knobs*) to change the sets of pipes that sound.

Artists loved to paint lutes and lutenists: This is *A Young Man Playing a Lute* by the great early Baroque painter Michelangelo Merisi da Caravaggio (1573–1610).

Organ The **pipe organ** has a great many sets of tuned pipes through which a complex wind system blows air, again activated from a keyboard. The pipes have different tone colors; a large organ is capable of an almost orchestral variety of sound. Most organs have more than one keyboard to control different sets of the pipes. There is also a pedal board—a big keyboard on the floor, played with the feet—to control the lowest-sounding pipes.

Each set of tuned pipes is called a *stop;* a moderate-sized organ has forty to fifty stops, but much bigger ones exist. (The biggest organ on record, at Atlantic City, has 1477 stops, for a total of 33,112 pipes.) Called "the king of instruments," the pipe organ is certainly the largest of them. Organs need their size and power in order to provide enough sound to fill the large spaces of churches and cathedrals on a suitably grand scale.

The organ is not a member of the orchestra; but since the grandest occasions call for orchestra, chorus, vocal soloists, and organ combined (e.g., the *Messiah* at Christmastime: see page 156), a major symphony hall has to have its organ—usually an imposing sight.

Electronic Keyboard Instruments Today "keyboard" or "organ" generally means an electronic instrument. Synthesizers simulate the sound of organs, pianos, and harpsichords. Electronic pianos look like acoustic ones and sound quite like them, though the "feel" is different. They cost a great deal less.

Modern concert music, from the 1960s on, has occasionally used electronic keyboards. On the whole, however, synthesizers have been used more to compose concert music than to play it.

Plucked Stringed Instruments

Plucked stringed instruments figure much less in art music of the West than in Asian countries such as India and Japan, as we shall see. One exception is the orchestral harp: See page 37. The acoustic **guitar** and the **mandolin** are used very widely in Western popular music, but only occasionally in orchestras.

However, a now-obsolete plucked instrument, the **lute,** was of major importance in earlier times. One of the most beautiful-looking of instruments, the lute sounds rather like a gentle guitar. It differs in its rounded sound box, and in the way its pegboard is set nearly perpendicular to the neck. Large members of the lute family were the **theorbo** and the **archlute.**

Like keyboard instruments, plucked stringed instruments have been revolutionized by electronic technology. The **electric guitars** of rock music have rarely found their way into concert music.

Web: *Listen to individual instruments of the orchestra at* <bedfordstmartins.com/listen>.

Musical Form and Musical Style

F *orm* is a general word with a long list of dictionary definitions. As applied to the arts, **form** is an important concept that refers to the shape, arrangement, relationship, or organization of the various elements. In poetry, for example, the elements of form are words, phrases, meters, rhymes, and stanzas; in painting, they are lines, colors, shapes, and space.

1 Form in Music

In music, the elements of form and organization are those we have already discussed: rhythm, pitch and melody, dynamics, tone color, and texture. A musical work, whether a simple song or a symphony, is formed or organized by means of repetitions of some of these elements, and by contrasts among them. The repetitions may be strict or free (that is, exact or with some variation). The contrasts may be of many different kinds—the possibilities are virtually limitless—conveying many different kinds of feeling.

Over the centuries and all over the world, musicians have learned to create longer and more impressive pieces in this way: symphonies, operas, works for the Javanese gamelan or Japanese gagaku orchestras, and more. Each piece is a specific sound experience in a definite time span, with a beginning, middle, and end, and often with subtle routes between. Everyone knows that music can make a nice effect for a minute or two. But how does music extend itself—and hold the listener's interest—for ten minutes, or half an hour, or three whole hours?

This is one of the main functions of musical form. Form is the relationship that connects those beginnings, middles, and ends.

Form and Feeling

Form in art also has a good deal to do with its emotional quality; it is a mistake to consider form as a merely structural or intellectual matter. Think of the little (or big) emotional "click" we get at the end of a limerick, or a sonnet, where the accumulated meanings of the words are summed up with the final

Keep two things in mind, then. Remember the general outlines of the [outer form], and remember that the content of the composer's thought forces him to use that formal mold in a particular and personal way—in a way that belongs only to the particular piece that he is writing.

Aaron Copland, *What to Listen For in Music*

Music: an art of sound in time that expresses ideas and emotions *in significant forms* through the elements of rhythm, melody, harmony, and dynamics.

Webster's College Dictionary, 1991 (our italics)

rhyme. This is an effect to which form—limerick form or sonnet form—contributes. Similarly, when at the end of a symphony a previously heard melody comes back, with new orchestration and new harmonies, the special feeling this gives us emerges from a flood of memory; we remember the melody from before, in its earlier version. That effect, too, is created by musical form.

How easy is it, actually, to perceive form in music and to experience the feelings associated with form? Easy enough with a short tune, such as "The Star-Spangled Banner"—that's what our analysis on page 25 was all about. The various phrases of this tune, with their repetitions, parallel features, contrasts, and climax, provide a microcosm of musical form in longer pieces. A large-scale composition like a symphony is something like a greatly expanded tune, and its form is experienced in basically the same way.

To be sure, a symphony requires more from the listener—more time and more attention—than a tune does. Aware of the potential problem here, composers scale their musical effects accordingly. The larger the piece, the more strongly the composer is likely to help the memory along by emphasizing the repetitions and contrasts that determine the musical form.

Form and Forms

Like the word *rhythm* (see page 10), the word *form* has its general meaning and also a more specific one. "Form" in general refers to the organization of elements in a musical work, but "*a* form" refers to one of many standardized formal patterns that composers have used over the centuries.

Form in Poetry

Fleas:
Adam
Had 'em.

Poet Ogden Nash creates rhyme and meter to add a little lift, and a smile, to the prose observation "Adam had fleas" (or "Ever since Adam, we've all suffered").

Form in Painting

A Madonna by Raphael Sanzio (1483–1520), built out of two cunningly nested triangles. To balance the boys at the left, the Virgin faces slightly to the right, her extended foot "echoing" their bare flesh. On a larger scale, the activity at the left is matched by a steeper landscape.

Forms in this latter sense can be referred to as "outer" forms; the ones treated later in this book are listed in the margin. In most periods, artists in all media have tended to employ such outer forms. The fixed elements in them provide a welcome source of orientation for listeners, but they are always general enough to allow composers endless possibilities on the detailed level. The quality and feeling of works in the same outer form can therefore vary greatly. Or, to put it another way, any work adhering to a common "outer form" can also have an individual "inner form" of its own.

Musical forms, as standardized patterns, are conventionally expressed by letter diagrams, such as **A B A** or **a b a** (small letters tend to be used for shorter sections of music). More complicated forms come about through "nesting":

<table>
<tr><td>**A**</td><td>**B**</td><td>**A**</td></tr>
<tr><td>a b a</td><td>c d c</td><td>a b a</td></tr>
</table>

Two basic factors create musical form: *repetition* and *contrast*. In **A B A** form, one of the simplest and most familiar, the element of repetition is **A** and the element of contrast is **B**. Some sort of tune or theme or other musical section is presented at the beginning (**A**), then another section (**B**) that contrasts with the first, and then the first one again (**A**). If **A** returns with significant modification, a prime mark can be added: **A'**.

But this tells us only so much. With any particular work, what about the inner form: Is **B** in a different mode? A different key? Does it present material that contrasts in rhythm, texture, or tone color—or does it work its contrast by ringing changes on the original material, on **A**? The returns in **A B A'** form, too, can convey very different feelings. One return can sound exciting, another tricky, while yet another provides a sense of relief.

So identifying "outer forms"—getting the letters right—is just a preliminary step in musical appreciation. The real point about great music is the way composers refine, modify, and personalize outer forms for their own expressive purposes.

Form in Architecture

The central, contrasting unit of this building seems almost to flow into the unit at the right. The musical analogy would be to an interesting **A B A'** form, in which **A** comes back after **B** in an expanded version (**A'**), and that version includes some new rhythm or instrument that we first heard during **B**.

LISTEN
for musical form

13, 14-16

"The Star-Spangled Banner" is in one of simplest possible forms, **a a b**. See page 25. "Oh, say can you see . . . twilight's last gleaming" is **a**, "Whose broad stripes . . . gallantly streaming" is the second **a**, and the rest of the anthem is **b**. Section **b** makes a definitive contrast with **a** by means of its new melody and higher range.

When sections of music are not identical but considered essentially parallel, they are labeled **a, a′, a″**, etc., with prime marks. Small sections can be nested in larger ones that are marked with capital letters: **A A′**. Our example comes from *The Nutcracker* by Pyotr Ilych Chaikovsky, said to be America's favorite piece of classical music. Thousands attend performances of this childhood ballet every year, as a Christmas ritual.

Act II includes a set of delightful little dances, in contrasting styles. The first of these is the Dance of the Sugar-Plum Fairy (a sugar plum is a hard candy). Chaikovsky used this dance essentially to show off the celesta, a rare instrument hardly ever featured in this way (see page 41). The piece is in **A B A′** form, breaking down into **a a′ b b a a′**.

13	0:00		Introduction—the **2/4** meter is previewed by low string instruments.
	0:08	**A a**	Solo for celesta with comments by a bass clarinet
	0:23	**a′**	Like **a**—only the ending is different, on a new pitch and harmony
	0:37	**B b**	Contrasts with **a**
	0:44	**b**	
	0:51		Transition—the music has a preparatory quality
	1:07	**A′ a**	Celesta an octave higher—a very striking new sound—with a quiet new click in the violins
	1:22	**a′**	

This **A B A′** form gets its prime mark from the new orchestration, not from changes in melody or harmony, as is often the case. (More strictly, we could mark this form as **a a′ b b** *transition* **a″ a‴**, but these letter diagrams are only used to show broad outlines.)

For a longer example, listen to the whole third movement of Beethoven's Fifth Symphony. It's now necessary to listen on a much longer time scale, passing by the phrases to experience larger spans of music. Section **A**, for example, includes two very different themes and other material. And here section **A′** is very different from **A**, abbreviated and reorchestrated much more radically than in *The Nutcracker*. See page 231.

14	0:00	**A**	Includes two different themes: one *p* (string instruments), one *f* (brass instruments)
15	0:00	**B**	B contrasts radically with A; starting with the tone color of the double basses, virtually all of the musical elements differ—melody, rhythm, texture, and more—except for the **3/4** meter.
	1:03	*Transition*	
16	0:00	**A′**	Another radical contrast—a shortened version of **A**, with the motives and themes of A played very quietly and with different tone colors: *pizzicato* (plucked) strings, bassoon, and oboe instead of bowed strings and loud French horns
	1:16		The movement is over; another passage of transition to the next movement begins.

Musical Genres

One often hears symphonies, sonatas, and operas referred to as "forms" of music. Actually this is loose terminology, best avoided in the interests of clarity, because symphonies and other works can be composed in completely different forms ("outer forms")—that is, their internal orders or organizations can be of quite different kinds. Thus, the last movement of Joseph Haydn's Symphony No. 95 is in rondo form, whereas the last movement of Hector Berlioz's *Fantastic* Symphony follows no standard form whatsoever.

The best term for these general categories of music is *genre* (jáhn-ruh), borrowed from French. A genre can be defined by its text (a madrigal has Italian verses of a specific kind), or by its function (a Mass is written for a Roman Catholic service), or by the performing forces (a quartet is for four singers or instrumentalists). The main genres of Western music are listed in the margin. Other genres from other musical traditions will be encountered in the Global Perspectives sections.

2 Musical Style

Style, like *form,* is another of those broad, general words—general but very necessary. The style of a tennis player is the particular way he or she reaches up for the serve, swings, follows through on the forehand, hits the ball deep or short, and so on. A lifestyle means the whole combination of things one does and doesn't do: the food one eats, the way one dresses and talks, one's habits of thought and feeling.

The style of a work of art, similarly, is the combination of qualities that make it distinctive. One composer's style may favor jagged rhythms, simple harmonies, and tunes to the exclusion of other types of melody. Another may prefer certain kinds of tone color; still another may concentrate on a particular form. The type of emotional expression a composer cultivates is also an important determinant of musical style.

One can speak of the lifestyle of a generation as well as the lifestyle of a particular person. Similarly, a distinction can be made between the style of a particular composer and the style of a historical period. For example, to a large extent George Frideric Handel's manner of writing falls within the parameters of the Baroque style of his day. But some features of Handel's style are unique, and perhaps it is those features that embody his musical genius.

Musical Style and Lifestyle

In any historical period or place, the musical style bears some relation to the lifestyle in general; this seems self-evident. Perhaps the point is clearest of all with popular music, where distinct (and distinctly different) worlds are evoked by rock, rap, and country music, to say nothing of earlier styles such as 1950s rhythm and blues or 1930s swing.

Older styles of music, too, relate to total cultural situations, though how this works in detail is not fully understood. We can, however, at least suggest some of these musical-cultural relationships for music of the various historical periods. For each period, we will sketch certain aspects of the culture, history, and lifestyle of the time. We will then briefly outline the musical style and, wherever possible, suggest correlations. Then the musical style will be examined in more detail through individual composers and individual pieces of their music.

Even *where* people listen to music reflects their lifestyle. The Hollywood Bowl, which has been known to hold 26,000 people, flaunts both the superb topography of Los Angeles and also the blockbuster mentality that is the hallmark of the movie industry.

These individual pieces are our principal concern—not history, or culture, or concepts of musical style in the abstract. Learning the basic concepts of music (as we have tried to do in this unit) is useful only insofar as it focuses and sharpens the process of listening to actual music. This book is called *Listen,* and it rests on the belief that the love of music depends first and foremost on careful listening to particular pieces. But such listening never happens in a cultural vacuum. It always takes place in a vivid, experienced context of some kind. The general information we present here on history, culture, styles, and genres is intended to remake, in some small way, our own listening contexts—and hence reshape our listening experiences.

Coming to the end of Unit I, after a lot of prose and a number of hasty musical excerpts, we should listen to a whole composition at some length. A convenient one at this point is *The Young Person's Guide to the Orchestra,* by the English composer Benjamin Britten (1913–1976).

This is *the* ideal piece for learning the tone colors of the Western orchestra. Britten, who wrote a lot of music for children, undertook this *Guide* as a pedagogical responsibility—and as a challenge to his ingenuity—but he also set out to create a coherent and interesting musical composition. Listen to it primarily to come to know instrumental sounds, but also as a review of several concepts introduced in Unit I.

The work uses one basic theme—a short, rather bouncy tune by an earlier English composer, Henry Purcell (see page 102). After first displaying the grand sound of the full orchestra playing this tune, Britten has each of the four orchestral choirs play it: woodwinds, brass, strings . . . but he knew he had to cheat with the percussion. It was clever, then, to prepare for the not-very-thematic percussion statement at 1:21 by freeing up the theme a little in the preceding brass and stringed statements, and afterwards to remind us of the original tune, played by the full orchestra again. (Britten makes up for his cheat by a particularly brilliant percussion episode later.)

So far everything has been in the minor mode and in triple meter. But next comes a series of *variations* on the theme—versions of the theme varied in melody, rhythm, texture, mode, tempo, everything. We study variation form on page 132. The first section of the piece has given us a theme in the minor mode and its repetitions, but the first variations already switch to the major mode. Variation 3, in a swinging triple meter, is followed at once by a variation in duple meter. Many variations—variations 1, 3, and 4, to begin with—involve a great deal of repetition of a single motive. There are variations in fast tempo that last for hardly more than half a minute, and others in slow tempo that take nearly three times as long.

In variation form, variety is the order of the day. This central, variation section of the *Guide* offers, in addition to the catalogue of instrumental sounds, an equally dazzling catalogue of the endlessly varied moods that can be represented in music. Some variations are hardly more than half a minute long, others are slowed down to nearly three minutes.

At the end, Britten writes an extremely vigorous *fugue*, based on yet another version of the Purcell tune. We study fugue on page 105. For now, notice that this section of the *Guide* provides an excellent example of imitative polyphony.

And our virtuoso composer has still one more trick up his sleeve: He brings the tune back triumphantly just before the end, unvaried, while the fugue is still going on. Both can be heard simultaneously. This is non-imitative polyphony. The return of the tune wraps up the whole long piece very happily as a unique variety of **A B A′** form.

Web: *To test your understanding of musical form and style, take an online quiz at* <bedfordstmartins.com/listen>.

---

theme, page 26

tune, page 24
orchestral choirs, page 43

major and minor mode,
    page 32

duple and triple meter,
    pages 11–12
motive, page 26
tempo, page 14

polyphony, page 28

form, page 46

LISTENING CHART 2

Britten, *The Young Person's Guide to the Orchestra*   SG

17 min., 13 sec.   17-22

17	0:00 **THEME**	Full orchestra	Note the prominent *sequence* in the middle of the Purcell tune. You will hear snatches of this in some of the variations.
	0:19 Transition		*Diminuendo* (getting softer). Further transitions occurring between thematic statements and variations will not be indicated on this chart.
	0:23 Theme	WOODWIND choir	
	0:45 Theme	BRASS choir	Ending is changed.
	1:04 Theme	STRING choir	Theme is changed further.
	1:21	PERCUSSION	"Theme" only in principle; only some rhythms remain
	1:36 **THEME**	Full orchestra	Same as the first time
18	1:55 Variation 1	Flutes and piccolo	(harp accompaniment)
0:11	2:06		Piccolo and flute play in thirds.
0:35	2:30 Variation 2	Oboes	Beginning of the tune transformed into a slow, romantic melody in oboe 1; oboe 2 joins in two-part *polyphony.*
1:42	3:37 Variation 3	Clarinet family	Solos for bass clarinet (1:42), clarinet (1:57), and E-flat clarinet (1:46)
2:21	4:16 Variation 4	Bassoon	Typical qualities of the bassoon: *staccato* (comic effect) and *legato* (melodious)
19	5:15 Variation 5	Violins	With chordal accompaniment—particularly clear *homophonic* texture
0:33	5:48 Variation 6	Violas	Slower
1:53	7:08 Variation 7	Cellos	Another slow, romantic melody: falls into a a′ form (clarinet in the background)
2:53	8:08 Variation 8	Double bass	Solo—humorous
3:47	9:02 Variation 9	Harp	In the background is a string *tremolo,* caused by bowing a single note extremely rapidly, so that it sounds like a single "trembling" note.
20	10:01 Variation 10	French horns	
0:51	10:52 Variation 11	Trumpets	With snare drum, suggesting a fast military march
1:22	11:23 Variation 12	Trombones, tuba	Typical qualities of the trombone: humorously pompous, and mysterious chords
21	12:33 Variation 13	PERCUSSION	Timpani and bass drum (heard throughout the variation), cymbals (0:15), tambourine (0:26), triangle (0:29), snare drum (0:38), Chinese block (0:42), xylophone (0:48), castanets (1:00), gong (1:06), whip (1:14), marimba and triangle (1:40)
			Percussion instruments are described on page 40.
22	14:28 **FUGUE**		*Imitative polyphony* starts with flutes, then oboe, clarinet (same order as above!).
1:53	16:21 **THEME**		Climax: slower than before. The TUNE is superimposed on the fugue.

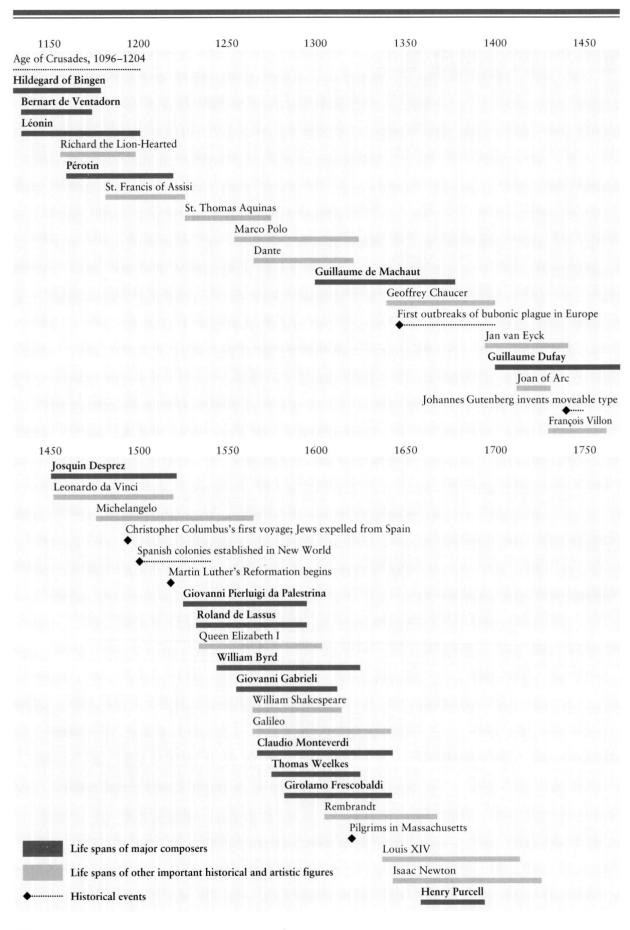

1150 1200 1250 1300 1350 1400 1450

Age of Crusades, 1096–1204

Hildegard of Bingen

Bernart de Ventadorn

Léonin

Richard the Lion-Hearted

Pérotin

St. Francis of Assisi

St. Thomas Aquinas

Marco Polo

Dante

Guillaume de Machaut

Geoffrey Chaucer

First outbreaks of bubonic plague in Europe

Jan van Eyck

Guillaume Dufay

Joan of Arc

Johannes Gutenberg invents moveable type

François Villon

1450 1500 1550 1600 1650 1700 1750

Josquin Desprez

Leonardo da Vinci

Michelangelo

Christopher Columbus's first voyage; Jews expelled from Spain

Spanish colonies established in New World

Martin Luther's Reformation begins

Giovanni Pierluigi da Palestrina

Roland de Lassus

Queen Elizabeth I

William Byrd

Giovanni Gabrieli

William Shakespeare

Galileo

Claudio Monteverdi

Thomas Weelkes

Girolamo Frescobaldi

Rembrandt

Pilgrims in Massachusetts

Louis XIV

Isaac Newton

Henry Purcell

Life spans of major composers

Life spans of other important historical and artistic figures

◆········· Historical events

Early Music: An Overview

W estern art music extends from the great repertory of Gregorian chant, assembled around the year 600 C.E., to electronic compositions that were programmed yesterday and today. One does not have to be a specialist to have some feeling for the sheer scope, variety, and bewildering richness of all this music. Some of it was developed to maintain Christianity through centuries of barbarism, some to glorify great monarchs such as Queen Elizabeth I of England or Louis XIV of France. Some of it is being produced in today's recording studios for the enjoyment, mainly, of connoisseurs. The field ranges from music attributed to the shadowy figures Léonin and Pérotin in the twelfth century, through compositions by familiar masters such as Bach and Beethoven, to work in progress saved on the hard drives at computer music centers in Paris or Berkeley, California. All of this music has fascinated, moved, and inspired its listeners.

Certainly there is too much here to cover in a single semester or quarter course—too much, that is, if one is going to do more than skim the music, picking up a few frantic facts and figures about it without really listening. It cannot be said often enough that listening to particular pieces again and again is the basic activity that leads to the love of music and to its understanding. A hurried survey does justice to none of the world's significant music; we have to make choices. We have: The essential coverage of this book begins in the eighteenth century, with Unit III and the music of Bach and Handel, who are the first composers with a long-standing place in the "standard repertory" of concert music. This phrase refers to a large but not limitless body of music from which concert artists and conductors usually draw their programs.

As an optional introduction to all of this, Unit II presents a brief overview of music before the eighteenth century. So-called Early Music was forgotten for centuries, and is still seldom performed at standard concerts. But in today's music world, less attuned to concerts than to recordings, Early Music has become familiar. It has its own musical institutions, its own specialist performers, and its own devotees, and through recordings it has also found its way into the musical mainstream.

CHAPTER 5

The Middle Ages

"The Middle Ages" is a catch-all term for nearly a thousand years of European history, extending from the collapse of the Roman Empire in the fifth century C.E. to the advent of new learning, technology, and political organization in the age of Columbus. Even though life and culture changed slowly in those days, this is obviously too broad a span of time to mean much as a single "period."

Nowhere is this clearer than in music. Music changed radically from the beginning to the end of the medieval era, more than in any other historical period. Two of the central principles of later Western music, *tune* and *polyphony*, originated around the middle of this long period.

Medieval musicians: The boy appears to be tuning his *vihuela*—a Spanish plucked stringed instrument—to the pitch being played by the older man (his teacher?).

1 Music and the Church: Plainchant

The early history of Western music was determined by the Christian Church to an extent that is not easy for us to grasp today. The church cultivated, supported, and directed music as it did art, architecture, poetry, and learning. All composers were in holy orders, and all musicians got their training as church choirboys. (Exception must be made for popular musicians—called minstrels and <u>jongleurs</u>—but we know next to nothing about their lives or their music. The only people who wrote music down were monks and other clerics, who could not have cared less about preserving popular music.)

The music cultivated by the church was the singing or chanting of sacred words in services, and we might pause for a moment to ask why singing was so important for Christian worship. One could point to traditions of singing in older religions from which Christianity borrowed much—especially the singing of psalms in the ancient Jewish synagogue. But this merely shifts the question: Why did ancient worshipers *sing* at all?

Singing is, first of all, a way of uttering words that sets them apart from ordinary speech. Words denote concepts, and singing words gives concepts in prayer or doctrine a special status, a step above merely speaking them. Music provides words with special emphasis, force, mystery, credibility, and even magic. Throughout human history, this heightening by music has served the basic aim of religion: to bring humans into beneficial contact with unseen spirits, with deities, or with a single God.

All the largest world religions—Islam, Hinduism, and Buddhism as well as Christianity and Judaism—possess and prize old and complex systems of chant. Most other, smaller religions do, too. (See Global Perspectives 1, pages 70–72.)

Music and Church Services

Sacred texts were sung at church services—and the life of the church centered in its services. The music that has come down to us was sung in monasteries and cathedrals, not humble parish churches; the services were conducted by and for the higher ranks of Christendom: monks, nuns, and cathedral clergy. And monks and nuns spent an amazing amount of their time in prayer. Besides the Mass, a lengthy ceremony that might happen more than once a day, there were no fewer than eight other services through the day and night, known collectively as the Divine Office. Large portions of these services were sung.

Though each service had its standard format, many details in the verbal texts for them changed according to the church calendar (Christmas, Easter, various saints' days, and so on). As a result, there were literally thousands of religious texts specified for the Mass and the Office throughout the year.

All these texts required music, but providing such music was less a matter of free invention than of small additions and adjustments to a sacrosanct, traditional prototype. And listening to it was not so much listening as worshiping, while allowing music to expand the devotional experience. Hearing Gregorian chant or later medieval music today, one feels less like a "listener" in the modern sense than like a privileged eavesdropper, someone who has been allowed to attend a select occasion that is partly musical, but mainly spiritual. The experience is an intimate and tranquil one, cool and, to some listeners, especially satisfying.

A psalm is the work of the Angels, the incense of the Spirit. Oh, how wise was that Teacher who found a way for us to sing psalms and at the same time learn worthwhile things, so that in some mysterious way doctrine is more deeply impressed upon the mind!

St. Basil, fourth century C.E.

Plainchant

The official music of the Catholic Church in the Middle Ages, and far beyond the Middle Ages, was a great repertory of melodies designated for the many religious texts to be sung at services throughout the year. This is the system of **plainchant** (or plainsong), widely known as Gregorian chant.

Clerics singing plainchant, depicted within an illuminated initial letter C in a late medieval manuscript. The whimsical little viol player is definitely outside the C, for instrumental music was taboo in church.

It is called "plain" because it is unaccompanied, monophonic (one-line) music for voices, without fixed rhythm or meter. And it is called "Gregorian" after the famous pope and church father Gregory I (c. 540–604); Gregory is reputed to have assembled and standardized all the basic chants required for the church services of his time. Many medieval plainchants were composed later, however, and so cannot strictly speaking be called "Gregorian." And even with truly Gregorian chant, we only know it by extrapolating backwards from later manuscripts. Notation for music of the Middle Ages did not begin to develop until around the ninth century C.E., long after Gregory.

Characteristics of Plainchant

Plainchant has many genres, differing widely in melodic style, depending on their religious function. Some plainchants consist of simple recitation on a monotone, with only slight deviations from that single pitch; in monasteries, the entire set of 150 psalms had to be sung in this fashion every week. Other chants are intricate songs with hundreds of notes ranging well over an octave. And still others count as the first real tunes that are known in Western music.

In whatever style or genre, all plainchants share two characteristic features. First, they are *nonmetrical*; they have no clearly established meter, and therefore the rhythm is free. Not only is a distinctive beat lacking in this music, but rhythms may change from one performance (rather, one service) to the next.

Second, plainchant is not construed in the major/minor system, but according to one of the **medieval modes.** As discussed in Unit I, the original scale of Western music was the diatonic scale—the "white-note" scale on the piano—and this is still the basic scale today. We use this scale oriented around the pitches C or A as "home" or tonic (see pages 31–32). Oriented around C, the music is said to be in the major mode, oriented around A, in the minor mode.

Musicians of the Middle Ages organized the scale differently—not around C or A, but around D, E, F, or G. The result was music in other modes, different from the modern major or minor. These modes were given numbers or Greek names (since medieval scholars traced them back to the modes of ancient Greek music, as discussed by Plato and others). The medieval modes are these:

Multicultural medieval music: At a time when half of Spain was in Arab (Moorish) hands, a Moor and a Spaniard are shown playing large vihuelas together. Plucked stringed instruments like the vihuela were an important novelty brought to medieval Europe from Arab countries.

The essential difference between the modern major and minor modes comes in the different arrangement of half steps and whole steps in their scales. The medieval modes provide four other arrangements. (Compare the preceding diagram with the one on page 31.) In this respect, then, medieval plainchant is actually richer and more subtle than music in the major/minor system. The artistic effect of plainchant—music without harmony or definite rhythm—is concentrated in melody, melody built on this rich and subtle modal system.

Gregorian Recitation

As we have said, the huge repertory of Gregorian chant ranges from simple recitation on a single pitch, with scarcely any variation, to long melodies that can make one dizzy by their endless, ecstatic twists and turns. Recitation was used for texts considered fairly routine in the services, such as lengthy readings from the Bible. Melody was used on more significant occasions, such as solemn church processions. (We will see an example of this use later.)

In Gregorian recitation, the pitch on which the text is sung, called the **reciting tone,** is held except for small, formulaic variations at beginnings and ends of phrases. These punctuate the text and make it easier to understand (and sing, since they give the singers time for a breath).

ANONYMOUS
Preface for Mass on Whit Sunday, "Vere dignum"

Our example is the music for a relatively minor text in the Mass, the Preface, which serves to introduce a much more important element in the service.* This

---

*The preface introduces the Elevation of the Host, where the priest celebrating Mass displays the bread and wine that is or represents the body and blood of Christ. By tasting these things, the faithful reaffirm their communion with Christ—the basic purpose of this service.

text consists of three sentences, recited in the same way. Each sentence is divided into three or four phrases, and the last of them changes to a new, second reciting tone, lower than the one at the start of the sentence. All the phrases have a little opening formula sliding up to the reciting tone—launching it, as it were—and a closing formula sinking down again. These are indicated only approximately on the chart below.

LISTEN   Preface for Mass on Whit Sunday, "Vere dignum"

The three sentences of the Preface text, each containing three or four phrases (a, b, c, d), are printed with their pitches roughly indicated by different levels. The **reciting tone** is shown in regular type, the opening and closing formulas in *italic*.

0:00   1[a] *Vere* dignum et justum est, aequum et salutare [b] *nos tibi* semper et ubique gratias *agere,*

0:24   [c] *Domine* sancte Pater, omnipotens aeterne Deus, [d] per Christum *Dominum nostrum.*

0:47   2[a] *Qui* post resurrectionem suam omnibus discipulis suis manifestus *apparuit,*

[b] *et* ipsis cernentibus est elevatus in coelum, [c] ut nos divinitatis suae tribueret *esse participes.*

1:29   3[a] *Et ideo cum* Angelis et *Archangelis,* [b] *cum* Thronis et Dominationibus, cumque omnia militia caelestis

exercitus [c] hymnum gloriae tuae canimus *sine fine dicentes:* [Sanctus, Domine Deus Sabaoth —not included in the recording]

1. It is truly meet and just, right and for our salvation, that we should at all times and in all places give thanks to Thee, O Lord, holy Father, almighty and eternal God, through Christ our Lord.

2. Who after His resurrection appeared openly to all His disciples, and while they looked on, was raised up into heaven, so that He might let us share in His own divinity.

3. And therefore with the Angels and Archangels, with the Thrones and Dominations, and with all the hosts of the heavenly army, we sing the hymn of Thy glory evermore, saying: ["Holy, holy, holy, Lord God of Sabaoth"]

Gregorian Melody

In addition to recitation, melody abounds in many different genres of plainchant. We will look first at one of the simplest genres, the **antiphon.**

ANONYMOUS
Gregorian antiphon, "In paradisum"

In the liturgy for the dead, this antiphon is sung in procession on the way from the final blessing of the corpse in church to the graveyard where burial takes place. "In paradisum" is in the Mixolydian (G) mode. Modal cadences are heard in lines 4 and 5, "Chorus An*gel*orum" and "quondam pau*pere.*"

The way to experience "In paradisum" is to place track 2 on repeat, and imagine yourself a medieval monk or nun who has lost a brother or sister. Candles have all been extinguished in the church after the Requiem Mass (so called because you have prayed for the soul's eternal rest—in Latin, *requiem aeternam*). As the coffin is lifted up, the priest begins "In paradisum," and then the entire religious community joins in. You sing this brief antiphon again and again, for as long as it takes the slow procession to reach the graveyard.

Notice that the beginning of "In paradisum" reveals its ultimate derivation from recitation; afterwards the music grows more and more melodic. The melodic highpoint comes in line 5, where the text refers to Lazarus, the poor man raised up from the grave by Christ—a point of identification for the humble mourners. This haunting melodic figure was etched in the memory of the Middle Ages through an endless succession of last rites.

| LISTEN | Gregorian antiphon, "In paradisum" | |

| | | 2 | 2 |

| 2 2 | 0:00 | In paradisum deducant te Angeli:
in tuo adventu suscipiant te Martyres,
et perducant te in civitatem sanctam Jerusalem. | May the Angels lead you to paradise,
and the Martyrs, when you arrive,
escort you to the holy city of Jerusalem. |
| | 0:39 | Chorus Angelorum te suscipiat,
et cum Lazaro quondam paupere
aeternam habeas requiem. | May the Angel choir sustain you,
and with Lazarus, who was once poor,
may you be granted eternal rest. |

HILDEGARD OF BINGEN (1098–1179)
Plainchant sequence, "Columba aspexit"

Abbess Hildegard of the little convent of Bingen, in western Germany, was one of the most remarkable figures of the Middle Ages. Most famous for her book relating her religious visions, she also wrote on natural history and medicine; she gained such renown that popes and emperors sought her counsel.

Five hundred years after Gregory I, the first compiler of Gregorian chants, Hildegard composed plainchant melodies in her own highly individual style to go with poems that she wrote for special services. "Columba aspexit" honored one of the many minor saints venerated in those days, Saint Maximinus. It belongs to a late medieval plainchant genre called the **sequence**.

The sequence is a much more elaborate kind of melody than the antiphon. It consists of a series of short tunes sung twice, with some variation (and an extra unit at the end: **A A′ B B′ C C′ . . . N**). A soloist sings **A**, the choir **A′**, and so on. "Modal" cadences—Mixolydian, once again—at the beginning of the melody ("fe*nes*trae," "*ei*us") give it a deceptively humble quality that contrasts with its ecstatic soaring later.

A miniature illustration of Hildegard, in one of her manuscripts, shows the miracle by which fire came down from heaven to engulf and inspire her.

Our recording includes an instrumental *drone*—a single two-note chord running continuously. Drones are known from music around the world as well as from European folk music, and there is evidence that drones were used to accompany plainchant, although medieval manuscripts do not confirm this. The drone, the mystical words of Hildegard's poem, and the free, surging rhythm of her music work together to produce a feeling of serene yet intense spirituality.

LISTEN			Hildegard of Bingen, "Columba aspexit"	

3	0:02	A	Columba aspexit	The dove entered
			Per cancellos fenestrae	Through the lattices of the window,
			Ubi ante faciem eius	Where, before its face,
			Sudando sudavit balsamum	Balm emanated
			De lucido Maximino.	From incandescent Maximinus.
	0:28	A′	Calor solis exarsit	The heat of the sun burned
			Et in tenebras resplenduit;	And dazzled into the gloom,
			Unde gemma surrexit	Whence a jewel sprang forth
			In edificatione templi	In the building of the temple
			Purissimi cordis benevoli.	Of the most pure loving heart.
	0:56	B	Iste turis . . .	He is the high tower of Lebanon . . .
	1:29	B′	Ipse velox . . .	The swift hart sped to the fountain . . .
	2:03	C	O pigmentarii . . .	O you makers of incense . . .
	3:15	D	O Maximine . . .	O Maximinus . . .

(two more stanzas)

2 Music at Court

Over the long span of the Middle Ages, kings and barons gained political power at the expense of the church. They also gradually assumed leadership in artistic matters. In the later Middle Ages, the princely courts joined the monasteries and cathedrals as major supporters of music.

Troubadour and Trouvère Songs

Large groups of court songs have been preserved from the twelfth and thirteenth centuries, the Age of Chivalry. The noble poet-composers of these songs—who, we are told, also performed the songs themselves—were called **troubadours** in the south of France, **trouvères** in the north, and **Minnesingers** in Germany (*Minne* means ideal or chivalric love). Among them were knights and princes, even kings—such as the most famous of all chivalric heroes, Richard I of England, "the Lion-Hearted." Troubadour society (but not trouvère society) also allowed for women troubadours, such as Countess Beatriz of Dia, Maria di Ventadorn, and others.

Perhaps some of these noble songwriters penned the words only, leaving the music to be composed by *jongleurs,* the popular musicians of the time. The music is relatively simple—just a tune, in most cases, with no indication of any accompaniment. We hear of jongleurs playing instruments while the trouvères sang; perhaps they improvised some kind of accompaniment, or played a drone, such as we heard in Hildegard's "Columba aspexit."

There are some very beautiful troubadour poems—crusaders' songs, laments for dead princes, and especially songs in praise of the poets' ladies, or complaints of their ladies' coldness. One interesting poetic type was the *alba,* the "dawn song" of a knight's loyal companion who has kept watch all night and now warns him to leave his lady's bed before the castle awakes. Another was the *pastourelle,* a (typically unsuccessful) seduction dialogue between a knight on horseback and a country maid.

My love and I keep state
In bower,
In flower,
Till the watchman on the
　　　　tower
Cry:
　"Up! Thou rascal, Rise,
　I see the white
　　　　Light
　　　And the night
　　　　　Flies."

—Troubadour alba

Left: More than a hundred German Minnesingers, from around 1200, are pictured in a later manuscript. The jongleurs directed by Heinrich Frauenlob (Henry Praiselady) play medieval equivalents of a drum, flute, oboe, viola, violin, harp, and bagpipe (left to right). The illustration on the right shows the Countess of Dia, one of a small number of women troubadours.

How Did Early Music Sound?

There is a special problem about old music, a problem that is less troublesome with music of more recent times: Although we have the scores of Early Music, often we do not have a clear idea of how it actually sounded.

One reason for this is that musical instruments have changed greatly over the centuries. Obsolete instruments have survived in an imperfect condition, and we can try to reconstruct them; but figuring out how they were actually played is much more speculative. As for singing, who can guess what a cathedral choir sounded like in the late Middle Ages, to take just one example? Since then, language itself has changed so much that it is hard enough to read a fourteenth-century poet such as Geoffrey Chaucer, let alone imagine how the words that he wrote were pronounced—or sung.

Composers of Early Music never indicated the tempo and rarely specified the instrumental or vocal forces that they anticipated for their music. With vocal pieces, they did not say whether a single singer or a whole choir was to sing. It has taken generations of patient research and experiment to "reconstruct," as it were, the probable sounds of Early Music.

The earliest music taken up in this book, Gregorian chant, is usually sung today in a performance style that was thought to be "historical" in the nineteenth century—this was the first of all Early-Music "reconstructions," in fact. Our recording of the antiphon "In paradisum" (page 60) adopts this familiar style.

In recent years, however, scholar-musicians have taken another look at history and proposed a different style—austere, less refined, and closer to other traditions of religious chanting that go back as far as Gregorian chant, such as the Qur'anic chanting discussed on pages 70–71. We hear this new "reconstruction" in the Preface "Vere dignum" (page 59).

BERNART DE VENTADORN (c. 1135–1194)
Troubadour song, "La dousa votz"

Bernart was one of the finest troubadour poets and probably the most important musically; other troubadour and trouvère songs were derived from some
of his pieces. Originally of humble background, he came to serve the powerful
Queen Eleanor of Aquitaine, wife of Henry II of England.

Like hymns and folk songs, troubadour songs set all their stanzas to the
same melody, resulting in what is called *strophic* form (**A A A . . .**); often each
stanza is in **a a′ b** form. "La dousa votz" is in the G (Mixolydian) mode:

La dousa votz ai au-zi - da Del rosin - ho-let sau - va-tge Et es m'insel cor salhi - da Si que tot lo co-si - rer

The performance on the recording stresses "secular" aspects of Bernart's song,
including an imaginative reconstruction of a possible instrumental accompaniment to it. It sounds far removed indeed from the spiritual atmosphere of
Hildegard of Bingen.

The language the troubadours spoke and wrote was Provençal, now almost
extinct. It combines elements from Old French and Old Spanish.

LISTEN		Bernart de Ventadorn, "La dousa votz"	

4 | 0:07 | *St. 1:* La dousa votz ai auzida | I have heard the sweet voice
| | Del rosinholet sauvatge | Of the woodland nightingale
| | Et es m'insel cor salhida | And my heart springs up
| | Si que tot lo cosirer | So that all the cares
| | E'ls mals traihz qu'amors me dona, | And the grievous betrayals love has given me
| | M'adousa e m'asazona. | Are softened and sweetened;
| | Et auria'm be mester | And I would thus be rewarded,
| | L'autrui joi al meu damnatge. | In my ordeal, by the joys of others.

| 0:48 | *St. 2:* Ben es totz om d'avol vida | In truth, every man leads a base life
| | C'ab joi non a son estatge . . . | Who does not dwell in the land of joy . . .

| 1:28 | *St. 3:* Una fausa deschauzida | One who is false, deceitful,
| | Trairitz de mal linhage | Of low breeding, a traitress
| | M'a trait, et es traida . . . | Has betrayed me, and betrayed herself . . .

The Estampie

There also survive a few—a very few—dances from the same court circles that
produced the chivalric trouvère repertory. Called **estampies,** they are unassuming
one-line pieces in which the same or similar musical phrases are repeated many
times in varied forms. (This suggests that these estampies may have been written-
down jongleur improvisations.) Estampies are marked by lively and insistent
rhythms in triple meter. Modern performers often add a touch of spice with
the help of percussion instruments.

This is a modest beginning to the long and important history of European
dance music. We shall pick it up again in the next chapter.

3 The Evolution of Polyphony

Polyphony—the simultaneous combination of two or more melodies—must have arisen in early Europe because people took pleasure in the sensuous quality of music, in the rich sounds of intertwining melodic lines with their resulting harmony. Many cultures all over the world have developed some kind of improvised polyphony, polyphony that is made up on the spot without the aid of written scores. (If you and someone you know can "sing in thirds" together, that is improvised polyphony.) Some other cultures, also, have traditions of complex, preplanned polyphony involving little or no improvisation.

We know about early European polyphony only from its uses within the church (for, once again, all we know about very early music comes from the writing of monks and other clerics). And within the church, the sensuous aspect of polyphony had to be rationalized away. Polyphony was seen as a way of embellishing Gregorian chants—that is, as yet another way of enhancing the all-important services.

More scenes of medieval music making. These and other miniatures in this chapter are from *Songs of the Virgin Mary,* written (or perhaps compiled) by King Alphonso X of Spain, "The Wise" (1252–1284), renowned for his support of learning and the arts.

Organum

The earliest type of polyphony is called **organum** (plural *organa*). First described theoretically in treatises around 900 C.E., actual organum has survived in musical notation from around 1000. Organum consists of a traditional plainchant melody to which a composer/singer/improviser has added another melody in counterpoint, sung simultaneously to the same words.

The history of organum between about 1000 and 1200 C.E. provides a fascinating record of growing artistic ambition and technical invention. We can trace a number of steps:

❧ Originally, each note of the chant was accompanied by another single note in the added melody (referred to as "the counterpoint"); the two melodies moved along with the same distance, or interval, between them. The rhythm of this early, so-called "parallel" organum was the free rhythm of Gregorian chant.

❧ Soon the counterpoint was treated more independently—it would sometimes go up when the chant went down, and vice versa.

❧ Next, the counterpoint began to include several notes at the same time as each single chant note. The embellishment process was growing richer. As more and more notes were crowded in, making richer and richer added melodies, the single chant notes were slowed down to surprising lengths, sounding finally like long drones.

❧ The next step was a radical one. Two counterpoints were added to the chant—which required much more skill from the composer, since the second counterpoint had to fit both the chant and also the first counterpoint.

Does the medieval word *organum* imply that early polyphony was accompanied by the organ? We do not know; but churches of the time certainly had organs. The keyboard of this medieval organ seems to have heavy levers rather than keys.

Notre Dame Cathedral in Paris. Flying buttresses—the great medieval engineering feat that made such high buildings possible—support the main structure (the nave). With its lofty front towers and its spire, Notre Dame seems to reach up to heaven itself.

¶   Equally radical was the idea of introducing definite rhythms controlled by meter. First the counterpoints and then the chant itself were set in lively rhythms. Fragments of the chant, too, were sometimes isolated and repeated many times, one after another.

Organum of these last, highly developed kinds flourished at the Cathedral of Notre Dame in Paris, which was built slowly over the period 1163–1235. The names of two composers of the so-called Notre Dame school are recorded: Master Léonin and his follower Pérotin (called "the Great"). Pérotin astonished thirteenth-century Paris by creating impressive organa for as many as four simultaneous voices.

PÉROTIN (c. 1200)
Organum, "Alleluia. Diffusa est gratia"

Many organa were composed for services devoted to the Virgin Mary, the patron saint of Notre Dame Cathedral. Our example is added to a chant for the Mass, "Alleluia. Diffusa est gratia." The music was probably written by Pérotin, though we cannot be certain.

At first the chant is sung—in the usual Gregorian way:

The whole chant is much longer, but this opening "Alleluia" section is the most important part—it comes back twice before the chant is over—and the most beautiful. The joyful exclamation "alleluia" is often set to **melismas,** passages of pure vocalism with many notes to a single syllable. The melisma on the syllable -*lu* rouses itself and then springs up still higher; then this melodic climax is balanced by a quiet, sinking "low climax" in phrase 3. After this (relative) excitement, phrase 4 stays within a calm range of four notes. This alleluia is a beautiful example of the characteristics of tunes discussed in Unit I: See page 25.

Then the organum starts. The voices begin with a strange, static harmony—which starts to sway, as it were, when the upper voices intertwine in various (triple-time) rhythms of the kind shown in the right margin of this page. They are singing long melismas on the syllables *Dif- fu- sa*, and so on.

Underneath, the lowest voice is singing the rest of the chant—but no longer in the characteristic free rhythm of Gregorian chanting. Sometimes the chant plods along in a stiff, regular rhythm (as at 1:21). Sometimes it is slowed down enormously (at 0:37, 1:07, and 1:33); at these points the chant is unrecognizable—it has been reduced to a series of lengthy drones. The plainchant has become a sort of musical scaffolding. Singers of organum need not attempt to bring out the chant voice. No longer perceivable as a melody, it is simply a constructive element supporting the ecstatic upper-voice melodies, which are the main focus of interest in this music.

Our recording takes a cut in this lengthy organum (the section indicated by italics below). It ends with a huge melisma on *de-* and a sort of shudder on the final syllable *-us*. Then plain, monophonic chanting is resumed, as the original "Alleluia" music returns with new words, *in aeternum* (with another big melisma on *-um*). The melody is then repeated for the word *Alleluia*.

LISTEN		Pérotin, "Alleluia. Diffusa est gratia"	

5	0:00	**Chant**	ALLELUIA, ALLELUIA——	Hallelujah.
	0:37	**Organum**	Diffusa est gratia in labiis tuis; *propterea benedixit te* deus	Grace has been poured out upon your lips; therefore, God has blessed you
	2:36	**Chant**	in aeternum.	eternally.
	3:05		ALLELUIA, ALLELUIA——	

4 Later Medieval Polyphony

After 1200 C.E. the most significant development in polyphonic music was its gradual distancing from church services. Music's foundation was still Gregorian chant; to this extent, the church still ruled. But the chant was now handled more abstractly. Composers had already made up new rhythms for the plainchants they were using; they now set only fragments of the chants, and often repeated these fragments.

In another radical development, the upper lines were now given their own words. This sort of polyphony is no longer an organum but a **motet**, from the French word *mot* ("word"). At first, motets were set to sacred poems in Latin, then to sacred poems in French. Later motets began to use love poems or political satires for their texts. It is clear that by now a church genre had been taken over by the courts; some motets even included bits of actual trouvère songs. But almost all motets still used a fragment of Gregorian chant for the notes of their bottom line.

Ars Nova

After 1300 the technical development of polyphony reached new heights of sophistication. Composers and music theorists of the time began to speak of an *ars nova*, a "new art," or "new technique." The organum and motets of the Notre Dame composers were now regarded as "ancient art," *ars antiqua*.

Some historians have compared the fourteenth century with the twentieth, for it was a time of the breakup of traditions—an age of anxiety, corruption, and worse. Bubonic plague, the "Black Death," carried away an estimated 75 million people, at a time when the papacy had been thrown out of Rome and two rival popes claimed the allegiance of European Christendom. The motet grew increasingly secular, intricate, and even convoluted, like the painting, architecture, and poetry of the time.

The new intricacy of the motet was mainly in the area of rhythm. The *ars antiqua* composers had introduced fixed rhythms and meter into organum and the motet, as we have seen; the composers of the *ars nova* carried their innovations much further. Rhythm seems to have obsessed them. They superimposed complex rhythmic patterns in the various voices so as to produce extraordinary combinations. Rhythms of such complexity are standard in much African music, but in Europe we have to go all the way up to 1950 to find anything like the dizzy rhythms of the advanced "new music" of 1400.

The leading composers, Philippe de Vitry (1291–1361) and Guillaume de Machaut (c. 1300–1377), were both churchmen—Vitry ended his life as a bishop—but they were political churchmen serving the courts of France and Luxembourg. Machaut was also the greatest French poet of his time, admired (and imitated) by his younger English contemporary, Geoffrey Chaucer.

Of instruments of strings
   in accord
Heard I so play a ravish-
   ing sweetnéss
That God, that Maker is of
   all, and Lord,
Ne heard never better, as
   I guess.

—Geoffrey Chaucer, 1375

GUILLAUME DE MACHAUT (c. 1300–1377)
Motet, "Quant en moi"

Following tradition, Machaut based this motet on a repeated fragment of plainchant, taken from the Eastertide services. On the recording, it is played on a viol, an early bowed stringed instrument.

Above this, he wrote two faster counterpoints set to love poetry (very artificial and elegant poetry, in both form and content: see opposite page). To the medieval mind, there was nothing sacrilegious about combining these sacred and secular elements. Notice the exceedingly complicated rhythm of these upper voices, the nervous, hyperelegant way in which they utter the words, and the spiky harmonies they produce in combination:

Quant en moi vint premierement Amours, si tres doucette - ment Me vost mon cuer enamourer Que d'un regart

As the voices stop abruptly, rest, and start up again, they create an intriguing texture—perforated, sparkling, asymmetrical. To make things even more intricate, the two singers actually sing two different poems simultaneously.

Each of these poems contains several stanzas with the same syllable counts and rhyme schemes, but Machaut (unlike a troubadour composer such as Bernart) does not repeat the same melodies for each stanza. A more esoteric system of repetition is at work. Successive stanzas are set to entirely different melodies in each voice—but these melodies have basically *the same overall rhythms*, complex patterns of over eighty notes in the soprano, forty notes in the tenor.

This technique of writing successive lengthy passages in identical rhythms but with distinct melodies is called **isorhythm**. Isorhythm represents the height of late medieval ingenuity and artifice, and it is hard to know whether anyone was ever expected to hear such purely rhythmic repetitions.

There are fast echoes between the soprano's two words in line 7 of her poem and the tenor's two words in line 2 of his, thus: "doubter—espoir—celer—d'avoir." This amusing device is called **hocket** (compare our word *hiccup*). Isorhythmic repetitions of rhythmic patterns are easiest to hear at hocket points.

Hocket is a cut-up song, composed for two or more voices. This kind of song is pleasing to the hot-tempered and to young men on account of its fluidity and speed.

From a fourteenth-century treatise on music

LISTEN	Guillaume de Machaut, "Quant en moi"

(The soprano's poem and the tenor's poem start together, and are sung simultaneously, stanza by stanza.)

6

0:00   STANZA 1: SOPRANO
        Quant en moi vint premierement   When I was first visited by
        Amours, si tres doucettement   Love, he so very sweetly
        Me vost mon cuer enamourer   Enamored my heart;
        Que d'un regart me fist present,   A glance is what he gave me as a gift,
        Et tres amoureus sentiment   And along with amorous sentiments
        Me donna avuec doulz penser,   He presented me with this delightful idea:

0:19   Espoir   d'avoir   To hope   to have

        Merci sans refuser.   Grace, and no rejections.
        Mais onques en tout mon vivant   But never in my whole life
        Hardement ne me vost donner.   Was boldness a gift he meant for me.

        TENOR
        Amour et biauté parfaite   *Thanks to love and consummate beauty,*

            Doubter,   celer   *Fearing,   feigning*

        Me font parfaitement.   *Are what consume me entirely.*

Hocket

Es-poir   d'avoir

Doubter,   celer

0:33   STANZA 2: SOPRANO
        E si me fait en desirant   And if, in my passion,
        Penser si amoureusement   He makes me think so amorously
        Que, par force de desirer,   That, thanks to desire
        Ma joie convient en tourment   My joy turns into torment—
        Muer, se je n'ay hardement.   Must turn, since I am not bold.
        Las! et je n'en puis recouvrer,   Alas! I cannot save myself—

0:51   Qu'amours   secours   For Love   no help

        Ne me vuet nul prester,   Will lend me—
        Qui en ses las si durement   Love, who holds me so tightly
        Me tient que n'en puis eschaper.   In his grasp that I cannot escape.

        TENOR
        Et vrais desirs, qui m'a fait   *And true desire, that has made me*

           De vous,   cuer doulz   *Love you,   dear heart,*

        Amer sans finement,   *For ever and ever,*

Qu'a-mours se-cours

De vous   cuer doulz

1:05   STANZA 3: SOPRANO
        Ne je me weil, qu'en attendant   Nor do I wish to escape, but awaiting
        Sa grace se weil humblement   Your mercy, I humbly
        Toutes ces dolours endurer.   Endure all these sorrows.

           Je says   de vrai . . .   I know,   in truth . . .

        TENOR
        Et quant j'aime si finement,   *And since I love you so perfectly,*

           Merci   vous pris . . .   *For mercy   I pray you . . .*

1:38   STANZA 4: SOPRANO
        Mais elle attend . . .

        TENOR
        Sans votre honeur . . .

Web: *Research and test your understanding of music in the Middle Ages at* <bedfordstmartins.com/listen>.

GLOBAL PERSPECTIVES 1

Sacred Chant

28, 29   40

The vast number of cultures that exist or that have existed in this world all generated their own music—or, as we say, their own different "musics." Often they are very different indeed; the first time South African Zulus heard Christian hymn-singing they were amazed, just as much as the missionaries were when they first heard Zulu music. Yet for all their diversity, the musics of the world do show some parallels, as we are going to see in the Global Perspectives sections of this book. There are parallels of musical function in society, there are parallels of musical technique, and sometimes there are parallels of both together.

Often these parallels come about as the result of influences of one culture on another—but influences are never accepted without modification and the blending of a foreign music with music that is indigenous. At other times parallels appear in musics that have nothing whatsoever to do with one another. Considering all these parallels, we have to believe that certain basic functions for music and certain basic technical principles are virtually universal in humankind.

One of these near-universal features—and one of the most fundamental—is the role of music in the service of religion. Singing serves across the world as an essential means of marking off the rituals of worship,

signaling their special status and their difference from other, secular, pursuits. The repertory of Gregorian chant developed in the Christian Church of the Middle Ages (see pages 56–62) is only one of many traditions of monophonic religious chant, albeit one of the more elaborate.

ISLAM

Islam: Reciting the Qur'an

Another highly elaborate tradition of chant is found in Islam, practiced today by about a fifth of the world's population, and the dominant religion in some fifty nations. Across all of Islam, the revelations of the prophet Muhammad gathered in the Qur'an (or Koran) are chanted or sung in Arabic. Muhammad himself is said to have enjoyed this melodic recitation.

Usually **Qur'anic recitation** is rigorously distinguished from all types of secular music making. It is thought of as "reading" the sacred text aloud, not "singing" it; it is not even considered to be the same sort of activity as secular singing or playing instruments. These nonreligious activities might be referred to as "music" (*musiqi*), but reading the Qur'an is not.

Given these distinctions, it is not surprising that Qur'anic recitation, like Gregorian chant, is monophonic, nonmetric, and does not involve instruments. It aims, above all else, to convey the Qur'anic text in a clearly comprehensible manner. Unlike plainchant, it has been passed along in oral tradition down to the present day. It has resisted the written notation that came to be a part of the Gregorian tradition already in the Middle Ages. To this day, great Islamic chanters sing the whole 114-chapter Qur'an from memory.

Ya Sin

Our excerpt is the beginning of a long recitation of one of the most highly revered chapters from the Qur'an. It is titled "Ya Sin" and is recited in times of adversity, illness, and death. A skilled reciter, Hafíz Kadir Konya, "reads" the verses in a style midway between heightened speech and rhapsodic melody. His phrases corre-

A muezzin high in a minaret calls the faithful to prayer in Cairo, Egypt.

spond to lines of the sacred text, and he pauses after every one. He begins:

> In the name of Allah, the Beneficent, the Merciful.
> Ya Sin.
> By the wise Qur'an,
> Lo! thou art of those sent
> On a straight path,
> A revelation of the Mighty, the Merciful,
> That thou mayst warn a folk whose fathers were not
>   warned, so they are heedless.
> Already hath the word proved true of most of them, for
>   they believe not.

In his first phrases, Konya begins at a low tonic and gradually expands his range to explore pitches around it. By 0:38, he reaches a pitch central to his melody, a fifth above the tonic. The succeeding phrases circle around this pitch, reciting words on it and decorating it with ornamental melodic formulas of varying intricacy. In this regard, it is a bit like the Gregorian reciting tone we studied before (page 59), only more elaborate in its melodies.

The Azan

Like Gregorian chant, Islamic chanting has developed a wide variety of approaches and styles. The best-known type of Islamic chant employs a style related to recitation, though it does not take its words from the Qur'an: the singing of the *adhan* or **azan**. This is a call to worship issued five times daily by a special singer called *mu'adhdhin* or *muezzin*. That an entire society comes to a stop five times a day for prayer reveals the tremendous force of Islamic religion.

The muezzin traditionally delivers his azan from the minaret, a tower attached to the mosque, and later inside the mosque to begin the prayers. In Islamic cities today, the azan is often broadcast over loudspeakers to enable it to sound over modern urban noises.

Hawai'ian Chant

We should not be too surprised to find certain broad similarities between Qur'anic and Gregorian chant. Both Islam and Christianity emerged from the same region, the Middle East, and Muhammad drew on elements of Christian doctrine in forming his new religion. He counted Jesus Christ as one of the Islamic prophets.

It is more surprising to find some of the same features in religious chant from halfway around the globe, in Polynesia—in Hawai'ian prayer songs, or **mele pule** (mél-eh póol-eh). By reciting these prayers, Hawai'ians intended to bring to life images of their gods fashioned of wood, stone, or feathers, animating them with divine powers.

Our brief example shows a style similar in some general ways to our Gregorian Preface and Qur'anic recitation. It is monophonic, like all traditional Hawai'ian song. It is also almost monotonal, with only one prominent pitch other than the central reciting tone. In this it contrasts with more active melodic styles used in

Three Hawai'ian singers. They strike large, resonant gourds on the ground to accompany their song.

other Hawai'ian genres of song—especially love songs and *mele hula*, or hula-dance songs.

The mele pule takes its rhythms from the words and shows little trace of meter. Though nearly monotonal, it is ornamented subtly with various shifts of vocal delivery and divergences from its reciting tone. The most prominent of these is a clear, pulsating, almost sobbing *vibrato*, or wavering pitch, that the singer, Kau'i Zuttermeister, introduces on long syllables. This technique, called *i'i*, is a stylistic feature much prized in many types of traditional Hawai'ian song. It is felt to endow melodies with special, deep emotion.

A Navajo Song

One more example of chant comes to us from Native American traditions. In these, too, singing is closely allied with the sacred. It plays a role in healing, hunting, social rituals, and—embracing all these activities—in human relations with gods, spirits, and ancestors. Most Native North American song is monophonic, like the Hawai'ian, Arabic, and Western chants we have heard. Unlike them, it is usually accompanied by drums or rattles of one sort or another.

Our example comes from the Navajo nation of the Four Corners area of the American Southwest. It is called "K'adnikini'ya'," which means "I'm leaving," and it dates from the late nineteenth century.

Just as individual Gregorian chants have their assigned places in Catholic services, so this chant has its own special role. It is sung near the end of the Enemy Way ceremony, a central event of Navajo spiritual life. In this solemn ceremony, warriors who have come in contact with the ghosts of their enemies are purified and fortified. Such purification is still performed today, sometimes for the benefit of U.S. veterans of Vietnam or other wars.

"K'adnikini'ya'" falls into a group of Navajo sacred songs known as *ho'zho'ni* songs, and you will hear the related word *ho'zhon'go* ("beautiful," "holy") sung alongside *"k'adnikini'ya'"* to end each of the seven central phrases of the song. Every phrase of the song begins with the syllables "hé-yuh-eh, yáng-a-ang-a." These are *vocables*, syllables having no precise meaning. Vocables are sometimes called "nonsense syllables" and likened to the "tra-la-las" and "hey-diddle-diddles" of European nursery rhymes. But they are hardly nonsensical. Instead, as scholars have gradually realized, they can carry secret, venerable, and even mystical significance.

At a powwow in British Columbia

The melody of "K'adnikini'ya'," like the other chants we have examined, is organized around a prominent reciting tone (the pitch of "he-yuh-eh"); each phrase turns upward at its end (on "k'adnikini'ya'"). The song's meter, given the regular drumstrokes, is more pronounced than in any of our earlier examples. The formal plan consists of a refrain at the beginning and end, with a group of parallel phrases in between.

LISTEN		
"K'adnikini'ya'"		30 41
0:00	**a**	Refrain
0:12	**a**	Refrain repeated
0:22	**b**	7 parallel phrases, each of 11 drumstrokes
1:05	**a**	Refrain

CHAPTER 6

The Renaissance

Renaissance ("rebirth") is the name given to a complex current of thought that worked deep changes in Europe from the fourteenth to the sixteenth century. It began in Italy. By rediscovering and imitating their ancient Greco-Roman civilization, Italians hoped they could bring about the rebirth of their glorious past. It was a somewhat confused dream, which came to nothing in political terms. Instead of becoming a new Roman empire, Italy at the end of the Renaissance consisted of the same pack of warring city-states that had been at each other's throats all through the Middle Ages.

However, the revival of Greek and Roman culture provided a powerful model for new values, both in Italy and in the rest of Europe. In the words of a famous nineteenth-century historian, the Renaissance involved "the discovery of the world and of man." This was the age of Columbus and Magellan, Leonardo da Vinci, Copernicus, and Shakespeare. Medieval society was stable, conservative, authoritarian, and oriented toward God. The Renaissance laid the groundwork for the dynamic world we know today, a world in which human beings and nature, rather than God, have become the measure in philosophy, science, art, and sometimes even religion.

Accordingly, Renaissance artists strove to make their work more relevant to people's needs and desires. They began to reinterpret the world around them—the architect's world of space and stone, the painter's world of images, the musician's world of sound—in new ways to meet these ambitions.

The church singers in these famous panels by Florentine sculptor Luca della Robbia (1400–1482) are handsome boys who seem to be taking the same sensuous pleasure in their singing as Luca did in sculpting them.

1 New Attitudes

A good indication of the Renaissance mindset, in the early fifteenth century, was a new way of treating plainchant in polyphonic compositions. Medieval composers writing organum or isorhythmic motets seem to have felt that so long as they used a traditional plainchant, there was nothing wrong with distorting it. They lengthened its notes enormously underneath the added counterpoints. They recast the meterless chant into fixed, arbitrary rhythms.

Renaissance composers no longer felt obliged always to use plainchants; but when they did they tended to treat them as melodies to listen to, not as rock-solid foundations for polyphonic structures. They embellished chants with extra notes, set them in graceful rhythms, and smoothed out passages that struck them as awkward or antiquated. This procedure is known as **paraphrase**. A fifteenth-century plainchant paraphrase is shown below; dashed lines mark the notes taken directly from the chant (shown above the paraphrase):

Music is a thing which delighteth all ages and beseemeth all states; a thing as seasonable in grief as in joy. The reason hereof is an admirable facility which music hath to express and represent the very standing, rising, and falling, the very steps and inflections every way, the turns and varieties of all passions.

Anglican bishop and theologian Richard Hooker, 1593

Gregorian hymn, "Ave maris stella" (see page 75)

The emphasis was on the sonorous, sensuous aspect of the chant rather than on its function as structure and control—its authoritarian function, one might say. (Sonority means either tone color or, more loosely, rich tone color.) A new sensitivity to sonority and melody was perhaps the first sign of Renaissance attitudes toward music.

Having transformed plainchants into "modern" melodies with a more attractive profile, composers put them not at the bottom of the polyphony but on top, in the soprano, where they could be heard most clearly. And the soprano voice was probably already considered the most beautiful.

Early Homophony

The fifteenth century also saw the beginning of composed *homophony*—that is, music in a harmonic texture (see page 28). In the simpler plainchant paraphrases of the time, the melody is often highlighted by an accompaniment that does not really sound polyphonic. Though there are still several polyphonic voices, most of the time their independence vanishes because they move along together and form simple chords.

The result is a plainchant harmonization. Once again the emphasis is on sensuous effect, that of homophony, rather than on the more intellectual process of polyphony.

Guillaume Dufay (c. 1400–1474)

Guillaume Dufay (or Du Fay) was born and bred in the north of France near modern Belgium, a region that supplied the whole of Europe with musicians for many generations. For over twenty-five years he worked in Italy, where he

"Ave maris stella": The Virgin Mary was the subject of special veneration in the late Middle Ages and the early Renaissance. Countless plainchants, motets, paintings, and sculptures were created to honor her. Lost in her own thoughts, this serene, childlike Virgin by the German artist Stefan Lochner (1400–1451) seems oblivious to Jesus, even to God—and no doubt to the music played for her by the baby angels.

came to know artists and thinkers of the Renaissance and (equally important!) the princely patrons who supported them. His later years were spent in a glow of celebrity at the important French cathedral of Cambrai.

GUILLAUME DUFAY
Harmonized hymn, "Ave maris stella"

This is a homophonic setting of a Gregorian **hymn,** one of the most tuneful of plainchant genres. A Gregorian hymn consists of a short tune sung through many stanzas, followed by an Amen—much like a modern hymn, in fact. One of the loveliest of these hymns, "Ave maris stella," was also one of the best known, because it was addressed to the Virgin Mary and sung on all of the many special feasts in her honor, and on most Saturdays, too. Note how line 1 contains the words AVE MARI(*s stell*)A.

"Ave maris stella" is in the D (Dorian) mode. You may be able to hear at once that the third note in the tune (the sixth note of the scale) is higher than would be normal in the minor mode. The hymn itself has six or seven stanzas, but Dufay set only the even-numbered ones to his own music, leaving the others

Plainsong hymn, "Ave maris stella"

A - ve _ ma-ris _ stel-la, _____

De - i Ma - ter _ al - ma,

At-que sem-per Vir-go, _____

Fe - lix coe - li por - ta.

to be sung Gregorian-style in alternation. This makes it fairly easy to hear how he embellished the plainchant.

His music for stanzas 2, 4, and 6 is the same each time—almost entirely homophonic and quite suave. The top voice sings a paraphrased, somewhat longer version of the hymn tune, as shown on page 75. The embellishment consists of a few extra notes and extensions, with the free rhythm of Gregorian chant channeled into a graceful triple meter.

| LISTEN | Dufay, "Ave maris stella" | |

7 0:00 STANZA 1: Plainchant

Ave maris stella,   Hail, star of the ocean,
Dei Mater alma,   Kind Mother of God,
Atque semper Virgo,   And also still a virgin,
Felix coeli porta.   Our blessed port to heaven.

STANZA 2: Dufay's paraphrase

0:22 Sumens illud Ave   May that blessed "Ave"
Gabrielis ore,   From Angel Gabriel's mouth
Funda nos in pace,   Grant us peace,
Mutans Hevae nomen.   Reversing the name "Eva."

STANZA 3: Plainchant

1:12 Solve vincla reis . . .

STANZA 4: Paraphrase

1:34 Monstra te esse matrem . . .

STANZA 5: Plainchant

2:26 Virgo singularis . . .

STANZA 6: Paraphrase

2:48 Sit laus Deo Patri,   Praise be to God the Father,
Summo Christo decus,   To Christ on high,
Spiritui Sancto,   To the Holy Spirit:
Tribus honor unus.   Three honored as one.
    Amen.   Amen.

There does not exist a single piece of music, not composed within the last forty years, that is regarded by the learned as worth hearing. Yet at this present time there flourish countless composers who glory in having studied the divine art under John Dunstable, Gilles Binchois, and Guillaume Dufay, recently deceased.

Composer and music theorist Johannes Tinctoris, 1477

Dufay and another fifteenth-century composer, Gilles Binchois (c. 1400–1460). Portable small organs (called *portatives*) were in use at the time.

This counts as a rather simple composition for Dufay, whose fame was and is based on longer, more elaborate pieces; he wrote some of the first polyphonic Masses, for example. Still, plainsong harmonizations make up an appreciable proportion of his output, and they show the new Renaissance attitudes with particular clarity.

The Mass

The new treatment of traditional plainchant, as in the technique of paraphrase, shows Renaissance composers taking a relaxed attitude toward medieval authority. The same can be said of their reaction to medieval intricacy, as represented by that most intellectual of musical devices, isorhythm. Fourteenth-century composers such as Machaut had used isorhythm even when writing love songs. Composers now cultivated a much simpler style for their polyphonic songs, or <u>chansons</u>: simpler, gentler, and more supple. The modest style of these new chansons was sometimes used for sacred texts, including portions of the Mass.

The rejection of isorhythm did not mean, however, that composers abandoned the technical development of their craft, which had taken such impressive strides from the early days of organum. Rather, such efforts were focused on large-scale musical construction. For the first time, compositions were written to last—and to make sense—over twenty or thirty minutes.

The problem of large-scale construction that fascinated fifteenth-century composers was how to write music that would in some sense unify the <u>**Mass.**</u> As the largest and most important of all church services, the Mass included some twenty musical items, originally sung in plainchant. By around 1450, composers settled on these five items for their polyphonic settings:

Kyrie	a simple prayer:	"Lord have mercy, Christ have mercy"
Gloria	a long hymn, beginning:	"Glory to God in the highest"
Credo	a recital of the Christian's list of beliefs, beginning:	"I believe in one God, the Father almighty"
Sanctus	another, shorter hymn:	"Holy, holy, holy, Lord God of hosts"
Agnus Dei	another simple prayer:	"Lamb of God . . . have mercy on us"

The polyphonic Mass thus was standardized into a five-section form, and the Mass has retained this form down to the present day, in settings by Palestrina, Bach, Mozart, Liszt, Stravinsky, and many others.

The five sections of the Mass are very different in the lengths of their texts, they serve different liturgical functions, and they come at widely separated times in the actual service. Various musical schemes were invented to unify the sections. Similar music could be used to signal the beginning of all five movements, for example. Or all the movements could paraphrase the same Gregorian chant.

So large and complex a structure presented composers with a challenge, and they took this up in a spirit of inventiveness and ambition characteristic of the Renaissance. What the symphony was to nineteenth-century composers and their audiences, the Mass was to their fifteenth-century counterparts: a brilliant, monumental test of artistic prowess.

Functional, commercial: Compare this Mass printed around 1500 with the manuscript on page 79. The circulation of music (as of books, maps, images, and data in general) skyrocketed with the great Renaissance invention of the printing press.

2 The "High Renaissance" Style

Around 1500 a new style emerged for Masses, motets, and chansons that would hold sway for much of the sixteenth century. The chief characteristic of this "High Renaissance" musical style was a careful blend of two vocal techniques, *imitative counterpoint* and *homophony* (see pages 28–29).

Imitation

Most polyphony at the beginning of the fifteenth century was non-imitative; most polyphony at the end of the century was imitative. This remarkable change is due partly to the fact that imitative polyphony, or imitation, reflects the ideals of moderation and balance that also characterize the visual arts of the High Renaissance. In the Raphael Madonna on page 47, the calm, dignified repose expressed by the figures and faces is as striking as the beautiful balance among all the pictorial elements.

By its very nature, imitative texture depends on a carefully controlled balance among multiple voice parts. A first voice begins with a motive (see page 26) designed to fit the words being set. Soon other voices enter, one by one, singing the same motive and words, but at different pitch levels; meanwhile the earlier voices continue with new melodies that complement the later voices without swamping them. Each voice has a genuinely melodic quality, and all the melodies are drawn from a single source. None is mere accompaniment or "filler," and none predominates for very long.

We can get an impression of the equilibrium of imitative polyphony from its look on the page, even without reading the music exactly. The following excerpt is from the score of Josquin Desprez's *Pange lingua* Mass:

Compare two Madonnas shown in this book: One (page 75) is a late medieval masterpiece from Northern Europe, the other from the new world of Renaissance Italy (page 47; painted only fifty years later). Uncrowned, uncluttered, a mother holds her child, smiles, the children play . . . God and His angels do not encircle this Madonna by Raphael as they do Lochner's.

Homophony

Almost all polyphony involves some chords, as a product of its simultaneously sounding melodies. But in the music of Machaut, for example, the chords are more of a by-product. Late medieval composers concentrated on the "horizontal" aspects of texture at the expense of "vertical" ones, delighting in the separateness of their different voice parts. Chordal sonority was a secondary consideration.

A major achievement of the High Renaissance style was to create a rich chordal quality out of polyphonic lines that still maintain a quiet sense of independence. Composers also used pure homophony—passages of "block chord" writing. They learned to use homophony both as a contrast to imitative texture and as an expressive resource in its own right.

Other Characteristics

The ideal tone color at this time, especially for sacred music, becomes *a cappella* performance—that is, performance by voices alone. Tempo and dynamics change little in the course of a piece. The rhythm is fluid, without any sharp accents, and shifting unobtrusively all the time, so that the meter is often obscured. The melodies never go very high or very low in any one voice; the ups and downs are carefully balanced. This music rarely settles into the easy swing of a dance rhythm or into the clear patterns of an actual tune.

Music in the High Renaissance style can sometimes strike modern listeners as vague, but if we listen more closely—and always listen to the words as well as the music—its flexibility, sensitivity, and rich expressive potential may come clear. Does it remind us of a wonderfully musical and subtle speaking voice? The sixteenth century would have been pleased to think so.

Josquin Desprez (c. 1450–1521)

The first master of the High Renaissance style was Josquin Desprez. Like Dufay, he was born in the north of France, and like Dufay and many other of his countrymen, in early life he traveled to Italy. The list of Josquin's patrons reads like a Renaissance *Who's Who:* Pope Alexander VI, the notorious Sforza family of Milan, the Estes of Ferrara, Louis XII of France.

An amazingly imaginative composer, Josquin brought the fifteenth-century Mass to a brilliant climax and pioneered whole new expressive genres, such as the sixteenth-century chanson and motet. He was famous both for his technical

Josquin Desprez

A Kyrie (one voice part) from a dazzling illuminated manuscript book of Mass music. Did singers actually sing from such precious books? The man who commissioned it is shown here praying with the help of an angel, who also (below) seems to be giving a seal of approval to the family coat of arms.

prowess and for his expressive innovations—for the childlike serenity of his motet "Ave Maria," as well as the grief-stricken accents of "Planxit autem David," a setting of King David's lament for his dead son Absalom.

JOSQUIN DESPREZ
Pange lingua Mass (c. 1510)

Josquin wrote eighteen different settings of the Mass—all large pieces in the standard five-section form. The *Pange lingua* Mass, one of his masterpieces, derives its melodic material largely from a hymn called "Pange lingua." This is a Gregorian hymn of the same kind as "Ave maris stella," which we have heard in Dufay's harmonized setting. "Pange lingua" (and hence Josquin's Mass) is designed for Corpus Christi, a feast celebrating the Holy Eucharist.

This is a four-part Mass (that is, a Mass for a choir with four separate voice parts). In Josquin's day, boys sang the high parts and men the lower ones; Josquin probably started his musical career as a choirboy. Today women usually substitute for boys in music of this period.

We shall examine the first two sections of Josquin's *Pange lingua* Mass.

Kyrie   The men in the choir sing line 1 of the hymn "Pange lingua" before the first section of the *Pange lingua* Mass. This first section, the Kyrie, is an elemental prayer consisting of three subsections:

Kyrie I: Kyrie eleison.   Lord have mercy.
Christe: Christe eleison.   Christ have mercy.
Kyrie II: Kyrie eleison.   Lord have mercy.

For Kyrie I, Josquin wrote a **point of imitation**—a brief passage of imitative polyphony covering one short phrase of a composition's verbal text, and using a single musical motive. This motive, which enters many times, is a paraphrase (see page 74) of line 1 of the hymn:

Gregorian hymn, "Pange lingua"

TENORS   Ky - ri -   e   e - le   -   i - son

(The order of the voice entries is tenor, bass, *wait*, soprano, alto, *wait*, bass, tenor, soprano.) Josquin did not invent this motive—it was derived from the plainchant hymn, as shown above—but his paraphrase is very beautiful, especially at the end.

The Christe has two points of imitation, also derived from the hymn, for the words *Christe* and *eleison;* the motives of these points are rhythmically similar. Kyrie II has a new point of imitation for the words "Kyrie eleison," followed by free (that is, nonhymn) material—a descending sequence and, prior to the drawn-out final cadence, a powerful oscillating passage.

Plainsong hymn, "Pange lingua"

Pan-ge lin-gua _ glo-ri-o - si

Cor - po-ris mys-te-ri-um, _

San-gui-nis-que pre-ti - o - si,

Quem in mun-di pre-ti - um _

Fruc-tus ven-tris gen-ne-ro-si

Rex ef-fu-dit _ gen - ti-um.

LISTEN		Josquin, *Pange lingua* Mass, Kyrie	

8

8	0:08	Kyrie eleison	Lord have mercy.
	0:53	Christe eleison	Christ have mercy.
	2:10	Kyrie eleison	Lord have mercy.

Gloria   The four remaining sections of the Mass—the Gloria, Credo, Sanctus, and Agnus Dei—introduce countless new points of imitation, which are interspersed with occasional text phrases set in homophony.

In the second subsection of the Gloria, beginning with the words *Qui tollis,* polyphony and homophony are contrasted in a highly expressive way. At the beginning, we can almost envisage one or two persons timidly invoking Him "who takes away the sins of the world" (polyphony), and then the whole congregation—or, symbolically, the whole of Christendom—urgently responding together with a plea for mercy and relief: "have mercy" (homophony). This music gives a dramatic sense of communal worship.

The "Qui tollis" as a whole includes eight points of imitation and four homophonic or nearly homophonic phrases. (The point for "Tu solus Dominus" is illustrated on page 78.) In the imitative phrases, the vocal lines fit together smoothly into chords, and while the sequence of these chords seems hard to predict, at least for modern ears, it does not seem arbitrary. The remarkable mood of Josquin's music—at once sober, quietly energetic, and reverential— owes much to its Phrygian (E) mode. Like the hymn "Pange lingua," the *Pange lingua* Mass is in this mode.

Throughout the motet ["Planxit autem David," by Josquin] there is preserved what befits the mourner, who at first is inclined to cry out constantly, then murmur to himself, then quiet down or—as passion breaks out anew—raise his voice again in a loud cry. All these things we see most beautifully observed in this composition.

An admirer of Josquin, writing a quarter century after his death

---

LISTEN	Josquin, *Pange lingua* Mass, from the Gloria	1 9

(Capital letters indicate phrases sung in homophony.)

9 | 0:00 | Qui tollis peccata mundi,
    MISERERE NOBIS. | You who take away the sins of the world,
    have mercy upon us.
| 0:34 | Qui tollis peccata mundi,
    SUSCIPE DEPRECATIONEM NOSTRAM.
Qui sedes ad dexteram Patris,

    miserere nobis. | You who take away the sins of the world,
    hear our prayer.
You who sit at the right hand of the
    Father,
have mercy upon us.
| 1:18 | Quoniam tu solus sanctus,
    tu solus Dominus,
    tu solus altissimus,
    Jesu Christe,
cum sancto spiritu,
    in gloria Dei Patris.
AMEN. | For you alone are holy,
    you alone are the Lord,
    you alone are the most high,
    Jesus Christ,
With the Holy Spirit,
    in the glory of God the Father.
Amen.

3 Music as Expression

In parts of Josquin's *Pange lingua* Mass, as we have just seen, the music does not merely enhance the service in a general way, but seems to address specific phrases of the Mass text and the sentiments behind them. Music can be said to "illustrate" certain words and to "express" certain feelings. The exploration of music's power to express human feelings was a precious contribution by musicians to the Renaissance "discovery of the world and of man."

Renaissance composers derived inspiration for this exploration from reports of the music of ancient Greece, just as artists, architects, and writers of the time were also looking to ancient Greece and Rome for inspiration. Philosophers such as Plato had testified that music was capable of arousing emotions in a very powerful way. In the Bible, David cures Saul when he is troubled by an "evil spirit" by playing on his harp; there are similar stories in Greek myth and Greek history. How modern music could recapture its ancient powers was much discussed by music theorists after the time of Josquin.

They reasoned somewhat as follows. If poets wish to arouse feelings, they do so by writing about them—by describing, depicting, expressing feelings in words. By doing this poets can arouse similar feelings in their readers. What is the analogy in music? How is it possible for composers to arouse feelings in their listeners?

The Renaissance answer was that this could be done indirectly, by illustrating or otherwise enhancing words. If words can express feelings and music can illustrate words, then music can express feelings and also arouse them, in conjunction with a text. Through this new link to the world of human emotions, Renaissance music sought to gain new relevance to humanity.

Devotion to the ideal of musical expression, by way of a text, was one of the main guiding ideas for composers of the later Renaissance. This led them to a new sensitivity to the words they were setting, which manifested itself in two important developments.

First, composers wanted the words of their compositions to be clearly heard. They strove for accurate **declamation**—that is, they made sure that words were sung to rhythms and melodies that approximated normal speech.

This may seem elementary and obvious, but it is simply not true of most medieval organum and motets (or of many plainchants). The pronunciation of words set to music mattered less than the structure of the music. The Renaissance was the first era when words were set to music naturally, clearly, and vividly. The little example below shows this (try singing it).

Second, composers began matching their music to the *meaning* of the words that were being set. The term **word painting** is used for this musical illustration of the text. Words such as "fly" and "glitter" were set to rapid notes, "up" and "heaven" to high ones, and so on:

Fly,   Love, a - loft   to heav'n to seek out   for - tune . . .

Sigh was typically set by a motive including a rest, as though the singers have been interrupted by sighing. *Grief, cruel, torment, harsh,* and exclamations such as *alas*—words found all the time in the language of Renaissance love poetry—prompted composers to write dissonant or chromatic harmony.

Word painting could become mechanical and silly—as for example, when the Italian word for "eyes," *occhi,* was set to two whole notes. But when used sensitively, it could intensify the emotion inherent in words and phrases in a striking way, as Renaissance doctrine demanded. First developed seriously in the sixteenth century, word painting has remained an important expressive resource of all later vocal music. For examples from the Baroque period, when it was especially important, see pages 101, 104, 157, and 161.

oc - chi

4 Late Renaissance Music

As we noted above, the High Renaissance style established by the generation of Josquin Desprez proved remarkably stable. Yet it was also flexible enough so that composers were able to do new things with it all the way up to the end of the sixteenth century. While its use was clearest in the church music of the time, important new secular genres also made use of this style, in a modified form.

My Lord, if in our century there is any more excellent music than that of Orlande Lassus, I leave that judgment to masters of that art. I will say only this: that Plato, who liked so much to teach political harmony through musical proportions, would have taken his examples from Orlande had they lived at the same time.

Publisher's dedication (like a jacket blurb) in a Lassus edition, 1575

Music at court: singers of the Bavarian Court Chapel in 1565, under Roland de Lassus. Each man and boy is carefully and solemnly depicted. With this imposing picture (and another, of an equally large group of court instrumentalists), the Duke showed off the size and distinction of his retinue—a reflection, of course, of his own glory.

The universality of the style is symbolized by the geographical spread of its four most famous masters, Palestrina, Lassus, Victoria, and Byrd. *Giovanni Pierluigi da Palestrina* (c. 1525–1594) was born just outside Rome and worked in the Holy City all his life. *Roland de Lassus* (c. 1532–1594), also known as Orlando di Lasso, was a worldly and much-traveled Netherlander who settled at the court of Munich. His output was enormous. *Tomás Luis de Victoria* (c. 1548–1611), a Spanish priest, spent many years in Rome working for the Jesuits but ended up in Madrid. *William Byrd* (1543–1623) was organist of England's Chapel Royal under Queen Elizabeth I but also a member of the English dissident Catholic minority, who wrote Masses for illegal and highly dangerous services held in secret in barns and attics.

GIOVANNI PIERLUIGI DA PALESTRINA (c. 1525–1594)
Pope Marcellus Mass (1557)

Palestrina was a singer in, or choirmaster of, many of Rome's most famous churches and chapels, including the Sistine (Papal) Chapel. He lived in the repressive atmosphere of the Counter-Reformation movement, which was launched by the papacy in 1545 to combat the threat of the Reformation. Palestrina wrote secular compositions in his youth, some of which were widely popular, but later he recanted and apologized for them. He wrote over a hundred Masses and published his first examples with a highly symbolic frontispiece, which shows the kneeling composer presenting the pope with a special papal Mass.

Because singing is so powerful a force in religion, as we noted on page 56, societies have felt a need to control it carefully. Christianity has witnessed periodic reforms to prune church services of musical features that were seen as abuses. The Counter-Reformation staged just such a reform. Palestrina's most famous composition, the *Pope Marcellus* Mass, was supposed to have convinced the pope and his council that composers of complicated polyphonic church music could still set the sacred words clearly, with clear enough declamation so that the congregation could hear them. Partly because of this legend, and partly because of the particular calmness and purity of his musical style, Palestrina became the most revered Renaissance composer for later centuries. His works are still treasured by Catholic choir directors today.

The frontispiece of Palestrina's *First Book of Masses*, 1554, announces to all the world that this music has the Pope's blessing. The page is open to the papal Mass *Ecce Sacerdos magnus* ("Behold the great priest").

Gloria   A part of the Gloria of the *Pope Marcellus* Mass, the "Qui tollis," shows how the High Renaissance *a cappella* style changed after the time of Josquin. Compared with Josquin's setting of these same words in his *Pange lingua* Mass (see page 81), Palestrina's setting employs much more homophony. Apart from some fuzziness on a few individual words, only the last, climactic line of Palestrina's composition uses polyphony.

Beyond this, we will notice at once that vocal sonority is of major importance in Palestrina's setting. He uses a larger and richer choir than Josquin— six vocal parts, rather than four—and keeps alternating between one choral group, or semichoir, drawn from the total choir, to another. Thus the first phrase, in high voices, is answered by the second, in low voices, and so on. The total choir does not sing all together until the word *suscipe*.

What matters most to Palestrina are the rich, shifting tone colors and harmonies, which he uses to produce a generalized spiritual aura, sometimes ethereal, sometimes ecstatic. And with the dictates of the Counter-Reformation in mind, he is certainly careful to declaim the words very clearly.

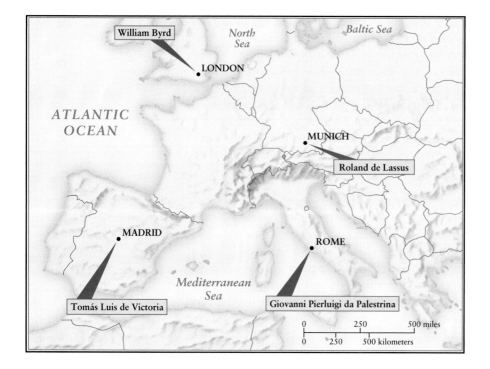

The dispersion of the High Renaissance style across Europe.

| LISTEN | Palestrina, *Pope Marcellus* Mass, from the Gloria |

10

(Capital letters indicate phrases sung in homophony.)

0:00	QUI TOLLIS PECCATA MUNDI,	You who take away the sins of the world,
	MISERERE NOBIS.	have mercy upon us.
	QUI TOLLIS PECCATA MUNDI,	You who take away the sins of the world,
	Suscipe DEPRECATIONEM NOSTRAM.	hear our prayer.
1:23	QUI SEDES AD DEXTERAM PATRIS,	You who sit at the right hand of the
	MISERERE NOBIS.	Father, have mercy upon us.
2:00	QUONIAM TU SOLUS SANCTUS,	For you alone are holy,
	TU SOLUS DOMINUS,	you alone are the Lord,
	TU SOLUS ALTISSIMUS,	you alone are the most high,
	JESU CHRISTE,	Jesus Christ,
2:36	CUM SANCTO SPIRITU,	With the Holy Spirit,
	in gloria Dei Patris.	in the glory of God the Father.
	Amen.	Amen.

The Motet

The term *motet* has been applied to very different kinds of music over the ages; thus motets by Palestrina or Byrd have little in common with motets by Machaut or even Dufay. The sixteenth-century **motet** is a relatively short composition to Latin words made up of short sections in the homophony and imitative polyphony that were the staples of the High Renaissance style. The words are nearly always religious, taken from a variety of sources—sometimes directly from the Bible. Thus, as compared with the Mass of the same time, the motet is basically similar in *musical style,* but different in *scope* and, of course, in text.

It was the variety of the text possibilities in the motet, as contrasted to the invariable Mass, that recommended it to sixteenth-century composers. By providing them with new words to express, motets allowed church composers to convey religious messages in their music with more verve and power than ever before.

The Italian Madrigal

It was in the secular field, however, that the Renaissance ideal of music as expression made the greatest inroads. This took place principally in an important new Italian genre, after around 1530, called the **madrigal.**

The madrigal is a short composition set to a one-stanza poem—typically a love poem, with a rapid turnover of ideas and images. Ideally it is sung by one singer per part, in an intimate setting. The music consists of a sometimes equally rapid turnover of sections in imitative polyphony or homophony. Essentially, then, the plan is the same as that in High Renaissance sacred works such as Masses and motets.

But with secular words came a decisive change of emphasis. The points of imitation were shorter, and the imitation itself less strict; there was generally much more homophony; and the words assumed more and more importance. Both declamation and word painting were developed with great subtlety. For three generations a line of Italian madrigal composers, or *madrigalists,* pioneered an amazing variety of techniques to make words more vivid and to illustrate and illuminate them by musical means.

If therefore you will compose madrigals, you must possess yourself of an amorous humor, so that you must be wavering like the wind, sometimes wanton, sometimes drooping, sometimes grave and staid, otherwise effeminate; and show the very uttermost of your variety, and the more variety you show the better shall you please.

From a music textbook by madrigal composer Thomas Morley, 1597

The English Madrigal

A genre like the madrigal, tied so closely to its words—Italian words—would seem difficult to transplant. All the same, Italian madrigals became all the rage in Elizabethan England and led to the composition of madrigals in English. This popularity may well have reflected the taste and interests of Queen Elizabeth I herself. The Virgin Queen not only maintained a splendid musical establishment, like all other ambitious monarchs and nobles of the time, but she was also an accomplished musician in her own right.

Queen Elizabeth I playing the lute. This miniature portrait is reproduced at almost exactly its original size.

In 1601, twenty-three English composers contributed madrigals to a patriotic anthology in her honor, called *The Triumphs of Oriana*. All the poems end with the same refrain: "Then sang the shepherds and nymphs of Diana: Long live fair Oriana!" Oriana was a pseudonym for Elizabeth, and the nymphs and shepherds of Diana—the goddess of virginity—were her subjects. The *Triumphs* was obviously a court-inspired project, and as such it reminds us vividly of one of the main functions of court music of all times: flattery.

THOMAS WEELKES (c. 1575–1623)
Madrigal, "As Vesta Was from Latmos Hill Descending" (1601)

Thomas Weelkes never rose beyond the position of provincial cathedral organist-choirmaster; in fact, he had trouble keeping even that post in later life, when the cathedral records assert that he became "noted and found for a common drunckard and notorious swearer and blasphemer." Although he is not a major figure, as are the other composers treated in this unit, he is one of the best composers of madrigals in English.

Written in better days, Weelkes's contribution to *The Triumphs of Oriana* is a fine example of a madrigal of the lighter kind. (Weelkes also wrote serious and melancholy madrigals.) After listening to the music of Josquin and Palestrina, our first impression of "Vesta" is of the sheer exuberant brightness of the musical style. Simple rhythms, clear harmonies, crisp melodic motives—all look forward to music of the Baroque era and beyond. This music has a modern feel about it.

The next thing likely to impress the listener is the elegance and liveliness with which the words are declaimed. We have already stressed the importance of declamation in the Renaissance composers' program of attention to verbal texts. Weelkes nearly always has his words sung in rhythms that would seem quite natural if the words were spoken, as shown at the right (where — stands for a long syllable, ⌣ for a short one). The declamation is never less than accurate, and it is sometimes expressive: The rhythms make the words seem imposing in the second phrase shown, dainty in the third.

Leav-ing their God-dess all a-lone

Then sang the shep-herds and nymphs of Di-a-na

To whom Di-a-na's dar-lings

As for the word painting, that can be shown in a tabular form:

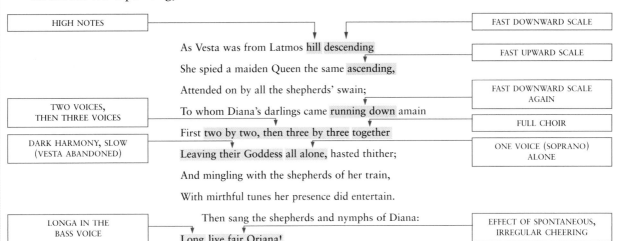

(The "maiden Queen" is Elizabeth, and "Diana's darlings" are the Vestal Virgins, priestesses of Vesta, the Roman goddess of hearth and home. The archaic word *amain* means "at full speed.")

This brilliant six-part madrigal uses two sopranos, alto, two tenors, and bass. Weelkes makes particularly good use of this group in his extended imitative setting of the poem's last line. Here we can easily imagine many more than six loyal voices endlessly cheering their Queen in a spontaneous, irregular way, one after another. Shakespeare and his contemporaries, Weelkes among them, were very fond of puns. Weelkes has the word "long" sung by the bass voice on a note four times the duration of a whole note—a note whose Latin name was *longa*. So this madrigal has its esoteric, in-joke side for musicians, as well as its public, political side for Elizabeth's subjects.

5 Instrumental Music: Early Developments

The best sixteenth-century composers concentrated almost entirely on vocal genres, on music with words. Except for the English master William Byrd, none of them devoted much attention to music for instruments alone. We have spoken above of the Renaissance preoccupation with expression in music, expression through the association of music with words.

Nevertheless, instruments and music for instruments developed significantly during this period. The first violins and harpsichords date from the sixteenth century; also perfected were the lute—a guitar-like instrument, originally from the Near East, that was perhaps the most popular of all at the time—and many other instruments. Instrumental music was to become one of the great glories of the Baroque era, and the basis for this was laid in the Renaissance.

Around 1500, hardly any music was written specifically for instruments. Instrumentalists would either play along with singers in vocal music, or else play motets, chansons, and other vocal genres by themselves, without words. The principal vocal genre after 1550, however, the madrigal, would not have made much sense performed without its words. By this time, in any case, new genres had been developed for instrumental performance.

Renaissance Dances

The most widespread of Renaissance instrumental genres was the dance, a reflection of the great popularity of dancing at the time.

Many dance types are described in detail in sixteenth-century instruction
books—the steps themselves, and also their order or sequence. (In this regard,
old dances were closer to square dances than to some modern social dancing,
where there is no fixed order for steps or movements.) One of the most popular was the **pavane** (paván), a solemn dance in duple meter, with the partici-
pants stepping and stopping formally. The pavane was usually paired with the
triple-meter **galliard.**

Simpler, less formal Renaissance dance types include the Italian *saltarello,*
the Irish *jig,* known also in Scotland and the north of England, and the French
bransle—whose name is related to our word *brawl.* The Renaissance also saw
elaborately choreographed ballets, court dances in which kings and nobles
could participate.

Conforming to the dance steps, dance music was written in easy-to-follow
phrases, almost always four to eight bars long. Ending with especially clear
cadences, the phrases were each played twice in succession to produce forms
such as **a a b b** or **a a b b c c.**

ANONYMOUS
Galliard, "Daphne"

12

The title of this melodious Elizabethan dance suggests that originally it may
have been a song. But if so, at some point the song was pressed into galliard
form, **a a b b c c,** and this is the only way it has survived.

Played in our recording by an early violin ensemble, "Daphne" is mainly
homophonic. The meter is kept very clear, and the distinct quality of the
phrases ending **a, b,** and **c** makes it easy for the dancers to remember the place
in the dance step sequence. The first violin provides extensive ornamentations
at the second playing.

ANONYMOUS
"Kemp's Jig"

13

Will Kemp was an Elizabethan actor, comedian, and song-and-dance man,
immortalized for having created comic roles in Shakespeare, such as Dogberry
the Constable in *Much Ado About Nothing.* Kemp specialized in a type of
popular dance number, called a jig, that was regularly presented in Elizabethan
theaters after the main play. He accompanied himself with pipe and tabor—a
type of simple flute, blown like a recorder, and a snare drum.

Dance Stylization

"Kemp's Jig" can lead us to an important topic that extends past the Renaissance. An oddity of this particular dance is that in phrase **a**, the cadence—a stopping place (see page 25)—comes in the fourth bar, whereas in phrase **b**, a cadence comes in the fifth. Though the motion does not stop at this point, the tonic is reached in a very solid way in measure 9. Another cadence comes three bars later, in measure 12. A dancer might be confused, even thrown off by this.

A listener, on the other hand, might well enjoy the interesting effect caused by this irregularity in the cadences. If we like to think that this little dance puts us in touch with true "folk music," we must also suspect that a musician of some sophistication has been tinkering with it.

"Kemp's Jig" is not as simple as it seems, then. It illustrates a tendency that will gain more and more importance later: the tendency to make dance music more and more elaborate and "artistic." Composers (and performers making it up on the spot) provided dance music with elements of a more strictly musical interest over and above the dancers' basic needs. Such elements are irregular cadences, as in "Kemp's Jig," subtle phrase lengths, unusual harmonies, and even counterpoint.

This was the first stage of a process that we can call the *stylization* of dance music. Already well established in the sixteenth century, dance stylization was to attain new heights in the dance suites by Bach and the symphony minuets of Haydn and Mozart. In the twentieth century, fox-trot tunes were (and sometimes still are)

Not Will Kemp of Kemp's Jig, but another famous comic of Shakespeare's time: Richard Tarleton, with the traditional tools of his trade, the pipe and tabor.

"stylized" into jazz numbers. Louis Armstrong and Charlie Parker did not expect that people who came to listen to them were going to dance to such stylized versions.

"Kemp's Jig" is a lively—perhaps "perky" is the right word—and seemingly simple dance tune in **a a b** form. It is played several times on our recording, first by a recorder and then by a viol, an early string instrument in the cello range; ornaments are piled on, first to the repeated phrase **a** and then to all the repetitions. A lute accompanies.

Web: *Research and test your understanding of Renaissance music at* <bedfordstmartins.com/listen>.

GLOBAL PERSPECTIVES 2

Music and Early European Colonialism

In introducing the Renaissance, on page 73, we echoed the words of a historian who saw in it "the discovery of the world and of man." But we have not yet said much about the *world* part of this formulation.

The period from 1480 to 1620 marks the first great phase of European expansion into other parts of the world. The most famous European voyages of exploration, by Bartolomeu Dias, Vasco da Gama, Columbus, and Magellan, were followed by countless others. Trade routes to Africa and the "New World" were quickly established—so quickly that from 1492 on, only one year passed without European journeys to the Americas.

The voyages of exploration were more than sheer adventurism or innocent trading ventures. They were also expeditions of military conquest and territorial expansion. They marked the beginning of an aggressive European colonization of large portions of the rest of the globe that would last almost half a millennium, well into the 1900s, and would profoundly shape the modern world.

A European depiction from the 1590s of the song and dance of the Tupi Indians of Brazil. At the bottom you can see an attempt to render Tupi singing in European music notation.

Cultural Conquest and Music

The European attempt to conquer was cultural as well as military. In the immediate wake of European soldiers and *conquistadors* came missionaries aiming to convert the native peoples to Christian beliefs—whether by patient persuasion or forcible coercion. Wherever they went, soldiers, missionaries, and merchants reported the novelties they found back to a fascinated Europe.

These reports—some precise and evidently accurate, others fanciful—very often made room for descriptions of music. They inform us of musical traditions that today are at least much changed and, in many cases, simply extinct. From the 1590s comes a description of African music in the Congo (for discussion of West African drumming, see page 398). English mariners report on Native North American song and dance (see page 72), and Dutch explorers tell about the elaborate gong orchestras, or *gamelans,* still played today in Indonesia (see page 214). The Jesuit Father Matteo Ricci, the first European allowed to reside in the imperial capital of Beijing, was scandalized by Chinese opera, "a curse," in his view, "more prone to vice" than any other activity (for more on Chinese opera, see page 310).

Music of the Aztecs and Incas

The Aztec and Inca empires were the greatest civilizations Europeans came upon in the New World. They amazed their conquerors with their cultural achievements and complexity, their riches, and their astonishing capitals: Tenochtitlán, in the middle of a Mexican lake that has long since disappeared, and Cuzco, built so high up in the Andes that the Spaniards had to establish Lima, a low-lying city on the coast, for themselves.

Since they had elaborate religious institutions of their own, the Mexicans and Andeans presented the European missionaries with their first great challenges for religious conversion in the New World. The missionaries systematically studied Aztec and Incan culture to determine how best to achieve their goal, and they taught the natives all the elements of a Christian life as they saw it. Prominent among their studies was native music; central to their teachings was European music.

A church procession in seventeenth-century Cuzco, with the Virgin Mary atop a wagon carrying musicians (not painted to scale). The aristocrat walking in front of the wagon wears traditional Inca garb.

Inevitably, the two musics were thrust into confrontation. A Mexican church council of the sixteenth century ruled that native musicians "shall sing polyphonic music only when their singing conforms to standards we consider acceptable . . . and they shall not be permitted to sing songs that remind people of their old idolatrous customs." A church council at Lima sought to abolish singing and dancing at native harvest festivals and to destroy the instruments and costumes used. Yet at the same time, the missionaries *encouraged* native song and dance in *Christian* festivals, hoping that they would hasten the Andeans' acceptance of the new, foreign religion.

These efforts could not succeed completely. We know that native singers preserved their traditional songs, often singing them secretly, away from the eyes and ears of the authorities. At the same time they easily learned and adopted the European music the missionaries pressed on them. (They sometimes had incentives: In Mexico the quickest learners had their taxes waived.) By the mid-seventeenth century Native Latin Americans were composing European-style church music in more than one newly built cathedral.

oring her. Imagine the scene in 1630 in front of the still unfinished cathedral of Cuzco, built on the sturdy foundations of an Inca palace: Native singers march in procession across the plaza, wearing the traditional garb still permitted for Christian festivals, singing Quechua words set to European-style music, and accompanying themselves on Andean flutes and drums. As they enter the church, they regroup as a choir for services including Gregorian chant (perhaps "Ave maris stella," the widely used hymn to the Virgin that we have already studied) and also polyphonic music, now with Latin words. Such are the cultural mixes that arise in colonial situations.

Our performance of "Hanaq pachap kusikuynin" is tamer than this—no instruments are used. The music is simple but moving. It sets the phrases of the Quechua text one by one, in the straightforward homophonic texture we have heard in Dufay's harmonization of "Ave maris stella" and Palestrina's *Pope Marcellus* Mass (see pages 75 and 83). Listen for the touch of expressive dissonance, reminiscent of European genres such as the madrigal, at the end of the third phrase.

Inca Processional Music

The song "Hanaq pachap kusikuynin" is a fascinating case of the musical merging of two cultures. Published in 1631 by a Franciscan friar named Bocanegra, it is the first piece of elaborate music to be published anywhere in the New World. The words of the song are in the native Andean language Quechua (*ket*-chwa). Was it the work of Bocanegra himself, or one of the new Indian composers?

The song is a hymn to the Virgin Mary. Bocanegra says that it was sung during religious processions hon-

LISTEN	"Hanaq pachap kusikuynin"	

Hanaq pachap kusikuynin	Bliss of heaven,
Waranqakta much'asqayki	A thousand times I adore you.
Yupay ruru puquq mallki	Tree of myriad fruits,
Runakunap suyakuynin	Hope of peoples,
Kallpannaqpa q'imikuynin	Pillar of the weak:
Waqyasqayta	Hear my cry.
	(one more stanza)

CHAPTER 7

The Early Baroque Period

At the end of the sixteenth century, music was undergoing rapid changes at the sophisticated courts and churches of northern Italy. Composers began to write motets, madrigals, and other pieces more directly for effect—with a new simplicity, in some respects, but also with the use of exciting new resources. A new style, the style of the early Baroque period, took hold rapidly all over Italy and in most of the rest of Europe.

1 From Renaissance to Baroque

As we have seen, the madrigal was the most "advanced" form in late Renaissance music. Toward the end of the sixteenth century, the thirst for expression led madrigal composers to increasingly esoteric kinds of word painting. Extreme dissonances and rhythmic contrasts were explored in order to illustrate emotional texts in a more and more exaggerated fashion.

At the same time, a reaction set in *against* the madrigal. In Florence, an influential group of intellectuals mounted an attack on the madrigalists' favorite technique, word painting. Word painting was artificial and childish, they said, and the many voices of a madrigal ensemble could not focus feeling or express it strongly. Whatever the madrigalists thought, a choir singing counterpoint could only dilute strong emotions, not concentrate them.

True emotionality could be projected only by a single human agent, an individual, a singer who would learn from great actors and orators how to move an audience to laughter, anger, or tears. A new style of solo singing was developed, *recitative,* that was half music, half recitation. This led inevitably to the stage and, as we shall see, to opera. Invented in Florence around 1600, opera became one of the greatest and most characteristic products of the Baroque imagination.

Music in Venice

Meanwhile, there were important developments in Venice, the city of canals. The "Serene Republic," as Venice called itself, cultivated especially brilliant styles in all the arts—matched, it seems, to the city's dazzling physical appearance. Wealthy and cosmopolitan, Venice produced architects whose flamboyant,

Why cause words to be sung by four or five voices so that they cannot be distinguished, when the ancient Greeks aroused the strongest passions by means of a single voice supported by a lyre? We must renounce counterpoint and the use of different kinds of instruments and return to simplicity!

A Florentine critic, 1581

Venice, the most colorful of European cities, and one of the most musical. Several major painters made a speciality of Venetian scenes, which were very popular; this one, of the Rialto Bridge over the Grand Canal, is by Francesco Guardi (1712–1793).

varied buildings were built out of multicolored materials, and painters—the Bellinis, Titian, Tintoretto—who specialized in warm, rich hues. Perhaps, then, it is more than a play on words to describe Venetian music as "colorful."

From the time of Palestrina's *Pope Marcellus* Mass, sixteenth-century composers had often subdivided their choirs into low and high "semichoirs" of three or four voice parts each. The semichoirs would alternate and answer or echo each other. Expanding this technique, Venetian composers would now alternate two, three, or more whole choirs. Homophony crowded out polyphony as full choirs answered one another stereophonically, seeming to compete throughout entire motets and Masses, then joining together for climactic sections of glorious massed sound.

The resources of sonority were exploited even further when sometimes the "choirs" were designated for singers on some parts and instruments on others. Or else whole choirs would be made up of instruments. As the sonorous combinations of Venetian music grew more and more colorful, the stately decorum of the High Renaissance style was forgotten (or left to musical conservatives). Magnificence and extravagance became the new ideals, well suited to the pomp and ceremony for which Venice was famous.

Extravagance and Control

Wherever they looked, knowledgeable travelers to Italy around 1600 would have seen music bursting out of its traditional forms, styles, and genres. Freedom was the order of the day. But they might have been puzzled to notice an opposite tendency as well: In some ways musical form was becoming more rigorously controlled and systematic. As composers sought to make music more untrammeled in one respect, they found they had to organize it more strictly in another so that listeners would not lose track of what was happening.

The control composers exercised over Baroque form, in other words, was an appropriate response to Baroque extravagance, exaggeration, and emotionality. We shall see similar forces and counterforces at other points in musical history later in this book.

GIOVANNI GABRIELI (c. 1555–1612)
Motet, "O magnum mysterium" (published 1615)

The most important composers in Venice were two Gabrielis, Andrea and his nephew Giovanni. (Andrea's dates are c. 1510–1586). As organists of St. Mark's Cathedral, both of them exploited the special acoustics of that extraordinary building, which still impress tourists today. By placing choirs of singers and instrumentalists in different choir lofts, they obtained brilliant echo effects that even modern audio equipment cannot duplicate.

Giovanni's "O magnum mysterium," the second part of a longer motet, was written for the Christmas season. The text marvels that lowly animals—the ox and the ass—were the first to see the newborn Jesus.

And the music marvels along with the text. Quite in the manner of a madrigal, the exclamation, "O" is repeated like a gasp of astonishment. Then lush chord progressions positively make the head spin, as the words *O magnum mysterium* are repeated to the same music, but pitched higher (that is to say, in sequence: see page 25). A momentary change in the meter, which slips from duple (**2/2**) into triple (**3/2**), provides a new feeling of majesty, as much as astonishment:

Gabrieli uses two "choirs," each with three voice parts and four instrumental parts, plus organ, though at first all we hear is a sumptuous blend of brass instruments and voices. Solo voices emerge at the word *sacramentum*. First solo tenors, then boy sopranos echo one another during the line *iacentem in presepio*, where a new rapid figure bounces back and forth from tenors to sopranos to brass.

Gabrieli really unleashes his musical resources at the choral *alleluia* section. The music moves in quick triple meter, matching the jubilation of repeated *alleluias*, and the two choirs echo back and forth across the sound space:

	FAST—triple meter									SLOW—duple meter	
	1 2 3	1 2 3	1 2 3	1 2 3	1 2 3	1 2 3	1 2 3	1 2 3	1 2 3 4	1 2 3 4	1
CHOIR 1	Al-le-	lu-ia,	al-le-lu-	ia;		al-le-lu-	ia,	al-le-lu-	ia: ⎡Al - - le- lu- - - - -		ia
CHOIR 2			Al-le-	lu-ia,	al-le-lu-	ia,	al-le-lu-	ia,	⎣Al - - le- lu- - - - -		ia

To make a grand conclusion, the choirs come together again. There is another wash of voice-and-brass sonority as the tempo slows and the meter changes to duple for a climactic *alleluia*. For yet another *alleluia*, the music adds a solemn extra beat, the meter changing once again:

And for still more emphasis, Gabrieli repeats the entire *alleluia* section, comprising the fast triple-time alternations and the massive slow ending.

Notice that there are certain parallels between the beginning and the end of "O magnum mysterium." These include the tempo and meter (slow, changing from **2/2** to **3/2**), the texture (massed choirs), and the musical technique (sequence). Gabrieli has imposed a kind of organization and control on the flamboyant chords and the solo rhapsodies. This is an example of the combination of extravagance and control in early Baroque music that we discussed above.

LISTEN	Giovanni Gabrieli, "O magnum mysterium"

0:00	O magnum mysterium,	O, what a great mystery,
0:30	et admirabile sacramentum	and what a wonderful sacrament—
0:53	ut animalia viderunt Dominum natum	that animals should see the Lord new born
1:18	iacentem in presepio:	lying in the manger.
1:56	Alleluia, alleluia.	Hallelujah, hallelujah.

2 Style Features of Early Baroque Music

Music from the period of approximately 1600 to 1750 is usually referred to as "baroque," a term that captures its excess and extravagance. (It was originally a jeweler's term for large pearls of irregular shape.) A number of broad stylistic features unify the music of this long period.

Rhythm and Meter

Rhythms become more definite, regular, and insistent in Baroque music; a single rhythm or similar rhythms can be heard throughout a piece or a major segment of a piece. Compare the subtle, floating rhythms of Renaissance music, changing section by section as the motives for the imitative polyphony change. (Renaissance dance music is an exception, and in the area of dance music there is a direct line from the Renaissance to the Baroque.)

Related to this new regularity of rhythm is a new acceptance of meter. One technical feature tells the story: Bar lines begin to be used for the first time in music history. This means that music's meter is systematically in evidence, rather than being downplayed as it was in the Renaissance. The strong beats are emphasized by certain instruments, playing in a clear, decisive way. All this is conspicuous enough in Gabrieli's motet "O magnum mysterium."

Texture: Basso Continuo

Some early Baroque music is homophonic and some is polyphonic, but both textures are enriched by a feature unique to the period, the **basso continuo.**

As in a Renaissance score, in a Baroque score the bass line is performed by bass voices or low instruments such as cellos or bassoons. But the bass part in Baroque music is also played by an organ, harpsichord, or other chord instrument. This instrument not only reinforces the bass line, it also adds chords continuously (hence the term *continuo*) to go with it. The basso continuo—or just "continuo"—has the double effect of clarifying the harmony and of making the texture bind or jell.

One can see how this device responds to the growing reliance of Baroque music on harmony (already clear from Gabrieli's motet). In the early days, the continuo was simply the bass line of the polyphony reinforced by chords; but later the continuo with its chords was mapped out first, and the polyphony adjusted to it. Baroque polyphony, in other words, has systematic harmonic underpinnings.

This fact is dramatized by a musical form that is characteristically Baroque, the **ground bass.** This is music constructed literally from the bottom up. In ground bass form, the bass instruments play a single short figure many times, generating the same set of repeated harmonies (played by the continuo chord instruments). Above this ground bass, upper instruments or voices play (or improvise) different melodies or virtuoso passages, all adjusted to the harmonies determined by the bass.

Baroque ground-bass compositions discussed in this book are "Dido's Lament" from the opera *Dido and Aeneas* by Henry Purcell (page 102), a passacaglia by Girolamo Frescobaldi (page 106), and Vivaldi's Violin Concerto in G, Op. 4, No. 12 (page 130).

Another name for the ground bass comes from Baroque Italian musicians: **basso ostinato,** meaning "persistent" or "obstinate" bass. By extension, the term *ostinato* is also used to refer to any short musical gesture repeated over and over again, in the bass or anywhere else, especially one used as a building block for a piece of music. Ostinatos are found in most of the world's musical traditions (see page 108). This is not surprising, since the formal principle they embody is so very fundamental: Set up a repeating pattern and then pit contrasting musical elements against it.

Functional Harmony

Inevitably, in view of these new techniques, the art of harmony evolved rapidly at this time. Whereas Renaissance music had still used the medieval modes, although with important modifications, Baroque musicians developed the modern major/minor system which we discussed on pages 31–34. Chords became standardized, and the sense of tonality—the feeling of centrality around a tonic or "home" pitch—grew much stronger.

A ground bass
(the Pachelbel Canon)

Andante

= repeated
many times

Music is a roaring-meg against melancholy, to rear and revive the languishing soul; affecting not only the ears, but the very arteries, the vital and animal spirits, it erects the mind and makes it nimble.

Robert Burton, 1621

A torchlight concert in a German town square. The harpsichord continuo is at the center of the action. Notice the big music stands or racks, and the two timpani sunk in a panel, like a double sink.

Composers also developed a new way of handling the chords so that their interrelation was felt to be more logical, or at least more coherent. Each chord now assumed a special role, or function, in relation to the tonic chord (the chord on the "home" pitch). Thus when one chord follows another in Baroque music, it does so in a newly predictable and purposeful way. "Functional" harmony, in this sense, could also be used as a way of organizing large-scale pieces of music, as we will see later.

In a Baroque composition, as compared with one from the Renaissance, the chords seem to be going where we expect them to—and we feel they are determining the sense or the direction of the piece as a whole. Harmonies no longer seem to wander, detour, hesitate, or evaporate. With the introduction of the important resource of functional harmony, Baroque music brings us firmly to the familiar, to the threshold of modern music.

3 Opera

Opera—drama presented in music, with the characters singing instead of speaking—is often called the most characteristic art form of the Baroque period. For Baroque opera combined many different arts: not only music, drama, and poetry, but also dancing, highly elaborate scene design, and spectacular special effects. Incredibly ingenious machines were contrived to portray gods descending to

Stage designers of Baroque opera specialized in rapidly moving scenery for their most dazzling effects. Shown here is the machinery for one such set and a drawing of the intended realization.

earth, shipwrecks, volcanos, and all kinds of natural and supernatural phenomena. Scene designers often received top billing, ahead of the composers.

The early Florentine operas were court entertainments put on to celebrate royal weddings and the like. But an important step was taken in 1637 with the opening of the first public opera theater. First in Venice and then in the whole of Italy, opera soon became the leading form of entertainment. By the end of the century, seven opera houses in Venice fulfilled much the same function as movie theaters in a comparable modern city (around 145,000 people).

Opera was a perfect answer to the general desire in the early Baroque era for individual emotionalism. For opera provided a stage on which the single individual could step forward to express his or her feelings in the most direct and powerful fashion. Indeed, composers felt a need to relieve the constant emotional pressure exerted on their characters by the ever-changing dramatic action. They had to contrive moments of relaxation, moments when the characters could stop and reflect. This led to a standard dualism that has been with opera ever since: *recitative* and *aria*. This dualism between tension and repose reflects that other Baroque dualism, between freedom and strictness, extravagance and control.

Recitative

Recitative (re-si-ta-téev), from the Italian word for "recitation," is the technique of declaiming words musically in a heightened, theatrical manner. The singing voice closely follows the free rhythm of highly emotional speech; it mirrors and exaggerates the natural ups and downs that occur as an actor raises his or her voice at a question, lowers it in an "aside," or cries out in distress. The accompaniment is usually kept to a minimum. This allows the singer-actor to interpret the dialogue or the action as spontaneously as possible, and also ensures all the words can be heard clearly.

Recitative—the "free" side of the operatic dualism—is used for plot action, dialogue, and other situations in the drama where it is particularly important for the words to be brought out. On the other hand, where spoken drama would call for soliloquies or meditations, opera uses arias.

Aria

An **aria** is an extended piece for solo singer that has much more musical elaboration and coherence than a passage of recitative. The vocal part is more melodic, the rhythm is more consistent, and typically the accompaniment includes the entire orchestra. Here the singer-actor mulls over his or her feelings at some leisure, instead of reacting moment by moment, as in recitative. Emotion is controlled and "frozen" into a tableau. Paradoxically, when the music gets more elaborate, the emotion stands still.

Recitative required great singing actors, and arias required artists who could convert the notes of a score into these tableaus of furious, sensuous, or tragic expression. Opera houses in the seventeenth century became showcases of vocal virtuosity—as they still are today. Ever since the Baroque era, musical drama and vocal display have vied with one another as the driving force of opera.

Claudio Monteverdi (1567–1643)

One figure stood out above all others in music around 1600, just as Josquin Desprez had around 1500. Claudio Monteverdi, an enormously imaginative and innovative composer, also has the dubious distinction of being the first great composer whose music was attacked publicly for being too radical. Radical it was. Monteverdi has aptly been called "the last great madrigalist and the first great opera composer"; indeed, while his earliest madrigals are close enough in style to those of Thomas Weelkes, some of his later ones are more like small opera scenes.

Monteverdi first worked at the music-loving court of Mantua, in northern Italy. There he wrote his first stage work, *Orfeo* (1607), famous in music history as the first masterpiece of opera. He was then appointed choirmaster of St. Mark's Cathedral in Venice, the most prestigious musical position in Europe. At the end of his life, in the 1640s, he helped inaugurate public opera, Venice's greatest contribution to the history of music.

CLAUDIO MONTEVERDI
The Coronation of Poppea (1642)

After his first opera, *Orfeo*, none of Monteverdi's operas were printed, and some have been completely lost—a grievous loss indeed. All we have left of his *Arianna* is the heroine's big lament, one of the greatest hits of the day, which Monteverdi published by itself in several different arrangements. Fortunately, two late masterpieces have survived: *The Return of Ulysses* and *The Coronation of Poppea*. After slumbering for three hundred years, *Poppea* has recently proved to be a "sleeper" in opera houses around the world.

Monteverdi as a young man, and as pictured on a commemorative edition of poems honoring him, published in Venice ("in VENE-TIA") just after his death. The design includes a fine collection of old instruments, including four lutes, shown in front and back views.

Background   Even today, the story of *The Coronation of Poppea* can shock by its startling and cynical dramatic realism. Poppea, mistress of the notorious Roman Emperor Nero, schemes to get his wife, Ottavia, deposed and his eminent adviser, Seneca, put to death. She succeeds in both. In a counterplot, Ottavia blackmails Ottone, Poppea's rejected lover, into an attempt on Poppea's life. He tries but fails. The counterplotters are all exiled. As an added cynical touch, Poppea's ruthless maneuvering to be crowned empress of Rome is shown to be aided by the God of Love and the Goddess of Fortune.

After a prologue sung by the mythological characters, Act I begins with Ottone arriving at Poppea's house at daybreak, and retreating in dismay after he sees Nero's guards outside it. In an ironic alba (see page 62), the guards curse military life and exchange scurrilous gossip about Poppea's scheming. This is a vivid prelude to the first of the opera's several steamy love scenes.

Recitative   Enter Nero and Poppea, who tries to wheedle Nero into staying with her. Delaying his departure as long as possible, she makes him promise to return. Accompanied by a lute as continuo instrument—a voluptuous sound, in this context—she repeats the question "*Tornerai?*" ("Won't you return?") in increasingly seductive accents until Nero stops evading the issue and agrees: "*Tornerò*" ("Yes, I will return"). Notice how the vocal line does not form it-self into real melodies, but goes up or down or speeds or slows, following the words in speechlike fragments.

Nero's most extended evasion is a short aria-like fragment, called an **arioso.** Then the recitative resumes. On the final *addios*—some of them melting, others breathless—the singers say goodbye, improvising delicate vocal ornaments.

Aria   As soon as Nero leaves, Poppea shows her true colors in a jubilant aria, a sort of victory dance. It is accompanied by a small orchestra, and contains

Many men's roles in early opera were written for castrati, male soprano singers (see page 152). On our recording, Nero is sung by a female mezzo-soprano, Della Jones, whose lower, more "focused" voice contrasts with that of the soprano singing Poppea.

three short sections. The first is an orchestral tune (strings and recorder) to which Poppea sings her first two lines of text:

Allegro
POPPEA (with strings, recorder)

Speran - za _____ tu mi va - i   il core ac - ca - rez - zando _____

Note that a moment of uncertainty ("a mantle that is . . . illusory") is marked by a momentary lapse into recitative. Her mood becomes harder and more determined in the aria's second section. Finally, in section 3, she sings lighthearted, fast military fanfares—this is word painting in the madrigal tradition—as she crows that the gods are fighting on her behalf.

Mercurial, manipulative, fearless, dangerously sensual: Poppea has been characterized unforgettably by Monteverdi's music in this scene.

LISTEN	Monteverdi, *The Coronation of Poppea,* from Act I	

15-16

(Italics indicate repeated words and lines. For a word about singing Italian, see page 102.)

RECITATIVE

15	0:00	**Poppea:**	Tornerai?	Won't you return?
		Nero:	Se ben io vò,	Though I am leaving you,
			Pur teco io stò, *pur teco stò . . .*	I am in truth still here . . .
		Poppea:	Tornerai?	Won't you return?
		Nero:	Il cor dalle tue stelle	My heart can never, never be torn away
			Mai mai non si disvelle . . .	from your fair eyes . . .
		Poppea:	Tornerai?	Won't you return?

ARIOSO

	0:24	**Nero:**	Io non posso da te, *non posso da te,*	I cannot live apart from you
			da te viver disgiunto	
			Se non si smembra l'unita del punto . . .	Unless unity itself can be divided . . .

RECITATIVE

	0:56	**Poppea:**	Tornerai?	Won't you return?
		Nero:	Tornerò.	I will return.
		Poppea:	Quando?	When?
		Nero:	Ben tosto.	Soon.
		Poppea:	Ben tosto, me'l prometti?	Very soon—you promise?
		Nero:	Te'l giuro.	I swear it!
		Poppea:	*E me l'osserverai?*	And will you keep your promise?
		Nero:	*E s'a te non verrò, tu a me verrai!*	If I do not come, you'll come to me!
	1:23	**Poppea:**	Addio . . .	Farewell . . .
		Nero:	Addio . . .	
		Poppea:	Nerone, Nerone, addio . . .	
		Nero:	Poppea, Poppea, addio . . .	
		Poppea:	Addio, Nerone, addio!	Farewell, Nero, farewell!
		Nero:	Addio, Poppea, ben mio.	Farewell, Poppea, my love.

16	2:25	ARIA	(Section 1)	
0:10	2:35	**Poppea:**	Speranza, tu mi vai	O hope, you
			Il core accarezzando;	Caress my heart;
			Speranza, tu mi vai il genio lusingando;	O hope, you entice my mind;
			E mi circondi intanto	As you cloak me
			Di regio si, ma immaginario manto.	In a mantle that is royal, yes, but illusory.
			(Section 2)	
0:46	3:11		No no, non temo, no,	No, no! I fear no adversity:
			no no, non temo, no di noia alcuna:	
			(Section 3)	
:03	3:28		Per me guerreggia, *guerreggia,*	I have fighting for me,
			Per me guerreggia Amor, *guerreggia*	I have fighting for me Love
			Amor e la Fortuna, *e la Fortuna.*	and Fortune.

Singing Italian

The Coronation of Poppea is the first of many Italian texts printed in this book. To follow the recordings, it will help to know a few simple rules about Italian pronunciation and singing conventions.

⁊   The consonants *c* and *g* are soft (pronounced "ch" and "j") when followed by *e* or *i* (cello, Genoa, cappuccino, DiMaggio). They are hard when followed by other letters, including *h* (Galileo, spaghetti con Chianti).

⁊   In poems, when an Italian word *ending* with a vowel is followed by another word *beginning* with a vowel, the two vowels are elided, run together as one.

⁊   In Italian (and German) *z* is pronounced *dz* or *tz* (pizza, Mozart).

Lines from our selection from *The Coronation of Poppea* are sung as indicated below:

3 Pur teco io stò	= Pur téc'yo stó
18 **tu a** me verrai	= tw'a méh verrah-ee
26 Il core **accarezzando**	= Il cór'accaretzándo
28 E mi **circondi** intanto	= E mi chircónd'intánto
33 Per me **guerreggia** Amor	= Per méh gwerréj'Amór

Henry Purcell (1659–1695)

Italy was the undisputed leader in music throughout the seventeenth century. However, music also flourished in France, Germany (or what is now Germany), and other countries, always under Italian influence.

The greatest English composer of the Baroque era, Henry Purcell, was the organist at Westminster Abbey and a member of the Chapel Royal, like several other members of his family. In his short lifetime he wrote sacred, instrumental, and theater music, as well as twenty-nine "Welcome Songs" for his royal masters. Purcell combined a respect for native traditions, represented by the music of William Byrd, Thomas Weelkes, and others, with a lively interest in the more adventurous French and Italian music of his own time. He wrote and published the first English examples of a new Italian genre, the sonata.

HENRY PURCELL
Dido and Aeneas (1689)

Though Purcell wrote a good deal of music for the London theater, his one true opera, *Dido and Aeneas,* was performed at a girls' school (though there may have been an earlier performance at court). The whole thing lasts little more than an hour and contains no virtuoso singing roles at all. *Dido and Aeneas* is an exceptional work, then, and a miniature. But it is also a work of rare beauty and dramatic power—and rarer still, it is a great opera in English, perhaps the only great opera in English prior to the twentieth century.

Background   Purcell's source was the *Aeneid*, the noblest of all Latin epic poems, written by Virgil to celebrate the glory of Rome and the Roman Empire. It tells the story of the city's foundation by the Trojan prince Aeneas, who escapes from Troy when the Greeks capture it with their wooden horse. After many adventures and travels, Aeneas finally reaches Italy, guided by the firm hand of Jove, king of the gods.

In one of the *Aeneid*'s most famous episodes, Aeneas and the widowed Queen Dido of Carthage fall deeply in love. But Jove tells the prince to stop dallying and get on with his important journey. Regretfully he leaves, and Dido kills herself—an agonizing suicide, as Virgil describes it.

Henry Purcell

In Acts I and II of the opera, Dido expresses apprehension about her feelings for Aeneas, even though her courtiers keep encouraging the match in chorus after chorus. Next we see the plotting of some witches—a highly un-Virgilian touch, but ever since Shakespeare's *Macbeth*, witches had been popular with English theatergoers, perhaps especially with school-age ones. For malicious reasons of their own, these witches make Aeneas believe that Jove is ordering his departure.

In Act III, Aeneas tries feebly to excuse himself. Dido spurns him in a furious recitative. As he leaves, deserting her, she prepares for her suicide.

Recitative   Dido addresses this regal, somber recitative to her confidante, Belinda. Notice the imperious tone as she tells Belinda to take her hand, and the ominous setting of the word *darkness*. Purcell even contrives to suggest a kind of tragic irony when Dido's melodic line turns to the major mode on the word *welcome* in "Death is now a welcome guest."

Aria   The opera's final aria, usually known as "Dido's Lament," is built over a slow ground bass or ostinato (see page 96), a descending bass line with chromatic semitones repeated a dozen times. The bass line sounds mournful even without accompaniment, as in measures 1–4. Violins in the string orchestra imitate this line while Dido is singing, and especially after she has stopped.

As often happens in arias, the words are repeated a number of times; Dido has little to say but much to feel, and the music needs time to convey the emotional message. We experience an extended emotional tableau. Whereas recitative makes little sense unless the listener understands the exact words, with arias a general impression of them may be enough. Indeed, even that is unnecessary when the song is as poignant as Purcell's is here.

The most heartbreaking place comes (twice) on the exclamation "ah," where the bass note D, harmonized with a major-mode chord during the first six appearances of the ground bass, is shadowed by a new minor chord:

Chorus   The last notes of this great aria run into a wonderful final chorus. We are to imagine a slow dance, as groups of sorrowful cupids (first-graders, perhaps) file past the bier. Now Dido's personal grief and agony is transmuted into a communal sense of mourning. In the context of the whole opera, this chorus seems even more meaningful, because the courtiers who sing it have matured so much since the time when they thoughtlessly and cheerfully urged Dido to give in to her love.

The general style of the music is that of the madrigal—imitative polyphony and homophony, with some word painting. (The first three lines are

Our Songs and our Musick
Let's still dedicate
To *Purcell*, to *Purcell*,
The Son of *Apollo*,
'Till another, another,
Another as Great
In the Heav'nly Science
Of Musick shall follow.

—Poet Thomas d'Urfey, seventeenth century (Apollo was the Greek god of music.)

Dec. 6, 1665. *Here the best company for musique I ever was in, in my life, and I wish I could live and die in it, both for the musique and the face of Mrs. Pierce, and my wife, and Mrs. Knipp, who is pretty enough and sings the noblest that ever I heard in my life.*

London civil servant Samuel Pepys, from his diary (first published in 1825) mostly imitative, the last one homophonic.) But Purcell's style clearly shows the inroads of functional harmony and of the definite, unified rhythms that had been developing in the seventeenth century. There is no mistaking this touching chorus for an actual Renaissance madrigal.

Like "Dido's Lament," "With drooping wings" is another emotional tableau, and this time the emotion spills over to the opera audience. As the courtiers grieve for Dido, we join them in responding to Dido's tragedy.

LISTEN	Purcell, *Dido and Aeneas*, Act III, final scene

17-18

(Italics indicate repeated words and lines.)

RECITATIVE

17 0:00 **Dido:**   Thy hand, Belinda! Darkness shades me;
    On thy bosom let me rest.
    More I would—but death invades me:
    Death is now a welcome guest.

ARIA

0:58 **Dido:**   When I am laid, *am laid* in earth
    May my wrongs create
    No trouble, *no trouble* in thy breast; *(repeated)*
    Remember me . . . *remember me,* but ah, forget my
        fate;

2:17   *Remember me, but ah, forget my fate.*
        (stabs herself)

CHORUS

18 4:01 **Courtiers:** With drooping wings, ye cupids come
        (words repeated)
    And scatter roses, *scatter, scatter roses* on her tomb.
    Soft, *soft* and gentle as her heart.

1:30 5:31   Keep here, *here* your watch;
    Keep here, here, keep here your watch,
        and never, *never, never,* part.

Colored type indicates words treated with word painting.

4 The Rise of Instrumental Music

The development of instrumental music—music without words, music that does not depend on words—counts as one of the most far-reaching contributions of composers in the early Baroque period. Broadly speaking, we can trace instrumental music to three main sources.

¶ *Dance,* the first of these sources, is one we have already discussed. In the Baroque period dance received a special impetus from opera, the genre that most fascinated people at the time. The reason is that opera was firmly linked to ballet, as we have seen in *Dido and Aeneas.* Musicians, especially in France, the center of ballet at the time, would put together sets of dances selected from operas or ballets. These dance **suites,** as they were called—groups of dances— could then be played by an orchestra and enjoyed apart from an actual stage performance.

Composers also wrote many dances and suites for harpsichord. These are "stylized" dances (see page 89), pieces written in the style or the form of dance music but intended for listening rather than dancing, for mental rather than physical pleasure.

⅂ *Virtuosity* was the second source from which composers of instrumental music drew. As long as instruments have existed there have surely been virtuoso players ready to show them off—and audiences ready to applaud the show. But the art of early virtuosos was improvised and scarcely ever written down; only in the sixteenth and seventeenth centuries was some of their art incorporated systematically into written-out compositions. Even then, not all the virtuosity on which the compositions depended for their effect was notated. Much was left to be improvised, and so modern performers often have to play a good deal more than what appears in the old scores.

⅂ *Vocal music* was the third source for instrumental music. More specifically, the principal technique of vocal music, imitative polyphony (imitation), was transferred to the instrumental medium. In fact, this happened already in the Renaissance, which developed several instrumental genres by modeling on vocal music in this way. Each genre consists of a series of points of imitation (see pages 78, 80) built on different motives, like a motet or a madrigal.

From these genres developed the characteristic polyphonic genre of the Baroque era, the **fugue.** A typical fugue uses only one theme throughout—like a single gigantic point of imitation—and often treats that theme with a considerable display of contrapuntal ingenuity and learning. The art of improvising and writing fugues was practiced especially by keyboard players: organists and harpsichordists. We will discuss fugue more fully in Chapter 9.

Vocal music influenced instrumental music in another way as well. It gave instrumentalists a fund of materials they could use as the basis for sets of **variations**—that is, sectional pieces in which each section repeats certain musical elements while others change around them.

Girolamo Frescobaldi (1583–1643)

The three main sources of instrumental music are all evident in the keyboard works of Girolamo Frescobaldi. Frescobaldi was the foremost organ virtuoso of the early seventeenth century, famed through much of Europe for his expressive and even extravagant improvising and composition. Organist of St. Peter's in Rome, he was an influential teacher, and his influence reached far beyond his own pupils. A century later Johann Sebastian Bach—keyboard virtuoso in his own right and composer of an immense body of organ and harpsichord works—carefully studied Frescobaldi's music.

We will hear Frescobaldi's music on an organ specially modeled on an instrument of his own time. The player employs four different *registrations,* that is, different combinations of the organ's many sets of pipes: See page 44. Frescobaldi's works represent several distinct genres:

⅂ **Toccatas,** free-formed pieces meant to capture the spirit of Frescobaldi's own improvisation (*toccata* means "touched" in Italian, as in the touching of keys);

⅂ **Canzonas,** more rigorously organized works emphasizing imitative texture— the ancestors of later fugues;

⅂ Stylized dances, formed of two phrases each, one or both of them repeated to yield the pattern **a a b** or **a a b b** (for similar Renaissance patterns, see page 88); these dances are sometimes grouped together in small suites; and

⅂ Sets of variations on melodic or harmonic patterns borrowed from vocal music.

Even that vulgar and tavern music, which makes one man merry, another mad, strikes in me a deep fit of devotion, and a profound contemplation of the first Composer; there is something in it of divinity more than the ear discovers.

Physician-author Sir Thomas Browne, 1642

Girolamo Frescobaldi

GIROLAMO FRESCOBALDI
Suite (Canzona, Balletto, Corrente, and Passacaglia) (1627–1637)

LISTEN

Frescobaldi, Suite

0:00 **Canzona**
0:27   new theme

0:00 **Balletto** a
0:08   a
0:16 (0:30) **b b**

0:00 **Corrente** a
0:10   a
0:21 (0:36) **b b**

0:00 **Passacaglia**
0:14   Variation 2
1:37   Variation 14

Frescobaldi's Balletto, Corrente, and Passacaglia is a miniature suite made up of two short dance movements followed by a set of variations. We introduce it, as Frescobaldi himself might have done, with the opening section of one of his canzonas.

19 *Canzona*   This piece opens with a point of imitation (see page 80) using a theme that begins with long leaps followed by running sixteenth notes:

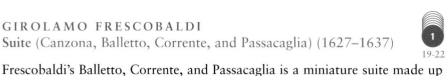

After four entries of this theme the music comes to a cadence. Then a new theme enters at the top of the texture, this one marked by three repeated notes at its start. Frescobaldi immediately combines the second theme in counterpoint with the first, pitting the two against each other until he brings the music to a solid cadence.

20, 21 *Balletto and Corrente*   Each of these dance movements consists of two phrases, both of which are repeated: **a a b b.** Careful listening reveals that the two dances are related, especially by their bass lines:

While sharing a bass line, however, the dances also contrast strongly in their meters, the first duple, the second triple. Such metrical contrast from one dance to the next was a basic principle of suites from the late Renaissance on. (Compare the pavane and galliard on page 88.)

22 *Passacaglia*   This mellifluous term (pronounced *pas-sa-cáhl-ya*) refers to a set of variations on a brief series of chords and also the bass line associated with the chords. Both the harmonies and the bass line were at first associated with vocal music. Because of their repeating bass lines, **passacaglias** bear a close kinship to slower ostinato pieces like "Dido's Lament." But usually the bass line of a passacaglia is repeated less strictly than is the ostinato of Purcell's work; it can even disappear entirely, leaving only the general chord progression to mark the variations. New at the time of Frescobaldi, the passacaglia remained popular a century later in the age of Bach and Handel.

The bass line of this passacaglia (and many others) runs in its simplest form something like the example to the right. Its length determines the length of each variation: four measures of fairly quick triple meter. (Get used to the main beat of the piece and then count **1** 2 3|**2** 2 3|**3** 2 3|**4** 2 3.) You can hear the bass line in its original, descending form in the first four measures, the theme, and many times more thereafter. Already in the second variation, however, and several times later, Frescobaldi plays a trick on the listener, composing an *ascending* bass line instead of the descending one while maintaining essentially the same progression of harmonies.

Violins are varnished and sun dried in Cremona, a little town in northern Italy famous for its violin makers since the 1600s. Violinist-composers such as Vivaldi (see page 132) wrote for instruments by Antonio Stradivarius and other master craftsmen. See page 128.

Frescobaldi seems able to milk endless variety from this simple material; this facility is the essence of skillful composing of variations. He is especially fond of coloring his music with piquant flashes of unexpected half steps, or **chromaticism** (especially piquant on this historical organ). At the same time he devises many different rhythmic patterns, some with fast running notes, others slower, some even and flowing, some dotted and jaunty.

Listen also for one more clever twist near the end of the movement: Frescobaldi changes key, or modulates, and at the same time shifts from major to minor mode. There are eighteen quick variations in all; the last five of them take place in this new key.

The instrumental music of the early seventeenth century was the quiet precursor to an explosion of new instrumental styles and genres in the late Baroque era. We go on to discuss this in Unit III, after an introductory "Prelude" chapter dealing with aspects of the history and culture of the time.

Web: *Research and test your understanding of early Baroque music at* <bedfordstmartins.com/listen>.

GLOBAL PERSPECTIVES 3

Ostinato Forms

32, 33

Though we borrow the term *ostinato* from Italian Baroque music, the technique is much older than the seventeenth century and is dispersed around the globe. The organizational principle at stake is, indeed, basic: Set up a brief repeating musical unit and use it as the foundation for other more varied melodies and harmonies.

Musical forms built according to this principle come in a wide variety of shapes and patterns. We have already begun to appreciate this variety in comparing "Dido's Lament" by Purcell with Frescobaldi's Passacaglia: The first presents a free-flowing melody over an unchanging bass line, while the second rings changes on an underlying harmonic pattern.

African Ostinatos

Nowhere in the world is ostinato form more prominent, or practiced with a richer array of techniques, genres, and instruments, than in Africa. From northern African nations, with their traditions of troubadour-

A Sudanese lyre (compare with the ancient Greek lyre on page 7).

like singers accompanying themselves on a single instrument, all the way to South Africa, with its electrified, rock'n'roll–derived Township Jive—up and down the continent, ostinato forms multiply in fascinating variety. (Rock itself is a great repository of ostinato forms.)

On our CD we hear two examples of African ostinato form, one from the Sudan, a nation lying along the Nile River to the south of Egypt, and the other from the Mbuti pygmies of the rainforests of Congo in central Africa.

A Minstrel's Song   In the first, Sudanese excerpt we hear a virtuosic singer-reciter named Doogus Idris accompanying himself on a plucked-string instrument called a *jangar,* a type of lyre. Two upright bars extend from a resonating sound box and are fastened to a crossbar at the top; five strings are stretched between the crossbar and the bottom of the sound box. Traditions of solo song accompanied by the lyre reach back very far in history in the cultures around the Mediterranean Sea, whether in Europe, the Middle East, or Africa. Homer's *Iliad* and *Odyssey* were sung to the lyre, but for some reason in most of Europe the lyre has not survived to the present day.

In Africa, the singers in these traditions fulfill a wide variety of social roles. They sing the praises of powerful leaders, narrate historical or legendary events, contribute to social rituals such as weddings, or simply provide informal entertainment. In all these functions they are not so different from the troubadours and trouvères of medieval France (see page 62).

In our example, the singer declaims in lively fashion a song about a young man and woman in love and the dowry he must pay to have her as his bride:

Doia, ben uli Kana	Kana, he comes!
Kaya ba cuzon nabore	Kaya desires her brown lover;
turi koleth Ebasel gnalek	she admired the knife on his shoulder.
bungur ley agamat ben	When he arrived at the house, he said:
ering-ei-yama kol mal.	"I need a large goat."

To accompany himself the singer plays a brief ostinato on the jangar. He alters it at times from a chordal strumming to a more melodic presentation—treating it, in other words, with the same freedom

Frescobaldi used in altering the bass line and texture of his Passacaglia. But the ostinato never loses its clear, repetitious identity.

Over this rigid scaffolding, Doogus Idris sings a relatively free melody. He presents the same stanza of words twice, repeating many individual words along the way: Listen at 0:53 on track 32 when, after a brief break for the jangar alone, he begins the whole text over again. Through each stanza his melody gradually and gracefully falls from the high pitches at its beginning to the low cadence at its end.

Pygmy Polyphony   Since it was first recorded in the 1950s, Mbuti communal singing has become famous for its delicate and complex polyphony. You may recognize the style, even if you have not heard recordings of pygmies before, since it has often been imitated by pop and world-beat singers such as Madonna and the group Zap Mama.

Pygmy polyphony is created in improvised group singing, sometimes in rituals central to the society, sometimes to accompany work, sometimes for simple pleasure and relaxation. It involves a technique common to many kinds of African music: *interlocking ostinatos*. In a pygmy chorus, various voices form an intricate, repetitive texture by singing over and over again their own short melodic lines—often only one or two notes—in quick alternation. (This technique may remind us of the *hocket* we encountered in the isorhythmic motet of the Middle Ages; see page 69.) The overall effect is of a multistranded, hypnotically

recycling ostinato. This choral ostinato can be savored on its own or else, as in our example, used as the foundation for freer melodies of lead singers.

A Hunting Song for Chorus   Two exclamations for the whole chorus announce the beginning of a song describing the bravery and daring of an elephant hunt. At first, we hear no clear ostinato. Instead, the two lead singers alternate prominent melodic phrases while, underneath them, we can hear the chorus singing softly—almost murmuring—an indistinct, ostinatolike melody.

Then something marvelous happens: At about 0:47 on track 33 the individual melodic motives of a polyphonic ostinato begin to crystallize in the chorus. We hear the polyphony taking shape. (How many distinct components of the ostinato can you make out?) By 1:30 the choral ostinato is fully formed and clearly articulated; it continues through to the end of the song (not heard here) underneath the soloists.

The singing is underlaid throughout by the simplest of instrumental accompaniments: two sticks struck together to mark the beat. The Mbuti rarely employ more elaborate instruments in their choral singing, though in other, individual contexts they regularly play on drums, flutes, musical bows, and other instruments.

This song was recorded in the mid-1950s by Colin Turnbull, a British anthropologist who was among the first to study the pygmies. He described their society poetically and lovingly in a book still read today, *The Forest People*, but he didn't give the names of the singers of this song.

Mbuti villagers, singing and dancing to tall drums

1700   1750   1800

Louis XIV

Isaac Newton

Antonio Vivaldi

Jean-Antoine Watteau

Johann Sebastian Bach

George Frideric Handel

Salem witch trials
◆

Voltaire

John Wesley

Benjamin Franklin

Leonhard Euler

David Hume

Jean-Jacques Rousseau

Frederick the Great

Christoph Willibald von Gluck

Carl Philipp Emanuel Bach

Adam Smith

Immanuel Kant

Franz Joseph Haydn

George Washington

Antoine Laurent Lavoisier

Thomas Jefferson

Francisco Goya

Jacques-Louis David

Johann Wolfgang von Goethe

First modern encyclopedia published in France
◆⋯⋯⋯⋯⋯

James Madison

Wolfgang Amadeus Mozart

William Blake

Napoleon Bonaparte

British industrialization begins
◆⋯⋯⋯⋯⋯⋯⋯⋯⋯⋯⋯⋯⋯⋯⋯⋯

Ludwig van Beethoven

Declaration of Independence, U.S. Constitution
◆⋯⋯⋯

Jane Austen

French Revolution begins
◆

           Life spans of major composers

           Life spans of other important historical and artistic figures

◆⋯⋯⋯⋯   Historical events

The Eighteenth Century

The first body of music this book takes up in some detail is the music of the eighteenth century, the earliest music we hear regularly in concerts and on the radio. The eighteenth century in music covers two very different style periods: the late Baroque era and the era of Viennese Classicism. In the following pages we will need to clarify the differences between these periods and their music.

In spite of these differences, the music of the eighteenth century can be thought of as a unit. The reason is not a matter of musical style, at least not directly, important as style may be. Rather, it has to do with a certain quality of musical expression, a certain objectivity in the feelings this music seems to express or depict. Even when it is powerful and moving, it keeps its distance from the listener. Music of the nineteenth century is more demonstrative, more personal, more obviously intense; this music is called "romantic." In drawing the broadest distinctions, then, it is fair to put Baroque and Classical music on one side, Romantic music on the other. Romantic music often seems to want to share—even impose—feelings. Eighteenth-century music seems rather to demonstrate feelings.

A fair distinction, and also a functional one, it seems. In one large American metropolitan area, not long ago, two radio stations used to broadcast what they called "good music" around the clock; and most of the time, eighteenth-century music was played on one of the stations, nineteenth-century music on the other. On some basic level, there must be a distinction between the music of these two centuries; these stations, their advertisers, and their audiences were responding to it. Some listeners are temperamentally attuned to one kind of music, some to the other. Probably still other listeners punch buttons on the car radio depending on their mood of the moment.

The social and economic conditions under which the music was originally produced are behind this broad distinction in expressive quality. In our "Prelude" chapters, Chapters 8 and 11, we look at the cultural background and the social setting of eighteenth-century music, and suggest how these factors influenced musical style and expression. The other chapters in this unit look into specific works by the leading late Baroque composers Bach, Handel, and Vivaldi, and the Classical composers Haydn and Mozart.

Prelude
The Late Baroque Period

M usic from the period of approximately 1600 to 1750 is usually referred to as "baroque," a term borrowed from art history. Art historians themselves borrowed the term from seventeenth-century jewelers, who applied it to large pearls of irregular shape. At one time, then, Baroque art was considered imperfect, bizarre, or at least erratic. With changing taste over the centuries, however, what was originally a negative implication has turned positive.

And over the last fifty years, with the help of recordings, Baroque music has grown more and more popular. Instruments of the period have been revived to play it, among them the harpsichord, the recorder, and a special high-pitched trumpet without valves. (Some of these instruments were discussed on pages 38–45.) Most of the Baroque music heard today dates from the eighteenth century—from around 1700 to 1750, a subperiod sometimes classified as the "late Baroque." Johann Sebastian Bach and George Frideric Handel were the greatest composers of this period, and among their most important contemporaries were Alessandro Scarlatti and Antonio Vivaldi in Italy, François Couperin and Jean Philippe Rameau in France, Domenico Scarlatti (the son of Alessandro) in Spain, and Georg Philipp Telemann in Germany.

1 Absolutism and the Age of Science

"Baroque" is a period term used by art historians and musicologists. Historians are more likely to speak of the period from 1600 to 1750 as the Age of Absolutism, a time when the doctrine of the "divine right of kings" ensured the absolute rule of "God-chosen" monarchs. This was the time when Louis XIV of France became the most powerful monarch in all of European history, and also one of the most ruthless. The pomp and splendor of his court were emulated by a host of lesser kings and nobles.

Students of the history of ideas, on the other hand, speak of this as the Age of Science. In this era, the telescope and the microscope revealed their first secrets; Newton and Leibniz invented calculus; Newton developed his laws of

Louis XIV's palace of Versailles, with a procession of carriages arriving in the great courtyard. Note the formal gardens and canal.

mechanics and the theory of gravity. These discoveries stimulated both technology and philosophy—not only the formal philosophy of the great empiricist thinkers Descartes, Locke, and Hume, but also philosophy in a more informal sense. People began to think about ordinary matters in a new way, affected by the newly acquired habits of scientific experimentation and proof. The mental climate stimulated by science significantly affected the music and the art we call Baroque.

Absolutism and science were two of the most vital currents that defined life in the seventeenth and early eighteenth centuries. The result was an interesting dualism that can be traced throughout Baroque art: pomp and extravagance on the one hand, system and calculation on the other. The same dualism can be traced in Baroque music.

Art and Absolutism

Though there had always been royalty in Europe who practiced the arts of peace as well as the arts of war, sponsorship of the arts rose to new heights in the Baroque era. In earlier years, the artistic glories of the Renaissance were supported by powerful merchant-princes, such as the Medici family in Florence, who were determined to add luster to the city-states they ruled. But never before the seventeenth century did one state loom so large in Europe as did France under Louis XIV (1638–1715), the so-called Sun King.

Art in the service of royalty: a *very* idealized portrait of Louis XIV by the greatest sculptor of the day, Gianlorenzo Bernini (1598–1680).

Design for an opera stage set by G. G. Bibiena. This astonishing scene was intended for an opera at the court of Dresden in Germany.

All of French life orbited around the royal court, like planets, comets, and cosmic dust in the solar system. Pomp and ceremony were carried to extreme lengths: The king's *levée*—his getting-up-in-the-morning rite—involved dozens of functionaries and routines lasting two hours. Artists of all kinds were supported lavishly, so long as their work symbolized the majesty of the state (and the state, in Louis's famous remark, "is me"—*"l'état, c'est moi"*).

The influence of this monarch and his image extended far beyond France, for other European princes and dukes envied his absolute rule and did everything they could to match it. Especially in Germany—which was not a united country, like France, but a patchwork of several hundred political units—rulers vied with one another in supporting artists who built, painted, and sang to their glory. Artistic life in Europe was kept alive for many generations by this sort of patronage, and the brilliance and grandeur of much Baroque art derives from its political function.

Art was to impress, even to stupefy. Thus Louis XIV built the most enormous palace in history, Versailles, with over three hundred rooms, including an eighty-yard-long Hall of Mirrors, and great formal gardens extending for miles. Many nobles and prelates built little imitation-Versailles palaces, among them the archbishop of Würzburg, whose magnificent residence was built in Bach's lifetime. The rooms were decorated by the Venetian artist Giovanni Battista Tiepolo (1696–1770), a master of Baroque ceiling painting.

Looking up at the ceiling shown on page 115, and trying to imagine its true dimensions, we are dazzled by figures in excited motion, caught up in great gusts of wind that whirl them out of the architectural space. Ceiling painting provides a vivid example of the extravagant side of the Baroque dualism.

The Music of Absolutism

Just as painting and architecture could glorify rulers through color and designs extending through space, music could glorify by sound extending through time. The nobility demanded horn players for their ceremonial hunts, trumpeters for their battles, and orchestras for balls and entertainments. They required smaller groups of musicians for *Tafelmusik* ("table music"), background music for their lengthy banquets. A special "celebratory" or "festive" orchestra featuring military instruments—trumpets and drums—was used to pay homage to kings and princes; by extension, it also glorified God, the "King of Kings," as he is called in Handel's "Hallelujah" Chorus. The words sung by the chorus in this famous work praise God, but the accompanying orchestra with its trumpets also pays splendid homage to King George II of England (see pages 158–59).

The main musical vehicle of Baroque absolutism was opera. Opera today is an expensive entertainment in which a drama is presented with music and elaborate stage spectacle. So it was in the Baroque era. The stage set shown opposite was created by a member of the Bibiena family, the foremost set designers of the time. It conveys the majestic heights and distances of an ideal Baroque palace by means of perspective, though the stage was actually quite shallow. The figures gesture grandly, but they are dwarfed by pasteboard architecture that seems to whirl as dizzily as does the painted architecture on Tiepolo's ceiling.

Baroque grandeur: a ceiling painting by Giovanni Battista Tiepolo (1696–1770). The oval measures 30 feet by 60 feet.

One aspect of Baroque opera is unlike opera today: The stories were allegorical tributes to the glory and supposed virtue of those who paid for them. For example, one favorite Baroque opera story tells of the Roman Emperor Titus, who survives a complicated plot on his life and then magnanimously forgives the plotters. This story was set to music by dozens of different court composers. It told courtiers that if they opposed their king, he might well excuse them out of the godlike goodness of his heart (for he claimed to rule by divine right). But it also reminded them that he was an absolute ruler—a modern Roman tyrant—who could do exactly the reverse if he pleased. Operas flattered princes while at the same time stressing their power and, not incidentally, their wealth.

Art and Theatricality

Opera was invented in Italy around the year 1600. Indeed, opera counts as Italy's great contribution to the seventeenth century's golden age of the theater. This century saw Shakespeare and his followers in England, Corneille and Racine in France, and Lope de Vega and Calderón in Spain.

The very term *theatrical* suggests some of the extravagance and exaggeration we associate with the Baroque. But the theater is first and foremost a place where strong emotion is on display, and it was this more than anything else that fueled the Baroque fascination with the theater. The emotionality that we generally sense in Baroque art has a theatrical quality; this is true even of much Baroque painting. Compare Raphael's calm Renaissance Madonna on page 47 with the early Baroque Madonna by Guercino. Jesus seems to be falling out of the picture as he twists toward his mother; she gestures in theatrical fashion, clenching with one hand while pointing delicately with the other; and the stagey lighting contrasts bright patches of flesh with dark shadows.

Madonna and Child with the Young St. John the Baptist, by Giovanni Francesco Barbieri (1591–1666), known as Il Guercino.

View of Delft, by Jan Vermeer (1632–1675)

Science and the Arts

All this may seem some distance away from the observatories of Galileo and
Kepler, and the laboratories where Harvey discovered the circulation of the
blood and Leeuwenhoek first viewed microorganisms through a microscope.
And indeed, the scientific spirit of the time had its most obvious effect on
artists who were outside the realm of absolutism. The Dutch were citizens of
free cities, not subjects of despotic kings. In Jan Vermeer's painting of his own
city, Delft, the incredibly precise depiction of detail reflects the new interest in
scientific observation. The painter's analysis of light is worthy of Huygens and
Newton, fathers of the science of optics. There is something scientific, too, in
the serene objectivity of this scene.

Man's control over nature is also symbolized by Baroque formal gardens.
Today, landscape architecture is not usually regarded as one of the major arts,
but it was very important in the age of the Baroque palace. Baroque gardens
regulate nature strictly according to geometrical plans. Bushes are clipped,
lawns tailored, and streams channeled, all under the watchful eye of big
statues of Venus, Apollo, Hercules, and the rest, lined up in rows. Such gardens spell out the new vision of nature brought to heel by human reason and
calculation.

Below the surface, furthermore, science is at work in even the most
grandiose and dazzling of Baroque artistic efforts. The perspective of Tiepolo's
ceiling painting or Bibiena's stage set depends on the use of very sophisticated
geometry. (Bibiena published a manual detailing the mathematics behind his
scene designs.) This dual influence of extravagance and scientism, of the splendid and the schematic, can also be traced in Baroque music.

The Age of Absolutism and the Age of Science converge: Louis XIV founding the Academy of Sciences.

Science and Music

Various aspects of Baroque music reflect the new scientific attitudes that developed in the seventeenth century. Scales were tuned, or "tempered," more precisely than ever before, so that for the first time all the twenty-four major and minor keys were available to composers. Their interest in exploring this resource is evident from collections such as Bach's *The Well-Tempered Clavier*, containing preludes and fugues in every key. Harmony was systematized so that chords followed one another in a logical and functional way.

Regularity became the ideal in rhythm, and in musical form—the distribution of sections of music in time—we find a tendency toward clearly ordered, even schematic plans. Whether consciously or not, composers seem to have viewed musical time in a quasi-scientific way. They divided it up and filled it systematically, almost in the spirit of the landscape architects who devised Baroque formal gardens.

In the important matter of musical expression, too, science was a powerful influence. Starting with the philosopher-mathematician René Descartes, thinkers applied the new rational methods to the analysis and classification of human emotions. It had always been felt that music has a special power to express and arouse emotions. Now it seemed that there was a basis for systematizing—and hence maximizing—this power.

Thus scientifically inclined music theorists compiled checklists of musical devices and techniques corresponding to each of the emotions. Grief, for example, was projected with a specific kind of melodic motive and a specific kind of rhythm—even with a specific key. By working steadily with these devices and saturating their pieces with them, composers believed they could achieve the maximum musical expressivity.

The emotions of Hope and Fear, as represented in a Baroque scientific treatise. Like composers of the time, the artist felt that feelings could be isolated and depicted in the abstract.

2 Musical Life in the Early Eighteenth Century

The eighteenth century was a great age for the crafts—the age of Chippendale in furniture, Paul Revere in silver, Stradivarius in violin making, to name just a few. Though attitudes were changing, composing music was also regarded as a craft. The Romantic idea of the composer—the lonely genius working over each masterpiece as a long labor of love expressing an individual personality— was still far in the future. Baroque composers were more likely to think of themselves as servants with masters to satisfy. They were artisans with jobs, rather than artists with a calling, and they produced music on demand to fill a particular requirement.

This is why many Baroque pieces seem relatively anonymous, as it were. They are not so much unique masterpieces as satisfactory examples of their style and genre, of which there are many other equally satisfactory examples.

There were three main institutions where composers could make a living by practicing their craft. In order of increasing glamour, these were the church, the court, and the opera house.

¶   The church. In the cathedrals, monasteries, and town churches of the Baroque era, the general assumption was that the organists or choirmasters would compose their own music, then play and conduct it. Organists had to improvise or write out music to accompany especially solemn places in the church services. They played long pieces to see the congregation out when the service was over.

At large institutions, important occasions called for elaborate music scored for chorus, soloists, and instruments: a Catholic Mass for the installation of an archbishop, or a Lutheran Church cantata for the anniversary of the Reformation. Church musicians were also responsible for training the boys who sang in their choirs, often in special choir schools.

¶   The court. Under the patronage of kings or members of the lesser nobility, a musician was employed on the same terms as a court painter, a master of the hunt, or a head chef. Though musicians had to work entirely at the whim of their masters, they could nevertheless count on a fairly secure existence, a steady demand for their services, and a pension.

Naturally, conditions varied from court to court, depending on the ruler's taste. For some, music was a good deal less interesting than hunting or banqueting. Others could not have enough of it. Frederick the Great of Prussia was a very keen flutist, so at his court concertos and sonatas for flute were composed at an especially healthy rate (see page xiv). He wrote many himself.

Court musicians kept in better touch with musical developments than church musicians, since they were required to travel with their employers. There were extended trips to major cities, where diplomacy was eased along by music they composed for the occasion.

¶   The opera house. Although many opera houses were attached to courts, others were maintained by entrepreneurs in major cities. (The public opera house existed before the public concert hall; in the Baroque era, public concerts were not a regular feature of musical life.) Audiences were alert to the most exciting new singers, and it was part of the composer's job to keep the singers well supplied with music that showed off their talents. Composers traditionally conducted their own operas, sitting at the harpsichord.

The revival of an older opera—usually because a favorite singer liked his or her part in it—was nearly always the occasion for massive recomposition, because another singer might want *her* part redone, too. If the opera's original

A Baroque opera performance (Turin, 1740). The stage set represents a great palace hall; the characters are striking various extravagant attitudes. Note the orchestra, a boy selling oranges, and a security guard.

composer had moved to the next town, other musicians would have no hesitation about rewriting (or replacing) some of the music. It was an exciting, unpredictable life, promising great rewards as well as humiliating reverses.

The life stories of the two greatest composers of the late Baroque period show a good deal about the interaction between musicians, the patrons who supported them, and the institutions that required music. Johann Sebastian Bach labored as a church organist, a court musician, and then a major composer-administrator for the Lutheran Church. George Frideric Handel, who also had a court position, became an independent opera composer and opera promoter. Their biographies are given on pages 138 and 155.

3 Style Features of Late Baroque Music

If any one characteristic can be singled out as central to the music of the late Baroque period, it would be its thorough, methodical quality. After listening to a short Baroque piece, or to one section of a longer piece, we may be surprised to realize, first, how soon all the basic material is set forth, and second, how much of the music after that consists of inspired repetition and variation.

It is as though the composers had set out to draw their material out to the maximum extent and wring it dry, as it were.

Indeed, the shorter pieces we will be examining in Chapters 9 and 10—pieces like Contrapunctus 4 from Bach's *The Art of Fugue* and the aria "La giustizia" from Handel's opera *Julius Caesar*—contain little if any notable contrast in rhythm, dynamics, melody, texture, or tone color (see pages 141 and 153). Baroque composers preferred thoroughness and homogeneity.

With longer pieces, Baroque composers tended to break them up into blocks of music that contrast with one another in obvious ways, but are still homogeneous in themselves. This is the case with Bach's *Brandenburg* Concerto No. 5, for example, where the orchestral and solo sections contrast clearly enough. Within each orchestral or solo section, however, things are usually quite regular (page 135).

Rhythm

Baroque music is brimming with energy, and this energy is channeled into a highly regular, determined sort of motion. Like jazz and other popular music, Baroque music gets its rhythmic vitality by playing off distinctive rhythms against a very steady beat. The meter nearly always stands out, emphasized by certain instruments in the ensemble. Most characteristic of these "marking-time" instruments is the busy, crisp harpsichord.

Another common feature that hammers home the beat is the so-called **walking bass,** a bass part that moves in absolutely even notes, usually eighths or quarters. In the Air from Bach's Suite No. 3 in D (see page 146), the bass keeps going for 138 "walking" eighth notes, plus 8 sixteenth notes and one half note (at the final cadence, of course). Rhythmic variety in the upper instruments is heard in reference to absolute regularity below.

Attentive listening will also reveal another aspect of regularity in the steady *harmonic rhythm*—that is, a Baroque piece tends to change chords at every measure or at some other set interval. (This must not be taken absolutely literally, but it is the tendency, and it is often the case.)

Dynamics

Another steady feature of Baroque music is dynamics. Composers rarely used loud and soft indications (*f* and *p*) in their scores, and once a dynamic was chosen or set, it remained at about the same level for the whole section—sometimes even for the whole composition.

Neither in the Baroque period nor in any other, however, have performers played or sung music at an absolutely even level of dynamics. Instrumentalists made expressive changes in dynamics to bring out rhythmic accents, and singers certainly sang high notes louder than low ones. But composers did not go much beyond natural variations of these kinds. Gradual buildups from soft to loud, and the like, were rarely used.

Abrupt dynamic contrasts were preferred—again, between fairly large sections of a longer piece, or whole movements. A clear *forte/piano* contrast is built into the concerto genre, with its alternating blocks of music for the full orchestra and for one or more quieter solo instruments. When, exceptionally, a Baroque composer changed dynamics in the middle of a section or a phrase of music, he could count on the great surprise—even the amazement—of his listeners. A famous sudden *forte* in Handel's "Hallelujah" Chorus has been known to electrify the audience, to bring them to their feet (page 158).

We spoke earlier of a characteristic dualism between extravagance and order that can be detected in various aspects of Baroque culture (page 113). The methodical, regular quality of Baroque musical style that we are tracing here clearly reflects the orderly, quasi-scientific side of this dualism. But Baroque music can also be highly dramatic, bizarre, or stupendous—a reflection of the other side of the dualism. Indeed, the magnificent momentary effects that occur occasionally in Handel and Bach are all the stronger because of the regular music around them.

Tone Color

Tone color in Baroque music presents something of a contradiction. On the one hand, the early part of the period evinced a new interest in sonority, and the end of it echoed with some very sophisticated sounds: Handel's imaginative orchestration in his operas, Bach's notably sensitive writing for the flute, and the refined harpsichord textures developed by several generations of composers in France. There are distinctive and attractive "Baroque sounds" that we do not hear in other periods: the harpsichord, the bright Baroque organ, the virtuoso recorder, and what we will call the "festive" Baroque orchestra, featuring high trumpets and drums.

On the other hand, a significant amount of music was written to allow for multiple or alternative performing forces. Thus it was a regular practice to designate music for harpsichord *or* organ, for violin *or* oboe *or* flute. Bach wrote a sonata for two flutes and rewrote it as a sonata for viola da gamba (a cello-like instrument) and harpsichord. Handel took solo arias and duets and rewrote them as choruses for his oratorio *Messiah*. In the last analysis, then, it seems the original tone color was often not critical.

The Baroque Orchestra

The core of the Baroque orchestra was a group of instruments of the violin family. The famous orchestra maintained by Louis XIV in the late seventeenth century was called "The Twenty-Four Violins of the King"; it consisted of six violins, twelve violas, and six cellos. A great deal of Baroque music was written for such an orchestra or a similar one—what would today be called a "string orchestra": violins, violas, cellos, and one or two bass viols.

To this was added a keyboard instrument as continuo (see page 124)—usually a harpsichord in secular music and an organ in church music.

Woodwinds and brass instruments were sometimes added to the string orchestra, too, but there was no fixed complement, as was to be the case later. For special occasions of a festive nature—music celebrating a

Eighteenth-century instruments: flute, violin, lute (back view), and *cornetto*—a wooden instrument played with a trumpet-like mouthpiece, with the pitch controlled by finger holes, as in a flute.

military victory, for example, or Christmas music ordered for a great cathedral—composers augmented the "basic Baroque orchestra" with trumpets or French horns, timpani, bassoons, and oboes and/or flutes. This "festive orchestra" has a particularly grand, open, and brilliant sound.

THE BASIC BAROQUE ORCHESTRA as in Vivaldi's Concerto in G (page 130)		THE FESTIVE BAROQUE ORCHESTRA as in Bach's Orchestral Suite in D (page 145)				
STRINGS	KEYBOARD	STRINGS	WOODWINDS	BRASS	PERCUSSION	KEYBOARD
Violins (divided into two groups, called violins 1 and violins 2) Violas Cellos Bass viol (playing the same music as the cellos an octave lower)	Harpsichord or organ	Violins 1 Violins 2 Violas Cellos Bass viol	2 Oboes 1 Bassoon	3 Trumpets	2 Timpani (kettledrums)	Harpsichord or organ

Melody

Baroque melody tends toward complexity. Composers liked to push melodies to the very limits of ornateness and luxuriance. As a rule, the range of Baroque melodies is extended; they use many different rhythmic note values; they twist and turn in an intricate way as they reach high and low. It can be maintained that in the European classical tradition, the art of melody reached a high point in the late Baroque era, a point that has never been equaled since.

These long, intricate melodies, with their wealth of "decorations" added to the main direction of the line, are not easy to sing, however. They hardly ever fall into any simple pattern resembling a tune; even their appearance on the page seems to tell the story:

One easily recognized feature of Baroque melodies is their frequent use of sequence (see page 25; a sequence is shaded on the melody above). Baroque melodies repeatedly catch hold of a motive or some longer section of music and play it again and again at several pitch levels. Sequences provide Baroque music with one of its most effective means of forward motion.

Ornamentation

Not all melodies of the time are as ornate as the one shown above, however, and some, such as the simpler Baroque dances, are exceptions to the rule. On the other hand, the most highly prized art of the elite musicians of the era, opera singers, was improvising melodic extras in the arias they sang night after night in the theater. This practice is called **ornamentation.**

Before the present era of sound amplification, when volume does much of the work, audiences thrilled to brilliant, fast, very high (or very low) music played and especially improvised by singers and instrumentalists. This is still very much the case with jazz. In the Baroque era, enough improvisations were written down, as guides for musicians who were not the most imaginative, to give us some idea of the art of the great virtuosos—such as the singers Bordoni and Cuzzoni (page 157) and the violinist-composer Vivaldi (page 132). They

There is nothing uniquely Baroque about musical ornamentation. If you heard Mariah Carey at Superbowl XXXVI, you heard "The Star-Spangled Banner" sung with ornaments added, not absolutely "straight."

would spontaneously add all kinds of ornaments (jazz players would call them "riffs" or "licks") to whatever scores composers placed before them. Artists today have re-created Baroque ornamentation, or something like it; for a superb example, listen to Handel's aria "La giustizia," page 153.

Texture

The standard texture of Baroque music is polyphonic (or contrapuntal). Even many Baroque pieces that consist of just melody and bass count as contrapuntal because of the independent melodic quality of the bass. And large-scale pieces spin a web of contrapuntal lines filling every nook and cranny of musical spacetime. While cellos, bass viols, bassoons, and organ pedals play the lowest line, the other string instruments stake out their places in the middle, with oboes and flutes above them and the trumpets piercing their way up into the very highest reaches of the sound universe. The density achieved in this way is doubly impressive because the sounds feel alive—alive because they are all in motion, because they are all parts of moving contrapuntal lines.

Again, some exceptions should be noted to the standard polyphonic texture of Baroque music. Such are the homophonic orchestra sections (the *ritornellos*) in the concerto, and Bach's highly expressive harmonizations of old German hymns (chorales: see page 160). But it is no accident that these textures appear *within pieces that feature polyphony elsewhere.* The ritornello in Bach's *Brandenburg* Concerto No. 5 alternates with polyphony played by the solo flute, violin, and harpsichord (see page 135). The harmonized hymn in his Cantata No. 4 comes at the very end, where it has the effect of calming or settling the complex polyphony of the preceding music (see page 161).

The Continuo

Yet all this polyphony is supported by a solid scaffold of harmony. The central importance of harmony in Baroque music appears in the universal practice of the *basso continuo*, or just **continuo.**

The continuo is a bass part (the lowest part in polyphonic music) that is always linked to a series of chords. These chords are played by a harpsichord, organ, or lute as support or accompaniment for the important melodies in the other instruments. Indeed, we might say "mere accompaniment," for composers did not bother to write the chords out in detail, but only notated them in an abstract way by a numerical shorthand below the bass part.

This left continuo players with a good deal to do, even though their role was considered subsidiary. By reading the basso continuo part, the harpsichordist or organist would play along with the cellos or bassoons—this with the left hand, which "doubles" the bass line. But the right-hand chords could be played in many ways: high or low, widely or closely spaced, smoothly connected or not. A certain amount of quick, on-the-spot improvisation was (and still is) required to "realize" a continuo, that is, to derive actual chords from abstract numbers. Another name for continuo, **figured bass,** derives from this numerical shorthand.

Continuo part, as written: cello and harpsichord, left hand

Simple "realization" of chords: harpsichord

More ornate "realization": harpsichord

Continuo chords provide the basic harmonic framework against which the contrapuntal lines of Baroque music trace their airy patterns. Under the influence of the continuo, Baroque texture may be described as "polarized"—a "polarity of voices" between a strong bass and a clear, high (soprano) range, the domain of the melody. Less clearly defined is a middle space containing the improvised chords. In Baroque works on the largest scale, this space is also filled in by polyphonic lines drawn from the median range of the orchestra and chorus, such as violas, tenors, and altos. In more modest works a characteristic texture is a hollow one: one or two high instruments (violins, flutes) or voices, a bass instrument, and subsidiary chord improvisation in the middle.

Baroque music is usually easily identified by the presence of the continuo—by the continuous but discreet sound of the harpsichord or organ playing continuo chords in the background. Indeed, the Baroque era in music was once called the "basso continuo" era, not a bad name for it.

Musical Form

Musical forms are clearer and more regular in the Baroque period than in most other historical periods. Two factors that appear to have contributed to this, one of them social, the other intellectual, were mentioned earlier.

The social factor is the patronage system, whereby the court and the church demanded a large amount of music and expected it to be produced in a hurry, almost as soon as it was ordered. Therefore composers needed to rely on formulas that could be applied quickly and efficiently. What is amazing about the church cantatas that Bach wrote at Leipzig, one a week, is how imaginatively he varied the standard forms for the various components of a cantata. But it was very helpful—in fact, it was absolutely necessary—for him to have those standard forms in place as a point of departure.

The other factor is the scientific spirit of the age, which affected composers only indirectly, but affected them nonetheless. One can detect the composer's ambition to "map" the whole range of a piece of music and to fill it in systematically in an orderly, logical, quasi-scientific way. This ambition seems to have

In a typical Baroque texture, singers and violins in the upper register are supported by the *continuo*, played by three musicians in this performance. A cello plays the bass, and the middle range is filled in by two chord-playing instruments (harpsichord and lute).

been based on the conviction that musical time could be encompassed and controlled at man's will, an attitude similar to that of scientists, philosophers, and craftsmen of the time.

The music of Bach, in particular, shows this tendency on various levels. Look, for example, at the symmetrical arrangement of the seven sections of his Cantata No. 4, diagrammed on page 161. The last fugue in his *Art of Fugue* (he died before finishing it) is a more famous example. An ordinary fugue, as we shall see, is a polyphonic composition that deals exclusively with a single theme. This fugue deals with *four* themes, one after another, in four sections; then in the last section all four themes combine in four-part counterpoint. Theme No. 4 spells "Bach" in a musical code (!). A simpler Bach fugue may still have a ground-plan that is highly symmetrical (see page 140).

4 The Emotional World of Baroque Music

All music, it seems safe to say, is deeply involved with emotion. But in the music of different cultures, and also in the music of different historical eras within a single culture, the nature of that involvement can be very different. The emotional effect of Baroque music strikes the modern listener as very powerful and yet, in a curious way, also impersonal. Baroque composers believed firmly that music could and should mirror a wide range of human feelings, or "affects," such as had been analyzed and classified by the scientifically oriented psychology of the day. Composers did not believe, however, that it was their task to mirror feelings of their own. Rather, they tried to isolate and analyze emotions in general and then depict them consistently.

The exhaustiveness of their musical technique made for a similar exhaustiveness of emotional effect. A single movement or aria was usually restricted to depicting one specific emotion, feeling, or mood. As the rhythms and themes are repeated, the music intensifies and magnifies a single strong feeling. Sadness in Baroque music is presented as the deepest gloom, calmness as profound quiet, brightness as pomp and splendor, happiness as jubilation.

These are extreme sentiments; the people who can be imagined to experience them would have to be almost larger than life. All this fits perfectly into place with the Baroque fascination with the theater. The Baroque theater concentrated on grand gestures and high passion, on ideal emotions expressed by ideal human beings. Kings and queens were shown performing noble actions or vile ones, experiencing intense feelings, delivering thunderous speeches, and taking part in lavish stage displays. How these personages looked and postured can be seen in the picture on page 120.

Theatrical emotion has the virtues of intensity, clarity, and focus; it has to have, if it is to get past the footlights and reach its audience. Actors analyze the emotion they are asked to depict, shape it and probably exaggerate it, and then methodically project it by means of their acting technique. It is not their personal emotion, though for the moment they *make* it their own. We may come to feel that Baroque composers worked in a similar way, not only in their operas—actual stage works set to music—but also in their oratorios and church cantatas, and even in their instrumental concertos and sonatas.

Web: *Research and test your understanding of late Baroque music at* <bedfordstmartins.com/listen>.

CHAPTER 9

Baroque
Instrumental Music

In most cultures, music with words is the norm; strictly instrumental music is less common or less important. So it is with popular music today, and so it was with the early music of Europe. In the Middle Ages, Gregorian chant was sung by monks and nuns to texts for the church services, and later some of these same texts were set to new polyphonic music for cathedral choirs and royal chapels. Troubadours set their love poems as solo songs. In the Renaissance, love poetry was set to music as madrigals, intricate part-music for a few solo singers. Vocal music was still very important in the late Baroque era, as we shall see in Chapter 10.

But part of the importance of the Baroque era was that for the first time, listeners and musicians began to take instrumental music much more seriously. A momentous change was set in motion, and the reasons for it are not entirely clear. It can hardly be a coincidence, however, that the rise of instrumental music took place at the same time as a similar development in the technology of instrument making. The name of Antonio Stradivarius (1644–1737) is known to many because of auctions where prices soar into the millions for one of his violins, unmatched after three hundred years. (They rarely come on the market. "Strad" cellos are even rarer.) Instruments by other master builders of the era, less well known, can still sound glorious: the organs of Gottfried Silbermann, the harpsichords of François Étienne Blanchet, the viols of Barak Norman (a viola da gamba is pictured on page 133 and also to the right).

In any case, the rise of instrumental music meant that there had to be a basic understanding between composers and audiences about instrumental forms and genres. To pose the most basic question: When the music starts, how long should the composer keep going, and what should the listener expect? With vocal music, the answer was (roughly speaking): until the words end—when the sense of the sentence, paragraph, or total text is completed with a punctuation mark, a summing-up, or a concluding passage. For instrumental music, there was no such "sense." Conventional forms and genres had to supply it.

In this chapter we shall look at the most important instrumental forms and genres established, developed, and refined in the Baroque era. Baroque vocal music will be treated in Chapter 10.

An early instrument that has now been revived, the viola da gamba is like a cello, with a quieter but also a rather husky sound. The beautiful viols by the Baroque maker Barak Norman have elaborately carved pegboards.

1 Concerto and Concerto Grosso

The **concerto** and the **concerto grosso** (plural: concerti grossi) are the most important orchestral genres of the Baroque era. The basic idea underlying these genres is contrast between an orchestra and a soloist (in the concerto) or a small group of soloists (in the concerto grosso). Indeed, the word *concerto* comes from the Latin word *concertare*, to contend—an origin that accurately indicates a sort of contest between solo and orchestra.

This contest pits the brilliance of the soloist or soloists—and brilliance often involves improvisation—against the relative power and stability of the orchestra. Contrast comes to these genres naturally, then; a good deal of Baroque music is more uniform, as we shall see. But people soon tire of music that stays more or less the same. Composers who wanted to develop large-scale forms had to find ways of bringing contrast into their music; they wanted large-scale forms because audiences, then as now, were more impressed by extended compositions than by short ones.

Movements

One way to extend a composition was and is to lay it out in several movements (or, to put it another way, join together several movements as a single composite work). A **movement** is a self-contained section of music that is part of a larger work; movements can be compared to chapters in a book. Movements in a multimovement work will always show some variety in tempo, meter, key, mood, and musical form.

The typical late Baroque concerto has three movements. The *first* movement is a bright, extroverted piece in a fast tempo. After this, the *second* movement strikes an obvious contrast: It is quieter, slower, and more emotional. The *third* movement is fast again—if anything, faster than the first. In the first concerto we study, Vivaldi's Violin Concerto in G, the first and last movements are in ritornello form, the second movement in ground bass form.

Ritornello Form

Many concerto movements are in *ritornello form,* from **ritornello,** the name for the orchestral music that typically starts the movement off. Contrast is basic to the concerto, and ritornello form focuses on contrast between two musical ideas, or groups of ideas—one belonging to the orchestra and the other to the soloist. The orchestral material (the ritornello) tends to be solid and forceful, the solo material faster and more brilliant.

Ritorno, the Italian word for "return," tells us that the function of the ritornello in ritornello form is to return many times as a stable element of the form. Usually it returns only in part, and usually it is played in different keys as the movement proceeds. As for the "musical ideas" for the solo, sometimes these are virtuoso passages, sometimes themes, sometimes larger sections including themes and other material. To end the movement, the orchestral ritornello returns in the tonic key and, often, at full length.

Ritornello form can be diagrammed as shown at the top of page 130, where RIT stands for the entire ritornello, [RIT] for any part of the ritornello, and Solo 1, 2, 3, etc. for the solo sections.

We need not worry too much about the exact number of ritornello fragments, the keys, and other details shown in such form diagrams. More important is

If the first movement [of a concerto] takes five minutes, the Adagio five to six, and the last movement three to four, the whole is of the proper length. And it is in general better if listeners find a piece too short rather than too long.

J. J. Quantz (1697–1773), court composer to Frederick the Great, 1752

RIT		[RIT]		[RIT]		[RIT]		RIT
	Solo 1		Solo 2		Solo 3		Solo 4	

Tonic key ——————————————— Other keys ——————————————— Tonic key

the general impression that the form gives: the sense of a sturdy, reliable support in the orchestra for rapid and sometimes fantastic flights by the solo or solo group. As a condition for the quasi-improvisational freedom of the solo instruments, the ritornello is always there, ready to bring them back down to earth and remind us of the original point of departure.

ANTONIO VIVALDI (1678–1741)
Violin Concerto in G, *La stravaganza,* Op. 4, No. 12 (1712–13)

The undisputed champion of the concerto was the Venetian composer Antonio Vivaldi. Vivaldi wrote hundreds of concertos, but published relatively few of them, in sets of six or twelve; each set was given a work number (*opus* is Latin for "work"). To some opuses he gave titles which evoke the "extravagant" side of the Baroque dualism (see page 113), such as "Harmonic Whims" (*L'estro armonico,* opus 3) and "Extravagance" (*La stravaganza,* opus 4). This Concerto in G is the last and one of the best of his opus 4.

It is a concerto for solo violin and the "basic" Baroque orchestra of strings and continuo (see page 123); on our recording the continuo chords are played by a large lute (an *archlute*). The orchestra is quite small. In the age of Antonio Stradivarius, violin-maker supreme, a great deal of music was composed at least partly to show off this favorite instrument. The violin's brilliance was especially prized, as was its ability to play expressively.

The Concerto in G begins and ends with movements in ritornello form.

Archlute, heard in the Vivaldi slow movement

First Movement (Spiritoso e non presto)   Read the following material about the first movement, checking the various points with the entries in Listening Chart 3. Then listen to the music, following along with the Listening Chart—see page xvi if anything about the chart (or the icons) is not clear. Read again, listen again.

"Spirited, not too fast" writes Vivaldi at the start of this triple-meter movement. The first and second violins of the orchestra echo one another brightly. The opening ritornello—with its typical loud, extroverted sound—consists of three parts. The first begins with a couple of loud chords to catch the audience's attention and set the tempo (**a**); then comes a central section with sequences (**b**), and then a cadential section featuring loud/soft echoes (**c**):

LISTENING CHART 3

Vivaldi, Violin Concerto in G, first movement

Ritornello form. 2 min., 46 sec.

0:00	**Ritornello**	a
0:11		b
0:18		c
0:26	**Solo 1**	Contrasting solo violin music
0:41	**Ritornello 2**	c
0:49	**Solo 2**	Virtuoso solo violin music; several different sections
		Continuo drops out for a short time
1:18	**Ritornello 3**	Part of this is derived from **b** and **c**; the rest is free.
		CADENCE in a minor key
1:34	**Solo 3**	More expressive
1:52	**Ritornello 4**	Even freer than Ritornello 3
2:11	**Solo 4**	Very fast
2:24	**Ritornello 5**	b c

Once the ritornello ends with a very solid cadence (another typical feature of Baroque ritornellos), the solo violin enters, first with music moving at about the same speed as the ritornello, but soon speeding up. Virtuosity for the Baroque violinist meant jumping from the high strings to the low, executing fast scales, in fact any and all kinds of fast playing.

Ritornello 2 is an exact repetition of **c**. The second solo has several sub-sections, which makes it much longer than any of the others; in one section the continuo drops out entirely. Ritornello 3 begins with derivatives of **b** and **c** but then wanders off freely and ends in a minor key. This provides a springboard for some expressive playing in the next solo. Ritornello 4 is freer still; it takes just enough from the original ritornello (part **b**) so that it seems to fit in with it and, indeed, to grow out of it spontaneously.

Vivaldi seems to have wanted his first four ritornellos to feel freer and freer, before he finally pulls the piece back in line. After the last solo (following Ritornello 4) cuts in very energetically, he ends the movement with a literal statement of **b** and **c**. (Absent is **a**, perhaps because its "wake-up" function is no longer needed.) Compare the "inner form" of this movement with the standard "outer form" shown in the previous diagram.

RIT a b c		[RIT 2] c		[RIT 3] (b c)		[RIT 4] free		[RIT 5] b c
	Solo 1		Solo 2		Solo 3		Solo 4	

Antonio Vivaldi (1678–1741)

The son of a Venetian violinist, Antonio Vivaldi was destined to follow in his father's footsteps. He entered the priesthood—where his bright red hair earned him the nickname of the "Red Priest"—and in 1703 became a music teacher at the Seminario Musicale dell'Ospedale della Pietà, a Venetian orphanage for girls. The Ospedale was one of several such institutions in Venice that were famous for the attention they paid to the musical training of their students. A large proportion of Vivaldi's works were composed for the school, whose concerts were a great tourist attraction.

The Ospedale allowed him frequent leaves of absence, so Vivaldi toured a good deal, but the composer's contract specified that he should write two concertos a month for the pupils and rehearse them if he was in town. Near the end of his life, Vivaldi left Venice permanently to settle in Vienna.

Internationally renowned as a virtuoso violinist, Vivaldi is remembered today chiefly for his brilliant concertos. He wrote more than four hundred of these, including concertos for harp, mandolin, bassoon, and various instrumental combinations; we know of more than 250 solo violin concertos, including our Concerto in G from *La stravaganza*. Critics of the day complained that Vivaldi's music was thin and flashy and that the composer was always playing for cheap effects. But the young Bach, before writing his *Brandenburg* Concertos, carefully copied out pieces by Vivaldi as a way of learning how to write concertos himself.

Vivaldi's most famous work—it has been recorded well over a hundred times—is also one of his most unusual: *The Four Seasons*, a set of four violin concertos which illustrate, in one way or another, spring (bird songs, gentle breezes, and so on), summer (a nap in the sun), fall (a tipsy peasant dance at a harvest festival), and winter ("the horrible wind," says the score). Baroque composers were fond of musical illustration, especially with the words of vocal music, as we shall see; but they seldom pursued it this far.

Since no reliable portrait seems to exist of Vivaldi, we show a contemporary caricature.

Chief Works: Solo concertos for many different instruments, including the very famous *Four Seasons* ▪ Concerti grossi for various instruments ▪ 21 extant operas; oratorios; cantatas

Encore: After the Violin Concerto in G, listen to *The Four Seasons*; Concerto for Two Violins in A Minor, Op. 3, No. 8.

Baroque Variation Form: The Ground Bass

Variation forms are among the simplest and most characteristic of Baroque forms. Although they are not as common as other forms, they project the Baroque desire for systematic, thorough structures in a very direct way. This is because **variation form** entails the successive, uninterrupted repetition of one clearly defined melodic unit, with changes that rouse the listener's interest without ever losing touch with the original unit, or theme.

That theme may be a complete melody in the soprano range or a shorter melodic phrase in the bass. Given the emphasis in the Baroque era on the basso continuo, it is not surprising that Baroque variations tend to occur above stable bass patterns; a name for such patterns is **basso ostinato,** meaning "persistent" or "obstinate" bass. Sometimes the bass itself is slightly varied—though never in such a way as to hide its distinctive quality. Dynamics, tone color, and some harmonies are often changed in variations. Tempo, key, and mode are changed less often.

There are a number of names for compositions in variation form, which seem to have grown up independently all over Europe, first as improvisations and then as written-out compositions. Besides the French *chaconne* and the Italian *passacaglia* (passa-cáhlia), there was the old English term *ground* (the repeating bass figure being called the **ground bass**). One seventeenth-century Italian composer left a passacaglia for organ with exactly a hundred variations.

As this child appears to be finding out, music lessons can often serve as a cover for lessons in something else—a fact which helps explain the popularity of "music lesson" pictures.

More compact examples of variation form sometimes appear as one movement in a larger Baroque genre, such as a concerto.*

Note that the term *ostinato* is also used to refer to any short musical unit repeated many times, in the bass or anywhere else, especially one used as a building block for a piece of music. Ostinatos are by no means unique to European music of the Baroque; in some form they are found in almost all musical traditions (see, for example, pages 108 and 217).

ANTONIO VIVALDI
Violin Concerto in G, *La stravaganza*, Op. 4, No. 12 (1712–13)

Second Movement (Largo)   As is typical, Vivaldi's Concerto in G has three contrasting movements—the first vigorous and brilliant, the second gentle and slow. This slow movement is in variation (ground bass) form.

Our first impression of this music is probably of its texture—the gentle throbbing, the ingenious weaving in and out of the orchestral violins and the solo violin, and the delicate, subsidiary continuo sounds. There is, however, not much melody to listen to in the violin's music. There is less, in fact, as the movement goes along and the texture changes.

Sooner or later we notice that the only real melody is in the bass, where a solemn, quiet theme (the ground bass) is heard repeatedly in the cellos and bass viol. The theme sinks down and down, ending with a strong cadence:

Theme, Variations 1–4, 7   Variations 5–6

etc.

*We examine earlier examples of variation (ground bass) form on pages 103 and 106: Dido's Lament, from *Dido and Aeneas* by Henry Purcell, and a Passacaglia by Girolamo Frescobaldi.

LISTENING CHART 4

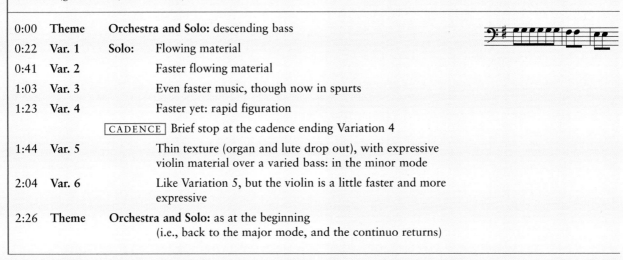

Vivaldi, Violin Concerto in G, second movement

Variation (ground bass) form. 2 min., 59 sec.

0:00	Theme	Orchestra and Solo: descending bass
0:22	Var. 1	Solo: Flowing material
0:41	Var. 2	Faster flowing material
1:03	Var. 3	Even faster music, though now in spurts
1:23	Var. 4	Faster yet: rapid figuration
		CADENCE Brief stop at the cadence ending Variation 4
1:44	Var. 5	Thin texture (organ and lute drop out), with expressive violin material over a varied bass: in the minor mode
2:04	Var. 6	Like Variation 5, but the violin is a little faster and more expressive
2:26	Theme	Orchestra and Solo: as at the beginning (i.e., back to the major mode, and the continuo returns)

We develop a sort of "double listening" for music like this, listening simultaneously to the unchanging theme and to the changing material presented above that theme. (This is no harder to do than taking in a distant view while also watching someone in the foreground.) After the theme's initial statement, four more statements with violin variations follow, during which the solo violin plays faster and faster material above the unvaried ground bass. In its quiet way, this movement is showing off the violinist's ability to play music that is fast and sleek.

After Variation 4, however, there is a marked stop. Variation 5 makes a grand contrast of the kind relished by Baroque composers and audiences (especially in music designed to be "extravagant," as this concerto was). The continuo stops, and since the texture is now thin and ethereal, the bass (played by the orchestral violins) can be heard more clearly—and what we hear is that the theme itself has been varied. It is now in the minor mode.

The mood becomes muted and melancholy; the violin is now showing off not its speed, but its expressive capabilities. The mood deepens in Variation 6. Rather abruptly, after this, the original theme returns in the full orchestra and continuo, played just as it was at the beginning.

The construction of this movement as a set of variations over a ground bass exemplifies the thorough, methodical quality of so much Baroque music. The effect of the contrast that Vivaldi has added with Variations 5 and 6 is not diminished by the steadily repeating, even obsessive bass. On the contrary, "double listening" can make the contrast seem richer and more interesting.

Third Movement (Allegro)   Like the first movement, the third movement of the Concerto in G is a fast one in ritornello form. This time ritornello form is treated much more freely—or, as Vivaldi might have said, "extravagantly."

He begins with a long solo passage for the violin—and when the orchestra finally breaks in, all it can offer by way of a ritornello is a sort of hasty fanfare, interrupted by a short solo. The second ritornello is a much longer, very spirited

LISTEN

Vivaldi, Violin Concerto in G, third movement

0:00	**Introduction** solo
0:16	**Ritornello 1** interrupted by solo
0:30	**Solo**
1:15	**Ritornello 2**
2:08	**Ritornello 3**
2:53	**Ritornello 4**
3:46	**Ritornello 5**

passage of new music. "Extravagant" features of this movement would include the eviction of the orchestra from its customary place at the beginning; the fact that the lively second ritornello has nothing whatsoever to do with the "official" ritornello, namely the fanfare; and the way the solo violin keeps darting around and changing the kind of virtuoso material it plays throughout the movement.

However, order is asserted when the third ritornello takes the original fanfare as its point of departure (in the minor mode). And the final ritornello returns to its origins almost literally, as in the first movement.

JOHANN SEBASTIAN BACH (1685–1750)
Brandenburg Concerto No. 5, for Flute, Violin,
Harpsichord, and Orchestra (before 1721)

A concerto grosso is a concerto for a group of several solo instruments (rather than just a single one) and orchestra. In 1721 Johann Sebastian Bach sent a beautiful manuscript containing six of these works to the margrave of Brandenburg, a minor nobleman with a paper title—the Duchy of Brandenburg had recently been merged into the kingdom of Prussia, Europe's fastest-growing state. We do not know why this music was sent (if Bach was job-hunting, he was unsuccessful) or if it was ever performed in Brandenburg.

To impress the margrave, presumably, Bach sent pieces with six different combinations of instruments, combinations that in some cases were never used before or after. Taken as a group, the *Brandenburg* Concertos present an unsurpassed anthology of dazzling tone colors and imaginative treatments of the Baroque concerto contrast between soloists and orchestra.

Brandenburg Concerto No. 5 features as its solo group a flute, violin, and harpsichord. The orchestra is the "basic" Baroque string orchestra (see page 123). The harpsichordist of the solo group doubles as the player of the orchestra's continuo chords, and the solo violin leads the orchestra during the ritornellos.

First Movement (Allegro)   In ritornello form, the first movement of *Brandenburg* Concerto No. 5 opens with a loud, bright, solid-sounding orchestral ritornello. The melody is attractive and easily recognized but, like so many Baroque melodies, becomes more complicated as it proceeds:

(For simplicity's sake, the music example above omits the note-repetitions on the eighth notes.) You could probably learn to sing phrase **a** easily enough, but **b** and **c** are much harder. There is no clear stop between them, and the melody begins to wind around itself in an intricate way. Yet it is undoubtedly just these features that give the ritornello its strength and its flair and keep it fresh when fragments of it return later in the movement.

Once the ritornello ends with a solid cadence, the three solo instruments enter with rapid imitative polyphony. They dominate the rest of the movement.

I shall
1. set the boys a shining example of an honest, retiring manner of life, serve the School industriously, and instruct the boys conscientiously
2. Bring the music in both the principal Churches of this town [Leipzig] into a good state, to the best of my ability
3. Show to the Honorable and Most Wise Town Council all proper respect and obedience . . .

Bach's contract at Leipzig, 1723—the first three of fourteen stipulations

LISTENING CHART 5

2   1
1-5   5-9

Bach, *Brandenburg* Concerto No. 5, first movement

Ritornello form. 9 min., 56 sec.

1 5	0:00	**Ritornello**	Complete ritornello is played by the orchestra, **forte:** bright and emphatic.	
	0:21	**Solo**	Harpsichord, flute, and violin in a contrapuntal texture (often in trio style). Includes faster rhythms; the soloists play new themes and also play some of the motives from the ritornello.	
	0:46	**Ritornello (first phrase)**	Orchestra, *f*	
	0:51	**Solo**	Similar material to that of the first solo	
	1:12	**Ritornello (middle phrase)**	Orchestra, *f*	
	1:18	**Solo**	Similar solo material	
	1:40	**Ritornello (middle phrase)**	Orchestra, *f;* minor mode	
	1:45	**Solo**	Similar solo material at first, then fast harpsichord runs are introduced.	
2 6	2:28	**Ritornello (middle phrase)**	Orchestra, *f*	
0:06	2:34	**Solo**	This solo leads directly into the central solo.	
0:32	3:00	**Central solo**	Quiet flute and violin dialogue (accompanied by the orchestra, *p*) is largely in the minor mode. The music is less motivic, and the harmonies change less rapidly than before.	
0:58	3:26		Detached notes in cello, flute, and violin; sequence	
1:35	4:03		Long high notes prepare for the return of the ritornello.	
3 7	4:18	**Ritornello (first phrase)**	Orchestra, *f*	
0:04	4:22	**Solo**		
0:50	5:08	**Ritornello (first and second phrases)**	Orchestra, *f;* this ritornello section feels especially solid because it is longer than the others and in the tonic key.	
1:02	5:20	**Solo**		
1:30	5:48	**Ritornello (middle phrase)**	Orchestra, *f*	
1:37	5:55	**Solo**	Fast harpsichord run leads into the cadenza.	
4 8	6:33	Harpsichord cadenza	*Section 1:* a lengthy passage developing motives from the solo sections	
1:56	8:29		*Section 2:* very fast and brilliant	
2:15	8:48		*Section 3:* long preparation for the anticipated return of the ritornello	
5 9	9:30	**Ritornello**	Orchestra, *f,* plays the complete ritornello.	

This painting is thought to depict Bach and three of his musician sons. It is a symbolic painting: The kindly, soberly dressed father is shown holding a cello—a basso continuo instrument—ready to support the treble lines of the boys, who are decked out in the frothy costumes of a later generation.

They introduce new motives and new patterns of figuration, take over some motives from the ritornello, and toss all these musical ideas back and forth between them. Every so often, the orchestra breaks in again, always with clear fragments of the ritornello, in various keys. All this has a very, very different effect from that of Vivaldi's Violin Concerto in G, not only because of the sheer length of the movement and its elaborate form, but because of the richness of the counterpoint and the harmony.

During a particularly striking solo section in the minor mode, the soloists abandon their motivic style and play Baroque mood music, with even richer harmonies and intriguing, special textures. After this, you may be able to hear that all the solos are closely related to solos heard before the minor-mode section—all, that is, except the very last. Here the harpsichord gradually outpaces the violin and the flute, until finally it seizes the stage and plays a lengthy virtuoso passage, while the other instruments wait silently.

An improvised or improvisatory solo passage of this kind within a larger piece is called a **cadenza.** Cadenzas are a feature of concertos in all eras; the biggest cadenza always comes near the end of the first movement, as in *Brandenburg* Concerto No. 5.

In this cadenza, the harpsichord breaks out of the regular eighth-note rhythms that have dominated this long movement. Its swirling, unexpectedly powerful patterns prepare inexorably for the final entrance of the orchestra. The whole ritornello is played, exactly as at the beginning; at last we hear it as a complete and solid entity, not in fragments.

Second Movement (Affettuoso)   After the forceful first movement, a change is needed: something quieter, slower, and more emotional (*affettuoso* means just that, *emotional*). As often in concertos, this slow movement is in the minor mode, contrasting with the first and last, which are in the major.

Johann Sebastian Bach (1685–1750)

During the Baroque era, crafts were handed down in family clans, and in music the Bach clan was one of the biggest, providing the region of Thuringia in central Germany with musicians for many generations. Most of the Bachs were lowly town musicians or Lutheran Church organists; only a few of them gained court positions. Johann Sebastian, who was himself taught by several of his relatives, trained four sons who became leading composers of the next generation.

Before he was twenty, Bach took his first position as a church organist in a little town called Arnstadt, then moved to a bigger town called Mühlhausen. Then he worked his way up to a court position with the Duke of Weimar. As a church organist, Bach had to compose organ music and sacred choral pieces, and at Weimar he was still required to write church music for the ducal chapel, as well as sonatas and concertos for performance in the palace.

The way his Weimar position terminated tells us something about the working conditions of court musicians. When Bach tried to leave Weimar for another court, Cöthen, the duke balked and threw him in jail for several weeks before letting him go. At Cöthen the prince happened to be a keen amateur musician who was not in favor of elaborate church music, so Bach concentrated on instrumental music.

In 1723 Bach was appointed cantor of St. Thomas's Church in Leipzig, a center of Lutheran church music in Germany. He not only had to compose and perform, but also organize music for all four churches in town. Teaching in the choir school was another of his responsibilities. Almost every week, in his first years at Leipzig, Bach composed, had copied, rehearsed, and performed a new cantata—a religious work for soloists, choir, and orchestra containing several movements and lasting from fifteen to thirty minutes.

Bach chafed under bureaucratic restrictions and political decisions by town and church authorities. The truth is he was never appreciated in Leipzig. Furthermore, at the end of his life he was regarded as old-fashioned by modern musicians, and one critic pained Bach by saying so in print. Indeed, after his death Bach's music was neglected by the musical public at large, though it was admired by composers such as Mozart and Beethoven.

Bach had twenty children—seven with his first wife, a cousin, and thirteen with his second, a singer, for whom he prepared a little home-music anthology, *The Note-*

Book of Anna Magdalena Bach. The children were taught music as a matter of course, and also taught how to copy music; the performance parts of many of the weekly cantatas that Bach composed are written in their hands. From his musical response to the sacred words of these cantatas, and other works, it is clear that Bach thought deeply about religious matters. Works such as his Passions and his Mass in B Minor emanate a spirituality that many listeners find unmatched in any other composer.

Bach seldom traveled, except to consult on organ construction contracts (for which the customary fee was often a cord of wood or a barrel of wine). Blind in his last years, he continued to compose by dictation. He had already begun to assemble his compositions in orderly sets: organ chorale preludes, organ fugues, preludes and fugues for harpsichord. He also clearly set out to produce works that would summarize his final thoughts about Baroque forms and genres; such works are the Mass in B Minor, the thirty-three *Goldberg* Variations for harpsichord, and *The Art of Fugue,* an exemplary collection of fugues all on the same subject, left unfinished at his death.

Bach was writing for himself, for his small devoted circle of students, perhaps for posterity. It is a concept that would have greatly surprised the craftsmen musicians who were his forebears.

Chief Works: More than 200 sacred and secular cantatas; two Passions, with words from the gospels of St. Matthew and St. John; *Christmas Oratorio;* Mass in B Minor; *Magnificat;* motets ▪ *The Well-Tempered Clavier,* consisting of 48 preludes and fugues in all major and minor keys for harpsichord or clavichord ▪ Three sets of suites (six each) for harpsichord—the French and English Suites and the Partitas; *Goldberg* Variations ▪ Organ works: many fugues (including the *St. Anne* Fugue) and chorale preludes ▪ *Brandenburg* Concertos, other concertos, orchestral suites, sonatas ▪ Late composite works: *A Musical Offering* and *The Art of Fugue* ▪ Chorale (hymn) harmonizations

Encore: After *Brandenburg* Concerto No. 5, listen to the Concerto for Two Violins; Mass in B Minor (Gloria section).

Bach's musical handwriting—the most beautiful and intricate of any composer's.

Baroque composers had a simple way of reducing volume: They could omit many or even all of the orchestra instruments. So here Bach employs only the three solo instruments—flute, violin, and harpsichord—plus the orchestra cello playing the continuo bass.

Third Movement (Allegro)   The full orchestra returns in the last movement, which, however, begins with a lengthy passage for the three soloists in fugal style (see below). The lively compound meter with its triple component — ONE two three *four* five six—provides a welcome contrast to the duple meter of the two earlier movements.

2 Fugue

Fugue is one of the most impressive and characteristic achievements of Baroque music, indeed of Baroque culture altogether. In broad, general terms, fugue can be thought of as systematized imitative polyphony (see page 29). Composers of the Middle Ages first glimpsed imitative polyphony, and Renaissance composers developed it; Baroque composers, living in an age of science, systematized it. The thorough, methodical quality that we pointed to in Baroque music is nowhere more evident than in fugue.

A **fugue** is a polyphonic composition for a fixed number of instrumental lines or voices—usually three or four—built on a single principal theme. This theme, called the fugue **subject,** appears again and again in each of the instrumental or vocal lines.

The term *fugue* itself comes from the Latin word *fuga,* which means "running away"; imagine the fugue subject being chased from one instrument to another. Listening to a fugue, we follow that chase. The subject stays the same, but it takes on endless new shadings as it turns corners and surrounds itself with different melodic and rhythmic ideas.

Fugal Exposition

A fugue begins with an **exposition** in which all the voices present the subject in an orderly, standardized way. (The contrapuntal lines in fugues are referred to as *voices,* even when the fugue is written for instruments. We shall be speaking of the lines in a Bach fugue for strings as the *soprano, alto, tenor,* and *bass.*)

First of all, the subject is announced in the most prominent fashion possible: It enters in a single voice without any accompaniment (usually), while the other voices wait. Any voice can begin; in the diagram below, we follow the regular order of the example on our CD (soprano, alto, tenor, bass), but any order is possible. After leading off, voice 1 continues with new material of its own while the subject enters in voice 2. Next, the subject arrives in voice 3—with 1 and 2 continuing in counterpoint with it (and with each other), using more new material, and so on. This section of a fugue, the exposition, is over when all the voices have stated the subject.

SOPRANO   Subject — New material — — — — — — — — — — — →

ALTO   Subject — New material — — — — — — — — — →

TENOR   Subject — New material — — — — — — — →

BASS   Subject — New material — — — — — →

After the exposition, the subject enters at intervals, spaced out by passages of other music. It may come at the top of the texture (in the soprano), the bottom (bass), or else half hidden away in the middle; see the diagram below. Some of these later **subject entries** come in different keys. Although the modulations to these other keys may not be very obvious—less so than in music of the Classical era, for example—without them the music would be dull and stodgy.

The passages of music separating the later subject entries are called **episodes.** They provide a contrast to the subject entries. This is true even though their material is often derived from the subject: In such cases, the episodes sound less distinct and solid than the subject entries, and so stand apart from them. A regular feature of fugal episodes is the use of sequences (see page 25).

After the exposition, the form of a fugue falls into an alternating pattern: Episodes of various lengths come between subject entries in various keys. Here is a diagram of a typical short fugue:

Exposition	Episode	Entry	Episode	Entry	Longer Episode	Entry
Subject						Subject
Subject		Subject				
Subject				Subject		
Subject						
TONIC KEY		ANOTHER KEY		ANOTHER KEY		TONIC KEY

Fugues, Free and Learned

Fugue is a somewhat complicated concept. We need to think of fugue not always as a genre ("a fugue"), but also as a style or a procedure (just "fugue," or fugal style), which is not always used strictly over the full length of a composition.

For in fact, full-scale fugues were very seldom written for public performance, at concerts (of which there were few in the Baroque era, anyway) or courts. Fugues occur as parts of French overtures—curtain-raisers for operas—but such fugues are invariably "free," in that the individual voice lines are not maintained all the way through, as in virtually all of Bach's freestanding fugues. Since Bach is unquestionably the greatest master of fugue, there is a tendency to think of strict fugues as the main kind.

Nonetheless, "free" fugues are the more common and important. They can be free in the sense that they take up only part of a composition, not the whole of it (sometimes called *fugato*). They can be free by constantly slipping out of polyphony—the true texture of fugue—into homophony and then back again.

As for Bach, his greatest fugues are keyboard works written for study purposes, not for public performance: Such are *The Well-Tempered Clavier,* his very famous collection of preludes and fugues in each of the twelve major and twelve minor keys, and *The Art of Fugue.*

And in the study context, fugues developed technical refinements, showing off the composers' contrapuntal skill and treating the subject in various learned, seemingly intellectual ways. Some of these *fugal devices* are:

✻ **countersubject**   The name given to the "new material" in the diagram on page 139 when it sticks with the subject, accompanying it one way or another throughout the fugue (i.e., the countersubject is the melodic line in voice 1 that is heard while the subject enters in voice 2).

✻ **stretto**   One subject entry overlaps another entry in time, with the second jumping in before the first is complete.

✻ **augmentation, diminution**   All note lengths in the subject are multiplied or divided (usually by two): A half note becomes a whole note, etc.

✻ **inversion**   All intervals in the subject are reversed: Steps up become steps down, and so on.

Sometimes these fugal devices sound as academic and dry as their descriptions, but the Baroque masters of fugue could make wonderful music out of such technical procedures. *The Well-Tempered Clavier* includes "learned" fugues that are moving and serene, airy and even comical. Some sound very much like dance music.

Contrapunctus 4 from *The Art of Fugue*, from the first edition of 1751. The fugue subject can be seen entering on lines 1, 2, 3, and 8.

JOHANN SEBASTIAN BACH (1685–1750)
The Art of Fugue, Contrapunctus 4 (published 1751)

Bach wrote *The Art of Fugue* at the end of his life, as a testament to his astonishing skill in writing fugues of all kinds, and with all shades of feeling. This huge work consists of twenty different canons and fugues—Bach uses the archaic and slightly pompous term *contrapunctus*—all on the same fugue subject. The number is not quite certain; Bach did not finish *The Art of Fugue,* and the heirs made something of a muddle when they published whatever they could find, soon after his death.

As a demonstration of his "art of fugue," Bach showed off the fugal devices mentioned in the box on page 140 in most of the fugues. But in Contrapunctus 4, one of the most melodious, he seems more interested in the long, smooth, and attractive episodes that come between the subject entries. These episodes are derived mainly from two sources, one from art—the rapid ending of the fugue subject, marked *x* on the music below—and the other from nature, it seems: a cuckoo figure, used repeatedly yet never sounding silly.

By comparison, the subject itself sounds restrained and serious, and it is presented in a very orderly way. The exposition brings the voices in a regular order from high to low (soprano, alto, tenor, bass). After an episode, four more entries follow the same order, modulating to a major key. After another episode, another four entries arrive in the reverse order, which is more climactic—and meanwhile the pitch range of the subject is expanded, as shown below:

The bearer, Monsieur J. C. Dorn, *student of music, has requested the undersigned to give him a testimonial to his knowledge in musicis . . . As his years increase it may well be expected that with his good native talent he will develop into a quite able musician.*

JOH. SEB. BACH (a tough grader)

LISTENING CHART 6

Bach, *The Art of Fugue*, Contrapunctus 4

Fugue form. 3 min., 30 sec.

26	0:00	**Exposition**	*Fugue subject in:*
			S (soprano; violin 1)
	0:06		A (alto; violin 2)
	0:15		T (tenor; viola)
	0:21		B (bass; cello)
	0:28	**Episode**	Uses a cuckoo figure, in sequence, then motive *x*, going up and down
	0:39	**Subject Entries**	S Major mode
	0:45		A Major
	0:51		T Minor mode
	0:56		B Minor
	1:03	**Long Episode**	Similar material, plus lead-up to the cadence ⟶
			CADENCE minor mode
			Similar material
27	1:34	**Entries**	B ⎫
0:06	1:39		T ⎪ Climactic: expanded form of the fugue subject, modulating
0:17	1:51		A ⎬
0:23	1:57		S ⎭
0:29	2:03	**Long Episode**	
0:38	2:12		CADENCE major mode (different key)
			Similar material, plus lead-up to the cadence ⟶
1:01	2:35		CADENCE minor mode (different key)
			Similar material
1:08	2:42	**Entries**	T
1:13	2:47		A (with a very close *stretto* in the S)
1:19	2:53	**Episode**	Episode material becomes more and more fluid.
1:40	3:14	**Final Entries**	T Expanded form of subject
1:46	3:20		A

This automatically makes the subject sound more intense, and also lets the music modulate naturally, increasing the intensity even more. This climax is recalled by the fugue's imposing conclusion.

The Art of Fugue was written for harpsichord, but it is often played by an instrumental group of some kind, which allows the individual voices to be heard more clearly. Mozart and Beethoven both arranged Bach fugues for string ensembles. We use an arrangement for string quartet by the English composer Robert Simpson (1921–1997).

3 The Dance Suite

Dance music was popular in the Baroque era, as has been true in every era, including of course our own. Dance music also inspired the greatest composers of the time to some of their best efforts.

The custom was to group a collection of miscellaneous dances together in a genre called the **suite.** Composers usually wrote "stylized" dances, that is, their music was intended for listening rather than dancing. Compared with music written for the actual dance floor, stylized dances naturally allowed for more musical elaboration and refinement, while still retaining some of the special features of the various dances.

Suites were written for orchestra, for chamber music combinations, or even for solo instruments such as the harpsichord or lute. Harpsichord suites are some of the very finest. Which dances occurred in a suite was not subject to any general rule, nor was there any specified order. All the dances in a suite were kept in the same key, and the last of them was always fast—frequently a **gigue,** a dance in compound meter that may have been derived from the Irish jig. Otherwise there was no standard overall structure to a suite.

Baroque Dances

Many different dances existed in the Baroque era. What distinguished them were features originally associated with the dance steps—a certain meter, a distinctive tempo, and some rhythmic attributes. The dance called the *gavotte,* for example, always begins with a double *upbeat,* two weak beats preceding the first strong beat (the *downbeat*) of a measure.

These are the main Baroque dances and their distinguishing features:

Dance	Usual Meter	Tempo	Some Rhythmic Characteristics
Allemande	4/4	Moderate	Upbeat sixteenth note; flowing motion
Courante	3/2	Moderate	Occasional substitution of **6/4** measures
Sarabande	3/4	Slow	Often a secondary accent on beat 2 (no upbeat)
Minuet	3/4	Moderate	Rather plain in rhythm (upbeat optional)
Gavotte	4/4	Moderate	Double upbeat of two quarter notes
Bourrée	2/2	Rather fast	Short upbeat
Siciliana	12/8	Moderate	Gently moving uneven rhythms; minor mode
Gigue	6/8	Fast	Short upbeat; uneven rhythms; lively movement

Baroque Dance Form

Although the number, type, and arrangement of dances in a suite varied widely, the *form* of dances was standardized. The same simple form was applied to all types, and it is an easily recognized feature of Baroque dance music.

A Baroque dance has two sections, **a** and **b.** Each ends with a strong cadence coming to a complete stop, after which the section is immediately repeated. Both sections tend to include the same motives, cadences, and other such musical details, and this makes for a sense of symmetry between them, even though **b** is nearly always longer than **a.** In the Baroque era there is usually no full-scale, clear repeat of the whole of **a** after **b,** as we shall see happen in later dances.

Hence Baroque dance form is diagrammed

               a a b b   *abbreviated as:*   **|: a :||: b :|**

Royals perform a Baroque
court dance.

where the signs |: and :| indicate that everything between them is to be repeated.
This form is also called **binary form**.

Trio   With shorter dances, composers tended to group them in pairs of the same
type, with the first coming back after the second. The result was a large-scale
A B A form. The **B** dance in such a pair was called the **trio**, because in seventeenth-
century orchestral music it had often been scored for only three instruments.

This made for a simple, agreeable contrast with the full orchestration of
the **A** dance. Even when the trio is scored for full orchestra, the idea of contrast between the two dances was always kept; the second is quieter than the
first, or it changes mode. (As for the term *trio*, to indicate a contrasting, subsidiary section, that was still used in the waltzes of Johann Strauss and the
marches of John Philip Sousa.)

Thus a Baroque minuet and trio, to choose this dance as an example, consists of one minuet followed by a second, quieter minuet, after which the first
is heard again. This time, however, the repeats are normally omitted:

	MINUET	TRIO	MINUET
	A	B	A
	a a b b	c c d d	a b
abbreviated as:	|: a :||: b :|	|: c :||: d :|	a b

The French Overture

A dance suite begins not with the first dance but with a special preparatory
number called a **French overture**. *Overture* is of course a general term for any
substantial piece of music introducing a play, opera, or ballet. The French
overture was a special type developed by the court orchestra of Louis XIV, de-

Concerts began late in the Baroque era. They were sometimes given in parks, where music accompanied gossip, flirtation, and food.

signed to symbolize the pomp and majesty of his court. Even after the French overture style had become antiquated, it was kept alive for the benefit of lesser rulers outside of France who aped everything associated with the Sun King.

The French overture consists of two sharply contrasted sections, an **A** section and a faster **B** section. They are typically arranged in an **A B A′** pattern, where **A′** stands for a variant—often an abbreviated variant—of **A**.

The slow **A** section is the one that is distinctively "French"; dotted rhythms (see page 20), sweeping scales and heavy accents, and other such features give it a majestic, pompous gravity that is easily recognized (and was easily imitated). This section was often labeled with the French word *Grave* (*grahv*).

The fast **B** section is in imitative polyphony. In some overtures this section amounts to a full-scale fugue.

JOHANN SEBASTIAN BACH
Orchestral Suite No. 3 in D (c. 1730)

It is thought that Bach wrote this suite for the Collegium Musicum of the University of Leipzig, a student music organization that seems to have provided a congenial outlet for his later work. The Suite in D is scored for the "festive" Baroque orchestra diagrammed on page 123: strings, two oboes, three trumpets, two timpani, and harpsichord. Bach carefully varied the orchestration from number to number.

This suite, like others written all over Europe, uses French titles as an acknowledgment of French leadership in ballet and the dance. After the overture, its movements are cast in the Baroque dance form described above.

Ouverture   The French overture that starts the suite is scored for all the instruments, and in fact it is the only movement in which the oboes have (slightly) independent parts that do not always double the violins. What is more, a solo violin emerges unexpectedly to dominate two passages during the **B** part of the overture, which is a full-scale fugue.

The form of this overture is **A B A′**. Shown below are the beginning of the **A** section, the "Grave," with its arresting drum roll and the obligatory "French" dotted rhythms, and part of the fugal exposition in **B**:

The episodes in this fugue are played by the solo violin. Indeed, this **B** part of the movement can be understood in two ways: as a fugue with solo violin episodes, or as a Baroque concerto with a fugal ritornello.

Following the overture come four pieces in dance form. Three of them follow the Baroque pattern |: **a** :||: **b** :|. Notice the "full stop" effect after each playing of all the **a**'s and **b**'s. Only the gavotte, the second of the dances, has a trio and so falls into **A B A** (gavotte and trio) form.

Air   *Air* is the French word for "aria"—and Bach composed this "instrumental song" in dance form, since it has to take its place in a dance suite. It is perhaps Bach's most famous and beloved melody. Only the strings and continuo play, as the quiet melody in the first violins is accompanied by a regular,

Eighteenth-century debates on the merits of French and Italian music could become catty. In this French cartoon, Italy's greatest composers—each playing the instrument he was famous for—join "Le chat de Caffarelli" in an aria (Caffarelli was a leading castrato).

downward-moving, soothing bass line in the cellos and bass viols (a **walking bass**: See page 121). And there are subsidiary but highly expressive counterpoints in the second violins and violas.

¶   The exquisite fluidity of this melody is a function of its rhythmic variety—variety that is set off by the regularity of the "walking" bass. Most of the basic two-beat (half-measure) units in the melody have rhythms not duplicated elsewhere. Therefore when measures 13–14 do repeat a rhythmic figure several times, they gain a special kind of climactic intensity. This intensity is underpinned by quiet *upward* motion in the bass, which had generally been moving downward, and by a newly prominent second violin part.

¶   Anticipated by some melodic figures in **a,** the figures in **b** keep reaching ever upward, in a wonderfully spontaneous way. This sense of aspiration is balanced by the graceful falling cadences ending **a** and **b.**

¶   To counteract all the rhythmic and melodic variety, Bach puts in several beautiful sequences, whose repetitive quality ensures a sense of organization: See measures 3–4, 13–14, and 15–16.

Gavotte   The wind instruments and timpani return in this number; the trumpets make this dance sound more like a march, as the festive orchestra evokes the military conquests that formed the basis of Baroque princely power. Trumpets deliver the strong two-quarter-note upbeat that characterizes the gavotte (see page 143). Then Bach inverts the bold opening melody of **a**

to obtain the opening of **b.** This inversion may *look* academic—a technical trick to be appreciated by the Collegium Musicum connoisseurs—but it *sounds* fresh and natural, another product of Bach's endlessly fertile melodic imagination:

The trio, or second gavotte, also fully orchestrated, sounds even more military than the first. Strings and oboes play fanfares to begin both **c** and **d.**

Bourrée   The lightest dance in this suite, a bourrée, is scored for full orchestra; the wind instruments and timpani are used mainly to underscore the sharp, exhilarating rhythms.

Gigue   Another drum roll (as in the French overture) launches this vigorous gigue, the most common dance for the last movement in a suite. The violins, doubled by the oboes, play almost continuous eighth notes in **6/8** time.

Web: *Research and test your understanding of Baroque instrumental music at* <bedfordstmartins.com/listen>.

LISTEN

Bach, Suite No. 3 in D, Gavotte

0:00 Gavotte (**A**): a
0:15   a *repeated*
0:30   **b**
0:56   **b** *repeated*
1:21 Trio (**B**): c c
2:10   d d
3:02 **A** (**a b**)

Baroque Vocal Music

Vocal music—music for solo voices, choruses, or both—formed a major part of the output of virtually all Baroque composers. We have seen that composers were supported by three main institutions: the church, the opera house, and the court. Each of these demanded vocal music. Indeed, of the three, only the court was a major source of instrumental music—and every court had its chapel, for which the court composers were also required to provide vocal music. Courts had their own opera theaters, too.

Words and Music

Theories of musical expression in the Baroque era were touched on in Chapter 8 (page 118). It was believed at the time that emotions could be isolated, categorized, and listed in a fairly simple way, and that music could enhance or even arouse each emotion by means of certain musical devices applied consistently, even single-mindedly, throughout a piece. Theorists developed checklists of musical devices corresponding to each of the "affects," as they called emotions conceived in this way.

It was particularly in vocal music—where the words that are sung define or suggest a specific emotion—that this musical "vocabulary of the emotions" was applied most consistently. If a text refers to "rejoicing," for example, a Baroque composer would match this with fast, lively runs; a mention of "victory" would probably require trumpets and drums to evoke battle music. More literally, when a text speaks of "high" or "low," a setting in high or low voices was likely, and so on.

1 Opera

The principal genre of secular vocal music of the Baroque era was opera. Introduced around the year 1600, opera flourished mightily all over Europe, and soon became the most glamorous and probably the most adventurous and influential artistic genre of the Baroque era.

In characterizing the emotional world of Baroque art (see page 116), we stressed its theatrical quality. The Baroque was fascinated by the theater, and especially by opera—the ultimate multimedia experience of its day, combining

A German opera house of the Baroque era. Notice that the best seats were actually on the stage.

poetry, drama, music, vocal virtuosity, scenic splendor, dance, and more. Spectacular singing was of the essence in Baroque opera, and so was spectacular stage architecture, featuring amazing transformation scenes and the like. Systems of pulleys and counterweights could rapidly change the set from a palace to a magic garden, with gods and goddesses descending from the heavens in a fiery chariot. Opera offered a wealth of satisfactions, then—most obviously, no doubt, for the vocal connoisseurs of the day, the fans of great singers. They are said to have gossiped and played cards in the boxes while waiting for their favorites to sing their special arias.

But opera's ability to project emotion was the real basis of its appeal. First and foremost, opera erected a stage on which individual singers could step forward to express feelings in the most direct and powerful fashion. Since the singers were portraying actual characters in a drama, they were repeatedly thrown into situations which made it natural for them to experience (and express) intense emotions.

Such emotions were intensified, of course, by music. Emotion could be intensified by great vocal virtuosity, too. The most obvious kind of vocal virtuosity is *coloratura* singing—fast brilliant runs, scales, high notes, vocal cadenzas, and so on, stressing technique for its own sake. But the legendary singers of old moved their audiences not only by singing faster than anyone else, but by singing more beautifully, more delicately, and more emotionally.

Italian Opera Seria

The principal type of Italian Baroque opera was **opera seria**, or serious opera. The plots—mostly derived from ancient history, with all kinds of alterations and additions—were designed to stir up powerful emotions, such as passion, rage, grief, and triumph. Such plots gave the singers many opportunities to excel in one kind of expression or another. Opera seria consists mainly of solo singing by sopranos and mezzo-sopranos, including castrati (see page 152). Tenors and basses play subordinate roles; there are few duets or choruses.

The text of an opera is called the *libretto* ("little book"), and the author of the text is the *librettist*. Librettists had to build up the drama as a whole from a series of texts, alternating with one another, for *recitatives* and *arias*.

Recitative

Recitative (resita-téev), from the Italian word for "recite," is a technique of declaiming words musically in a heightened, theatrical manner. There is always an instrumental accompaniment. The singing voice closely follows the free rhythm of emotional speech; it mirrors and indeed exaggerates the natural ups and downs that occur as an actor raises his or her voice at a question, lowers it in "asides," or cries out angrily. The composer makes no effort to organize these speechlike utterances into real melodies.

Recitative was used for plot action, dialogue, and other places in the drama where it is particularly important for the words to be brought out. Text phrases and individual words are not ordinarily repeated, of course, any more than they would be in speech.

Most of the time, recitative accompaniment was kept to a minimum—basso continuo (cello and harpsichord) alone—so that the singer could interpret

A much more informal picture of a Baroque opera performance—evidently during a recitative, to judge from the interaction of the characters on stage and the inattention of the audience. (The painting is perhaps by Antonio Longhi, 1702–1785.)

The Castrato

Intimately tied up with Italian opera seria was the castrato singer (plural: *castrati*). The starring male roles in opera were hardly ever sung by tenors or basses but rather by men who had submitted to castration as young boys in order to preserve their voices in the soprano or alto range. At its best, the castrato voice was a prized virtuoso instrument, more powerful and brilliant than a woman's soprano.

This practice seems an outrage to us today, as it did to everybody outside Italy at the time (and to many in Italy itself). It has been pointed out that for an intelligent peasant boy, the classic way to avoid a lifetime of labor in the fields was to enter the priesthood, with its vow of chastity, and that becoming a castrato provided another, similar option.

In any case, in Italy and all over Europe — though France was a notable exception — castrati were gladly accepted because of their wonderful singing and given top billing, along with women prima donnas. But the presence of frankly unnatural men in the main opera roles, which were of course usually romantic roles, made it hard to believe in the ideal of opera as serious drama in music. Often it was closer to "concert in costume." Contributing to the side-show quality, it was common for male characters to disguise themselves as women (and vice versa). The male soprano voice was used for female impersonation.

Farinelli

The most famous castrati were international stage figures. Some were pampered stars and objects of ridicule at the same time, such as Caffarelli (see page 146), who was once jailed for indecent gestures during an opera performance. Others were serious artists. Carlo Broschi, whose stage name was Farinelli, the most famous of all, was also a composer and later in life an influential figure at the court of Spain.

Many more castrati worked out of the limelight, in Italian churches. The last known castrato, a member of the Sistine Choir in Rome, made a recording in 1902; the voice has been described as "penetrating and curiously disembodied."

For a 1995 film about Farinelli, a virtual castrato voice was invented by digital wizardry.

---

the dialogue or the action as spontaneously as possible. A name for recitative with continuo accompaniment is **secco recitative**, from the Italian word *secco*, meaning "dry" (think of the sound of the harpsichord).

In every opera, however, one or two of the most excited, emotion-filled recitatives were provided with orchestral accompaniment of one kind or another. This type is called **accompanied recitative**.

Aria

An **aria** is a set piece for solo singer that has much more musical elaboration and coherence than a passage of recitative. The vocal part is more melodic, and ordinarily the accompaniment includes the orchestra, not just the continuo, as in secco recitative. Here the singer-actor is mulling over his or her emotions at some leisure, "getting his feelings out," instead of reacting moment by moment, as in recitative. Consequently in arias the repetition of poetic phrases or words is common and, in principle, appropriate.

The standard form for the Baroque Italian opera aria is **da capo** form, **A B A** (less usual is free da capo form, **A B A'**). Both the words and music of **A** are repeated after **B**; *da capo* ("from the head") is a direction on scores meaning repeat from the beginning. The composer wrote the music for **A** and **B** only, leaving the performers to do the rest. Indeed, the singer would do more than just repeat **A**. He or she would also ornament the music with improvised runs, cadenzas, and so on, so as to create an exciting enhanced effect the second time around.

If we can neither get [the famous castrato] Senesino, nor Carestini, then Mr. Handel desires to have a man soprano and a woman contralto, and the price (for both) must not exceed 1100 guineas, and that the persons must set out for London the latter end of August, and that no engagement must be made with one without a certainty of getting the other.

Letter from one of Handel's agents, 1730

For connoisseurs of the day, a great deal depended on the **A** repeats, since it was there that the singers really dazzled their audiences. Many modern singers have relearned the lost improvisational art of the Baroque era, and we can recapture some of the original excitement on recordings.

GEORGE FRIDERIC HANDEL
Julius Caesar (Giulio Cesare in Egitto) (1724)

As a young man, Handel wrote a few German operas for the Hamburg opera company (most of the music is lost) and a few Italian operas for theaters in Florence and Venice; in his maturity he wrote as many as forty Italian operas for London. Probably the most famous of them is *Julius Caesar,* one of a trio of Handel masterpieces written in the years 1724–25, the others being *Rodelinda* and *Tamerlano.*

Background Like most opera seria plots of the late Baroque era, *Julius Caesar* draws on Roman history. Cleopatra, the unprincipled Queen of Egypt, applied her formidable charms to Julius Caesar and then, after Caesar's assassination, also to his successor Mark Antony. Shakespeare deals with the second of these famous affairs in *Antony and Cleopatra;* Handel tackles the first.

But Handel's librettist added a great deal of nonhistorical plot material that Shakespeare would have shaken his head at. History tells that Pompey—who comes into the story because he waged war on Caesar and lost and fled to Egypt—was murdered by his centurion, but in the opera the murderer is Cleopatra's brother Ptolemy. Pompey's widow Cornelia is thrown into Ptolemy's harem and has to resist his advances (among others'). Her son Sextus rattles around the opera swearing vengeance on Ptolemy and finally kills him. In actuality Ptolemy was poisoned by Cleopatra, but her character is whitewashed, and she gets to sing some of the opera's most ravishing music, seductive indeed, while she is disguised as her maid.

Although the role of Sextus, for mezzo soprano, was presumably meant for a castrato, at the first performance it was sung by a woman singer who was one of Handel's regulars.

Aria, "La giustizia" Sextus promises revenge on Ptolemy, not for the first time, in the aria "La giustizia" (Justice). This aria is preceded or, rather, set up by a recitative (as usual). Since it makes more sense to study recitative when the words are in English, we leave that discussion until we get to Handel's *Messiah.*

The aria starts with a ritornello played by the string orchestra, establishing the mood right away:

The "affect" Handel means to covey by this strenuous, vigorous music is anger, and Sextus starts up with the same music. We will hear this ritornello three more times, abbreviated one time, prior to the second **A** section.

Apart from this abbreviation, "La giustizia" is in strict **A B A** (da capo) form. In the **A** section Handel goes through the words three times, with short ritornellos in between to allow the singer to catch her breath. (These short spacers are not marked on the Listening Chart.) Notice how the music tends to explode angrily on certain key words, principally by the use of *coloratura* (fast scales and turns), as on "ven-*det*-ta" (vengeance) and "tradi-*tor*" (traitor). Even more vivid are the sudden high notes on "pu-*ni*-re" (punish) and a suspense-making long note on "tradi-*tor*."

There is a flamboyant effect typical of the Baroque near the end of **A**, where Sextus pauses dramatically for effect. After a breathless fermata (see page 14), he moves on to make a very forceful final cadence. Revenge is nigh!

The aria's **B** section introduces some new keys for contrast; otherwise it is brief and seems rather subdued—the strings drop out, leaving only the continuo as accompaniment. What the audience is waiting for is the da capo of **A**, where we can forget about Sextus and get to admire a display of vocal virtuosity. Lorraine Hunt Lieberson, the singer on our recording, adds brilliant improvised flourishes to the high notes on "pu-*ni*-re" and the long note on "tradi-*tor*." When she gets to the fermata in **A** she fills it in with a cadenza, and her (ornamented) final cadence sweeps us away. Anyone who can carry off a feat like this, the aria seems to say, will be more than a match for Ptolemy.

Vocal cadenzas at the time were short, because they were supposed to be sung in a single breath—thus showing off virtuoso breath control as well as vocal technique and inventiveness.

Lorraine Hunt Lieberson in another Handel opera role

LISTEN			Handel, *Julius Caesar*, Aria "La giustizia"	

8

0:00	**A**	RITORNELLO		
0:16		**St. 1:** first time	La giustizia ha già sull' arco Pronto strale alla vendetta Per punire un traditor	Justice now has in its bow The arrow primed for vengeance To castigate a traitor!
0:50		**St. 1:** second time	*La giustizia . . . etc.*	
1:10		**St. 1:** third time	*La giustizia . . . etc.*	
1:31		RITORNELLO		
1:47	**B**	**St. 2:**	Quanto è tarda la saetta Tanto più crudele aspetta La sua pena un empio cor.	The later the arrow is shot The crueler is the pain suffered By a dastardly heart!
2:15	**A**	RITORNELLO		
2:22		(abbreviated)	*La giustizia . . . etc.*	Justice . . . etc.

For a note on Italian pronunciation, see page 102: "La joostidzia (ah) jah sool arco."

2 Oratorio

Sacred, or religious, vocal music of the Baroque era exhibits considerable diversity in style and form. Most of it was written directly for church services, and so its style and form depend first of all on whether those services were of the Roman Catholic, Lutheran, or Anglican rite. Every service has places where music is appropriate, even if they are not actually specified by the liturgy. In principle, each place gives rise to a different musical genre.

There are, however, two general factors that are important for all Baroque sacred-music genres—oratorio and passion, cantata, Mass, and motet. One of these factors is traditional in origin; the other is specific to the Baroque era.

The traditional factor is the participation of the choir. Choral music has had a functional place in the religious music of virtually all rites and ages. For

George Frideric Handel (1685–1759)

Georg Friedrich Händel—he anglicized his name to George Frideric Handel after settling in England—was one of the few composers of early days who did not come from a family of musicians. His father was a barber-surgeon and a valet at a court near Leipzig. He disapproved of music, and the boy is said to have studied music secretly at night, by candlelight. In deference to his father's wishes, Handel studied law for a year at Halle, one of Germany's major universities, before finally joining the orchestra at Hamburg, Germany's leading center of opera.

From then on, it was an exciting, glamorous life. Still in his teens, Handel fought a duel with another Hamburg musician about which was to get top billing. In 1706 he journeyed to the homeland of opera and scored big successes in Venice, Florence, and Rome. Though he became a court musician for the Elector of Hanover, in northern Germany, he kept requesting (and extending) leaves to pursue his career in London, a city that was then beginning to rival Paris as the world capital.

Here Handel continued to produce Italian operas, again with great success. He also wrote a flattering birthday ode for Queen Anne and some big pieces to celebrate a major peace treaty; for this he was awarded an annuity. In 1717, after the Elector of Hanover had become George I of England, Handel got back into his good graces by composing music to be played on boats in a royal aquatic fete on the River Thames—the famous *Water Music* (two suites for the Baroque festive orchestra).

As an opera composer, Handel had learned to gauge the taste of the public and also to flatter singers, writing music for them that showed off their voices to the best advantage. He now became an opera impresario—today we would call him a promoter—recruiting singers and negotiating their contracts, planning whole seasons of opera, and all the while composing the main attractions himself: an opera, every year, on average, between 1721 and 1743. He also had to deal with backers—English aristocrats and wealthy merchants who supported his opera companies, and persuaded their friends to take out subscriptions for boxes.

Handel made and lost several fortunes, but he always landed on his feet, even when Italian opera went out of style in Britain, for he never lost a feel for his audience. After opera had failed, he popularized oratorios—retellings of Bible stories (mostly from the Old Testament) in a semioperatic, semichoral form. Opera audiences had always been ready to identify opera's virtuous Roman emperors with local princes. Now they were delighted to identify oratorio's virtuous People of Israel with the British nation.

Handel was a big, vigorous man, hot-tempered but quick to forget, humorous and resourceful. When a particularly temperamental prima donna had a tantrum, he calmed her down by threatening to throw her out the window. At the end of his life he became blind—the same surgeon operated (unsuccessfully) on both him and Bach—but he continued to play the organ brilliantly and composed by dictating to a secretary.

Chief Works: 40 Italian operas, including *Giulio Cesare* (Julius Caesar) ▪ Near-operatic works in English: *Semele* and *Acis and Galatea* ▪ Oratorios, including *Messiah, Israel in Egypt, Samson,* and *Saul* ▪ Concerti grossi and organ concertos ▪ *Water Music,* written for an aquatic fete on the River Thames, and *Royal Fireworks Music,* celebrating the end of the War of the Austrian Succession, in 1747 ▪ Sonatas for various instruments; variations ("The Harmonious Blacksmith") for harpsichord

Encore: After *Messiah,* listen to the *Royal Fireworks Music;* Concerto Grosso in B-flat, Op. 6, No. 7.

---

when one person utters a religious text, he or she speaks as an individual, but when a choir does so, it speaks as a united community. A church choir can be said to speak for the whole church, even for the whole of Christianity.

⁊ The other important fact about Baroque sacred vocal music is its strong tendency to borrow from secular vocal music—which is to say, from opera. In an era fascinated by the theater, the church grew more and more theatrical. Arias inspired by Italian opera seria appear even in Baroque settings of the Catholic Mass. Solo singers could display their vocal prowess at the same time as they were presenting parts of the divine service.

The most operatic of all religious genres was oratorio, which existed in Catholic and Protestant countries alike. An **oratorio** is basically an opera on a religious subject, such as an Old Testament story or the life of a saint. It has a narrative plot in several acts, real characters, and implied action—even though oratorios were not staged, but presented in concert form, that is, without scenery, costumes, or gestures. Oratorio takes over such operatic features as recitatives and arias. On the other hand, it also makes much use of the chorus—a major difference from Italian opera of the time.

Unlike most other religious genres, an oratorio was not actually part of a church service. Indeed, in opera-crazed Italy, the oratorio was prized as an entertainment substituting for opera during Lent, a season of abstinence from opera as well as other worldly diversions.

In England, the oratorio was also a substitute for opera, though in a different sense. Thanks largely to Handel, Italian opera became very popular in London for a quarter of a century, but finally audiences tired of it. At that point, Handel, already in his mid fifties, began composing oratorios, and these turned out to be even more popular yet, the pinnacle of his long career.

> *On Tuesday the 2nd day of May will be performed, the Sacred Story of Esther, an Oratorio in English. Formerly composed by Mr. Handel, and now revised by him, with several Additions . . . N.B. There will be no Action on the Stage . . .*
>
> London newspaper announcement, 1731

GEORGE FRIDERIC HANDEL
Messiah (1742)

Handel's oratorio *Messiah*, his most famous work, is also one of the most famous in the whole of Western music. It is the only composition of its time that has been performed continuously—and frequently—since its first appearance. Today it is sung at Christmas and Easter in hundreds of churches around the world, as well as at symphony concerts and *"Messiah* sings," where people get together just to sing along with the Hallelujah Chorus and the other well-known choral numbers, and listen to the well-loved arias.

Unlike most oratorios, *Messiah* does not have actual characters acting out a biblical story in recitative and arias, although its text is taken from the Bible. In a more typical Handel oratorio, such as *Samson,* for example, Samson sings an aria about his blindness and argues with Delilah in recitative, while choruses represent the People of Israel and the Philistines. Instead, *Messiah* works with a group of anonymous narrators, relating episodes from the life of Jesus in recitative. The narration is interrupted by anonymous commentators who react to each of the episodes by singing recitatives and arias.

All this is similar in many ways to opera in concert form (that is, not staged); but in addition, the chorus has a large and varied role to play. On one occasion, it speaks for a group of angels that actually speaks in the Bible. Sometimes it comments on the story, like the soloists. And often the choristers raise their voices to praise the Lord in Handel's uniquely magnificent manner.

We shall first examine two numbers in *Messiah* covering the favorite Christmas story about the announcement of Christ's birth to the shepherds in the fields. Included are a recitative in four brief sections and a chorus.

***Recitative** Part 1 (secco)*   Sung by a boy soprano narrator accompanied by continuo (cello and organ), this recitative has the natural, "proselike" flow typical of all recitatives. Words that would be naturally stressed in ordinary speech are brought out by longer durations, higher pitches, and pauses: "*shepherds,*" "*field,*" "*flock,*" and "*night.*" No words are repeated.

Part 2 (accompanied)   Accompanied recitative is used for "special effects" in operas and oratorios—here the miraculous appearance of angels. The slowly pulsing high-string background furnishes the angel with a sort of musical halo. It is also a signal for more vigorous declamation: The words *lo, Lord,* and *glory*

Women in Music

Before the twentieth century, opportunities for women were limited. Though some women worked as teachers, nurses, and laborers, society viewed women's primary role as that of wife and mother. Occasionally accidents of royal succession placed a woman in a position of great power, and the eighteenth century saw two amazingly long-lasting cases: Catherine the Great, empress of Russia, who ruled from 1762 to 1796, and Maria Theresa, de facto empress of the Austrian Empire from 1740 to 1780. But what we now think of as "careers" were simply not open to women, with few exceptions.

Music provided one of those exceptions. It did so by way of the theater, because an opera singer, like an actress or a ballet dancer, could attain fame and fortune and the opportunity to develop her talents in the same way as men in those same fields. Indeed, opera depended on women singers; without them the genre could never have developed or survived.

The names—although not, alas, the voices—of opera's legendary prima donnas have come down to us, along with those of opera's great composers: from **Anna Renzi** (c. 1620–c. 1660), who sang in Monteverdi's *Poppea* (see page 99), to the notorious rival sopranos **Faustina Bordoni** (1700–1781) and **Francesca Cuzzoni** (1698–1770) in the age of Handel,

Bordoni

Cuzzoni

and beyond. Cuzzoni sang in the star-studded premiere of Handel's *Julius Caesar* (see page 153).

Women of the theater paid a price for their career opportunities, of course. They were displaying themselves—their legs or their voices—for the enjoyment of, mainly, men, who paid for the privilege. There was always a question about the respectability and marriageability of opera singers.

While women opera singers were a fixture in the musical workplace of the Baroque, women instrumentalists were much rarer. Women composers were simply flukes. We noted on page 138 that Baroque music was often the product of clans, like the Bachs; but next to none of these clans ever thought to make one of its daughters into a composer.

One that did was the Jacquet family, harpsichord makers in Paris for at least four generations. **Elizabeth-Claude Jacquet** (1667–1729) was a Mozart-style prodigy who was sponsored by Louis XIV himself. Famous as a harpsichordist, she composed music of all kinds, including an opera which was put on at the forerunner of the Paris Opéra—then as now the grandest venue for opera in Europe.

There was no respectability problem with Elizabeth-Claude Jacquet; by the time she was seventeen she was married to an organist, one Marin de la Guerre, whose name is usually hyphenated with hers.

---

are brought out with increasing emphasis. The end of this brief accompanied recitative is heavily punctuated by a standard cadence formula, played by the continuo. This formula is an easily recognized feature of recitatives.

Part 3 (secco)   Notice that the angel speaks in a more urgent style than the narrator. And in *Part 4 (accompanied),* the excited, faster pulsations in the high strings depict the beating wings, perhaps, of the great crowd of angels. When Handel gets to what they will be "saying," he brings the music to a triumphant high point, once again over the standard recitative cadence.

Chorus, "Glory to God"   "Glory to God! Glory to God in the *highest!*" sing the angels—the *high* voices of the choir, in a bright marchlike rhythm. They are accompanied by the orchestra, with the trumpets prominent. The *low* voices alone add "and peace on *earth,*" much more slowly. Fast string runs following "Glory to God" and slower reiterated chords following "and peace on earth" recall the fast and slow string passages in the two preceding accompanied recitatives.

After these phrases are sung and played again, leading to another key, the full chorus sings the phrase "good will toward men" in a fugal style. The

good will to-ward men

sequence
good will . . .

important words are *good will*, and their two-note motive is happily sung (in imitation) again and again by all the voices of the angel choir. To conclude, the "good will" motive is singled out in an enthusiastic ascending sequence.

The whole chorus is quite concise, even dramatic; the angels do not stay long. At the very end, the orchestra gets quieter and quieter—a rare effect in Baroque music, here indicating the disappearance of the shepherds' vision.

9   11

| LISTEN | Handel, *Messiah*, Recitative "There were shepherds" and Chorus, "Glory to God" |

*(Bold **italic** type indicates accented words or syllables. Italics indicate phrases of text that are repeated.)*

RECITATIVE PART 1 (secco)
0:01   There were **shep**herds abiding in the **field**, keeping **watch** over their **flock** by **night**.

PART 2 (accompanied)
0:13   And *lo!* the angel of the **Lord** came upon them, and the glo**ry** of the Lord shone round about them; and they were sore afraid.   Standard cadence

PART 3 (secco)
0:34   And the angel said unto **them: Fear** not, for be**hold**, I bring you good **ti**dings of great **joy**, which shall **be to all peo**ple.   Standard cadence
For unto you is born this **day** in the city of **Da**vid a **Sa**viour, which is **Christ** the **Lord**.   Standard cadence

PART 4 (accompanied)
1:08   And *sud*denly there was with the **an**gel a **mul**titude of the heavenly **host**, praising **God, and saying:**   Standard cadence

CHORUS
1:20   Glory to God, *glory to God*, in the highest, and peace on earth,
2:02   good will toward men *good will*
2:21   *Glory to God*

Hallelujah Chorus   This famous chorus brings Act II of *Messiah* to a resounding close. Like "Glory to God," "Hallelujah" makes marvelous use of monophony ("King of Kings"), homophony (the opening "Hallelujah"), and polyphony ("And he shall reign for ever and ever"): almost a textbook example of musical textures. Compare "And peace on earth," "Glory to God," and "Good will toward men" in the earlier chorus.

In a passage beloved by chorus singers, Handel sets "The Kingdom of this world is become" on a low descending scale, *piano*, swelling suddenly into a similar scale in a higher register, *forte*, for "the Kingdom of our Lord, and of his Christ"—a perfect representation of one thing becoming another thing, similar but newly radiant. Later the sopranos (cheered on by the trumpets) solemnly utter the words "King of Kings" on higher and higher long notes as the other voices keep repeating their answer, "for ever, Hallelujah!"

George II of England, attending the first London performance of *Messiah*, was so moved by this chorus that he stood up in his box—prompting everyone else to stand in honor of the King of Kings, no doubt, but also reminding everyone of his own majesty, which was being acclaimed by the typical Baroque festive orchestra. Audiences still sometimes stand during the "Hallelujah" Chorus.

An oratorio performance, caught by the satirical pen of Handel's contemporary William Hogarth (1697–1764). Note the words. Is nothing sacred?

LISTEN   Handel, *Messiah*, Hallelujah Chorus

(Italics indicate phrases of text that are repeated.)

0:07   Hallelujah, *Hallelujah!*
0:26   For the Lord God omnipotent reigneth. *Hallelujah!*
       For the Lord God omnipotent reigneth.
1:17   The Kingdom of this world is become the kingdom
          of our Lord and *of his Christ.*
1:35   And He shall reign for ever and ever, *and he shall reign for ever and ever.*
1:58   KING OF KINGS *for ever and ever, Hallelujah!*
       AND LORD OF LORDS *for ever and ever, Hallelujah!*

3 The Church Cantata

Second in importance to oratorio among Baroque sacred-music genres is the **church cantata.** *Cantata* is a general name for a piece of moderate length for voices and instruments, and in Germany church cantatas were written to be performed during Lutheran Church services. Lutheran Churches had (and still have today) fixed readings and hymns specified for every Sunday of the year, as well as for special occasions such as Easter and Christmas. The words of cantatas addressed the religious content of the day in question. Sung before the sermon, the cantata was in effect a second, musicalized sermon.

As cantor, or music director, of Leipzig's biggest church (the Thomaskirche), Bach was required to produce cantatas for the entire year—a stupendous task that kept him very busy indeed for years after he was appointed. Over two hundred cantatas by Bach have survived, each of them with several movements, including some secular cantatas written for court or civic celebrations.

The Lutheran Chorale

The content and structure of the church cantata were quite various. One kind, for example, has singers who represent Hope, Fear, the Soul, and so on, discussing Christian issues in operatic arias and recitatives, like a short scene from an oratorio. A special feature of nearly all Lutheran cantatas is their use of traditional congregational hymns. Lutheran hymns are called **chorales** (coráhls), from the German word for hymn (*Choral*).

Martin Luther, the father of the Protestant Reformation, placed special emphasis on hymn singing when he decided on the format of Lutheran services. Two hundred years later, in Bach's time, a large body of chorales served as the foundation for Lutheran worship, both in church services and also at informal pious devotions in the home. Everybody knew the words and music of these chorales. You learned them as a small child and sang them in church all your life. Consequently when composers introduced chorale tunes into cantatas (and other sacred-music genres), they were drawing on a rich source of association.

Just how were tunes "introduced"? There were many ways. The last movement of a Bach cantata is usually a single hymn stanza sung straight through, in much the same simple way as the congregation would sing it, but with the orchestra playing.

Longer cantata movements present the individual lines or phrases of the chorale one by one, with gaps in between them, while other music runs on continuously, both during the chorale phrases (that is, in counterpoint with them) and during the gaps. In a **gapped chorale,** the chorale melody is delivered in spurts. It can be sung, or it can be played by one prominent instrument—an oboe, say, or a trumpet—while the continuous music goes along in the other instruments and/or voices.

I have always been very fond of music. Whoever is proficient in this art is a good man, fit for all other things. Hence it is absolutely necessary to have it taught in the schools. A schoolmaster must know how to sing or I shan't tolerate him.

Martin Luther, 1538

Chorale, sung simply (phrases):

Gapped chorale movement:

JOHANN SEBASTIAN BACH (1685–1750)
Cantata No. 4, "Christ lag in Todesbanden"
(Christ Lay in Death's Dark Prison) (1707)

In his posts as an organist and cantor, Bach made multiple settings of many hymns, both in cantatas and also as chorale preludes for organ (see page 162). We shall study just a few of his settings of the Easter chorale "Christ lag in Todesbanden" (Christ Lay in Death's Dark Prison).

This rugged old tune had been fitted with even more rugged words by Martin Luther himself, in 1524. The seven stanzas of the chorale, each ending with "Hallelujah!," tell in vivid language of mankind's struggle with Death and the victory achieved through Christ's sacrifice. The fact that this hymn is in the minor mode throws a tough, sober shadow over all the rejoicing; the mood is unforgettable.

We cannot recapture the associations that Bach's contemporaries would have brought to this tune, but we can begin to learn it by singing the first stanza:

There - fore   let   us __   thank - ful   be   And   praise   our   Sa - viour   joy - ful - ly,
All' __   sein   Recht   und __   sein'   Ge - walt,   Da   blei - bet   nichts   denn   Tod's   Ge - stalt,

So   sing   we, __   Hal - le - lu - jah,   Hal - le - lu - jah!
Den   Stach'l   hat __   er   ver - lo - ren.   Hal - le - lu - jah!

The cantata based on "Christ lag in Todesbanden" is one of Bach's earliest. It employs simple forces: voices and a string orchestra, with continuo.* The words of the seven movements are the words of the seven stanzas of the famous Easter chorale.

Bach set these seven stanzas with a sharp eye (or ear) for symmetry. Not all of the voices sing in all of the stanzas; the diagram below tallies the voices that sing in each one:

SINFONIA	STANZA 1	2	3	4	5	6	7	
Orchestra	Soprano	S		S		S	S	*Color shading indicates which voice sings the chorale melody.*
	Alto		A		A		A	*(In stanza 6, it is divided between two voices.)*
	Tenor			T	T		T	T	
	Bass				B	B		B	

After a short orchestral prelude—Bach calls it "sinfonia"—all the stanzas except the last are set as "gapped" chorales of some sort.

Stanza 3   The tenor sings the "gapped" chorale tune; follow him along with the music, above. Accompanied by the continuo (played on the organ), a violin plays an urgent melody at both ends of the piece and in the gaps between the lines. At the word *nichts* ("nothing") the music comes to a wrenching stop and a slowdown, a quite astonishing effect. Then the violin starts up again as though nothing had happened. The sudden absence of music tells us what is left of Death's power: *nichts*, zilch!

Stanza 4   Here it is the alto (doubled by an organ stop) that sings the gapped chorale tune, more slowly than the tenor of stanza 3. The "continuous" music is assigned to other voices singing faster imitative polyphony to the same words, always using fragments of the chorale melody. (Compare the music to the right with the chorale melody.) Perhaps all this busy imitative polyphony makes a good illustration of the warfare described with such gusto in this stanza. Perhaps, too, the jaunty rhythm at *ein Spott* can indeed be heard as mocking Death who has lost his sting.

Stanza 7   No longer gapped, this is a straightforward presentation of the hymn as it might be sung by the congregation. Bach's rich harmonies below the soprano melody are sung by the lower voices, doubled by the instruments. The cantata comes to a restful conclusion at last, as the text turns from battles to the confidence of faith. Even "hallelujah" can now be uttered simply.

*When Bach wrote Cantata No. 4 he was a young small-town organist, and probably could not count on more than one singer to a part, as on our recording—which compensates, however, by adding reverberation to suggest an echoing church.

A Leipzig church service

STANZA 4

line 1 Es war ein wunder . . .

line 5 Die Schrift hat . . .

line 6 Wie ein Tod . . .

line 7 Ein Spott . . .

| LISTEN | Bach, "Christ lag in Todesbanden" | 11-13 |

11 **Stanza 3:** Jesus Christus, Gottes Sohn, Jesus Christ, the Son of God,
An unser Statt ist kommen, Has come on our behalf,
Und hat die Sünde weggetan, And has done away with our sins,
Damit den Tod genommen Thereby robbing Death
All' sein Recht und sein' Gewalt; Of all his power and might;
Da bleibet *nichts*—denn Tod's Gestalt; There remains nothing but Death's image;
Den Stach'l hat er verloren. He has lost his sting.
Hallelujah! Hallelujah!

12 **Stanza 4:** Es war ein wunderlicher Krieg, It was a marvelous war
Da Tod und Leben rungen; Where Death and Life battled.
Das Leben da behielt das Sieg, Life gained the victory;
Es hat den Tod verschlungen. It swallowed up Death.
Die Schrift hat verkündiget das Scripture has proclaimed
Wie ein Tod den andern frass; How one Death gobbled up the other;
Ein Spott aus dem Tod ist worden. Death became a mockery.
Hallelujah! Hallelujah!

13 **Stanza 7:** Wir essen und leben wohl We eat and live fitly
Im rechten Osterfladen. On the true unleavened bread of Passover;
Der alter Sauerteig nicht soll The old yeast shall not
Sein bei dem Wort der Gnaden. Contaminate the word of grace.
Christus will die Koste sein Christ alone will be the food
Und speisen die Seel' allein, To feed the soul:
Der Glaub' will keins andern leben. Faith will live on nothing else.
Hallelujah! Hallelujah!

4 The Organ Chorale

German churches took special pride in their organs, both in their appearance and their acoustic quality. Organ technology developed prodigiously in the Baroque era. The **chorale prelude** or *organ chorale,* an important genre of keyboard music at the time, is an organ composition incorporating a hymn (chorale) tune.

Like cantatas, organ chorales incorporated hymn tunes in many ways. The "gapped" method (see page 160) was common. Played on the organ, the tune could also be ornamented with scales, trills, and so on, for expressive purposes—much the same technique as was applied to opera melodies.

In religious terms, the effect of an organ chorale was probably not very different from a sung one. Lutherans knew their hymns by heart, so the tune on the organ would automatically bring to mind the hymn text and its message or lesson.

When Bach seated himself at the organ, he used to choose some theme and treat it in all the various forms of organ composition. First, he used this theme for a prelude and fugue, with the full organ. Then he showed his art of using the stops for a trio, quartet, etc., on the same theme. Afterwards followed a chorale, the melody of which was playfully surrounded by the same theme in three or four contrapuntal parts . . .

From the first biography of Bach, 1802

JOHANN SEBASTIAN BACH
Chorale Prelude, "Christ lag in Todesbanden"
(Christ Lay in Death's Dark Prison) (1715)

14

At certain points in a Lutheran service, the organist would play chorale preludes based on seasonal hymns. On Easter Sunday, Bach might well have played this organ prelude on "Christ lag in Todesbanden."

The music is powerful and triumphant—a wordless hallelujah for the miracle of Easter. The chorale tune can be heard on the high organ pipes, played without any gaps, but with a vigorous faster motive accompanying it, a motive that clatters away splendidly in the organ pedals. The rich harmonies are formed

ORGAN PEDALS

Lavishly decorated in Baroque style, the splendid organ of St. John's Church in Lüneburg, northern Germany, may have been played by the young Bach; Bach is thought to have studied with its organist, Georg Böhm. Böhm was an important composer of organ music.

by dense counterpoint. Perhaps next in the service the hymn would have been sung by the congregation.

This piece comes from the *Orgelbüchlein*, a "Little Organ Book" of 162 short chorale preludes that Bach planned for use in different services throughout the entire church year. This not-so-little collection bears witness to both sides of Bach's temperament: encyclopedic on the one hand and on the other strictly practical.

Web: *Research and test your understanding of Baroque vocal music at* <bedfordstmartins.com/listen>.

CHAPTER 11

Prelude
Music and
the Enlightenment

In the second part of the eighteenth century, a new musical style emerged in Europe. Called the Classical style, it had important pioneers in Italy and northern Germany; one of them was Carl Philipp Emanuel Bach, a son of Johann Sebastian. But the Classical style was developed particularly by several great composers active in Vienna, capital of Austria. Here conditions seem to have been ideal for music. Geographically, Austria stands at the crossroads of four other musical nations—Germany, Bohemia (now the Czech Republic), Hungary, and Italy—and Vienna was also central in political terms. As the capital of the powerful Hapsburg empire, Vienna was plunged into every European conflict of the time and exposed to every new cultural and intellectual current.

Vienna's golden years were from 1780 to 1790, during the reign of Emperor Joseph II, the most enlightened of the long line of Hapsburg monarchs. Joseph emancipated the peasantry, furthered education, and reduced the power of the clergy; he supported music and literature with his patronage and encouraged a free press. In a city of only 150,000 people, there were three hundred newspapers and journals during Joseph's reign, representing every shade of opinion.

In this liberal atmosphere, Franz Joseph Haydn of nearby Eisenstadt became recognized as the principal composer of Europe; his symphonies were commissioned from far-off Paris and London. The young Wolfgang Amadeus Mozart was drawn to the capital in 1781 from Salzburg, a hundred miles to the west, to spend his brilliant last decade there. And in 1792 a young musician from the other end of Germany, who had composed a long cantata mourning Emperor Joseph's death, decided to come to this great musical center to launch his career. His name was Ludwig van Beethoven.

1 The Enlightenment and Music

To describe Joseph II as an "enlightened" ruler is both to commend him and also to locate him in European intellectual history. Like a number of other rulers of the time, Joseph II derived his principles of governance from an important intellectual movement of the eighteenth century known as the Enlightenment, a movement that also helped to define the music that flourished under his reign.

Centered in France, the Enlightenment had strong roots in English philosophy and strong offshoots in Germany and Austria. Its original source was the faith in reason that led to the great scientific discoveries of the Baroque period. Now, however, the emphasis veered away from the purely intellectual and scientific toward the social sphere. People were less intent on controlling natural forces by science than on turning these forces to human benefit. People also began to apply the same intelligence that solved scientific problems to problems of public morality, education, and politics.

Social injustice came under especially strong fire in the eighteenth century; so did established religion. For the first time in European history, religion ceased to be an overriding force in many people's minds. There were currents

Emperor Joseph II

The phrase "Viennese Classical style" brings to mind Haydn, Mozart, and Beethoven; each of them came to the capital city from other, smaller centers.

of agnosticism and even outright atheism—to the outrage of the English poet and mystic William Blake:

> Mock on, mock on, Voltaire, Rousseau:
> Mock on, mock on, 'tis all in vain!
> You throw the sand against the wind,
> And the wind blows it back again.

The two French philosophers named by Blake are always mentioned in connection with the Enlightenment: François Marie Arouet, whose pen name was Voltaire (1694–1778), tireless satirist and campaigner for justice and reason, and the younger, more radical, more disturbing Jean-Jacques Rousseau (1712–1778). Rousseau is one of the few major figures of European philosophy who had a direct effect on the history of music, as we shall see.

"The Pursuit of Happiness"

The Enlightenment was also the occasion for the first great contribution to Western civilization from America. In colonial days, the austere Puritan spirit was hardly in step with the growing secularization of European society, but the Declaration of Independence and the Federalist Papers proved to be the finest flowers of Enlightenment idealism. The notion that a new state could be founded on rational principles, set down on a piece of paper, and agreed to by men of good will and intelligence—this could only have emerged under the influence of the political and philosophical writings of the eighteenth century.

"Life, liberty, and the pursuit of happiness": The last of these three famous rights, too, was very much of its time. One can imagine the medieval barons who forced King John to accept the Magna Carta insisting on life and liberty, of a sort, but it would never have occurred to them to demand happiness as a self-evident right for all. Voltaire and Rousseau fought passionately for social justice so that people might live good lives according to their own convictions.

Voltaire, by Jean-Antoine Houdon (1740–1828), master sculptor of the neo-Roman busts that were much favored at the time. (All the other portrait busts in this chapter are also by Houdon.)

In the Classical era, lighter entertainments took over the stage, in place of the heavy drama characteristic of the Baroque. Compare this picture (a London ballet of 1791) with the opera seria shown on page 120.

A French Rococo
ceramic plaque

The eighteenth century was an age of good living, then, an age that valued intelligence, wit, and sensitivity. The age cultivated elegant conversation, the social arts, and hedonism. One of its inventions was the salon—half party, half seminar: a regular gathering in a fashionable lady's home where notables would discuss books, music, art, and ideas. Another innovation of the time was the coffee house. Another was the public concert.

Art and Entertainment

Entertainment, for most people, contributes to the good life—though certainly Thomas Jefferson was thinking of more than entertainment when he wrote of "the pursuit of happiness." However, the pursuit of entertainment was not something that the eighteenth century looked down upon at all. The arts were expected to *please* rather than to instruct, impress, or even express, as had been the case in the Baroque era. The result of this attitude is evident in the style of all the arts in the eighteenth century.

For a time at midcentury a light and often frothy style known as *Rococo* was fashionable in painting, decoration, furniture and jewelry design, and so on. Our illustration—a ceramic plaque—catches the spirit of this entertainment art with special charm. Wreathed in leaves that fit in with the border, two well-dressed court gentlemen cavort in an ideal countryside; one plays the flute while the other dances. The subject, the feathery designs on the frame, even the pretty rim itself, are all characteristic of the light art of the Rococo.

Music at midcentury, just before the formation of the Viennese Classical style, was also very light—charming at best, but often frivolous and empty. A genre that was typical of the time was the **divertimento,** a piece designed to divert, amuse, and entertain. Elegant figurines of musicians and ornamented music boxes, playing little tunes, were extremely popular (see page 176).

Thomas Jefferson

The Viennese Classical music of Haydn and Mozart is far from this light style, yet these composers never put pen to paper without every expectation that their audiences were going to be "pleased." Every historical era, of course, has had its entertainment music. But only in the Classical era was great music of the highest quality put forth quite frankly and plainly as entertainment.

Jean-Jacques Rousseau and Opera

Rousseau is remembered today as Europe's first "alienated" intellectual. Whatever his subject, he always came around to blasting the social institutions of his day as stifling to the individual. Passionately devoted to nature and to personal feeling, he disseminated the very influential idea of "natural man," born good but corrupted by civilization. This interest, incidentally, caused Rousseau to think hard and sympathetically about the so-called primitive peoples in the Americas, peoples whom Europeans had colonized and enslaved for over two hundred years.

Jean-Jacques Rousseau

To the great French *Encyclopédie* of 1751–65, which was the bible of Enlightenment thought, Rousseau contributed articles on two subjects: politics and music. For Rousseau was also a self-taught composer, who made his living for years as a professional music copyist.

Both by means of his fiery writings and by actual example, Rousseau launched a devastating attack on the aristocratic opera of the late Baroque era. And to attack opera—the most important, extended, and glamorous musical genre of the time—was to throw Baroque music itself into question. For Rousseau, the complicated plots of Baroque operas were as impossibly artificial as their complicated music. He demanded a kind of opera that would portray real people in actual life—simple people, close to nature, singing "natural" music.

Thus Rousseau acclaimed a famous Italian comic opera of the time that played in Paris, Giovanni Battista Pergolesi's *La serva padrona* ("The Maid as Mistress," 1733). The music is lively and catchy, with no elaborate coloratura singing, rich harmonies, or exaggerated emotional outpourings. And the story could scarcely be more down-to-earth or rudimentary: A servant girl uses a simple ruse to trick a rich old bachelor into marriage.

Thanks to Pergolesi and Rousseau—and to Mozart—comic opera became the most progressive operatic form of the later part of the century. It dealt not with Roman emperors and their idealized noble sentiments, but with contemporary middle- and lower-class figures expressing everyday feelings in a relatively vivid and natural way. *Opera buffa*, as Italian comic opera was called, will be discussed on pages 206 and 207.

The Novel

In its ideals, this new kind of opera was comparable to the most important new literary genre that grew up at the same time. This was the novel, which—together with the symphony—counts as the Enlightenment's greatest artistic legacy to the nineteenth and twentieth centuries.

Precursors of the novel go back to ancient Rome, but the genre did not really capture the European imagination until around 1750. Among the best-known early novels are Henry Fielding's *Tom Jones*, the tale of a rather ordinary young man and his adventures in town and country, and Samuel Richardson's *Pamela*, a domestic drama that manages to be sexually explicit, sentimental, and moralistic all at the same time. Just before the end of the century, Jane Austen began her subtle explorations of the social forces at work on the hearts of her very

Rousseau himself composed a very successful opera of the uncomplicated kind he recommended. Pictured are the shepherdess Colette, with sheep, and her lover Colin from Rousseau's *Le Devin du village (The Village Soothsayer)*, 1752.

A late eighteenth-century court musician surrounded by the tools of his trade. However, he is depicted not in a palace of the era, but in a sober imitation classical temple—amusing testimony to the Neoclassical enthusiasms and aspirations of the time.

sensitive (and sensible) characters in novels such as *Pride and Prejudice*, *Emma*, *Persuasion*, and others. These novels still provide plots for Hollywood films today.

Sharp, realistic observation of contemporary life, and sensitive depiction of feeling—these are the ideals shared by late eighteenth-century opera and the novel. It is no accident that within a few years of their publication, both *Tom Jones* and *Pamela* were turned into major operas, one French, the other Italian.

In Mozart, opera buffa found a master comparable to Jane Austen in the sensitive response to feeling and action. In his opera *Don Giovanni*, for example, the three women romantically involved with the hero—the coquettish country girl, Zerlina, the steely aristocrat, Donna Anna, and the sentimental Donna Elvira—are depicted in music with the greatest human sympathy and psychological acumen. One can come to feel that the same qualities are reflected in Mozart's symphonies and concertos.

Neoclassicism

It is from the standpoint of "the natural," that great rallying cry of the Enlightenment, that we should understand Neoclassicism, an important movement in the visual arts at this time influenced by the Greek and Roman classics. The classics have meant many things to many eras; to the eighteenth century, they meant a return to simple, natural values. They meant a rejection of the complex solemnities of the Baroque on the one hand, and of the pleasant frivolities of the Rococo on the other. Shown throughout this chapter, the portrait busts (modeled on Roman busts) by Jean-Antoine Houdon are prime examples of eighteenth-century Neoclassical art.

Christoph Willibald von Gluck (1714–1787), an important composer active in both Vienna and Paris, used austere classical subjects in a determined effort to "reform" (that is, simplify and ennoble) eighteenth-century opera. His *Orfeo ed Euridice* (1762) is based on the Greek myth of Orpheus, his *Alceste* (1767) on a classical Greek drama. When *Alceste* reached Paris, it was greeted enthusiastically by the aging Rousseau.

Christoph Willibald von Gluck

Apart from the operas of Gluck, however, Neoclassical art has little direct connection with music in what is traditionally called the Classical style. One can perhaps see that a taste inclined toward moderation, simplicity, and balance would also appreciate the order and clarity of late eighteenth-century music, but the traditional label is not a very happy one. "Classicism" was a label coined in the nineteenth century to distinguish the music of Haydn and Mozart from the "Romanticism" that came after it.

2 The Rise of Concerts

A far-reaching development in the sociology and economics of music was the rise of public concerts. Occasional concerts had been put on before, in taverns, private homes, palaces, and theaters, but it was only in the middle of the eighteenth century that they became a significant force in musical life. Concert series, financed by subscription, were put on by the forerunners of today's promoters. Concerts for the benefit of charity were set up on a regular basis as major society events.

In 1748 Europe's first hall designed especially for concerts was built in a college town, Oxford. Still in use, the Holywell Music Room holds about 150 people.

Music of all kinds was presented at these new public concerts; one major series—the Parisian *Concert spirituel,* founded in 1725—originally concentrated on sacred vocal music. But orchestral music was the staple. The importance of concerts lay mainly in the impetus they gave to the composition of orchestral music—symphonies and concertos. For there were, after all, other public forums for church music (churches) and opera (opera houses). Now purely orchestral music, too, moved into the public domain, and its importance and prestige grew rapidly.

However, the livelihood of musicians still depended principally on court patronage, the opera house, and the church (see page 119). Concerts were certainly a factor in the careers of both of the masters of Classical style already mentioned: Haydn wrote his last symphonies, the "London" symphonies, for concerts on two celebrity tours to that city, and Mozart wrote most of his

For the Benefit of Mr. F L A G G.
This Evening,
A public CONCERT of
Vocal and Inftrumental MUSIC,
Will be performed at Concert Hall in Queen-ftreet.
The Vocal part to be performed by Four Voices, and to conclude with the B R I T I S H G R E N A D I E R S.——N. B. *TICKETS* to be had at the Printers, or at the London Book-ftore, at *HALF a DOLLAR* each.—To begin precifely at half after feven.
⁎⁎ The laft Concert this Seafon.

The rise of concerts: With only around 15,000 inhabitants, pre-revolutionary Boston already had a concert hall and a concert promoter (bandmaster Josiah Flagg). This advertisement is from the *Boston Chronicle* of 1769.

piano concertos—among his greatest works—for concerts he himself put on in Vienna. But concerts were a resource that Haydn did not draw upon significantly until the end of his long life, and they were not an adequate resource, alas, to sustain Mozart.

3 Style Features of Classical Music

In discussing the musical style of the late Baroque period, we started with a single guiding concept. There is a thorough, even rigorous quality in the ways early eighteenth-century composers treated almost all aspects of music, and this quality seems to underpin the expressive gestures of grandeur and overstatement that are characteristic of the Baroque.

Classical music cannot be discussed quite as easily as this. We have to keep two concepts in mind for its understanding, concepts that were constantly on the lips of men and women of the time. One was "natural," and the other was "pleasing variety." In the late eighteenth century, it was taken for granted that these two artistic ideals went hand in hand and provided mutual support.

Today we can see that sometimes they pulled in opposite directions. For although "variety" was invoked as a guard against boredom, it was also an invitation to complexity, and complexity would seem to run counter to "natural" simplicity and clarity. In any case, in Classical music one or the other—and sometimes both—of these qualities can be traced in all the elements of musical technique: in rhythm, dynamics, tone color, melody, texture, and form. A new expressive quality developed in this music as a result of its new technique.

Rhythm

Perhaps the most striking change in music between the Baroque and the Classical periods came in rhythm. In this area the artistic ideal of "pleasing variety" reigned supreme. The unvarying rhythms of Baroque music came to be regarded as dreary, obvious, and boring.

Classical music is highly flexible in rhythm. Throughout a single movement, the tempo and meter remain constant, but the rhythms of the various themes tend to differ in both obvious and subtle ways. In the first movement of Mozart's Symphony in G Minor, for example, the first theme moves almost entirely in eighth notes and quarters, whereas the second theme is marked by longer notes and shorter ones—dotted half notes and sixteenths.

Audiences wanted variety in music; composers responded by refining the rhythmic differences between themes and other musical sections, so that the differences sound like more than differences—they sound like real contrasts. The music may gradually increase or decrease its rhythmic energy, stop suddenly, press forward by fits and starts, or glide by smoothly. All this gives the sense that Classical music is moving in a less predictable, more interesting, and often more exciting way than Baroque music does.

Dynamics

Variety and flexibility were also introduced into dynamics. Passages were now conceived more specifically than before as loud, soft, very loud, and so on, and marked *f, p, ff, mf* by composers accordingly. Again, concern for variety went along with a new sensitivity to contrast. By insisting on the contrast between

Domestic music making in the eighteenth century: a group portrait by Johann Zoffany (1733–1810), one of many fashionable painters in Britain (and British India). It was not uncommon for members of the gentry—including, here, an earl—to order pictures showing off their musical accomplishments.

loud and soft, soft and very soft, composers made variety in dynamics clearly perceptible and, we must suppose, "pleasing."

Furthermore, instead of using the steady dynamics of the previous period, composers now worked extensively with gradations of volume. The words for growing louder (*crescendo*) and growing softer (*diminuendo*) first came into general use in the Classical period. Orchestras of the mid-eighteenth century were the first to practice long crescendos, which, we are told, caused audiences to rise up from their seats in excitement.

The clearest sign of the new flexibility in dynamics was the rise in popularity of the piano, at the expense of the ever-present harpsichord of the Baroque era. The older instrument could manage only one sound level, or at best a few sound levels, thanks to its two or three separate sets of strings. The new pianoforte could produce a continuous range of dynamics from soft to loud (the name, in fact, means "soft-loud" in Italian). It attracted composers because they wished their keyboard instruments to have the same flexibility in dynamics that they were teaching to their orchestras.

Tone Color: The Orchestra

Classical composers also devoted increasing attention to tone color. The clearest sign of this was the emergence of the Classical orchestra. The orchestra standardized in this period formed the basis of the symphony orchestra of later times.

The heart of the Classical orchestra was still (as in the Baroque orchestra) a group of stringed instruments: violins, divided into two groups, first violins and second violins; violas; and cellos, with a few basses playing the same music as the cellos an octave lower. As we saw on page 123, there was a "basic" Baroque orchestra consisting of just these instruments, plus the continuo, and various other possibilities, including the "festive" Baroque orchestra:

THE BASIC BAROQUE ORCHESTRA

STRINGS	KEYBOARD
Violins (divided into two groups, called violins 1 and violins 2) Violas Cellos Bass viol (playing the same music as the cellos, an octave lower)	Harpsichord or organ

THE FESTIVE BAROQUE ORCHESTRA

STRINGS	WOODWINDS	BRASS	PERCUSSION	KEYBOARD
Violins 1 Violins 2 Violas Cellos Bass viol	2 Oboes 1 Bassoon	3 Trumpets	2 Timpani (kettledrums)	Harpsichord or organ

In the Classical orchestra, however, the woodwind and brass instruments were given clearly defined, regular roles. With the strings as a framework, woodwind instruments were added: in the high range, pairs of flutes, oboes, and (a bit later) clarinets; in the low, bassoons. These instruments provided "pleasing variety" by playing certain melodies and other passages; each of the woodwinds contributed its own characteristic tone color or timbre. They also strengthened the strings in loud sections.

THE CLASSICAL ORCHESTRA

STRINGS	WOODWINDS	BRASS	PERCUSSION
Violins 1	2 Flutes	2 French horns	2 Timpani
Violins 2	2 Oboes	2 Trumpets*	
Violas	2 Clarinets*		
Cellos	2 Bassoons		
Bass viols		*Optional	

Brass instruments were added in the middle range. The function of French horns and trumpets was mainly to provide solid support for the main harmonies, especially at points such as cadences when the harmonies needed to be made particularly clear. The only regular percussion instruments used were two timpani, which generally played along with the brass.

The great advance in the orchestra from the Baroque to the Classical era was in flexibility—flexibility in tone color and also in rhythm and dynamics. The orchestra now became the most subtle and versatile musical resource that composers could employ, as well as the grandest.

Melody: Tunes

The Enlightenment ideal of "pleasing variety" was a secondary issue with Classical melody. Rather the demand was for simplicity and clarity, for relief from the complex, richly ornamented lines of the Baroque period. When people at the time demanded "natural" melodies, what they meant were tunes: uncomplicated, singable melodies with clear phrases (and not too many of them), melodies with easily grasped parallelisms and balances.

Confronted with a Baroque work such as Bach's Suite No. 3 in D (see page 145), a late eighteenth-century audience might have tolerated the fairly straightforward Gavotte, but would have been unmoved by the beautiful Air.

Its elegant winding lines and the mere fact of its great length would have struck them as completely "unnatural":

In their move toward melodic simplicity, composers of the Classical period moved much closer to popular music, and some varieties of folk music, than their Baroque predecessors had. There is an unmistakable popular lilt in Haydn's music that people have traced to the Croatian folk melodies he heard in childhood. Short tunes—or, more often, attractive little phrases that sound as though they might easily grow into tunes—are heard again and again in Classical symphonies, quartets, and other pieces. Tunes are not the only melodic material to be heard in these works, as we shall see in a moment. Nonetheless, by comparison with a Baroque concerto, a Classical symphony leaves listeners with a good deal more to hum or whistle as they leave the concert.

Often entire tunes were worked into larger compositions. For example, variation form (theme and variations) grew popular both for separate pieces improvised by virtuosos and for movements in multimovement genres. Haydn wrote variations on the Austrian national anthem (he also wrote the tune), and Mozart wrote variations on "Twinkle, Twinkle, Little Star," in its original French version, "Ah vous dirai-je, maman" ("Oh mama, I must tell you"). Occasionally, popular songs were even introduced into symphonies. There is a contemporary opera tune in Mozart's *Jupiter* Symphony, the last he composed.

Texture: Homophony

The predominant texture of Classical music is homophonic. In Classical compositions, melodies are regularly heard with a straightforward harmonic accompaniment in chords, without counterpoint and without even a melodic-sounding bass line. Again, this was thought (not unreasonably) to be a more "natural," clearer way of presenting a melody than polyphony.

All this made, and still makes, for easy listening. The opening of Mozart's famous Symphony No. 40 in G Minor proclaims the new sonorous world of the late eighteenth century:

A single quiet chord regrouped and repeated by the violas, the plainest sort of bass support below, and above them all a plaintive melody in the violins—this simple, sharply polarized texture becomes typical of the new style.

Homophony or melody with harmony was not, however, merely a negative reaction to what people of the time saw as the heavy, pedantic complexities of Baroque counterpoint. It was also a positive move in the direction of sensitivity. When composers found that they were not always occupied in fitting contrapuntal parts to their melodies, they also discovered that they could handle other elements of music with more "pleasing variety." In particular, a new sensitivity developed to harmony for its own sake.

One aspect of this development was a desire to specify harmonies more precisely than in the Baroque era. The first thing to go was the continuo, which had spread its unrelenting and unspecified (because improvised) chord patterns over nearly all Baroque music. Classical composers, newly alert to the sonorous quality of a particular chord, wanted it "spaced" and distributed among various instruments in just one way. They refused to allow a continuo player to obscure the chord with unpredictable extra notes and rhythms.

It may seem paradoxical, then, but the thrust toward simplicity in texture and melody led through the back door to increased subtlety in other areas, notably in rhythm and in harmony.

Classical Counterpoint

The rise of homophony in the Classical period represents a major turnaround in musical technique. For although Baroque composers did write some homophonic pieces, as we have seen, the predominant texture of music at that time was polyphonic. This turning point was, in fact, one of the most decisive in all of musical history, for polyphony had monopolized music since the Middle Ages.

Yet it is not the way of history to abandon important resources of the past completely, even when the past is discredited. Classical composers rejected Baroque music, but they cautiously retained the basic principle of counterpoint. They were able to do this by refining it into a more delicate, unobtrusive kind of counterpoint than that of the Baroque era. And there was a sharper awareness now of counterpoint's expressive possibilities. In a texture that was mostly "natural" and homophonic, counterpoint attracted special attention; this texture could be used to create the impression of tension, of one line rubbing against another. The more intense, "artificial" texture of polyphony stood out against "natural" homophonic texture.

Hence, as we shall see in the next chapter, the section in Classical sonata form called the development section, whose basic function is to build up tension, typically involves contrapuntal textures. Sonata form was the most important musical form of the time, and so counterpoint was often heard.

4 Form in Classical Music

How can a piece of music be extended through a considerable span of time when listeners expect everything to be "natural," simple, and easily understood? This was the problem of musical form that faced composers of the Viennese Classical era. They arrived at a solution of considerable elegance and power, involving several elements.

Repetitions and Cadences

First, themes in Classical music tend to be *repeated* immediately after their first appearance, so that listeners can easily get to know them. (In earlier music, this happened only in dance music, as a general rule.) Later in the piece, those same themes will be repeated again.

Porcelain musicians, c. 1770

Second, themes are *led into* in a very distinctive manner. The music features prominent transitional passages that do not have much melodic profile, only a sense of urgency about arriving someplace—the place where the real theme will be presented (and probably presented twice).

Third, after themes have been played, they are typically *closed off* just as distinctively. Often there are quite long passages consisting of cadences repeated two, three, or more times, as though to make it clear that one musical idea is over and another, presumably, is coming up. Composers would devise little cadential phrases, often with minimal melodic interest, that could be repeated and thus allow for such multiple cadences.

Multiple cadences are a characteristic and easily recognizable feature of Classical music, particularly, of course, at the very ends of movements. Two clear examples come from our CD set.

28   26

ℸ   *Haydn, Symphony No. 95 in C Minor, second movement:* This is rather formal-sounding, deliberate music, so repeated cadences at the end sound even a little pompous. It is as though each of the instruments of the Classical orchestra wants to make sure the movement ends properly: first the violins, playing ornamented cadences (thirty-second notes) with bassoons in the background; then the French horns alone; then the rest of the orchestra. For the dynamics at the very end (*pp* and *ff*), see page 189.

♪ *Aria "Ho capito" from* Don Giovanni: Near the end of this aria (1:11), the singer sings much the same cadence over and over again. (A few seconds later, the orchestra has its cadence, and the whole piece is over.) The situation is explained on page 209: Sputtering with rage at Zerlina, Masetto keeps reiterating his sarcastic taunts until he is finally chased away. This cadence, then, is even more solid than it needed to be—for Mozart, a comical effect:

fac-ciail no-stro ca - va - lie - re ca - va - lie-ra an-co - ra te,   ca - va - lie-ra an-co - ra te,   ca - va - lie-ra an-co - ra te.

Cadences 1 and 2   Cadence 3   Cadence 4

Classical Forms

A third feature designed to cope with the problem of musical form in Classical music is perhaps the most far-reaching. Composers and their audiences came to rely on a limited number of "forms," or standard formal patterns, the most important of which are *sonata form, minuet form, rondo,* and *theme and variations form.*

These provided a commonly understood frame of reference for composing music and appreciating it. Broadly speaking, after listening for just a short time to some new piece, an eighteenth-century music lover could always tell what sort of themes and keys it would include, when they would return, and about how long the piece would last. This frame of reference is not so obvious today, so the four Classical forms just mentioned will be taken up in some detail in Chapter 12.

The repetitions, self-conscious transitions, and emphatic cadences that are so characteristic of the Classical style all help clarify the forms. And the forms themselves were a special necessity at a time when composers were filling their compositions with contrasts of all kinds. It is a mark of the aesthetic success of Classical music that the contrasts don't sound too drastic, because the forms control and, in effect, tame them. The seemingly inexhaustible emotional range of Classical music is directly proportional to the extent of those contrasts, on the one hand, and, on the other, to the elegance of their control by musical form.

Web: *Research and test your understanding of music during the Enlightenment at* <bedfordstmartins.com/listen>.

Houdon's most unclassical portrait bust—of his wife

The Symphony

T he genres of music that arose in the Classical period, replacing those of the Baroque era, continued to hold their own in the nineteenth century. Indeed, they are still in use today, at least in the sense that their names are still encountered. Not surprisingly, the style, the number of movements, and the forms employed today will bear little relation to norms from two hundred and more years ago. But it is still true that if you compose a large, impressive concert piece for orchestra, the best way to convey that fact to conductors, musicians, and audiences is to name it a **symphony**.

One reason for the prominence of the symphony in the Classical era is its close association with a crucial development in the sociology of music, discussed in Chapter 11: the growth of public concerts. As concerts became more and more frequent, people felt a need for some genre that would make an effective, substantial focus for these occasions. Symphonies filled the bill—and in turn, required more variety and flexibility of sound than anything orchestras of the early eighteenth century could provide. The symphony spurred a major technical development within music, the evolution of the Classical orchestra (see page 173).

The symphony, then, is rightly viewed as the crowning achievement of Viennese Classical music—but when any musician acknowledges this, he or she wants to add a plea in the same breath: Please don't forget the other genres that grew up alongside the symphony, for these genres accommodate music that you will find just as beautiful, and that has become for us, sometimes, just as precious. In Chapter 13 we shall study the sonata, the Classical concerto, the string quartet, and—in the field of opera—Italian *opera buffa*.

Movements of the Symphony

Opening Movement
> tempo: fast/moderate
> form: sonata form (sometimes preceded by a slow **Introduction**)

Slow Movement
> tempo: slow/very slow
> form: sonata form, variations, rondo, other

Minuet (with Trio)
> tempo: moderate
> form: minuet form

Closing Movement
> tempo: fast/very fast
> form: sonata form or rondo form

1 The Movements of the Symphony

As with Baroque genres, works in the Classical period consist of several movements, which contrast in tempo and are composed in different musical forms. The outline in the margin of this page gives the particulars for the four movements of a typical symphony. Compare the following brief description with the description given on page 129 for the Baroque concerto:

❧ The *first* opening movement of a symphony is a substantial piece in fast or moderate tempo, written in the most important new form of the time: sonata form (which we will study in the next section). Sometimes this fast music is preceded by a short but solemn *introduction* in a slower tempo.

¶   The *second* movement strikes an obvious contrast with the first by its slow tempo and its quiet mood.

¶   The *third* movement contrasts in another way, by its persistent dance rhythms: It is always a minuet and trio. A minuet is a moderately paced dance in triple meter: See page 143.

¶   The *fourth,* closing movement is fast again—if anything, faster than the first. It may also be in sonata form, like the first movement.

If we compare the symphony table shown on the previous page with a parallel table for the Baroque concerto, on the right, we see many differences, but also certain similarities. The forms used for the movements are entirely different, and there is the extra minuet. However, in the broadest terms, the sequence from *fast/complex* to *slow/quiet* to *fast/brilliant* is the same.

A word of caution: The symphony table on page 178 represents the norm, but there are always exceptions. Some famous ones are Mozart's *Prague* Symphony, lacking a minuet, and Haydn's *Farewell* Symphony with an extra slow movement—five movements in all. (Likewise, Bach's First *Brandenburg* Concerto has two dance movements added to the "normal" three for the concerto.)

Movements of
the Baroque Concerto

Opening Movement
  tempo: fast/moderate
  form: ritornello form

Slow Movement
  tempo: slow/very slow
  form: no standard form

Closing Movement
  tempo: fast/very fast
  form: ritornello form

2   Sonata Form

A new form developed at this time, called **sonata form,** is closely associated with the symphony—even though it turns up in much other music of the time. The opening movement of every symphony is in sonata form, and this movement counts as the intellectual and emotional core of the whole work. Many Classical works have two or even three movements in this same form.

The reason for this wide use, perhaps, was that more than any other form, sonata form exploited what was the overriding interest of Classical composers. This was an interest in contrasts of every kind—especially contrast of thematic material and contrast of key, or tonality. In any case, whatever the reason, composers found sonata form particularly rich and flexible in its expressive application. It was something they could use for forceful, brilliant, pathetic, even tragic opening movements, gentle or dreamy slow movements, and lively, often humorous closing movements.

Viewed on the highest level, sonata form is simple enough—a very large-scale example of **A B A′** form, usually with repetitions: |: **A** :||: **B A′** :| or |: **A** :|| **B A′**. What is less simple, and what makes sonata form different from other **A B A** forms, is the nature and the function of the musical material in each letter-section. This is implied by the special terms that are used for them: **A** is called the *exposition,* **B** the *development,* and **A′** the *recapitulation.* We need to look more closely at what each of these terms entails.

Exposition (A)

The **exposition** of a sonata-form movement is a large, diverse section of music in which the basic material of the movement is presented (or "exposed"). The material always consists of the following elements:

¶ To begin, a main theme is presented in the first key, the tonic key (see page 31; this key is the key of the piece as a whole—in Mozart's Symphony in G Minor, the tonic is G minor). This **first theme** may be a tune, a group of small phrases that sound as though they are about to grow into a tune, or just a motive or two (see page 26) with a memorable rhythmic character.

¶ After the first theme is firmly established, often with the help of a repetition, there is a change in key, or *modulation*. The subsection of the exposition that accomplishes the change is called the **bridge,** or the *transition*.

¶ The modulation in the bridge is an essential feature (even *the* essential feature) that gives sonata form its sense of dynamic forward movement. With a little experience, it is not hard to hear the contrast of key and sense the dynamism, for the idea is not to make the crucial modulation sound too smooth. There has to be a sense of tension in the way the new themes, now to be introduced, "set" in the new key.

¶ Next comes a group of themes or other musical ideas in the new key, called the **second group.** At least some of these new themes contrast with the first theme in melody, rhythm, dynamics, and so on, as well as in key. Usually one new theme stands out by its melodious quality; this is called the **second theme.**

¶ The last theme in the second group, the **cadence theme,** or *closing theme*, is constructed so as to make a solid ending prior to a full stop and the big repeat. The very end of the exposition is marked by a loud series of repeated cadences, as though the composer wanted listeners to know exactly where they are in the form. This **A** (exposition) section is almost always repeated.

Development (B)

The following section, the **development,** heightens the tonal-thematic tension set up by the contrasting themes and keys of the exposition. The themes are "developed" by being broken up, recombined, reorchestrated, extended, and in general shown in unexpected and often exciting new contexts.

Eighteenth-century English spinet, a type of small harpsichord. Especially away from the main musical centers, the harpsichord continued in use along with the piano.

Most development sections use counterpoint to create a sense of breakup and turmoil. This section moves around restlessly from key to key; there are frequent modulations that can easily be heard. The music sounds unstable.

After considerable tension has been built up in this way, the last modulation of the development section returns to the first key. The passage that accomplishes this, called the **retransition,** has the function of discharging the tension and preparing for the recapitulation to come. Classical composers were amazingly inventive in devising ways to make this crucial juncture of the form seem both fresh and inevitable.

Recapitulation (A′)

With a real sense of relief or resolution, we now hear the first theme again, followed by all the other themes and other elements of the exposition. There may be minor changes, but in principle everything comes back in its original order. Hence the name for this section—the **recapitulation** (meaning a step-by-step review).

But there is an important difference: The music now remains in the same key, the tonic key. (In practical terms, this means that the whole second group is relocated in the tonic. To allow for this, the bridge has to be rewritten—often in a very interesting way.) Stability of key in the recapitulation is especially welcome after the instability of the development section. Basically, as we have said, sonata form depends on a strong feeling of balance between exposition and recapitulation (**A B A′**). But it is a weighted balance, because **A′** has achieved a new solidity.

The entire **B A′** sequence may be repeated. Whether this happens or not, another section in the tonic is often added at the end, a post mortem or wrap-up for the main action. This optional section is called the **coda** (coda is a general term for a concluding section in any musical form).

In the following schematic diagram for sonata form, changes of key (tonality) are shown on a continuous band. Notice the tonal stability of the recapitulation, where the steady horizontal band contrasts dramatically with the fluctuations of the exposition and development sections.

I compare a symphony with a novel in which the themes are the characters. We follow their evolution, the unfolding of their psychology. . . . Some of these characters arouse feelings of sympathy, others repel us. They are set off against one another or they join hands; they make love; they marry or they fight.

Swiss composer Arthur Honegger, 1951

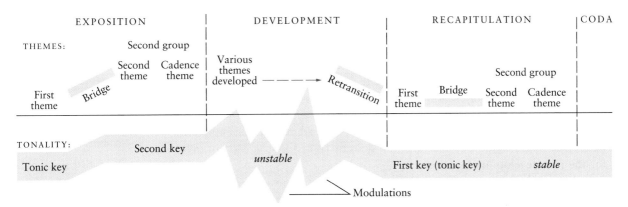

It may not be accidental that the terms used in discussing sonata form resemble those used in discussions of drama. We speak of the "exposition" of a play, where the initial situation is set forth, and of the "development" of the plot. Indeed, sonata form has a "dramatic" quality compared with the more "architectural" quality of Baroque music such as a fugue. In a Classical symphony, the themes seem almost like characters in a play or a novel to whom things are happening. They seem to change, take part in various actions, and react to other themes and musical processes.

WOLFGANG AMADEUS MOZART (1756–1791)
Symphony No. 40 in G Minor, K. 550* (1788)

Mozart's Symphony in G Minor is one of the most famous and admired of all his works. The opening movement, with its sharp contrasts and clear demarcations, makes an arresting introduction to sonata form.

Not many Classical compositions convey as dark and uneasy a mood as does this symphony. (Not many Classical symphonies are in the minor mode.) It suggests some kind of muted struggle against inescapable restraints. Mozart's themes alone would not have created this effect; expressive as they are in themselves, they only attain their full effect in their setting. Mozart needed sonata form to manage these expressive themes—in a sense, to give them something to struggle against.

First movement (Molto allegro)   We have already cited this movement's opening texture—melody with a strictly homophonic accompaniment—as characteristic of the Viennese Classical style (see page 174). So also are the delicate dynamic changes toward the end of the theme and the loud repeated cadences that terminate it. The unique nervous energy of this theme, a blend of refinement and subdued agitation, stamps the first movement unforgettably.

Exposition   The first theme is played twice. The second playing already begins the modulation to the exposition's second key, and a forceful bridge passage completes this process, after which the music comes to an abrupt stop. Such stops will come again and again in this movement.

The second theme, in the major mode, is divided up, measure by measure or phrase by phrase, between the strings and the woodwinds:

Then it is repeated with the role of the instruments reversed, the strings taking the notes originally played by the winds, and vice versa. These instrumental alterations contribute something absolutely essential to the character of the theme, and show Mozart's fine ear for tone color.

The second appearance of the second theme does not come to a cadence, but runs into a series of new ideas which make up the rest of the second group. Since all of them are so brief, and leave so little impression on the rest of the movement, it is best not to consider them actual "themes." One of these ideas begins to develop the motive of the first theme—a premature development process, one might think; but once again, it goes by so fast that we do not take it for the real development section.

A short cadence theme, *forte,* and a very insistent series of repeated cadences bring the exposition to a complete stop. (We still hear the rhythm of theme 1.) After one dramatic chord, wrenching us back from major to the original minor key, the whole exposition is repeated.

Original

Fragmented

Development   Two more dramatic chords—and then the development section starts quietly. The first theme is accompanied as before. It modulates at

*Mozart's works are identified by K numbers, after the chronological catalog of his works compiled by Ludwig von Köchel. The first edition (1862) listed 626 works composed by Mozart in his short lifetime; later editions add many more that may have come to light since then.

Freemasonry in the eighteenth century was a high-minded society of intellectuals and aristocrats, promulgating ideas that were often radical. "Enlightened" Emperor Joseph II tolerated them, barely. Mozart joined the group and wrote a good deal of music for their secret meetings; this extraordinary painting shows him at the far right.

once, and seems to be losing itself in grief, until the rest of the orchestra bursts in with a furious contrapuntal treatment of that tender, nervous melody.

The music seems to exhaust itself, and comes to another stop. But in the following *piano* passage, the modulations continue, with orchestral echoes based on smaller and smaller portions of the melody, as shown at the bottom of page 182. Breaking up a theme in this way is called *fragmentation*.

Passion breaks out anew in another *forte* passage; but the modulations, we notice, have finally ceased. The fragmentation reaches its final stage, as shown. At last the harmony seems to be waiting or preparing for something, rather than shifting all the time. This passage is the *retransition*.

Recapitulation   After its fragmentation in the development section, the first theme somehow conveys new pathos when it returns in its original form, and in the original tonic key. The bassoon has a beautiful new descending line.

And pathos deepens when the second theme and all the other ideas in the second group—originally heard in a major-mode key—are now recapitulated in the tonic key, which is minor. The result is a great many small alterations of the exposition material—small, but they change the mood decisively. There should be no problem hearing that the recapitulation is more stable than the exposition, because both the first and second groups are now in the same mode (minor), as well as in the same key. The bridge theme, much expanded, also hammers away at the minor mode, recalling the contrapuntal outburst of the development section. It is a passage of great power.

Coda   In a very short coda, Mozart refers one last time to the first theme. It sounds utterly disheartened, and then battered by the usual repeated cadences.

The Mozart children as prodigies. Both seem to have been great talents, but—inevitably for that time—it was the boy who went ahead. Nannerl grew up to be a rather straitlaced woman, married, and took care of her father in his old age.

Wolfgang Amadeus Mozart (1756–1791)

Mozart was born in Salzburg, a charming town in central Austria, which today is famous for its music festivals. His father, Leopold, was a court musician and composer who also wrote an important book on violin playing. Mozart showed extraordinary talent at a very early age. He and his older sister, Nannerl, were trotted all over Europe as infant prodigies; between the ages of six and seventeen, Wolfgang never spent more than ten successive months at home. His first symphony was played (at a London concert) when he was only eight years old.

But mostly Wolfgang was displayed at courts and salons, and in a somewhat depressing way, this whole period of his career symbolizes the frivolous love of entertainment that reigned at midcentury. The future Queen Marie Antoinette of France was one of those for whose amusement the six-year-old prodigy would name the keys of compositions played to him, and sight-read music at the piano with a cloth over his hands.

It was much harder for Mozart to make his way as a young adult musician. As usual in those days, he followed in his father's footsteps as a musician at the court of Salzburg, which was ruled by an archbishop. (Incidentally, one of their colleagues was Joseph Haydn's brother Michael.) But the archbishop was a disagreeable autocrat with no patience for independent-minded underlings. Mozart hated working for him. In 1781, he extricated himself from his court position, not without a humiliating scene, and set himself up as a freelance musician in Vienna.

It seems clear that another reason for Mozart's move was to get away from his father, who had masterminded the boy's career and now seemed to grow more and more possessive as the young man sought his independence. Leopold disapproved of Wolfgang's marriage around this time to Constanze Weber, a singer. (Mozart had been in love with her older sister, Aloysia—a more famous singer— but she rejected him.)

Mozart wrote his greatest operas in Vienna, but only the last of them, *The Magic Flute*, had the success it deserved. Everyone sensed that he was a genius, but his music seemed too difficult—and he was a somewhat "difficult" personality, too. He relied for his living on teaching and on the relatively new institution of concerts. Every year he set up a concert at which he introduced one of his piano concertos. In addition, the program might contain arias, a solo improvisation, and an overture by somebody else.

But as happens with popular musicians today, Mozart seems (for some unknown reason) to have suddenly dropped out of fashion. After 1787, his life was a struggle, though he did receive a minor court appointment and the promise of a church position, and finally scored a really solid hit with *The Magic Flute*. When it seemed that financially he was finally getting out of the woods, he died suddenly at the age of thirty-five.

He died under somewhat macabre circumstances. He was composing a Requiem Mass, that is, a Mass for the dead, commissioned by a patron who insisted on remaining anonymous. Mozart became ill and began to think he was writing for his own demise. When he died, the Requiem still unfinished, a rumor started that he had been poisoned by the composer Antonio Salieri.

Unlike Haydn, the other great master of the Viennese Classical style, Mozart allowed a note of disquiet, even passion, to emerge in some of his compositions (such as the Symphony in G Minor). The Romantics correctly perceived this as a forecast of their own work. Once we recognize this, it is hard not to sense something enigmatic beneath the intelligence, wit, and sheer beauty of all Mozart's music.

Chief Works: The comic operas *The Marriage of Figaro, Don Giovanni, Così fan tutte* (That's What They All Do), and *The Magic Flute* ▪ *Idomeneo,* an *opera seria* ▪ Church music: many Masses, and a Requiem (Mass for the Dead) left unfinished at his death ▪ Symphonies, including the *Prague,* the G minor, and the *Jupiter* ▪ String quartets and four superb string quintets; a quintet for clarinet and strings; a quartet for oboe and strings ▪ Concertos: nearly twenty much-loved concertos for piano; also ones for French horn, violin, and clarinet ▪ Piano sonatas; violin sonatas ▪ Lighter pieces (such as divertimentos, etc.), including the famous *Eine kleine Nachtmusik*

Encore: After Symphony No. 40, listen to the Clarinet Quintet and *The Marriage of Figaro* (Act I).

Mozart's musical handwriting

LISTENING CHART 7

Mozart, Symphony No. 40 in G Minor, first movement

Sonata form. 8 min., 16 sec.

15 **13**	**EXPOSITION**	
	0:01 **Theme 1** **(main theme)**	Theme 1, *p*, minor key (G minor); repeated cadences *f*
	0:25	Theme 1 repeats and begins the modulation to a new key.
	0:34 **Bridge**	Bridge theme, *f*, confirms the modulation.
		CADENCE Abrupt stop
	Second Group	
16 **14**	0:53 **Theme 2**	Theme 2, *p*, in major key; phrases divided between wood-winds and strings
0:11	1:04	Theme 2 again, division of phrases is reversed
0:29	1:22	Other shorter ideas, *f*, and *p*: echoes of theme 1 motive
0:55	1:48 **Cadence theme**	Cadence theme, *f*, downward scales followed by repeated cadences
		CADENCE Abrupt stop
1:11	2:03 *Exposition repeated*	
	DEVELOPMENT	
17 **15**	4:10 **Theme 1** **developed**	Theme 1, *p*, modulating
0:16	4:26 **Contrapuntal** **passage**	Sudden *f*: contrapuntal treatment by the full orchestra of theme 1
0:44	4:54 **Fragmentation**	Sudden *p*: beginning of theme 1 echoes between strings and woodwinds; theme fragmented from ♩♩ | ♩ ♩♩ | ♩ ♩ to ♩♩ ♩ | ♩♩ | ♩ ♩ and finally to ♩♩ | ♩
1:01	5:11	Retransition *f* (full orchestra), *p* (woodwinds), which leads into the recapitulation
18 **16**	**RECAPITULATION**	
	5:26 **Theme 1**	Theme 1, *p*, G minor, as before
0:24	5:50	Theme 1, modulating differently than before
0:33	5:59 **Bridge**	Bridge, *f*, longer than before
		CADENCE Abrupt stop
	Second Group	
19 **17**	6:41 **Theme 2**	Theme 2, *p*, this time in the minor mode (G minor)
		All the other second-group themes are in the tonic key (minor mode); otherwise much the same as before
1:00	7:41 **Cadence theme**	Scale part of the cadence theme, *f*
20 **18**	**CODA**	
	7:54	New imitative passage, *p*, strings; based on theme 1 motive
0:10	8:03	Repeated cadences, *f*
		Stop, this time "confirmed" by three solid chords

3 Classical Variation Form

Variation form, as we saw on page 132, entails the successive, uninterrupted repetition of a clearly defined melodic unit, the *theme*, with various changes at each repetition. In the Baroque era, the theme was usually a bass pattern (sometimes called a ground bass). The same basic principle is at work in Classical variation form, but now the theme is a tune in the upper register.

We can understand why the Baroque era, which developed the idea of the basso continuo supporting harmonies from below, would have cultivated variations on a bass pattern, whereas the Classical era, with its emphasis on simple melody, preferred variations on short tunes in the upper register.

The point of variations is to create many contrasting moods with the same theme, which is transformed but always somehow discernible under the transformations. Nothing distracts from this process, at least until the end, where composers usually add a coda. There are no contrasting themes, modulations, transitions, cadence sections, or development sections, as there are in sonata form movements (and in many rondos).

© Jasper Johns/VAGA, NY, NY.

Variations in the visual arts: three monotypes (from a total of seventeen) by the contemporary American artist Jasper Johns. While the variations all differ from the "theme"—an actual coffee can with paint brushes, all bronzed—they never lose it entirely.

A Classical **theme and variations** movement begins with a theme that is typically in |: **a** :||: **b** :| or |: **a** :||: **ba** :| or |: **a** :||: **b′** :| form. This miniform "nests" within the larger variation form:

Theme	Variation 1	Variation 2 . . .	Coda
|: **a** :||: **b** :|	|: **a¹** :||: **b¹** :|	|: **a²** :||: **b²** :|	(free)

Variations were part of the stock-in-trade of virtuosos of the Classical era. At a musical soirée, someone might suggest a popular opera tune, and the pianist would improvise variations on the spot, for as long as his or her imagination held out. Twelve was a common number for these variations when they were published; virtuosos piled them up for maximum effect.

In symphonies and concertos, theme and variations movements are less extended, since they have to fit into a time scale with all the other movements. For our example we turn to Joseph Haydn, since tuneful, witty variations movements in symphonies were a specialty of his.

FRANZ JOSEPH HAYDN (1732–1809)
Symphony No. 95 in C Minor (1791)

During the last twenty years of his active career, from around 1780 to 1800, Joseph Haydn averaged better than one symphony a year, nearly all of them masterpieces.

The most famous of them are the last twelve, written for concerts in London, where Haydn enjoyed enormous success on two tours after his retirement from the court of the Esterházy princes. Symphony No. 95 is one of these "London" symphonies, composed on the first tour in 1791.

First movement (Allegro moderato) Symphonies always begin with movements in sonata form, and since we have already worked on this form with Mozart's Symphony in G Minor, we will not go through Haydn's movement in the same detail. (Follow the mini–Listening Chart at the right.) The music starts in the minor mode, in a rather somber mood, but this all clears up when it turns cheerfully to the major, for good, in the recapitulation. Compare Mozart's first movement, which ends in the minor. In lighter moods, Haydn is every bit the equal of Mozart, but in his late years, at least, he avoids the beautiful shadows that occasionally—and unforgettably—darken Mozart's music, as in the G-minor Symphony.

Coming out of a long, eventful development section, Haydn slips into the expanded recapitulation before we even notice. Where Mozart's recapitulation mostly mirrors the exposition, Haydn's is more like an imaginative rewrite, treating the exposition material quite freely.

Second movement (Andante) The second movement of a symphony is the slow movement—a restful episode to contrast with the vigorous first movement. There is no standardized form for slow movements (in symphonies or in other genres, such as sonatas or concertos). Mozart, in his late symphonies, preferred sonata form or some derivative of sonata form. Haydn favored his own version of variation form.

In Symphony No. 95 the variation theme is a graceful tune in |: **a** :||: **b** :| form. Whereas **a** is rather simple, the melody of **b** melts into counterpoint for a time, before ending peacefully in the low register.

Haydn, Movements of Symphony No. 95

Opening Movement
tempo:　fast
form:　sonata form

Slow Movement
tempo:　slow
form:　variations

Minuet (with Trio)
tempo:　moderate
form:　minuet form

Closing Movement
tempo:　fast
form:　rondo

LISTEN

Haydn,　21-23　19-21
Symphony No. 95,
first movement

EXPOSITION
0:00 Theme 1: minor
0:49 Theme 2, etc.: major
1:44 *Repeated*

DEVELOPMENT
0:00 Uses theme 1
0:42 Uses theme 2
0:59 Back to theme 1

RECAPITULATION
0:00 Theme 1: minor
0:42 Theme 2, etc. major
End expanded: major

Now the variations start; the music example on page 189 shows the key melody notes that each of them preserves, while much else is varied. The normal expectation would be the scheme shown in the margin, as discussed on page 187. Haydn wrote dozens of variation movements like this—though not, interestingly, in symphonies. He seems to have felt it would be boring for a concert audience, and he needed to do something freer and more interesting. For example, instead of repeating the **a** and **b** phrases in the variations exactly, he sometimes writes "variations within variations," as indicated by prime marks on the chart below:

THEME	|: a :||: b :|
Variation 1	|: a_1 :||: b_1 :|
Variation 2	|: a_2 :||: b_2 :|
Variation 3	|: a_3 :||: b_3 :|

	"NORMAL" VARIATIONS	HAYDN, SYMPHONY NO. 95
THEME	a a b b	a a b b
Variation 1	a_1 a_1 b_1 b_1	a_1 a_1' b_1 b_1
Variation 2	a_2 a_2 b_2 b_2	a_2 b_2 b_2' —— transition ——→
Variation 3	a_3 a_3 b_3 b_3	a_3 a_3' b_3

Variation 1 starts with a cello solo that stays very close to the theme itself, with new material in the other strings above. It is as though the composer wants to remind us of the original **a,** one more time, before varying it in a_1'.

Esterháza, where Haydn spent most of his life—a huge palace built by Esterházy princes in imitation of Versailles. It cannot compare with the real item, however: See page 113.

LISTENING CHART 8

Haydn, Symphony No. 95, second movement (Andante cantabile)

Variation form. 4 min., 17 sec.

24 22	**THEME**		Strings only
	0:00 **a**		
	0:13 **a**		
	0:26 **b**		
	0:46 **b**		
25 23	**VARIATION 1**		
	1:06 **a**	Cello solo—begins with the melody of **a**	
0:12	1:18 **a**₁′	Triplet sixteenth notes	
0:24	1:30 **b**₁	Cello—now in triplets, then violins	
0:41	1:47 **b**₁		
26 24	**VARIATION 2** Minor mode		
	2:06 **a**₂		
0:12	2:18 **b**₂		Winds: *f*
0:32	2:38 **b**₂′	Ends with a transition to variation 3	Winds: *f*
27 25	**VARIATION 3** Back to the major mode		
	2:58 **a**₃	(= **a**; unvaried)	Strings
0:12	3:10 **a**₃′	Thirty-second notes, *f*	More use of winds
0:24	3:22 **b**₃		Still more
28 26	**CODA**		
	3:40 **a**₄	New, expressive harmony	Strings
		Continuation: extra cadences	Wind solos
0:30	4:10 *Surprise!* *ff*		

Haydn's musical handwriting

Franz Joseph Haydn (1732–1809)

Joseph Haydn was born in Austria, the son of a village wheelwright who was a keen amateur musician. Another of his sons, Michael, also became a composer. As a boy Joseph had a beautiful voice, and at the age of eight was sent to Vienna to be a choirboy in St. Stephen's Cathedral. After his voice broke, he spent several difficult years as a freelance musician in Vienna before obtaining the position of Kapellmeister with Prince Paul Anton Esterházy, one of the most lavish patrons of music at the time.

After this, Haydn's career reflects the changing social situation in the later eighteenth century, when the old system of court patronage coexisted with an early form of the modern concert system. Indeed, there is no finer tribute to the system of court patronage than Haydn's thirty-year career with the Esterházys. The post of Kapellmeister involved managing and writing music not only for the prince's chapel (the *Kapell*), but also for his private opera house, his marionette theater, and for palace chamber music and orchestral performances. Haydn had a good head for administration. Hiring his own musicians, he was able over many years to experiment with the symphony and other genres and develop his style under ideal conditions.

Haydn's output was staggering. He composed 104 symphonies, 83 string quartets, numerous divertimentos, trios, and sonatas, and over 20 operas. He also had to write a great deal of music for baryton—a bizarre archaic instrument fancied by the next Esterházy prince, Nikolaus, which was something like a cello with extra strings that could be plucked, like guitar strings.

The Esterházys had a splendid estate some miles outside of Vienna, but Haydn's duties there did not prevent him from spending a good deal of time in the capital. In the 1770s his string quartets made a particularly strong impression in the metropolis. In the 1780s he befriended Mozart, and the two actually played together in an amateur string quartet.

Meanwhile the spread of Haydn's international fame was accelerated by the growth of public concerts. At first his symphonies were picked up by French concert organizers (who paid Haydn nothing). Then in the 1780s his six *Paris* symphonies were commissioned for concerts in that city, and in the 1790s twelve *London* symphonies were written for two highly successful tours to Britain.

Toward the end of his life Haydn turned to choral music: six impressive Latin Masses for soloists, chorus, and orchestra, and two German oratorios inspired by Handel, *The Creation* and *The Seasons,* admired by his contemporaries as the apex of an exemplary career in music.

One of the most attractive personalities in the gallery of the great composers, Haydn was shrewd but generous-minded, humorous, always honorable, and though fully aware of his own worth, quite ready to praise his young, "difficult" colleague, Mozart. "Friends often flatter me that I have some genius," he once said—without contradicting them—"but he stood far above me."

Haydn's music combines good-humored simplicity of melody with a very sophisticated delight in the manipulations of musical form and technique. No composer has ever enjoyed a (musical) joke more. In his reasonableness, his wit, and his conviction that his art should serve humanity (a conviction he both expressed and acted upon), Haydn is the true musical representative of the Enlightenment.

Chief Works: 104 symphonies; the last twelve, composed for London in 1791–1795, include the *Surprise, Clock, Drum Roll,* and "London" symphonies ▪ A cello concerto and a delightful trumpet concerto ▪ Over 80 string quartets; piano trios and piano sonatas ▪ Choral music in his late years: six Masses and the oratorios *The Creation* and *The Seasons*

Encore: After Symphony No. 95, listen to Symphony No. 102; Trumpet Concerto.

Baryton

In $a_1{'}$ and the two b_1 phrases, the variation is supplied by fast-moving violins that effectively swamp the melody. Still, the melody's phrases and its harmonic pattern are clear.

Variation 2 goes to the minor mode; the mood shifts from melancholy (in a_2) to blustering and then apprehensive (in b_2). Perhaps we need a moment to recover from all this, before returning to the major mode and the original feeling. Haydn provided a short transition passage to ease the way.

Variation 3 begins with a_3, equivalent to **a** in its original, unvaried form—another reminder of the fundamental source of all the variations. Then $a_3{}'$ and b_3 sound like a more intense version of Variation 1, with the violins moving faster. There is a hush, and a lovely new harmonization of **a** suggests the arrival of another variation. But instead of continuing with the theme, repeated cadences marked *p* and *pp* begin guiding the music to its close. It is an utter surprise, then, when the very last chords are jolted by a sudden *ff*.

Haydn used this kind of effect on more than one occasion. Is he making fun of the repeated cadences, which do sound a bit heavy-handed, or is the joke on this whole elegant movement—or even on the whole Classical style itself? Haydn can write serious, profound music, yet there are times when he seems to make a point of not taking himself too seriously.

Notice that at first this slow movement is scored for strings alone, and that the wind instruments play a larger and larger role, until they solo in the coda.

The admirable and matchless HAYDN! *From whose productions I have received more pleasure late in my life, when tired of most Music, than I ever received in the ignorant and rapturous part of my youth.*

English music historian
Charles Burney, 1776

4 Minuet Form (Classical Dance Form)

Stylized dances—music of considerable elaboration in the style and form of dances, but intended for listening rather than dancing—reached a state of high development in the Baroque era. In Chapter 9 we saw how various dance types such as the gavotte and the bourrée were assembled into suites. Unlike the Baroque era, which developed a single genre made up of different dances, the Classical era brought a single stylized dance into many different genres.

The sole dance type from the Baroque suite to survive in the multimovement genres of the Classical period was the **minuet**. One reason for its endurance was simply that the dance itself, originally popularized at the court of Louis XIV in the seventeenth century, continued as one of the major fashionable social dances during the eighteenth. The minuet movement of a symphony was always a reminder of the aristocratic courts which had originally established orchestras.

Another reason was more technical. As a moderately paced piece in triple meter, the minuet makes an excellent contrast to the quick duple meter that was by far the most common meter in the opening and closing movements of Classical symphonies, quartets, and the like.

Works with four movements—symphonies and string quartets—always included a minuet, usually as a light contrast after the slow movement. Mozart even managed to fit a minuet into some of his piano concertos, though traditionally the concerto, as a three-movement genre, did not leave room for one.

Baroque and Classical Dance Form

A Baroque minuet consists of two sections; each comes to a complete stop and is immediately repeated (|: **a** :||: **b** :|). See page 144. Minuets tend to come in pairs, alternating in an **A B A** pattern. The second dance, **B**, is called the **trio**, because in early days it was often played by only three instruments.

A Baroque minuet movement can be diagrammed as follows. (Remember that |: :| means repeat, and that in the second **A** the parts are not repeated.)

MINUET	TRIO	MINUET
A	B	A
|: a :||: b :|	|: c :||: d :|	a b

Classical composers extended the internal form of minuets (and trios) by developing internal **a b a** structures according to one of the following schemes:

MINUET	TRIO	MINUET		MINUET	TRIO	MINUET
A	B	A	or (more often)	A	B	A
|: a :||: b a :|	|: c :||: d c :|	a b a		|: a :||: b a′ :|	|: c :||: d c′ :|	a b a′

Prime marks (a′ and c′) indicate significant changes or extensions to the original **a** and **c** sections. It is easy to see why Classical dance form is sometimes called **ternary form.**

And indeed, changes of this kind were a major element in the dance "stylization" of this time. Haydn and Mozart could fashion a microcosm of the art of Classical music out of the basic elements of minuet form, always remaining within earshot of the ballroom with its easy, regular dance beat. (Mozart makes particularly creative use of minuet form in his Symphony in G Minor.)

FRANZ JOSEPH HAYDN
Symphony No. 95 in C Minor, third movement (Menuetto)

The minuet movement of Symphony No. 95 takes a small mental journey from the ballroom to the countryside, and then back again. Perhaps it is not a real countryside but a "stylized" one, like the one shown on page 167.

Be assured, my D. H., that among all your numerous admirers NO ONE *has listened with more* PROFOUND *attention, and no one can have such veneration for your* MOST BRILLIANT TALENTS *as I have. Indeed, my D. H., no tongue* CAN EXPRESS *the gratitude I* FEEL *for the infinite pleasure your Music has given me . . .*

Letter to Haydn from another, more intimate English admirer, 1792

LISTENING CHART 9

29-31 27-29

Haydn, Symphony No. 95, third movement (Menuetto)

Minuet form. 4 min., 56 sec.

MINUET (A)			
0:00	a	Theme	
0:09		Theme again, moving to the major mode	
0:25	a	*Repetition*	
0:50	b	(Picks up a motive introduced for the previous cadence)	
1:00	a′	Theme (back in the minor)	
1:13		Unexpected pause, with fermata ⌒	
1:20		Strong return to the minor	
1:30	b a′	*Repetition*	
TRIO (B)			
2:12	c	Slower tempo, major mode: cello solo	
2:25	c	*Repetition*	
2:38	d		
2:51	c′		
2:58		Violins	
3:11	d c′	*Repetition*	
MINUET (A)			
3:46		*Repetition of* a b a′	

(left margin:)
29 / 27
30 / 28
0:13
0:26
0:39
0:46
0:59
31 / 29

Minuet   Although the minuet starts with a quiet and weakly accented theme, it soon switches into the easy, energetic swing of a real ballroom dance, as **a** switches from the original minor to the major mode.

If you count the triple-meter bars, you will find almost all of them fit into the four- and eight-bar phrases that are necessary for the dance floor, if the dancers are to keep going. However, this is a stylized minuet, ripe for one of Haydn's jokes, and in phrase a′ he suddenly puts in a long rest, with a fermata. The music starts up again coolly, with a mysterious harmony, and goes on to a solid conclusion, but any in-the-flesh dancers would be thrown off completely.

Trio   As happens quite often in Haydn, this trio sounds less like a court dance, even of a muscular kind, than like some sort of country dance, with a suggestion of none-too-competent peasant musicians. The tempo slows, the mode changes from minor to major, and a somewhat awkward tune, all in even eighth notes, is played by a solo cello (who also starred, we remember, in the slow movement). Haydn knew that London audiences liked solo turns in symphonies.

Phrase **c′** is another joke: The cello player seems to forget how to go on, and has to be given his cue by the violins. Then he apparently has to play for time by repeating the cue over and over again, before finding a way to the cadence.

Minuet   The minuet returns unchanged, except for omission of the repeats. But coming after the quiet trio, there is an interesting new feel to the minuet's quiet opening.

Unlike a recapitulation in a sonata-form movement, the return of **A** after the trio in minuet form does not give the impression of emerging out of previous musical events and completing them. Minuet returns are more formal than organic. We probably listen to them less reflectively than to recapitulations, remembering their origin in the ballroom, where dances are played as many times as the dancers need them and are always gratefully received.

Informal pencil drawing of Haydn, which he once singled out as the best likeness he had ever seen: not the choice of a vain man. Compare page 190.

The minuet movement of Mozart's Symphony in G Minor—another "stylized" minuet—is not on our CD set, but it is easy to find and fascinating to compare with the minuet from Haydn's Symphony No. 95. There are no jokes in Mozart, and if there is anything rustic about his trio, the quality is laced with nostalgia, even romanticism.

The minuet itself is even more highly stylized than Haydn's. Full of raging music in three-bar phrases with grating counterpoint—both features guaranteed to confuse ballroom dancers—it never modulates so as to depart from the gloom of the minor mode (beyond four bars of major at the start of the **b** section). In this extraordinary minuet, the mood of Mozart's symphony intensifies, from nervous agitation and distress in the first movement to near-tragedy in the third.

5 Rondo Form

The **rondo** is a relatively simple form with popular leanings. In the symphonies and other multimovement genres of the Classical era, it was used mainly for closing movements, which tend to be relatively light.

The basic principle of the rondo is simply repetition, repetition of a full-fledged tune. The main tune (**A**) recurs again and again after *episodes* that serve as spacers between its appearances. If **A** falls into the favorite |: **a** :||: **b a′** :| pattern of the time, the recurrences of **A** may present only **a b a′** or **a b**, or **a**, but there is always enough of the tune for one to recognize.

In the simplest rondos, the episodes are little tunes much like **A**; we shall see such a rondo in Mozart's Piano Sonata in B-flat, on page 198. In more elaborate works such as symphonies, the episodes may contain transitions to new themes, cadence formulas, and even sonata-form style developments. (Rondos of these kinds are sometimes called *sonata rondos*.) Various schemes are possible; often a coda is added. Whatever the specific structure, the regular return of the main tune **A** is the critical feature of rondo form.*

Rondo schemes:

A B A C A coda
A B A C A B A
A B A C A D A
—and others

Symphony No 95:
A B A B C A coda

*In some ways, rondo form resembles ritornello form (see page 129), but the differences are worth noting. Ritornello form usually brings back its ritornello in fragments and in different keys; rondo form usually brings back its theme complete and in the same key.

LISTENING CHART 10

Haydn, Symphony No. 95, fourth movement (Finale. Vivace)

32-35   30-33

Rondo. 3 min., 41 sec.

32 **30**	0:00	**A (Tune)**	a	Dynamic is *p*	
	0:08		a		
	0:15		b		
	0:22		c	Long extension (winds)	
	0:36		b c		
33 **31**	0:58	**B (Episode 1)**	Fugal exposition, *f:*	First subject entry	
0:06	1:04			Second entry (rapid counterpoint in the bassoons)	
0:10	1:08			Third entry (stretto)	
0:14	1:12		Further material: many new, non-fugal ideas		
0:19	1:17		Seems to head for a big cadence; trumpets		
0:40	1:38		Fugue resumes:	Subject entry	
0:48	1:46			Final entry—in the bass	
1:04	2:02		Expectant STOP		
34 **32**	2:05	**A**	a b c ⌒		*p*
0:28	2:33	**B (Episode 2)**	Fugue starts up again, *f:* seems to almost *reach* a cadence		
0:41	2:46	**C**	*Surprise! sudden stormy section in the minor mode, ff*		
1:00	3:05		Transition (in several short stages)		
35 **33**	3:14	**A**	a	New, expressive harmony	*p*
0:12	3:26	**Coda**	Brass fanfares		*f*

FRANZ JOSEPH HAYDN
Symphony No. 95 in C Minor, fourth movement (Finale. Vivace)

The rondo theme, **A,** starts out as a rather delicate, airy tune played by the strings. The form could be diagrammed |: **a** :||: **b** :|, but |: **a** :||: **b c** :| better represents what we actually hear. Phrases **a, a,** and **b** are played by the strings alone. Then, when **b** seems to have answered **a** and rounded it off with a full cadence, the wind instruments enter much less delicately, adding **c** as a lively appendage lasting as long as **a** and **b** together. A three-note figure ♩♩♩𝄾 appears in **a** and **c** and *under* **b.**

The first episode, **B**, starts with a bang right on the last note of **A**. It is a fugue on a subject derived from **A** (the beginning of **a** played in sequence):

We spoke earlier of free and learned fugues (page 140). This one is *very* free; once the exposition of only three (instrumental) voices is over, the polyphonic texture changes to homophony and even monophony, in sweeping downward scales.

Theme **A** returns, this time without the repeats, and the next episode starts much like **B**, that is, with the same fugue—which turns out to be a feint. After a few bars the mode changes suddenly from major to minor and the dynamic rises from *f* to *ff* for a passage of furious, stormy music that would have jolted—and also delighted—the London audience during Haydn's first triumphant tour.

They would have been delighted because they would have recognized it as another of Haydn's jokes, similar in spirit to the sudden fortissimo ending of this symphony's slow movement (see page 191). For the music here is not just noisy and furious, it is disproportionately noisy and furious, a manic explosion that rattles the orderly Classical style of the rest of the finale.

The harmony soon turns to the major mode and the storm subsides (the audience knew this would happen, too). We touch base on **A** one more time, with its **a** phrase in a newly harmonized version, and the piece comes quickly to a close.

Thinking back on Haydn's Symphony No. 95, we might ask if there is any aesthetic quality that derives from the combination of the particular four movements we have heard. Is the whole greater than the sum of the parts?

If so, this is not something that musicians or musicologists have been able to elucidate with any consistency. It seems, rather, that Classical composers wrote symphony movements to fit together only in a general way, without thinking very much about connections between them, or any greater whole. This is as true of Mozart's agitated G-minor Symphony as of Haydn's more cheerful Symphony No. 95.

Indeed, the question only comes up because later, nineteenth-century symphonies often *do* make such connections. Symphony No. 5 by Ludwig van Beethoven seems to trace a psychological process from turmoil to triumph. The *Fantastic* Symphony by Hector Berlioz literally traces a story line written by the composer. See pages 227 and 265.

Web: *Research and test your understanding of the symphony at* <bedfordstmartins.com/listen>.

Haydn's most famous composition is a simple Austrian patriotic song:

It appears with variations in his *Emperor* Quartet, Op. 76 No. 3 (1797). The tune was adopted for the German national anthem, "Deutschland über Alles," and for the hymn "Glorious Things of Thee Are Spoken."

CHAPTER 13

Other Classical Genres

In Chapter 12 we examined the symphony as exemplified by Haydn's Symphony No. 95 in C Minor and the first movement of Mozart's Symphony No. 40 in G Minor. We go on in this chapter to examine the other main genres of music in the Viennese Classical era: the sonata, the Classical concerto, the string quartet, and opera buffa, the name for Italian comic opera of the time.

It would be impractical to spend the same amount of detail on each of these genres as on the symphony, and also somewhat redundant, for many features of the symphony are duplicated in these other genres. Indeed, for Classical instrumental music, the symphony can be used as a sort of prototype. With this use in mind, the symphony outline given on page 178 is reprinted on this page.

In the following pages we select a sonata, a concerto, and a string quartet and then discuss a single movement in each (using recordings and Listening Charts, as usual). The discussions will emphasize generic specificity—that is, the specific features that differentiate the music in question from the symphony. In the case of opera buffa, two numbers will serve as samples of the whole.

Movements of the Symphony

Opening Movement
   tempo: fast/moderate
   form: sonata form
      (sometimes preceded by
      a slow **Introduction**)

Slow Movement
   tempo: slow/very slow
   form: sonata form,
      variations, rondo, other

Minuet (with Trio)
   tempo: moderate
   form: minuet form

Closing Movement
   tempo: fast/very fast
   form: sonata form or
      rondo form

1 The Sonata

The term **sonata** has multiple meanings. We know its adjectival use in the term "sonata form," the scheme employed in the first movements of Classical overtures, symphonies, quartets, and also (as it happens) most sonatas. As a noun, *sonata* refers to a piece for a small number of instruments or a single one. And whereas in the Baroque period there were trio sonatas and solo sonatas—solo plus continuo, usually—in the Classical period the term was restricted to compositions for one or two instruments only.

Sonatas were not designed for concerts, which in any case were still rare at this time, but for private performance, often by amateurs. The symphony is a public genre, the sonata a domestic one. Given their destination in social life, some (not all!) sonatas are easy to play and may be limited in expression.

Piano sonatas were composed for solo piano, the favorite new instrument of the time, and *violin sonatas* were composed for violin and piano. In Classical

The sonata was said by a German critic to be intended by its earliest writers to show in the first movement what they could do, in the second what they could feel, and in the last how glad they were to have finished.

Philadelphia musician
P. H. Goepp, 1897

sonatas with violin or (less frequently) another instrument, the piano is not a mere accompaniment but an equal partner; it holds its own in such combinations in a way that the earlier harpsichord did not.

Compare the movement plan for the sonata, shown to the right, with the symphony prototype on the previous page. But also note that sonatas are much less uniform than symphonies, concertos, or quartets. In Mozart's sonatas, for example, only 65 percent follow the plan, leaving many exceptions. None of them has more than three movements, however, and the movements are always shorter than those of a symphony.

Movements of the Sonata

Opening Movement
   tempo: fast/moderate
   form: sonata form

Slow Movement
   tempo: slow/very slow
   form: sonata form, variations, rondo, other

Closing Movement
   tempo: fast/very fast
   form: often rondo

WOLFGANG AMADEUS MOZART (1756–1791)
Piano Sonata in B-flat, K. 570 (1787)

This sonata finds Mozart in a sunny mood—a more frequent mood for him than the sometimes painful agitation that we recall from Symphony No. 40. The first movement, a lively work in the major mode, is in sonata form. The second is in simple rondo form (see page 194), and the third in an irregular, compressed form similar to a rondo.

First Movement (Allegro)   As is usual with Mozart's movements in sonata form, all the formal articulations—bridges, cadences, and the like—are signaled clearly, in fact almost flaunted. There is one novelty, however. After a long bridge that clearly announces the second key, the "second theme" turns out to be the first theme in the left hand with a faster counterpoint in the right:

As always, the recapitulation remains in the tonic key, rather than moving to a new one. Otherwise it stays very close to the exposition (closer than in either of the symphony first movements we have heard). There is no coda.

From the late eighteenth century on, musical accomplishment was regarded as a highly desirable social asset for women worldwide: for a French princess (painted by Elizabeth Vigée-Lebrun, a fashionable court painter, 1755–1842) or an American First Lady—Louise C. (Mrs. John Quincy) Adams—at a later period.

LISTENING CHART 11

Mozart, Piano Sonata in B-flat, third movement (Allegro)

A B C A form. 3 min., 35 sec.

2

36-38

36	0:00	**A**	a	
	0:14		b	
	0:24		a	
	0:38	**B**	c	
	0:52	(Episode 1)	c	*Repetition*
	1:06		d	
	1:14		c′	
	1:28		d c′	*Repetition*
	1:50			Short transition
37	1:54	**C**	e	In a new key
		(Episode 2)	e	*Repetition*
0:13	2:07		f	
0:20	2:14		e′	
0:27	2:21		f e′	*Repetition*
0:40	2:34			Short transition = end of **b**
38	2:45	**A**	a	Back in the tonic key
0:13	2:58	Coda		Refers to **d** (or **c**), then **f**
0:34	3:19			⎡CADENCE⎤ Trill and strong cadence
				New cadence motive

Second Movement (Adagio)   Mozart is at his most melodious in this lovely slow movement. The first rondo episode, **B**, in the minor mode, offers a whiff of agitation that may recall the G-minor Symphony. The coda looks back nostalgically to **C** and **f**. The rondo form can be diagrammed as follows:

      A   **B**   short   **A**   **C**   short   **A** **Coda**
|: a :||: b a :| |: c :||: d c′ :| transition a′ |: e :||: f :| transition a′

Third Movement (Allegretto)   There is a sharp edge, almost a bite, to this movement; one thing that contributes to this is the set of tart little syncopations (see page 13) within the **a** and **b** phrases of the main tune, **A.**

Syncopations are also heard in the first episode, **B**, together with a repeated-note figure in the left hand, which Mozart takes over for the beginning of the second episode, **C**. This rather simple-minded repeated-note figure, originally meant for a routine accompaniment function, is soon combined with spiky

Mozart's fortepiano, the eighteenth-century version of a pianoforte—smaller than today's instrument, with strings strung less tightly because iron was not used in the frame. Hence the volume was lower, but the fortepiano made up for this by its responsive touch and delicate tone. Compare the sound of a fortepiano in our recording of this sonata with the modern piano in Mozart's A-major Concerto, page 202.

counterpoints (in phrase **f**). Some charming little ornaments in the last **A** are not written in the score—they were improvised by the pianist in our recording.

The coda makes witty references to both episodes, and arrives at its cadence with a small flourish and a trill—except that this is not quite the end: Mozart adds a new motive for a doubly emphatic, self-satisfied conclusion.

The form has the feel of a simple rondo because of the structure of the main tune and of the episodes: Compare the Adagio. But there is no central **A**:

A	**B**		short	**C**		short	**A**	**Coda**
a b a	|: **c** :||: **d c′** :|		transition	|: **e** :||: **f e′** :|		transition	**a**	

2 The Classical Concerto

On page 129 we discussed the Baroque concerto and concerto grosso at the time of Bach and Vivaldi in terms of the basic concerto idea—the contest between soloist and orchestra. This basic idea was refined and sharpened by the Viennese Classical composers.

Instrumental virtuosity remained a central feature of the Classical concerto. At the same time, the orchestra was growing. With its well-coordinated string, woodwind, and brass groups, the Classical orchestra was much more flexible than the Baroque concerto orchestra could ever be.

So the balance between the two contesting forces—soloist and orchestra—presented a real problem, a problem that Mozart worked out in a series of seventeen superb piano concertos written during his years in Vienna, mostly for his own concert use. He pitted the soloist's greater agility, brilliance, and expressive capability against the orchestra's increased power and variety of tone color. The contestants are perfectly matched; neither one can ever emerge as the definite winner.

Compare the movement plan for the Classical concerto with the symphony prototype in the margin of page 197. Concertos have long opening movements—see below—and no minuet movements.

*Movements of
the Classical Concerto*

Opening Movement
tempo: fast/moderate
form: double-exposition
          sonata form
cadenza near the end

Slow Movement
tempo: slow/very slow
form: sonata form,
          variations, rondo, other

Closing Movement
tempo: fast/very fast
form: rondo form
          (occasionally variation
          form)

Double-Exposition Form

For the first movements of concertos, Mozart developed a special form to capitalize on the contest that is basic to the genre. Though the diagram for **double-exposition form** may look rather cluttered, it is in fact simply an extended variant of sonata form. Compare the sonata-form diagram, page 181:

In sonata form, the exposition is repeated; here each of the competing forces presents the thematic material in its own somewhat different version. Note that unlike the exposition in a symphony, in a concerto the **orchestra exposition** does not modulate—an important difference. The point is to save the change of key (which counts for so much in all sonata-form compositions) until the **solo exposition**. The listener senses that the orchestra can't modulate and the soloist can—evidence of the soloist's superior range and mobility. This is demonstrated spectacularly by the soloist playing scales, arpeggios, and other brilliant material, making the solo exposition longer than the orchestral one.

The recapitulation in double-exposition form amounts to a composite of the orchestral and solo versions of the exposition. Typically the orchestra's cadence theme, which has been crowded out of the solo exposition to make room for virtuoso activity, returns at the end to make a very satisfactory final cadence.* Shortly before the end, there is a big, formal pause for the soloist's **cadenza** (see page 137). The soloist was supposed to improvise at this point—to show his or her skill and flair by working out new thematic developments on the spot, and also by carrying off brilliant feats of virtuosity.

---

*Double-exposition form, like sonata form, may also have a coda—a feature exploited by Beethoven more than Mozart and Haydn.

WOLFGANG AMADEUS MOZART (1756–1791)
Piano Concerto in A, K. 488 (1786)

This favorite Mozart concerto proceeds from one of his most gentle and songful first movements to a second movement that is almost tragic followed by an exuberant, sunny finale. The first movement might almost have been intended as a demonstration piece for double-exposition form, except for one unique feature: a new theme introduced halfway through.

First Movement (Allegro)   No fewer than four themes in this movement could be described as gentle and songful—though always alert. For a work of this character, Mozart uses a reduced orchestra, keeping the mellow clarinets but omitting the sharper-sounding oboes as well as trumpets and timpani.

Orchestra Exposition   Theme 1, played *piano* by the strings and repeated by the woodwinds, is answered by a vigorous *forte* passage in the full orchestra.

This "response" idea returns many times, balancing the quiet themes, and often leading to something new—here, theme 2, another quiet melody, full of feeling. A somewhat agitated passage interrupts, touching on two different minor keys, but this is only a momentary deflection from the basic tonality of this section. It is all in the major tonic key, without any actual modulation. The cadence theme that ends the section maintains the gentle mood.

Solo Exposition   The solo exposition expands on and illuminates the orchestra exposition, with the piano taking over some of it, while also adding fast-moving scales or other figuration of its own. The main difference comes at the bridge; the modulation, needed to give the music a lift, is engineered by the piano. The orchestral second theme sounds especially intimate and lovely when played on the piano—as Mozart planned. And at the end, instead of the gentle cadence theme, the piano has a moment of brilliant passage work, culminating in a drawn-out, triumphal cadence with a long trill.

Showy cadences of this kind are a regular feature of Classical concertos; the orchestra always answers with loud music of its own, like a cheer. Here it is the orchestra's "response" passage again. But this time it stops in mid-course, as though the music has suddenly remembered something intimate and a little serious. A new theme in the orchestra (yet another quiet, gentle melody, this time with a thoughtful character) appears out of nowhere:

New theme

Development
CLARINET

upbeat

PIANO

upbeat

After the orchestra plays the new theme, the solo repeats it in an elaborated version, and we slip into the development section.

Development   The basic idea behind concertos, the contest between orchestra and soloist, is brought out wonderfully here. Mozart sets up a rapid-fire dialogue between the two contestants; fragments of the new theme in the wood-

These piano concertos are a happy medium between too easy and too difficult; they are very brilliant, pleasing to the ear, and natural, without being simple-minded. There are passages here and there which only connoisseurs will be able to appreciate, but less learned listeners will like them too, without knowing why.

Letter from Mozart to his father, 1782

Richter, the piano virtuoso, is giving six Saturday concerts . . . The nobility subscribed, but remarked that they really did not care much about going unless I played too. So Richter asked me to do so. I promised to play three times—and then arranged three concerts for myself, to which they all subscribed.

Letter from Mozart to his father, 1784

LISTENING CHART 12

Mozart, Piano Concerto in A, K. 488, first movement

Double-exposition form. 11 min., 16 sec.

On this chart, the column arrangement distinguishes the main orchestra and solo sections.

1 | ORCHESTRA EXPOSITION

0:00	Theme 1, *p*	Orchestra	Strings; woodwinds for the second playing
0:33	*f* response		
0:56	Theme 2, *p*		
1:26	"Deflection" passage		Two minor-mode keys are suggested
1:57	Cadence theme, *p*		

Cadence theme

2 | SOLO EXPOSITION

2:06	Theme 1		SOLO: melody is increasingly ornamented
:29 2:35	*f* response	Orchestra, with SOLO cutting in	
:37 2:43	Bridge—modulates		
:59 3:05	Theme 2		
:28 3:34	"Deflection" passage		
:57 4:03	Solo virtuoso passage		
3 4:17	*f* response, leads to		
:12 4:29	*new theme*	Orchestra	
:23 4:40			SOLO *ornaments* the new theme

DEVELOPMENT

:36 4:53		Orchestra and SOLO: *dialogue* around the new theme; modulations	
:18 5:35	Retransition		
:38 5:55	Short cadenza		in free time; ends with a fermata

4 | RECAPITULATION

6:12	Theme 1, *p*	Orchestra, with SOLO cutting in for the second playing	
:29 6:41	*f* response	Orchestra, with SOLO cutting in again	
:37 6:49	Bridge		
:57 7:09	Theme 2		
:27 7:39	"Deflection" passage		
5 8:12	*New theme*		(the first time the SOLO plays it without ornaments)
	(longer virtuoso passage)		
:42 8:54	*f* response, leads to		
:54 9:06	*new theme*		
:11 9:23	Main CADENZA		SOLO free, improvised passage
:30 10:42	*f* response	Orchestra	
:45 10:56	Cadence theme, *p*		
:52 11:04	Brief ending *f* ⟶ *p*		

Doodle on a Mozart concerto score

winds seem to discuss or argue with the piano, as the music modulates to minor-mode keys and the material is developed. (A changeable upbeat attaches itself to the new theme: See the music example on page 202).

The new theme turns unexpectedly anxious in the retransition (see the music in the margin, to the right). Finally, with a brief cadenza, the piano pulls out of the dialogue and steers the way to the recapitulation.

STRINGS

upbeat

Recapitulation   At the start of the movement, the songful first theme was claimed in turn by the orchestra and the solo in their respective expositions. In the recapitulation, a composite of the two expositions, they share it.

The recapitulation resembles the solo exposition, though the bridge is altered so that the whole remains in the tonic key. There is a beautiful extension at the end, and when the "response" passage comes again, it leads to a heavy stop, with a fermata—the standard way for the orchestra to bow out, after preparing for the soloists's grand re-entrance for the main cadenza. Compared to the cadenza in Bach's *Brandenburg* Concerto—see page 135—this one is much more varied. Written out by Mozart himself, it includes mild improvisatory moments as well as brilliant ones.

The solo's showy cadence after the cadenza is cheered along once again by the orchestra's "response" passage, which we have heard so many times before. This time it leads to something we have *not* heard many times—only once, nine minutes back: the quiet cadence theme of the orchestra exposition. Do you remember it? It makes a perfect ending for the whole movement, with an extra twist: a little flare-up to *forte* that subsides almost at once.

3 The String Quartet

Developed in the Classical era, the **string quartet** is a genre for four instruments: two violins, a viola, and a cello. ("String quartet" is also the name for a group of four musicians who work together playing quartets.) The plan for a string quartet, with its four movements, is close to that of the symphony; compare page 197. Indeed, next to the symphony the quartet counts as the most important genre of Classical music.

The quartet may have as many movements as the symphony, but of course it doesn't have as many instruments, and it cannot match the symphony's range of volume and tone color. This can disappoint listeners today. For the eighteenth century, however, volume was no issue, because quartets were never intended for concert listening. They were intended primarily for the performers, with small, informal audiences—or none at all.

As for range of tone color, the quartet compensates for this by its own special qualities: nuance, delicacy, and subtlety. Without any conductor, the quartet players are partners responding to one another as only old, close associates can. As developed by Haydn, the four instruments of the quartet grow more and more similar in their actual musical material, and more and more interdependent. There is a fine interplay as they each react to musical gestures by the others, sometimes supporting them, sometimes countering.

This interplay has been aptly compared to the art of cultivated conversation—witty, sensitive, always ready with a perfectly turned phrase—that was especially prized in eighteenth-century salons (page 167).

There are dozens of wonderful string quartets by Haydn and ten, equally wonderful, by Mozart. We could have chosen any one of these for the example

Movements of the String Quartet

Opening Movement
  tempo: fast/moderate
  form: sonata form

Slow Movement
  tempo: slow/very slow
  form: sonata form,
     variations, rondo, other

Minuet (with Trio)
  tempo: moderate
  form: minuet form

Closing Movement
  tempo: fast/very fast
  form: sonata form or
    rondo form

String quartets, then and now (left, below, and next page). Nineteenth-century quartets were often led by celebrated violin soloists; shown here is a group led by a virtuosa of the time, Wilma Norman-Néruda (1838–1911). From left to right: two violins, viola (slightly larger), and cello.

on our CD set. However, since Haydn and Mozart are already well represented in this book, we will use an example by a somewhat later composer. If you like, jump ahead to page 232 for Ludwig van Beethoven's String Quartet in F, Op. 135.

Chamber Music

The string quartet was the main but not the only genre developed at this time for small forces in relatively intimate circumstances. **Chamber music** is a term for music designed to be played in a room (a chamber)—in a palace drawing room or in a small hall. Chamber music can be taken as encompassing compositions for from two to nine players. Other types are the piano trio (violin, cello, piano: a favorite of Haydn) and string quintets (string quartet plus another low instrument; Mozart wrote four superb quintets with two violas, and one of Schubert's great masterpieces is a quintet with two cellos).

The Juilliard Quartet, perhaps the leading American quartet, was formed at the Juilliard School in New York in 1946 and is still active. Two violins, cello, and viola.

The Kronos Quartet, based in San Francisco, plays almost exclusively contemporary music, including jazz arrangements and other "crossover" items. They have commissioned more than 400 new works in their 25-year history. Two violins, viola, and cello.

Broadly speaking, what has been said above about the intimate character of the quartet applies to all chamber music, though it is probably obvious that a string octet must be less subtle and more "orchestral" than a string trio.

4 Opera Buffa

In the late eighteenth century, comic opera grew to equal in importance the serious opera that was a hallmark of the Baroque era (see page 150). Roman emperors and their courtly confidants gave way to contemporary peasant girls and soldiers; castratos were edged aside by basses specializing in comical diatribes and exasperated "slow burns," the so-called *buffo* basses (*buffone* is

In an opera buffa ensemble, characters register different feelings musically, by singing contrasting melodies. In this production of a Haydn opera buffa, they also do so visually—by their contrasting grimaces and gestures.

Italian for "buffoon"). Happy endings were the result of pranks, rather than issuing from the decrees of magnanimous princes.

Comic opera stars had to be funny; they had to act, not just sing. The new flexibility of the Classical style was perfectly suited to the casual, swift, lifelike effects that are the essence of comedy. As much as its humor, it was this "natural," lifelike quality of comedy that appealed to audiences of the Enlightenment. Enlightened monarch Joseph II of Austria actively promoted comic opera.

Italian comic opera was the most important, though there were also parallel developments in Germany, France, and England. Serious Italian opera was called *opera seria;* comic Italian opera was called **opera buffa.** Just as Italian opera seria was very popular in London in Handel's time, so Italian opera buffa was in Vienna at the time of Haydn and Mozart. Thus Haydn, whose court duties with the Esterházys included running their opera house, wrote twelve comic operas—all in Italian. Mozart in his mature years wrote six comic operas, three in German (one is a one-acter) and three in Italian.

The Ensemble

Baroque opera seria, as we have seen (page 151), employs two elements in alternation: recitatives for the dialogue and the action, and numbers that are fully musical—almost always arias—for static meditation and "tableaus" of emotional expression. Classical opera buffa works with the same elements, except that the fully musical numbers include *ensembles* as well as solo arias.

An **ensemble** is a number sung by two or more people. And given the Classical composers' skill in incorporating contrast into their music, they were able to make their ensembles depict the different sentiments of the participating characters simultaneously. This meant that sentiments could be presented much more swiftly and vividly: swiftly, because we don't have to wait for the characters to sing whole arias to find out what they are feeling, and vividly, because the sentiments stand out in sharp relief one against the other.

The music also depicts these sentiments in flux. For in the course of an ensemble, the action proceeds and the situation changes. This is usually projected by means of new musical sections with different tempos, keys, and themes. A Classical opera ensemble, then, is a sectional number for several characters in which the later sections represent new plot action and the characters' new reactions to it.

In short, whereas the aria was essentially a static number, the ensemble was a dynamic one. At the end of a Baroque da capo aria (see page 152), the return of the opening music tells us that the dramatic situation is just where it was when the aria started. But at the end of a Classical ensemble, the drama has moved ahead by one notch or more, and the music, too, has moved on to something different. The ensemble transformed opera into a much more dramatic genre than had been possible within the Baroque aesthetic.

WOLFGANG AMADEUS MOZART
Don Giovanni (1787)

Mozart wrote *Don Giovanni* in 1787 for Prague, the second largest city of the Austrian empire, where his music was enjoying a temporary spurt in popularity. While technically it counts as an opera buffa, *Don Giovanni* is neither a wholly comic drama nor wholly tragic. A somewhat enigmatic mixture of both—what might be called today a "dark comedy"—it seems to convey

Chamber music never sounds as well as when one is close to it. Probably the ideal place is directly in the middle of the players. Retreat forty feet, and at once the thing begins to be thin and wheezy. Go back sixty feet, and one may as well leave the place altogether.

H. L. Mencken, famously skeptical American critic, 1930

On Monday the 29th the Italian opera company gave the eagerly awaited opera by Maestro Mozard, Don Giovanni, or The Stone Guest. Connoisseurs and musicians say that Prague had never heard the like. Herr Mozard conducted in person; when he entered the orchestra he was received by three-fold cheers, as also happened when he left. The opera is extremely difficult to perform . . .

Prague newspaper, 1787

24th [of August, 1787]
A Piano Sonata with accompanying violin

28th of October
in Prague
The Reprobate Punished, or Don Giovanni: opera buffa in 2 acts.
24 musical numbers. Actors. Ladies: Teresa Saporitti, Bondini,
and Micelli. Gentlemen: Papi, Ponziani, Taglioni and Lolli.

3rd of November
Scena [operatic scene] for Mad.ᵐᵉ Dušek. Recitative: "My lovely
flame." Aria: "Stay, dearest." Accompaniment:

		6th	
A Song	—	—	"Little Frederick's Birthday"
		ditto	
A Song	—	—	"The Phantom"

Mozart's feeling that events have both comical and serious dimensions, and
that life's experiences cannot be pigeonholed.

Background   Don Giovanni is the Italian name for Don Juan, the legendary
Spanish libertine. The tale of his endless escapades and conquests is meant to
stir up incredulous laughter, usually with a bawdy undertone. Certainly a subject of this kind belongs to opera buffa.

But in his compulsive, completely selfish pursuit of women, Don Giovanni
ignores the rules of society, morality, and God. Hence the serious undertone of
the story. He commits crimes and mortal sins—and not only against the
women he seduces. He kills the father of one of his victims, the Commandant,
who surprises Giovanni struggling with his daughter.

This action finally brings Don Giovanni down. Once, when he is hiding
from his pursuers in a graveyard—and joking blasphemously—he is re-
proached by the marble statue that has been erected over the Commandant's
tomb. He arrogantly invites the statue home for dinner. The statue comes, and
when Giovanni refuses to mend his ways drags him off to *its* home, which is
hell. The somber music associated with the statue was planted ahead of time by
Mozart in the orchestral overture to *Don Giovanni*, before the curtain rises.

Thanks to Mozart's music, our righteous satisfaction at Don Giovanni's
end is mixed with a good deal of sympathy for his verve and high spirits, his
bravery, and his determination to live by his own rules, not those of society,
even if this dooms him. The other characters in the opera, too, awaken ambivalent feelings. They amuse us and move us at the same time.

Act I, scene iii   The opera's third scene begins with a chorus of peasants,
celebrating the betrothal of Masetto and Zerlina. Don Giovanni enters with
his manservant Leporello and immediately takes a fancy to Zerlina. He promises Masetto various favors, and then tells him to leave—and tells Leporello to
take him away by force if necessary.

From the scary final scene of
Don Giovanni:
"Repent, tell me you will live
a new life: this is your last
chance!"
"No, never, let me alone!"
"Repent, villain!"
"Never, old fool!"

Mozart kept a little notebook in which he entered every new composition when it was finished. On the right-hand page he wrote the first few measures of the music, and on the left the title and date. The pages shown include *Don Giovanni* (under its subtitle *The Reprobate Punished*) and an operatic scene for a soprano named Josefa Dušek.

Mozart first met Dušek in the 1770s, before moving to Vienna, and may have been involved with her in the 1780s.

Aria, "Ho capito"   This opera buffa aria, sung by Masetto, shows how vividly (and rapidly!) Mozart could define character in music. Singing almost entirely in very short phrases, Masetto almost insolently tells Don Giovanni that he will leave only because he has to, because great lords can always bully peasants. Then he rails at Zerlina in furious, fast asides; she has always been his ruin. He sings a very sarcastic little tune when he promises her that Don Giovanni is going to make her into a fine lady:

Fac-cia il nostro ca-va-lie-re   Ca-va-lie-ra ancora te,   ca-va-liera ancora   te!

Toward the end of the aria he forgets Don Giovanni and the opening music he used to address him, and thinks only of Zerlina, repeating his furious words to her and their sarcastic tune. He gets more and more worked up as he sings repeated cadences, so characteristic of the Classical style. A variation of the tune, played by the orchestra, ends this tiny aria in an angry rush.

The total effect is of a simple man (judging from the music he sings) who nonetheless feels deeply and is ready to express his anger. There is also a clear undercurrent of class conflict: Masetto the peasant versus Don Giovanni the aristocrat. Mozart was no political radical, but he had indeed rebelled against court authority; and the previous opera he had written, *The Marriage of Figaro*, was based on a notorious French play that had been banned because of its anti-aristocratic sentiments. Two years after *Don Giovanni* was composed, the French Revolution broke out in Paris.

Recitative   Next comes an amusing secco recitative, sung with just continuo accompaniment, as in Baroque opera (see page 151). Giovanni invites Zerlina up to his villa, promising to marry her and make her into a fine lady, just as Masetto had ironically predicted.

17 MAY 1788. *To the Opera. Don Giovanni. Mozart's music is agreeable and very varied.*

Diary of a Viennese opera buff, Count Zinzendorf

Duet, "Là ci darem la mano"   Operas depend on memorable tunes, as well as on musical drama. The best opera composers are able to write melodies that are not only beautiful in themselves, but also further the drama at the same time. Such a one is the most famous tune in *Don Giovanni,* in the following **duet** (an ensemble for two singers) between Don Giovanni and Zerlina.

Section 1 (Andante)   Don Giovanni sings his first stanza to a simple, unforgettable tune that combines seductiveness with a delicate sense of banter. When Zerlina sings the same tune to *her* first stanza, we know she is playing along, even though she hesitates (notice her tiny rhythmic changes, and her reluctance to finish the tune in eight measures—she delays for two more).

Là ci darem la   mano,   Là mi di-rai di si;   Ve - di, non è lon - ta - no, Par-tiam, ben mio, da   qui.

In stanza 3, as Don Giovanni presses more and more ardently, yet always gently, Zerlina keeps drawing back. Her reiterated "non son più forte" ("I'm weakening") makes her sound very sorry for herself, but also coy. When the main tune comes back—section 1 of the ensemble falls into a **A A′ B A″ coda** form—Giovanni grows more insistent, Zerlina more coquettish. The words they sing (from stanzas 1–3) are closer together than before, and even simultaneous. The stage director will place them physically closer together, too.

Section 2 (Allegro)   Zerlina falls happily into Don Giovanni's arms, echoing his "andiam" ("let us go"). The "innocent love" they now mean to celebrate is depicted by a little rustic melody (Zerlina is a peasant girl, remember) in a faster tempo. But a not-so-innocent sensuous note is added by the orchestra after the singers' first phrase in this section.

How neatly and charmingly an ensemble can project dramatic action; the whole duet leads us step by step through Don Giovanni's successful "technique." By portraying these people through characteristic action or behavior—Don Giovanni winning another woman, Zerlina playing her own coy game—Mozart exposes their personalities as convincingly as any novelist or playwright.

Don Giovanni and Zerlina, in an early engraving; page 211, a modern production.

LISTEN   **Mozart, *Don Giovanni:* from Act I, scene iii**

(Italics indicate phrases of the text that are repeated.)

39   ARIA: "Ho capito"

0:03 **Masetto:**	Ho capito, *signor, si!*	I understand you, *yes sir!*
(to Don Giovanni)	Chino il capo, e me ne vò	I touch my cap and off I go;
	Ghiacche piace a voi così	Since that's what you want
	Altre repliche *non fò.* . . .	I have nothing else to say.
	Cavalier voi siete già,	After all, you're a lord,
	Dubitar non posso affè,	And I couldn't suspect you, oh no!
	Me lo dice la bontà,	You've told me of the favors
	Che volete *aver per me.*	You mean to do for me!
0:30 *(aside, to Zerlina)*	(Briconaccia! malandrina!	(You wretch! you witch!
	Fosti ognor la mia ruina!)	You have always been my ruin!)
(to Leporello)	Vengo, vengo!	Yes, I'm coming—
(to Zerlina)	(Resta, resta!	(Stay, why don't you?
	È una cosa molto onesta;	A very innocent affair!
0:45	Faccia il nostro cavaliere	No doubt this fine lord
	cavaliera ancora te.)	Will make you his fine lady, too!)

(last seven lines repeated)

RECITATIVE (with continuo only)

40	1:32	**Giovanni:**		Alfin siam liberati,	At last, we're free,
				Zerlinetta gentil, da quel scoccione.	My darling Zerlinetta, of that clown.
				Che ne dite, mio ben, so far pulito?	Tell me, my dear, don't I manage things well?
		Zerlina:		Ma signore, io gli diedi	But sir, I gave him
				Parola di sposarlo.	My word that we would be married.
		Giovanni:		Tal parola	That word
				Non vale un zero! voi non siete fata	Is worth nothing! You were not made
				Per esser paesana. Un'altra sorte	To be a peasant girl. A different fate
				Vi procuran quegli occhi bricconcelli,	Is called for by those roguish eyes,
				Quei labretti sì belli,	Those beautiful little lips,
				Quelle dituccie candide e odorose,	These slender white, perfumed fingers,
				Parmi toccar giuncata, e fiutar rose.	So soft to the touch, scented with roses.
		Zerlina:		Ah, non vorrei—	Ah, I don't want to—
		Giovanni:		Che non voreste?	What don't you want?
		Zerlina:		Alfine	To end up
				Ingannata restar! Io so che raro	Deceived! I know it's not often
				Colle donne voi altri cavalieri	That with women you great gentlemen
				siete onesti e sinceri.	Are honest and sincere.
		Giovanni:		È un' impostura	A slander
				Della gente plebea! La nobiltà	Of the lower classes! The nobility
				Ha dipinta negli occhi l'onestà.	Is honest to the tips of its toes.
				Orsù non perdiam tempo; in quest'istante	Let's lose no time; this very instant
				Io vi voglio sposar.	I wish to marry you.
		Zerlina:		Voi?	You?
		Giovanni:		Certo io.	Certainly, me;
				Quel casinetto è mio, soli saremo;	There's my little place; we'll be alone—
				E là, gioella mio, ci sposeremo.	And there, my precious, we'll be married.

DUET "Là ci darem la mano"

SECTION 1 Andante, **2/4** meter

41	3:17	**Giovanni:**	A	Là ci darem la mano	There [in the villa] you'll give me your hand,
				Là mi dirai di si!	There you'll tell me yes!
				Vedi, non è lontano;	You see, it isn't far—
				Partiam, ben mio, da qui!	Let's go there, my dear!
		Zerlina:	A'	Vorrei, e non vorrei;	I want to, yet I don't want to;
				Mi tremo un poco il cor.	My heart is trembling a little;
				Felice, è ver, sarei,	It's true, I would be happy,
				Ma può burlarmi ancor.	But he could be joking with me.
0:40	3:57	**Giovanni:**	B	Vieni, mio bel diletto!	Come, my darling!
		Zerlina:		Mi fa pietà Masetto . . .	I'm sorry for Masetto . . .
		Giovanni:		Io cangierò tua sorte!	I shall change your lot!
		Zerlina:		Presto non son più forte . . .	All of a sudden I'm weakening . . .

(repetition of phrases [both verbal and musical] from stanzas 1–3)

1:01	4:18	**Giovanni:**	A″	Vieni, vieni! Là ci darem la mano
		Zerlina:		Vorrei, e non vorrei . . .
		Giovanni:		Là mi dirai di si!
		Zerlina:		Mi trema un poco il cor.
		Giovanni:		Partiam, ben mio, da qui!
		Zerlina:		Ma può burlarmi ancor.
1:28	4:45	**Giovanni:**	coda	Vieni, mio bel diletto!
		Zerlina:		Mi fa pietà Masetto . . .
		Giovanni:		Io cangierò tua sorte!
		Zerlina:		Presto *non son più forte* . . .
		Both:		Andiam!

SECTION 2 Allegro, **6/8** meter

1:57	5:14	**Both:**		Andiam, andiam, mio bene,	Let us go, my dear,
				A ristorar le pene	And relieve the pangs
				D'un innocente amor.	Of an innocent love.

(words and music repeated)

Web: *Research and test your understanding of Classical music genres at* <bedfordstmartins.com/listen>.

GLOBAL PERSPECTIVES 4

Musical Form: Three Case Studies from Asia

As we have seen, musical forms in the Classical style become quite elaborate. It is certainly no accident that these intricate designs emerged across the eighteenth century, just when independent instrumental music was gaining unprecedented prestige in the Western classical tradition. Instrumental music often seems to require such complexities. It is as if the removal of other determinants of form—a poem set to music, a specific religious ritual, or a pattern of dance steps—calls for a different, more abstract musical organization.

If we take the broadest view of these complex forms, however, we can see that they work changes through a simple process. Composers state a tune and then repeat it throughout a movement, joining with it contrasting elements that might be either more complex (sonata form, first-movement concerto form) or simpler (minuet and trio, most rondos and slow movements). Such a basic concept may be realized in myriad ways, according to the imagination and inclination of the composer, resulting in an unlimited array of individual styles.

Many other traditions of instrumental music around the world also start from this simple idea and elaborate it, building intricate forms. In this segment we will take a historical snapshot of three Asian instrumental traditions, from Japan, Indonesia, and India, and then examine music from each.

1. Japan

JAPAN

The European symphony orchestra as we know it emerged in the seventeenth century as a reflection of the power and splendor of various courts (see page 122). In Japan, a court orchestra had been established a thousand years earlier. This was the period in Japanese history, from the sixth century C.E. to the eighth, when the first centralized government of the islands was created. The new Japanese central government, many of its institutions, and even its newly constructed capital city of Nara were modeled on the greatest empire in Asia, China. In the process, many elements of Chinese culture were imported to Japan—most importantly Buddhism, which had in turn been imported to China from India centuries before.

The new Japanese court also imported various musical styles from continental Asia. These were altered and developed into an independent Japanese tradition, which came to play an important role in the court's ceremony and ritual. Altogether, these styles are known as **gagaku** (gáh-gáh-koo), from Chinese characters meaning "elegant music," though their sources are more than just Chinese.

The gagaku repertory is divided into two parts. One, known as *togaku* (tóh-gáh-koo), consists of music derived from Chinese styles (with ingredients from India and Southeast Asia as well). The other, *komagaku* (ko-máh-gáh-koo), is made up of works of Korean and Manchurian origin. Further distinctions are made when gagaku accompanies dance, which is often the case, just as with European Baroque orchestral music.

The Japanese Togaku Orchestra   The togaku orchestra is so distinctive, and so different from any European orchestra, that we should spend a moment getting to know the various instruments. While European orchestras are dominated by strings, all gagaku orchestras feature wind instruments. The instruments all have specific functions:

❧   The sliding, wailing double-reed *hichiriki* (hée-chee-ree-kée) carries the main melody. Several are heard on our recording, playing together.

The togaku orchestra: *kakko, biwa, sho,* and *hichiriki* (back left).

The togaku orchestra: *tsuridaiko* suspended on the large stand, back right, and, in the fore-ground, *gakuso, ryuteki,* and a small suspended gong not heard on our recording, called *shoko.*

⁊ The side-blown flute called *ryuteki* (ree-óo-tay-kée) is the first instrument heard. It plays the melody along with the hichirikis, though in a slightly different version. Thus it produces a *heterophonic* texture with the hichirikis (see page 28); heterophony is an important feature in many non-Western musics.

⁊ The *sho,* a mouth reed-organ with seventeen pipes, plays chordal clusters of tones derived from the main melody. This unusual instrument contributes a haunting background of harmonic haze to the texture.

⁊ The *kakko,* a two-headed barrel drum played with sticks, is used for single strokes or short rolls. It is the first drum heard.

⁊ A deep, larger barrel drum *tsuridaiko* (tzóo-ree-díe-koh; its first beat is heard at 0:13) marks off long phrases of the melody with two successive strokes, the first soft and the second louder.

⁊ A *biwa* or four-stringed lute (bée-wah, first plucked at 1:11) strums across several strings quickly, punctuating the melody.

⁊ A *gakuso,* a zither with thirteen strings (gáh-kóo-so, first heard at 1:31), plays short motives, mainly of three notes related, again, to the melody. Both the biwa and the gakuso take a more active role as this performance proceeds, finally even playing some of the main melody.

Etenraku   *Etenraku* is the most famous piece for the togaku orchestra. Its name means "music of divinity," and it emanates a deep, powerful calm associated with Buddhist contemplation. This is the oldest music on our CD set; its origins reach back almost to the origins of gagaku itself.

The musical form of this piece exhibits three characteristics of gagaku music. *First,* the piece as a whole is constructed from a single melody, according to a predetermined plan and without improvisation. The melody is played through by some of the instruments and punctuated by others, as described above. It consists of three phrases, labeled **a, b,** and **c** in the musical example and Listening Chart on page 214. Each phrase is 32 beats long. The beats move by slowly at first, so slowly that the phrases can be hard to discern; but as you get used to the melody you will be able to follow their repetitions.

Second, the instruments of the orchestra are introduced gradually and in a predetermined order as they fulfill their various functions.

Third, the beat quickens, the meter is more clearly marked, and the general musical activity increases as the performance proceeds. At first, while the flute alone carries the melody, the beats are very slow and flexible—the music seems almost to have no meter at

Sho

Etenraku   8 min., 4 sec.

0:00	a	Ryuteki, kakko, tsuridaiko only
0:51		Sho and hichirikis enter.
1:11	a	Biwa enters.
1:31		Gakuso enters, completing the orchestra.
2:18	b	
3:15	b	
4:04	c	Paired beats of tsuridaiko every 8 beats
4:46	c	Gakuso and biwa gradually play more and more fragments of main melody, joining in heterophony of hichirikis and ryuteki.
5:25	a	
6:02	a	
6:37	b	
7:11	b	After the phrase is completed (at 7:55), biwa and gakuso end the piece with a brief coda.

all. (Each pair of beats on the tsuridaiko drum, however, coming 16 very slow beats after the last, provides a certain sense of regularity and meter.) When the double-reed hichirikis enter, they play the melody along with the flute to a more prominent beat. Then, at the **c** phrases of the melody, the tsuridaiko doubles its pace, beating twice every 8 beats instead of every 16.

Meanwhile the tempo gradually quickens: At the outset the beats come every 2–3 seconds (*very* slow!), while at the close they move by at about one per second.

Even at this relatively quick tempo, the music never loses its sense of restraint. Virtuosic playing is strictly avoided. *Etenraku*'s aura of quiet, inward-looking Buddhist contemplation characterizes the gagaku repertory as a whole.

2.   Indonesia

The Southeast Asian Republic of Indonesia consists of some six thousand islands in all, half of them inhabited. The central island is Java. Across Indonesia, ensembles playing traditional musics thrive—alongside, these days, many kinds of pop, rock, and world beat ensembles, especially in large urban centers such as Jakarta. A traditional musical ensemble in Indonesia is called a **gamelan**.

The Indonesian Orchestra: Gamelan   Gamelans assume a wide, even bewildering variety of shapes and sizes, as we might expect of musical traditions that extend back many centuries and that have served an

Phrase **a**

Phrase **b**

Phrase **c**

array of religious, political, and social functions. Gamelans may involve three or four musicians or they may involve dozens. They may or may not include singers. They frequently accompany drama or dance: sacred temple dances, danced dramas, or the famous Indonesian shadow-puppet plays enacting stories from Hindu epics. The music gamelans play may have been passed down over hundreds of years or it may be recently composed.

At the heart of gamelan music stands a great variety of gongs and **metallophones** (instruments like a xylophone, with metal keys). These make Indonesia the home of the most highly developed of the so-called gong-chime musical cultures prominent throughout Southeast Asia. Indeed the word *gong* itself comes to us from Java, where it names (and also evokes the sound of) the largest gamelan instrument.

Balinese Gamelans Nowhere in Indonesia are gamelans more prevalent than on Bali, a good-sized island to the east of Java. In 1980 it was estimated that there was a gamelan for every 350 inhabitants of the island—a staggering number, in a population of around two million!

Gamelans seem to have come to Bali in the sixteenth century, brought from Java by aristocratic refugees when their Hindu kingdom fell to Islamic invaders from the Asian mainland. Balinese gamelans, at least the elaborate ones with many instruments, were associated especially with temples and princely courts. When Bali came under colonial control of the Netherlands, in 1906, the courts declined, but their traditions of gamelan music did not simply disappear. Instead they were taken over more and more by village gamelan clubs, and these comprise the main venue in which Balinese gamelan music thrives today.

INDONESIA

Gamelan Pelegongan *Gamelan pelegongan*, heard on our recording, is a type of Balinese orchestra used primarily to accompany elaborate dance-dramas. It takes its name from this dance, called *legong*. The primary instruments in gamelan pelegongan are:

⅂ two hand-beaten drums; the drummers direct the ensemble in the manner of a Western orchestra conductor.

⅂ several gongs of varying sizes

⅂ a large group of metallophones, some low-pitched, some high. Most of these have five metal keys each, with a range of a single octave, while some have thirteen keys and a wider range. The sounds, construction,

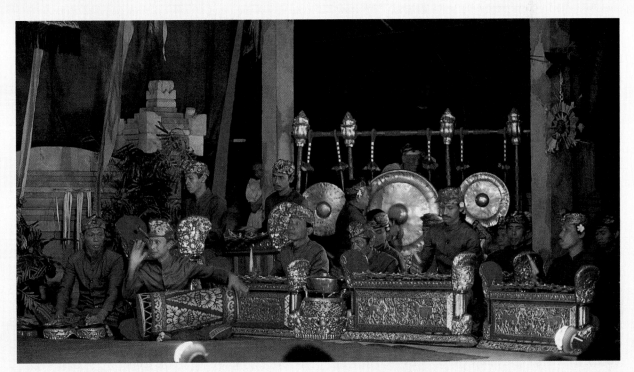

Gamelan pelegongan, with floor gongs, drum, gangsas, and, in the rear, large suspended gongs.

A *legong* dancer and part of the *gamelan pelegongan*: a drum, a small floor gong, and a thirteen-key gangsa are prominent.

and names of these metallophones vary, but all of them can be called by the umbrella term *gangsa,* "bronze."

¶ one or two bamboo flutes. What Western ears might hear as "out of tune-ness" in their playing is a quality recognized and prized by Balinese musicians.

Form in Gamelan Music A traditional piece for gamelan is usually organized around the repetition of a long, symmetrical melody. This melody is made up of smaller, equal phrases, generally 8 or 16 beats long, so that the whole melody will last a multiple of these numbers, especially 64 or 128 beats. A central group of instruments in the gamelan presents this nuclear melody. At the same time it may be played by other instruments in a simpler version, mainly in even note values, creating a heterophonic presentation.

At the end of each statement of the melody, the largest, deepest gong in the orchestra sounds. The unit between one gongstroke and the next, known as a *gongan,* is considered the basic structural unit for the piece. The gongan is divided into smaller units by other instruments in the gamelan: first into two units by a higher-sounding gong, then into four by other gongs, then into eight, and so forth. A 64-beat melody, for example, breaks down audibly into units of 32 beats, 16 beats, 8 beats, 4 beats, and so on.

This process of division continues right through the rhythmic level of the main melody, so that certain instruments elaborate upon its pitches twice as fast, four times as fast, and perhaps even eight times as fast.

The whole texture, then, is an elaborately *stratified* polyphony, with rhythmic layers ranging from the gongan itself all the way down to subdivisions of individual beats. Each instrument or group of instruments plays a single role, occupying one of these rhythmic strata. In the midst of it all is the nuclear melody, presented in one version or simultaneously in distinct versions.

Bopong The piece on our recording, *Bopong,* is not a full dance piece but instead a sort of brief overture, played before the dancing begins. It was composed by I Lotring, a famous Balinese master musician born about 1900 and involved in many stylistic innovations of the 1920s and 1930s.

The 64-beat melody is played through three times; this is the traditional heart of the piece. Before it we hear introductory material, partly based on the main melody. After it comes a lengthy, separate section with an ostinato (see page 132), and then a new concluding melody played by the whole gamelan.

As you listen to the first statement of the nuclear melody itself, from 0:29 to 1:19, *count* the beats,

LISTENING CHART 14

I Lotring, *Bopong*   4 min., 33 sec.

0:00	Introduction: a few gangsas alone
0:04	Gong; introduction continues with fast gangsa figuration
0:29	Gong; **first** statement of melody begins
1:19	Gong; **second** statement of melody
2:06	Gong; **third** statement of melody
2:38	Melody truncated
2:41	Ostinato begins (fourteen times through); gong every eight beats
4:04	Syncopated, unison closing melody
4:20	Final gongstroke

A gamelan at a Balinese funeral. The large array of gongs in the foreground is not found in *gamelan pelegongan*.

counting slightly faster than one beat per second. The melody is 64 beats long and composed of four phrases of 16 beats each. The large gong sounds at the end of the 64-beat cycle.

The core melody, the most prominent melody you hear, is played by some of the gangsas and by two flutes, one high-pitched and one lower and less easy to hear. At the same time other gangsas play a simpler, unadorned version of this melody in slow notes. They are omitted from the beginning of the melody; listen for them starting at 0:42.

Around this melody is woven faster figuration, dividing each beat you count into four, played by a group of brittle-sounding gangsas. They fall silent at the start of each statement of the melody. Then they enter, softly at first, finally asserting themselves with a clamorous outburst (listen for the first instance at

0:58). Such outbursts are a famous hallmark of the newer, post-court styles of Balinese gamelan music.

The third statement of the melody speeds up toward the end but does not quite finish. An entirely new melodic phrase breaks in to start a different section or "movement" of the piece. Beginning at 2:41, some of the gangsas play a single, eight-beat ostinato, repeated many times; other gangsas and the flutes play along with a slightly elaborated version. Meanwhile the brittle-sounding gangsas contribute spectacular figuration, moving eight times as fast as the main beat. The large gong, sounding at the end of every ostinato—hence every eight beats instead of every 64—adds to the feeling of rhythmic climax.

Finally, all this rhythmic energy is channeled into a single closing melody with striking syncopations (see page 13), played in unison by most of the gamelan.

3. India

The classical music of India finds its ancient origins in the singing of the Vedas, sacred writings in Sanskrit from two thousand years ago. Here is another example, along with Christian plainchant and Qur'anic recitation, of sacred chant and its fundamental importance all over the globe (see pages 57 and 70).

Two traditions of Indian music emerged, and diverged, beginning in the thirteenth century: one Hindustani, associated with the Muslim and Hindu regions of north India, and the other Karnatak (or Carnatic), practiced in the mainly Hindu south. Though distinct in many ways, they share many features, the most important of which are *improvisation* and the *rag*. Improvising music—making it up on the spot according to certain prescribed guidelines—is something we know well from jazz but hear less often in Western classical music. (Remember, however, the improvised cadenzas and ornaments of Bach, Mozart, and others.) Improvisation has no place in Japanese gagaku and plays a limited role in Indonesian gamelan music. There is none to speak of in our gamelan pelegongan example. In India, however, it is basic to both classical traditions.

Melody: The Rag   Indian melody is based on the concept of **rag** (or *raga* or *ragam*). A rag is something like a Western scale, only much more: It is really a comprehensive kit or set of guidelines for producing melody. Each rag specifies not only a scale, but also a hierarchy of more and less important pitches, certain melodic gestures associated with those pitches, ways of ascending and descending the scale, characteristic patterns of ornamentation, and even snatches of melody used to improvise variations.

Rags carry broader implications also. They are felt to express particular emotional states and are associated with specific times of the day or seasons of the year. Indian musicians spend years mastering both the subtleties of technique and the "character" of rags. The best of them can improvise complex, beautiful, appropriate, and distinct melodies out of dozens of different rags.

The texture of Indian classical music is in principle monophonic. But a simple notion of monophony hardly does justice to what we hear in this music. In the first place, several resonant, continuous drone pitches sound against the melody. Second, the melody might be simultaneously presented by two instruments, or voice and instrument, in a loosely synchronized fashion; this creates a heterophonic texture. In addition, the melody unfolds most of the time in carefully prescribed interaction with complicated metrical patterns played by a drummer.

A Hindustani Ensemble   The typical north Indian performance ensemble consists of one instrument that carries the main melody—on our recording the most famous Indian melodic instrument today, the *sitar*, a long-necked lute with a characteristic buzzing, almost

The joy of dueling sitars: Ravi Shankar plays with his daughter Anoushka.

metallic resonance. (A lute is a plucked stringed instrument something like a guitar; see page 45.)

A second melodic instrument, as we have noted, may interact with the first in constructing the melody. In our performance this is the *sarod,* another lutelike instrument sounding less metallic than the sitar and a bit closer to an acoustic guitar. Yet another type of lute, a *tambura,* plays no melody but supplies the drone pitches.

Finally, a drummer plays *tabla,* two small, hand-beaten drums. These have very different sounds: one rather like a bongo drum, the other deep, with a sliding *whoop* to its tone.

A Performance of Rag Mauj-Khammaj   In the most famous and esteemed instrumental performances of rags, the musicians start from a tune, like the European, Japanese, and Indonesian musicians we have studied. The tune may be relatively fixed and unimprovised or freer, depending on the rag. Our rag, named *Mauj-Khammaj,* has a fixed melody.

Around this tune, the instrumentalists spin out a long, continuous performance that falls into several connected "movements" marked by different styles and tempos. The movements always involve much improvisation, but at the same time they develop according to broad outlines. (Vocalists perform several different genres of song based on rags, also according to elaborate guidelines.) Knowledgeable listeners savor the skill of the musicians for their adherence to the features of the particular rag performed, for their virtuosic elaborations of them, and for their gradual and skillful presentation of this multimovement form.

A performance such as this can last as long as an hour. We choose two excerpts from a condensed rag performance, excerpts that will help us understand the rag's multimovement format. The rag is played, in a spirit of friendly, virtuosic rivalry, by two of the most renowned Indian musicians of the twentieth century, Ravi Shankar on sitar and Ali Akhbar Khan on sarod. They are accompanied by tambura and tabla.

Excerpt 1   An **alap**—the first movement—opens the performance, without any clear meter. The drums do not play at all. The sarod and sitar begin to alternate phrases in a free, dreamy exploration of the rag's pitches and associated melodic gestures. Toward the end of the alap, the rhythmic activity quickens, but there is still no clear meter. (In a full performance, this leads to subsections of the alap, each quicker than the last and each announcing to the audience another stage of the musical form.) Finally, at 3:32, the sitar begins

---

LISTENING CHART 15

Rag *Mauj-Khammaj*   7 min., 15 sec.   28, 29

First excerpt

0:00   **Alap:** tambura, then sarod, then sitar

3:15   Rhythms quicken as the alap ends.

3:32   **First gat:** tune played by sitar and sarod in heterophony; tabla enter.

Second excerpt

0:23   Tempo quickens as **second gat** begins.

0:35   Tune from the first gat returns, faster.

---

a metrical melody and the sarod joins in. Quickly, the tabla player begins as well, marking a regular beat with complex rhythmic patterns.

This shift to metrical music marks the beginning of the second movement, the first **gat** (pronounced *gut*). In a moderate tempo, the first gat now introduces the basic tune of *Mauj-Khammaj.* Free variations on the tune follow, improvised according to the rag guidelines.

Excerpt 2   Our second excerpt picks up near the end of the first gat. At 0:23 the tempo quickens slightly, marking the beginning of the second gat, always faster than the first. If you listen closely, you will hear that the second gat begins with an up-tempo version of the melody that began the first. The tune basic to the rag introduces both metered movements. The quicker tempo results in especially dazzling improvisations by the sitar and sarod as well as the tabla. The pace continues to speed up through the second gat, bringing the performance, which ends after our excerpt, to a spectacular close.

One more, general point: We saw this same gradual quickening of tempo in Japanese gagaku, but without the flashy spirit of the Indian performance. If we think about it, indeed, this tendency to move faster and faster across a lengthy work applies to the European Classical genres we have studied: All save the fastest for last. There is, apparently, something deeply ingrained and satisfying about speeding up across a performance; perhaps it is the release of energy involved for both listeners and performers. It is a trait of countless musical repertories across the globe.

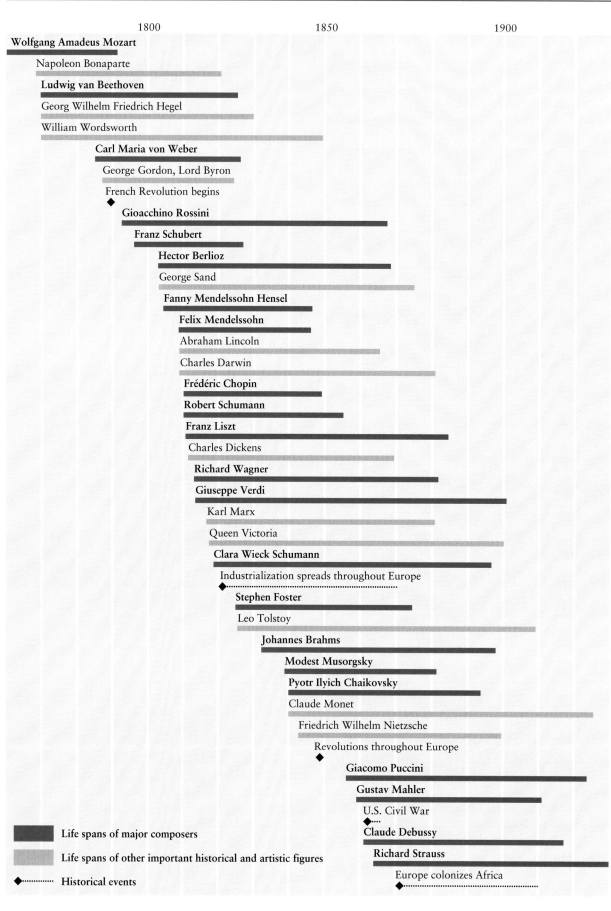

1800   1850   1900

Wolfgang Amadeus Mozart

Napoleon Bonaparte

Ludwig van Beethoven

Georg Wilhelm Friedrich Hegel

William Wordsworth

Carl Maria von Weber

George Gordon, Lord Byron

French Revolution begins ◆

Gioacchino Rossini

Franz Schubert

Hector Berlioz

George Sand

Fanny Mendelssohn Hensel

Felix Mendelssohn

Abraham Lincoln

Charles Darwin

Frédéric Chopin

Robert Schumann

Franz Liszt

Charles Dickens

Richard Wagner

Giuseppe Verdi

Karl Marx

Queen Victoria

Clara Wieck Schumann

Industrialization spreads throughout Europe ◆········

Stephen Foster

Leo Tolstoy

Johannes Brahms

Modest Musorgsky

Pyotr Ilyich Chaikovsky

Claude Monet

Friedrich Wilhelm Nietzsche

Revolutions throughout Europe ◆

Giacomo Puccini

Gustav Mahler

U.S. Civil War ◆····

Claude Debussy

Richard Strauss

Europe colonizes Africa ◆·············

Life spans of major composers

Life spans of other important historical and artistic figures

◆············ Historical events

The Nineteenth Century

I n Unit IV we take up music of the nineteenth century. Starting with the towering figure of Beethoven in the first quarter of the century, famous names now crowd the history of music: Schubert, Schumann, Chopin, Wagner, Verdi, Brahms, Chaikovsky, Mahler, and others. Nearly everyone, whether conscious of it or not, knows a fair amount of music by these masters, or at least some of their melodies. These tend to turn up as background music to movies and television; some of them are metamorphosed into pop tunes and advertising sound tracks.

The appeal of this music today in the symphony hall and the opera house, the classroom and the teaching studio, seems to rest on much the same grounds as those governing its great success a hundred years ago and more. It is important to realize, first of all, that nineteenth-century music was a great success story. For the first time in European history, music was taken entirely seriously as an art on the highest level. Composers were accorded a new, exalted role, to which they responded magnificently, writing music that sounds important and impressive; and listeners ever since have been thoroughly impressed.

Music and Individual Emotion

Music's prestige, in the Romantic scheme of things, derived first and foremost from the belief that music more than any other art mirrors one's inner emotional life. Music, then, should have a unique power to convey individual feeling. Again, composers rose to the challenge. Nineteenth-century music is more direct and unrestrained in emotional quality than the music of any earlier time. And for most audiences, full-blooded emotion in music—even exaggerated emotion—seems never to lose its powerful attraction.

The individuality of all artists, including composers, was accorded special value in the nineteenth century. Composers produced music with much more pronounced personal attributes than in the late Baroque period or the Classical period (when many pieces by Haydn and Mozart, for example, sounded rather similar in character). It is therefore a natural tendency to think of the history of nineteenth-century music in terms of great names, *such as those in the list given above. The prospect of getting to know all these distinct, unusual, and probably fascinating characters—meeting them, as it were, under the emotional conditions of Romantic music—surely contributes to the appeal of this particular body of music. And since the Romantic composers have such strong distinct personalities, it is not only natural but inevitable to find oneself drawn to certain of these individuals, and put off by others. There are music lovers who recoil from Wagner. Others cherish Schubert above even Beethoven and Bach.*

Like eighteenth-century music, music of the nineteenth century is not stylistically homogeneous, yet it can still be regarded as a larger historical unit. We shall take up the Romantic style, usually dated from the 1820s, after discussing the music of Beethoven, who was born in 1770 and as a young man traveled twice to Vienna, the city of Classicism—first to meet Mozart and then to study with Haydn.

But while in technique Beethoven was clearly a child of the eighteenth century, in his emotionalism, his artistic ambition, and his insistence on individuality he was a true inhabitant of the nineteenth. Indeed, Beethoven was the model, either direct or indirect, for many of the great nineteenth-century composers who came after him. Understanding Beethoven is the key to understanding Romantic music.

CHAPTER 14

Beethoven

If any single composer deserves a special chapter in the history of music, that composer is Ludwig van Beethoven (1770–1827). Probably no other figure in the arts meets with such a strong universal response. People may pity van Gogh, respect Michelangelo and Shakespeare, and admire Leonardo da Vinci, but Beethoven instantly summons up a powerful, positive image: that of the tough, ugly, angry genius staring down adversity and delivering himself of one deeply expressive masterpiece after another. Beethoven's music has enjoyed broad-based, uninterrupted popularity from his own day to the present. Today its place is equally secure with unsophisticated listeners and with the most learned musicians.

There is a sense, furthermore, in which music may be said to have come of age with Beethoven. For despite the great music that came before him—that of Bach, Mozart, and many other composers we know—the art of music was never taken so seriously until Beethoven's symphonies and sonatas struck listeners of his time as a revelation. They were almost equally impressed by the facts of his life, in particular his deafness, the affliction that caused him to retire from a career as a performing musician and become solely a composer.

A new concept of artistic genius was evolving at the time, and Beethoven crystallized this concept powerfully for his own age. He still exemplifies it today. No longer a mere craftsman, the artist suffers and creates; endowed not just with greater talent but with a greater soul than ordinary mortals, the artist suffers and creates for humanity. Music is no longer merely a function of bodily parts like the ear or the fingers. It exists in the highest reaches of the artist's spirit.

There is much to be done on earth, do it soon!

I cannot carry on the everyday life I am living; art demands this sacrifice too. Rest, diversion, amusement—only so that I can function more powerfully in my art.

From Beethoven's journal, 1814

1 Between Classicism and Romanticism

Beethoven is special in another sense, in the unique position he occupies between the eighteenth-century Viennese Classical style and nineteenth-century Romanticism. Beethoven's roots were firmly Classical. He was a student of Haydn when the latter was at the height of his fame. Beethoven remained committed to the principles of the Classical style until the end of his life.

Beethoven was committed to the *principles* of Classicism—but not to every one of its manifestations, and certainly not to the mood behind it. There is almost always a sense of excitement, urgency, and striving in Beethoven's music that makes it instantly distinguishable from that of Haydn and Mozart. These qualities emerged in response to Romantic stirrings that are the subject of our next chapter.

The French Revolution

Romanticism, as we shall see, was originally a literary movement. Though well under way by the beginning of the nineteenth century, it was not yet influential in Vienna; and, in any case, Beethoven did not have a very literary sensibility. At the root of Romanticism, however, there lay one great political event that made an enormous impact on the composer's generation. This was the French Revolution. Beethoven was one of many artists who felt compelled to proclaim their sympathy with the ideal of freedom symbolized by that cataclysmic event.

When the Parisian crowd stormed the Bastille in 1789, Beethoven was a highly impressionable eighteen-year-old, already grounded in liberal and humanistic ideals. More than a decade later, Beethoven's admiration for Napoleon Bonaparte as hero of the revolution led him to an extravagant and unprecedented gesture—writing a descriptive symphony called *Bonaparte*. Retitled the *Eroica* (Heroic) Symphony, it was the decisive "breakthrough" work of Beethoven's maturity, the first work to show his full individual freedom as an artist.

Before Beethoven could send the symphony to Paris, Napoleon crowned himself Emperor of France. Liberal Europe saw this as a betrayal of the revolution, and Beethoven scratched out the title in a fury. But idealism dies hard. To Beethoven, and to many of his contemporaries, the French Revolution still stood for an ideal of perfectibility—not so much of human society (as

Storming the Bastille, a contemporary engraving of the most famous event of the French Revolution.

The revolution betrayed: Napoleon's coronation as Emperor of France in 1803, as portrayed by Jacques-Louis David (1748–1825), the greatest practitioner of Neoclassical art (see page 169). Today this huge (20 by 30 feet) and pompous painting repels some viewers as much as the actual event it depicts enraged Beethoven.

Beethoven himself acknowledged by deleting Napoleon's name) as of human aspiration. That ideal, too, is what Beethoven realized by his own triumph over his deafness. The point was not lost on those of his contemporaries who were swept away by his music.

And that is what listeners have responded to ever since. Listening to the *Eroica* Symphony, we sense that it has less to do with Napoleon than with the composer's own self-image. The quality of heroic striving and inner triumph is what emerges so magnificently in Beethoven's most famous compositions.

2 Beethoven and the Symphony

As we have said, what sets Beethoven instantly apart from Haydn or Mozart is his mood of excitement and urgency. This he achieved by maximizing virtually all musical elements. Higher and lower registers, sharper syncopations, stronger accents, harsher dissonances yielding to more profound resolutions— all of these are found in Beethoven's music. He made new demands on instruments, expanded the orchestra, and stretched Classical forms to their limits.

Given all this, it is not surprising that this composer should be especially associated with the symphony, the most "public" of Classical genres, with the greatest range of expression, variety, and sheer volume. In fact, Beethoven wrote fewer symphonies (nine) than piano sonatas (thirty-two) or string quartets

His clothes were very ordinary and not in the least in the customary style of those days, especially in our circles. . . . He was very proud; I have seen Countess Thun, the mother of Princess Lichnowsky, on her knees before him begging him to play something—and he would not. But then, Countess Thun was a very eccentric woman.

An old lady remembers the young Beethoven (1867)

Ludwig van Beethoven (1770–1827)

Beethoven, like Mozart, followed his father as a court musician; the Beethovens served the archbishop-elector of Bonn in West Germany. But Ludwig's father—unlike Wolfgang's—was a failure and an alcoholic who beat the boy to make him practice. A trip to Vienna to make contacts (he hoped to study with Mozart) was cut short by the death of his mother. Still in his teens, Beethoven had to take charge of his family because of his father's drinking.

Nonetheless, Bonn was an "enlightened" court, ruled by the brother of the liberal Emperor Joseph II of Austria. The talented young musician had an opportunity to mix with aristocrats and intellectuals. The idealism that is so evident in Beethoven's later works—such as his Ninth Symphony, ending with a choral hymn to universal brotherhood—can be traced to this early environment.

Compared to Mozart, Beethoven was a slow developer, but by the age of twenty-two he had made enough of an impression to receive a sort of fellowship to return to Vienna, this time to study with Haydn. He was soon acclaimed as a powerful virtuoso pianist, playing his own compositions and improvising brilliantly at the palaces of the music-loving aristocracy of that city. He remained in Vienna until his death.

After the age of thirty, he became progressively deaf—a devastating fate for a musician, which kept him from making a living in the traditional manner, by performing. The crisis that this caused in Beethoven's life is reflected by a strange, moving document (called the "Heiligenstadt Testament," after the town where it was written, in 1802) that is half a proclamation of artistic ideals, half suicide note. But Beethoven overcame his depression and in 1803 wrote the first of his truly powerful and individual symphonies, the Third (Eroica).

Beethoven all but demanded support from the nobility in Vienna, who were awed by his extraordinarily forceful and original music as well as by his uncompromising character. An alarmingly brusque and strong-willed person, he suffered deeply and seemed to live for his art alone. His domestic life was chaotic; one anecdote has him pouring water over himself to cool off in summer and being asked by his landlord to leave. (He changed lodgings an average of once a year.) By the end of his life he was well known in Vienna as an eccentric, teased by street boys.

Probably the first musician to make a career solely from composing, Beethoven was regarded as a genius even in his lifetime. He had an immense need to receive and to give affection, yet he never married, despite various love affairs. After he died, passionate letters to a woman identified only as his "Immortal Beloved" were found; we now know she was the wife of a Frankfurt merchant, both members of Beethoven's circle. In his later years Beethoven adopted his own orphan nephew, but his attitude was so overprotective and his love so smothering that the boy could not stand it and attempted suicide.

Beethoven had always lived with ill health, and the shock of this new family crisis hastened his death. Twenty thousand attended his funeral; his eulogy was written, and delivered at the funeral, by Vienna's leading poet.

Taste in many matters has changed many times since Beethoven's lifetime, but his music has always reigned supreme with audiences and critics. The originality and expressive power of his work seem never to fade.

Chief Works: Nine symphonies, the most famous being the Third (Eroica), Fifth, Sixth (Pastoral), Seventh, and Ninth (Choral) ▪ The opera Fidelio (originally called Leonore), for which he wrote four different overtures; overtures to the plays Egmont, by Goethe, and Coriolanus ▪ Violin Concerto and five piano concertos, including the Emperor (No. 5) ▪ 16 string quartets ▪ 32 piano sonatas, including the Pathétique, Waldstein, Appassionata, and the late-period Hammerklavier Sonata ▪ Mass in D (Missa solemnis)

Encore: After Symphony No. 5, listen to the "Moonlight" Sonata; Sonata in A-flat, Op. 110; Symphonies No. 6 and 9.

(sixteen)—and no musician would rank these works any lower than the symphonies. But at the height of his career, from around 1800 to 1810, even many of his piano sonatas and string quartets sound like symphonies. The torrents of sound Beethoven summoned up in these works demanded whole new techniques of piano and string playing.

We can approach Beethoven's "symphonic ideal" through his Fifth Symphony, written in 1808. Three main features of this work have impressed generations of listeners: its rhythmic drive, its motivic consistency or unity, and the sense it gives of a definite psychological progression. The first feature is apprehended at once, the second by the end of the opening movement, and the third only after we have experienced all four of the symphony's movements.

❡   *Rhythmic drive.* Immediately apparent is the drive and blunt power of the rhythmic style. Beethoven hammers the meter, piles accent upon accent, and calculates long time spans with special power: a far cry from the elegance and wit of the Classical style.

❡   *Motivic consistency.* During the first movement of the Fifth Symphony, a single motive is heard constantly, in many different forms. They are not random forms; the motive becomes more and more vivid and significant as the work proceeds. People have marveled at the "organic" quality of such music, which seems to them to grow like a plant's leaves out of a simple seed.

❡   *Psychological progression.* Over the course of the Fifth Symphony's four movements, Beethoven seems to trace a coherent and dramatic psychological progression in several stages. "There Fate knocks at the door!" he is supposed to have said about the first movement—but after two eventful middle stages, Fate is nullified in the last movement, trampled under by a military march.

In Beethoven's hands, the multimovement symphony seems to trace an inspirational life process, one so basic and universal that it leaves few listeners unmoved. This was, perhaps, the greatest of all his forward-looking innovations.

The Scherzo

Another of Beethoven's technical innovations should also be mentioned. On the whole, Beethoven continued to use Classical forms for his symphonies and other multimovement works. As early as his Second Symphony, however, he substituted another kind of movement for the traditional minuet.

This was the **scherzo** (*scairtzo*), a fast, rushing movement in triple meter—inherited from the minuet—and in the basic minuet-and-trio form, **A B A**. With their fast tempo, Beethoven's scherzos sometimes need more repetitions to make their point; **A B A** is sometimes extended to **A B A B A**.

The word *scherzo* means "joke" in Italian. Beethoven's brand of humor is very different from, say, Haydn's: It is broad, brusque, jocular, even violent. Originally associated with the court of Louis XIV, the minuet at the time of the French Revolution still stood for eighteenth-century formality and elegance; one can see why Beethoven rejected it. The scherzo became an ideal vehicle for Beethoven's characteristic rhythmic drive. See page 234.

LUDWIG VAN BEETHOVEN (1770–1827)
Symphony No. 5 in C Minor, Op. 67 (1808)

Beethoven composed his Fifth Symphony together with his Sixth *(Pastoral)* for one of the rare concerts in which he showcased his own works. This concert, in December 1808, was a huge success, even though it lasted for five hours and the heating in the hall failed.

First Movement (Allegro con brio)   Motivic consistency, as we have said, is a special feature of Beethoven's work. The first movement of the Fifth Symphony is dominated by a single rhythmic motive, ♪♪♪ ♩ . This motive forms the first theme in the exposition; it initiates the bridge; it appears as a subdued

Beethoven striding through Vienna: a caricature by one of his contemporaries.

background to the lyrical, contrasting second theme; and it emerges again in the cadence material:

The motive then expands further in the development section and continues growing in the long coda.

How is this different from Classical motivic technique? In such works as Mozart's Symphony No. 40, a single motive is likewise developed with consistency and a sense of growth. But Beethoven's use of the same device—the use of a Classical device for non-Classical ends—gives the Fifth Symphony its particular gripping urgency. The difference is not in the basic technique but in the way it is being used—in the expressive intensity it is made to serve. Let us see how this works.

Exposition   The movement begins with an arresting presentation of the first theme, in the key of C minor (shown above). The meter is disrupted by two fermatas (see page 14), which give the music an improvisational, primal quality, like a great shout. Even after the theme rushes on and seems to be picking up momentum, it is halted by a new fermata, making three fermatas in all.

The horn-call bridge (see above) performs the usual function of a bridge in an unusually dramatic way. That function is to cement the new key—a major key—firmly and usher in the second theme with power and authority.

The second theme introduces a new gentle mood, despite the main motive rumbling away below it. But this mood soon fades—Beethoven seems to brush it aside impatiently. The main motive bursts out again in a stormy cadence passage, which comes to a satisfying, complete stop. The exposition is repeated.

Development   The development section starts with a new shout, as the first theme makes an immediate modulation, a modulation back to the minor mode. There is yet another fermata. It sounds like the crack of doom.

For a time the first theme (or, rather, its continuation) is developed, leading to a climax when the ♩♩♩♩ rhythm multiplies itself furiously, as shown to the right. Next comes the bridge theme, modulating through one key after another. Suddenly the *two middle pitches* of the bridge theme are extracted and echoed between high wind instruments and lower strings. This process is called **fragmentation** (for an example from Mozart, see page 183). The two-note figure breaks apart, and the echoing process focuses on just one note:

Went to a German charitable concert [the American premiere of Beethoven's Fifth Symphony]. . . . The music was good, very well selected and excellently well performed, as far as I could judge. The crack piece, though, was the last, Beethoven's Sinfonia in C minor. It was generally unintelligible to me, except the Andante.

Diary of a New York music lover, 1841

LISTENING CHART 16

Beethoven, Symphony No. 5 in C Minor, first movement

Sonata form. 7 min., 18 sec.

3 6-14   **2** 1-9

EXPOSITION

6 1	0:00	**Theme 1**	Main theme with *two fermatas,* followed by the *first continuation* (based on ♪♪♪ 𝅗𝅥); *another fermata (the third)*
	0:20		Main motive (♪♪♪ 𝅗𝅥), *ff,* is followed by a *second continuation:* timpani, crescendo
7 2	0:46	**Bridge theme**	French horn, *f*

Second Group

0:02	0:48	**Theme 2**	Major mode, *p,* strings and woodwinds (♪♪♪ 𝅗𝅥 in background)
8 3	1:17	**Cadence theme**	Based on ♪♪♪ 𝅗𝅥 motive
0:05	1:22		CADENCE
0:09	1:26	*Exposition repeated*	

DEVELOPMENT

9 4	2:52		First modulation, using ♪♪♪ 𝅗𝅥 motive; French horns, *ff;* minor mode
0:05	2:57		Development of *first continuation* of theme 1
0:29	3:21		Climactic passage of powerful reiterations: ♪♪♪ | ♪♪♪♪ | ♪♪♪♪ | 𝅗𝅥
0:36	3:28		Development of bridge theme
10 5	3:39		Fragmentation of bridge theme to two notes, alternating between strings and winds
0:09	3:48		Fragmentation of bridge theme to one note, alternating between strings and winds, *p*
0:29	4:08	**Retransition**	Based on ♪♪♪ 𝅗𝅥, *ff,* runs directly into the recapitulation

RECAPITULATION

11 6	4:13	**Theme 1**	Harmonized; *two fermatas. First continuation* of theme; woodwind background
0:18	4:31		*Slow oboe cadenza in place of the third fermata*
0:33	4:46		*Second continuation of* theme 1
0:53	5:06	**Bridge theme**	Bassoons, *f*

Second Group

12 7	5:09	**Theme 2**	Strings and winds, *p* (♪♪♪ 𝅗𝅥 in timpani); major mode
0:33	5:42	**Cadence theme**	This time it does not stop.

CODA

13 8	5:49		Another climax of reiterations (as in the development)
0:15	6:04		Returns to the minor mode. New expanded version of bridge theme, in counterpoint with new scale figure
0:30	6:19		New marchlike theme, brass; winds and strings build up
14 9	6:51		Theme 1: climactic presentation in brass. *Last fermatas*
0:08	6:59		*First continuation* of theme 1, with a pathetic coloration; oboe and bassoon figures
0:13	7:04		Strong conclusion on ♪♪♪ 𝅗𝅥

Beethoven is famous for the tension he builds up in retransitions, the sections in sonata form that prepare for the recapitulations (see page 181). In the Fifth Symphony, the hush at this point becomes almost unbearable. Finally the whole orchestra seems to grab and shake the listener by the lapels, shouting the main motive again and again until the first theme settles out in the original tonic key.

Recapitulation   The exposition version of the main theme was jolted by three fermatas. Now, in the recapitulation, the third fermata is filled by a slow, expressive passage for solo oboe, a sort of cadenza in free rhythm. This extraordinary moment provides a brief rest from the incessant rhythmic drive. Otherwise the recapitulation stays very close to the exposition—a clear testimony to Beethoven's Classical allegiance.

Coda   On the other hand, the action-packed coda that follows is an equally clear testimony to Beethoven's freedom from Classical formulas.

In the exposition, we recall, the stormy cadence passage had been defused by a satisfying "Classical" cadence and a complete stop. At the end of the recapitulation, the parallel passage seems to reject any such easy solution. Instead, after a violent climax reminiscent of the development section, a new contrapuntal idea appears:

STRINGS, FRENCH HORNS

Compare the bottom contrapuntal line of this example with the first theme, as shown on page 228. Here the four main-theme *pitches* (G E♭ F D) are played in the bridge *rhythm* (♪♪♪| ♩♩| ♩), so that GGG–E♭ FFF–D becomes GGG–E♭ F D. Then the two middle notes E♭ and F—the common ground between the themes—are emphasized by a long downward sequence.

The sequence evolves into a sort of grim minor-mode march—a moment of respite from the endless thematic evolutions of the main motive. A final appearance of the original theme leads this time to continuations that are unexpectedly poignant. But the very end of the movement consists of affirmative, defiant-sounding cadences, built once again out of the main motive.

The Remaining Movements   The defiant-sounding final cadence of the first movement feels like a standoff at the end of a heroic struggle. Beethoven now builds on this feeling to give the impression of a dramatic psychological progression, another characteristic feature of his symphonic writing.

The later movements of the Fifth Symphony feel like responses to—and, ultimately, a resolution of—all the tension Beethoven had summoned up in the first movement. We are never allowed to forget the first movement and its mood, not until the very end of the symphony, mainly because a form of the first movement's rhythmic *motive*, ♪♪♪♩, is heard in each of the later movements. This motive always stirs uneasy recollections. Furthermore, the later movements all refer to the *key* of the first movement. Whenever this key returns in its original minor mode (C minor), it inevitably recalls the struggle that Beethoven associated with "Fate knocking at the door." When it returns in the major mode (C major), it signifies (or foretells) the ultimate resolution of all that tension—the triumph over Fate.

A New Year's card from Beethoven to Baroness Ertmann, one of many women with whom his name has been romantically linked.

You need not worry about recognizing C major or distinguishing it from any other major-mode key. Almost any time you hear a very loud, triumphant theme in the later movements, it is in the key of C major. As important as the melody of those themes and their orchestration (often with brass) is the fact that they come in C major, thus negating the first movement's struggle.

A special abbreviated Listening Chart for the entire symphony is provided on page 233. All the C-major sections are indicated.

Second Movement (Andante con moto)   The first hint of Beethoven's master plan comes early in the slow movement, after the cellos have begun with a graceful theme, which is rounded off by repeated cadences. A second placid theme commences, but is soon derailed by a grinding modulation—to C major, where the second theme starts again, blared out by the trumpets, *ff*.

This shattering fanfare or near-fanfare fades almost immediately into a mysterious passage where the ♪♪♪♩ rhythm of the first movement sounds quietly. Beethoven is not ready to resolve the C-minor turmoil of the first movement just yet. Variations of the first theme follow (one is in the minor mode), but there is something aimless about them. What stays in the memory from this movement are two more enormous brass fanfares in C major.

Third Movement (Allegro)   This movement, in **3/4** time, is one of Beethoven's greatest scherzos (though the composer did not label it as such, probably because its form is so free). There are two features of the smooth, quiet opening theme (**a**) that immediately recall the mood of the first movement—but in a more muted, apprehensive form. One is the key, C minor. The other is the interruption of the meter by fermatas.

Then a very forceful second theme (**b**), played by the French horns, recalls in its turn the first movement's rhythmic motive. The two themes alternate and modulate restlessly, until the second makes a final-sounding cadence.

When now a bustling and somewhat humorous fugal section starts in the major mode—in C major—we may recognize a vestige of the old minuet and trio form, **A B A** (though the **A** section, with its two sharply contrasted themes **a** and **b**, has nothing in common with a minuet beyond its triple meter). **B**, the major-mode "trio," is in the traditional |: c :| |: d c':| form, but with an important modification. The second **d c′** is reorchestrated, becoming quieter and quieter.

After this, the opening minor-mode music, **A′**, returns quietly—almost stealthily—with the tone color transformed. Hushed *pizzicato* (plucked) strings for **a** and a brittle-sounding oboe for **b** replace the smooth and forceful sounds heard before. Everything now breathes a quite unexpected mood of mystery.

Fourth Movement (Allegro)   The point of this reorchestration appears when the section does not reach a cadence but runs into a doubly mysterious transition passage, with timpani tapping out the rhythm of **b** over a strange harmony. The music grows louder and clearer until a forceful military march erupts—in the key, needless to say, of C major.

Minor cedes to major, *pp* to *ff*, mystery to clarity; the arrival of this symphony's last movement has the literal effect of triumph over some sort of adversity. This last movement brings in three trombones for the first time in the symphony. (They must have really awakened the freezing listeners at that original 1808 concert.)

The march turns out to be the first theme of a sonata-form movement; the second theme includes a speeded-up version of the ♪♪♪♩ rhythm, with a

First movement:

Third movement (**b**):

slower, upward-stepping bass which will drive the development section. The bridge and the cadence theme are wonderfully gutsy. The end of the development offers another example of Beethoven's inspired manipulation of musical form. The second theme (**b**) of the previous movement, the scherzo, comes back quietly once again, a complete surprise in these surroundings (there is even a change from the **4/4** meter of the march back to **3/4**). This theme now sounds neither forceful nor mysterious, as it did in the scherzo, but rather like a dim memory. Perhaps it has come back to re-mind us that the battle has been won.

All that remains is a great C-major cele-bration, in the recapitulation and then later in a huge accelerating coda. "There Fate knocks at the door"—but fate and terror alike yield to Beethoven's optimistic major-mode vision.

A modern impression of Beethoven in his later years. The artist has cap-tured both the famous scowl of defiance, and also the chaotic state of Beethoven's household—the broken piano strings, the sheets of musical sketches all over the place, and the useless ear trumpets.

3 Beethoven's "Third Period"

Beethoven's output is traditionally divided into three style periods. The first period (until 1800, in round numbers) covers music building on the style of Haydn and Mozart. The middle period contains characteristically "heroic" works like the *Eroica* and Fifth Symphonies.

In the third period (from around 1818 to 1827) Beethoven's music loses much of its earlier tone of heroism. It becomes more abstract, introspective, and serene, and tends to come framed in more intimate genres than the sym-phony, such as the piano sonata and the string quartet. (However, Beethoven's mightiest symphony, the Ninth, also dates from this period.) His control of contrast and musical flow becomes more potent than ever, and a new freedom of form leads to a range of expression that can only be called miraculous. All the strength of his earlier music seems to be encompassed together with a new gentleness and spirituality.

While disruption was always a feature of Beethoven's music—think of the fermatas in the first movement of the Fifth Symphony, and the C-major trum-pets in the second—now the breaks and breaches in the musical fabric can be almost frightening. At any rate, they proved incomprehensible in his own time and for many years thereafter. Today these features seem if anything to in-crease the power of Beethoven's late music.

LUDWIG VAN BEETHOVEN
String Quartet in F, Op. 135, second movement (Vivace) (1826)

Three blind mice, see how they run. The tiny and very quiet **a** phrase in this extraordinary movement skitters through the pitches A (three), G (blind), and F (mice) nearly thirty times before the piece is over.

Phrase **b,** consisting of just two pitches, is even simpler. Pitch-wise, it contrasts with **a,** but resembles it in its constant use of syncopation (see the

LISTENING CHART 17

Beethoven, Symphony No. 5 in C Minor (complete work)

31 min., 31 sec.

3 6-20   2 1-15

	FIRST MOVEMENT (Allegro con brio, 2/4; sonata form)		C minor, *ff*	
	See Listening Chart 16.			
15 **10**	**SECOND MOVEMENT** (Andante, 3/8; variations)		A♭ major, *p*	
	0:00 **Theme 1**	Ends with repeated cadences		
	1:03 **Theme 2**	Played by clarinets and bassoons		
	1:26	Trumpets enter	(goes to C MAJOR, *ff*)	
	2:12 **Theme 1**	Variation 1, played by strings		
	3:06 **Theme 2**	Clarinets and bassoons		
	3:29	Trumpets enter	(goes to C MAJOR, *ff*)	
	4:16 **Theme 1**	Variations 2–4 (without repeated cadences), ending *f*; then a long, quiet transition: woodwinds		
16 **11**	6:13 **Theme 2**	Trumpets	C MAJOR, *ff*	
	6:59 **Theme 1**	Variations 5 (minor; woodwinds) and 6 (full orchestra); cadences		
:30	8:29 **Coda**		A♭ major	
	THIRD MOVEMENT (Allegro, 3/4; A B A′)		C minor, *pp*	
	Scherzo (A)			
17 **12**	0:00 **a b**			
	0:40 **a′ b′**			
	1:21 **a″ b″**	Ends with a loud cadence built from **b**		
	Trio (B)		C MAJOR, *ff*	
18 **13**	1:52 |: **c** :|	Fugal		
:33	2:25 **d c′**			
:03	2:55 **d c′**	*Reorchestrated, p*; runs into scherzo (goes back to C minor, *pp*)		
	Scherzo (A′)			
:37	3:29	Scherzo repeated, shorter and *reorchestrated, pp*		
:54	4:46 **Transition**	Timpani; leads directly into the fourth movement		
			(goes to C MAJOR, *ff*)	
	FOURTH MOVEMENT (Allegro, 2/2; sonata form)		C MAJOR, *ff*	
	Exposition			
19 **14**	0:00 Theme 1	March theme		
	0:34 Bridge theme	Low horns and bassoons		
	1:00 Theme 2			
	1:27 Cadence theme			
	Development			
	1:57	Development begins; modulation		
	2:02	Theme 2 and its bass developed		
20 **15**	3:31 **Retransition**	Recall of the scherzo (**A′, 3/4** meter)	(recall of C minor, *pp*)	
	Recapitulation		C MAJOR *ff*	
:32	4:03 Theme 1			
:07	4:38 Bridge theme			
:36	5:07 Theme 2			
:02	5:33 Cadence theme			
	Coda			
:30	6:01	Coda; three sections, accelerating; uses parts of the bridge, cadence theme, and theme 1	C MAJOR, *ff*	

ff

p

f   TRUMPETS

a   CELLOS

p

b   FRENCH HORNS

f

c   DOUBLE BASSES

f   fugue subject

with TROMBONES

ff

ff

bass:

music example below). It is this rhythmic feature, syncopation, that makes the motion seem like a strange skittering, rather than just running fast.

Though Beethoven did not label this movement a scherzo (his heading was simply Vivace, meaning vivacious), that is what it is: a fast triple-meter movement, full of surprises, jolts, and even violent shocks, in **A B A** form. *Scherzo*, as we have seen, means "joke," and this scherzo is all smiles at first. Later, however, it taps into a level of ferocity that not even this composer had scarcely touched before.

For he appears to have determined to carry the traditional contrast between minuet and trio to the breaking point. Whereas section **A** uses only a few adjacent pitches, as we have seen, at least up to the cadential **c** segment, **B** takes off like a rocket. Scales shoot up through the octaves, starting—significantly!—first from F, then from G, then from A. In **B** the traditional |: **a** :||: **b a** :|-type form of **A** is thrown overboard—nothing like |: **c** :||: **d c** :| happens here. After each of the upward scales has started with a *forte* jolt (Beethoven writes *fp,* meaning *f* followed directly by *p*), the dynamic swells up to an almost insane *ff* explosion, as the instruments get stuck sawing away at repeated figures. The beat is relentless, counteracting all the syncopation that came before.

This episode of turmoil, or terror, depending on how you react, could hardly make a greater contrast to **A.** As though to make the point, **A** now comes back without change—"vivacious," very quiet, smiling through its syncopations as though nothing has happened. But a brief coda ends with one final *f* jolt.

We have not said anything yet about the string quartet as a medium, and its special sounds and textures. The subtlety and variety of these should be evident after listening to Beethoven's Vivace movement. For example, take first of all the delicate counterpoint of the various instruments in **a,** which allows the original bass line in the cello *below* "Three blind mice" to rise and shine later *above* it in the two violins (at the end of **a′**):

LISTEN

Beethoven,
String Quartet in F,   21
Op. 135: Vivace

A (SCHERZO)
0:00 |:**a**:| (A G F G A . . .)
0:08 |:**b a′c**:|

B (TRIO)
0:56 *fp* scales up from F
1:10 . . . from G, then A
1:31 *ff* explosion
1:55 *ppp* A G F G A

A (SCHERZO)
1:58 *pp* **a** |:**b a′c**:| **coda**

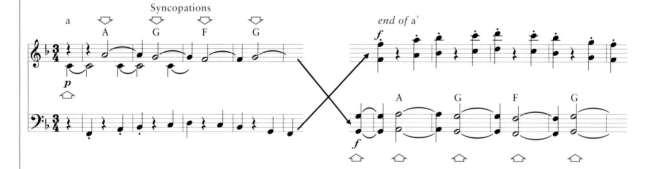

Only now are we really sure of the beat. In **c** and in the first of **B**'s scale passages, notice the interplay between high and low, the two violins answered back and forth by the cello and viola. The retching sound of the *ff* explosion passage in **B**—Beethoven's prediction of Heavy Metal—fades into ghostly syncopated octaves, with all four instruments playing the same pitches (which are A, G, and F, once again) in the unusual dynamic *ppp*.

Web: *Research and test your knowledge of the works of Beethoven at* <bedfordstmartins.com/listen>.

Prelude
Music after Beethoven: Romanticism

Baroque, as a designation for an historical style period in music, was adopted by musicologists from the field of art history many years after the period in question. The term *Romantic* was adopted from literature—and it was adopted by the literary Romantics themselves. When the first Romantic composers began their careers in the 1820s, their literary contemporaries were already excitedly talking about "Romantic" music.

This may seem like just one more footnote to history, but it tells us two important things about music after the time of Beethoven. One is that largely thanks to Beethoven, people had become highly aware of music as a major art. Music was treated with a new respect in cultivated circles; it was taken seriously in a way it never had been before.

The other is that it seemed quite natural for observers of the time to link up developments in music with parallel developments in literature. From Homer and Virgil to Shakespeare and Milton, literature had always been considered the most important and most convincing of the arts. The prestige and power of literature were now freely extended to music.

This fact is illustrated in a highly Romantic—not to say romanticized—painting that was popular at midcentury, showing a group of celebrities of the time listening to Franz Liszt at the piano (page 236). Their expressions tell us how profoundly the music moves them; their aesthetic experience is very different, clearly, from the casual enjoyment of eighteenth-century listeners pictured on page 145. For the nineteenth century, Beethoven's symphonies had been a revelation of music's profundity. It is no accident, then, that in the Liszt painting a larger-than-life bust of Beethoven rests on the piano, and that Liszt gazes on it so soulfully.

1 Romanticism

Romantic literature and literary theory flourished particularly in and around the first two decades of the nineteenth century. In England, this was a great age of poetry: Wordsworth, Coleridge, Shelley, Keats, and Byron. There was also a brilliant outpouring of German Romantic literature during the same period,

The power of Romantic music: Liszt as the inspiration for novelists Alexandre Dumas, Victor Hugo, George Sand, Daniel Stern (on the floor), legendary violinist Niccolò Paganini, and opera composer Gioacchino Rossini. Daniel Stern was the pseudonym of the Countess d'Agoult (see page 263).

though the names of its writers are less familiar in the English-speaking world: Tieck, Novalis, Kleist, Hölderlin, and E. T. A. Hoffmann.

For us, the word *romantic* refers to love; this usage dates from the nineteenth century and derives from the literary movement. But the glorification of love was only one of the many themes of Romantic literature, themes that were also central to the music of the nineteenth century.

The Cult of Individual Feeling

Striving for a better, higher, ideal state of being was at the heart of the Romantic movement. Everyday life, to the Romantics, seemed harsh, dull, and meaningless; it could be transcended only through the free exercise of individual will and passion. The rule of feeling, unconstrained by convention, religion, or social taboo (or anyone else's feelings, often enough)—this became the highest good, and emotional expression became the highest artistic goal. "Bohemians," as they were disparagingly called at the time, proclaimed romantic love, led irregular lives, and wore odd clothes. We have the Romantics to thank for one familiar image of the artist that is still around today.

These attitudes may be laid at the door of Jean-Jacques Rousseau—the same Enlightenment philosopher who had spoken up in the mid-eighteenth century for "natural" human feelings, as opposed to the artificial constraints imposed by society. Hailed as the ideological father of the French Revolution, Rousseau provided the Romantics with the ideal of individual, as well as political, freedom and fulfillment. (We have also seen Rousseau as a proponent of a "natural" music, and indeed his own music was still being played at French revolutionary rallies and pageants.)

But there was more than philosophy behind the new attitudes. The Industrial Revolution had already begun its inexorable course, and increasingly as the nineteenth century went on, people felt their helplessness in the face of the factories, slag heaps, and inhumane working conditions of developing capitalism. The smokestacks of what William Blake called "these dark, Satanic mills" now loomed over the European landscape. Understandably there was an element of escapism in Romantic striving.

Romanticism and Revolt

In the wake of the Industrial Revolution came actual revolution—the central fact in the politics of the age. It began with our own American Revolution. The French Revolution of 1789 rocked Europe as deeply in the nineteenth century as did the Russian Revolution of 1917 in the twentieth. It was followed by a whole set of aftershocks up to 1848, a year of major traumatic upheavals in France, Germany, Austria, and Italy.

The Romantics were inevitably cast in the role of rebels against the established order. Many musicians (like many poets and painters) associated themselves with libertarian politics, starting with Beethoven, who wrote a symphony named *Bonaparte* (which he renamed the *Eroica:* See page 224). In a later generation, Liszt briefly espoused a strange half-communistic, half-religious movement founded by a French priest, Father Felicité Lamennais. Giuseppe Verdi's name became an acronym for the Italian liberation movement. Richard Wagner was thrown out of Germany in 1849 for inflammatory speeches he made from the revolutionary barricades in the town of Dresden.

Along with political revolution went social revolution. The barriers of hereditary nobility were breached, and the lower and middle classes assumed more social mobility. Thus Franz Liszt, who was the son of an estate foreman, could conduct glamorous liaisons—one stormy, the other stable—with a French countess and a Russian princess. The importance of this was not lost on Liszt's contemporaries; the countess is another of the celebrities included in the picture of Liszt at the piano (though the artist tactfully hid her face).

Music and the Supernatural

The supernatural—often linked to the macabre—loomed large in the Romantic firmament, as we might expect of a movement so intent on transcending the ordinary. In *Nightmare,* a weird picture by the early Romantic painter Henry Fuseli, dream is made concrete, visible, and public in the figure of a horrible incubus (see page 238). Faust pledging his soul to the Devil for a single moment of transcendent happiness

La Marseillaise, the great rallying song of the French Revolution.

Nightmare, by Henry Fuseli (1741–1825), an eighteenth-century pre-Romantic painter, poet, and revolutionary who emigrated from Switzerland to England for political reasons.

became the subject of the greatest poem of the time, Goethe's *Faust.* Franz Schubert wrote "The Erlking," about a demon who claims a terrified child, in 1816 (see page 250); Mary Shelley wrote *Frankenstein* in 1818. The titles of some of the most famous operas of the time—*Robert the Devil, The Vampire, The Magic Bullet*—speak for themselves.

Composers cultivated strange harmonies and sinister orchestral sounds as their contribution to this aspect of Romanticism; the sounds they dreamed up can still be heard on some television soundtracks today. A famous scene of devilish conjuration in a deep forest, the Wolf's Glen scene in Carl Maria von Weber's opera *Der Freischütz* (*The Magic Bullet*, 1821), was the first impressive musical monument to Romanticism in music. Spooky music was devised by Verdi for the witches in his Shakespeare opera *Macbeth,* and by Wagner for the ghost ship and its spectral crew in *The Flying Dutchman.* And in his *Fantastic* Symphony, Hector Berlioz wrote a movement called "Dream of a Witches' Sabbath" that bears comparison with Fuseli's *Nightmare* (see page 268).

Artistic Barriers

The Romantics' search for higher experience and more intense expression provoked a reaction against the restraints of artistic form and genre. Artists resisted all rules and regulations. They distrusted abstract notions of "beauty" or "decorum" that they felt might hamper their spontaneity.

Eighteenth-century drama, for example, was hemmed in by such rules until the Romantics overturned them, citing the works of Shakespeare. Locations change scene by scene in Shakespeare's plays, as tragedy clashes with farce, rich poetry with bawdy prose, and noble characters with clowns. The lifelike turbulence and the loose, casual form of these plays made Shakespeare enormously popular in the nineteenth century. The list of composers who wrote music associated with them is practically endless, from Mendelssohn and Berlioz to Chaikovsky, Wagner, and Verdi.

In music itself, composers worked to break down barriers of harmony and form. All the Romantic composers experimented with chords, or chord progressions, that had previously been forbidden by the textbooks. From the time of Schubert on, their music was enriched by imaginative new harmonies. And sonata form, the hallmark of Classicism, was treated so freely in Robert Schumann's piano sonatas, written in the 1830s, that he finally labeled the last (and greatest) of them "Fantasy"—a proclamation of his spontaneity on the one hand, and insurance against accusations of "breaking the rules" on the other.

Music and the Other Arts

"Shakespearean," open-ended, sometimes fragmentary, and above all contemptuous of formal barriers are the characteristics of Romantic art. Efforts were made to blend the arts together: poetry became more "musical," paintings and musical works were given "poetic" titles, and poetry, drama, music, and stagecraft merged in Wagner's unique and enormously influential "total artwork," or *Gesamtkunstwerk*. Within individual arts, blurred effects were cultivated— half-obscure verbal meanings, ambiguous shapes and color blends, and musical sounds that are imprecise but rich and evocative.

No one went further in this respect than the English landscape painter J. M. W. Turner. In one of his most famous pictures, *The "Fighting Téméraire,"* the

The "Fighting Téméraire" Tugged to Her Last Berth to Be Broken Up, 1838 by J. M. W. Turner (1775–1851).

Two Romantic depictions of nature: *Mountainous Landscape* by Caspar David Friedrich (left) and *The Bard* by John Martin (right). In each, man is dwarfed by nature—nature depicted as both menacing and thrilling.

grandeur of nature and the horrors of industrialization merge in dizzy, almost abstract swirls of color. Whereas Rousseau had admired nature for its simplicity, Turner captured what was called at the time its "sublime" quality: the majesty and mystery of nature, its boundlessness, even its menace. The great Romantic artists stared unblinkingly at the infinite, and tried to set it down in their art.

And it was exactly the boundless quality of music that gave it its special prestige and status. Music, people felt, could express inner experience more deeply than the other arts because the musician's imagination is not tied down to the meaning of words (like the poet's) or to the representation of things (like the painter's). The special place of music in the Romantic scheme of things was forcefully expounded by Arthur Schopenhauer, a much-read German philosopher of the time. Wagner's opera *Tristan und Isolde* practically spells out Schopenhauer's philosophy, as we will see.

"All art aspires to the condition of music," wrote a famous Victorian critic, Walter Pater. All Romantic art tried to capture music's depth and freedom of emotional expression and its continuous, "infinite" quality.

2   Concert Life in the Nineteenth Century

First introduced in the Baroque era, during the age of aristocratic patronage of the arts, public concerts grew more important in the days of Haydn, Mozart, and Beethoven. As the nineteenth century progressed, the concert hall together with the opera house came to dominate the presentation of music.

Every town of any size had its symphony association, organized by merchants, government officials, lawyers, and other members of the middle class. Concert halls built to accommodate symphony concerts were also expressions of civic pride. In 1891 the New York Symphony, that city's second orchestra (the New York Philharmonic was founded in 1842), proudly presented a five-concert music festival led by Chaikovsky in brand-new Carnegie Hall.

By the end of the century even intimate, "domestic" musical genres, designed for the drawing room or the studio, were presented on the concert stage. Concerts of *Lieder* (German songs) and string quartet concerts became established, though they were never as important as orchestral concerts. Concerts made more music available to more and more people. Improved transportation brought musicians on tour to remote areas, such as the American west.

However, the institutionalization of concert life also had its negative aspect, in that audiences gradually became more conservative in their musical tastes. The old aristocratic system had actually been more neutral in this respect. While many aristocratic patrons cared less about music than display, and some exercised the most whimsical of tastes, others actually encouraged composers to pursue new paths, or at least left them alone to do so. On the other hand, the concert public tended to conservatism. The mainly middle-

Groundbreaking ceremony for Carnegie Hall in New York. The bearded man visible behind one of the vertical ropes is the famous railroad and steel baron Andrew Carnegie, the donor.

class buyers of concert tickets naturally wanted "value," as with anything else they bought. What counted as value was something already established as a "masterpiece," something that they already knew and liked.

The Artist and the Public

For the reasons above, composers with an interest in innovation—and that includes every composer discussed in this unit—felt at one time or another that their work was being neglected by the concert world. A paradoxical situation developed. The composer's dependence on the public was tinged with resentment, and the public's admiration for composers was tinged with distrust, even hostility.

Thus the composer Robert Schumann started an important magazine to campaign for Romantic music in the face of public indifference to serious art and preference for what he regarded as flashy trivia. Editor Schumann invented a "League of David" to slay the "Goliath" of the concert audience. (Goliath was the champion of the Philistines; it was around this time that the adjective "philistine" came to mean "uncultured.") Later, the music of Liszt and Wagner was attacked by hostile critics as formless, dissonant, and overheated. Later still, the symphonies of Gustav Mahler were repeatedly rejected in Vienna, in spite of Mahler's important position as head of the Opera there.

The gap between innovative music and a conservative concert public, which opened up in the nineteenth century, widened in the twentieth, as we shall see. Here as elsewhere, the nineteenth century set the tone for modern musical life.

3 Style Features of Romantic Music

Since the main artistic value in the Romantic era was the integrity of personal feeling, every genuine artist was expected to have a personal style. Many artists cultivated styles that were highly personal and even eccentric. Furthermore, Romanticism's constant striving after ever-new states of consciousness put a premium on innovation; this could be seen as an exciting breaking down of artistic barriers on the one hand, and as a heroic personal breakthrough on the other. Consequently it is harder to define the Romantic style in general than to spot innovations, novelties, and individual peculiarities.

To be sure, nineteenth-century composers were united by some common interests, which will be discussed below: technical interests concerning melody, harmony, tone color, and, perhaps especially, musical form. But it is important to remember that one such common interest was to sound different from everybody else.

Rhythm: Rubato

The general Romantic tendency to blur all sharp edges found its musical counterpart in the rhythmic practice of *tempo rubato*, or just **rubato**. Rubato means that in musical performance the rhythm is handled flexibly; the meter itself may waver, or else the beat is maintained strictly in the accompaniment while the melody is played or sung slightly out of phase with it. (Literally *tempo rubato* means "robbed time"—that is, some time has been "stolen" from the beat— but the beat is likely to be slowed and the time "given back" a moment later.)

Rubato was practiced in the service of greater individual expressivity. Though seldom indicated in a score—indeed, no one has ever found an accurate way to indicate rubato in musical notation—its practice is documented by old recordings, made around 1900 by musicians who were close to the Romantic composers (or even by the composers themselves). Improvisation, in the sense of adding ornaments or other notes to a score, was all but abolished by the end of the nineteenth century. Let no mere performer tamper with notes which had been set down by a composer of transcendent genius! But performers of the time improvised *rhythmically,* in that they applied rubato freely to nearly every score they played.

Considered a sign of bad taste in Baroque or Classical music, at least when applied extensively, rubato is an essential expressive resource in the playing, singing, and conducting of Romantic music. A musician's sensitivity and "feeling" depends to a great extent on his or her artistic use of rubato.

Romantic Melody

The most instantly recognizable feature of Romantic music is its melodic style. Melody in the Romantic era is more emotional, effusive, and demonstrative than before. Often the melodic lines range more widely than the orderly, restrained melodies of the Classical era; often, too, they build up to more sustained climaxes. Melodies became more irregular in rhythm and phraseology, so as to make them sound more spontaneous.

A fine example is the so-called Love theme of Chaikovsky's Overture-Fantasy *Romeo and Juliet* (page 290). It begins with a great outburst—a climax, at the very start—and then sinks down an octave and more, in melodic curves whose yearning quality grows more and more sensuous. Especially striking is the second part of the melody, where a rhythmic figure surges up, seven times in all, before exploding into a free return of the first part:

When one thinks of Romantic melody, what comes first to mind is the grand, exaggerated emotionality of Chaikovsky, perhaps, or Mahler. Some Romantic melodies are more intimate, however—and they are no less emotional for sparing the handkerchief, as it were. Each in an individual way, Romantic composers learned to make their melodies dreamy, sensitive, passionate, ecstatic, or whatever shade of feeling they were able to express.

Romantic Harmony

Harmony was one of the areas in which Romantic music made the greatest technical advances. On the one hand, composers learned to use harmony to underpin melody in such a way as to bring out its emotionality. Romantic melody is, in fact, inseparable from harmony. In the *Romeo and Juliet* Love theme, for example, a rich new chord goes hand in glove with the warm upward scoop of the melodic line in measure 5.

On the other hand, harmony was savored for its own sake, and composers experimented freely with new chord forms and new juxtapositions of chords.

These, it was found, could contribute potently to those mysterious, sinister, rapturous, ethereal, or sultry moods that Romantic composers sought to evoke. There are even some themes and motives in Romantic music that gain their memorable quality from harmony, rather than from melody and rhythm, as in earlier music (see page 284).

Chromaticism is a term for a style that liberally employs all twelve notes of the chromatic scale (see page 17). Baroque and Classical style is not "chromatic" in this sense, but all Romantic composers pursued chromaticism to some extent, in order to expand the expressive range of both their melodies and their harmony. If you look at the *Romeo and Juliet* theme, you will find nearly all twelve notes of the chromatic scale included—something that seldom if ever happens in earlier music. Chromaticism was carried furthest in the nineteenth century by Richard Wagner, and further yet by the early twentieth-century modernists.

The Expansion of Tone Color

While tone color had been treated with considerable subtlety by the Viennese Classical composers, the Romantics seized on this aspect of music with particular enthusiasm. For the first time in Western music, the sheer sensuous quality of sound assumed major artistic importance on a level with rhythm, melody, and musical form.

All instruments went through major technical developments during the nineteenth century—the piano not least. As orchestral instruments reached their present-day forms, the orchestra was expanded, soon reaching its present standard makeup. The chart below for a typical Romantic orchestra, when compared with the Classical orchestra chart on page 173, shows how the ranks of the brass, woodwind, and percussion sections were filled out:

The increased chromaticism of nineteenth-century music spawned this bizarre experimental harp, which is really two harps, crisscrossed, to accommodate all the notes of the chromatic scale.

A TYPICAL ROMANTIC ORCHESTRA

STRINGS	WOODWINDS	BRASS	PERCUSSION
First violins (12–16 players)	2 Flutes	4 French horns	3 Timpani
Second violins (12–16)	1 Piccolo	2 Trumpets	Bass drum
Violas (8–12)	2 Oboes	3 Trombones	Snare drum
Cellos (8–12)	1 English horn	1 Bass tuba	Cymbals
Bass viols (6–10)	2 Clarinets		Triangle
	1 High E♭ clarinet		Tubular bells
	1 Bass clarinet		
Note: Each string section is sometimes divided into two or more subsections, to obtain richer effects.	2 Bassoons		
	1 Contrabassoon		
2 Harps			Piano

What such charts cannot show, however, are the ingenious new *combinations* of instruments that were now investigated. Composers learned to mix instrumental colors with something of the same freedom and virtuosity with which painters mix actual colors on a palette. The clear, sharply defined sonorities of the Classical era were replaced by multicolored shades of blended orchestral sound.

Romantic composers and audiences alike were fascinated by the symphony orchestra, and for the first time conductors came to the fore—conductors wielding batons. In earlier times, orchestras had simply followed the first violinist or the continuo player, but now they needed experts to control and balance out those special blended effects. The orchestra also became increasingly important in nineteenth-century opera. Major opera composers, such as Weber, Meyerbeer, and Wagner, specialized in orchestral effects that sometimes even threatened to put the voices in the shade. If today the symphony orchestra comes to mind almost automatically when one thinks of "classical music," that is a holdover from the Romantic nineteenth century.

4 Program Music

Program music is a term for nonvocal music written in association with a poem, a story, or some other literary source—or even just a highly suggestive word or two. While program music was certainly not new in the Romantic era, it gained new importance and prestige, for program music answered the general Romantic demand for transcending inter-art boundaries. Music could be made even more expressive, it was felt, by linking it to poetry and ideas.

The term *program music* is sometimes restricted to music that tells or at least traces a story, the story being the "program." In 1829, at the premiere of his *Fantastic* Symphony, Hector Berlioz actually handed out a pamphlet containing his own made-up program, and the music of the symphony behaves like a narrator a good deal of the time. From the weird shrieks and groans at the start of the symphony's last movement, through the riotous welcome of the heroine, to the final frenzied round dance, we feel we are treated to musical events that follow the incidents of the story step by step (see page 265).

Another type of program music adopts a different strategy. Instead of telling a story, it attempts to capture the general flavor of a mood associated with some extramusical condition, concept, or personality. In short piano pieces, Schumann drew portraits of his friends (and even of himself), under coded names. The single word "nocturne," as the title for a whole genre of such compositions by Frédéric Chopin, is enough to set up expectations of night-time romance—and the music does the rest (see page 261).

Program music sparked a great debate in the nineteenth century, a debate that still goes on. Does the music *really* illustrate or represent the program? Suppose the music is played without listeners being given the program—could they tell it from the music? Should not the music make complete sense on its own terms, even if we grant that the program provides an added dimension to it?

But the point is that the Romantics did not *want* to be without the program. They did not necessarily *want* the music to "make sense on its own terms." And it seems they were prepared to live with this apparent inconsistency: On the one hand they revered purely instrumental music as the highest form of art; on the other hand, they embraced music that is less "pure" because of its admixture with nonmusical elements, that is, program music.

5 Form in Romantic Music

Individual spontaneity was an important goal of the Romantic movement. And if there was any area in which the composer wanted to seem particularly free and spontaneous, it was the area of musical form. The music should bubble out moment by moment, irrepressible and untrammeled, like churning emotion itself. . . . But composers faced a problem: how to control that spontaneity? They had to provide their music with enough sense of coherence so that listeners could follow it.

More and more complex orchestras required conductors, and conductors required batons. Before sticks came into use, the German opera composer Carl Maria von Weber (see page 272) seems to have made do with a tight scroll of paper.

In their use of standard forms or form-types, nineteenth-century composers broke with classical norms. To return to a distinction made earlier, on page 48, the Romantics wanted each work of art to express its own individual "inner form"; they distrusted "outer forms" as dry and conventional. Even when they followed forms such as sonata form, rondo, and so on, they tended to follow them so loosely that it becomes a matter of opinion whether they are doing so at all. Themes tend to blend into one another, and there is much less of the neat, clear cadencing of Classical music.

Some Romantic compositions deliberately break down the boundary between music and nonmusical silence. Robert Schumann's song "Im wunderschönen Monat Mai" (page 254) begins hesitantly, as though already in the middle of a transition; we feel we have just begun hearing music that started long ago. Instead of ending with a decisive cadence, the song comes to a questioning dissonance, then—silence. The vague, atmospheric quality at the start, and the suggestion of "infinity" at the end—again, these are typically Romantic.

Yet the music had to avoid real formlessness if it was to hold the attention of an audience. Once again, for romantic composers the problem was how to create the impression of spontaneous form while at the same time giving the listener some means of following the music. They developed a number of interesting and characteristic solutions.

"Miniature" Compositions

While many Romantic compositions last for about as long as works from the eighteenth century, special classes of music arose with quite different dimensions.

First of all, composers cultivated what we will call **miniatures,** pieces lasting only a few minutes. Mostly songs and short piano pieces, these were designed to convey a particularly pointed emotion, momentary and undeveloped. In this way the composer could commune with the listener intensely but intimately, as though giving him or her a single short, meaningful glance. The meaning might well be hinted at by a programmatic title.

Though short pieces were also written in earlier times, of course—think of minuet movements in classical symphonies—usually they were components of larger units, where their effect was balanced by other, longer movements.

The man has put down his violin to sit with the woman at the piano; we can imagine the four-hand music they are playing, perhaps, but we cannot see their faces. This picture catches both the intimacy and privacy of the Romantic "miniature" and also its characteristic location, the middle-class living room.

Romantic "miniatures," though they were often published in sets, as we will see, nevertheless were composed so as to stand out as individuals in their own right, apart from their sets. Miniatures for piano were sometimes given general titles, such as Schubert's Impromptus (Improvisations) and Brahms's Capriccios (Whims). Sometimes they masqueraded as dances, like Chopin's Mazurkas (a Polish dance). Often they were given more suggestive, "programmatic" titles: *Years of Pilgrimage* by Franz Liszt, *Spring Song* by Felix Mendelssohn, *To a Wild Rose* by Edward MacDowell, America's leading late Romantic composer. Schumann was something of a specialist in such titles: *The Poet Speaks, Confession, The Bird as Prophet,* and—*Why?*

As for the problem of musical form, in such pieces this was not so much solved as bypassed. They are over before the listener begins to wonder where the music is going, what the next effect will be, and why.

"Grandiose" Compositions

Another Romantic tendency was diametrically opposed to the "miniatures." Many composers wrote "grandiose" compositions—larger and larger symphonies, cantatas, and so on, with more and more movements, increased performing forces, and a longer (sometimes much longer) total time span. For example, Hector Berlioz's "dramatic symphony" *Romeo and Juliet* of 1839 lasts for nearly an hour and a half. (Haydn's Symphony No. 95 lasts twenty minutes.) Starting with an augmented symphony orchestra, Berlioz added soloists and a chorus in certain of the movements and a narrator between them, and then threw in an off-stage chorus for still other movements.

In the field of opera, Richard Wagner's *The Ring of the Nibelung* is an opera that goes on for four evenings with a huge orchestra including specially invented instruments, a cast of thirty, and fifteen separate stage sets (see page 283). The total effect of these "grandiose" compositions was laced with poetry, philosophical or religious ideas, and (in operas) dramatic action. Listeners were impressed, even stupefied, by a combination of opulent sounds, great thoughts, powerful emotions, and sheer length.

These works met what we have called the problem of musical form in their own way. The bigger the work, the bigger the problem, but to help solve it com-

The "grandiose" compositions of the nineteenth century occasioned many cartoons—amusing enough, but not in the last analysis friendly to the advanced music of the time.

posers could draw on extramusical factors—on the text of a vocal work, or the program of an instrumental one. Music could add emotional conviction to ideas or stories; in return these extramusical factors could supply a rhyme and reason for the sequence of musical events, that is, for the musical form.

The Principle of Thematic Unity

An important general principle developed by Romantic composers was that of thematic unity. There was an increasing tendency to maintain some of the same thematic material throughout whole works, even (or especially) when these works were in many movements.

In nineteenth-century symphonies and other such works, several different levels of thematic unity can be distinguished:

⁊   Most obviously, themes from one movement may come back literally and quite clearly in other movements. We have already heard this happen in Beethoven's Fifth Symphony, when the scherzo theme returns in the last movement.

⁊   In other compositions, new *versions* of a single theme are used at important new points in the music, either later in the same movement or in later movements. While these new versions are really nothing more than variations of the original theme, this procedure differs fundamentally from Classical theme-and-variations form (see page 187). In Classical variation form, the "theme" is an entire tune, and the variations follow one another directly. In the new Romantic procedure, the theme is (generally) much more fragmentary than a tune, and the new versions of the theme appear at irregular intervals.

The term **thematic transformation** is used for this variationlike procedure in Romantic music, whereby short themes are freely varied at relatively wide and unpredictable intervals of time. A precedent for it can be traced to works such as Beethoven's Fifth Symphony, where the ♪♪♪♩ motive of the first movement is evoked freely in each of the later ones.

⁊   In still other nineteenth-century pieces, we hear themes with even looser relationships among them. Clearly different, they nonetheless seem to exhibit mysterious inner similarities—similarities that seem to help unify the music, though they are too shadowy to count as transformations in the Romantic definition, let alone as variations in the Classical style. Wagner's operas are famous for such themes. In the Prelude to *Tristan und Isolde*, for example, the family resemblance between some of the motives can't be missed—yet it can scarcely be pinned down, either (see page 283).

Of all the levels of thematic unity employed by nineteenth-century composers, this last is the most typical of all. Vague similarity rather than clear likeness, suggestion rather than outright statement, atmosphere rather than discourse, feeling rather than form: All these go to the heart of Romanticism. We cannot appreciate Romantic music fully if we approach it in too literal a frame of mind. In much of this music, the "inner form"—the special spontaneous form of the individual piece, as distinct from standard "outer forms" such as sonata form and rondo—is tied to the principle of thematic unity. Listening to Romantic music requires ears that are not only attentive but also imaginative, exploratory, and more than a little fanciful.

Web: *Research and test your understanding of Romanticism at* <bedfordstmartins.com/listen>.

The Early Romantics

Perhaps the most brilliant generation of composers in the entire history of music was that of the early Romantics. Franz Schubert was born in Vienna in 1797; then the ten-year period between 1803 and 1813 saw the birth of Robert Schumann, Frédéric Chopin, Felix Mendelssohn, Franz Liszt, Hector Berlioz, Richard Wagner, and Giuseppe Verdi. It was a brilliant generation, but not a long-lived one. Only the last four of these composers survived to continue their major work into the second half of the century.

Two general points are worth making about this early Romantic galaxy. First, Beethoven's music had a profound effect on them, though this was naturally felt more strongly by German composers than by non-Germans. Schubert, who lived in Vienna under Beethoven's shadow, was influenced by the older master much more directly than Chopin, a Pole who lived in Paris.

The second important point is that these composers were deeply influenced by literary Romanticism, which had flourished some decades before their time. Schubert wrote many songs to texts by Romantic poets such as Goethe, Novalis, and Friedrich Schlegel, and Schumann's enthusiasm for the German Romantic novelist Jean Paul Richter was reflected in his music, as well as in his own prose writings. We have mentioned that Shakespeare was particularly admired by the Romantics; nearly all the composers mentioned here wrote music associated with Shakespeare's plays.

1 The Lied

The ordinary German word for song is *Lied* (plural, *Lieder*—pronounced "leader"). The word also has a special application: the lied is a particular type of German song that evolved in the late eighteenth century and flourished in the nineteenth. As such, the lied is one of the most important "miniature" genres of Romanticism.

Though one cannot generalize about the melodies of these songs—some consist of little more than a tune, others are melodically much more complex—they share certain other characteristic features.

Accompaniment. A lied is nearly always accompanied by piano, and the accompaniment contributes significantly to the artistic effect. Indeed, the pianist becomes more of a discreet partner to the singer than a mere accompanist.

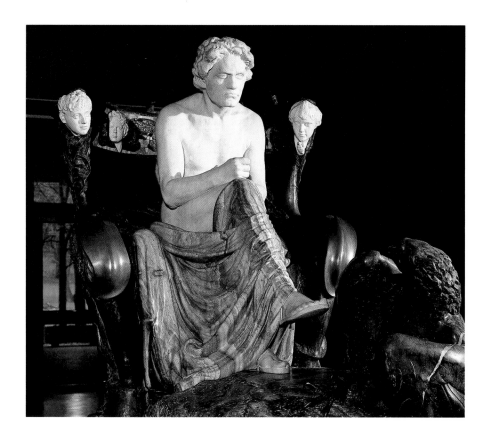

Beethoven: a late Romantic view. The awesome, ideal figure—nude, and carved in marble, like a Greek statue—sits, kinglike, on a superb throne. He seems to be both reigning over and deploring the music that was written after his own time.

❧ *Poetry.* The text of a lied is usually a Romantic poem of some merit (at least in the composer's estimation). Hence, although we need to understand the words of almost any vocal music, with the lied we should also try to appreciate how the poem's words and meanings fit together as poetry. The art of the lied depends on the sensitivity of the composer's response to the poetic imagery and feeling.

❧ *Mood.* A third characteristic, harder to explain, is the intimacy of expression that is captured by these pieces. The singer and the pianist seem to be sharing an emotional insight with just you, rather than with an entire audience; words and music are uttered softly, inwardly. Composers intended lieder for the intimacy of a living room, not a formal concert hall, and that is where they are best heard.

Is not music the mysterious language of a distant realm of spirits, whose lovely sounds re-echo in our soul and awaken a higher, more intensive life? All the passions, arrayed in shining armor, vie with each other, and ultimately merge in an indescribable longing that fills our breast.

Arch-Romantic novelist, critic, and composer E. T. A. Hoffmann, 1816

FRANZ SCHUBERT
"Erlkönig" ("The Erlking") (1815)

The earliest and (for most musicians) greatest master of the lied is Franz Schubert. He wrote close to seven hundred songs in his short lifetime. In his eighteenth year, 1815, he averaged better than a song every two days! Many of these are quite short tunes with simple piano accompaniments, but Schubert's tunes are like nobody else's; he was a wonderfully spontaneous melodist. Later in life his melodies became richer but no less beautiful, and taken together with their poems, the songs often show remarkable psychological penetration.

One of those songs from 1815 was an instant hit: "The Erlking," published as the composer's opus 1, and still today Schubert's best-known lied. In those early years, Schubert wrote a considerable number of long, narrative songs, though this one stands out from the others in its dramatic intensity.

Franz Schubert (1797–1828)

Schubert was the son of a lower-middle-class Viennese schoolmaster. There was always music in the home, and the boy received a solid musical education in the training school for Viennese court singers. His talent amazed his teachers and also a number of his schoolmates, who remained devoted to him throughout his career. Schubert began by following in his father's footsteps as a schoolteacher, without much enthusiasm, but soon gave up teaching to devote all his time to music.

Schubert was an endearing but shy and unspectacular individual who led an unspectacular life. However, it was the sort of life that would have been impossible before the Romantic era. Schubert never married—he was probably gay—and never held a regular job. He was sustained by odd fees for teaching and publications and by contributions from a circle of friends who called themselves the Schubertians—young musicians, artists, writers, and music lovers. One of the Schubertians, Moritz von Schwind, who became an important painter, has left us many charming pictures of the group at parties, on trips to the country, and so on.

It was an atmosphere especially conducive to an intimate musical genre such as the lied. Schubert wrote nearly seven hundred lieder and many choral songs. For a time he roomed with a poet, Johann Mayrhofer, who provided him with gloomy texts for about fifty of them.

It is unfortunate that Schubert's wonderful songs have tended to overshadow his symphonies, sonatas, and chamber music. Starting out with Classical genres, Schubert in his very short lifetime transformed them under the influence of Romanticism. He never introduced himself to Beethoven, even though they lived in the same city; perhaps he instinctively felt he needed to keep his distance from the overpowering older master. It speaks much for Schubert that he was able to write such original and powerful works as the "Unfinished" Symphony, the so-called *Great* Symphony in C, and others, right under Beethoven's shadow.

A few of Schubert's instrumental works include melodies taken from his own songs: the popular *Trout* Quintet, the String Quartet in D Minor (*Death and the Maiden*), and the *Wanderer* Fantasy for piano.

Schubert died in a typhoid fever epidemic when he was only thirty-one. He never heard a performance of his late symphonies, and much of his music came to light only after his death.

Our portrait shows Schubert around the time he wrote *The Erlking*.

Chief Works: Lieder, including the song cycles *Die schöne Müllerin, Winterreise,* and *Schwanengesang,* "The Erlking," "Gretchen at the Spinning Wheel," "Hedgerose," "Death and the Maiden," "The Trout," and hundreds of others ▪ "Character" pieces for piano; waltzes ▪ Symphonies, including the "Unfinished"—Schubert completed only two movements and sketches for a scherzo—and the *Great* Symphony in C ▪ Many piano sonatas—five (plus an "Unfinished Sonata") in his mature years; *Wanderer* Fantasy for piano ▪ Four mature string quartets; a string quintet; the genial *Trout* Quintet for piano and strings (including double bass)

Encore: After "The Erlking," listen to the "Unfinished" Symphony and songs from *Winterreise.*

The poem is by Johann Wilhelm von Goethe, the greatest literary figure of the day—by turns a Romantic and a Classic poet, novelist, playwright, naturalist, philosopher, and a favorite source of texts for many generations of lied composers. Cast in the old ballad form, which enjoyed a vogue in the Romantic era, and dealing with death and the supernatural, the poem is famous in its own right.

Though Goethe's ballad poem consists of eight parallel stanzas, they are not set to the same music. Schubert provided the later stanzas with different or modified music; such a song is said to be **through-composed**. (A song that uses the same music for all its stanzas is called **strophic**: See page 64.) In mood, the poem changes so much as it goes along that it almost demands this kind of musical setting. A father rides furiously through the night with a child who is presumably running a high fever, for he claims to see and hear a murderous demon. The Erlking first beckons the child, then cajoles him, then threatens and assaults him. The father—uncomprehending, even impatient—tries to quiet the boy, but by the time they reach home the boy is—dead!

ERLKÖNIG

BALLADE VON GOETHE.

In Musik gesetzt

Title page of the first edition of "The Erlking" (1821). Note the stunted tree; the literal meaning of "Erlkönig" is King of the Alders, or birches—in effect, a forest troll.

The opening piano introduction sets the mood of dark, tense excitement. The right hand hammers away at harsh repeated notes in triplets, representing the horse's hooves, while the left hand has an agitated motive:

Schubert invented different music for the poem's three characters (and also the narrator). Each "voice" characterizes the speaker in contrast to the others. The father is low, stiff, and gruff, the boy high and frantic. Marked *ppp,* and inaudible to the father, the ominously quiet and sweet little tunes crooned by the Erlking, offering his "schöne Spiele," add a chilling note.

The triplet accompaniment keeps the whole song alive and gives it more unity, as it were; yet one could wish that Herr Schubert had occasionally transferred it to the left hand; for the ceaseless striking of one and the same note in triplets tires the hand, if the piece is to be played at the rapid pace demanded by Herr Schubert.

Review of "Erlkönig," 1821

Schubert playing at an evening with the Schubertians. To the left is Johann Vogel, an older singer, one of his main supporters. Their friend Moritz von Schwind started this picture but didn't quite finish it.

Two things help hold this long song together as an artistic unity. First, the piano's triplet rhythm continues ceaselessly, until the very last line, where recitative style lets us know that the ride is over. (The triplets are muffled during the Erlking's speeches—because the child is hearing him in a feverish daze?) Second, there are some telling musical repetitions: the agitated riding motive (stanzas 1–2 and 7–8), and a desperately strained phrase sung higher and higher as the boy appeals to his father (stanzas 4, 6, and 7).

LISTEN	Schubert, "Erlkönig"

22   34

0:22	Wer reitet so spät, durch Nacht und Wind? Es ist der Vater mit seinem Kind; Er hat den Knaben wohl in dem Arm, Er fasst ihn sicher, er hält ihn warm.	Who rides so late through the night and wind? It is the father with his child. He holds the youngster tight in his arm, Grasps him securely, keeps him warm.
0:55	"Mein sohn, was birgst du so bang dein Gesicht?" "Siehst, Vater, du den Erlkönig nicht? Den Erlenkönig mit Kron' und Schweif?" "Mein Sohn, est ist ein Nebelstreif."	"Son, what makes you afraid to look?" "Don't you see, Father, the Erlking there? The King of the forest with his crown and train?" "Son, it's only a streak of mist."
1:28	*"Du liebes Kind, komm, geh mit mir! Gar schöne Spiele spiel' ich mit dir; Manch' bunte Blumen sind an dem Strand; Meine Mutter hat manch' gülden Gewand."*	*"Darling child, come away with me! I will play some lovely games with you; Many bright flowers grow by the shore; My mother has many golden robes."*
1:52	"Mein Vater, mein Vater, und hörest du nicht Was Erlenkönig mir leise verspricht?" "Sei ruhig, bleibe ruhig, mein Kind: In dürren Blättern säuselt der Wind."	"Father, Father, do you not hear What the Erlking is softly promising me?" "Calm yourself, be calm, my son: The dry leaves are rustling in the wind."
2:14	*"Willst, feiner Knabe, du mit mir gehn? Meine Töchter sollen dich warten schön; Meine Töchter führen den nächtlichen Reihn Und wiegen und tanzen und singen dich ein."*	*"Well, you fine boy, won't you come with me? My daughters are ready to wait on you. My daughters lead the nightly round, They will rock you, dance for you, sing you to sleep!"*
2:31	"Mein Vater, mein Vater, und siehst du nich dort Erlkönigs Töchter am düstern Ort?" "Mein Sohn, mein sohn, ich seh es genau: Es scheinen die alten Weiden so grau."	"Father, Father, do you not see The Erlking's daughters there in the dark?" "Son, my son, I see only too well: It is the gray gleam in the old willow trees."
3:01	*"Ich liebe dich, mich reizt deine schöne Gestalt, Und bist du nicht willig, so brauch' ich Gewalt."* "Mein Vater, mein Vater, jetzt fasst er mich an! Erlkönig hat mit ein Leids getan!"	*"I love you, your beauty allures me, And if you're not willing, then I shall use force."* "Father, Father, he is seizing me now! The Erlking has hurt me!"
3:26	Dem Vater grauset's, er reitet geschwind, Er hält in Armen das ächzende Kind, Erreicht den Hof mit Müh and Not; In seinen Armen das Kind war tot.	Fear grips the father, he rides like the wind, He holds in his arms the moaning child; He reaches the house hard put, worn out; In his arms the child was—dead!

The Song Cycle

A **song cycle** is a group of songs with a common poetic theme or an actual story connecting all the poems. Composers would either find whole coherent groups of poems to set, or else make their own selections from a larger collection of a poet's work. Schubert, who wrote two great song cycles relatively late in his career, was able to use ready-made groups of poems published by a minor Romantic poet named Wilhelm Müller: *Die schöne Müllerin* ("The Fair Maid of the Mill") and *Winterreise* ("Winter Journey").

The advantage of the song cycle was that it extended the rather fragile expression of the lied into a larger, more comprehensive, and hence more impressive unit. It was, in a sense, an effort to get beyond "miniaturism." The "unity" of such larger units, however, is always loose, even when the songs are related by melodic or rhythmic means, as occasionally happens. The individual songs can often be sung separately, as well as in sequence with the rest of the cycle.

ROBERT SCHUMANN (1810–1856)
Dichterliebe ("A Poet's Love") (1840)

"Schubert died. Cried all night," wrote the eighteen-year-old Robert Schumann in his diary under a date in 1828. Yet living in Zwickau, Germany, far from Schubert's Vienna, Schumann did not know many of the older composer's best-known works, his lieder. He loved Schubert's piano music, and indeed, for the first ten years of his own career as a composer, Schumann wrote only piano music.

To cast light into the depths of the human heart—the artist's mission!

Robert Schumann

Then in 1840, the year of his marriage, he suddenly started pouring out lieder. Given this history, it is not surprising that in Schumann's songs the piano is given a more complex role than in Schubert's. This is particularly true of his most famous song cycle, *Dichterliebe,* the first and last songs of which (nos. 1 and 16) we shall examine here. *Dichterliebe* has no real story; its series of love poems traces a psychological progression from cautious optimism to disillusionment and despair. They are the work of another great German poet, Heinrich Heine, a man who reacted with bitter irony against Romanticism, while acknowledging his own hopeless commitment to its ideals.

"Im wunderschönen Monat Mai" ("In the wonderfully lovely month of May") The song begins with a piano introduction, halting and ruminative in quality—which seems at first to be a curious response to the "wonderfully lovely" month of May. The piano part winds its way in and out of the vocal line, ebbing and flowing rhythmically and sometimes dwelling on quiet but piercing dissonant harmonies.

What Schumann noticed was the hint of unrequited longing in Heine's very last line, and he ended the song with the piano part hanging in midair, without a true cadence, as though in a state of reaching or yearning: a truly Romantic effect. Technically, the last sound is a dissonance that requires resolution into a consonance but does not get it (until the next song).

In this song, both stanzas of the poem are set to identical music. As mentioned earlier, such a song is called *strophic;* strophic setting is of course familiar from folk songs, hymns, popular songs, and many other kinds of music. For Schumann, this kind of setting had the advantage of underlining the similarity in the text of the song's two stanzas, both in meaning and in actual words. Certainly his music deepens the tentative, sensitive, hope-against-hope quality of Heine's understated confession of love.

The qualities of intimacy and spontaneity that are so important to Romantic miniatures can be inhibited by studio recording. Our recording of Schumann's song was made at a concert (you will hear applause as the artists enter).

LISTEN	Schumann, "Im wunderschönen Monat Mai"

23   35

0:28	Im wunderschönen Monat Mai,	In the wonderfully lovely month of May,
	Als alle Knospen sprangen,	When all the buds were bursting,
	Da ist in meinem Herzen	Then it was that in my heart
	Die Liebe aufgegangen.	Love broke through.
1:05	Im wunderschönen Monat Mai,	In the wonderfully lovely month of May,
	Als alle Vögel sangen,	When all the birds were singing,
	Da hab' ich ihr gestanden	Then it was I confessed to her
	Mein Sehnen und Verlangen.	My longing and desire.

"Die alten, bösen Lieder" ("The hateful songs of times past")   After many heart-wrenching episodes, the final song in the *Dichterliebe* cycle begins strongly. The very insistent rhythm in the piano part sounds a little hectic and forced, like the black humor of Heine's poem. Although basically this is a through-composed song, there are musical parallels between many of the stanzas, and the music of stanza 1 comes back even more forcefully in stanza 5.

But there is a sudden reversal of mood in stanza 6, as the poet suddenly offers to tell us what this morbid action is about. In the music, first the accompaniment disintegrates and then the rhythm. All the poet's self-dramatization vanishes when he speaks of his grief in recitative-like accents; the end of the song would be a whimper if Schumann at the piano were not quietly and firmly in control. In a lovely meditative piano solo, music takes over from words. The composer comments on and comforts the frantic poet.

Not only does the composer interpret the poet's words with great art, both in the hectic early stanzas and the self-pitying final one, but he adds something entirely his own in the final solo. The sixteen vignettes by Heine and Schumann in *Dichterliebe* add up to a memorable anthology of the endless pains and pleasures of love celebrated by the Romantics.

During the night of October 17, 1833, I suddenly had the most frightful thought a human being can possibly have: "What if you were no longer able to think?" Clara, anyone who has been crushed like that knows no worse suffering, or despair.

Letter from Robert Schumann, 1838

LISTEN   Schumann, "Die alten, bösen Lieder"

0:05	Die alten, bösen Lieder,	The hateful songs of times past,
	Die Träume bös' und arg,	The hateful, brutal dreams,
	Die lasst uns jetzt begraben:	Let's now have them buried;
	Holt einen grossen Sarg.	Fetch up a great coffin.
0:23	Hinein leg' ich gar Manches,	I've a lot to put in it—
	Doch sag' ich noch nicht, was.	Just what, I won't yet say;
	Der Sarg muss sein noch grösser	The coffin must be even bigger
	Wie's Heidelberger Fass.	Than the Great Cask of Heidelberg.
0:41	Und holt eine Todtenbahre	And fetch a bier,
	Und Bretter fest und dick,	Boards that are strong and thick;
	Auch muss sie sein noch länger	They too must be longer
	Als wie zu Mainz die Brück'.	Than the river bridge at Mainz.
0:59	Und holt mir auch zwölf Riesen,	And fetch me, too, twelve giants
	Die mussen noch stärker sein	Who must be stronger
	Als wie der starke Christoph	Than St. Christopher, the great statue
	Im Dom zu Köln am Rhein.	At the Cathedral of Cologne on the Rhine.
1:17	Die sollen den Sarg forttragen	It's they that must haul the coffin
	Und senken in's Meer hinab,	And sink it in the sea,
	Denn solchem grossen Sarge	For a great coffin like that
	Gebührt ein grosses Grab.	Deserves a great grave.
1:49	Wisst ihr, warum der Sarg wohl	Do you know why the coffin really
	So gross und schwer mag sein?	Has to be so huge and heavy?
	Ich senkt' auch meine Liebe	Because I sank all my love in it,
	Und meinen Schmerz hinein.	And all of my grief.

Robert Schumann (1810–1856)

Robert Schumann's father, a bookseller and writer, encouraged the boy's musical talent and started him studying the piano at the age of six. When his father died, his mother wanted him to go into law; he attended the University of Leipzig, but finally persuaded her to let him pursue the career of a piano virtuoso. He had to give this up, however, after an injury sustained when he tried to strengthen his fingers with a mechanical device.

Besides his musical talent, Schumann had a great flair for literature, no doubt inherited from his father. When he was only twenty-three, Schumann founded a magazine to campaign for a higher level of music, *Die Neue Zeitschrift für Musik* ("The New Music Journal"— it is still being published). For several years he wrote regular music criticism, often couched in a fanciful romantic prose style. For example, he signed some of his reviews with the names "Florestan" or "Eusebius," representing the opposite (but both thoroughly romantic) sides of his character—the impetuous side and the tender, dreamy side. He encouraged fledgling composers such as Chopin and (later) Brahms.

Schumann's piano works—among his most important music—are mostly "character pieces," often with imaginative titles, and occasionally signed "Eu." or "Fl." at the end. They are arranged in loosely organized sets, with titles such as *Butterflies, Kreisleriana* (after a character in a Romantic novel), *Scenes from Childhood*, and *Carnaval*.

Schumann fell in love with Clara Wieck, the daughter of his piano teacher; at the age of fifteen she was already a famous pianist. Thanks to her father's fanatical opposition—he did not think Robert was a very savory character—they had to wait until she was twenty-one (minus one day) before getting married, in 1840. A charming outcome of the marriage was that Robert, whose early compositions were almost entirely for the piano, suddenly started to write love songs for Clara. Nearly 150 songs were composed in this "song year."

A little later, he also turned to the composition of larger works: concertos, symphonies, chamber music, choral music, and one opera. Thereafter he worked as a teacher and conductor, but his withdrawn personality made him less than successful. Schumann suffered from mood swings and had experienced breakdowns in his youth, and now he began to show tragic signs of insanity. In 1854, tormented by voices, hallucinations, and loss of memory, he tried to drown himself in the River Rhine and was committed to an asylum. He died two years later.

Chief Works: Sets of "miniatures" for piano, among them *Scenes from Childhood, Album for the Young, Papillons* (Butterflies), and *Carnaval* ■ Songs (lieder) and song cycles: *Woman's Life and Love, Dichterliebe* ■ Piano Fantasy (a free sonata); Piano Concerto and the first important concerto for cello; four symphonies ■ Chamber music: a quintet and a quartet for piano and strings ■ An opera, *Genoveva*; incidental music to Byron's *Manfred* and Goethe's *Faust*; choral works

Encore: After *Dichterliebe* and *Carnaval*, listen to the Piano Concerto in A Minor.

CLARA SCHUMANN
"Der Mond kommt still gegangen" ("The moon has risen softly") (1843)

This lied is another perfect Romantic miniature, in spite of the cliché-filled poem, with its moonlight, its dreams of love, and its downhearted lover. Both melody and piano accompaniment are very plain, but the slightly unusual chords chosen by Schumann create a unique pensive mood. The form, too, is simple: modified strophic form, **A A A′**. Some modification, however slight, had to occur in stanza 3, where the poem's speaker, catching sight of the lit-up windows in the house, registers his excitement by crowding his poetic lines with extra words and extra syllables—which require extra notes.

There is an obvious, banal way of setting such crowded lines: See page 259, in the margin. But instead Schumann very skillfully pulls the words out of phase with the musical phrases, achieving beautiful rhythmic matches for some of the extra words: slower for *drunten* (down), livelier for *funkeln* (light—literally, sparkle), and very slow for *still* (silently):

Clara Wieck (Clara Schumann) (1819–1896)

Clara Wieck was the eldest child (she had two younger brothers) of a highly ambitious music teacher named Friedrich Wieck (pronounced *Veek*). Wieck had his own piano method, and he determined to make Clara a leading pianist. By the age of fifteen she was widely known as a prodigy. Like most virtuosos of the time, she also composed music to play at her own concerts: variations on popular opera arias, waltzes, a piano concerto.

Robert and Clara Schumann figure in what must be music's greatest love story. Still, there seems to have been just a little friction between them because she was so much better a pianist; she, on her part, felt diffident about composing under his shadow, though he did encourage her to some extent, and they published one song cycle jointly, containing music by both of them. Clara often wrote songs to give Robert on his birthdays. The last of these is dated 1853, the year before he was committed to an insane asylum.

Even before that, Robert's depression and instability made life difficult for Clara. She continued her career as best she could, but more and more, she had to take care of the family. During the 1848 revolution in Leipzig, for example, it was up to her to get the five Schumann children out of town (three more were born later).

Things were difficult in another way when Robert died. At the age of thirty-seven, after losing the husband whom she loved and revered, Clara found herself more than half in love with his twenty-two-year-old protégé Johannes Brahms (see page 298). It is not known which of them withdrew from the relationship. They remained close friends; Brahms was a lifelong bachelor, and she did not remarry.

Today we tend to regret that Clara decided to give up composing, for she left enough good pieces to make us wish there were more of them. But she knew it would have been an uphill battle, given the all too common nineteenth-century view that great music couldn't be written by a woman. With so many children to support, she can hardly be blamed for concentrating instead on activities that had already earned her admiration and respect—and a good living: playing and teaching.

Clara Schumann went on to further establish herself as one of Europe's leading pianists and a much-sought-after pedagogue. She concertized and toured widely. Brahms (who always asked her to critique his new compositions) was just one in the eminent circle of her friends and associates. Outliving Robert by forty years, Clara became a major force in late nineteenth-century music.

Chief Works: Miniatures for piano, with names such as *Romances* and *Soirées musicales* ("Musical Evenings"); songs ▪ A piano concerto and a trio for piano, violin, and cello ▪ *Piano Variations on a Theme by Robert Schumann* (Brahms wrote a set of variations on the same theme)

Encore: After "Der Mond," listen to *Romances* for piano and the Piano Concerto.

St. 1: ¹The moon has ri - sen soft - ly ²With gleaming rays of gold, ³Be - neath its shin-ing splendor ⁴The wea - ry earth's at rest.
St. 2: ¹And on the drifting breez-es ²From man - y faith-ful minds ³Endearing thoughts by the thousand ⁴Waft down on those who sleep.

St. 3: ¹Und drun-ten im Ta-le, da funkeln ²Die Fenster von Lieb - chens Haus; ³Ich a - ber blicke im Dunkeln ⁴Still . . .
¹And down in the val-ley, a light can ²Be seen in my loved _ one's house; ³But I keep staring, in darkness, ⁴Silently

Three things help make the climactic word *Liebchens* (loved one) radiant: the new long high note, the new harmony, and the expansive phrase (five bars in place of four). Schumann's piano postlude adds a wistful minor-mode aftertaste. As with many great lieder, music here far transcends the words.

An amazing nineteenth-century score of Schumann lieder. The poems are given in ornate calligraphy and illustrated in the richest, most opulent Romantic style. The picture might well be for Clara Schumann's "The Moon Has Risen Softly" (page 256; actually, it is for Robert's similar song "Moonlit Night").

LISTEN   **Clara Schumann, "Der Mond kommt still gegangen"**

0:03	*St. 1:* ¹Der Mond kommt still gegangen ²Mit seinen goldn'en Schein, ³Da Schläft in holdem Prangen ⁴Die müde Erde ein.	The moon has risen softly With gleaming rays of gold, Beneath its shining splendor The weary earth's at rest.
0:30	*St. 2:* ¹Und auf den Lüften schwanken ²Aus manchem treuen Sinn ³Viel tausend Liebesgedanken ⁴Über die Schläfer hin.	And on the drifting breezes From many faithful minds Endearing thoughts by the thousand Waft down on those who sleep.
0:58	*St. 3:* ¹Und drunten im Tale, da funkeln ²Die Fenster von Liebchens Haus; ³Ich aber blikke im Dunkeln ⁴Still in die Welt hinaus.	And down in the valley, a light can Be seen in my loved one's house; But I keep staring, in darkness, Silently out to the world.

Obvious (i.e., unmodified strophic) setting:

St. 3 ¹And down in the val-ley, a   light can

²Be seen in my loved one's house; _

2 The "Character Piece" for Piano

Besides the lied, the other chief type of Romantic miniature composition was the short piano piece. Such pieces were written in great profusion in the nineteenth century, and they appeared under many names. Frédéric Chopin preferred simple genre titles such as Nocturne, Waltz, Scherzo, or **Étude** (study). Robert Schumann preferred descriptive titles. Piano miniatures were composed at all levels of difficulty, ranging from virtuoso tours de force, which hardly anyone but their composers could negotiate, to unassuming pieces playable (and enjoyable) by beginning students.

A good general name for these short Romantic piano pieces (one sometimes used by the Romantics themselves) is **character pieces,** for the essential point about them is that each portrays some definite mood or character. In principle, at least, this is as true of the brilliant virtuoso works as of the simple ones. Each conveys an intense, distinct emotion—an emotion often hinted at by an imaginative title supplied by the composer.

This explains why the Romantic character piece can be thought of as analogous to the Romantic song, or lied, though without its poem. Indeed, six books of such piano pieces by Felix Mendelssohn—pieces that were very popular in Victorian times—are entitled *Songs Without Words.* Some of them have subtitles that stress still further their similarity to lieder: "Spinning Song," "Venetian Boat Song," and the famous "Spring Song."

FRANZ SCHUBERT
Moment Musical No. 2 in A-flat (1827?)

Creative publishers gave Franz Schubert's piano miniatures their titles: "Momens musicals" (spelled wrong) and "Impromptus" (improvisations—Johannes Brahms would later call some of *his* miniatures "caprices"). We heard No. 3 from the published set of "musical moments" on the CD-ROM for Unit I (page 35). No. 2 is the most romantic of its companions.

The main idea, **A,** is a gentle rocking figure, with a nostalgic mood characteristic of Schubert. The mood deepens when **A′** is provided with a relatively long coda, which seems reluctant ever to let go. In between comes **B,** a sad melody in the minor mode; the piano texture changes from cloudy chords in **A** to plain melody with a steady moving accompaniment in **B.** As usual in piano miniatures, the form is simple, at least on the surface: **A B A′ B′ A″.**

LISTEN

Schubert, Moment
Musical No. 2

A
0:00 a, *p*
0:35 a′
B
1:20 b: minor, *p*
A′
2:23 a″ (longer)
3:17 coda
B′
3:57 b′: minor, *ff*
     Turns to the major
A″
4:54 a‴, *p*
5:36 coda

But in fact this is an excellent example of how much these impersonal form diagrams can hide. After **A B A′**, especially with its coda, and after four minutes, we think that the piece must be over—except, perhaps, for a hint when the piano moves to an unusually high register at the coda's final cadence. And indeed **B** returns—*fortissimo,* in the high register, no longer sad but terribly anguished, a cry of pain. In the wake of this climax, there is a momentary switch from the minor mode to the major, a Schubert fingerprint we also noted in Moment Musical No. 3. Does this change heal the pain? By the end of **A″** the high register no longer hints at anything. It simply hovers at the border of hearing, a Romantic evocation of the ineffable.

ROBERT SCHUMANN
Carnaval (1833–35)

2-3   38-39

Schumann's style of piano writing has a warmth and privacy that set it apart from the music of any of the other pianist-composers of his day. A favorite marking on his scores is the German word *innig,* meaning "inward," "intimate," or "heartfelt." Schumann typically assembled his piano pieces into collections with some general title and, often, some interesting musical means of connection among them. If the Romantic character piece for the piano is analogous to the Romantic lied, these collections are analogous to song cycles.

Such a collection is *Carnaval,* a set of twenty short character pieces that really *are* characters—musical portraits of masked guests at a Mardi Gras ball. After the band strikes up an introduction, the sad clown Pierrot arrives, followed by the pantomime figures Harlequin and Columbine, Schumann himself, two of his girlfriends masquerading under the names Estrella and Chiarina, a Coquette, and even the composers Paganini and Chopin. This diverse gallery provided Schumann with an outlet for his whimsy and humor, as well as all his Romantic melancholy and passion.

"Eusebius"   "Eusebius" was Schumann's pen name for his tender, dreamy self, and this little piece presents him at his most introspective. In the passage below, the yearning effect of the high notes (shaded) is compounded by the vague, languorous rhythm:

Eusebius: "In sculpture, the actor's art becomes fixed. The actor transforms the sculptor's forms into living art. The painter turns a poem into a painting. The musician sets a picture to music." Florestan: "The aesthetic principle is the same in every art; only the material differs."

Robert Schumann, 1833

The right-hand triplets and quintuplets blur with the left-hand quarter notes, especially when played with Romantic rubato. The somewhat unusual form is **aa ba b′a′ ba**, in which **b′a′** stands out although it differs from **ba** only in its much thicker chords and its use of the pedal.

"Florestan"   After "Eusebius" ends very tentatively, Schumann's impetuous other self makes his entrance. "Florestan" is built out of a single explosive motive; the piece moves in fits and starts. It gets faster and faster, almost madly, ending completely up in the air. This non-cadence is resolved only in the next number.

Frédéric Chopin (1810–1849)

Chopin was born near Warsaw, where his father, a Frenchman who had emigrated to Poland and married a Polish lady, ran a private school for young gentlemen. In this atmosphere Fryderyk—later he adopted the French form Frédéric—acquired his lifelong taste for life in high society. Provided with the best teachers available, he became an extraordinary pianist. There are many reports of the exquisite delicacy of his playing, and his miraculous ability, as it seemed at the time, to draw romantic sounds out of the piano.

Furthermore, his set of variations on Mozart's "Là ci darem la mano" (see page 210), written when he was seventeen, was already an impressive enough composition to earn a rave review from Robert Schumann.

Chopin settled in Paris, where he found ready acceptance from society people and from other artists and intellectuals, such as the novelist Honoré de Balzac and the painter Eugène Delacroix, who produced a famous portrait of the composer. Chopin made his way as a highly fashionable piano teacher and by selling his music to publishers. The facts that he was Polish and that Poland was being overrun by Russia at that time seem to have made him even more glamorous to the French. Among Chopin's piano miniatures are over fifty Mazurkas and sixteen Polonaises, which are stylized Polish dances.

Chopin was a frail and fastidious personality. Though he sometimes played in public, he truly disliked the hurly-burly of concert life and preferred to perform for select audiences in great houses. More than any other of the great composers, he restricted his work to music for *his*

instrument, the piano. Even his works for piano and orchestra—two concertos and a few other works—were all from his pre-Paris days.

The major event of his personal life was his ten-year romance with Madame Aurore Dudevant, an early feminist and a famous novelist under the pen name George Sand. (They were introduced by Liszt, who wrote an admiring book about Chopin after his death.) The relationship was a rocky one; Sand sketched some unkind scenes from their life together in one of her novels. After the affair broke up in 1847, Chopin's health declined with his spirits. He toured England and Scotland unhappily in 1848 and died the next year, aged thirty-nine, of tuberculosis, a major killer in the nineteenth century.

Chief Works: Character pieces for piano: Preludes (including the "Raindrop" prelude), Nocturnes, Études, Ballades, Waltzes (including the "Minute" waltz), and Polish Mazurkas and Polonaises ▪ Three piano sonatas, including one with a famous funeral march as the slow movement ▪ Two piano concertos ▪ A cello sonata; a few Polish songs

Encore: Listen to some other Chopin Nocturnes, the Fantasy-Impromptu, and Ballade in G Minor.

"Chiarina"   As we are probably meant to guess from the letters in the name, this is a musical portrait of then sixteen-year-old Clara Wieck. The heading is "Passionato," and by the end the dynamic has risen to *fortissimo.* Robert did not see his future wife as a shrinking violet.

FRÉDÉRIC CHOPIN
Nocturne in F-sharp, Op. 15, No. 2 (1831)

4   37

Chopin's twenty-one **nocturnes,** meaning "night pieces," written throughout his career, are as different as twenty-one different nights. But each features a particularly striking tune—a languid serenade, for example, or a dark, secret lament. Something else is usually heard or overheard in the night, too, such as a distant procession, a passionate encounter, or even a fragment of a dance or a folk song.

The opening tune in Chopin's Nocturne in F-sharp has an elegance unique to the composer—an elegance that stems partly from the wonderfully graceful rhythm, partly from the Romantic turns of harmony, and partly from the pianistic decorations of the melodic line. We have seen decorated melodies before,

LISTEN

Chopin, Nocturne in F-sharp

0:00 **a**
0:27 **a′** ornamented
0:58 **b**
1:28 **c**
2:13 **a″**
2:55 **coda**

Was this striking painting, by a minor late nineteenth-century artist, done with Chopin's nocturnes in mind? Called *Notturno*, its cool elegance, faint sensuality, and vaguely apprehensive quality might suggest so.

but Chopin's have an almost liquid quality, caused partly by chromaticism— by the free use of all the notes of the chromatic scale, as in this fragment:

Romantic form contributes to the Romantic effect. Chopin avoids sharp demarcations and literal returns; the music seems to grow spontaneously, in an almost improvisational way. The main tune, **A** (**a a′ b**), does not really end; it is interrupted by plaintive sounds emerging out of nowhere, which surge up to a moment of real passion. Then the return of the tune (**a″**) is fragmentary, though in a way more intense, and the whole is capped by an unexpected little coda: delicious right-hand arpeggios over a bolero rhythm in the left. Free rhythm in the performance (rubato) mirrors the freedom of form.

"That's not your own fingering, is it?" he asked, in his melodious little voice. "No, Liszt's" I said. "Ah, that one has ideas, I tell you!" And Chopin began to try this fingering. "But one could go down the whole keyboard this way like a crayfish scuttling back to his stream. It is perfect, your fingering! I shall use it!"

Reminiscence by a student of Chopin, 1859

3 Early Romantic Program Music

The lied and the character piece for piano—the two main forms of early Romantic miniature compositions—were intimately tied up with nonmusical, usually poetic, ideas. Furthermore, in a work such as Schumann's *Carnaval*, the various piano portraits are juxtaposed in such a way as to hint at their interaction—hint, that is, at a shadowy story line. Poems, stories, and nonmusical ideas in general were also associated with large-scale instrumental pieces.

Liszt's phenomenal virtuosity as a pianist inspired many a cartoonist. The sword here refers to his many decorations; he has a halo because he had turned to religion and become an unordained priest. "The Abbé Liszt" was known to break, if not pianos, piano strings, and this helped ruin one Viennese piano maker (Graf).

Liszt was the greatest piano virtuoso of the nineteenth century; greatest in the twentieth century was the Russian-American pianist Vladimir Horowitz (1904–1989).

Franz Liszt (1811–1886)

There are some important composers whose music we unfortunately have to pass over in this book, because of space limits. In this box and the one on page 264 we give the biographies of three of them, together with some account of their roles in the history of Romantic music.

Franz Liszt learned music from his father on the Hungarian estate of the princes Esterházy, whom Haydn had once served. At age eleven, the boy gave his first piano concert in Vienna, where he met Beethoven. He later settled in Paris, home of another great pianist-composer, Chopin.

Liszt's dashing looks and personality and his liaisons with married noblewomen—Countess d'Agoult and, later, Princess Sayn-Wittgenstein—dazzled Europe as much as his incredible pianistic technique. No one had heard such virtuosity. He drew crowds like a modern rock star and cultivated a lifestyle to match.

After his relationship with d'Agoult came to a stormy end in 1839, Liszt spent a few years giving sensational concerts all over Europe. Tiring of concert life, he then took a position as conductor and director of the theater at Weimar, in Germany, where there was still a court that supported the arts in the eighteenth-century manner. There he wrote his most radical and influential music.

Like many other Romantic composers, Liszt was a writer of note, as well as a musician. He was a strong advocate of the music of Richard Wagner; the two men learned from each other. Both friend and foe linked Wagner's "music dramas" with Liszt's symphonic poems as "Music of the Future." In his personality, however, Liszt was as generous as Wagner was self-centered and devious.

Liszt really had two major careers. The first, at Paris, his career as a fantastic piano virtuoso, underpins a musical ideal that was still alive and well in the 1997 movie *Shine*. It left a mass of fiercely difficult piano music, including the *Transcendental Études* (the name says it all!) and the popular *Hungarian Rhapsodies*—important early products of nationalism in music (see page 292).

Liszt's second career, at Weimar, focused on orchestral music: program symphonies and symphonic poems. We will take up these genres on pages 265 and 290.

Felix Mendelssohn (1809–1847)

Felix Mendelssohn may be the only great composer who has ever come from an upper-class family, a family of converted Jews who were in banking. Their home was a meeting place for artists and intellectuals over generations. Felix and his sister Fanny were brought up with music and every other advantage that came with a life of privilege. (Felix also became a fine amateur painter.)

By the time he was fifteen Felix was conducting the family orchestra in his own music. He went on to a stellar career, not only as an enormously successful composer, but as a pianist, organist, conductor, educator—he founded the Leipzig Conservatory of Music—and even as a musicologist. His performance of Bach's *St. Matthew Passion* was a landmark in the revival of "early music."

This action was typical, for from the start Mendelssohn showed a great respect for, even deference toward, the classics. His music never goes as far as, say, Schumann or Chopin in acceding to Romantic tendencies, but always keeps a firm foundation of Classical technique.

One of Mendelssohn's most significant fields of activity was the concert overture, an early **genre** of Romantic program music; see below. In his lifetime he was admired even more for his oratorios *St. Paul* and *Elijah*, and for popular sets of piano miniatures he called *Songs Without Words*. His Violin Concerto is a special favorite.

Fanny Mendelssohn (1805–1847)

Fanny Mendelssohn, Felix's older sister, was also a highly prolific composer. The siblings were always very close; music was one of their bonds, for Fanny showed as much talent as her brother. Married to a painter named Wilhelm Hensel, she devoted herself to weekly concerts at the Mendelssohn home in Berlin, for which she composed music of all kinds, including even oratorios.

However, Fanny's music did not pass beyond the threshold of the Mendelssohn mansion. Only a small percentage of it found its way into print, at the end of her short life. Fanny is often seen as a victim of patriarchal society and of the general refusal in the past to take women composers seriously. Like Mozart's sister Nannerl, she watched as her younger brother built a great career while she was expected—indeed, conditioned—to put motherhood and family first, music second. But we should remember that unlike other successful women composers of the nineteenth century—from Louise Farrenc (1804–1875) to Clara Schumann (1819–1896) to Cécile Chaminade (1857–1944) and Ethel Smythe (1858–1944)—Fanny Mendelssohn belonged to the upper class. Few members of this class, male or female, had ever pursued public careers in the arts. They didn't need the rat race. Workaholic Felix was an exception.

Fanny's sudden death at age forty-one devastated Felix, and hastened his own death six months later.

As we have seen, *program music* is a term used for instrumental compositions associated with poems, stories, and the like. Program music grew up naturally in opera overtures, for even in the eighteenth century it was seen that an overture might gain special interest if it referred to moods or ideas in the opera to come by citing (or, rather, forecasting) some of its themes.

This happens in Mozart's *Don Giovanni*, in which the next-to-last scene has Don Giovanni carried off to hell by the statue of the murdered Commandant (see page 208). The somber music associated with the Statue is first heard in the opera's overture, even before the curtain has gone up. Lively, effervescent music follows; but the half-serious, half-comical mood of Mozart's opera is already manifest in the overture.

The Concert Overture: Felix Mendelssohn

A further step, conceptually, was the **concert overture,** never intended to be followed by a stage play or an opera—never intended, indeed, for the theater. Robert Schumann wrote an overture to *Hermann und Dorothea*, by Goethe, which is not a play but an epic poem. Hector Berlioz wrote overtures to literary works of various kinds: plays (Shakespeare's *King Lear*), long poems (*The Corsair* by Lord Byron, a special hero for the Romantics), and novels (*Waverly* by Sir Walter Scott).

Probably the best-known and best-loved concert overtures are by Felix Mendelssohn. His concert overture to *A Midsummer Night's Dream* was written at the age of seventeen; the play was a special favorite with both Felix and Fanny. He had no theatrical occasion in mind, though years later the overture was indeed used in productions of the Shakespeare play. At that time Mendelssohn also added other music, and a suite derived from this piece (see page 143) has become a popular concert number.

A work in sonata form, following Classical models quite clearly, the overture to *A Midsummer Night's Dream* nonetheless includes some representational features. Music illustrates the delicate, fluttering fairies in the service of King Oberon and Queen Titania, the sleep induced by Puck's magic flower, and even the braying of Bottom the Weaver when he is turned into a donkey.

Another fine example by Mendelssohn is the *Hebrides* Overture, an evocative, moody depiction of lonely Scottish islands rich in romantic associations. Surging string music suggests the swell and the spray of waves; woodwind fanfares suggest seabird calls, perhaps, or romanticized foghorns. This is evidently program music, but what makes it an overture? Nothing more than the fact that it follows the standard scheme for overtures at the time—namely, a single movement in sonata form.

The Mendelssohns

The Program Symphony: Hector Berlioz

PROGRAM OF THE SYMPHONY: A young musician of unhealthy sensibility and passionate imagination poisons himself with opium in a fit of lovesick despair. Too weak to kill him, the dose of the drug plunges him into a heavy sleep attended by the strangest visions, during which his sensations, emotions, and memories are transformed in his diseased mind into musical thoughts and images. Even the woman he loves becomes a melody to him, an *idée fixe* [an obsession], as it were, that he finds and hears everywhere.

So begins a long pamphlet that the French Romantic composer Hector Berlioz distributed at performances of his first symphony—a symphony which he could justifiably call *Fantastic,* and which to this day remains his most famous work. It certainly represents a more radical approach to program music than that of the concert overture. Berlioz, too, had written several concert overtures, but he now felt the need for a broader canvas. In his **program symphonies**— entire symphonies with programs, spelled out movement by movement, in this case—Berlioz set the tone for the "grandiose" compositions that were to become as characteristic of Romanticism as its musical miniatures.

HECTOR BERLIOZ
Fantastic Symphony: Episodes in the Life of an Artist (1830)

Clearly Berlioz had a gift for public relations, for the program of his *Fantastic* Symphony was not a familiar play or novel, but an autobiographical fantasy of the most lurid sort. Here was music that encouraged listeners to think it had been written under the influence of opium, the drug of choice among the Romantics, which shocked society at large. What is more, half of Paris knew that Berlioz was madly in love (from afar) with an Irish actress, Harriet Smithson, who had taken the city by storm with her Shakespearean roles.

Audiences have never been quite sure how seriously to take it all, but they continue to be bowled over by Berlioz's effects of tone color. He demanded an orchestra of unprecedented size, which he used in incredibly original and imaginative ways. Also highly original was the notion of having a single theme recur in all the movements as a representation of the musician's beloved—his **idée fixe.**

Love or music—which power can uplift man to the sublimest heights? It is a large question; yet it seems to me one should answer it in this way: Love cannot give an idea of music; music can give an idea of love. But why separate them? They are the two wings of the soul . . .

From the *Memoirs of Hector Berlioz,* 1869

Here is the *idée fixe* theme as it first appears:

This typically Romantic melody seems like a passionate struggle to inch higher and higher up the scale: E–F (measure 2), F♯–G (measure 7), G–A♭, G–A♮, A–B♭, B♮–C. Near the end, measure 19 provides a positive shudder of emotion. Notice how many dynamic, rubato, and other marks Berlioz has supplied, to ensure just the right expressive quality from moment to moment.*

To illustrate his drastic mood swings, Berlioz subjects the *idée fixe* to thematic transformation (see page 248) for all its other appearances in the opium dream. The last movement, for example, has a grotesque parody of the theme; its new jerky rhythm and squeaky orchestration (using the small E-flat clarinet) thoroughly undermine the original Romantic mood.

First Movement: Reveries, Passions (Largo—Allegro agitato e appassionato assai)   We first hear a short, quiet run-in—a typically Romantic touch suggesting that the music has grown up imperceptibly out of silence. Then the "soul-sickness" mentioned in the program is depicted by a halting, passionate melody. A faster section begins with the *idée fixe,* and the music picks up energy (the "volcanic love" of the program).

This fast section follows sonata form, but only very loosely indeed. The *idée fixe* is the main theme, and a second theme is simply a derivative of the first. Some of the finest strokes in this movement run counter to Classical principles—for example, the arresting up-and-down harmonized chromatic scale that arrives in the development section without any logical connection to anything else. The recapitulation, too, is extended in a very un-Classical fashion; it actually includes a whole new melody for the oboe.

Near the end, beginning an outsized coda, the *idée fixe* returns noisily at a faster tempo—the first of its many transformations. At the very end, slower music depicts the program's "religious consolations."

Second Movement: A Ball (Allegro non troppo)   A symphony needs the simplicity and easy swing of a dance movement, and this ballroom episode of the opium dream conveniently provided one. The dance in question is not a minuet or a scherzo, but a waltz, the most popular ballroom dance of the nineteenth

THE PROGRAM CONTINUES: First he recalls the soul-sickness, the aimless passions, the baseless depressions and elations that he felt before first seeing his loved one; then the volcanic love that she instantly inspired in him; his jealous furies; his return to tenderness; his religious consolations.

WOODWINDS STRINGS

He encounters his beloved at a ball, in the midst of a noisy, brilliant party.

*The music example has been simplified to facilitate reading. *Canto espressivo* = expressive song; *dolce* = sweetly; *poco* = somewhat; *poco a poco* = bit by bit; *animato* = animated; *ritenuto* = slowed down (ritardando); *a tempo* = back to the original tempo.

century. The *idée fixe*, transformed into a lilting triple meter, first appears in the position of the trio (**B** in the **A B A** form) and then returns hauntingly in a coda.

Third Movement: Scene in the Country (Adagio)   Invoking nature to reflect human emotions was a favorite Romantic procedure. The "pastoral duet" is played by an English horn and an offstage oboe (boy and girl, perhaps?). At the end, the English horn returns to the accompaniment of distant thunder sounds, played on four differently tuned timpani. Significantly, the oboe can no longer be heard.

In this movement the *idée fixe* returns in a new, strangely agitated transformation. It is interrupted by angry sounds swelling to a climax, indicative of the anxieties chronicled in the program.

On a summer evening in the country, he hears two shepherds piping in dialogue. The pastoral duet, the location, the light rustling of trees stirred gently by the wind, some newly conceived grounds for hope— all this gives him a feeling of unaccustomed calm. But she *appears again . . . what if she is deceiving him?*

Fourth Movement: March to the Scaffold (Allegretto non troppo) This movement is the exciting march that you (may) have heard as the Overture to this book. See Listening Chart 1, on page 4. Adding a fifth movement to the traditional four of the Classical symphony was a typical Berlioz innovation (though it can be traced back to the Beethoven he so much admired). **SG** 1-3

There are two main themes: a long downward scale ("gloomy and wild") and a blaring, ominous military march ("brilliant and grand"). Later the scale theme appears divided up in its orchestration between plucked and bowed strings, woodwinds, brass, and percussion—a memorable instance of Berlioz's novel imagination for tone color. The scale theme also appears in a truly shattering inverted form (that is, moving up instead of down).

As we noted on page 5, Berlioz had written the march itself or something like it several years earlier. As he revised it to go into the *Fantastic* Symphony, he added a coda that uses the *idée fixe* and therefore only makes sense in terms of the symphony's program. The final fall of the axe is illustrated musically by the sound of a guillotine chop and a military snare-drum roll, right after bars 1–2 of the *idée fixe*. "Berlioz tells it like it is," conductor Leonard Bernstein once remarked. "You take a trip and you end up screaming at your own funeral."

He dreams he has killed his beloved, that he is condemned to death and led to execution. A march accompanies the procession, now gloomy and wild, now brilliant and grand. Finally the idée fixe *appears for a moment, to be cut off by the fall of the axe.*

Fifth Movement: Dream of a Witches' Sabbath (Larghetto—Allegro)   Now the element of parody is added to the astonishing orchestral effects pioneered

Witches' Sabbath (detail), by Francisco Goya (1746–1828)

Hector Berlioz (1803–1869)

If the deaf Beethoven was the first great composer who made his living actually as a composer, rather than as a performer, Berlioz was the first composer who played no standard instrument like violin or piano at all. His father, a country doctor, sent him to medical school in Paris. But, as Berlioz told it, he was so horrified when he entered the dissecting room, where the rats were nibbling at the scraps, that he leaped out the window and went to the Paris Conservatory of Music instead.

The anecdote is typical of his emotional and utterly Romantic personality. More than any other composer of his generation, except Wagner, Berlioz "thought the unthinkable" in music; his "grandiose" program symphonies had simply no precedent and were not matched in ambition until the time, about 1900, of Gustav Mahler. The only instrument he played well was the guitar, but his imagination for orchestral tone color was extraordinary. Like almost all the Romantic composers, he was inspired by literary models, including especially Shakespeare—his *Lélio* is a meditation on *Hamlet,* and his opera *Béatrice et Bénédict* is taken from *Much Ado about Nothing*—and Virgil. *The Trojans* (1858), his long two-part opera derived from Virgil's *Aeneid,* was seldom performed until modern times, but it is now regarded as his masterpiece.

Berlioz had two unhappy marriages, the first to the Irish Shakespearean actress Harriet Smithson, who is immortalized as the *idée fixe* in the *Fantastic* Symphony. In spite of suffering from constant ridicule from the musical establishment on the one hand, and wretched health on

the other, it was a triumph of his impetuous personality that Berlioz ultimately managed to have most of his enormous compositions performed and to gain a good measure of recognition in musically conservative Paris.

Throughout his life, he was obliged to support himself with musical journalism, at which he was a master; his *Memoirs* is one of the most delightful books ever written about music. He also wrote important treatises on orchestration and conducting. One of the first great conductors, Berlioz toured extensively as a conductor of his own music, especially in Germany, where he was welcomed in progressive circles.

His last years were spent in physical pain and depression. After 1862 he listened to little music and composed none. Berlioz died in Paris in 1869.

Chief Works: Program symphonies: *Fantastic* Symphony, *Harold in Italy, Romeo and Juliet* ▪ Concert overtures: *King Lear, The Corsair, The Roman Carnival* ▪ Operas: *Benvenuto Cellini, The Trojans* (after Virgil's *Aeneid*) ▪ Oratorios: *The Damnation of Faust, The Childhood of Christ* ▪ A great Requiem Mass for orchestra, chorus, and four brass bands, and a *Te Deum*

Encore: After the *Fantastic* Symphony, listen to the Symphony *Harold in Italy;* Overture *The Corsair.* Read the *Memoirs.*

---

earlier in the symphony. First we hear the unearthly sounds of the nighttime locale of the witches' orgy. Their swishing broomsticks are heard, and some kind of distant horn calls summon them. Mutes are used in the brass instruments—perhaps their first "poetic" use ever.

As Berlioz remarks, the "noble and timid" *idée fixe* sounds thoroughly vulgar in its last transformation, played in a fast jig rhythm by the shrill E-flat clarinet. (Compare the music examples on page 266.) The treatment of the *idée fixe* here is strictly "programmatic": When the theme first arrives, only two phrases are played before the orchestra breaks in, with a "roar of joy" welcoming Harriet Smithson to the orgy.

As the merriment is brought to an end by a dramatic funeral bell, Berlioz prepares his most sensational stroke of all—a burlesque of one of the most solemn and famous of Gregorian chants, the *Dies irae* (Day of Wrath). This chant is the centerpiece of Masses for the dead, or Requiem Masses; in Catholic France, any audience would have recognized the *Dies irae* instantly. Three segments of it are used. Its distorted rhythms and grotesque orchestral sounds paint a blasphemous, shocking picture of the witches' black mass.

He finds himself at a Witches' Sabbath. . . . Unearthly sounds, groans, shrieks of laughter, distant cries echoed by other cries. The beloved's melody is heard, but it has lost its character of nobility and timidity. It is *she* who comes to the Sabbath! At her arrival, a roar of joy. She joins in the devilish orgies. A funeral knell; burlesque of the *Dies irae.*

LISTENING CHART 18

5-11 16-22

Berlioz, *Fantastic* Symphony, fifth movement

9 min., 59 sec.

	INTRODUCTION		
5 16	0:00		Mysterious orchestral effects
	0:28	*Fanfare*	Like a distant summons: trombones, then flutes plus piccolo echoed by muted French horns
	0:58		Free repetitions: mysterious sounds, fanfare
	IDÉE FIXE		
	1:40		Prefatory statement: two phrases (only) of the *idée fixe;* note the bass drum. Riotous orchestral response, *ff*
6 17	1:59	*Idée fixe*	Entire tune presented in a grotesque transformation, in 6/8 meter, played by "squeaky" E-flat clarinets
:30	2:29	*Crescendo*	Big climax—the first of many
:51	2:50	Upward motive	A short, expectant motive (later this motive initiates the fugue subject of the "Round Dance")
:54	2:53	*Transition*	Quiet descending passage
:12	3:11	Funeral bells	**Three sets of three bells (the third set is muted); the upward motive also appears**
	DIES IRAE		
7 18	3:37	Segment 1	Segment 1 of the plainchant is played in three versions:
			(1) tubas and bassoons—slow
:22	3:59		(2) horns and trombones—faster
:32	4:09		(3) woodwinds—faster still (the rhythm here recalls that of the *idée fixe*)
:37	4:14	Segment 2	Segment 2 of the plainchant, same three versions
:01	4:38	Segment 3	Segment 3 (begins like segment 1), same three versions
:34	5:11	*Transition*	The upward motive is developed; crescendo
8 19	**WITCHES' ROUND DANCE (free fugue)**		
	5:29	**Exposition**	Four entries of the fugue subject
:27	5:56	*Episode 1*	
:46	6:15	**Subject entries**	*Three more entries, in stretto*
9 20	6:31	*Episode 2*	A passage starting with a loud rhythmic motive, derived from the subject, comes four times.
:20	6:51		The music dies down.
:40	7:11		Fragments of the *Dies irae*
:55	7:26		Long transition; crescendo over a drum roll
:35	8:06	**Subject entry**	The original subject returns.
10 21	8:13	**Subject plus** *Dies irae*	The two themes together in a polyphonic combination. This is a climax; trumpets play the *Dies irae* for the first time.
:31	8:44	**Subject entry**	Final appearance of subject: over strings *col legno* (played with the wood, that is, the back of the bow). Some notes are lengthened.
11 22	9:19	*Dies irae*	Segment 1 of the *Dies irae* hastily recollected; big drum strokes
:09	9:28	Conclusion	Final passage of cadences: very loud

The final section of the movement is a "Witches' Round Dance." Berlioz wrote a free fugue—a traditional form in a nontraditional context; he uses counterpoint to give a feeling of tumult. The subject is an excited one:

The climax of the fugue (and of the symphony) comes when the Round Dance theme is heard together with the *Dies irae*, played by the trumpets. Berlioz wanted to drive home the point that it is the witches, represented by the theme of their round dance, who are parodying the church melody. The *idée fixe* seems at last to be forgotten. But in real life Berlioz did not forget; he married Smithson and both of them lived to regret it.

Web: *Research and test your understanding of early Romantic music at* <bedfordstmartins.com/listen>.

Romantic Opera

An important theme of Romanticism was the transcendence of artistic barriers. The idea of combining music with poetry and other forms of literature, and even with philosophy, made perfect sense to Romantic composers and their audiences. The age that produced the lied—a German song with an important poetic dimension—was also committed to the union of music and drama. The nineteenth century was a golden age of opera, which flourished all over Europe from Germany, France, and Italy to Bohemia and Russia.

Opera in the nineteenth century was affected by another important Romantic theme: the celebration of music as the most profound of all the arts. Opera composers and librettists began thinking seriously about the meaning and "message" of their work; they came to view opera as a type of serious

Carve this into your head, in letters of brass: An opera must draw tears, cause horror, bring death, by means of song.

Opera composer Vincenzo Bellini, 1834

The Wolf's Glen Scene from Weber's *Der Freischütz*, most famous of early German Romantic operas (see page 272).

Early Romantic Opera

Romantic opera made its serious start in the 1820s, after the end of the Viennese Classical period. It did not, however, start or flourish in the heartland of Classical music, which was Vienna. In that city, both Beethoven and Schubert felt threatened by the popular rage for the operas of Gioacchino Rossini, a young Italian whose meteoric career left a mark on the whole of Europe.

Gioacchino Rossini (1792–1868)

Rossini is most famous today for crisp, elegant opera buffas in a style that is not all that far from Mozart—the immortal *Barber of Seville* among them. The overtures of these operas, which are popular as concert pieces, are even written in sonata form, the true trademark of Classicism in music.

But in his own day Rossini was admired equally for his serious operas, which established the style and form of Italian Romantic opera. This is called *bel canto* opera because of its glorification of beautiful singing *(bel canto* means just that—"beautiful song"). Rossini's operas provided models of Romantic emotional melodic expression, such as Desdemona's "Willow Song" from his Shakespeare opera *Otello*. The same operas are also well stocked with coloratura arias, showcases for the legendary virtuoso singers of that era.

To everyone's astonishment, Rossini gave up opera after the success of *William Tell,* his greatest work, in 1829.

Gaetano Donizetti (1797–1848)

Donizetti, who dominated Italian *bel canto* opera after Rossini's sudden retirement in 1830, moved decisively in the direction of simple, sentimental arias and blood-and-thunder "action" music. Enormously prolific, he wrote more than sixty operas in his short lifetime.

The most famous are *Lucia di Lammermoor,* based on the historical novel by Scott mentioned on page 273, and *Don Pasquale,* a very late example of opera buffa. In the 1970s, the American soprano Beverly Sills starred in

a Donizetti trilogy featuring famous queens of English history: *Anna Bolena* (Anne Boleyn, the ill-fated second wife of Henry VIII), *Maria Stuarda* (Mary Stuart—Mary, Queen of Scots), and *Roberto Devereux* (about Queen Elizabeth I and Robert Devereux, Earl of Essex).

Vincenzo Bellini (1801–1835)

Vincenzo Bellini strikes listeners today as the most refined among the three early *bel canto* composers. He wrote many fewer operas than the others, and his most beautiful arias have a unique Romantic sheen. The title role in *Norma,* his finest work, is the final testing ground for sopranos, for it demands highly expressive singing, coloratura fireworks, and great acting, all in unusual quantities.

Verdi often expressed his admiration for the supremely melodious Bellini. All the same, he learned more from the more robust and dramatic Donizetti.

Carl Maria von Weber (1786–1826)

Weber was the founder of German Romantic opera. His most important work, *Der Freischütz* (The Magic Bullet), has the quality of a German folktale or ballad put to music. Max, a somewhat driven young huntsman, sells his soul to the devil for seven magic bullets, but is redeemed by the sacrifice of his pure, blond fiancée, Agatha.

Two spiritual arias sung by Agatha in this opera show Romantic melody at its best. There are German choruses in folk-song style. A famous scene of devilish conjuration in the Wolf's Glen features sensational orchestral writing of a kind previously unknown to opera.

Supernatural subject matter, with its strongly moral overtone—quite unlike the historical subjects chosen by Donizetti, for example—and emphasis on the orchestra became characteristic of German Romantic opera, features still evident in the mature music dramas of Richard Wagner, who started out in the 1830s as an opera composer in Weber's mold. Otherwise, however, Wagner's music dramas leave early Romantic opera far behind.

Legendary singers of the *bel canto* era: Pauline Viardot (1821–1910), Maria Malibran (1808–1836), and Giulia Grisi (1811–1869), along with a playbill for one of their favorite showcases, the opera *Norma* by Vincenzo Bellini.

drama in music, not just a vehicle for song, spectacle, and entertainment, as had often been the case before. Richard Wagner is famous for embracing, publicizing, and indeed co-opting this notion. He put it into action with his "music dramas"—works that fascinated the later nineteenth century. Nonetheless, Wagner was building on new attitudes toward opera that were developing all over Europe even when he was still an unknown provincial conductor.

Thus many operas took their subjects from highly regarded Romantic novels, such as *Ivanhoe*, *The Lady of the Lake*, and *The Bride of Lammermoor*, by Sir Walter Scott. Since poets and playwrights were turning with new enthusiasm to Shakespeare's plays, opera composers, too, drew on them widely. Giuseppe Verdi set versions of Shakespeare's tragedies *Macbeth* and *Othello* as well as the comedy *The Merry Wives of Windsor*. Over his long career, Verdi developed his own form of musical drama, which bears comparison with that of Wagner or anyone else for seriousness and power.

1   Verdi and Italian Opera

Giuseppe Verdi, the greatest of Italian opera composers, was the dominant figure in nineteenth-century opera houses. For while Wagner's "music dramas" and his theories of opera attracted much excited attention, Verdi's operas got many more performances. Then as now, people were inevitably drawn to compare and contrast these two masters.

The heart of the contrast lies in Verdi's unswerving commitment to the human voice. In this, he was a faithful follower of the *bel canto* principles of Rossini, Donizetti, and Bellini. Verdi never allowed the voice to be overshadowed by the orchestra, and over the course of his long career he learned to write more and more beautiful melodies. Opera was a singing art to Verdi, and generations of Italians before, during, and after his lifetime have enthusiastically agreed with him.

But while audiences have always loved Verdi's melodies, what he himself cared most about was the dramatic quality of his operas. First and foremost, Verdi was interested in people, people placed in situations in which strong exciting actions bring out equally strong emotions. He sought out dramatic subjects full of stirring action, and he had a genius for finding just the right vocal melody to enhance a dramatic situation.

Recitative and Aria: The Orchestra

As an opera composer, Verdi never wavered in his commitment to the human voice. That said, however, it must also be said that the orchestra plays a much richer role in Verdi's operas than in those of any of his Italian predecessors. This was all but inevitable in the orchestra-intoxicated nineteenth century.

The role of the orchestra was especially expanded in passages of recitative or near-recitative—the relic or descendant of the recitatives of Baroque opera seria and Classical opera buffa. Italian opera still held roughly to the old division of declamation (recitative) for the action and dialogue portions of an opera, and melody (arias) for reflective, emotional expression. (Ensembles encompassed both.) But plot action and dialogue were now always accompanied by the full orchestra. The orchestra is usually not restricted to the simple chords that were normal in earlier recitative styles; it plays more active, motivic, and excited music that points up the words and urges the singers on.

Giuseppe Verdi (1813–1901)

The son of a storekeeper in a tiny village in northern Italy, Verdi had a spotty education. He played church organ and conducted the band of the neighboring little town. A local merchant, Antonio Barezzi, who became a patron and almost a second father to the young man, sent him to Milan to study music.

In those days, the center of musical life in Italy was Milan's famous opera house, La Scala. After several discouraging years in that city, Verdi scored a huge success with his biblical opera *Nabucco* (Nebuchadnezzar) when he was twenty-nine years old. For the next ten years he composed operas at a furious rate for opera houses in Italy, Paris, and London. Three great hits in the early 1850s are still his most popular works: *Rigoletto,* which chronicles cynical and deadly court intrigues (the original play was banned), *Il trovatore,* a grisly tale in the age of chivalry, and—entirely up to date—*La traviata,* about a courtesan with a noble heart. After this Verdi took more time with his operas, and his later works became richer and more subtle.

Verdi was an ardent supporter of the Risorgimento, or Italian liberation movement, and many of his early operas had patriotic themes. The most beloved number in *Nabucco* was a nostalgic hymn of the Hebrew slaves in Babylon—a clear reference to the Italians under the heel of the Austrian empire. In the year of revolution, 1848,

Verdi wrote the rousing *Battle of Legnano.* "Verdi" actually became a patriotic acronym for the popular choice for king—Vittorio Emmanuele, *Re d'Italia.* After independence was achieved, the composer was made an honorary deputy in the first Italian parliament.

A dour character and a tough businessman, Verdi drove hard bargains with opera impresarios, bullied his librettists, and insisted on supervising the production of his new operas. When he had accumulated enough money, he retired to a fine country estate near his birthplace and spent his later years hunting and raising livestock. After fifteen years of this life, he was coaxed out of retirement by his canny publisher and by an eminent librettist, Arrigo Boito. In his seventies, Verdi wrote his two greatest operas with Boito on Shakespearean subjects: the tragedy *Otello* and the comedy *Falstaff.*

Verdi's first marriage, to the daughter of his early patron Barezzi, ended when his young wife and two babies died within two years. The composer bore the emotional scars of this tragedy all his life, and it may be that the many moving scenes between fathers and daughters in Verdi's operas served to channel his feelings about fatherhood. He later married a remarkable woman, Giuseppina Strepponi, a singer who had assisted him in his early career and starred in his first success, *Nabucco.* She had been Verdi's mistress for many years.

By the time he died, at the age of eighty-eight, Verdi was a national institution, and he was mourned throughout Italy. Schools closed. Eulogies were delivered in a special session of the senate in Rome. Nearly 300,000 people saw the old man to his grave. His operas remain the most popular of all in the international repertory.

Chief Works: Twenty-four operas, including *Nabucco, Macbeth, Rigoletto, Il trovatore, La traviata, Don Carlo, The Force of Destiny, Aida* ■ Two great Shakespeare operas composed in his seventies, *Otello* and *Falstaff* ■ A Requiem Mass, and a few other choral works; a string quartet

Encore: After *Aida* (Act IV), listen to *Otello* (Act I); *Rigoletto* (Act III).

A popular graffito of the Italian revolution: "Viva VERDI" (meaning "Long live Victor Emmanuel, King of Italy").

"Recitative" is no longer a satisfactory name—though no other name exists—for this action music in Verdi's operas. Highly melodramatic, it is always on the point of merging into a full-fledged melodic style. What distinguishes this music from actual arias is that arias are formally complete and distinct. Unlike passages of Verdian recitative, Verdian arias can be (and often are) extracted and sung separately, as concert numbers.

In arias and duets, the orchestra's role is smaller; here, however, Verdi uses another Romantic resource, that of rich harmonies underpinning melodic high points and climaxes. Many—though by no means all—of Verdi's arias might be described as simple strophic songs in his own exuberant style of Romantic melody. Some of his most famous music consists of timeless tunes such as the tenor aria "La donna è mobile" from *Rigoletto*, the choral hymn "Va pensiero" from *Nabucco,* and the duet "O terra, addio" from *Aida,* which we will examine next.

GIUSEPPE VERDI
Aida (1871)

Aida is one of the most frequently performed of all operas. It includes gorgeous arias—including a tenor favorite, "Celeste Aida"—and grandiose stage display, including elephants. Egypt is the locale; this work was commissioned for a new opera house in Cairo, for an enormous sum. Egypt was very much in the news at the time, on account of a milestone in the history of nineteenth-century capitalism and commerce, the opening of the Suez Canal in 1869. Constructed by the visionary French entrepreneur Ferdinand-Marie de Lesseps, this 100-mile freshwater canal opened a seafaring trade route from the Mediterranean to India and the Far East, vastly superior to going all the way around Africa.

In view of his commission, Verdi chose an Egyptian subject and wrote some exotic and (as he thought) Egyptian-sounding music. In other hands, perhaps, all this might have been pretty vulgar. But Verdi's arias, display, and exoticism are coupled with an absorbing drama, a drama of credible human beings destroyed by powerful political forces and equally powerful emotions.

Background   The plot of *Aida* is thoroughly romantic (in the sense of amorous). A tragic love triangle is acted out against the background of a war between ancient Egypt—controlled by a sinister priesthood—and Ethiopia.

Acts I and II introduce a young Egyptian general, Radames, and a captive Ethiopian slave girl, Aida, who are secretly in love. (The Egyptians don't know that Aida is the daughter of Amonasro, King of Ethiopia.) Unfortunately, Radames has also attracted Amneris, a passionate and jealous Egyptian princess.

In Act III, by a turn of the plot that we need not follow here, Radames is tricked into revealing his country's battle plans to Aida. Amneris discovers their tryst, and in a jealous rage she turns Radames over to the all-powerful priests for judgment as a traitor. Aida escapes in the confusion.

In Act IV Amneris offers to save Radames if he will return her love. To her dismay, he says he would rather die than live without Aida; Amneris realizes too late that she has assured the doom of the man she loves. His trial by the priests, in Act IV, scene i, which she witnesses, is one of the most dramatic in the entire opera. Radames makes no defense and is condemned to be buried alive in a tomb under the temple, sealed in by a huge stone.

Tomb Scene (Act IV, scene ii)   Radames has just been entombed. Verdi called for a very striking stage set, divided horizontally: below, a cramped cell containing Radames; above, the Temple of Vulcan, complete with altar, colossal statue of Osiris, and other grandiose Egyptian paraphernalia. Although the impact of Verdi's music seldom fails, outside of the theater a special effort is required to envisage the stage and the action, so as to appreciate the full range of Verdi's dramatic art.

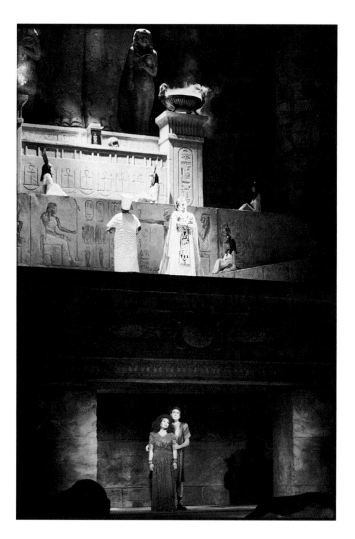

Recitative   The scene opens with quiet, ominous music in the strings—already, in its understated way, a forecast of doom. The first singing consists of three short passages of recitative. Each follows the same general plan. In each recitative passage, simple declamatory singing (with very light orchestral accompaniment) leads to an intense moment of genuine melody, with rich harmonic and orchestral support.

Radames begins singing on a lengthy monotone, but works up some emotion when he thinks of Aida and hopes she will be spared knowledge of his fate. Then his more excited second speech is still fragmentary, up to the point when he discovers that Aida has hidden in his tomb to see him once again and die with him. He cries out "You, in this tomb!" on a high note, picking up from an anguished downward scale in the orchestra.

The third recitative passage, Aida's reply, begins simply, over a knell-like orchestral accompaniment. It melts into a beautiful and sensuously harmonized melodic phrase when she tells him she wants to die in his arms.

Ariosos   There follow two concise tunelike sections, or *ariosos* (see page 100). In the first of them, sung by Radames, notice the subdued, subservient role of the orchestra. The next arioso is more tuneful yet, with Aida's phrases falling into an almost Classical **a a′ b a′ c** pattern. The harmony is fully Romantic, however, especially in phrase **b**.

Take great pains with the contrast between the two levels! The lower one is gloomy, with stark colors, bathed in a grey-green light; the temple [above] glows with light, warm colors.

Columns will serve very well to mask the lighting mechanism, which should preferably be gas jets.

Verdi on the visuals in *Aida*

Duet (with Chorus)   Then Verdi mounts his impressive final scene. At the top level of the stage, priests and priestesses move slowly as they sing a hymn with an exotic, Near Eastern flavor. They are invoking the great god Ptah:

CHORUS OF PRIESTS AND PRIESTESSES (with harp accompaniment)

Im - - menso, immenso Ftha, del mon - - do _ spirito ani - ma - tor _____
Great Ptah, the world's creative spirit

At the bottom level, Aida and Radames begin their final duet, a farewell to the sorrows of earth and a welcome to eternity. It is a famous instance of Verdi's simple and yet expansive melodic style:

Andante
AIDA, then RADAMES

O terra ad - dio addi - o, val - le di pianti,   Sogno di gaudio che in do - lor   sva - nì;   A noi si
Farewell to earth, farewell, vale of tears,   *Dream of happiness which vanishes in grief;*   *The*

schiude, si schiude il   ciel, ___ si schiude il ciel e l'alme erran - ti ____ Volano al   raggio dell' eter - no dì.
heavens open and our fleeing souls   *Escape to the rays of eternal day.*

There is an exquisite Romantic harmony at the climax of the melody, in **c** of the **a a′ b a′ c** form—and the final climax, on nearly the highest note in the tenor's range, has to be sung very softly. This gives the melody a uniquely ethereal effect, as befits a couple who are about to die from lack of oxygen.

Other features reinforce this effect: the melodic line that focuses on just a few notes (high and low G♭ and D♭), and the high accompanying haze of string instruments that later swell up ecstatically. We sense that Aida and Radames are already far out of this world, perfectly attuned to each other (they sing the same tune in octaves) in a love that transcends death itself.

LISTEN   Verdi, *Aida*, Tomb Scene, Act IV, scene ii

4   2

12-15   23-26

RECITATIVE: Radames alone, then Aida

Part 1: Radames reflects *Quiet orchestral introduction (strings) sets the mournful mood. Radames sings his first three lines on a monotone. Accompaniment: slow and halting.*

0:26	**Radames:**	La fatal pietra sopra me si chiuse;	The fatal stone closes over me;
		Ecco la tomba mia.	This is my tomb.
		Del dì la luce più non vedro . . .	The light of day I'll never see again.
		Non rivedrò più Aida.	I'll never see Aida.
		Aida, dove sei tu? possa tu almeno	Aida, where are you?
1:51		Viver felice, e la mia sorte orrenda	Live happily, and never know
		Sempre ignorar!	Of my terrible death.

Part 2: Radames hears a sound *Accompaniment: the rhythm picks up*

2:04	**Radames:**	Qual gemito—una larva—un vision . . .	What sound was that? a ghost? a vision?
		No! forma umana è questa . . . Ciel, Aida!	No, a human form . . . Aida!
	Aida:	Son io . . .	Yes . . .
	Radames:	Tu, in questa tomba!	You, in this tomb!

(12 / 23 in left margin)

Part 3: Aida explains *Accompaniment: mournful low notes*

2:41	**Aida:**	Presago il core della tua condanna,	A presentiment of my heart foretold your sentence;
		In questa tomba che per te s'appriva	This tomb awaited you—
		Io penetrai furtiva,	I hid secretly in it,
		E qui lontana da ogni umano sguardo	And here, far from any human gaze,
		Nelle tue braccia desiai morire.	I wanted to die in your arms.

ARIOSO I

13
24

Radames reacts in despair *"Con passione"—passionately*

3:33	**Radames:**	Morir! si pura e bella!	Dying, so innocent and beautiful,
		Morir per me d'amore,	Dying, for love of me!
		Degli anni tuoi nel fiore,	So young,
		degli anni tuoi nel fiore fuggir la vita!	so young to give up life!
		T'avea in cielo per l'amor creata,	You were made in heaven for love
		Ed io t'uccido per averti amata!	And I have killed you by loving you!
		No, non morrai, troppo t'amai, troppo	You cannot die! I love you too much,
		sei bella!	you are too beautiful!

ARIOSO II

Aida, "almost in a trance" *Ethereal high strings*

14
25

4:50	**Aida:**	Vedi? di morte l'angelo	See, the angel of death
		Radiante a noi s'appressa,	Approaches us in radiance,
		Ne adduce a eterni gaudii	Leading to eternal joys
		Sovra i suoi vanni d'or.	On his golden wings.
		Già veggo il ciel dischiudersi;	I see the heavens open;
0:40	5:30	Ivi ogni affano cessa,	Here pain ceases,
		Ivi *comincia l'estasi*	Here begins the ecstasy
		D'un immortal amor.	Of immortal love.

CHORUS (on the upper stage) with interjections by Radames and Aida
Modal harmonies, harp, and flute

1:13	6:03	**Aida:**	Triste canto!	Mournful chant!	**Chorus** *(simultaneously):*
		Radames:	Il tripudio dei sacerdoti . . .	The priestly rites . . .	Immenso Ftha,
		Aida:	Il nostro inno di morte.	Our funeral hymn.	del mondo spirito animator,
		Radames:	Nè le mie forti braccia	All of my strength cannot	noi t'invocchiamo.
			Smuovere ti potranno, o fatal pietra!	Move that fatal stone!	
		Aida:	Invan—tutto e finito	In vain—all is finished	Great Ptah,
			Sulla terra per noi.	For us on earth.	the world's creative spirit,
		Radames:	È vero, è vero!	True, it is true.	we invoke thee.

DUET: First Aida, then Radames with Aida *With quiet high strings*

15
26

6:44	**Aida and**		
	Radames:	O terra, addio, addio, valle di pianti,	Farewell to earth, vale of tears,
		Sogno di gaudio che in dolor svanì,	Dream of happiness which vanishes in grief;
		A noi *si schiude* il ciel,	The heavens open,
		si schiude il ciel e l'alme erranti	And our fleeing souls
		Volano al raggio dell'eterno dì.	Escape to the rays of eternal day.

CHORUS (on the upper stage) singing with Aida and Radames
DUET continues: Aida and Radames together (same music) with Amneris and the Chorus

2:39	9:23	**Aida and**			
		Radames:	O terra addio, addio valle di pianti,		**Chorus** *(simultaneously):*
			Sogno di gaudio che in dolor svanì,		Immenso Ftha,
			A noi *si schiude* il ciel,		del mondo spirito animator,
			si schiude il ciel e l'alme erranti		noi t'invocchiamo.
			Volano al raggio dell'eterno dì.		
4:18	11:02	**Amneris:**	Pace t'imploro, salma adorata,	Rest in peace, I pray, beloved spirit;	Great Ptah,
			Isi placata, *Isi placata* ti schiuda il ciel,	May Isis, placated, welcome you to	the world's creative spirit,
4:34	11:18		*pace t'imploro, pace* . . .	heaven . . . peace, peace . . .	we invoke thee.

*Ends with violins playing the "O terra" tune, Amneris singing "Pace, pace," and the Chorus
repeating "Immenso Ftha!"*

Conclusion   Before the final curtain, a figure in mourning enters the temple above the tomb to pray. Drained of all the emotion that she poured out in earlier scenes, Amneris can only whisper on a monotone, "Peace, rest in peace, I pray" *(Pace t'imploro)*. The different psychic states of the characters are made more vivid by simultaneous contrast, a principle we saw at work in Mozart's opera buffa ensembles (see page 206). Amneris's grief is set directly against the ecstatic, otherworldly togetherness of Radames and Aida.

High violins take over the duet melody; one can almost visualize the souls of Aida and Radames ascending to "eternal day." And by giving the last words to the priests—the judges of Radames and the proponents of Egypt's wars—Verdi hands them the ultimate responsibility for the threefold tragedy.

2 Wagner and "Music Drama"

Richard Wagner was, after Beethoven, the most influential of all nineteenth-century composers. His strictly musical innovations, in harmony and orchestration, revolutionized instrumental music as well as opera. In terms of opera, Wagner is famous for his novel concept of the "complete work of art" (*Gesamtkunstwerk*; see below) and his development of a special operatic technique, that of the "guiding motive" (leitmotiv).

Unlike earlier innovative composers, it seems Wagner could not just compose; he had to develop elaborate theories announcing what art, music, and opera ought to be like. (Indeed, he also theorized about politics and philosophy, with very unhappy results.) Wagner's extreme self-consciousness as an artist was prophetic of attitudes toward art of a much later period.

His theory of opera had its positive and negative sides. First, Wagner wanted to do away with all the conventions of earlier opera, especially the French and Italian varieties. Opera, he complained, had degenerated from its original form as serious drama in music—Wagner was thinking of ancient Greek drama, which he knew had been sung or at least chanted—into a mere "concert in costume." He particularly condemned arias, which were certainly at the heart of Italian opera, as hopelessly artificial. Why should the dramatic action keep stopping to allow for stretches of pretty but undramatic singing?

The "Total Work of Art"

The positive side of Wagner's program was the development of a new kind of opera in the 1850s, for which he reserved a special name: **music drama**. Music, in these works, shares the honors with poetry, drama, and philosophy—all furnished by Wagner himself—as well as the stage design and acting. Wagner coined the word **Gesamtkunstwerk**, meaning "total work of art," for this powerful concept. He always insisted on the distinction between music drama and ordinary "opera."

Since words and ideas are so important in the *Gesamtkunstwerk*, the music is very closely matched to the words. Yet it is also unrelievedly emotional and intense, as Romantic doctrine required. The dramas themselves deal with weighty philosophical issues, or so at least Wagner and his admirers believed, and they do so under the symbolic cover of medieval German myths and legends.

This use of myths was another Romantic feature, one that strikingly anticipated Freud, with his emphasis on myths (for example, the myth of Oedipus)

Richard Wagner (1813–1883)

Wagner was born in Leipzig during the turmoil of the Napoleonic wars; his father died soon afterward. His stepfather was a fascinating actor and writer, and the boy turned into a decided intellectual. Wagner's early interests, literature and music (his idols were Shakespeare and Beethoven), later expanded to include philosophy, mythology, and religion.

As a young man he worked as an opera conductor, and he spent an unhappy year in Paris trying to get one of his works produced at the very important opera house there. The virulent anti-French sentiments in his later writings stemmed from this experience. Back in Germany, he produced the first of his impressive operas, *The Flying Dutchman* and *Tannhäuser,* and wrote *Lohengrin.* Though these works basically adhere to the early Romantic opera style of Carl Maria von Weber, they already hint at the revolutionary ideal for opera that Wagner was pondering.

This he finally formulated after being exiled from Germany (and from a job) as a result of his part in the revolution of 1848–49. He wrote endless articles and books expounding his ideas—ideas that were better known than his later operas, for these were extremely difficult to stage. His book *Opera and Drama* set up the principles for his "music drama" *The Rhinegold,* the first segment of the extraordinary four-evening opera *The Ring of the Nibelung.* He also published a vicious essay attacking Felix Mendelssohn, who had just died, and other Jews in music. Fifty years after Wagner's death, his anti-Semitic writings (and his operas) were taken up by the Nazis.

Wagner's exile lasted thirteen years. His fortunes changed dramatically when he gained the support of the young, unstable, and finally mad King Ludwig II of Bavaria. Thanks to Ludwig, Wagner's mature music dramas were at last produced (*The Rhinegold,* completed in 1854, was not produced until 1869). Wagner then promoted the building of a special opera house in Bayreuth, Germany, solely for his music dramas—an amazing concept! These grandiose, slow-moving works are based on myths, and characterized by high-flown poetry of his own, a powerful orchestral style, and the use of *leitmotivs* (guiding or leading motives). To this day the opera house in Bayreuth performs only Wagner, and tickets are almost impossible to get.

A hypnotic personality, Wagner was able to spirit money out of many pockets and command the loyalty and affection of many distinguished men and women. His first marriage, to a singer, ended in divorce. His great operatic hymn to love, *Tristan und Isolde,* was created partly in response to his love affair with the wife of one of his patrons. His second wife, Cosima, daughter of Franz Liszt, had been married to an important conductor, Hans von Bülow, who nonetheless remained one of Wagner's strongest supporters. Cosima's diaries tell us about Wagner's moods, dreams, thoughts, and musical decisions, all of which he shared with her. After the death of "the Master," Cosima ruled Bayreuth with an iron hand.

Half con man and half visionary, bad poet and very good musician, Wagner created a storm of controversy in his lifetime that has not died down to this day. He was a major figure in the intellectual life of his time, a thinker whose ideas were highly influential not only in music but also in other arts. In this sense, at least, Wagner was the most important of the Romantic composers.

Wagner, Cosima, and their son Siegfried, who followed Cosima as director of the Wagner festivals at Bayreuth.

Chief Works: Early operas: *The Flying Dutchman, Tannhäuser,* and *Lohengrin* ▪ Mature "music dramas": *Tristan und Isolde, The Mastersingers of Nuremberg* (a brilliant comedy), *Parsifal,* and *The Ring of the Nibelung,* a four-opera cycle consisting of *The Rhinegold, The Valkyrie, Siegfried,* and *The Twilight of the Gods* ▪ *Siegfried Idyll,* for small orchestra (based on themes from *Siegfried;* a surprise birthday present for Cosima after the birth of their son, also named Siegfried)

Encore: After selections from *Tristan,* listen to "Wotan's Farewell" from *Die Walküre* (Act III); *Siegfried Idyll.*

as embodiments of the deepest unconscious truths. Wagner employed the old romance of Tristan and Iseult, the saga of the Nordic god Wotan, and the Arthurian tale of Sir Perceval to present his views on love, political power, and religion, respectively. Wagner's glorification of Germanic myths in particular made him the semiofficial voice of German nationalism, paving the way for Hitler.

One of the first great conductors and a superb orchestrator, Wagner raised the orchestra to new importance in opera, giving it a role modeled on Beethoven's symphonies with their motivic development. Leitmotivs (see below) were among the motives he used for this "symphonic" continuity. The orchestra was no longer used essentially as a support for the singers (which was still the situation, really, even in Verdi); it was now the orchestra that carried the opera along. Instead of the alternation of recitatives, arias, and ensembles in traditional opera, "music drama" consisted of one long orchestral web, cunningly woven in with the singing.

Leitmotivs

A **leitmotiv** (guiding, or leading, motive) is a musical motive associated with some person, thing, idea, or symbol in the drama. By presenting and developing leitmotivs, Wagner's orchestra guides the listener through the story.

Leitmotivs are easy to ridicule when they are used mechanically—when, for example, the orchestra obligingly sounds the Sword motive every time the hero reaches for his weapon. On the other hand, leitmotivs can suggest with considerable subtlety what the hero is thinking or feeling even when he is saying something else. Wagner also became very skillful in thematic transformation—the characteristic variation-like technique of the Romantic composers (see page 248). By transforming the appropriate motives, he could show a person or an idea developing and changing under the impact of dramatic action.

And since, for the Romantics, music was the undisputed language of emotion, leitmotivs—being music—could state or suggest ideas in *emotional* terms, over and above the intellectual terms provided by mere words. This was Wagner's theory, a logical outcome of Romantic doctrine about music. Furthermore, the complex web of leitmotivs provided his long music dramas with the thematic unity that Romantic composers sought. On both counts, psychological and technical, leitmotivs were guaranteed to impress audiences of the nineteenth century.

Mathilde Wesendonck

RICHARD WAGNER
Tristan und Isolde (1859)

Two major life experiences helped inspire Wagner's first completed music drama, *Tristan und Isolde.* One was his discovery of the Romantic philosophy of Arthur Schopenhauer, and the other was his love affair with Mathilde Wesendonck, the wife of one of his wealthy patrons.

Schopenhauer had made his own philosophical formulation of the Romantic insight into the central importance of music in emotional life. All human experience, said Schopenhauer, consists either of emotions and drives—which he called "the Will"—or of ideas, morals, and reason, which he downgraded by the term "Appearance." He insisted that the Will always dominates Appearance, and that our only direct, unencumbered sense of it comes through music.

For the philosopher, the inevitable domination of the Will was a source of profound pessimism. But a composer could read another message in Schopen-

In Act II of Wagner's opera, Isolde signals Tristan that all is clear for their fatal meeting.

hauer's work. It reinforced Wagner's conviction that music was specially privileged for emotional representation, that the deepest truths—those to do with the Will—could indeed be plumbed by music, in a music drama. And what would exemplify the Will better than the most exciting human drive that is known, sexual love? As usual, the story itself would be taken from a medieval legend.

Tristan und Isolde is not just a great love story, then, but something more. It is a drama that presents love as the dominant force in life, one that transcends every aspect of worldly Appearance. Many love stories hint at such transcendence, perhaps, but Wagner's story makes it explicit, on the basis of an actual philosophy that the composer espoused.

Background   Written by Wagner himself, though derived from a medieval legend, the story of *Tristan und Isolde* shows step by step the growing power of love. In Act I, when Tristan and Isolde fall in love by accidentally drinking a love potion, the Will overpowers Isolde's fierce pride, which had previously made her scorn Tristan as her blood enemy. It also dissolves Tristan's heretofore perfect chivalry, the machismo of the medieval knight, which had demanded that he escort her safely to her marriage to King Mark of Cornwall, his uncle and liege lord.

In Act II, love overcomes the marriage itself when the two meet adulterously (in the longest unconsummated love scene in all of opera). The lovers' tryst is discovered, and Tristan is mortally wounded—but love seems to overcome the wound, too. In Act III he simply cannot or will not die until Isolde comes to him from over the seas. Then, after Isolde comes and he dies in her arms, she herself sinks down in rapture and expires also. For both of them, death is not a defeat but an ecstatic expression of love.

At this point (if not earlier) the plot passes the bounds of reality—which was exactly Wagner's point. Tristan and Isolde, representing Schopenhauer's

Music never expresses outer phenomena, but only mankind's inner nature, the "in-itself" of all phenomena: the Will itself.

Philosopher Arthur Schopenhauer, 1818

Will, move in a realm where conventional attitudes, the rules of society, and even life and death have lost their powers. Transcendence is a recurring theme of Romanticism; here love becomes the ultimate transcendent experience, beyond reality. Indeed, the opera's transcendental quality brings it close to mystical experience.

Incidentally, Wagner and Mathilde did not live up to their operatic ideals. After a while, Wesendonck—the King Mark in this triangle—put his foot down and the affair came to an end.

Prelude   Given Wagner's emphasis on the orchestra in his music dramas, it is not surprising that the strictly orchestral Prelude (or Overture) to *Tristan und Isolde* is already a magnificent depiction of romantic love. Or at least one aspect of romantic love: not the joys of love, but love's yearning.

The Prelude opens with a very slow motive whose harmonies create a remarkably sultry, sensual, yearning feeling. The motive is actually made up of two fragments in counterpoint, easily heard because x is played by the cellos

Wagner's *Ring of the Nibelung*

Four evenings long and nearly thirty years in the making, Richard Wagner's mega-opera *The Ring of the Nibelung* is one of the towering artworks of all time, comparable to the Taj Mahal, the *Iliad* and the *Odyssey*, and Michelangelo's Sistine Chapel (comparisons which the megalomaniac Wagner would have enjoyed). Its story, of epic scope, spans many generations. It relates a myth originating in the Middle Ages, one with powerful resonance for Wagner's own time and ours, too—as witness its clear echoes in *Star Wars* and *Lord of the Rings*. Wotan, King of the Gods, has attained absolute power by subterfuge. But as the price, he has lost—along with an eye—the golden ring that ultimately dooms his kin and his enemies and brings down his empire. First, though, they and he experience fantastic adventures.

Water spirits and the Earth mother, giants and dwarfs, dragons, toads, and prophetic birds, magic swords and magic potions mix it up with some of the most psychologically complex characters in all of opera. The music of the *Ring* paints a wide range of emotions: innocence, spite, rage, regret, love at first sight, passion, sympathy, exuberance, and wonder. In its leitmotivs, matched flexibly with people and events in the drama, it also paved the way for the composers of today's sound tracks.

See the *Ring* on DVD, in the Bayreuth production conducted by Pierre Boulez.

Medieval themes on a monumental, mythic scale were a specialty of Wagner and remain a staple of recent epic films. Shown here are a stage set from 1893 for the castle of the gods in Wagner's *Ring* and the Argonauth, statues of ancient kings, from *Lord of the Rings* (2001).

and *y* by an oboe. Fragment *x* includes four *descending* notes of the chromatic scale. Fragment *y* consists of four *ascending* chromatic notes.

Langsam und schmachten (*"Slowly and languishing"*)

Often treated (as here) in a threefold sequence (see page 25), motive **a** turns out to be the opera's chief leitmotiv. It becomes associated with a rich compound of meaning, including passion, yearning, and release in death. At the risk of oversimplification, we can label it the Love-Death Motive.

This Love-Death Motive is an example of a Romantic theme that derives its essential character from harmony, rather than from melody or rhythm. The harmony is dissonant and complex: It does not feel at rest, and we expect it to proceed to some other harmony. After the slow opening sequence, the music stretches up and up—still very slowly!—but when the dissonance finally resolves, it resolves in the "wrong" place and still sounds decidedly uneasy.

In other words, the cadence has been undercut; instead of the chord we expect (because it has been clearly prepared by the upward motion), we hear a different chord. This is called a *deceptive cadence*. Deceptive cadences were not new with Wagner, of course; we have heard many of them in works studied in this book. But Wagner used them continuously in order to keep his music surging ahead. When the music stops, it stops "deceptively" at an unexpected place. Those places sound unstable, and so they motivate further surging.

Here, near the beginning of the Prelude, a flowing melodic theme follows, played by the cellos. This passionate theme is heard again and again:

As new themes emerge—yet are they new, or are they subtle transformations of earlier themes?—we realize that Wagner is never going to let the music rest. A marvelous dark churning of emotion is produced by the many sequences, by Wagner's orchestration, and by his characteristic way of avoiding true cadences in favor of deceptive cadences. The music constantly shifts in key (modulates); every time it seems ready to stop, it starts moving forward restlessly.

In form, the total Prelude amounts to a gradual, irregular crescendo, reaching a climax with a *fortissimo* return of the original threefold sequence on the Love-Death Motive. (Nineteenth-century listeners heard this as climactic in another sense, but they did not say so in print.) Then there is a hush. The motive is heard again in brooding new versions, growing quieter, so that when the curtain goes up the orchestra has fallen entirely silent, without ever having come to a cadence.

It is not easy to make a Listening Chart for music that sets out to create the sense of formless waves of emotion, as this Prelude does. In addition to motive **a** and the surging cello theme **B**, we are using the symbol **d/c** to refer to specially prominent deceptive cadences.

LISTENING CHART 19

Wagner, Prelude to *Tristan und Isolde*
10 min., 31 sec.

16-20

*(Note: **d/c** stands for deceptive cadence.)*

16	**MAIN THEMATIC GROUP** (**a d/c B**): dynamics *pp*, surge to *f*, back to *p*			
	0:00	**a** in threefold sequence	With fermatas (long gaps)	
	1:33	**d/c**	Deceptive cadence, *f*: French horn	
17	1:37	**B**	B followed by extension: cellos	
:46	2:23	**C**	Descending sequence	
:04	2:41		Somber trombone motive	
18	**B WITH NEW EXTENSIONS**			
	3:06	**B**	B followed by extension: woodwinds	
:23	3:29		Quieter material; strings answered by strings and woodwinds	
:05	4:10	**d/c**		
:10	4:16	**C**	Descending sequence: woodwinds, horn	
:21	4:27		Trombone motive, louder now	
:32	4:38		Big surge begins	
:03	5:09	**B**		
19	**RETRANSITION PASSAGE** (bass is more static)			
	5:54		New, yearning string music	
:15	6:09	*y*, 4 times	(*y* is first heard in the oboe)	
:51	6:45	**d/c - B** overlaps	Louder and louder: *ff*	
20	7:17	*x*, played twice ⟶	Climactic horn calls, in preparation for:	
	ENTIRE THEMATIC GROUP		Dynamics *ff*, then down to *p* and *pp*	
:11	7:26	**a** in threefold sequence	Varied, and with the gaps filled in	
:23	8:38	**d/c**	Deceptive cadence, as at first, but *p*	
:27	8:42	**B** fragments	Varied; minor-mode coloration. Drum roll	
:07	9:24	**a** in twofold sequence	Varied (English horn) ⟶ curtain goes up	

OBOE

a

CELLOS

B CELLOS

C VIOLAS

"Philter" Scene from Act I   A short segment from *Tristan und Isolde* will show how Wagnerian music drama works, and how it makes dramatic use of previously introduced leitmotivs—in this case, the Love-Death Motive and its threefold sequence, featured in the opera's Prelude. In Act I, a bleak shipboard scene, Isolde is being escorted by Tristan to Cornwall, the kingdom of King Mark. To her maid and confidante, Brangaene, Isolde furiously denounces Tristan, bewails her coming marriage to King Mark, and mutters something about a loveless marriage.

The "Philter" Scene has three subsections:

Brangaene's Song   "Loveless?" answers Brangaene. "But anyone would love you; and if he doesn't, we have our magic potions."

First, we hear a short solo passage that is about as close as Wagner got to writing a clear-cut aria, at least in his later years. The music is seductive and

Never in my life having enjoyed the true happiness of love, I shall build a monument to this most beautiful of dreams, in which love will for once find utter, complete fulfillment, from first to last. I have devised in my mind a Tristan und Isolde . . .

Letter from Wagner to his friend Liszt, 1854

sweet, but though Brangaene certainly sings rich melodic phrases, they do not fall together into a tune. Her melody follows the words closely, without word repetitions. Such repetition, which was taken for granted in all Baroque and Classical arias and ensembles, and most Romantic ones, Wagner would have called an "artificial" feature. The orchestra develops its own seductive motive more freely and more consistently than does the singer.

Dialogue   Lowering her voice, and glancing meaningfully at Isolde, Brangaene asks her if she has forgotten the golden chest containing her mother's magic love potion. (Isolde's mother was a famous sorceress.) Here her singing line is like heightened recitative. In the orchestra the Love-Death Motive sounds three times, in a sequence, as in the Prelude. Through the orchestra, then, Brangaene is hinting about the love potion.

Isolde answers her by imitating or parodying her recitative: No, she has not forgotten her mother's magic; and the Love-Death Motive sounds again. But whatever Brangaene was hinting about, Isolde in her despair is thinking instead of the "death philter," a poison. She recalls a special philter that she marked for just such an occasion as this. At the thought (not even the mention!) of death, a sinister new Death Motive emerges in the trombones. And when Isolde actually *mentions* the death philter and Brangaene realizes that she means to kill herself, the orchestra practically explodes. A harsh, intense passage paints Brangaene's horror.

Wagner's time scale is often enormously slow, as we recall from the Prelude. He can, however, move fast enough when he chooses. Before Brangaene can fully absorb the enormity of the situation, she is cut off by a rousing sailors' sea chantey announcing that land is in sight—the Cornwall so hated and feared by Isolde. The women's moody talk is dramatically interrupted.

Kurvenal's Song   Tristan's squire, Kurvenal, enters and tells them roughly to get ready for landing. Again, this passage for Kurvenal is not really a song or an aria. Exactly the same points can be made about it as about Brangaene's speech. Though Kurvenal's song is melodious enough, the main musical idea is an orchestral motive, not the singer's melody; no one will leave the theater humming Kurvenal's music. Yet its bluff accents characterize the man sharply, especially by comparison with the more sensitive, more impassioned women.

Isolde's suicide never takes place, of course. Brangaene switches the philters, and Isolde and Tristan drink the aphrodisiac, setting the opera's slow, inexorable action into motion.

Web: *Research and test your understanding of Romantic opera at* <bedfordstmartins.com/listen>.

Sept. 27 1878 R. *had a restless night, he dreamed of a clarinet that played by itself. . . . Toward the end of the evening, he sits down at the piano and plays* Tristan; *he does this so beautifully, in a way so far above the ordinary bounds of beauty, that I feel the sounds I am hearing will bless me when I die.*

From Cosima Wagner's diary

LISTEN Wagner, *Tristan und Isolde*, "Philter" Scene, from Act I

21-23

(Note: The English translation attempts to reproduce the "antique" quality of Wagner's poetry.)

BRANGAENE'S SONG

21 0:10 **Brangaene:** Wo lebte der Mann, | Where lives a man
Der dich nicht liebte? Der Isolden säh' | Who does not love you? Who sees you
Und Isolden selig nicht ganz verging'? | And sinks not into bondage blest?
Doch, der dich erkoren, wär' er so kalt, | And, if any bound to you were cold,
Zög ihn von dir ein Zauber ab, | If any magic drew him from thee,
Den Bösen wüsst' ich bald zu binden | I could soon draw the villain back
Ihn bannte der Minne Macht. | And bind him in links of love.

ORCHESTRA

DIALOGUE *(Secretly and confidentially)*

Love-Death Motive, three times:

22 1:26 Kennst du der Mutter Künste nicht? | Mind'st thou not thy mother's arts?
Wähnst du, die alles klug erwägt, | Do you think that she, the all-wise,
Ohne Rath in fremdes Land | Helpless in distant lands
Hätt' sie mit dir mich entsandt? | Would she have sent me with you?

0:46 2:08 **Isolde:** Der Mutter Rath gemahnt mich recht; | My mother's counsel I mind aright;
Willkommen preis' ich ihre Kunst; | And highly her magic arts I hold:
Rache für den Verrath, | Vengeance for treachery,
Ruh' in der Noth dem Herzen! | Rest for the broken heart!
Den Schrein dort bring' mir her! | Yon casket hither bear!

Love-Death Motive, three times:

1:34 2:56 **Brangaene:** Er birgt was heil dir frommt, | It holds a balm for thee:

(Brings out a golden medicine chest)

So reihte sie die Mutter, | Your mother filled it with
Die mächt'gen Zaubertränke: | The most potent magic philters;
Für Weh' und Wunden Balsam hier, | For pain and wounds there's salve,
Für böse Gifte Gegengift; | For poisons, antidotes;
Den hehrsten Trank, ich halt' ihn hier. | The noblest draught is this one—

(Takes out a flask)

2:51 4:13 **Isolde:** Du irrst, ich kenn' ihn besser; | Not so, you err: I know a better;
Ein starkes Zeichen schnitt ich ihm ein. | I made a mark to know it again:
Der Trank ist's, der mir taugt! | Here's the drink that will serve me!

New, ominous motive– Death Motive

TROMBONE

(Seizes another flask)

3:26 4:48 **Brangaene:** Der Todestrank! | The death philter!

3:32 4:54 **Sailors** *Ho, he, am Untermast!* | *Ho, heave ho! Watch the lower mast!*
(offstage): *Die Segel ein! Ho, he!* | *The mainsail in! Heave ho!*

Isolde: Das deute schnelle Fahrt. | They tell of a swift journey;
Weh' mir, Nahe das Land! | Woe's me! Near to the land!

Ho! he! ho! he!

KURVENAL'S SONG *(Kurvenal enters, boisterous and insolent)*

23 5:17 **Kurvenal:** Auf, auf, ihr Frauen! | Up, up, ye ladies!
Frisch und froh! Rasch gerüstet! | Look lively, now! Bestir you!
Fertig nun, hurtig und flink! | Be ready, and quick, prepare!
Und Frau Isolden, sollt' ich sagen | Dame Isolde, I'm told to tell you,
Von Held Tristan, meinem Herrn: | By Tristan our hero, my master:
Vom Mast der Freude Flagge | The mast is flying the joyful flag;
Sie wehe lustig ins Land; | It waveth landwards aloft;
In Marke's Königschlosse | From King Mark's royal castle
Mach' sie ihr Nahen bekannt. | It makes our approach be seen.
Drum Frau Isolde bät' er eilen, | So, Dame Isolde, he bids you hasten
Für's Land sich zu bereiten | For land to prepare you,
Dass er sie könnt' geleiten. | So that he may there conduct you.

CHAPTER 18

The Late Romantics

The year 1848 in Europe was a year of failed revolutions in France, Italy, and in various of the German states. Political freedom, which for the Romantics went hand in hand with freedom of personal expression in life and art, seemed further away than ever. While not all the early Romantics lived in free societies, at least by today's standards, freedom was an ideal they could take seriously as a hope for the future. We recall Beethoven's enthusiasm for Napoleon as a revolutionary hero, reflected in the *Eroica* Symphony of 1803, one of the landmarks of nineteenth-century music. In the 1820s, artists and intellectuals thrilled to the personal role of one of them—Lord Byron, a poet— in the struggle for Greek independence. Then they lamented his death near the field of battle.

But the failure of the revolutions of 1848 symbolized the failure of so many Romantic aspirations. In truth, those aspirations had had little to nourish them since the days of Napoleon. Romanticism lived on, but it lived on as nostalgia.

The year 1848 is also a convenient one to demarcate the history of nineteenth-century music. Some of the greatest early Romantic composers— Mendelssohn, Chopin, and Schumann—died between the years 1847 and 1856. By a remarkable coincidence of history, too, the 1848 revolution transformed the career of Richard Wagner. Exiled from Germany for revolutionary activity, he had no opera house to compose for. Instead he turned inward and—after a long period of philosophical and musical reflection—worked out his revolutionary musical ideas. Wagner's music dramas, written from the 1850s on, came to dominate the imagination of musicians in the second part of the century, much as Beethoven's symphonies had in the first part.

Romanticism and Realism

European literature and art from the 1850s on was marked not by continuing Romanticism, but by realism. The novel, the principal literary form of the time, grew more realistic from Dickens to Trollope and George Eliot in Britain, and from Balzac to Flaubert and Zola in France. In French painting, there was an important realistic school led by Gustave Courbet. Thomas Eakins was a realist painter in America; William Dean Howells was our leading realist novelist.

Realists in the arts of the nineteenth century tended toward glum or grim subject matter. The Philadelphia artist Thomas Eakins was so fascinated by surgery that he painted himself in among the students attending a class by a famous medical professor, Dr. S. D. Gross *(The Gross Clinic,* 1875).

Even more important as regards realism in the visual arts, no doubt, was that powerful new invention, the camera.

There was a move toward realism in opera at the end of the nineteenth century, in France as well as in Italy. On the other hand, the myth-drenched music dramas of Wagner were as unrealistic as could be. And what would "realism" in orchestral music be like? Given music's nature, it was perhaps inevitable that late nineteenth-century music assumed a sort of inspirational and emotional escape function—an escape from political, economic, and social situations that were not romantic in the least.

Perhaps, too, music serves a similar function for many listeners of the late twentieth century. Significantly, concert life as we know it today, with its emphasis on great masterpieces of the past, was formed for the first time in the late nineteenth century.

1 Late Romantic Program Music

Late Romantic program music took its impetus from an important series of works called "symphonic poems," composed in the 1850s by Franz Liszt. A **symphonic poem** is a one-movement orchestral composition with a program, in a free musical form. By using the word "poem," Liszt insisted on the music's programmatic nature.

It is not often that a great virtuoso pianist such as Liszt, who started out composing études and other miniatures of the kind cultivated by Chopin and Schumann, turns himself into a major composer of large-scale orchestral works. Liszt's formula was simply to write a one-movement piece for orchestra associated in one way or another with a famous poem, play, or narrative poem. Though obviously inspired by the earlier genres of program music (see page 262), Liszt departed from them in musical form, as well as in style. Unlike a Berlioz program symphony, a symphonic poem was in one movement. Unlike a Mendelssohn concert overture, it was not written in sonata form or some clear derivation of sonata form. Although the term failed to gain universal acceptance, symphonic poems under that or some other name became very popular in the later nineteenth century.

Among Liszt's symphonic poems are *Hamlet, Orpheus, Prometheus,* and *Les Préludes,* the latter loosely connected with a poem by the French Romantic poet Alphonse de Lamartine. But except for *Les Préludes,* these works are heard less often today than other symphonic poems written by composers influenced by Liszt's example. The most popular of later symphonic poems are those by Pyotr Ilyich Chaikovsky and Richard Strauss (see page 353).

PYOTR ILYICH CHAIKOVSKY
Overture-Fantasy, *Romeo and Juliet* (1869, revised 1880)

Chaikovsky wrote several symphonic poems, including one on a subject already used by Liszt and Berlioz, Shakespeare's *Hamlet*. Rather than "symphonic poem," he preferred the descriptions "symphonic fantasia" or "overture-fantasy" for these works. They are lengthy pieces in one movement, with free forms adopting some features from sonata form, rondo, and so on.

In his *Romeo and Juliet,* Chaikovsky followed the outlines of the original play only in a very general way, but one can easily identify his main themes with elements in Shakespeare's drama. The surging, romantic string melody clearly stands for the love of Romeo and Juliet. The angry, agitated theme suggests the vendetta between their families, the Capulets and the Montagues. More generally, it suggests the fate that dooms the two "star-cross'd lovers," as Shakespeare calls them. The hymnlike theme heard at the very beginning of the piece (later it sounds more marchlike) seems to denote the kindly Friar Laurence, who devises a plan to help the lovers that goes fatally wrong.

Slow Introduction   The slow introduction of *Romeo and Juliet* is already heavy with drama. As low clarinets and bassoons play the sober Hymn theme, the strings answer with an anguished-sounding passage forecasting an unhappy outcome. The wind instruments utter a series of solemn announcements, interspersed by strumming on the harp, as though someone (Friar Laurence?) was preparing to tell the tale. This sequence of events is repeated, with some variation, and then both the woodwind and string themes are briefly worked up to a climax over a dramatic drum roll.

The kernel of a new work usually appears suddenly, in the most unexpected fashion . . . All the rest takes care of itself. I could never put into words the joy that seizes me when the main idea has come and when it begins to assume definite shape. You forget everything, you become a madman for all practical purposes, your insides quiver . . .

Chaikovsky writes to Mme. von Meck about his composing, 1878

Pyotr Ilyich Chaikovsky (1840–1893)

The composer's name is usually spelled Tchaikovsky, but it is time to retire this French spelling, which exists only because "ch" sounds like "sh" in that language. We spell it "ch," as in Chekhov the author, Chernobyl the nuclear site, Chomsky the linguist, etc.

Chaikovsky was born in the Russian countryside, the son of a mining inspector, but the family moved to St. Petersburg when he was eight. In nineteenth-century Russia, a serious musical education and a musical career were not accorded the social approval they received in Germany, France, or Italy. Many of the famous Russian composers began in other careers and only turned to music in their mature years, when driven by inner necessity.

Chaikovsky was fortunate in this respect, for after working as a government clerk for only a few years, he was able to enter the brand-new St. Petersburg Conservatory, founded by another Russian composer, Anton Rubinstein. At the age of twenty-six he was made a professor at the Moscow Conservatory. Once Chaikovsky got started, after abandoning the civil service, he composed prolifically—six symphonies, eleven operas, symphonic poems, chamber music, songs, and some of the most famous of all ballet scores: *Swan Lake, Sleeping Beauty,* and *The Nutcracker.*

Though his pieces may sometimes sound "Russian" to us, he was not a devoted nationalist like some other major Russian composers of the time (see page 295). Of all the nineteenth-century Russian composers, indeed, Chaikovsky had the greatest success in concert halls around the world. His famous Piano Concerto No. 1 was premiered in 1875 in Boston, and he toured America as a conductor in 1891.

Chaikovsky was a depressive personality who more than once attempted suicide. He had been an extremely delicate and hypersensitive child, and as an adult he worried that his homosexuality would be discovered and exposed. In an attempt to raise himself above suspicion, he married a highly unstable young musician who was in love with him. The marriage was a fiasco; in a matter of weeks, Chaikovsky fled and never saw his wife again. She died in an asylum.

For many years Chaikovsky was subsidized by a remarkable woman, Nadezhda von Meck, a wealthy widow and a recluse. She not only commissioned compositions from him but actually granted him an annuity. By mutual agreement, they never met; nevertheless, they exchanged letters regularly over the thirteen years of their friendship. This strange arrangement was terminated, without explanation, by Madame von Meck.

By this time Chaikovsky's position was assured, and his music widely admired. By a tragic mishap, he died after drinking unboiled water during a cholera epidemic.

Chief Works: Symphonies No. 4, 5, and 6 *(Pathétique)*; Violin Concerto; piano concertos ▪ Operas: *The Queen of Spades* and *Eugene Onegin,* based on works by the Russian Romantic poet Aleksandr Pushkin ▪ Symphonic poems: *Romeo and Juliet, Hamlet, Francesca da Rimini, Overture 1812* (about Napoleon's retreat from Russia in that year) ▪ Ballet scores: *Swan Lake, Sleeping Beauty, The Nutcracker*

Encore: After *Romeo and Juliet,* listen to the *Nutcracker* Suite; Symphony No. 4; Violin Concerto.

Allegro   The tempo changes to allegro, and we hear the Vendetta or Fate theme. It is made up of a number of short, vigorous rhythmic motives, which Chaikovsky at once begins to develop. Then the Vendetta theme returns in a climax punctuated by cymbal claps.

The highly romantic Love theme (illustrated on page 243) is first played only in part, by the English horn and violas—a mellow sound. It is halted by a curious but affecting passage built out of a little sighing figure:

The Love theme, now played at full length by the French horn, is made doubly emotional by a new two-note accompaniment derived from the sighing motive (marked with a bracket above).

A famous Juliet of Chaikovsky's time: Mrs. Patrick Campbell in an 1895 London production of Shakespeare's play.

After the Love theme dies down at some length, a lively development section begins (a feature suggesting sonata form). Confronted by various motives from the Vendetta theme, the Hymn theme takes on a marchlike character. We may get the impression of a battle between the forces of good and evil.

The Vendetta theme returns in its original form (suggesting a sonata-form recapitulation). The sighing motive and the lengthy Love theme also return, but the end of the latter is now broken up and interrupted—a clear reference to the tragic outcome of the drama. At one last appearance, the Vendetta theme is joined more explicitly than before with the Hymn theme.

Coda (slow)   A fragment of the Love theme appears in a broken version over funeral drum taps in the timpani. This seems to depict the pathos of Romeo's final speeches, where he refers to his love before taking poison. A new, slow theme in the woodwinds is really a transformation of the sighing motive heard earlier.

But the mood is not entirely gloomy; as the harp strumming is resumed, the storyteller seems to derive solace and inspiration from his tale. Parts of the Love theme return for the last time in a beautiful new cadential version, surging enthusiastically upward in a way that is very typical of Chaikovsky. Doesn't this ecstatic surge suggest that even though Romeo and Juliet are dead, their love is timeless—that their love transcends death? The influence of Wagner's *Tristan und Isolde* was felt here as everywhere in the later nineteenth century.

2 Nationalism

One legacy of Romanticism's passion for freedom played itself out all through the nineteenth century: the struggle for national independence. The Greeks struggled against the Turks, the Poles rose up against Russia, the Czechs revolted against Austria, and Norway broke free of Sweden.

As people all over Europe became more conscious of their national character, they also came to prize their distinctive artistic heritages more and more.

LISTENING CHART 20

Chaikovsky, Overture-Fantasy, *Romeo and Juliet*

18 min., 39 sec.

4 24-35   2 27-38

INTRODUCTION (Andante)

24 27	0:00	**Hymn theme**	Low woodwinds, *pp*
	0:34	**String motives**	Anguished quality; contrapuntal
	1:26	**Strumming harp**	With "announcements" in the high woodwinds
25 28	2:07	**Hymn theme**	High woodwinds with pizzicato strings. Followed by the string motives and harp; the "announcements" are now in the strings.
:50	3:57	**Buildup**	Ends with drum roll, *f*
26 29	4:32	**Preparation**	Prepares for the main section; *p*, then *crescendo*

MAIN SECTION (Allegro)

27 30	5:01	**Vendetta theme**	Full orchestra, *f*
:22	5:23		Development of the Vendetta theme; contrapuntal
:46	5:47		Reaches a climax: cymbals
:58	5:59	**Vendetta theme**	Full orchestra, *ff*
:17	6:18		Relaxes, in a long slowdown
:57	6:58		Prefatory statement of Love theme (English horn): phrase **a**
28 31	7:13		"Sighing" theme; muted strings, *pp*
29 32	7:52	**Love theme**	Form is **a b a**, in woodwinds, with the sighing motive played by the French horn.
:58	8:50		Harp. Cadences; the music dies down and nearly stops.

DEVELOPMENT

30 33	9:53	**Developmental combination**	Vendetta theme fragments are combined with the Hymn theme, which now sounds more like a march than a hymn.
31 34	11:07		This works up to a climax, marked by a cymbal clash.
:23	11:30	**Hymn theme**	Played by trumpets; syncopated rhythm in the cymbals

CYMBALS

FREE RECAPITULATION (abbreviated)

32 35	11:58	**Vendetta theme**	Full orchestra, *ff*
:22	12:20		Sighing theme
:00	12:58	**Love theme**	**a b a**; ecstatically in the strings, with the sighing motive again in the French horn; the last **a** is *ff*.
33 36	14:01		Fragments of the Love theme
:25	14:26	**(Love theme)**	Sounds like another ecstatic statement, but is interrupted.
:35	14:36		Interruption by the Vendetta theme: conflict! Cymbals
:49	14:50	**Developmental combination**	Vendetta theme fragments combined with the Hymn theme Builds up to *fff*
:21	15:22		Then dies down, rather unwillingly; ends on drum roll, *f*

CODA (Moderato)

34 37	15:59	**Love theme**	A broken version of the Love theme, with muffled funeral drums. The music seems to be ending.
35 38	16:37	**New theme**	Woodwinds; ends with a transformation of the sighing motive
:05	17:43	**Love theme**	Section **a** in a slow cadential "transcendent" version. The strumming harp of the slow introduction has returned.
:40	18:17		Final cadences; a drum roll and solemn ending gestures

pp

Nationalism: Finnish myths inspired both the composer Jean Sibelius and his compatriot the painter Akseli Gallen-Kallela. The wounded hero Lemminkaïnen is tended by his mother, who sends bees to fetch a healing balm from a magic fountain.

This gave rise to a musical movement, **nationalism** in music. The characteristic feature of this movement is simply the incorporation of national folk music into concert pieces, songs, and operas. Symphonic poems or operas were based on programs or librettos that took up national themes—a hero of history such as Russia's Prince Igor; a national literary treasure such as the Finnish Lemminkaïnen legends; or a beloved river such as the Vltava (Moldau) in Bohemia. Such national themes were reinforced by actual musical themes taken from folk song. The result was music that stirred strong emotions at home, and often made an effective ambassador abroad.

Although in the nineteenth century political nationalism was certainly a major factor all over Europe, composers in Germany, Italy, and France are not categorized with the musical nationalists. For musical nationalism also strove to make local music independent of Europe's traditional cultural leaders. Nationalist composers often deliberately broke the traditional rules of harmony, form, and so on. They did this both in a spirit of defiance and also in an effort to develop new, genuinely local musical styles.

The art of music is above all other arts the expression of the soul of a nation. The composer must love the tunes of his country and they must become an integral part of him.

Nationalist composer Ralph Vaughan Williams

Exoticism

Audiences came to enjoy hearing folk music at symphony concerts, whether it was their own folk music or somebody else's. We have seen that Verdi wrote Egyptian music, in the priest's hymn in *Aida*. French composers wrote Spanish music, Russians wrote Italian music, and Czechs wrote American music (George Bizet's opera *Carmen*, Chaikovsky's orchestra piece *Capriccio Italien*, and Antonín Dvořák's famous *New World* Symphony, with its reference to spirituals). Such music cannot be called nationalistic, since its aim was not national self-definition. Perhaps the best name for it is "exotic."

Yet even this nonpolitical, exotic music had the effect of emphasizing the unique qualities of nations. In the later nineteenth century, Romantic individuality had become a national ideal as much as a personal one.

Modest Musorgsky (1839–1881)

Musorgsky (pronounced MOO-sorgsky) was the son of a well-to-do landowner. The social class into which he was born dictated that he become an officer in the Russian Imperial Guard. Musorgsky duly went to cadet school and joined a regiment after graduation, but he could not long ignore his deep-seated desire to become a composer.

In the meantime, the emancipation of the serfs and other political-economic changes in Russia caused the liquidation of his family estate. For a time Musorgsky tried to help run the family affairs, but in his twenties he was obliged to work at a clerical job. Meanwhile, he experimented with musical composition, struggling to master the technique of an art that he had come to late in life. It was around this time that he joined the circle of Russian nationalist composers that was dubbed the *kuchka* (the Group).

Musorgsky never felt secure in his technique, and relied on his skillful *kuchka* friend, Nikolai Rimsky-Korsakov, to criticize his work. But his intense nationalism formed his vision of what he wanted his work to be—truly Russian music. His masterpiece, the opera *Boris Godunov*, is based on the story of the sixteenth-century tsar as told by the great Russian poet Alexander Pushkin. It hardly had the success it deserved when it was finally revised and put on in St. Petersburg. Indeed, this and other works by Musorgsky only succeeded some time later, after their orchestration had been touched up (some say glamorized) by Rimsky-Korsakov.

Musorgsky led a rather grim life; his was a personality filled with doubts, and his instability was a constant concern to his friends. He became an alcoholic early in life. Musorgsky died of alcoholism and epilepsy in an army hospital at the age of forty-two.

Chief Works: Operas: *Boris Godunov* and *Khovanschina* ▪ Orchestral program compositions: *Pictures at an Exhibition* (originally for piano) and *Night on Bald Mountain* ▪ Songs, including the very impressive song cycles *The Nursery* and *Songs and Dances of Death*

Encore: After *Pictures*, listen to *Boris Godunov*, Coronation Scene (scene ii).

The Russian *Kuchka*

A close group of five Russian nationalist composers were nicknamed (by one of their critic friends) the *kuchka*—sometimes translated as the "Mighty Five," but actually meaning a group or clique. They were an interesting and exceptionally talented group—even though they included only one trained musician, Mily Balakirev (1837–1910). Alexander Borodin (1833–1887) was a distinguished chemist, César Cui (1835–1918) an engineer, Nikolai Rimsky-Korsakov (1844–1908) a navy man, and Modest Musorgsky (1839–1881) an officer in the Russian Imperial Guard.

What held this group together were their determination to make Russian music "Russian," their deep interest in collecting folk song, and their commitment to self-improvement as composers, relatively late in life.

MODEST MUSORGSKY
Pictures at an Exhibition (1874)

1-4   1-4

The title of this interesting work refers to a memorial exhibit of pictures by a friend of Musorgsky's who had recently died, the Russian painter Victor Hartmann. Like Musorgsky, Hartmann cared deeply about getting Russian themes into his work. *Pictures at an Exhibition* was originally written for piano solo, as a series of piano miniatures joined in a set, like Robert Schumann's *Carnaval*. In 1922 the set was orchestrated by the French composer Maurice Ravel, and this is the form in which it has since become popular.

Promenade [1]   To provide some overall thread or unity to a set of ten different musical pieces, Musorgsky hit upon a plan that is as simple and effective as it is ingenious. The first number, "Promenade," does not refer to a picture, but depicts the composer strolling around the picture gallery. The same music returns several times in free variations, to show the promenader's changes of mood as he contemplates Hartmann's varied works.

The promenade theme recalls a Russian folk song:

Ravel orchestrated this forceful theme first for brass instruments, later for woodwinds and strings. Quintuple meter (**5/4**: measures 1, 3, and 5) is a distinct rarity, and having this meter alternate with **6/4** (measures 2, 4, and 6) rarer still. The metrical anomaly gives the impression of blunt, unsophisticated folk music—and perhaps also of walking back and forth without any particular destination, as one does in a gallery.

Gnomus   "Gnomus" is a drawing of a Russian folk-art nutcracker. The gnome's heavy jaws crack the nut when his legs (the handles) are pulled together; the same grotesque figure, which could frighten a little child, comes to life and dances in Chaikovsky's well-known Christmas ballet *The Nutcracker*. Musorgsky writes music that sounds suitably macabre, with a lurching rhythm to illustrate the gnome's clumsy walk on his handle-legs, and striking dissonant harmonies.

The lurching rhythms and dissonance of "Gnomus" and the **5/4** meter of "Promenade" are among the features of Musorgsky's music that break with the norms of traditional European art music, in a self-consciously nationalistic spirit.

Promenade [2]   Quieter now, the promenade music suggests that the spectator is musing as he moves along . . . and we can exercise our stroller's prerogative and skip past a number of Hartmann's pictures, pictures that are not nationalistic in a Russian sense. Some do refer to other peoples, and Musorgsky follows suit, writing music we would call "exotic": "Bydlo," which is the name of a Polish cattle-cart, and "Il Vecchio Castello," Hartmann's Italian title for a conventional painting of a medieval castle, complete with a troubadour serenading his lady.

The Great Gate at Kiev   The last and longest number is also the climactic one. It illustrates—or, rather, spins a fantasy inspired by—a fabulous architectural design by Hartmann that was never executed.

Musorgsky summons up in the imagination a solemn procession with clashing cymbals, clanging bells, and chanting Russian priests. The Promenade theme is now at last incorporated into one of the musical "pictures"; the promenader himself has become a part of it and has joined the inspiring parade. In addition, two real Russian melodies appear:

The ending is very grandiose, for grandiosity forms an integral part of the national self-image of Russia—and, unfortunately, of many other nations.

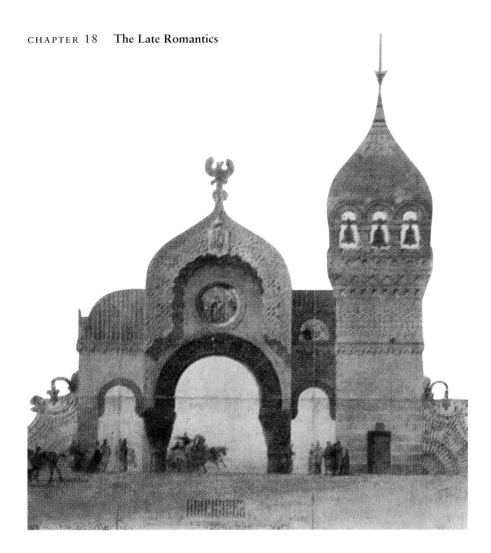

The Great Gate at Kiev

Other Nationalists

Nationalism enjoyed new life after the turn of the century. Some of the most impressive nationalists were also among the earliest modernists, among them Béla Bartók in Hungary and Charles Ives in the United States. We shall examine this "new nationalism" in Chapters 20 and 21, restricting ourselves here to a listing of some of the main nationalists outside of Russia.

❧ *Bohemia* Bohemia, as the Czech Republic was then called, produced two eminent national composers: Bedřich Smetana (1824–1884), who wrote the symphonic poem *Vltava* (The Moldau) and the delightful folk opera *The Bartered Bride,* and Antonín Dvořák (1841–1904), composer of the popular *Slavonic Dances* as well as important symphonies and other large-scale works.

❧ *Scandinavia* The Norwegian composer Edvard Grieg (1843–1907) wrote sets of piano miniatures with titles such as *Norwegian Mountain Tunes,* which were very popular at the time; also a well-known suite of music for *Peer Gynt,* the great drama by the Norwegian playwright Henrik Ibsen.

Jean Sibelius (1865–1957), a powerful late-Romantic symphonist, produced a series of symphonic poems on the folklore of his native Finland: *The Swan of Tuonela, Finlandia,* and others.

❧ *Spain* Among Spanish nationalists were Enrique Granados (1867–1916), Joaquín Turina (1882–1949), and Manuel de Falla (1876–1946), best known for his *Nights in the Gardens of Spain* for piano and orchestra. Spain was a favorite locale for "exotic" composition with a Spanish flavor written by Frenchmen—among them Bizet's opera *Carmen* and orchestral pieces by Emmanuel Chabrier *(España),* Claude Debussy *(Iberia),* and Maurice Ravel *(Boléro).*

❧ *Great Britain* The major English nationalist in music was Ralph Vaughan Williams (1872–1958). His *Fantasia on a Theme by Thomas Tallis* is a loving meditation on a psalm tune that was written by a major composer from Britain's national heritage at the time of Queen Elizabeth I.

Less well known is Irish composer Sir Charles Villiers Stanford (1852–1924), who wrote *Irish Ballads* for orchestra and the opera *Shamus O'Brien.*

Johannes Brahms (1833–1897)

The son of an orchestral musician in Hamburg, Brahms was given piano lessons at an early age. By the time he was seven, he was studying with one of Hamburg's finest music teachers. A little later he was playing the piano at dockside taverns and writing popular tunes.

A turning point in Brahms's life came at the age of twenty when he met Robert and Clara Schumann. These two eminent musicians befriended and encouraged the young man and took him into their household. Robert wrote an enthusiastic article praising his music. But soon afterward, Schumann was committed to an insane asylum—a time during which Brahms and Clara (who was fourteen years his senior) became very close. In later life Brahms always sent Clara his compositions to get her comments.

With another musician friend, Joseph Joachim, who was to become one of the great violinists of his time, the young Brahms signed a foolish manifesto condemning the advanced music of Liszt and Wagner. Thereafter he passed an uneventful bachelor existence, steadily turning out music—chamber music, songs, and piano pieces, but no program music or operas. Indeed, he was forty-three before his first symphony appeared, many years after its beginnings at his desk; it seemed that he was hesitating to invoke comparison with Beethoven, whose symphonies constituted a standard for the genre. In fact, this symphony's last movement contains a near-quotation from Beethoven's Ninth Symphony that is more like a challenge. When people pointed out the similarity, Brahms snarled, "Any jackass can see that," implying that it was the differences between the two works that mattered, not their superficial similarities.

Brahms would eventually write four symphonies, all harking back to forms used by Beethoven and even Bach, but thoroughly Romantic in their expressive effect.

For a time Brahms conducted a chorus, and he wrote much choral music, including *A German Requiem*, a setting of sober texts from the Bible. As a conductor, he indulged his traditionalism by reviving music of Bach and even earlier composers, but he also enjoyed the popular music of his day. He wrote waltzes (Johann Strauss, the "Waltz King," was a valued friend), folk song arrangements, and the well-known *Hungarian Dances*.

Chief Works: Four symphonies, *Tragic* Overture, and a rather comical *Academic Festival* Overture ▪ Violin concerto and two piano concertos ▪ Much chamber music, including a beautiful quintet for clarinet and strings, a trio for French horn, violin, and piano, as well as string quartets, quintets, and sextets ▪ Piano music and many songs ▪ Choral music, including *A German Requiem* and *Alto Rhapsody* ▪ Waltzes, *Hungarian Dances*

Encore: After the Violin Concerto, listen to the Clarinet Quintet; Symphony No. 3.

3 Responses to Romanticism

At the beginning of this chapter, we remarked that European art and literature after the 1850s were marked not by continuing Romanticism, but by realism, which was in fact a reaction against Romanticism. In music, an art that can hardly be realistic in the usual sense, the anti-Romantic reaction came later—at a time when realism was no longer an ideal in the other arts.

After 1850, music continued to develop along Romantic lines, but it seemed oddly out of phase with a no-nonsense world increasingly devoted to industrialization and commerce. In the world of Victorian morality, people devoted to the work ethic denied themselves and others the heady emotion that the Romantics had insisted on conveying in their art. There is probably some truth to the contention that late nineteenth-century music assumed the function of a sort of never-never land of feeling. Music was an emotional fantasy-world for a society that placed a premium on the suppression of feeling in real life.

The work of the two greatest late nineteenth-century German composers can be viewed in terms of their responses to this situation. Johannes Brahms, a devoted young friend of Robert Schumann, one of the most Romantic of composers, nonetheless turned back to the Classicism of the Viennese masters.

Evidently he saw this as a way of tempering the unbridled emotionalism of Romanticism, which he expressed only in a mood of restraint and resignation.

A younger man, Gustav Mahler, reacted differently. Lament was his mode, rather than resignation; his music expresses an intense, bittersweet nostalgia for a Romanticism that seems to have lost its innocence, even its credibility. The lament for this loss is almost clamorous in Mahler's songs and symphonies.

The Renewal of Classicism: Brahms

Born in the dour industrial port city of Hamburg, Johannes Brahms gravitated to Vienna, the city of Haydn, Mozart, and Beethoven. The move seems symbolic. For Brahms rejected many of the innovations of the early Romantics and went back to Classical genres, forms, and, to some extent, even Classical style.

Brahms devoted his major effort to traditional genres such as string quartets and other chamber music works, symphonies, and concertos. In these works, he employed and indeed found new life in the Classical forms—sonata form, theme and variations, and rondo. The only typical Romantic genre he cultivated was the "miniature"—the lied and the characteristic piano piece; he never contemplated "grandiose" works such as philosophical program symphonies or mythological operas. Almost alone among the important composers of his time, he made no special effort to pioneer new harmonies or tone colors.

What impels a great composer—and Brahms *was* a great composer, not a timid traditionalist—to turn back the clock in this way? One can only speculate that he could not find it in himself to copy or continue the enthusiastic, open-ended striving of the early Romantics. In the late nineteenth century, this type of response no longer rang true, and Brahms recognized it.

On the other hand, the nobility and power of Beethoven inspired him with a lifelong model. Seen in this way, Brahms's effort was a heroic one: to temper the new richness and variety of Romantic emotion with the traditional strength and poise of Classicism.

Brahms, without giving up on beauty and emotion, proved to be a progressive in a field that had not been cultivated in half a century [i.e., the Classical tradition]. He would have been a pioneer if he had simply returned to Mozart. But he did not live on inherited wealth; he made a fortune of his own.

Modernist composer
Arnold Schoenberg, 1947

Violinist Joseph Joachim, for whom Brahms wrote his Violin Concerto, playing with another Brahms friend, Clara Schumann (see page 257).

JOHANNES BRAHMS
Violin Concerto in D, Op. 77 (1878)

Concertos are always written to show off great virtuosos—who are often the composers themselves, as with Mozart, Chopin, and Liszt. Brahms wrote his one violin concerto for a close friend, Joseph Joachim, a leading violinist of the time and also a composer. Even this late in life—Brahms was then forty-five— he accepted advice about certain details of the composition from Joachim, and Joachim wrote the soloist's cadenza for the first movement.

We can appreciate Brahms's traditionalism as far as the Classical forms are concerned by referring to the standard movement plan for the Classical concerto, on page 201. Like Mozart, Brahms wrote his first movement in double-exposition sonata form; this must have seemed extremely stuffy to the many writers of Romantic concertos who had developed new and freer forms. Also, Brahms's last movement is a rondo—the most common Classical way to end a concerto. If it is a relatively simple movement, by Brahms's standards, that is because the last movements of Classical concertos were typically the lightest and least demanding on the listener.

Third Movement (Allegro giocoso, ma non troppo vivace)   *Giocoso* means "jolly"; the first theme in this rondo, **A,** has a lilt recalling the spirited gypsy fiddling that was popular in nineteenth-century Vienna. Imitating gypsy music in this work and others counts as an "exotic" feature in Brahms's music (see page 294).

The solo violin plays the theme (and much else in the movement) in *double stops,* that is, in chords produced by bowing two violin strings simultaneously. Hard to do well, this makes a brilliant effect when done by a virtuoso.

The theme falls into a traditional **a a b a′** form; in Brahms's hands, however, this becomes something quite subtle. Since the second **a** is identical to the first,

Brahms was a serious man; this is one of the few pictures of him smiling. He is sketched with some bachelor friends at his favorite Vienna tavern, the Red Hedgehog.

LISTENING CHART 21

5
5-10

Brahms, Violin Concerto, third movement

Rondo. 7 min., 43 sec.

5	0:00	**A (Tune)**	The entire tune is presented.
	0:00	**a**	Solo violin, with double stops
	0:11	**a**	Orchestra
	0:22	**b**	Solo violin
	0:35	**a′**	Orchestra
	0:46		The solo violin begins the cadences ending the tune, which lead into a transition.
	1:05		Fast scales prepare for **B**.
6	1:14	**B (Episode 1)**	Melody (emphatic upward scale) in the violin, with inverted motive below it, in the orchestra
0:21	1:35		Melody in the orchestra, with inverted motive above it
0:36	1:50		Cadential passage (orchestra), *f*
7	2:00	**A′**	
	2:00	**a**	Solo
0:11	2:11	**a″**	Orchestra
0:20	2:20		Transition (orchestra and solo), *p*
8	2:38	**C (Episode 2)**	Lyrical tune (solo and orchestra), *p*
0:33	3:11		Expressive climactic section, solo
0:44	3:22		Orchestra interrupts, *f*.
0:48	3:26		Scales prepare for **B**.
0:57	3:35	**B**	
9	4:23	**A″**	Starts with **b′** (solo)
0:20	4:43	**a‴**	In orchestra, extended; the real feeling of "return" comes only at this point.
0:45	5:08	**Short cadenza**	Solo, double stops again; orchestra soon enters.
1:02	5:25		Solo trills and scales; motive ♩♪♪♩
1:31	5:54		Passage of preparation: motive ♩♪♪♩ in low French horns
10	6:09	**Short cadenza**	
0:11	6:20	**Coda**	Mostly in **6/8** time. Starts with a marchlike transformation of phrase **a** (solo), over a drum beat.
0:35	6:44		References to **B**
1:07	7:16		Final-sounding cadences
1:19	7:28		The music dies down and ends with three loud chords.

From Brahms's score of his Violin Concerto

except in instrumentation, the last **a** (**a′**) might be dull unless it were varied in an interesting way. Brahms extends it and yet also makes it compressed and exciting by free diminutions of the basic rhythmic figure:

Such "cross-rhythms"—3/8 fitted in for a moment within 2/4—are a characteristic fingerprint of Brahms's style. There are other examples in this movement.

The first rondo episode, **B,** a theme with a fine Romantic sweep about it, begins with an emphatic upward scale played by the solo violin (high double stops in octaves). This is answered by a *downward* scale in the orchestra in a lower range. When the orchestra has its turn to play **B,** timpani are added; the upward scale is transferred down to the low register, and the downward scale up to the high register.

The second rondo episode, **C,** involves another rhythmic change; this charming melody—which, however, soon evaporates—is in **3/4** time:

The coda presents a version of the **a** phrase of the main theme in **6/8** time, in a swinging march tempo. Again the timpani are prominent. Most of the transitions in this movement are rapid virtuoso scale passages by the soloist, who is also given two short cadenzas prior to the coda.

Romantic Nostalgia: Mahler

If, like Brahms, Gustav Mahler felt ambivalent about the Romantic tradition, he expressed this ambivalence very differently. He eagerly embraced all the excesses of Romanticism that Brahms had shrunk from, writing huge program symphonies (though he vacillated on the question of distributing the programs to his audiences) and symphonies with solo and choral singing. Mahler once said that a symphony is "an entire world." Again and again his works set out to encode seemingly profound metaphysical or spiritual messages.

Yet it would appear that Mahler felt unable to enter freely into this Romantic fantasy world. There is an uneasy quality to his music that sets it apart from other late Romantic music. For while we may feel that the emotion expressed in Chaikovsky's music, for example, is exaggerated, we do not feel that Chaikovsky himself thought so. Mahler's exaggeration, on the other hand, seems deliberate and self-conscious.

Exaggeration spills over into another characteristic feature, distortion. Mahler tends to make more or less slight distortions of melody, motive, and harmony. Sometimes these distortions put a uniquely bittersweet touch on the musical material; sometimes they amount to all-out parody. The parody does not seem harsh, however, but affectionate, nostalgic, and ultimately melancholy. Distortion for Mahler was a way of acknowledging his inability—and the inability of his generation—to recapture the lost freshness of Romantic music.

A symphony must be like the world, it must embrace everything.

Famous dictum of Gustav Mahler

Mahler's Symphony No. 8, called "Symphony of a Thousand," represents a peak in the nineteenth-century tradition of "grandiose" compositions (see page 247). One early performance (in Philadelphia) did indeed reach 1,069 orchestral players, chorus singers, and soloists.

To give an example: The slow movement of his Symphony No. 1 quotes the cheerful children's round, "Frère Jacques," strangely distorted so as to sound like a funeral march. Mahler explained that this march was inspired by a well-known nursery picture of the time, *The Huntsman's Funeral Procession,* showing forest animals shedding crocodile tears around the hearse of a hunter. But an innocent children's song was not distorted in this way in order to mock childhood or childish things. If anything, Mahler used it to lament his own lost innocence, and that of his time.

GUSTAV MAHLER
Symphony No. 1 (1888)

Mahler's first symphony started out as a symphonic poem in one movement, grew to a five-movement symphony, and was finally revised into four movements. As is also true of several of his other symphonies, Symphony No. 1 includes fragments from a number of earlier songs by Mahler, songs about lost love. The program that Mahler once published for the whole symphony, but then withdrew, concerns the disillusion and distress of disappointed love, ending with the hero pulling himself together again.

An important general feature of Mahler's style is a special kind of counterpoint closely tied up with his very individual style of orchestration. He picks instruments out of the orchestra to play momentary solos, which are heard in counterpoint with other lines played by other "solo" instruments. The changing combinations can create a fascinating kaleidoscopic effect, for the various bright strands are not made to blend, as in most Romantic orchestration, but rather to stand out in sharp contrast to one another.

The Huntsman's Funeral Procession, inspiration for the slow movement of Mahler's Symphony No. 1.

Third Movement (Feierlich und gemessen, ohne zu schleppen—"With a solemn, measured gait; do not hurry")   This ironic funeral march is also a personal lament, for its trio is taken from an earlier song by Mahler about lost love. (Though the musical form of the movement is quite original, it is based on march and trio form, analogous to the Classical minuet and trio.)

Section 1   Mahler had the extraordinary idea of making his parody funeral march out of the French round "Frère Jacques," as we have said. He distorts the familiar tune by playing it in the minor mode at a slow tempo:

The mournful, monotonous drumbeat that accompanies the march is derived from the ending of the tune. (Note that Mahler slightly changed that ending of "Frère Jacques" as he transformed it into his march—he wanted only so much monotony.)

The slow march itself is played first by a single muted double bass playing in its high register—a bizarre, deliberately clumsy sonority. An additional figure that Mahler appends to his version of "Frère Jacques," played by the oboe, fits so naturally that we almost accept it as part of the traditional tune. The music dies out on the drumbeat figure (played by the harp), then on a single repeated note.

Section 2   This section is a study in frustration, as fragmentary dance-music phrases that sound distorted, parodistic, and even vulgar, give way to equally fragmentary recollections of the funeral march. One dance starts up in band instruments, with a faster beat provided by pizzicato strings; notice the exaggerated way in which its opening upbeat is slowed down. It is cut short by a new dance phrase—louder, more vulgar yet, scored with bass drum and cymbals. "With Parody," Mahler wrote on the score at this point:

This phrase, too, is cut short, and a varied repetition of the material introduced so far does not proceed much further. Instead, a long, grieving cadential passage is heard over the funeral-march drumbeat. Other fragments of "Frère Jacques" are recalled. Mourning gives way to utter exhaustion.

Section 3   A note of consolation is sounded by this contrasting "trio," beginning with warm major-mode sounds and a triplet accompaniment on the harp. (The funeral-march beat dissolves into a faster but gentler throb.) The melody introduced is the one that belonged originally to a nostalgic song about lost love. Played first by muted strings, then the oboe and solo violins, the song melody soon turns bittersweet.

The rhythm is halted by quiet but dramatic gong strokes. Flutes play a few strangely momentous new phrases, also taken from the song.

Section 4   The final section combines elements from both sections 1 and 2. Soon after the "Frère Jacques" round commences, in a strange key, a new counterpoint joins it in the trumpets—another parodistic, almost whining sound:

Mahler and his daughter: an informal photo.

Gustav Mahler (1860–1911)

Mahler's early life was not a happy one. Born in Bohemia to an abusive father, five of his brothers and sisters died of diphtheria, and others ended their lives in suicide or mental illness. The family lived near a military barracks, and the many marches incorporated into Mahler's music—often distorted marches—have been traced to his childhood recollections of parade music.

After studying for a time at the Vienna Conservatory, Mahler began a rising career as a conductor. His uncompromising standards and his authoritarian attitude toward the orchestra musicians led to frequent disputes with the authorities. What is more, Mahler was Jewish, and Vienna at that time was rife with anti-Semitism. Nonetheless, he was acknowledged as one of the great conductors of his day and also as a very effective musical administrator. After positions at Prague, Budapest, Hamburg, and elsewhere, he came to head such organizations as the Vienna Opera and the New York Philharmonic.

It was only in the summers that Mahler had time to compose, so it is not surprising that he produced fewer pieces (though they are very long pieces) than any other important composer. Ten symphonies, the last of them unfinished, and six song cycles for voice and orchestra are almost all he wrote. The song cycle *The Song of the Earth* of 1910, based on translated Chinese poems, is often called Mahler's greatest masterpiece.

He married a famous Viennese beauty, Alma Schindler, who after his death went on to marry the great architect Walter Gropius and later the novelist Franz Werfel and then wrote fascinating memoirs of her life with the composer. By a tragic irony, Gustav and Alma's young daughter died of scarlet fever shortly after Mahler had written his grim orchestral song cycle *Songs on the Death of Children*.

Mahler's life was clouded by psychological turmoil, and he once consulted his famous Viennese contemporary, Sigmund Freud. It has been said that his disputes with the New York Philharmonic directors, which discouraged him profoundly, may have contributed to his early death.

Chief Works: Ten lengthy symphonies, several with chorus, of which the best known are the First, Fourth, and Fifth ▪ Orchestral song cycles: *The Song of the Earth, Songs of a Wayfarer, The Youth's Magic Horn* (for piano or orchestra), *Songs on the Death of Children*

Encore: After Symphony No. 1, listen to the Adagietto from Symphony No. 5; *Songs of a Wayfarer.*

From the score Mahler was working on at his death—the unfinished Symphony No. 10.

One of the dance phrases from section 2 interrupts, picking up the tempo; and when "Frère Jacques" and the trumpet tune return, the tempo picks up even more for a wild moment of near chaos. But the mourning passage that ended section 2 returns, with its constant somber drumbeat. The movement ends after another series of gong strokes.

Web: *Research and test your understanding of late Romantic music at* <bedfordstmartins.com/listen>.

LISTENING CHART 22

Mahler, Symphony No. 1, third movement, Funeral March

10 min., 20 sec.

SECTION 1

11 5	0:00	**Funeral March**	Drum beat, then four main entries of the round "Frère Jacques" (minor mode), which is the march theme.
	0:07		Entry 1: Double bass, muted
	0:28		Entry 2: Bassoon (a subsidiary entry follows: cellos)
	0:48		Entry 3: Tuba
	1:02		("Additional" fragment: oboe)
	1:15		Entry 4: Flute in low register
	1:35		("Additional" fragment). The march gradually dies away; the drum beat finally stops.

SECTION 2

12 6	2:09	**Dance-Band Phrases**	**a** Oboes, *p*, repeated (trumpets in counterpoint); pizzicato string beat
0:30	2:39		**b** Faster, *mf;* high (E-flat) clarinets, bass drum, and cymbals
13 7	2:53		**a** Strings, with varied repeat (trumpets in counterpoint)
0:31	3:24		**b′** With new continuation
0:48	3:41	**Conclusion**	Descending cadential passage, a little slower, based on **a**
1:19	4:12	**Return to Funeral-March Motives**	The funeral-march drumbeat, which entered during the previous passage, continues in the background. The march dies away; the drumbeat almost stops.

SECTION 3

2:00	4:53	**Trio (Song)**	The rhythm gradually picks up: a gentle triplet accompaniment with a throbbing background
14 8	5:09		A songlike melody starts in muted strings, then moves to the flute, two solo violins, clarinet, and oboe.
1:16	6:25		The trio dies away (violins).
15 9	6:43		Gong strokes
0:07	6:50		Flutes play two new phrases, as though waiting.

SECTION 4

16 10	7:02	**March**	Drumbeat, faster, in a new key: march ("Frère Jacques")
0:16	7:18		("Additional" fragment: E-flat clarinet, strings, flute)
17 11	7:36		March theme with new, parodistic counterpoint: trumpets
0:23	7:59		Dance-band phrase **b**: clarinets, cymbals, drums
18 12	8:17		March theme with new trumpet counterpoint; new sudden speedup: clarinets, *ff*
0:19	8:36	**Conclusion**	Descending cadential passage, based on **a**, with drumbeat as in section 2; slower
1:21	9:38		("Additional" fragment, in low range: bassoon)
1:36	9:53		The music dies down; gong strokes

GLOBAL PERSPECTIVES 5

Musical Drama Worldwide

We saw earlier (page 56) that most religious traditions make substantial use of singing of one sort or another. Likewise, most traditions of drama worldwide do not consist of plain speech and little else, but instead incorporate chanting, singing, instrumental music, and dance. In this way they resemble the European opera we have studied and other kinds of Western drama, from ancient Greek tragedy and comedy to today's megamusicals on Broadway.

Perhaps, in fact, this connection of music and drama is related at a very deep level to the connection of singing and religion. Just as the heightening of prayer in song seems to give readier access to invisible divinity, so music seems somehow compatible with the illusory, real-and-yet-unreal enactment of actions and events onstage.

Whatever the reason, from the ancient beginnings of drama down to the present day, music has been joined with acting more often than not. The operatic notion of singing a play is more in line with world traditions than the purely spoken rendition of Shakespeare or Ibsen or Tom Stoppard. And where would the movies be without music?

Japanese Drama

Asia has developed particularly rich traditions of musical drama. These include the shadow plays of Indonesia, accompanied by gamelan music and relating

stories from lengthy epic poems by means of the shadows of puppets cast on a screen (see page 215). In India, religious dance-dramas reach back hundreds of years. Today the main form of musical drama is on screen: Movie musicals are the staple of the huge and lucrative Indian film industry. China, meanwhile, offers hundreds of regional styles of music theater, the most famous of which, Beijing (or Peking) opera, we will study on page 310.

In Japan, the main traditions of musical drama are these:

❧ **Noh** dramas emerged in the fourteenth and fifteenth centuries and were particularly prized in the elite shogun and samurai culture of the time. Noh dramas are steeped in Zen Buddhist philosophy. Their stage action consists of highly restrained, stylized, and symbolic gestures and movements. They involve singing (both by the actors and a chorus), dance, and complex, carefully predetermined instrumental accompaniment by a strictly limited ensemble: three percussion players and a flutist.

❧ **Bunraku** (bóon-ráh-koo) is a puppet theater, like the Indonesian shadow plays, but instead of casting shadows on a screen, large puppets are skillfully manipulated onstage, each by three puppeteers. Meanwhile one singer

Inside a kabuki theater, c. 1745

provides narration and the different voices for each of the puppets. He is accompanied by a single three-stringed Japanese lute called *shamisen* (shah-mée-sen).

Kabuki (kah-bóo-kee) theater arose in the seventeenth century and adopted features from both noh and bunraku. Kabuki played to an audience different from the samurai class that prized noh. It used more modern stories and appealed to a new public made up of members of the urban merchant class that was emerging in Japan at this time. In a strikingly similar way, Baroque opera in Europe evolved from its aristocratic origins to become a cherished entertainment of new, upper-middle-class audiences (see page 98).

Performing Kabuki Theater   Kabuki was first performed by women and young boys, but before long both of these types of performance were banned because of their associations with prostitution. Until recently, only men sang kabuki. Female roles were played by special female impersonators.

The musical forces in kabuki are particularly complex. In addition to the singing actors, they can involve three other musical groups. Onstage, the main group sits behind the actors and accompanies their dialogue and dances. This group consists of a chorus, a number of shamisen players, and the three percussionists and flute player of the noh orchestra.

A second orchestra is hidden in a room to the left of the stage. Its makeup is variable, and it performs many functions. It can create musical sound effects, provide appropriate "mood" music and musical interludes, accompany certain onstage actions, and even suggest unspoken thoughts of the actors onstage.

Finally, the singer-narrator and shamisen player of bunraku may also be present. They sit to the right of the stage.

Nagauta Music from Dojoji   The most famous genre of music involved in kabuki is the **nagauta** (náh-gah-

Kabuki. Behind the elaborately costumed actors are the stage musicians: the four noh players (lower row) and the chorus and shamisen players (upper row).

óo-ta), or "long song," which usually accompanies dance. It is an extended piece for a singer (or singers in unison) and the onstage orchestra of shamisens, percussion, and flute. Sometimes the offstage orchestra takes part too.

We hear part of a nagauta from the kabuki play *Dojoji*. The singer and shamisens carry the main melody in a free and complex heterophony—you will hear the voice lagging behind or running ahead of the same pitches played by the shamisens. The flute contributes either its own version of the main melody or, in the most striking fashion, an independent melody in the style of noh music that is often not even in the same tonality as the main melody.

Meanwhile the drummers play either rhythmic patterns synchronized with the shamisens and voice or independent, "out-of-sync" patterns, derived from noh music.

LISTEN

Nagauta Music from the Kabuki Play *Dojoji*   3 min., 30 sec.

0:02	Part 1	Instrumental: shamisens play the main melody, accompanied by drums and a bell-like gong. Flute plays an independent melody. Exclamations by percussionists can also be heard.
0:55	Part 2	Main melody in heterophony (singer, shamisens, flute), supported by percussion
1:55	Part 3	Singer pauses; main melody in shamisens and flute
2:12	Part 4	Main melody (singer, shamisens); flute plays independent melody.
3:07	Part 5	Free heterophony for singer and shamisen alone

Chinese Opera

What we know as Beijing opera, the most famous variety of Chinese musical drama, is in China called **jingju** (chéeng-chu), meaning "theater of the capital." It is one of more than three hundred different local varieties of traditional Chinese musical drama, each identified by the province or district of its origin. Beijing opera is a rich amalgam of song, spoken dialogue, instrumental music, dance, elaborate costume, and martial arts. In a nation of vast size and immense cultural diversity, the "theater of the capital" comes closest to being a national tradition of musical drama.

Beijing opera is a relatively recent product of a long, complex history. Some of its stylistic features were introduced to the capital by provincial theater troupes at the end of the eighteenth century, while others developed through much of the nineteenth. Only by the late 1800s did Beijing opera assume the form we know today, and even that form has more recently undergone striking changes, especially during the Communist period of the last half-century.

Voice Types in Beijing Opera

In European opera, different voice types have been habitually associated with specific character types. In Romantic opera, tenors usually play young, vital, and amorous characters (for example, Radames in Verdi's *Aida*), and sopranos play their female counterparts (Aida herself);

Beijing opera: a female character and a *jing*

most often the two are star-crossed lovers. The lower female voice is often reserved for a character who conspires against the soprano and tenor (Amneris), while the low male voices, baritone and bass, can variously have fatherly, comic, or evil associations.

Such conventional connections of voice and character type are highly developed in Beijing opera, too—but the voice types are different. Young men of romantic, dreamy inclination sing in a high register and usually in falsetto. Older, bearded men, trusted and loyal advisors of one sort or another, sing in the high baritone range. Warriors sing with a forced, throaty voice; in addition they must be skilled acrobats in order to enact lively, athletic battle scenes.

Two other special male roles are the male comic, who speaks more than he sings, and the *jing* or face-painted role, who may be a warrior, a dashing bandit, or even a god. His face is painted more elaborately than those of the other actors, with patterns whose colors symbolically reveal much about his character. The *jing* sings in a loud, hoarse manner that takes years to master, like the other voice types here—and like the equally artificial voice types of European opera.

The female roles in Beijing opera were, until the Communist era, almost always sung by male impersonators. They include a mature, virtuous woman, sung in a refined, delicate falsetto (when women sing these roles today, they imitate that male falsetto). A younger woman, lively and flirtatious, is sung in a suggestive, innuendo-laden falsetto. There is also an acrobatic female warrior.

The Orchestra

The small orchestra of Beijing opera consists of a group of drums, gongs, and cymbals, a few wind instruments, and a group of bowed and plucked stringed instruments. These are all played by a handful of versatile musicians who switch from one instrument to another during the performance.

The percussion group is associated especially with martial music, accompanying battle scenes. But it also fulfills many other roles: It can introduce scenes, provide special sound effects, use conventional drum patterns to announce the entrances and social status of different characters, and play along with the frequent songs. The most important function of the stringed instruments is to introduce and accompany the songs.

Beijing Opera Songs

In a way that is somewhat akin to the Western contrast of recitative and aria, Beijing opera shows a wide range of vocal styles, from full-fledged song through more declamatory song to heightened, stylized speech and even, for comic and

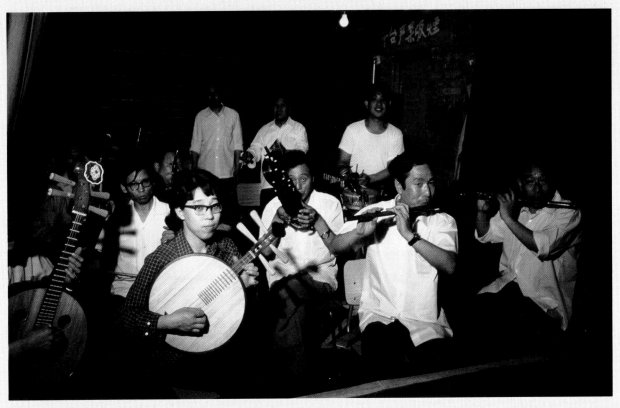

A Beijing opera orchestra: The player in front holds the banjo-like *yueqin;* behind him are an *erhu* player and, standing, percussion players.

minor characters, normal speech. In general, the songs of Beijing opera are like the arias of Italian opera. They are the musical heart of the drama, marked off from the other singing around them by their lyrical style. The songs suggest the feelings and internal psychological states of their singers.

Unlike Italian opera, however, these Chinese arias are not composed anew for each new opera. Instead, their music is chosen from a stock collection of melodies and percussion patterns and fitted to the song-texts of each new libretto added to the repertory. Sometimes whole songs are fitted to new texts in standard poetic forms; at other times, looser musical patterns are taken over and adapted to texts of freer poetry. The crucial concern in this fashioning of arias is to choose melodies and rhythms that convey effectively the emotional situation of a particular song-text.

The Prince Who Changed into a Cat

Our recording presents the beginning of a scene from *The Prince Who Changed into a Cat,* one of the most famous of Beijing operas. The story concerns an Empress who is banished from Beijing through the machinations of one of the Emperor's other wives. (Her newborn son, the prince of the title, is stolen from his cradle and replaced by a cat.) The present scene takes place many years later, when a wise and just Prime Minister meets the Empress and determines to restore her to her rightful position.

First the percussion plays, and then the string instruments, along with a wooden clapper, introduce an aria sung by the Prime Minister (0:25). There are only three strings: a high-pitched two-string fiddle played with a bow called a *jinghu* (chéeng-hoo), a similar but lower-pitched fiddle called *erhu* (ár-hoo), and a plucked lute called *yueqin* (yuéh-chin). All three play the same melody, the erhu doubling the jinghu an octave below while the yueqin adds characteristic repeated notes created by the quick, banjo-like strumming of a string.

Finally, the singer enters (0:41). He sings the same melody as the stringed instruments, though he pauses frequently while they continue uninterrupted. This heterophonic texture (see page 28) is typical of Beijing opera arias. The Prime Minister is a bearded old-man role and sings in the appropriate high baritone range.

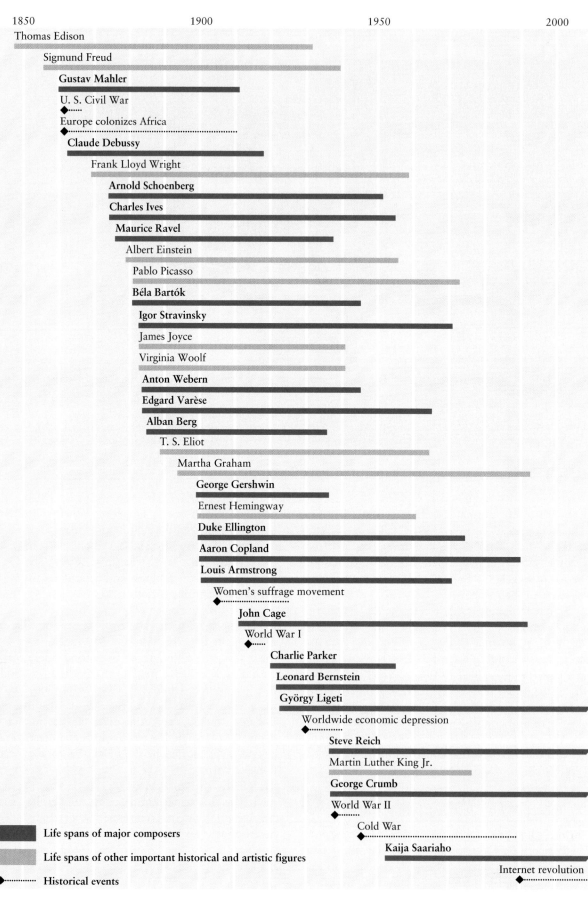

1850   1900   1950   2000

Thomas Edison

Sigmund Freud

Gustav Mahler

U. S. Civil War ◆·······

Europe colonizes Africa ◆···

Claude Debussy

Frank Lloyd Wright

Arnold Schoenberg

Charles Ives

Maurice Ravel

Albert Einstein

Pablo Picasso

Béla Bartók

Igor Stravinsky

James Joyce

Virginia Woolf

Anton Webern

Edgard Varèse

Alban Berg

T. S. Eliot

Martha Graham

George Gershwin

Ernest Hemingway

Duke Ellington

Aaron Copland

Louis Armstrong

Women's suffrage movement ◆·······················

John Cage

World War I ◆·······

Charlie Parker

Leonard Bernstein

György Ligeti

Worldwide economic depression ◆·········

Steve Reich

Martin Luther King Jr.

George Crumb

World War II ◆··········

Cold War ◆·······························

Kaija Saariaho

Internet revolution ◆··················

▬▬▬ Life spans of major composers

▬▬▬ Life spans of other important historical and artistic figures

◆············· Historical events

312

The Twentieth Century

T his unit, which deals with music from around 1900 on, brings our
survey up to the present. Looking back to the year 1900, we can
recognize today's culture in an early form. Large cities, industrialization,
inoculation against disease, advertising, processed food, the first auto-
mobiles, telephones, movies, and phonographs—all were in place by the
beginning of the twentieth century.

Hence many of the phenomena treated in this unit will strike us as fairly
familiar, compared to those of earlier centuries. For one thing, the wide availability of art to mass audiences—not just to the various select groups, as in
the past—is something we take for granted. The new mass audience emerged
because of sociological factors, as mobility between social classes became
easier and more common, along with technological factors—the amazing development of the phonograph, radio, television, and more. We also take for
granted the split that has occurred between classical music and popular music.
A rift that had widened in the nineteenth century became a prime factor of
musical life in the twentieth.

We are also aware of the force of American popular music—music whose
characteristic features emerged around the year 1900, once again. With the
evolution of ragtime and early jazz, a vital rhythmic spring derived from
African-American sources was brought into the general American consciousness. This led to a long series of developments: swing, bebop, rhythm and
blues, rock, rap. After World War II, when the United States began to play
a commanding political role in the world at large, our popular music became
a world language.

Modernism and Traditionalism

What was classical music like in this same period? Classical music itself experienced a split. On the one hand there was music that we shall call "modernist,"
on the other hand, music of a more traditional nature.

The term modernist requires a word of explanation. It is not the same as
contemporary or modern, terms that refer to anything at all that happens to
take place in the present; the -ist at the end of the word modern gives it an

extra twist. The modernists of 1900 were artists and intellectuals who insisted on their modernity—that is, their anti-traditionalism—and who formed a specific cultural movement marked by radical experimentation. Though its roots go back earlier, this movement peaked during the years 1890 to 1918— a period of breakthrough works by such novelists, poets, and painters as Marcel Proust and James Joyce, Ezra Pound and T. S. Eliot, Pablo Picasso and Henri Matisse.

The chief composers associated with the modernist movement were Claude Debussy, Arnold Schoenberg, and Igor Stravinsky. Sometimes they are referred to as members of the "avant-garde"; **avant-garde**—*"vanguard"—is a military or at least a militant term that has long been embraced by radical artists and intellectuals to denote the forefront of their activity.*

At the same time, some twentieth-century artists and composers resisted modernism, and some artists, after some experiments, turned back from it. They found they could comfortably continue in the general spirit of late Romanticism, or even look back to earlier styles. Though the avant-gardists often claimed that the old principles of art had been "used up," there was still plenty of potential left in more traditional methods.

In this unit we shall study the music of modernism and also the reaction against modernism. Our final chapter deals with America's characteristic music, jazz, and some of its consequences.

CHAPTER 19

Prelude
Music and Modernism

Modernism in art, literature, and music flourished especially from around 1890 to 1918, the end of World War I. It was an unusually brilliant movement. A sharp reaction to late nineteenth-century culture, especially to the accepted rules of art within that culture, modernism found amazing resources within the materials of the arts themselves. It is probably the case that the arts of Europe and the West had never before gone through such revolutionary developments together.

1 Industrialization and Progress

Industrialization is one of two overriding historical facts of the nineteenth century. The other one, the emergence of the modern nation-state, we spoke of earlier; see pages 292–94. Ever since the first so-called age of science in the seventeenth century, technological discoveries had come faster and faster, and industry was transformed. The harnessing of steam power in the eighteenth century was matched by the capturing of electricity in the nineteenth. Europe and America were crisscrossed with railroads, built for the benefit of industry and commerce. By the early twentieth century, automobile and air travel were in their early stages of development, as were telephones, movies, and sound recordings.

What had been essentially rural societies, controlled by stable aristocracies, turned into modern nations, dominated by urban societies and run by self-made entrepreneurs. These changes occurred at breakneck speed, as people saw at the time. Yet no one could have forecast how the stresses caused by such social changes would lead on the one hand to the disturbing artistic-intellectual movement known as modernism, and on the other to the catastrophe of World War I.

For at the heart of "official" nineteenth-century culture was a sense of confidence in progress. Progress in science and technology, it was thought, would be matched in due time by progress in human affairs. And although anyone could see evidence to the contrary—for example, in the appalling conditions of the new industrial poor, as exposed by the novels of Charles Dickens—this evidence was easily ignored by the rich and powerful who were profiting from technology's advances.

Another, dark side of progress became evident in the development of weaponry. The deadly novelty of the American Civil War was the rifle, effective over five times the range of previous shoulder weapons. In World War I, tanks, submarines, and chemical weapons showed technology's terrible potential for destruction: an estimated forty million military and civilian dead from war, famine, and epidemic, and twenty million wounded. With World War I, modern nation-states came into their own, pitting themselves against one another. Nineteenth-century confidence in progress—a response to the successes of technology—was thrown into question by technology itself.

Science and Uncertainty

By this time, however, the groundwork for such loss in confidence had already been laid by science in other areas. Men and women were shaken in their most basic assumptions about life by ominous advances in physics, biology, and psychology.

⅄   The impact of Einstein's theory of relativity (which later in the century made its own contributions to the technology of weaponry) was at first more philosophical than practical in nature. The idea that things depend on the standpoint of the observer, and cannot be counted on according to the "objective" rules of Newtonian physics, rocked people's sense of certainty.

⅄   For many, this uncertainty deepened a crisis in religion that the Victorians had already experienced as a result of scientific theories of evolution. Here the key figure was Charles Darwin. Were human beings created by God in God's image, as the Bible teaches, or did they evolve by an impersonal process from animals? The disturbance that this idea caused in people's sense of stability is still reflected in today's disputes about creationism and "creation science."

⅄   Meanwhile the psychological theories of Sigmund Freud suggested that in spite of what people thought they were doing or feeling, they were in fact controlled by unconscious drives. The idea of men and women in the grip of irrational forces of their own (or their parents') making was, again, very disturbing. At the same time, the prospect of "working out" one's problems through psychotherapy gave the new century its paradigm for personality change.

2 The Response of Modernism

If the traditional laws of physics, biblical authority, and psychological certainty could no longer be accepted, it seemed a small enough step to question the rules, assumptions, and prohibitions surrounding the arts.

One such assumption was that visual art had to represent something from the external world. Once this idea was questioned, and then abandoned, the materials of painting and the other arts could be used for themselves—and a whole world of abstract (or nonrepresentational) painting opened up. This general category includes cubism, abstract expressionism, op art, and other such subcategories.

Cubism was one of the earliest forms of abstract or near-abstract art, developed around the time of World War I by Pablo Picasso, Georges Braque, and others. In this painting by Braque, one can discern a guitar and the score of *Socrate*, by a leading modernist composer, Erik Satie.

In literature, the basic assumption was that poets and novelists would use ordinary sentence structure, syntax, and grammar. Freedom from these conditions opened up a whole new sphere of suggestion. Using the so-called stream-of-consciousness method, James Joyce ended his novel *Ulysses* of 1922 with a famous long section—forty pages, without punctuation or paragraphs—tracking the miscellaneous but not-so-idle thoughts of a character who hadn't even spoken until then, Molly Bloom, as she lies in bed.

In music, the basic assumptions were melody and its close associates harmony and tonality. These assumptions, too, were thrown into doubt. Arnold Schoenberg's song cycle *Pierrot lunaire* ("Moonstruck Pierrot") of 1912 traumatized the world of music by employing a kind of half-speaking, half-singing style that the composer called *Sprechstimme* (speech-song; see page 340) throughout all twenty-one of its numbers. Ranging from a throaty whisper to a near-hysterical shriek, *Sprechstimme* was an explicit—indeed aggressive—denial of melody.

New Languages for Art

Avant-garde artists developed whole new languages for art—for example, the "language" of cubism, shown in the painting by Georges Braque, above. If we take the word *language* literally, the most dramatic case is that of James Joyce whose last novel, *Finnegans Wake*, makes use of a language that is half English and half a construction of words he invented.

Schoenberg, once again, provides a striking analogue in music. His twelve-tone method, or **serialism,** developed in the 1920s, replaced the old "language" for music based on tonality (see page 326). By arranging the twelve notes of the chromatic scale into fixed patterns, and manipulating those patterns by means of mathematical operations, Schoenberg arrived at a radical new way of composing music—and hearing it, too. His experiments were continued with great energy after World War II, as we shall see in Chapter 22.

Broadway Boogie-Woogie by Piet Mondrian—a tribute to the "mechanical" rhythms of jazz (as he perceived them) by a premier abstract painter.

Art and Objectivity

The "new languages" for art were unquestionably (and unapologetically) difficult. To this day, few people understand *Finnegans Wake*. Few can follow Schoenberg's serial compositions. Avant-garde art became detached from music's ordinary public, and hence abstracted from a base in society.

At the same time, the modernists' concentration on artistic materials led to abstraction of another kind, the abstraction of technique from expression. This emphasis on technique was welcomed by some as a relief from the overheated emotionality of late Romantic music of Chaikovsky, Mahler, and the like. Especially in the 1920s, "objectivity" was an ideal espoused by many artists. Only too often, their works struck the public as "abstract" in a cold, dry sense.

Characteristic of this phase of the avant-garde were various experiments with schematic, even mathematical devices in the arts. The Dutch painter Piet Mondrian made pictures out of straight lines at right angles to one another, and juxtaposed planes of bright color. Among composers, Igor Stravinsky was known for his provocative statements extolling objectivity and attacking Romantic music—and certainly the brisk, mechanistic rhythms that characterize Stravinsky's style are diametrically opposed to rubato (see page 242), the rhythmic "stretching" that contributes so much to nineteenth-century music's emotionality.

Several lesser composers, fascinated by "machine" rhythms, even tried to evoke machinery in their works: the American George Antheil *(Ballet mécanique)*, the Russian A. V. Mosolov *(The Iron Foundry)*, and the Swiss Arthur Honegger *(Pacific 231—*a locomotive).

Cover for *The Blue Rider*, a magazine that promulgated modernist art and music.

3 Literature and Art before World War I

There was a tendency around this time for artists of various kinds to gravitate together in formal or informal groups, both for mutual encouragement and for the exchange of ideas. Thus Claude Debussy was friends with several avant-garde poets. Schoenberg, himself a painter as well as a musician, associated with a group of artists who set forth their ideas in *The Blue Rider*, a magazine named after a picture by the pioneer nonrepresentational painter Wassily Kandinsky (see page 323). Stravinsky and Maurice Ravel belonged to a group who called themselves the Apaches. With all this interchange, it is not surprising that one can sometimes detect similar tendencies in music and the other arts.

Impressionists and Symbolists

As we have already remarked, modernism got its start in the late nineteenth century and then peaked in the twentieth. The best-known modernist movement, **impressionism**, dates from the 1870s, when people were astonished by the flickering network of color patches used by impressionist painters to render simple scenes from everyday life (as in Edouard Manet's *In the Boat*; see page 320). These painters claimed that they had to develop such a technique to catch the actual, perceived quality of light. They proudly called themselves "realists," in reaction to the idealized and overemotional art of Romanticism.

    Symbolism, a consciously *un*realistic movement, followed soon after impressionism. Symbolist poets revolted against the "realism" of words being

With pure nails brightly
  flashing their onyx
Anguish at midnight
  holds up (Lucifer!)
A multitude of dreams
  burnt by the Phoenix
A mortuary urn
  cannot recover
On credence table,
  in empty hall: . . .

Opening of a symbolist
sonnet (Stéphane Mallarmé)

In the Boat, an impressionist painting by Edouard Manet (1832–1883).

Does nature imitate art? This snapshot of Debussy (second from the left) and some friends is startlingly similar in mood to the (earlier) impressionist painting by Manet shown above.

used for reference—for the purpose of exact definition or denoting. They wanted words to perform their symbolizing or signifying function as freely as possible, without having to fit into phrases or sentences. The meaning of a cluster of words might be vague and ambiguous, even esoteric—but also rich, "musical," and endlessly suggestive.

"Musical" was exactly what the symbolists called it. They were fascinated by the music dramas of Richard Wagner, where again musical symbols—Wagner's leitmotivs—refer to elements in his dramas in a complex, ambivalent, multi-layered fashion. All poets use musical devices such as rhythm and rhyme, but the symbolists were prepared to go so far as to break down grammar, syntax, and conventional thought sequence to approach the elusive nonreferential quality of music.

Claude Debussy is often called an impressionist in music, because his fragmentary motives and little flashes of tone color seem to recall the impressionists' painting technique. Debussy can also—and more accurately—be called a symbolist, since suggestion, rather than outright statement, is at the heart of his aesthetic. Famous symbolist texts inspired two famous Debussy works: the orchestral *Prelude to "The Afternoon of a Faun"* (a poem by Stéphane Mallarmé), and the opera *Pelléas et Mélisande* (a play by Maurice Maeterlinck), where Debussy's elusive musical symbols and Maeterlinck's elusive verbal ones combine to produce an unforgettable effect of mysterious suggestion.

Expressionists and Fauves

Symbolism is also the force behind powerful images in the work of Vincent van Gogh. In his *Thatched Roofs at Cordeville*, the distorted rooftop and the almost liquid trees are not there to represent objects, but to symbolize the artist's disturbing vision of the universe.

But even in van Gogh's most extreme works, the trees are still recognizably trees. In Paris and Vienna—artistic centers which were also centers of avant-

Thatched Roofs at Cordeville, by Vincent van Gogh, 1890.

Horses and riders, painted by Wassily Kandinsky over a four-year period, show his path toward nonrepresentational painting. In the first picture, the figures are quite clear; in the last, they could be missed entirely. Top left: *Couple on Horseback* (1907); top right: *Blue Mountain* (1909); bottom: *Romantic Landscape* (1911).

Picasso's famous shocker *Les Demoiselles d'Avignon* (1907). Picasso and other abstract painters designed sets for the Diaghilev Ballets Russes, sponsor of Stravinsky and other modernist composers.

garde music—two émigré artists pursued separate but parallel paths toward completely abstract painting.

Our horse-and-rider pictures on page 322 by the Russian-born Wassily Kandinsky (1866–1944) show step by step how the process was accomplished. (Where does the *Blue Rider* picture fit in?) Kandinsky belonged to a German movement in the arts called **expressionism**—not to be confused with impressionism—which sought to express the most extreme human feelings by divorcing art from everyday literalness. Anguish, even hysteria, could be conveyed by the harsh clashing of strong colors, irregular shapes, and jagged lines. What seems to be conveyed is not something external but the artist's inner turbulence—most violently in the last Kandinsky picture, *Romantic Landscape*, which is almost entirely abstracted from the outer world.

Parallel to the expressionists was a short-lived group in Paris dubbed *Les fauves*, "the wild beasts." The fauves experimented with distorted images bordering on the grotesque; they also employed motifs from what they called "primitive" art as though in defiance of a decadent European culture. In Pablo Picasso's famous painting *Les Demoiselles d'Avignon* of 1907 (Avignon is a street in the red-light district of Barcelona), the quality of abstraction is evident in the angular bodies and the African-mask-like heads—a complete break with the conventional rules of human portrayal. Picasso took a further step toward abstraction a little later when he turned to cubism (see page 317).

There is violence in both Kandinsky's and Picasso's work of this period. Certainly that is how it struck a generation used to the nonthreatening art of the impressionists—painters of flickering summer landscapes, soft-edged nudes, and diaphanous action pictures of the ballet. Composers, too, courted violence in their music. The Hungarian composer Béla Bartók wrote a "barbarous" piano piece entitled *Allegro barbaro*. Stravinsky, in his ballet *The Rite of Spring*, depicted human sacrifice in the fertility ceremonies of primitive Slavic tribes.

4 Music before World War I

The art of music never enjoyed (or suffered) a link to the tangible world that was comparable to representation in painting, or to reference in poetry. But it did have its own stable, generally accepted set of principles, its own traditional "internal logic." This rested upon elements that we have discussed many times in this book: tune, motive, harmony, tonality, tone color, and rhythm.

The music of Bach, Beethoven, and Brahms was based on this "logic," and so was the entire stream of Western European folk songs, popular songs, dances, military marches, and the rest. Avant-garde music moved away from this norm.

Music by Gustav Klimt, the leading modernist painter in Vienna in the years around 1900.

Like abstract, nonrepresentational painting, music worked out new principles based on the materials of the art itself.

With European music before World War I, we can lay our main emphasis on developments in melody, harmony, and tonality, for on the whole, these features were the main preoccupations of avant-garde composers in that period. Developments in tone color and rhythm—or, more broadly, musical sonority and musical time—dominated music after World War II.

Experiment and Transformation: Melody

Melody, harmony, and tonality all work closely together. In historical terms, harmony arose as a way of supporting and adorning melody, and tonality first arose as a means of clarifying both melody and harmony; later tonality functioned as a more general way of organizing music. Each of these functions was transformed in the early twentieth century.

We have seen the Viennese Classical composers bring tunes to the fore in their music, and the Romantics capitalize on tunes as the most emphatic means of conveying powerful emotion. Yet Wagner, despite the melodic quality of many of his leitmotivs, was criticized for the confusing quality of his singing lines, and Mahler's audiences were puzzled and irritated by the bittersweet distortions that he applied to folklike melodies. In his later works, such as his immense Ninth Symphony of 1909, Mahler wrote increasingly intricate and difficult melodic lines. The long melodies surge, swoop, and yearn in a strange, almost painful manner.

And by that time another Viennese composer, Arnold Schoenberg, was writing even more complex melodies that simply made no sense to contemporary listeners. The intense rhythms and the anguished intervals of Romanticism were there, but the actual notes did not appear to fit together at all.

Schoenberg, *Pierrot lunaire*

Outside of Vienna, the disintegration of traditional melody was accomplished in other ways. In many (not all) of his works, Claude Debussy used only the most shadowy motives—a constant suggestion of melody without clear tunes. A little later Igor Stravinsky, writing in Paris, seized upon Russian folk songs but whittled them down (or abstracted them) into brief, utterly simple fragments, blank and "objective," as his theories demanded.

New Horizons, New Scales

We have mentioned the influence of African masks on Picasso's *Demoiselles*. Non-Western musics, too, began to make inroads into Western classical music. At a World's Fair that fascinated Paris in 1889—the fair for which the Eiffel Tower was built—Debussy heard his first non-Western music played by native musicians, under simulated native conditions. He tried to recapture the sounds of the Indonesian gamelan (see page 214) in a number of his compositions, even taking a Balinese melody for the theme of a concerto finale.

Debussy sensed a resonance between his own music and the unique timbres of the gamelan, and also the scales used in Indonesian music. The traditional diatonic scale had served as the foundation of Western music for so long that

Schoenberg and Serialism

Of all early twentieth-century composers, Arnold Schoenberg (1874–1951) was the most keenly aware of the problem caused by ever-broadening dissonance and atonality. The problem, to put it simply, was the clear and present danger of chaos. In the early 1920s Schoenberg found a way that he felt would impose order or control over the newly "emancipated" elements of music.

This resulted in the **twelve-tone system,** defined by Schoenberg as a "method of composing with the twelve tones solely in relation to one another"—that is, *not* in relation to a central pitch, or tonic, which is no longer the point of reference for music. This method became known as **serialism.** Serialism can be regarded as a systematization of the chromaticism developed by Romantic composers, especially Richard Wagner (see pages 244, 328).

Schoenberg's "Twelve-Tone System"

Schoenberg developed a way of composing with the twelve pitches of the chromatic scale held to a *fixed ordering.* An ordered sequence of the twelve pitches is called a **twelve-tone row** or **series:** hence the term *serialism.* For any composition, he would determine a series ahead of time and maintain it (the next piece would have a different series).

What does "maintain" mean in this context? It means that Schoenberg composed by writing notes only in the order of the work's series, *or of certain carefully prescribed other versions of the series* (see below). As a general rule, he always went through the entire series without any repetitions or backtracking before starting over again. The pitches can, however, appear in any octave, high or low. They can stand out as melody notes or blend into the harmony. They can assume any rhythm.

And what are those "versions" of the series? The series can be used not only in its original form, but also

✓ *transposed,* that is, the same note ordering can start from any note in the chromatic scale: a series beginning A B D D♯ can appear as D E G G♯, or G A C C♯, or in nine other transposed forms.

✓ *inverted,* with the intervals between notes turned upside down:
A B D becomes A G E

✓ used in *retrograde,* played backwards:
A B D D♯ E F♯ C♯ G♯ A♯ C F G becomes G F C A♯, etc.

The basic idea of serialism may seem to impose order with a vengeance, putting very severe limits on what a

Arnold Schoenberg at forty, by Egon Schiele. Schoenberg was fifty before he developed the twelve-tone system.

composer can do. But once the versions are taken into consideration, an enormous number of options becomes available, especially since transposition and inversion can both occur at the same time (A B D becoming G F D, and so on).

Serialism and Unity

Part of the point of twelve-tone composition is that each piece has its own special "sound world" determined by its series. This permeates the whole piece. The next piece has a new series and a new sound world.

Indeed, serialism can be regarded as the end result of an important tendency in nineteenth-century music, the search for ever stronger means of unity within individual compositions. We have traced the "principle of thematic unity" in music by Berlioz, Wagner, and others, and mentioned the different "levels" on which it operated—actual recurring themes, thematic transformations, and subtler similarities between motives (see page 248).

A serial composition is, in a sense, totally unified, since every measure of it shares the same unique sound world. Thus, on its own special terms, Schoenberg's serialism seemed to realize the Romantic composers' ideal of unity.

Phrase of a Schoenberg melody using a twelve-tone series.

it was almost regarded as a fact of nature. But now composers were beginning to reconsider the basic sound materials of music. Notable among these experimenters was Charles Ives, in America (see page 348). New scales were employed for themes or even whole movements, first among them the **pentatonic scale,** a five-note scale playable on the black notes of the keyboard. Imported from folk song and Asian music, this scale was tried in all the usual genres, not only (as before) in nationalist or other folk-derived compositions.

Incidentally, Debussy was also intrigued by another "exotic" music: ragtime and a dance associated with it, the cakewalk, precursors of American jazz (see page 350). In a simple piano piece he dedicated to his young daughter, Debussy wrote a cakewalk up front and contrasted it with a little spoof of Wagner's *Tristan und Isolde*—a pretty clear pronouncement on the direction he saw music taking.

Three other new scales introduced at this time are (significantly enough) abstract constructions, which anyone can figure out by systematically analyzing the total chromatic scale. The **whole-tone scale** divides the octave into six equal parts—all of its intervals are whole steps; again, Debussy worked with this resource in many pieces. The **octatonic scale**—a specialty with Stravinsky—fits eight pitches into the octave by alternating whole and half steps.

Less used, the **quarter-tone scale** employs all the pitches of the chromatic scale plus the pitches that come halfway between each pair of them.

More important as a means of composition than the use of any of these scales was serialism, the "new language" for music invented in the 1920s by Arnold Schoenberg. As is explained in the box on the opposite page, serialism in effect creates something like a special scale for every serial composition.

"The Emancipation of Dissonance"

As melody grew more complex, more fragmentary, or more vague, harmony grew more and more dissonant. The concepts of consonance and dissonance, as we noted on page 27, rest on the fact that certain chords (consonant chords) sound stable and at rest, whereas others (dissonant chords) sound tense and need to resolve to consonant ones. In a famous phrase, Schoenberg spoke of "the emancipation of dissonance," meaning emancipation from that need to resolve. Dissonance was to be free from the "rule" that says it must always be followed by the appropriate consonance.

To be sure, dissonance and consonance are relative matters; there are mild dissonances (play A on the piano together with the G above it) and more tense, strident dissonances (play A and G and all the nine notes between them simultaneously). As early twentieth-century composers explored higher and higher levels of dissonance, they discovered that a kind of resolution could be obtained by proceeding not from dissonance to consonance, but from a harsh dissonance to a milder one. Slowly listeners began hearing this, too.

Tonality and Atonality

Tonality is the feeling of centrality, focus, or "homing" toward a particular pitch that we get from simple tunes and much other music. As melody grew more complex or fragmented, and harmony grew more dissonant and chromatic, tonality grew more indistinct. Finally, some music reached a point at which no tonal center could be detected at all. This is **atonal** music.

However, just as consonance and dissonance are not open-and-shut concepts, neither are tonality or atonality. Most Baroque music sounds firmly rooted in its key, for example, whereas certain Romantic music seems rather to hover around a general key area. Much early twentieth-century music that was once criticized as "atonal" can be heard on careful listening to have a subtle sense of tonality after all.

Wagner, as we recall, went further than other Romantic composers in the direction of *chromaticism*, the free use of all twelve pitches of the chromatic scale. For example, there are as many as ten different chromatic notes in this prominent phrase from his opera *Tristan und Isolde* (see page 284).

Since tonality depends on one pitch standing out from the others in the ordinary diatonic scale (for example, C in the C-major scale C D E F G A B), when all twelve chromatic pitches are used freely, the centrality of any single one is automatically diluted. Wagner's technique of chromaticism was a significant forecast of atonality, which was realized most systematically by Schoenberg's development of serialism.

Melody, harmony, tonality: All are closely related. Beleaguered conservatives around 1900 referred to them jokingly as the "holy trinity" of music. The "emancipation" of melody, harmony, and tonality all went together. This joint emancipation counts as the central style characteristic of the first phase of twentieth-century avant-garde music.

Web: *Research and test your understanding of music and modernism at* <bedfordstmartins.com/listen>.

The Twentieth Century: Early Modernism

The first major phase of avant-garde music—what we now call modernist music—took place in Paris and Vienna from around 1890 to 1914. Claude Debussy, Igor Stravinsky (a young Russian working in Paris), and Arnold Schoenberg were the leading figures in this brilliant era. And there were strong modernist rumblings in Russia, Hungary, Italy, and the United States.

It was a period of rapid development in all the arts, as we have seen, in which the basic tenets of nineteenth-century art were everywhere challenged. In particular, nineteenth-century ideas of melody, harmony, and tonality came under attack. Developments in tone color and rhythm—or, more broadly, musical sonority and musical time—dominated the second phase of modernism, which followed after World War II.

To be sure, musical elements such as melody, harmony, rhythm, and sonority affect each other intimately, and composers hardly ever think of them in isolation. Debussy, Stravinsky, and Schoenberg were all noted for their novel treatment of tone color and rhythm. In terms of historical impact, however, Stravinsky's rhythm, though widely imitated, really worked for him alone, and Debussy's concept of tone color was not fully absorbed until the post–World War II period. It was the revolution in tonality—which went along with a radical reconsideration of melody and harmony—that caught the imagination of the early twentieth century.

1 Debussy and Impressionism

Claude Debussy occupies the border area between late nineteenth- and early twentieth-century styles. His investigation of sensuous new tone colors for orchestra and for piano, his development of new rich harmonies, and his search for new ways to express emotion in music—all remind us of the Romantics. Yet while in some ways his work seems tied to Romanticism, in others it represents a direct reaction against it.

Debussy's tone colors avoid the heavy sonorities that were usual in late Romantic music, merging instead into subtle, mysterious shades of sound. His

(. . . Sounds and perfumes sway in the evening air)

Title of a Debussy "miniature" for piano; the parentheses and dots are his.

The map includes labels:

- North Sea
- ATLANTIC OCEAN
- PARIS
- VIENNA
- Adriatic Sea
- Mediterranean Sea

Box near Vienna:
20th century: Mahler, Schoenberg, Berg
19th century: Beethoven, Brahms, Mahler
18th century: Haydn, Mozart, Beethoven

Box near Paris:
20th century: Debussy, Ravel, Stravinsky
19th century: Berlioz, Chopin, the young Liszt

Paris and Vienna as musical centers.

themes and motives are usually fragmentary and tentative, his harmonies sound strangely vague, and the tonality of his music is often clouded. His themes often draw on the vague-sounding new scales mentioned in Chapter 19.

Debussy's orchestral sound differs sharply from that of his contemporary, Gustav Mahler, another great innovator in orchestration. Mahler treated the orchestra more and more contrapuntally; each instrument tends to stand out from the others like a Romantic hero striving for his own say in the world. Debussy's orchestra is more often a single, delicately pulsing totality to which individual instruments contribute momentary gleams of color. One thinks of an impressionist picture, in which small, separate areas of color, visible close up, merge into unified color fields as the viewer stands back and takes in the painting as a whole.

CLAUDE DEBUSSY
Three Nocturnes (1899)

Debussy's Three Nocturnes, like most of his orchestral works, might be described as impressionist symphonic poems, though without narrative programs. They evoke various scenes without attempting to illustrate them literally.

The title "nocturne" evokes a night-time scene, the great examples before Debussy being the piano nocturnes of Chopin (see page 261). But in fact Debussy's reference was to famous atmospheric paintings by an artist who was close to the impressionists, James McNeill Whistler (see page 331). The first of the nocturnes, *Clouds,* is a pure nature picture, the least nocturnal of the three. The second, *Festivals,* depicts mysterious night-time fairs and parades. The third Nocturne, *Sirens,* includes a women's chorus along with the orchestra, singing not words but just vowels, like an extra orchestral "choir" (see page 43). The women's voices evoke the legendary maidens of the title, who tempt lonely sailors and pull them into the deep.

The title "Nocturnes" should be taken here in a more general and especially in a more decorative sense. . . . Clouds: *the unchanging aspect of the sky, the slow, melancholy motion of the clouds, fading away into agonized grey tones, gently tinged with white.*

Claude Debussy

Nocturne—Grey and Gold by James McNeill Whistler (1834–1903). The American-born expatriate artist painted many more "Nocturnes" and other pictures with musical titles: "Symphony," "Harmony," and "Variations."

Clouds   We first hear a quiet series of chords, played by clarinets and bassoons, that circles back on itself repeatedly. They seem to suggest great cumulus clouds, moving slowly and silently across the sky.

As a "theme," however, these chords do not function conventionally. They make no strong declarations and lead nowhere definitive. This is also true of the next motive, introduced by the English horn—a haunting motive that occurs many times in *Clouds*, with hardly any change. (It is built on an octatonic scale: See page 327.) Yet even this muted gesture, with its vague rhythm and its fading conclusion, seems sufficient to exhaust the composition and bring it to a near halt, over a barely audible drum roll:

After this near stop, the "cloud" music begins again, leading this time to a downward passage of remarkably gentle, murmuring chords in the strings—chords all of the same structure (major ninth chords):

Claude Debussy (1862–1918)

Claude Debussy went through the strict curriculum of the famous Paris Conservatory of Music, which he entered at the age of ten. He did not do well in the piano exams, or at least not well enough, but won various awards in theory and composition. He was finally awarded the coveted Grand Prix (Top Prize)—a three-year fellowship to study in Rome.

Before this, Debussy took a job with Madame von Meck, the eccentric patron of Chaikovsky, playing in a trio at her house in Moscow. Russian music (music of the *kuchka:* see page 295) was one of several vivid influences on the young composer; another was the Indonesian gamelan (see page 214), which he encountered at the World's Fair in Paris in 1889. Visits to Bayreuth, the shrine of Wagner's music dramas, afforded another, even stronger influence. But Debussy soon turned against Wagner and German music in general. He felt it was a stifling influence on modern music in France.

Debussy settled into Parisian café life, becoming a familiar bearded figure in his broad-brimmed hat and flowing cape. A long-term relationship with a mistress came to a bad end, as did Debussy's first marriage, when he eloped with a married woman, who later became his wife. They had a daughter—Debussy wrote the well-known *Children's Corner* Suite for her before she was old enough to play the piano.

In his early thirties Debussy seems to have rather suddenly crystallized his musical style, reflecting the influences of the French symbolist poets and impressionist painters. One remarkable work after another was given its premiere, greeted with a flurry of controversy, and then generally accepted by the critics and the public. His one opera, *Pelléas et Mélisande* (1902), written directly to the words of a play by the prominent symbolist Maurice

Maeterlinck, exasperated the author. But today Maeterlinck's play is remembered mainly on account of Debussy's opera.

Debussy is famous for his innovations in orchestration and in piano writing; his Preludes and Études for the piano are the most impressive "miniatures" since the time of the early Romantics. Some would say the same for his songs. One of his later works, music for the ballet *Jeux* (Games), dissolves melody, theme, and rhythm so far that it was taken up as a model by the avant-garde after World War II.

For a short time Debussy wrote music criticism, in which he expressed in pungent prose the anti-German attitudes that were already manifest in his music. Debussy died of cancer in Paris during World War I, during a bombardment of his city by the Germans he hated.

Chief Works: For orchestra, *Prelude to "The Afternoon of a Faun"* (a famous poem by the French symbolist poet Mallarmé), Three Nocturnes, *La Mer* (The Sea), *Iberia, Jeux* (Games) ▪ The opera *Pelléas et Mélisande* ▪ For piano: Preludes and Études, *Children's Corner* Suite, and *Suite bergamasque,* including "Clair de lune" ▪ Songs to poems by Baudelaire, Verlaine, and Mallarmé ▪ A string quartet and other chamber music ▪ *Syrinx* for solo flute

Encore: After *Clouds,* listen to *Fêtes* (Festivals), *Prelude to "The Afternoon of a Faun,"* "Clair de lune."

These rich chords slip by without establishing a clear sense of tonality; gorgeous in themselves, they are not "functionally" significant. This use of parallel chords is one of Debussy's finest and most famous innovations.

Clouds might be said to fall into an **A B A′** form—but only in a very general way. Debussy shrinks from clear formal outlines; the musical form here is much more fluid than that of **A B A** structures observed in earlier music. This fluidity is something to bear in mind when following *Clouds* and other avant-garde music with Listening Charts. By design, avant-garde composers break down the sharp and (to them) oversimple divisions of older musical styles. If they avail themselves of form types such as rondo, sonata form, and so on, they do so in very free, imaginative ways.

In the **A** section of *Clouds,* the return of the "cloud" theme after a more active, restless passage suggests an internal **a b a′** pattern as well. The next idea, **B,** sounds at first like a meditative epilogue to **A;** it is built on a pentatonic scale (see page 327, again). But when the little pentatonic tune is repeated

LISTENING CHART 23

5 **2**
19-24 39-44

Debussy, *Clouds*

7 min., 0 sec.

19 39	0:00	**A a**	Cloud theme: clarinets and bassoons	
	0:15		English-horn motive	
	0:20		Quiet timpani roll—music almost stops	
	0:34		Cloud theme: high strings	
20 40	0:47		Downward chord passage	
0:15	1:02		Further development: strings	
0:34	1:21		English-horn motive, with a new echo in the French horn	
1:02	1:49		Downward chord passage	
21 41	2:10	**b**	Rising section, more restless: woodwinds added	
0:30	2:40		Brief climax	
0:38	2:48		English-horn motive (with new even-note rhythm accompaniment) is repeated several times, until it dies away.	
22 42	3:38	**a′**	Cloud theme, with new solo viola counterpoint	
0:16	3:54		Downward chord passage	
23 43	4:12	**B**	A new tune enters tentatively, but then repeats itself; flute and harp	
0:27	4:39		Tune in strings and solo violin	
0:44	4:56		Tune in flute and harp	
		(A′)	*Not a real "return" of* **A**, *only of selected elements standing in for* **A**	
24 44	5:19		English-horn motive, with its echo	
0:31	5:50		Quiet timpani and low strings—prominent until the end	
			Recollection of thematic fragments:	
0:54	6:13		Cloud theme: bassoons, then cellos	
1:13	6:32		**B** tune	
1:21	6:40		French-horn echo to the English-horn motive	

ENGLISH HORN

FLUTE

several times, it begins to feel like a substantial section of contrast. The "return," **A′**, is really just a reference to some of **A**'s material, notably the English-horn figure. Then at the end the bassoons play a dim, disturbed fragment of the cloud theme; the flute hovers for a moment on the **B** tune; and the drum roll is extended—so as to suggest distant thunder, perhaps.

2 Stravinsky: The Primacy of Rhythm

Stravinsky's earliest work followed from that of his teacher, the nationalist composer Rimsky-Korsakov. But in three famous ballet scores written for the Ballets Russes in Paris, Stravinsky rapidly developed his own powerful, hard-edged avant-garde style, a style that can be compared to the contemporary fauve style in French painting (see page 323). These ballets reveal a fascinating progression toward a more and more abstract use of folk material. Compare the development of abstraction in art by Kandinsky and Picasso, which we spoke of earlier.

The first ballet, *The Firebird* (1910), spins a romantic fairy tale about the magical Firebird, the ogre Kastchei, and Prince Ivan Tsarevitch, son of the tsar. Its rich, half-Asian setting is matched by beautifully colored folk music and orchestral sound worthy of Debussy himself. But in the next ballet, Stravinsky moved from the steppes to the urban marketplace, to Mardi Gras in St. Petersburg. *Petrushka* (1911), the story of a carnival barker and his puppet, encouraged him to put a hard, satirical edge on his folk material. Then in *The Rite of Spring* (1913), Stravinsky boldly and brutally depicted the fertility cults of prehistoric Slavic tribes. Here Russian folk music, broken down into repeated, fragmentary motives, is treated as the source of primitive rhythmic and sexual energy, rather than picture-postcard charm.

The musical style that Stravinsky brought to a head in the *Rite* has many features that struck listeners of the time as "barbaric," apart from its use of deliberately crude folk-tune fragments. The music was "abstract" in the sense that it sounded utterly unemotional, by Romantic standards. It was grindingly dissonant. It emphasized meter in a very heavy, exciting way, and the rhythms themselves were dazzling and unpredictable. Finally, the score is enormously loud: It demands a colossal orchestra, as though the composer wanted to show how he could control—and transform—the chief powerhouse of musical Romanticism.

Stravinsky, drawn by Picasso during the period when they were associated at the Ballets Russes.

IGOR STRAVINSKY
The Rite of Spring (1913): Part I, "The Adoration of the Earth"

The first performance of *The Rite of Spring* caused a riot; the audience was shocked and infuriated by the violent, dissonant sounds in the pit and the provocative choreography on the stage, suggesting rape and ritual murder.

The ballet has no real story, and Stravinsky even said that he preferred to think of the music as an abstract concert piece. However, inscriptions on the score specify a series of ancient fertility rites of various kinds, culminating in the ceremonial choice of a virgin for sacrifice. After this she is evidently danced to death in the ballet's second part, entitled "The Sacrifice."

Introduction   The halting opening theme is played by a bassoon at the very top of its normal register. Avant-garde composers strained all the elements of music, including the ordinary capabilities of instruments. The bleating bassoon is joined by odd hootings on other woodwinds, gradually building up an extraordinary texture that is highly dissonant. The instrumental parts sound rather like a static series of preliminary fanfares (or perhaps like the calls of prehistoric wildlife?).

"Omens of Spring"—"Dance of the Adolescents"   After a brief introduction, in which the dancers presumably "register" an awareness of spring's awakening, the "Dance of the Adolescents" commences with a famous instance of Stravinskian rhythmic irregularity. (Probably the original audience started their catcalls at this point.) A single very dissonant chord is repeated thirty-two times in even eighth notes—but with heavy accents reinforced by short, fat chords played by eight (!) French horns on the most unexpected beats:

My idea was that the Prelude should represent the awakening of nature, the scratching, gnawing, wiggling of birds and beasts.

Igor Stravinsky, reminiscing in 1960 about *The Rite of Spring*

BASSOON

These accents completely upset ordinary meter. Instead of eight standard measures of four eighth notes— **1** *2 3 4*, **1** *2 3 4*, etc.—Stravinsky makes us hear **1** *2 3 4*, **1** *2 3 4 5*, **1** *2*, **1** *2 3 4 5 6*, **1** *2 3*, **1** *2 3 4*, **1** *2 3 4 5*, **1** *2 3*. (For a truly bewildering experience, try beating time to this passage.) Yet these irregular rhythms are also exhilarating, and they certainly drive the music forward in a unique way.

The repeating chords are now overlaid with new motives, derived from Russian folk song. The motives are repeated with slightly different rhythms and at slightly different lengths. This is Stravinsky's distinctive type of ostinato, a technique we have met with in many other kinds of music (pages 96, 108, 132); the ostinato is indicated by brackets on the example below. Like Debussy, Stravinsky tends to concentrate on small melodic fragments, but whereas Debussy soon abandons his fragments, Stravinsky keeps repeating his in this irregular, almost obsessive way.

"The Game of Abduction"   New violence is introduced with this section, a whirlwind of brilliant rhythms, with much frantic pounding on the timpani.

The climax of *The Rite of Spring*

Igor Stravinsky (1882–1971)

The son of an important opera singer, Igor Stravinsky studied law and did not turn seriously to music until he was nineteen. He was fortunate to be able to study with Nikolai Rimsky-Korsakov, a survivor of the nationalist *kuchka* (see page 295) who was still composing actively.

Rimsky's brand of nationalism served young Stravinsky well in the famous (and still outstandingly popular) ballet scores *The Firebird, Petrushka,* and *The Rite of Spring,* which he wrote for the Ballets Russes, a Russian company centered in Paris. This enormously dynamic organization, run by a brilliant producer and man-about-the-arts named Sergei Diaghilev, astonished the blasé Parisian public with its exotic spectacles combining the newest and the most sensational in dance, music, scenery, and costume design. Among Diaghilev's dancers were Vaslav Nijinsky and George Balanchine; among his designers were Pablo Picasso and Henri Matisse.

After World War I Stravinsky composed more ballets for Diaghilev, as well as other works in a dazzling variety of styles, forms, and genres. One of the first classical composers, along with Debussy, to be interested in jazz, Stravinsky wrote *Piano Ragtime* in 1917 (and, much later, *Ebony Concerto* for clarinetist Woody Herman's jazz band). He became an outspoken advocate of "objectivity" in music, which meant to him the rejection of Romantic emotionality. For many years he modeled his music on pre-Romantic composers such as Bach, Handel, and Mozart, transforming the music by his own unique rhythmic and harmonic style.

His final work in this vein, called **Neoclassicism**, was an opera, *The Rake's Progress,* which is a modern transformation of Mozart's *Don Giovanni.* This was written in America (to English words), where Stravinsky moved in 1939. After World War II his music grew more abstract and formal in style. During the last twenty years of his life, Stravinsky had as his protégé the young American conductor and critic Robert Craft, who helped to manage his affairs, conducted and promoted his music, and introduced him to the music of Schoenberg and Anton Webern.

For a quarter of a century people had regarded Stravinsky (and he regarded himself) as the leading Neoclassical composer in the French orbit, at the opposite pole from Schoenberg and the Viennese serialists. So he created yet another sensation when, in his seventies, he produced a remarkable group of late compositions employing serial technique.

After some scary stays in American hospitals, on which the composer's comments were particularly sardonic, Stravinsky died at his home in New York in 1971. He is buried in Venice, near the grave of Diaghilev.

Chief Works: Ballet scores, including *The Firebird, Petrushka, The Rite of Spring, The Wedding, Orpheus, Agon* ▪ *The Soldier's Tale,* an unusual chamber-music piece with narrator ▪ An "opera-oratorio," *Oedipus the King; The Rake's Progress,* an opera in English (words by the poet W. H. Auden) ▪ Two symphonies; concertos; *Symphony of Psalms* for orchestra and chorus ▪ Other religious works: a Mass, *Requiem Canticles, Threni* (settings from the Lamentations of Jeremiah)

Encore: After *The Rite of Spring,* listen to *Petrushka* and *Symphony of Psalms.* Read *Conversations with Stravinsky* by Robert Craft.

"Round Dances of Spring"   After a moment of respite, a short, quiet introduction conveys a remarkably desolate, empty feeling, partly as a result of its novel orchestration: a high (E♭) clarinet and low (alto) flute playing two octaves apart. Then a slow dragging dance emerges, built out of the third folk-tune fragment from the "Dance of the Adolescents."

The strong downbeat makes the meter hypnotic—but one or two added or skipped beats have a powerful animating effect. The dance reaches a relentless climax with glissando (sliding) trombones, gong, cymbals, and big drum. After a sudden fast coda, the primordial introduction returns to conclude the section.

Four more sections follow our selection in Part I of *The Rite of Spring.* The dynamic "Games of the Rival Tribes" introduces two more folk-tune fragments. A huge masked figure is borne aloft by the male dancers in a slower section, the "Procession of the Sage"; the Sage then performs a brief ceremony,

LISTENING CHART 24

Stravinsky, *The Rite of Spring*, from Part I

Ballet score. 10 min., 41 sec.

25 **13**	0:00	**Introduction**	Bassoon "fanfare," *p*, twice interrupted by English horn
	1:04		Fanfares in oboe, high (E♭) clarinet, bass clarinet
	1:41		Buildup
26 **14**	2:04		New motive in the oboe and E♭ clarinet
0:29	2:33		Stop; return of the bassoon fanfare, *p*
0:37	2:41	**Omens of Spring**	Dance of the Adolescents is foreshadowed; the music stops and starts, ending with a high violin chord.
0:58	3:02		Tempo is established; trill, ♩♩♩♩ rhythm introduced
27 **15**	3:08	**Dance of the Adolescents**	Loud rhythmic passage with irregular accents (French horns); various motives are introduced
0:36	3:44		Rhythmic passage again
28 **16**	3:53		Folk-song fragment no. 1—bassoons and contrabassoon, etc.
0:28	4:21		Abrupt interruption of the regular rhythm
0:37	4:30		Return of the introductory "Omens" music
0:53	4:46		Folk-song fragment no. 2—French horn, flutes
1:27	5:20		Folk-song fragment no. 3—trumpets (triangle)
1:50	5:43		Folk-song fragment no. 2—piccolos; big buildup
29 **17**	6:16	**The Game of Abduction**	Faster; frantic rhythms. Brass is prominent; sliding horn calls
0:55	7:11		Ending passage: alternation between scurrying figures in the winds and heavy booms in the drums
30 **18**	7:33	**Round Dances of Spring**	Slower; introduction: flute trills, clarinet melody
0:34	8:07		The main slow dance rhythm is introduced; woodwind motive
31 **19**	8:45		Folk-song fragment no. 3 (slower than before)—violas, *mf*
0:54	9:39		Folk-song fragment no. 3, *ff*, with cymbals
1:15	10:00		Climactic passage—brass
1:33	10:18		Short coda: faster, with violent rhythmic interjections
1:49	10:34		Brief return of the slow introduction, *p*

Very fast

ff

Slow

mf

Musical sketches for
The Rite of Spring

"Adoration of the Earth." The concluding orgiastic "Dance of the Earth" is built on a fast and furious ostinato.

What is conspicuously absent from any of this is emotionality. Tough, precise, and barbaric, it is as far from old-line Romantic sentiment as it is from the delicate, shadowy vision of Debussy. In Stravinsky's later works the barbarism was tamed, but the dry, precise quality remained, and so did the exhilarating irregular rhythms. Throughout his long career they provided him with a powerful strategy for movement, unlike that of any other composer. It was the primacy of rhythm that produced Stravinsky's "new language" for music.

3 Expressionism

In Paris during the first decades of the twentieth century, Debussy's shifting musical shadows and Stravinsky's extroverted gestures were on display nightly at the Ballets Russes. Some analogies can be drawn between these composers in stylistic terms, but primarily what they had in common was their rejection, in their different ways, of the steamy emotions of late Romanticism.

In Austria and Germany, however, composers pressed forward with music that was increasingly emotional and complex. As though intent on taking Romantic fervor to its ultimate conclusion, they found themselves exploiting

Nightmarish images recur in expressionist art. Perhaps the most famous expressionist image is *The Scream*, by the Norwegian artist Edvard Munch (1863–1944).

Arnold Schoenberg (1874–1951)

The most conscious and self-conscious member of music's avant-garde was Arnold Schoenberg, who grew up in Europe's most intense musical environment, the Vienna of Johannes Brahms and Gustav Mahler. He was largely self-taught in music, though he found a mentor in the conductor and composer Alexander von Zemlinsky, whose sister became Schoenberg's first wife. (His second wife, also had a musical brother, the leader of an important string quartet—a quartet that featured Schoenberg's music.) A man of unusual versatility, Schoenberg produced important books on music theory, painted (and gave exhibitions of) pictures in expressionist style, and wrote the literary texts for many of his compositions.

His early music—notably *Transfigured Night* of 1899, still his best-known work—followed from the late Romantic tradition of Brahms and Mahler. But Schoenberg soon came to feel that he was destined to carry this tradition through to its logical modern development, by way of increasing chromaticism and atonality. Listeners felt otherwise, and Schoenberg's revolutionary compositions of the 1900s probably met with more hostility than any other works in the entire history of music. At the same time, they attracted the sympathetic interest of Mahler and Richard Strauss, and drew a coterie of brilliant young students to Schoenberg.

Schoenberg's music grew progressively more and more atonal, but he was nearly fifty before he developed the twelve-tone (or serial) system. Of all the "new languages" for music attempted by the early avant-garde composers, serialism was the most radical and also the most fruitful. After World War II, even though some leading radicals rejected Schoenberg's music, they still used his fundamental idea of a serial language for music.

As a Jew, Schoenberg was forced to leave Germany when the Nazis came to power, and he spent the rest of his life in Los Angeles, becoming a U.S. citizen in 1941.

His unfinished opera *Moses and Aaron* of 1933 is both a Judaic epic and an allegory of the problem of modernist communication with the public. *A Survivor from Warsaw* was written in memory of the slaughter that occurred in Warsaw's Jewish quarter when the Nazis crushed the uprising there in 1943.

Arnold Schoenberg was a strange personality: gloomy, uncompromising, inordinately proud, and also highly superstitious. Of all the major composers, he was the first great teacher since Bach; besides his close associates of the Second Viennese School, he strongly influenced many other musicians who sought him out as a teacher. At the end of his life he taught at UCLA. Though only some of his music has won popular approval, musicologists (and many musicians) regard Schoenberg as the most significant composer of the twentieth century.

Chief Works: An early "symphonic poem" for string sextet, *Transfigured Night;* Five Orchestral Pieces; two chamber symphonies, a piano concerto and a violin concerto ▪ *Erwartung* ("Anticipation"), an expressionist monodrama for one singer and orchestra; the unfinished opera *Moses and Aaron* ▪ Choral works, including *Gurrelieder,* the unfinished oratorio *Jacob's Ladder,* and *A Survivor from Warsaw* ▪ Songs, including *The Book of the Hanging Gardens,* to texts by the German symbolist poet Stefan George; *Pierrot lunaire* ("Moonstruck Pierrot"), a chamber-music piece with *Sprechstimme* singer ▪ Four string quartets and other chamber music

Encore: After *Pierrot lunaire,* listen to *Verklärte Nacht* ("Transfigured Night") and Five Orchestral Pieces.

---

extreme states, extending all the way to hysteria, nightmare, even insanity. This movement, *expressionism,* shares its name with important parallel movements in art and literature (see page 323).

These years also saw the publication of the first works of Sigmund Freud, with their bold new analysis of the power of unconscious drives, the significance of dreams, and the central role of sexuality. Psychoanalytic theory had a clear impact on German expressionism; a vivid example is *Erwartung* (Anticipation), a monologue for soprano and orchestra written by Arnold Schoenberg in 1909. In it, a woman comes to meet her lover in a dark wood and spills out all her terrors, shrieking as she stumbles upon a dead body she believes to be his. One cannot tell whether *Erwartung* represents an actual scene of hysteria, an allegory, or a Freudian dream fantasy.

Schoenberg was the leading expressionist in music. He pioneered in the "emancipation of dissonance" and the breakdown of tonality, and shortly after

World War I he developed the revolutionary technique of serialism (see page 326). Even before the war, Schoenberg attracted two brilliant Viennese students who were only about ten years his junior, and who shared almost equally in his path-breaking innovations. Schoenberg, Anton Webern, and Alban Berg are often referred to as the Second Viennese School, by analogy with the earlier Viennese triumvirate of Haydn, Mozart, and Beethoven.

ARNOLD SCHOENBERG
Pierrot lunaire (1912)

This highly influential song cycle sets text by a minor symbolist poet, Albert Giraud. Like many artists of the time—poets as well as composers—Giraud is not easy to figure out at once. Pierrot is the eternal sad clown, and hence perhaps also the alienated artist; but why is he called "lunar"? In poems that are dotted with Freudian imagery, we hear about his obsession with the moon, his amorous frustrations, his nightmarish hallucinations, his pranks and his adventures.

To match all this, Schoenberg wrote music which utterly lacks the tunes that one might expect to find in a set of songs. The soprano does not exactly sing or exactly speak, but performs in an in-between style of Schoenberg's invention called *Sprechstimme* ("speech-song"). **Sprechstimme** is an extreme example of the avant-garde composers' search through the most basic artistic materials—here, sound that is not even fully organized into pitches—for new

An expressionist Pierrot by Georges Rouault (1871–1958).

expressive means. Through *Sprechstimme*, Giraud's strange moonstruck poems are somehow magnified, distorted, parodied, and haunted all at the same time.

Pierrot lunaire calls for five instruments: flute, clarinet, violin, cello, piano. Three of their players double on other instruments; that is, the flutist sometimes switches to piccolo, the clarinetist to bass clarinet, and the violinist to viola. Not all the songs involve all the players, so nearly every song has its own unique accompaniment, ranging from a single flute in No. 7 to all eight instruments in No. 21 (the players switching within this one). Schoenberg's dazzling variety of instrumental effects compensates for the inherent sameness of the *Sprechstimme*.

We will examine two songs vastly different in expressive tone—both unsettling in their distinctive ways.

I only know that on the two occasions I heard Pierrot lunaire I was conscious of the most profound impression I have ever experienced from a work of art, and that the enigmatic power of these pieces has left permanent traces on my innermost being. But when I look at the score it still remains completely mysterious. . . .

Letter to Schoenberg from student Alban Berg, 1914

32 | *No. 8: "Night"* (voice, piano, bass clarinet, cello)   The poem presents the nightmarish aspect of expressionism; we could easily imagine the screaming figure of Edvard Munch's famous painting (see page 338) responding to a vision of this sort:

Finstre, schwarze Riesenfalter	Sinister giant black butterflies
Töteten der Sonne Glanz.	Eclipse the blazing disk of sun.
Ein geschlossnes Zauberbuch,	Like a sealed-up book of wizard's spells
Ruht der Horizont—verschwiegen.	Sleeps the horizon—secret silent.
Aus dem Qualm verlorner Tiefen	From dank forgotten depths of Lethe
Steigt ein Duft, Erinnrung mordend!	A scent floats up, to murder memory.
Finstre, schwarze Riesenfalter	Sinister giant black butterflies
Töteten der Sonne Glanz.	Eclipse the blazing disk of sun.
Und vom Himmel erdenwarts	And from heaven downward dropping
Senken sich mit schweren Schwingen	To the earth in leaden circles,
Unsichtbar die Ungetüme	Invisible, the monstrous swarm
Auf die Menschenherzen nieder…	Descends upon the hearts of men,
Finstre, schwarze Riesenfalter.	Sinister giant black butterflies.

Schoenberg used the lowest instruments of his ensemble to depict these ominous insects, weighty in a way utterly unlike real butterflies. Through the last section of the poem we can hear their swarm settling heavily downwards, blotting out the light of day and bringing on artificial night.

Schoenberg called this song a *passacaglia*, recalling a type of ostinato piece from the Baroque period (see page 106). If you listen closely you will hear that his music is dominated by the three-note ostinato shown in the margin.

The ostinato is announced at the very beginning by the piano, then taken up by the cello and bass clarinet; and is also the last thing you hear at the end of the song. Throughout, the instrumental accompaniment is largely constructed from overlapping versions of it, moved freely to various pitch levels. The soprano is even asked to sing it, at the eerie bottom of her range, on the word *verschwiegen* (secret silent)—the only moment in the entire song cycle when Schoenberg has her abandon *Sprechstimme* for conventional song.

Note, however, that the ostinato is chromatic in essence, its last pitch set a half-step below its first. From such simple materials, Schoenberg can both unsettle conventional tonality and match the scary tone of Giraud's words.

33 | *No. 18: "The Moonfleck"* (voice, piano, piccolo, clarinet, violin, cello)   The piano plays a short introduction, or transition from the previous number. Listen to this piano passage several times. Dense, dissonant, atonal, and alarmingly intense in its motivic insistence, the passage gives us Schoenberg's uncom-

promising version of musical modernism in a nutshell. It also seems devised to recall the loudest, scariest moments of "Night," one of many such musical connections across Schoenberg's cycle.

In the song itself, the tone shifts abruptly from this intensity; now it is not horror but the nagging bother of an obsession. Pierrot can neither forget nor bear the moonfleck that has soiled his tuxedo:

Einen weissen Fleck des hellen Mondes	With a fleck of white—bright patch of moonlight—
Auf dem Rücken seines schwarzen Rockes,	On the back of his black jacket,
So spaziert Pierrot im lauen Abend,	Pierrot strolls about in the mild evening air
Aufzusuchen Glück und Abenteuer.	On his night-time hunt for fun and good pickings.
Plötzlich stört ihn was an seinem Anzug,	Suddenly something strikes him as wrong,
Er beschaut sich rings und findet richtig—	He checks his clothes over and sure enough finds
Einen weissen Fleck des hellen Mondes	A fleck of white—bright patch of moonlight—
Auf dem Rücken seines schwarzen Rockes.	On the back of his black jacket.
Warte! denkt er: das ist so ein Gipsfleck!	Damn! he thinks, There's a spot of plaster!
Wischt und wischt, doch—	Rubs and rubs, but can't get rid of it.
bringt ihn nicht herunter!	
Und so geht er, giftgeschwollen, weiter,	So goes on his way, his pleasure poisoned,
Reibt und reibt bis an den frühen Morgen—	Rubbing and rubbing till dawn comes up—
Einen weissen Fleck des hellen Mondes.	At a fleck of white, a bright patch of moonlight!

In his setting Schoenberg explores timbres completely different from those of "Night." He uses high-pitched, quicksilver motives, scattered through the whole ensemble, to depict flickering moonlight. Simultaneous fugues and canons are at work, but what the listener perceives is a fantastic lacework of sounds, with hardly a hint of tonality, as Pierrot frantically but in vain brushes at himself. "The Moonfleck" uses extremely complicated technical means to achieve a unique sonorous effect.

ALBAN BERG (1885–1935)
Wozzeck (1923)

After Schoenberg, the most powerful exponent of expressionism in music was his student Alban Berg. Berg's opera *Wozzeck*, first conceived during World War I, was completed in 1923. In general plan, this opera can be described as Wagnerian, in that it depends on musical continuity carried by the orchestra. It uses leitmotivs, and contains no arias. Its musical style owes much to Schoenberg's *Pierrot lunaire*.

Background   Berg set a remarkable fragmentary play by the German dramatist Georg Büchner, a half-legible draft that was discovered after his death in 1837. In a series of brief, savage scenes spoken in the plainest vernacular, Büchner presents an almost paranoid vision of the helpless poor oppressed by society. Berg's music for the play's dialogue is all highly intense, and he kept the tension up by writing continuous orchestral interludes during the blackouts between all the scenes, five in each of the opera's three acts.

Franz Wozzeck is an inarticulate and impoverished soldier, the lowest cog in the military machine. He is troubled by visions and tormented for no apparent reason by his captain and by the regimental doctor, who pays him a pittance for serving as a human guinea pig in bizarre experiments. Wozzeck's lover, Marie, sleeps with a drum major, who beats Wozzeck up when he makes some objection. Finally Wozzeck murders Marie, goes mad, and drowns himself.

Act III; Interlude after Scene ii   Scene ii is the murder scene. When Wozzeck stabs Marie, she screams, and all the leitmotivs associated with her blare away in the orchestra. It is said that all the events of our lifetime flash before our eyes at the moment of dying.

A blackout follows, and the stark interlude between the scenes consists of a single pitch played by the orchestra in two gut-bursting crescendos. Don't turn the sound down if this passage hurts your ears—it is supposed to. (It is also pretty hard on the stagehands, who have less than half a minute for the scene change.)

Scene iii   The lights snap on again. In a sordid tavern, Wozzeck gulps a drink and seeks consolation with Marie's friend Margret. Berg's idea of a ragtime piano opens the scene—one of many signs that European music of the 1920s had woken up to American influences. But it is a distorted, utterly dissonant ragtime, heard through the ears of someone on the verge of a breakdown.

The music is disjointed, confused, shocking. When Margret gets up on the piano and sings a song, her song is distorted, too:

Suddenly she notices blood on Wozzeck's hand. It smells like human blood, she says. In a dreadful climax to the scene, the apprentices and street girls in the inn come out of the shadows and close in on Wozzeck. He manages to escape during another blackout, as a new orchestral interlude surges frantically and furiously.

An earlier scene from *Wozzeck*

The Second Viennese School

This is a phrase often applied to Schoenberg and his two closest associates, Anton von Webern and Alban Berg. Both studied with him in Vienna before World War I, and both followed him in adopting serialism in the 1920s. They were very different in musical personality, and serialism did not really draw them together; rather it seems to have accentuated the unique qualities of each composer.

Anton von Webern (1883–1945), who later dropped the aristocratic von, was an unspectacular individual whose life revolved around his strangely fragile artistic accomplishment. Despite his aristocratic background, he became a devoted conductor of the Vienna Workers' Chorus, as well as holding other rather low-profile conducting positions.

From the start, Webern reacted against the grandiose side of Romanticism, as represented by the works of Richard Strauss and Gustav Mahler. He turned his music about-face, toward abstraction, atomization, and quiet: so quiet, that listening to his music, one listens to the rests almost as much as to the notes themselves. His compositions are all extremely brief and concentrated (we will discuss one of them on page 370). Webern's entire musical output can be fitted on three CDs.

But both Webern's vision of musical abstraction and his brilliant use of serialism made him a natural link between the first phase of modernism, around World War I, and the second. Though he died in 1945, shot in error by a member of the American occupying forces in Austria, his forward-looking compositions caught the imagination of an entire generation of composers after World War II.

Alban Berg (1885–1935), in contrast, looked back; more than Schoenberg and certainly more than Webern, he kept lines of communication open to the Romantic tradition by way of Mahler. Berg's first opera, *Wozzeck,* was an immediate success on a scale never enjoyed by the other "Second Viennese" composers. His second opera *Lulu* (1935) is now also a classic, though it made its way slowly—Berg had only partly orchestrated Act III when he died, and both operas were banned by the Nazis.

Berg died at the age of 50 as a result of an infected insect bite. After his death, it came out that he had been secretly in love with a married woman, and had employed a musical code to refer to her and even to address her in his compositions—among them a very moving Violin Concerto (1935), his last work, which also refers to two other women.

The whole of scene iii is built on a single short rhythm, repeated over and over again with only slight modifications—*but presented in many different tempos.* This twitching "master rhythm" is marked above the two previous examples, first at a fast tempo, then at a slow one; we first heard it in the timpani in the interlude between scenes ii and iii. Another obvious instance comes when Margret first notices the blood:

Here is yet another kind of ostinato—very different from Stravinsky's kind (see page 335). Even though this master rhythm may elude the listener in a good many of its appearances, its hypnotic effect contributes powerfully to the sense of nightmare and fixation.

Scene iv   Fatefully, Wozzeck returns to the pond where he murdered Marie. The orchestra engages in some nature illustration, making strange macabre

For once, a composer picture that's different: Alban Berg looks out over a lifesized portrait of himself painted by Arnold Schoenberg.

sounds (so different from the nature illustration in Debussy's *Clouds*!). Wozzeck's mind has quite cracked. He shrieks for the knife (in powerful *Sprechstimme* reminiscent of *Pierrot lunaire:* see page 340), discovers the corpse, and sees the blood-red moon and the pond, too, seemingly filled with blood. He walks into the water, saying that he has to wash himself.

At this point, his principal tormenters walk by. The Captain and the Doctor hear the vivid orchestral gurgles and understand that someone is drowning, but like people watching a mugging on a crowded city street, they make no move to help. "Let's get away! Come quickly!" says the terrified Captain—in plain, naturalistic speech, rather than the *Sprechstimme* used by Wozzeck.

In the blackout after this scene, emotional music wells up in the orchestra, mourning for Wozzeck, Marie, and humanity at large. Here Berg adopts and even surpasses the late Romantic style of Gustav Mahler. Our recording fades after a few minutes of this great lament.

Scene v   Berg (following Büchner) has yet another turn of the knife waiting for us in the opera's final scene. Some children who are playing with Wozzeck's little son run off to view his mother's newly discovered corpse. Uncomprehending, he follows them. The icy sweetness of the music here is as stunning as the violent music of the tavern scene and the weird pond music. In turning Büchner's visionary play fragment into an expressionist opera, Berg created one of the great modernist theater pieces of the twentieth century.

LISTEN   Berg, *Wozzeck*, Act III, scenes iii and iv

SCENE iii: A tavern

34	0:29	**Wozzeck:**	Tanzt Alle; tanzt nur zu, springt, schwitzt und stinkt, es holt Euch doch noch einmal der Teufel!	Dance, everyone! Go on, dance, sweat and stink, the devil will get you in the end.

(Gulps down a glass of wine)
(Shouts above the pianist:)

		Es ritten drei Reiter wohl an den Rhein, Bei einer Frau Wirtin da kehrten sie ein. Mein Wein ist gut, mein Bier ist klar, Mein Töchterlein liegt auf der . . .	Three horsemen rode along the Rhine, They came to an inn and they asked for wine. The wine was fine, the beer was clear, The innkeeper's daughter . . .
		Verdammt! Komm, Margret!	Hell! Come on, Margret! *(Dances with her)*
		Komm, setzt dich her, Margret! Margret, Du bist so heiss. . . . Wart' nur, wirst auch kalt werden! Kannst nicht singen?	Come and sit down, Margret! Margret, you're hot! Wait, you too will be cold! Can't you sing?

(She sings:)

	1:43	**Margret:**	In's Schwabenland, da mag ich nit, Und lange Kleider trag ich nit. Denn lange Kleider, spitze Schuh, Die kommen keiner Dienstmagd zu.	But Swabia will never be The land that I shall want to choose, For silken dresses, spike-heeled shoes, Are not for servant girls like me.
		Wozzeck:	Nein! keine Schuh, man kann auch blossfüssig in die Höll' geh'n! Ich möcht heut raufen, raufen. . . .	No shoes! You can go to hell just as well barefoot! I'm feeling like a fight today!
35	2:29	**Margret:**	Aber was hast Du an der Hand?	But what's that on your hand?
		Wozzeck:	Ich? Ich?	Me? My hand?
		Margret:	Rot! Blut!	Red! Blood!
		Wozzeck:	Blut? Blut?	Blood? Blood? *(People gather around)*
		Margret:	Freilich . . . Blut!	Yes, it is blood!
		Wozzeck:	Ich glaub', ich hab' mich geschnitten, da an der rechten Hand. . . .	I think I cut myself, on my hand. . . .
		Margret:	Wie kommt's denn zum Ellenbogen?	How'd it get right up to the elbow, then?
		Wozzeck:	Ich hab's daran abgewischt.	I wiped it off there. . . .
		Apprentices:	Mit der rechten Hand am rechten Arm?	Your right hand on your right arm?
		Wozzeck:	Was wollt Ihr? Was geht's Euch an?	What do you want? What's it to you?
		Margret:	Puh! Puh! Da stinkt's nach Menschenblut!	Gross! It stinks like human blood! *(curtain)*

Confusion. The people in the Inn crowd around Wozzeck, accusing him. Wozzeck shouts back at them and escapes.

SCENE iv: A pond in a wood

36	3:41	**Wozzeck:**	Das Messer? Wo ist das Messer? Ich hab's dagelassen . . . Näher, noch näher. Mir graut's! Da regt sich was. Still! Alles still und tod . . . Mörder! Mörder! Ha! Da ruft's! Nein, ich selbst.	The knife! Where is the knife? I left it there, around here somewhere. I'm scared! Something's moving. Silence. Everything silent and dead . . . Murderer! Murderer! Ah, someone called! No, it was just me.
			Marie! Marie! Was hast Du für eine rote Schnur um den Hals? Hast Dir das rote Halsband verdient, wie die Ohrringlein, mit Deiner Sünde? Was hangen Dir die schwarzen Haare so wild?	Marie, Marie! What's that red cord around your neck? A red necklace, payment for your sins, like the earrings? Why is your dark hair so wild?

| | | | Mörder! Mörder! Sie werden nach mir suchen. . . . Das Messer verrät mich! Da, da ist's! | Murderer! Murderer! They will come look for me. . . . The knife will betray me! Here, here it is. |

:03 | 4:44

Mörder! Mörder! Sie werden nach mir suchen. . . . Das Messer verrät mich! Da, da ist's!

Murderer! Murderer! They will come look for me. . . . The knife will betray me! Here, here it is.

So! da hinunter! Es taucht ins dunkle Wasser wie ein Stein. Aber der Mond verrät mich . . . der Mond ist blutig. Will denn die ganze Welt es ausplaudern?!— Das Messer, es liegt zu weit vorn, sie finden's beim Baden oder wenn sie nach Muscheln tauchen.

There! Sink to the bottom! It plunges into the dark water like a stone. But the moon will betray me. . . . The moon is bloody. Is the whole world going to betray me? The knife is too near the edge— they'll find it when they're swimming or gathering mussels.

Ich find's nicht . . . Aber ich muss mich waschen. Ich bin blutig. Da ein Fleck . . . und noch einer.

I can't find it. But I have to get washed. There's blood on me. Here's one spot . . . here's another. . . .

Weh! Weh! Ich wasche mich mit Blut! Das Wasser ist Blut . . . Blut. . . .

Oh, woe! I am washing myself in blood! The water *is* blood . . . blood. . . .
(drowns)

37 | 6:21 | **Captain:** Halt! — Wait!

Doctor: Hören Sie? Dort! — Don't you hear? There!

Captain: Jesus! Das war ein Ton! — Jesus! What a sound!

Doctor: Ja, dort. — Yes, there.

Captain: Es ist das Wasser im Teich. Das Wasser ruft. Es ist schon lange Niemand entrunken. Kommen Sie, Doktor! Es ist nicht gut zu hören. — It's the water in the pond, the water is calling. It's been a long time since anyone drowned. Come away, Doctor! This is not good to hear.

Doctor: Das stöhnt . . . als stürbe ein Mensch. Da ertrinkt Jemand! — There's a groan, as though someone were dying. Somebody's drowning!

Captain: Unheimlich! Der Mond rot und die Nebel grau. Hören Sie? . . . Jetzt wieder das Achzen. — It's weird! the red moon, the gray mist. Now do you hear? . . . That moaning again.

Doctor: Stiller, . . . jetzt ganz still. — It's getting quieter—now it's stopped.

Captain: Kommen Sie! Kommen Sie schnell! — Let's get away! Come quickly! *(curtain)*

38 | 7:53 | ORCHESTRAL MUSIC (LAMENT)

4 Modernism in America: Ives

As we have seen, Paris and Vienna, centers of intense activity in all the arts, were also the first centers of modernist music. Echoes of modernism, some loud, some soft, were heard elsewhere in Europe: in Italy, where there was a short-lived movement called Futurism, and in Germany, Russia, Hungary, and England. We will discuss the case of two important modernist composers, Béla Bartók and Richard Strauss, in Chapter 21.

It is still amazing, however, that a major modernist composer should have emerged in the United States as early as around 1900; for at that time America had no rich tradition of classical music, and what we did have was resolutely conservative. "Emerged" is not quite the word, for what also amazes is that Charles Ives worked in isolation, composing in his spare time. His music was scarcely performed until the 1950s.

Many of Ives's compositions have American subjects, such as *Central Park in the Dark* and *Some Southpaw Pitching*. His *Holidays* Symphony includes

I remember, when I was a boy—at the outdoor Camp Meeting services in Redding (Conn.), all the farmers, their families and field hands, for miles around, would come afoot or in their farm wagons. I remember how the great waves of sound used to come through the trees . . . There was power and exaltation in those great conclaves of sound from humanity.

Charles Ives

Charles Ives (1874–1954)

Charles Ives was the son of a Civil War military band-master and music teacher from Danbury, Connecticut, near New York City. Ives senior was an extraordinary character who enjoyed musical games such as playing two tunes simultaneously in different keys. His father's unconventionality—and his association with popular music—left a lasting impression on Charles.

Ives was a church organist as a teenager, and then went on to Yale, where he was a popular undergraduate (with a D+ average). He absorbed everything that his professor, the eminent composer Horatio Parker, had to teach him. But the American musical climate in the 1890s was basically hostile to modern trends; Parker wrote in a dull, traditional style. For Ives, this was not only dull but somehow also unmasculine. His vision was of a much more vigorous, rough-grained, enthusiastic, experimental kind of music.

So when he got his B.A. he hedged his bets and took a job in insurance as well as another church organist position. After a few years he relegated music entirely to his spare time, while pursuing a very successful and innovative business career during the day. He seldom mixed with musicians and for years made little effort to get his works performed or published. (There is an interesting parallel here with Wallace Stevens, a major twentieth-century American poet, who also made a good living in insurance.)

All the while Ives was developing his unique mystical notions about music, notions that have been linked to nineteenth-century New England transcendentalism. To Ives, the actual sound of music seems to have counted less than the idea of music making as a basic human activity. All kinds of music were equally valid, then, whether popular or sophisticated, whether simple or wildly dissonant, whether played in or out of tune. What mattered was

people's communal joy in music making. Believing also that all musical experiments have equal validity, Ives launched into visionary projects that no other composer of the time would have considered.

Ives's late years were clouded by pathos, for after 1920 he gave up music almost entirely due to discouragement and bad health. He also sometimes tinkered with his old music to make it appear even more revolutionary than it was—though the music as he originally wrote it still amazes music historians. For his last thirty years Ives lived in quiet affluence with his wife, Harmony, the sister of a college friend—he had taken her to his junior prom; Harmony seems to have had a strong influence on her husband's ideas about music and life. They lived long enough to see his music admired first by a growing number of American musicians and then by the public at large.

Chief Works: For orchestra, 4 symphonies and the *Holidays* Symphony, several "Orchestral Sets," *Central Park in the Dark* and *The Unanswered Question* ■ *Concord* Sonata for piano (movements entitled "Emerson," "Hawthorne," "The Alcotts," "Thoreau") ■ *Variations on "America"* for organ (written at age 17; best known in its arrangement for orchestra) ■ Chamber music—many of the movements having programmatic titles ■ Church music, choral music, and important solo songs, among them "General William Booth enters into Heaven"

Encore: After Orchestral Set No. 2, listen to *The Unanswered Question, Putnam's Camp, The Fourth of July.*

---

movements titled "The Fourth of July," "Thanksgiving," and so on. These pieces regularly employ or quote American music: folk songs, popular songs by Stephen Foster, gospel hymns, ragtime—sometimes in great profusion. The hymns Ives remembered from his youth are especially favored.

Ives was our first important nationalist composer. But he was also more than that: a true American "original," a man with amazingly radical ideas about music, and an insatiable experimenter with musical materials. Ives anticipated many of the most talked-about musical innovations of the early part of the twentieth century—and of the later part, too.

Writing highly dissonant music was the least of it. He also wrote music for pianos tuned to quarter tones, and several works in which certain elements can be played, or not played, or played differently, depending on the performer's choice. For the whole length of his *Psalm 90*, for chorus, organ, and bells, low C sounds continuously in the organ pedals—for nearly eleven minutes. In one of his major works, the *Concord* Sonata of 1915, the pianist has to use his elbow and a special wooden block that holds sixteen notes down at a time.

To get an idea of the extraordinary range of Ives's work, we should examine two works—one of them little known, the other very famous.

CHARLES IVES
Second Orchestral Set, second movement: "The Rockstrewn Hills Join in the People's Outdoor Meeting" (1909)

This orchestral piece is the second of three that make up Ives's Second Orchestral Set. Ives wrote four symphonies; if his orchestral sets are thought of as (very) informal examples of the same genre, this movement would count as the scherzo. For all its obscurity, the title has a true Ivesian ring: The grandeur of nature joins a human festivity, apparently some sort of revival meeting.

The piece begins with several false starts, as though any effort to formulate a melody is bound to be defeated by other sounds, rhythms, and bits of tunes coming from this way and that. A dance fragment, first in the strings, then in the woodwinds, is interrupted by snatches of brass march music and piano ragtime. The hubbub gets more and more dissonant and atonal.

A revival meeting and a gospel hymn book of the time, open at the hymn used in Ives's Second Orchestral Set.

LISTENING CHART 25

Ives, "The Rockstrewn Hills"

4 min., 43 sec.

36 **20**	0:00	Introductory
	0:17	Dance fragment, strings; interrupted
	0:29	Dance fragment, woodwinds; interrupted
	0:49	Ragtime fragment, piano
		Kaleidoscopic array of fragmentary ideas; buildup
	1:27	Brass becomes prominent.
	1:58	Cakewalk fragment
	2:08	Climax: homophony
	2:34	Slowdown and pause (solo stringed instruments)
	2:44	March fragment, trombones
	3:00	The hymn is prefigured.
37 **21**	3:14	Hymn fragment—collapse
0:13	3:27	Hymn, clearer
0:44	3:58	At last the hymn emerges clearly: "I am coming, Lord!"
0:55	4:09	Fades: a fragmentary whole-tone scale in the piano

Gradually the kaleidoscopic array of "sound bites" builds up to a passage of forceful irregular rhythms. We catch a fragment of a cakewalk, a ragtime dance of the 1890s. At the climax, the confused superimposition of various ideas gives way for just a moment to homophony; the irregular pounding rhythms here remind us of Stravinsky's *The Rite of Spring*—a work written four years after Ives wrote this one. There is a slowdown and a quiet pause.

A new section begins with a fragmentary march in the trombones. Then at last a phrase of a hymn tune crystallizes out, as it were, in four tries. Only at the fourth try does the melody become clear. "I am coming, Lord!," the rousing chorus from one of Ives's favorite hymns, is orchestrated like a march:

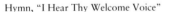

Hymn, "I Hear Thy Welcome Voice"

I am coming, Lord!   Com-ing now to Thee!   Wash me, cleanse me, in the blood That flowed on Calva - ry.

Ives

Slow, swinging tempo

After this collapses, the piano can be heard playing four-note segments of the whole-tone scale (a hallmark of Debussy—but Ives probably learned it from his inquisitive father, not from the French composer). The outdoor meeting ends on an intense but quiet dissonance that is strangely serious, even spiritual—a characteristic Ivesian feature.

Whole-tone scale

CHARLES IVES
The Unanswered Question (1906)

This famous work—utterly quiet, serene, and solemn—is as different as could be from the cheerful clatter of "The Rockstrewn Hills." It requires two conductors. We cannot describe it better than Ives did himself:

> The strings play *ppp* throughout, with no change in tempo. They represent "The Silences of the Druids" who know, see, and hear nothing. The trumpet intones "The Unanswered Question of Existence" and states it in the same tone of voice each time. But the hunt for "The Invisible Answer" undertaken by the flutes and other human beings [Ives is personifying the other woodwind instruments] gradually becomes more active and louder. The "Fighting Answerers" seem to realize a futility, and begin to mock "The Question"—the strife is over. . . . After they disappear, "The Question" is asked for the last time, and the "Silences" are heard beyond in "Undisturbed Solitude."

TRUMPET

What is so novel here is the concept of three distinct, independent levels of music. The smooth string choir, playing consonant harmonies, is one. Another is provided by the dissonant woodwinds, a sort of frustrated modernist challenge to the strings. Then there is the single trumpet, sounding like a voice, with its haunting Question.

These simultaneous levels do not fit together in the least, in terms of traditional polyphony. Their precise rhythmic or contrapuntal relationship is left to chance. Yet this unusual nondialogue between "Silences," "Questioner," and "Answerers" proves to be both coherent and poignant: a foretaste, perhaps, of our own age, an age marked by the quiet desperation of noncommunication.

Web: *Research and test your understanding of early modernism at* <bedfordstmartins.com/listen>.

CHAPTER 21

Alternatives to Modernism

I n music, as in all the arts, modernism was the main source of creative energy in the period from before World War I until after World War II. The vision of new "languages" to express the new conditions of modern life was a powerful one, even if the public at large often found those languages hard to understand. The success of many avant-garde works of art—Alban Berg's opera *Wozzeck*, for one—shows that they met with a deep response from minds and hearts battered by the events of the early twentieth century.

Not everyone was as successful as Berg, however; most modernist music played to a small, esoteric audience. A figure like Schoenberg, convinced that music's progress depended on his leadership, could accept this and hold uncompromisingly to modernist principles. Many others, too, never blinked—including, after Ives, several modernists here at home, chief among them Carl Ruggles (1876–1971), Roger Sessions (1896–1985), and Edgard Varèse (1883–1965; Varèse came to America from France).

Twentieth-Century Traditionalism

But other composers, both here and abroad, developed a more ambivalent attitude toward modernism. No one could escape its influence, and not many wanted to; but not everyone wanted to accept it fully. The force of Romantic tradition was still strong. Some famous twentieth-century names never joined the avant-garde at all and kept on mining the reliable quarries of Romanticism for their own private veins of (they hoped) musical gold.

Other composers worked with the ideas of Schoenberg or Stravinsky. They selectively adopted and adapted no more than they needed to fulfill their own creative needs. Still others started out wholeheartedly in the avant-garde, only to turn back to stylistic amalgams of one kind or another between the modern and the more traditional. American figures who fall somewhere in this spectrum are Charles Griffes (1884–1920), William Grant Still (1895–1978), Samuel Barber (1910–1981), and William Schumann (1910–1992), as well as Aaron Copland (1900–1990), whom we come to at the end of this chapter. Both Still, the first important African American composer in the concert music tradition, and Copland also recall nineteenth-century nationalism in their use of American musical idioms.

Opera in the Early Twentieth Century

As we have seen in Chapter 17, late nineteenth-century opera was dominated by the towering figures of Giuseppe Verdi in Italy and Richard Wagner in Germany. It is a remarkable fact that each country produced a younger opera composer, working under the shadow of these masters, whose works today are almost as much admired as theirs: Giacomo Puccini and Richard Strauss.

Both produced their main operas in the period from 1895 to 1915—the breakthrough years for Stravinsky, Schoenberg, and the rest of the avant-garde. Each found his own, very different alternative to modernism. Puccini kept his distance, selecting just a few modernist techniques that he could incorporate into his relatively conservative style. Strauss started out as a musical radical second to none, only to pull back later in life.

Giacomo Puccini (1858–1924)

Growing up in Italy, the land of opera, Puccini composed operas and not much else—like Verdi. For Italians, opera means melody, and Puccini was the only composer of his time whose melodies could stand comparison to Verdi's. This, together with an exceptional gift for all things theatrical, resulted in a stream of operas that bowled over international audiences in his day, and still do today.

Puccini is especially moving in his musical depiction of afflicted women: the abandoned Cio-Cio San (*Madame Butterfly*), Mimi, dying of consumption (*La Bohème*), and Floria Tosca, who fights off a lecherous police chief (*Tosca*).

Modernism, which arose in France and Germany, was never kind to melody. So the world of Italian opera paid it little attention. Nonetheless, Puccini found he was able to incorporate certain modernist techniques for striking effects in his operas. One such technique was harmony of the kind developed by Debussy (see page 329). It is prominent in two Puccini operas: *La Fanciulla del West* (*The Girl of the Golden West*, 1910) and *Il Tabarro* (*The Cloak*, 1918).

Puccini also made a careful study of non-Western music for use in operas set in Japan and China: *Madame Butterfly* (1904) and *Turandot* (completed after his death by another composer, 1926).

Richard Strauss (1864–1949)

The career of Richard Strauss could hardly have been more different. In the 1890s, when Schoenberg and Stravinsky were still youngsters, Strauss was *the* modernist discussed by everyone, resented by many, and attacked by some. He first raised eyebrows with sensational symphonic poems and symphonies, but the climax of his early career was a pair of operas that still have the power to shock, *Salome* (1905) and *Elektra* (1909).

They owe this power both to their librettos and to their music. *Elektra* revisits the most dreadful of all the old Greek myths: Clytemnestra, murderer of her husband Agamemnon, is slain in turn by her son Orestes, egged on by her almost maniacally vengeful sister Electra. The music is often violent and distorted. It verges on and sometimes slips into atonality.

But after 1909, to the astonishment of the musical world, Strauss pulled sharply back from such extremes. His later operas are either frankly Romantic or Neoclassical. *Der Rosenkavalier* (The Knight of the Rose, 1911), still another opera favorite, is a delightful, dizzy mixture of Mozart, Wagner, and Johann Strauss the Waltz King (no relation). With this opera, coming soon after *Elektra*, it feels as though the composer were bluntly criticizing modernism.

Yet the greatest modernist opera, Alban Berg's *Wozzeck*, followed soon after (see page 342).

Strauss ended his career in 1948 with some of the loveliest songs (for soprano and orchestra) ever written in the Romantic style.

Giacomo Puccini and Richard Strauss, with contemporary posters of *Madame Butterfly* and *Elektra*.

Ravel with the legendary dancer Vaclav Nijinsky, the star of his ballet *Daphnis and Chloé* in 1912. A year later Nijinsky was responsible for the riot-inducing choreography of Stravinsky's *Rite of Spring*.

1 Maurice Ravel

Of the many impressive composers active in the first half of the twentieth century, several have maintained and even increased their hold on audiences up to the present day. One is the opera composer Giacomo Puccini (1858–1924), discussed on page 353. The surprise Broadway hit of 2002 was Puccini's opera *La Bohème,* sung in its original language with English supertitles, over a hundred years after its premiere in Turin, Italy.

Two other composers were Russians who fled the Russian Revolution of 1917: Sergei Rachmaninov (1873–1943), who went to Switzerland and then to the United States, and Sergei Prokofiev (1891–1953), who relocated to Paris, but later returned home to a hard life in the Soviet Union under Stalin. Rachmaninov, one of the greatest pianists of all time, wrote extraordinarily popular piano concertos.* Prokofiev is known for a wider range of works—operas, including one based on *War and Peace* by Tolstoy, film scores, concertos, and his famous ballet *Romeo and Juliet.*

Maurice Ravel, born in 1875 in the south of France, was also attracted to Paris. From the very start, his music was marked by refinement, hyperelegance, and a certain coolness; musicians admire him for his superb workmanship and high style. As Debussy occupied the middle ground between Romanticism and modernism, Ravel carved out a place for himself between impressionism and Neoclassicism. While his harmonies and chord progressions often remind us of Debussy, he favored clarity, precision, and instant communication, qualities he found in earlier musical forms and styles.

Few composers have ranged as widely in imagination as Ravel. In his music he visited Spain, Madagascar, Asia, ancient Greece, America, and—again and again—the world of childhood. He even evoked Vienna, in a bitter anti-German parody of waltz music, *La Valse.*

---

*There is a section from Rachmaninov's *Rhapsody on a Theme by Paganini,* a concerto-like work for piano and orchestra, on our Student Guide CD-ROM.

MAURICE RAVEL
Piano Concerto in G (1931)

A light-hearted piece for piano and small orchestra, the Piano Concerto in G is Ravel's tribute to jazz (his most outspoken tribute, but not his first; like Debussy and Stravinsky, Ravel was fascinated by jazz long before he came to the United States in 1928 and haunted night-spots in Harlem). Americans like George Gershwin and Aaron Copland incorporate jazz accents in their compositions in a fairly direct way (see page 404). With Ravel everything is slightly skewed, as through a special filter, with a delicacy and elegance that we think of as characteristically French, perhaps, and that Ravel projects more clearly than any other composer.

First Movement (Allegramente)   The first theme is *not* jazzy. A long, lively, folk-like tune is presented in the sort of fabulous orchestration that is this composer's hallmark: After a whiplash—literally—a piccolo plays the tune with syncopated *pizzicato* (plucked) string chords and the piano shimmering in the background. But the tune really belongs to a special high trumpet (trumpet in C), with the syncopated chords barked out by the other brass.

PICCOLO

Maurice Ravel (1875–1937)

Maurice Ravel was born in a little town in the south of France, two miles from the Spanish border, and was brought to Paris at an early age. His mother came from the Basque region of Spain, and many of his compositions have "exotic" Spanish resonances—*Boléro,* most famously, also *Habanera, The Spanish Hour,* and others.

Ravel spent no fewer than sixteen lackluster years at the Paris Conservatory, the gateway to French musical life in those days, while his older contemporary Claude Debussy emerged as a leader in the music of modernism. When Debussy died in 1918, Ravel was acknowledged as the leading composer of war-ravaged France. Ravel despised Germany and German music, and he was young enough to volunteer for military service against the Germans in World War I, despite his frail and retiring personality.

From the time of his first major success, with the impressionistic piano piece *Jeux d'eau* (Fountains; 1901), it was clear Ravel had an amazing ear for sonority, and the magical sound of his music for piano or orchestra is unmatched. In the following years he belonged to a group of modernist artists and writers who called themselves the Apaches (a name with fauve overtones: see page 323), but he never really warmed to the modernist spirit. He was the most meticulous and exquisite of composers, and his aim was for clarity above all. Some of his most famous compositions make use of classical forms, such as the

Sonatine for Piano and the Piano Concerto in G.

Ravel never married, seems to have had no close relationships, and lived an uneventful life at his home in Paris. His one big trip, in 1928, was to America; here he met George Gershwin (and Charlie Chaplin) and came back with a small fortune. In 1932, Ravel succumbed to a rare brain disease; he died five years later. The Piano Concerto in G of 1931 was his last work but one.

Chief Works: Orchestral works: *Mother Goose Suite, La Valse,* two piano concertos, the ballet scores *Boléro* and *Daphnis and Chloé* ▪ One-act operas: *L'Heure espagnole* (The Spanish Hour) and *L'Enfant et les sortilèges* (The Child Bewitched), a delightful childhood fantasy ▪ *Gaspard de la nuit,* one of the hardest pieces ever written for piano; *Jeux d'eau;* and a charming piano *Sonatine* ▪ Songs; a string quartet ▪ Many arrangements for orchestra, including Musorgsky's *Pictures at an Exhibition* (see page 295)

Encore: After the first movement of the Piano Concerto in G, listen to the second movement; *Boléro; Sonatine* for Piano.

The piano now introduces a second theme that recalls the blues—not directly, but clearly enough. A third theme suggests romantic torch songs of the 1930s. Typical of early jazz is Ravel's use of short *breaks*, instrumental interludes between lines of a song lasting just one or two measures (see page 390). He catches this device perfectly with the high clarinet (E-flat clarinet) and a muted trumpet cutting into theme 2, with swishing sounds from the piano and the harp.

At a later point, the harp plays theme 2 itself, in a dreamlike episode that brings this busy movement to a state of near suspension.

After the piano and orchestra have presented themes 2 and 3, the piano engages in vigorous, propulsive music of the sort that often leads to cadences in concertos (see page 202). A new syncopated motive strongly implies that a cadence is coming, though the actual resolution is disguised.

Ravel uses the classical form for a concerto first movement (see page 201), but in the freest possible way. He skips both the orchestra exposition and the development section entirely. A passage that he labels "cadenza" resembles a true cadenza in that it comes near the end of a concerto first movement and the piano plays entirely solo, yet it feels nothing like a free improvisation; in fact, the unaccompanied piano plays theme 3. Ravel drew on classical tradition but at the same time invented his own super-clear and listener-friendly form for the Piano Concerto in G.

(At the very end of the first movement, Ravel borrows a favorite device invented by Debussy, a long series of parallel chords. The effect could hardly be more different: Debussy's chords—in *Clouds,* for example; see page 331—are *piano,* legato, silky, vague, and atmospheric; Ravel's are *fortissimo* and staccato, crisp and clear.)

2 Béla Bartók

Growing up in Hungary in the 1890s, the young Béla Bartók was first swept away by the international avant-garde leaders Debussy and especially Richard Strauss. Later in his career he was also influenced by his close contemporary Stravinsky. Bartók was, however, a man of multiple careers—pianist, educator, and musicologist as well as composer. His deep commitment to folk music—much deeper than Stravinsky's—and his professional involvement with it had a decisive impact on his music. Many would say that Bartók was more successful in integrating folk music into classical music than any other composer.

Folk music assured that Bartók's music would never (or seldom) become as abstract as much modernist music was. There is always an earthy feel to it; even at its most dissonant, there will be an infectious folk-dance swing or a touch of peasant melody. This is true even in works of his most modernist period, around 1925–1935. The austere String Quartet No. 4 of 1928 is often regarded as Bartók's masterpiece.

The right type of peasant music is most perfect and varied in its forms. Its expressive power is amazing, and at the same time it is devoid of all sentimentality and superfluous ornaments. It is simple, sometimes primitive, but never silly. . . . A composer in search of new ways cannot be led by a better master.

Béla Bartók

LISTENING CHART 26

Ravel, Piano Concerto in G, first movement

Free sonata form. 8 min., 12 sec.

39	**EXPOSITION**	
	0:00 **Theme 1,** piccolo, syncopated strings *pizzicato*	
	0:24 **Theme 1,** trumpet, syncopated brass	
	0:36 Sudden modulation	
	Second group	
	0:44 **Theme 2,** piano: slower; interrupted by the "break"	
40	1:40 **Theme 3,** piano	
:37	2:17 **Theme 3,** orchestra—bassoon, trumpet	
:55	2:35 Vigorous, driving music for the piano	
:14	2:54 Break	
:48	3:28 Approach to a cadence	
41	3:36 **Retransition:** upward scales in the piano	
	RECAPITULATION	
:09	3:45 **Theme 1,** piano, *ff;* returns to the tonic key	
:21	3:57 Sudden modulation	
	Second group	
:29	4:05 **Theme 2:** piano—with gong	
42	4:30 Dreamlike episode: **theme 2,** harp	
:38	5:08 Break; melody continues in the French horn	
:15	5:45 "Cadenza": **theme 3,** with extensive trills	
:04	6:34 **theme 3:** piano and orchestra	
:35	7:05 Piano: vigorous, brilliant	
:07	7:37 Approach to a cadence	
	CODA	
43	7:42 Orchestra (trumpet), *f,* in the original tonic key, with motives derived from **theme 1**	
:17	7:59 *ff*	

After that time Bartók's music gradually became more accessible, and the references to folk songs in it became more mellow and, often, more poignant. He now used established forms such as sonata form and rondo; this made his music easier to follow for listeners already accustomed to these forms from eighteenth- and nineteenth-century music. And many of his last works include passages reminiscent of Romanticism: Violin Concerto No. 2, the popular Concerto for Orchestra, and Quartet No. 6 of 1939—another good candidate for Bartók's greatest composition.

Music and Totalitarianism

European composers of the early twentieth century found their lives profoundly affected by the economic, political, and military upheavals of the time. Besides the sheer threat of annihilation in a time of war, other, more subtle difficulties loomed. Many institutions that composers' careers depended on—orchestras, opera companies, and the like—disappeared or fell into disarray. Some were victims of changing governments with new priorities. Others did not survive staggering inflation in parts of Europe in the 1920s, worldwide depression in the 1930s, or war in the 1940s.

Modernist composers in particular faced threats that were not only physical and social but also *ideological*— that is, threats made not on their lives or livelihoods but on their ideas, including musical ideas. This was most evident in (though not restricted to) the two most powerful repressive totalitarian regimes of the era. In Nazi Germany and Stalin's Soviet Union, artistic modernism in most of its guises was rejected and banned.

In each country the rationale for repression was the same distorted outgrowth of nineteenth-century nationalism: Art ought to speak straightforwardly to the national "folk" and give voice to its aspirations and history. This tenet was foreign to modernist art's emphasis on originality and individualism, its formal intricacies, and its questioning of the fundamental bases of artistic expression—its elitism, as the culture czars in Russia and Germany saw it. For Nazis and Stalinists alike, modernist art had no right to exist.

Nazi Germany

Hitler's regime promoted music of the great German masters; Beethoven and Wagner were special favorites. But it banned explicitly modernist music, supporting instead the latter-day romanticism of the aging Richard Strauss, for example (see page 353). Meanwhile Jewish composers and other musicians faced extermination. Those who could fled to countries all over the world, many of them to the United States. Arnold Schoenberg is the best known of these refugees (see page 339), but there were many others, including Kurt Weill, composer of "Mack the Knife," who established a second career on Broadway. Béla Bartók, who was not Jewish, but who also decided to emigrate when his native Hungary finally joined with Hitler, had a harder time (see page 359).

The Soviet Union

Perhaps the most famous victim of ideological muzzling was the greatest Russian composer after Stravinsky, Dmitri Shostakovich (1906–1975; Shostakóvitch). Growing up under Communism, he originally followed the dictates of the state without question. Shostakovich was certainly no radical modernist of the Schoenberg sort; but his music did show novel tendencies, including especially strong dissonant harmonies. A darling of the regime in the early 1930s, he nevertheless walked a perilous path.

With his opera *Lady Macbeth of the Mtsensky Region* of 1934, when he was twenty-eight, he went over the edge. Subject matter and music were equally shocking. The worldwide clamorous success of this work brought Stalin himself to see it. Two days later the official government newspaper *Pravda* condemned the work and issued a scarcely veiled threat to the composer: "The power of good music to affect the masses has been sacrificed to a petty-bourgeois, formalist attempt to create originality through cheap clowning. It is a game of clever ingenuity *that may end very badly.*"

In fact, Shostakovich was rehabilitated a year after the *Pravda* broadside. But his troubles were not over; he was condemned again ten years later—only to be rehabilitated once more when Stalin died. To what extent Shostakovich accommodated the regime, or criticized it by means of half-secret musical signals in his later compositions—signals recognized by his audiences—is a fascinating question still under debate.

Dmitri Shostakovich, on one of his rare trips to the West (1962). Looming over him is the Communist Party functionary who came along.

Bartók collecting folk songs: He was using recording equipment just a few years after commercial records began coming out. Around 1906, these rural Hungarians seem less amazed by the primitive phonograph than by the camera.

BÉLA BARTÓK (1881–1945)
Music for Strings, Percussion, and Celesta (1936)

This interesting composition can be thought of as an informal symphony in the usual four substantial movements, composed for a specially constituted small orchestra. Much of the time the instruments are divided into two sections that answer one another back and forth.* Besides strings, Bartók includes piano, harp, celesta (see pages 37 and 41), timpani—very important—and other percussion. We do not learn this all at once, however. The celesta makes its first entrance with an exquisite effect halfway through the first movement. The piano and harp arrive in the second, and the xylophone only in the third.

Second Movement (Allegro)   The music bubbles over with variety, an exhilarating rush of little melodic tags, rhythms, folk-dance fragments, and novel percussion sounds. It is all held together by sonata form.

A "preface" played by *pizzicato* (plucked) strings precedes theme 1:

The preface, theme 1, and the contrapuntal bridge passage—all are energized by motive **a.** One thinks of Beethoven's Fifth Symphony. This motive works especially well in the timpani, which play a powerful role in this movement.

We've rehearsed a lot . . . the conductor and orchestra have all worked with me showing the greatest affection and devotion; they claim to be very enthusiastic about the work (I am too!). A couple of spots sound more beautiful and startling than I had imagined. There are some very unusual sounds in it!

Bartók writes to his wife about rehearsals for the premiere of Music for Strings, Percussion, and Celesta

*This is a principle that goes back at least as far as Giovanni Gabrieli in the early Baroque era: See page 94.

Béla Bartók (1881–1945)

Béla Bartók showed unusual talent as a pianist and composer at an early age. Music was the avocation of his father, who was principal of an agricultural school in Hungary; after his death Bartók's mother worked as a piano teacher, tirelessly promoting her son's career.

Few musicians have ever had as varied a career as Bartók. He was a prolific composer and a fine pianist, as was his second wife; they appeared as a two-piano team. (Both of his wives had been his students.) In conjunction with another important Hungarian composer, Zoltán Kodály, he directed the Budapest Academy of Music, where the two men tried out new ideas in music teaching. An outcome of this side of Bartók's career is his *Mikrokosmos*, a series of 153 graded piano pieces starting with the very easiest. Well known to most piano students today, the *Mikrokosmos* has probably done more than any other work to introduce modernism to large numbers of musicians in their impressionable years.

Also with Kodály, Bartók undertook a large-scale investigation of Hungarian (and other) folk music, writing several standard books in the field of ethnomusicology, which is the scholarly study of folk music and the music of non-Western cultures. He published many folk-song and folk-dance arrangements, and his other compositions are saturated with folk elements such as rhythms, modes, and melodic turns. The outstanding nationalist composer of the twentieth century, Bartók left a body of work that equals or surpasses that of any nineteenth-century nationalist.

Bartók was strongly opposed to the Nazis. After they came to power in Germany, he refused to concertize there and switched away from his German publisher. And his liberal views caused him a good deal of trouble from right-wingers in Hungary. In 1940, after the outbreak of World War II, Bartók came to America, but he was not well known here and there was little interest in his music. His last years were a struggle to complete his Third Piano Concerto and the Viola Concerto. Ironically, his important works earned a wide, enthusiastic audience shortly after his death.

Chief Works: Concerto for Orchestra, 3 piano concertos, Violin Concerto, Music for Strings, Percussion, and Celesta (for small orchestra) ▪ Six string quartets; a fascinating Sonata for Two Pianos and Percussion ▪ An opera, *Bluebeard's Castle*, and a ballet, *The Miraculous Mandarin* ▪ *Cantata profana*, for chorus, soloists, and orchestra ▪ *Mikrokosmos* and other works for piano ▪ Many folk-song arrangements for various ensembles, including Six Rumanian Dances

Encore: After Music for Strings, Percussion, and Celesta, listen to the Violin Concerto and Quartet No. 6.

There is a full stop after the bridge, so self-conscious that one wonders if Bartók is making fun of sonata-form conventions. The second theme group contains at least three very short themes. Theme 3 has a folk-dance lilt about it:

Suddenly the piano enters with a theme containing odd note-repetitions. Since the pianist has hardly played at all up to this point, this new theme feels more like a beginning than like a conclusion. Still, it functions as a cadence theme; very soon the exposition ends with another exaggerated cadence.

The timpani introduce the ***development section.*** Motive **b,** played *pizzicato,* comes in for an extensive workout. After a moment the strings drop down into an accompaniment for an amazing passage for piano, snare drum, and xylophone,

LISTENING CHART 27

Bartók, Music for Strings, Percussion, and Celesta, second movement (Allegro)

Sonata form. 6 min., 59 sec.

1 22	**EXPOSITION** 0:00	Theme 1	With pizzicato "preface"	
	0:23		Held note, drum	
	0:26	**Bridge**		
			CADENCE Big stop, after drum beat	
2 23	Second group 0:56	**Theme 2**		
:14	1:10	**Theme 3**	Folklike tune, strong beat Developmental	
:36	1:32	**Theme 4**	Over a string trill	
:08	2:04	**Cadence theme**	Piano	
			CADENCE Exaggerated cadence; drum beat	
3 24	**DEVELOPMENT** 2:24	**Section 1**	Irregular rhythms: piano and percussion, leading to the Stravinskian passage (see below)	
:49	3:13	**Section 2**	Pizzicato scales, from the "preface"	
4 25	3:34		New folklike tune Drum prepares:	
:31	4:05	**Section 3**	Crescendo	
:21	4:55	**(retransition)**	Drum grows insistent; slowdown ⟶	
5 26	**RECAPITULATION** 5:10	**Theme 1**	With timpani; meter change	
:18	5:28	**Bridge**		
6 27	Second group 5:40	**Theme 2**	Transformation: triple meter	
:11	5:51		New continuations	
:24	6:04	**Theme 4**	Transformation: triple meter	
:44	6:24	**Cadence theme**	Piano, as before	
7 28	**CODA** 6:32		New fast dialogue on theme 1	

punching out syncopated notes. This must have been inspired by the riot-producing "Dance of the Adolescents" in Stravinsky's *The Rite of Spring* (see page 334).

PIANO, ORCHESTRA — FIRST SECTION

ORCHESTRA — SECOND SECTION
(with Harp)

Next, pizzicato string scales in imitative polyphony weave endless new knots and tangles. The scales blend into another folklike tune, similar to theme 3, which is repeated very freely. Introduced by the timpani, a fugue starts up in the lowest register, preparing for the recapitulation. The fugue subject is derived from theme 1, with the meter askew.

And when the *recapitulation* comes, after much signaling from the timpani, and after an expectant slowdown, the meter is changed throughout. Theme 1 vacillates between duple and triple meter, and the second group tips the balance: themes 2 and 4 each return in swinging triple meter (as shown in the examples on page 360). Theme 3 returns more freely. It takes the piano's odd "cadence theme" to bring us back to the solid duple meter of the start. As a *coda,* Bartók stages a fast, intense dialogue on theme 1.

What I like about music is its ability to be convincing, to carry an argument through to the finish, though the terms of the argument remain unknown quantities.

Poet John Ashbery, 1976

3 Aaron Copland

America's leading composer of the generation after Charles Ives was Aaron Copland. (Ives was active from around 1895 to 1920; Copland wrote his main works from 1925 to 1950.) Young composers after World War I found many more options open to them than Ives had around 1900. The musical climate was much more favorable to new ideas, partly because the United States had been growing more aware of all things European, including European new music. Like important American writers who lived abroad—Gertrude Stein, T. S. Eliot, Edith Wharton, Ernest Hemingway—composers now associated themselves with European modernism in a way that their predecessors never did.

The chief modernist influence on Copland was Stravinsky, and one of Copland's most impressive works is a strenuous set of twenty Variations for Piano (1930) that reflects Stravinsky's dry rhythmic style and his "objective"

It bothers me not at all to realize that my range as a composer includes both accessible and problematic works. To have confined myself to a single compositional approach would have enhanced my reputation for consistency, no doubt, but would have afforded me less pleasure as a creator.

Aaron Copland, 1941

Ben Shahn, *Trio,* 1955. © Estate of Ben Shahn/VAGA, NY, NY

A worker, a farmer, and a boss are shown "harmonizing": a political allegory by New York painter Ben Shahn (1898–1969), a friend of Copland.

Aaron Copland (1900–1990)

Aaron Copland was the son of Russian-Jewish immigrants living in Brooklyn. After a solid musical education at home, he went abroad to study in Paris. Like many other overseas students, Copland was fortunate to be able to work with a remarkable musician named Nadia Boulanger (1887–1979). For fifty years Boulanger was a revered teacher and mentor of composers, even though she gave up composition herself in deference to the talent of her sister Lili, also a composer, when Lili died tragically at the age of twenty-four. Boulanger encouraged Copland's interest in Stravinsky, whose avant-garde style influenced him greatly.

Back in America, Copland tirelessly promoted American music. He organized an important series of concerts (with another composer, Roger Sessions) to showcase new American scores, wrote articles and books, and formed a Composer's Alliance. Like many artists and writers of the 1930s, he was attracted by leftist ideology and the idea that art should "serve the people." Many works drawing on American folk materials stem from this period of Copland's career, as does his high-school opera *The Second Hurricane*. During World War II he wrote *A Lincoln Portrait* and *Fanfare for the Common Man*, patriotic works, and *Appalachian Spring*, a celebration of traditional American values.

After 1940 Copland headed up the composition faculty at the important summer school at Tanglewood, Massachusetts, in association with the Boston Symphony Orchestra, but his output as a composer decreased. Among his students was Leonard Bernstein. Devoid of the egoism characteristic of so many artists, Copland was one of the most beloved figures of modern American music.

Chief Works: For orchestra: 3 symphonies, *A Lincoln Portrait* (with a speaker), *El salón México* (incorporating South American jazz) ▪ Film scores: *Of Mice and Men* and *The Red Pony* (by John Steinbeck), *Our Town* (Thornton Wilder) ▪ Clarinet Concerto, written for jazzman Benny Goodman ▪ Operas: *The Second Hurricane* and *The Tender Land*; ballet scores *Billy the Kid*, *Rodeo*, *Appalachian Spring* ▪ For piano: Variations (Copland's outstanding modernist work; 1930), a sonata, Piano Fantasy (a fine late work; 1957) ▪ A song cycle to poems by Emily Dickinson

Encore: After *Appalachian Spring*, listen to *El salón México* and Clarinet Concerto.

aesthetic. But after this, Copland's music grew more traditional. Like Strauss, Bartók, and most other composers of the time, he held back from the most extreme manifestations of modernism and forged his own style using such elements of modernism as he needed.

Music for Americans

Again like Bartók, Copland adopted a nationalist agenda. From the start he felt that as an American, he should write music that would speak to his fellow Americans. Unlike Bartók, however, and unlike Ives, he did not focus on the music of his own immediate tradition—in the one case, Hungarian folk song and dance, and in the other, hymns and popular songs known in New England. Copland reached out for American music of all kinds, regions, and ages.

He first turned to jazz, in orchestral pieces called *Music for the Theater* and *El salón México*. Later he incorporated cowboy songs in the ballets *Rodeo* and *Billy the Kid*, an old Shaker melody in *Appalachian Spring*, and square dancing in *The Tender Land*, an opera about growing up in the corn belt. Old hymns make an appearance in his song cycle *Twelve Poems of Emily Dickinson*. In this eclectic attitude we can perhaps again trace the influence of Stravinsky, who over his long career also tapped many musical sources, from Russian folk song to Bach, Chaikovsky, and Schoenberg.

AARON COPLAND
Appalachian Spring (1945)

8-11   29-31

The ballet *Appalachian Spring* was choreographed and danced by Martha Graham, a towering figure in American modern dance. She conceived of "a pioneer celebration in spring around a newly built farmhouse in the Pennsylvania hills in the early part of the last century." From his ballet music, Copland arranged a concert suite in six continuous sections. Our recording is conducted by the composer.

8
29

Section 1   The ballet begins with a very still, clear, static passage of a kind that Copland made very much his own. It seems to catch the spirit of a vast silent landscape at dawn, perhaps, or just before dawn. Solo instruments play meditative figures in counterpoint; an occasional solemn pulse is heard in the harp.

9
30

Section 2   Here "the bride-to-be and the young farmer husband enact the emotions, joyful and apprehensive, their new domestic partnership invited." The celebration of their new house starts with a lively square dance. Soon a new slower melody—something like a hymn—looms up in counterpoint to the dance figures, first in the wind instruments and then in the strings:

'Tis the gift to be simple,
  'tis the gift to be free,
'Tis the gift to come down
  where you ought to be,
And when we find ourselves
  in the place just right
'Twill be in the valley of
  love and delight. . . .
When true simplicity is
  gained
To bow and to bend we
  shan't be ashamed,
Turn, turn will be our
  delight,
Till by turning, turning
  we come round right.

"Simple Gifts"

After a section of irregular rhythm, reminiscent of Stravinsky, the music dies down into a prayerful version of the hymn. We also hear little fragments of the dance.

Sections 3 and 4   The next two sections pick up the tempo: Section 3 evokes another whirling square dance and section 4 is a danced sermon by a revivalist and his followers. Both sections include quiet statements of the hymn.

10
31

Section 5   The next dance is choreographed to a set of variations on a Shaker song, "Simple Gifts." The Shakers, a religious sect adhering to celibacy and common ownership of property, founded scattered communities from New York to Kentucky in the late eighteenth century.

LISTEN

Copland, *Appalachian Spring* SECTION 5

0:00	5:14	Theme
0:37	5:51	Variation 1
1:05	6:19	Variation 2
1:51	7:05	Variation 3
2:31	7:45	Variation 4

The four variations are little more, really, than playings of the tune or part of the tune by different instruments, in different keys, and in different tempos. Sometimes melodic phrases are heard in imitation.

11 | ***Section 6***   Finally, after some music that the program says is "like a prayer," the hymn and the landscape music return once again. We realize that Copland has ingeniously made one grow out of the other. The ballet concludes very quietly. Perhaps the housewarming celebrations have gone on all night, and we are now experiencing another clear gray dawn, a reminder of the many lonely dawns the pioneer couple will face together in the years to come.

Web: *Research and test your understanding of alternatives to modernism at* <bedfordstmartins.com/listen>.

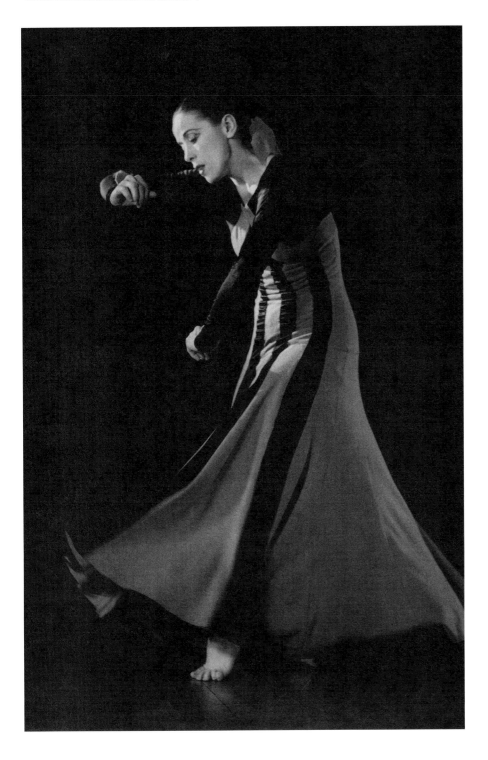

Modern dance is, with jazz, one of the great American art forms. Martha Graham (1894–1991), who commissioned and choreographed Copland's *Appalachian Spring,* was one of the legendary group of women who created modern dance in the early twentieth century.

The Late Twentieth Century

O nly twenty-one years, from 1918 to 1939, separated the two cataclysmic wars of the twentieth century. It was an uneasy period. The terrible devastation of World War I had stunned artists as well as everybody else, and the sorts of extravagant experimentation that had marked the prewar period no longer seemed appropriate. There was a new tendency toward abstraction, and also a search for standards and norms. At the time, Schoenberg's serialism and Stravinsky's Neoclassicism were seen as two different efforts to achieve some kind of consolidation, organization, and order.

But these efforts were undercut by a new round of devastating events. First came the economic depression, worldwide and protracted, that began in the late 1920s. Then, in the 1930s, the ominous rise of Hitler and the unbelievable (and, by many, disbelieved) tyranny of Stalin led to a second world war. With the attack on Pearl Harbor at the end of 1941, the United States was thrown into this war to an extent that made our involvement in World War I seem minor. The occupation of France, the siege of Leningrad, the bombings of London, Dresden, and Tokyo, the mass murders in the concentration camps, the detonation of atom bombs over Hiroshima and Nagasaki—these events were virtually impossible for human beings (including artists) to take in. History seemed to be showing that all human conceptions or representations of the world were illusory.

In the postwar world, artists in any medium faced greater uncertainties than ever before. One response to this among composers was to move toward a kind of absolute freedom. While some of them continued to write music according to models of the past, a radical generation of avant-garde composers invented new systems—or entertained the idea of destroying all systems.

1 Modernism in Music: The Second Phase

Modernism reemerged as the driving force in music during the third quarter of the twentieth century, but it was modernism in a new, more extreme phase. It was a fascinating phase—and no less fascinating because two of its main tendencies can seem almost contradictory.

First of all, highly intellectual constructive tendencies came to the fore, inspired by Schoenberg's serialism, but going far beyond it. There were even efforts to "serialize" rhythm, sonority, and dynamics—that is, to set up predetermined series of note durations or tone colors and compose with them in a fixed order. Never before had such complex mathematical theories been advanced to compose and explain music.

Meanwhile, other composers moved in the opposite direction, relinquishing control over some elements of musical construction and leaving them to chance. (We have already discussed an early anticipation of this move, *The Unanswered Question* by the ever-original Ives.) Some of these same composers also worked toward an extreme simplification of musical materials, offering a stark alternative to the cerebral complexities of post–World War II "total serialism."

It may seem strange to find composers who followed such different paths grouped together under the same general rubric of avant-garde modernism. However, both groups, the complex constructivists and the chance composers, pursued the same goal: They all wanted to question the most general premises that had guided music composition before them. Debussy might have blurred the identity of melodic themes, Stravinsky might have undermined the regularity of musical meter, and Schoenberg might have dispensed altogether with tonality. But mainstream modernism after 1945 questioned every one of these features of the musical tradition at once and others as well—to the point of even questioning the composer's role in structuring a work at all.

New Sound Materials

In this light another general tendency of modernist composers after World War II is not at all surprising: their demand for new sound materials. The ordinary orchestra, even as expanded by Debussy, Stravinsky, and others, now struck them as stiff and antiquated. They explored amazing new sonorities—nonmusical noises, unexpected new sounds squeezed out of old instruments, and an infinite range of musical materials produced not by instruments at all, but by electronics.

The search for new sonorities began when composers made new demands of the standard sources of music. Singers were instructed to lace their singing with hisses, grunts, clicks, and other "nonmusical" noises. Pianists had to stand up, lean over the piano, and pluck the strings or hit them with mallets. Using a special kind of breath pressure, clarinetists learned to play chords called *multiphonics*—weird-sounding chords by conventional standards but fascinating to those attuned to the new sound universe.

Western orchestras and chamber music groups had always been weak in percussion, as compared to their counterparts in many non-Western cultures, notably the gamelans of Indonesia, as we have seen (page 214). Even more to the point, Western art music had been weak in this respect as compared to jazz. Marimbas, xylophones, gongs, bells, and cymbals of many kinds—percussion instruments that had been used only occasionally in the art music of earlier times—became standard in the postwar era.

However, the truly exciting prospect for new sonorities in music emerged out of technology developed during the war: the production of music by electronic means.

Electronic Music

Recording equipment can *reproduce* sounds of any sort—music, speech, and all the sounds and noises of life. Electronic sound generators can *generate* sounds from scratch—in principle, any sounds that can be imagined, or calculated using formulas derived from the science of acoustics.

The Pianist by
Pablo Picasso

A technological breakthrough during World War II, the development of magnetic tape, made the storing and handling of sound much easier. It also opened up exciting possibilities for modifying it by manipulating the tape: making tape loops, changing speed, cutting and splicing, and so on. Across the second half of the twentieth century, we can discern three stages in the evolution of electronic music, each of them defined by new technological possibilities:

⸙ *Musique concrète*   Shortly after World War II composers began incorporating the sounds of life into their compositions. This they called "concrete" music because it used actual sound, as contrasted to the "abstract" products of electronic sound generators. Sounds (traffic noise was a favorite) were recorded, painstakingly manipulated in ways such as those mentioned above, and then (usually) put on phonograph discs.

Musique concrète lives on, in a sense, in *sampling*, now that technology has made it easy for anything that is recorded—traffic noise, commercial records, special effects—to be put under keyboard control for easy combination.

⸙ *Synthesizers*   In the early postwar period electronic sound-generation was unbelievably clumsy, requiring whole rooms full of radio equipment and complicated machinery to carry out tape manipulations. Only after the advent of transistors (silicon chips were still in the future) could viable equipment be envisaged. In the 1960s various *synthesizers* appeared, apparatus designed specifically for music, with arrays of sound-producing modules connected by "patch cords" to create complex sounds.

At first they worked one note at a time. Still, they allowed many composers to produce taped music, and also to combine music on tape with performed live music. It was still difficult to produce "customized" sound in real time.

Electronic music: from a synthesizer of the 1960s to a mixing board of the 2000s. Violinist Chee-Yun, left, and pianist Akira Eguchi, right, stand in front of the board.

❧ *Computer music* The amazing evolution of computers over the last twenty years has allowed for an equally amazing evolution in music. Today electronic music can be produced on a home computer, using sequencer software to record, edit, and reproduce digital sounds in patterns and sequences at will. Advanced synthesizers now produce their stuff in real time (as the simpler synthesizers of popular music have been doing for years). They can interact via computer with live musicians as they perform to produce today's cutting-edge interactive computer music.

On the Boundaries of Time

Sonority is one of two areas in which avant-garde music in its second post-war phase made the greatest breakthroughs. The other area was time and rhythm.

To understand one aspect of this development, let us try to contrast two radically different pieces of music. One is a tiny piece by Schoenberg's student and friend Anton Webern, the fourth of his *Five Orchestral Pieces* of 1913 (see page 344). The whole piece—it is all of six measures long—can be shown on one line of music:

12   32

Listen to it several times: The music feels exceptionally concentrated, because the relationship between the notes is so strained by the "atomized" orchestration and the complex network of pitches and rhythms. Each note somehow becomes a separate little source of tremendous energy. This might be described as a *very short* time segment of *very high* intensity.

Contrast this with *In C*, a famous avant-garde work from the 1960s by the American composer Terry Riley. *In C* lasts for about forty-five minutes. During this time the instruments repeat over and over again a set of fifty-three tiny melodic figures that spell out only three harmonies—three harmonies drawn out over the music's total span. The pitches and rhythms are simple, indeed deliberately soothing. This might be described as a *very long* time segment of *very low* intensity.

With both Webern and Riley, we measure time (because we have no other way) in the same units: minutes and seconds. Yet the *feeling* of time is very different in the two. It is like the difference between one minute at the end of a tied basketball game and one minute in the middle of an all-night truck run across South Dakota. Such contrasting perceptions of time were now widely explored and exploited by musicians of the avant-garde.

Webern's unique vision of time made him a major influence in the postwar years, even though he died at the end of World War II. Composers were fascinated by his intense, seemingly disconnected note patterns, with their flickering instrumental sounds and their highly complex rhythms. Riley's *In C* and works like it became prophetic of a later development in music which gathered force in the 1970s and 1980s, *minimalism* (see page 380).

Chance Music

In playing his fragmentary melodies, the instrumentalists in Riley's *In C* interacted with each other in ways largely unspecified by the composer. *In C* thus exemplifies the **chance music** we mentioned earlier. (It was also called *aleatoric music,* from *alea,* Latin for "dice.") This term covers a great variety of music in which certain elements are not precisely specified by the composer, but left to chance—in a way that usually *is* specified by the composer.

In an extreme case, a chance composer would work out a way of throwing dice so as to determine which instruments, which pitches, and so on were to be used in his or her music. In a less extreme case, a performer getting to a certain place in a piece would be told to play anything at all, so long as it was (for example) loud and fast. Strictly speaking, what would be heard would be determined by chance, but the composer could count on a type of controlled chaos for a limited span of time, a span situated between two passages of fully written-out music.

Whereas earlier modernists had questioned traditional assumptions about melody and dissonance, chance composers questioned even more basic assumptions about musical time. The musical forms we have studied throughout this book tend to mark off time as a clear linear progress and even make it goal-directed: Think of the recapitulation of a Beethoven sonata form. More generally, time is conventionally plotted on a graph in the same way that distance is— see page 20—and a "timer" tells us when to get things done.

Is time always (chance composers would ask: is it *ever*) actually experienced in this way? Must music convey such an experience? Could it instead mark time as a random sequence of events, or even as "timeless," like the suspended consciousness we experience in certain kinds of meditation? Such questions, and a passive sense of time that cuts against our goal-directed culture, lie at the root of chance music.

2   The Postwar Avant-Garde

After World War II, exciting composers seemed to appear like magic from almost every corner of the globe. Among the leaders from France, Germany, and Italy were Olivier Messiaen (1908–1994), Pierre Boulez (b. 1925), Karlheinz Stockhausen (b. 1928), and Luciano Berio (1925–2003). They were joined by the Poles Witold Lutosławski (1913–1994) and Krzysztof Penderecki (b. 1933), the Hungarian György Ligeti (b. 1923), the Greek Iannis Xenakis (1922–2001), the Americans Milton Babbitt (b. 1916), John Cage (1912–1992), and Elliott Carter (b. 1908), and the Japanese Tōru Takemitsu (1930–1996).

Many of these composers are still composing actively—and interestingly— fifty years later, in the new millennium. But fifty years later, it cannot be said that their music has gained a firm place in the musical repertory or in the hearts of most music listeners (at least, as far as the United States goes). Modernism's first phase—the phase just before World War I—produced works that now count as "classics": Berg's *Wozzeck*, a fixture in the opera house; Bartók's string quartets, played by every professional string quartet; and Stravinsky's *Rite of Spring*, an all-time favorite in the CD catalog, with more than fifty listings. For acknowledged masterpieces written after World War II, however—such as Boulez's fascinating song cycle *Le Marteau sans maître*, or Berio's moving and powerful *Sinfonia*—similar acceptance has been slow in coming.

György Ligeti (b. 1923)

György Ligeti studied at the Budapest Academy of Music, and as a young man was appointed professor there. Unable to pursue his unique sound visions under the Communist restrictions prevailing in Hungary, he left for the West in 1956. Ligeti was past thirty before his advanced music became known.

Ligeti typifies both the search for new sonorities that occupied the postwar avant-garde and also their new attitudes toward time. Some of his music uses no clear pitches, or chords; or, more accurately, while he may start with pitches and chords, he soon adds so many more pitches that all sense of consonance, dissonance, and even the quality of pitch itself is lost. What remain

Violet, Black, Orange, Yellow on White and Red, by the American painter Mark Rothko
(1903–1973). The overwhelming yet placid sheets of color merging into one another recall
the musical technique in compositions such as Ligeti's *Lux aeterna.*

are "sound complexes" that can be experienced better than they can be described, sound complexes that slowly change with time.

And in the time dimension, there is no discernible meter or rhythm. Rather there is a sense of gradual, almost glacial surging of the sound complexes, followed by a sense of receding—all the while revealing incredibly diverse new tone colors.

GYÖRGY LIGETI
Lux aeterna (1966)

Ligeti's *Lux aeterna* is written for sixteen solo singers and chorus; often they sing chords that include all twelve pitches of the chromatic scale. We need a new vocabulary even to talk about music such as this, and some new diagrams—our pitch-time graph on page 20, which indicated melodies by lines, doesn't work for Ligeti's sound complexes. To represent them and show how they develop over time, we have to use nonmusical figures:

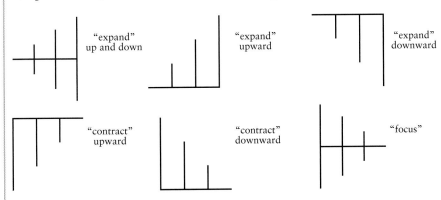

Lux aeterna starts with a single pitch, which Ligeti "expands" both upward and downward by slowly adding a dense mix of pitches above and below it. At other times he starts with a single pitch and expands it upward (adding mainly higher pitches) or downward (adding lower ones). Starting with a full-range sound, Ligeti can "contract" it: either downward (by removing notes till only a single low pitch remains), or upward, or to some pitch in the middle—an effect that can be called "focusing," on the analogy of a camera lens.

The interest of this music, as we have said, is in the astonishing rich sonorities that are revealed by the slow ebbing and flowing of the sound complexes. Once we have accustomed our ears to this, we can appreciate that the musical form of *Lux aeterna* is simplicity itself. Of the four lengthy sound surges that constitute the piece, No. 1 (going up) seems to be "resolved" by No. 4 (going down). Nos. 1 and 4 are parallel, too, in that a high pitch is added halfway through—in this music, a very dramatic effect.

The words of *Lux aeterna* are taken from the Requiem Mass, but they can scarcely be heard and understood; the piece is a study in sheer vocal sonority. Ligeti wrote other "sound complex" pieces employing other forces, such as *Atmosphères* for full orchestra; *Lux aeterna* is his most famous work, thanks to its use in the 1968 Stanley Kubrick film *2001: A Space Odyssey*.

In the years since, Ligeti has written music in different styles. With Luciano Berio, he now stands out as one of the most active and impressive figures of the brilliant postwar generation.

My idea was that instead of tension-resolution, dissonance-consonance, and other such pairs of opposition in traditional tonal music, I would contrast "mistiness" with passages of "clearing up." "Mistiness" usually means a contrapuntal texture, a micropolyphonic cobweb technique . . .

From an interview with György Ligeti, 1978

György Ligeti

Lux aeterna luceat eis, Domine, cum sanctis tuis in aeternum, quia pius es. . . .

May everlasting radiance shine upon them, O Lord, with thy saints in eternity: for you are merciful. . . .

LISTENING CHART 28

6
13-16

Ligeti, *Lux aeterna*
7 min., 52 sec.

13	0:00	WOMEN'S VOICES	Single pitch, high voices *(Lu)* The sound "expands," *up and down.*	
	1:39		A high pitch is added softly: SOPRANO.	
	2:02		The sound "contracts" *upward,* ending in . . .	
	2:22		a single pitch (octave).	
14	2:28	MEN'S VOICES	The high pitch stops, replaced by a chord *(Domine).* in the high men's voices.	
0:08	2:36		The sound expands *downward.*	
0:36	3:04		More lower voices; higher men's voices drop out; the sound slowly "focuses" to . . .	
1:30	3:58		a held, dissonant chord.	
15	4:03	MEN AND WOMEN	Complex sound, *f* (with a clear high, low, middle)	
1:30	5:33		The sound "contracts" *downward* to a lengthy focus, ultimately to a single pitch.	
16	5:45		Complex sound—low voices *(Domine)* Sound expands, *up.*	
0:28	6:13		A high note is added: SOPRANO.	
0:58	6:43		The high note is dropped, replaced by a very low note: BASS. Sound contracts *downward* to . . .	
1:45	7:30		a two-note dissonant chord.	

Edgard Varèse (1883–1965)

Edgard Varèse is an older composer who bridged both phases of modernism in twentieth-century music. Though he had started his career in France before World War I, he emigrated to America in 1915, and it was here that he found his voice (late in life, like Haydn).

The music Varèse wrote in the 1920s was among the most radical in the world at that time. He developed an approach to rhythm and especially to sonority that surpassed anything the other early avant-garde composers had attempted. *Hyperprism* is scored for seven wind instruments and seven percussion, and *Ionisation* is for percussion alone—thirteen percussionists playing forty-five instruments, including a siren. The manipulation of what had been thought of as "noise" into coherent musical patterns was a heady forecast of modernist music of the post–World War II era.

Edgard Varèse

EDGARD VARÈSE
Poème électronique (1958)

6
17

Indeed, it was after World War II that this veteran of many a modernist battle really came into his own. Around 1930, Varèse had unsuccessfully tried to persuade the Bell Telephone Company to set up a research center for electrically produced music. Now the introduction of electronic composing equipment was a vindication of his vision. His *Déserts* (1950–54), for instruments and tape, was one of the most ambitious early essays in electronic music. And his entirely electronic *Poème électronique* is recognized as one of the masterpieces of the genre.

Poème électronique (1958) (ending)   As we stroll within earshot of *Poème électronique* (see below), a heavy electronic crash is followed by various seemingly random rustles. Then a brilliant section displays a veritable anthology of electronic effects: low sliding groans, rattles, bell-like noises, and watery sounds. Suddenly something human joins these space-age sounds—a short vocal hum. This tells us that Varèse makes use of *musique concrète* in *Poème*: that is, he uses prerecorded sounds from real life, such as humming, singing, bells, and train noises, as well as material that is generated electronically.

The rhythm has been highly irregular. Now it slows down, and a sustained chord appears quietly, grows almost unbearably loud, and then fades. Varèse introduces isolated pitches that appear to be arbitrary, though in fact they merge into another sustained chord. We hear drum rhythms, too, and a *musique concrète* snare drum (remember Varèse's affection for percussion instruments).

Humanity seems to reassert itself in the form of a soprano solo—but this is manipulated electronically so as to shriek its way out of hearing in the high register. Sharp, explosive punctuations decimate the men's voices that follow. A mournful three-note motive (also heard earlier in *Poème*) is played twice with the notes sliding into one another. Then a momentous-sounding siren moves up, falters, and moves up again until it becomes a violent noise, which ceases abruptly and mechanically.

So ends the Varèse *Poème électronique*: for some, on a strange note of unspecified disquiet.

Modernist Music and Architecture

The *Poème électronique* of Edgard Varèse was just one part of an extraordinary multimedia experience. It was written for an exhibit at the 1958 Brussels World Fair by the Philips Radio Corporation, held in a pavilion designed by the famous modernist architect Le Corbusier (1887–1965). Corbu, as he was called, also designed a sequence of colored lights and images to be projected while Varèse's three-track tape was played from 425 speakers.

Here is another example of modernist artists of various kinds working in tandem (see page 319). Le Corbusier himself had been a painter in his youth.

As visitors entered the pavilion and walked around, the music came at them from various angles. Likewise, as they kept turning corners they kept seeing different parts of the superb building and of the light show. All this was very new at that time.

There was obviously an element of chance in the way one got to experience *Poème électronique*—an element that the composer of course encouraged. John Cage would have concurred enthusiastically. So it is quite in Varèse's spirit for us to take a quick tour of the pavilion, as it were, and happen to hear just the last few minutes of this music, rather than the entirety.

John Cage (1912–1992)

The most consistent radical figure of postwar music was John Cage, the father of chance music (Charles Ives has to count as the grandfather). He studied with Schoenberg, among others—when Schoenberg was teaching in California, Cage's home state—and early developed an almost bewildering variety of interests. Cage exhibited specially prepared prints, toured as music director of avant-garde dancer Merce Cunningham's dance company, and was a recognized mycologist (mushroom authority). In the 1950s, his study of Zen led him to a fresh attitude toward music, time, and indeed all experience.

John Cage

Cage posed questions that challenge all the assumptions on which traditional music rests. Why should music be different from the sounds of life? Why compose with "musical" sounds, rather than noises? Why work out music according to melodies, climaxes, twelve-tone series, or anything else that gives the impression of one thing following another in a purposeful order? Why not leave it to chance? The basic message that Cage has conveyed is that we should open our ears to every possible kind of sound and every possible sound conjunction.

JOHN CAGE
4' 33" (1952)

Often, indeed, the actual sounds Cage produced were less crucial than the "statement" he was making about sound by means of his music. This is the case with *4'33"*, perhaps his most celebrated work (or statement). Any number of players can perform it. They sit silently on the stage for 4 minutes and 33 seconds.

Is this just an exasperating hoax? What Cage is saying is that silence is an entity, too, as well as sound. When did you last really concentrate on silence? (Try it.) In fact, *4'33"* consists not of silence but of little bits of random audience noise, sounds from outside the hall, and the thump of the irate listener's heartbeat. And how does the experience of concentrating on near silence for exactly 4 minutes and 33 seconds compare with concentrating for exactly three minutes, or exactly five?

We seldom really analyze our experience freshly; life is unpredictable and full of surprises. Music should be, too. This is the philosophy represented by Cage and his music. It has had a major impact on avant-garde composers all over the world, and on some innovators in popular music, also (see page 416).

When you get right down to it, a composer is simply someone who tells other people what to do. I find this an unattractive way of getting things done.

John Cage

Score for a multilingual solo vocal work by John Cage, *Aria* (1958). Much is left to the singer's imagination!

3 Music at the End of the Century

It is not easy to characterize the confused, multivalent, multicultural music of our own time, at the beginning of the twenty-first century. A date comes to mind, 1971—not because anything as complex as music changes in a year, but because an event in it can symbolize a complex historical process. When Stravinsky died in 1971, at the age of eighty-eight, classical music lost its last great master, and a figure whose role in music history was uniquely comprehensive.

His first, Russian works were wholehearted essays in late nineteenth-century nationalism. Then works for Paris such as *The Rite of Spring* were prime monuments of modernism in its first, early twentieth-century phase. In Los Angeles, Stravinsky remained a major player in modernism in its second phase, the extreme phase following World War II.

Since the 1970s modernism has mellowed. The trauma of atonality is now a thing of the past. Not all composers relinquished tonal music with its clear harmonies and melodies, as we have seen in Chapter 21, and now it has returned gradually into the music of modernism. Works that we will now study absorb modernist ideas and ideals but also show more concern for communication than did music of the immediate postwar period.

I think composers are everything they've ever experienced, everything they've ever read, all the music they've ever heard. All these things come together in odd combinations in their psyche, where they choose and make forms from all their memories and their imaginings.

George Crumb, 1988

George Crumb (b. 1929)

A later representative of the American postwar avant-garde is George Crumb, a professor at the University of Pennsylvania. Unlike Cage, he is not a "chance" composer, and unlike Varèse or his followers, he does not write electronic or computer music—though he makes powerful use of amplification effects, as we shall see. Instead he has devised new ways of playing all kinds of standard and nonstandard instruments. In *Black Angels* he asks string quartet players to do things to their instruments that would make a traditional violin teacher turn pale. By such means Crumb obtains a predominantly violent, grotesque quality that could not be achieved in any other way.

In other works (and occasionally in this one), Crumb achieves remarkably delicate effects—quiet, precise, a controlled musical kaleidoscope of fascinating elegance. Like many American composers today, he has been much influenced by Asian music; thanks to such composers, Western music has for the first time employed large groups of percussion instruments with something of the subtlety known to East Asia.

George Crumb, 1988

6

18-22

GEORGE CRUMB
Black Angels, for Electric String Quartet (1970)

Subtitled "Thirteen Images from the Dark Land," *Black Angels* was inspired by the Vietnam War, if not directly, at least by way of the anguished mood that the war instigated. "There were terrifying things in the air," the composer has said recently. "They found their way into *Black Angels*."

This highly unconventional string quartet consists of thirteen short (often very short) sections arranged in three groups, of which we will hear the first. A sense of doom is conveyed partly by the titles—*threnody* means a funeral lamentation song—and partly by various quotations of earlier music with lethal associations. But of course it is the quality of the music itself that conveys the sense of stress most powerfully.

18 ***No. 1 Threnody I: Night of the Electric Insects***   The skittery, amplified string playing suggests some sort of menacing insect life. A loud clatter alternates with quiet scratching. Against this, the high violins play fast glissandos, or scooping effects. Crumb marks them *piangendo,* "crying."

The scores of Nos. 1, 3, and 4 of *Black Angels* are not written with barlines, and the music has no discernible meter. In contrast, Nos. 2 and 5 project dance rhythms quite clearly, and in No. 2, at least, one can often beat out a regular meter.

19 ***No. 2 Sounds of Bones and Flutes***   This section evokes Asian music. The players click their tongues and chant "Ka-to-ko to-ko" to illustrate the rattling of bones, and somehow imitate a flute by bowing their strings with the back of the bow, that is, with the wood *(col legno).*

20 ***No. 3 Lost Bells***   This duo for violin and cello mimics the mournful, bell-like noises characteristic of electronic music. Fragmentary melodies at the end remind us of the "flute" in No. 2.

21 ***No. 4 Devil-music***   An extremely vehement solo for the first violin is accompanied by the other players, one of whom also strikes a gong. The violinist produces what can only be called retching sounds; then the cellist, followed by the other players, rasps or grates by dragging the bow very slowly over the strings while applying maximum pressure. Toward the end there are some siren effects, and the electric insects put in another appearance.

22 ***No. 5 Danse Macabre***   Rhythmic energy picks up again, as the players tap on the wood of their instruments and jiggle maracas. Crumb borrowed the title for this section from a nineteenth-century concert piece by the French composer Camille Saint-Saëns, and he quotes bits of Saint-Saëns's music as well as *Dies irae,* from the Mass for the dead (see page 268). Isolated phrases of this plainchant appear high in the violin; they are vaguely reminiscent of the "flute" in No. 2 and the ending melodic fragments of No. 3.

The players end up with some mysterious chanting (actually, they count from one to seven in Hungarian).

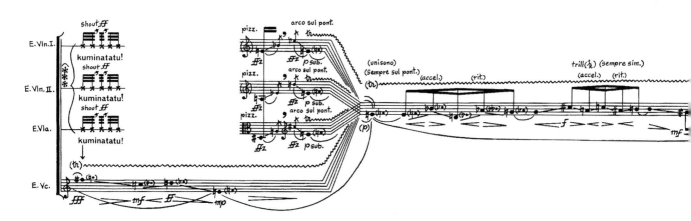

Avant-garde music has made obsolete the old "pitch–time" graph that forms the basis of traditional musical notation (see page 20). Composers often invent their own notations: George Crumb, above, and John Cage, page 376.

Kaija Saariaho (b. 1952)

The Finnish composer Kaija Saariaho is representative of a generation of European composers born after World War II who have carried on the experiments of earlier modernism. She regularly combines live performers with electronic and computer music, often working at IRCAM, a famous center for electronic music composition in Paris. While her long list of compositions exploits a wide variety of performing forces, her special interest is vocal music, and more specifically, the soprano voice. A major work, the opera *L'Amour de loin* (*Love from Afar*), received its U.S. premiere in 2002.

Kaija Saariaho

KAIJA SAARIAHO
From the Grammar of Dreams (1988)

From the Grammar of Dreams is a cycle of five songs for two unaccompanied sopranos. The songs set words of Sylvia Plath, a moving American poet who struggled with depression and took her own life at an early age in 1963. The words of the songs bring together prose excerpts from Plath's most famous work, the novel *The Bell Jar*, and a multistanza poem entitled "Paralytic." The poem recounts the impressions and sensations of a polio patient lying in an iron lung. (This was a huge medical machine, all too common in the years before vaccinations, that pumped air in and out of the lungs of patients paralyzed by polio.)

Saariaho departs in a number of ways from a conventional musical setting of these words. First, she scatters the stanzas of the poem unevenly across her five songs. Songs 1 and 3, which we will consider here, set stanzas 1–4 and 8, respectively. Second, Saariaho often superimposes two different texts sung simultaneously, a treatment rarely encountered in songs. (For one genre that did it as a matter of course, see the isorhythmic motet of the late Middle Ages, page 68.) Finally and most strikingly, Saariaho employs her restricted performing forces with great versatility, presenting a miniature catalogue of unorthodox—and highly expressive—vocal techniques.

Song 1   The more active soprano here sings stanzas 1–2 of "Paralytic" to a violent, leaping, swooping melody. At first she tears apart the words, as in some sort of bizarre verbal dissection, delivering the sounds of individual letters and word fragments with distorted emphasis: *huh—huh—appp—enzzzzzzz* for "happens," and so on. Meanwhile the other soprano unfolds a gentler line in counterpoint, filled with warbling trills, in which we gradually come to hear words from *The Bell Jar:* "A bad dream. I remembered everything." Is she casting the experience of the paralytic as a nightmare, and nothing more?

Finally, at about 1:20, the violent soprano begins to shift to her partner's more lyrical style (stanza 3). In the end, each soprano is reduced in turn to deliberate, monotonal speech, accompanied by a lingering trill from the other singer.

Song 3   This is the lyrical and emotional heart of the cycle—and also its most conventional song. Its words, the last stanza of "Paralytic," are sung by both voices. The singers, like the poetic image of their words, seem to convey a calm, quiet renunciation (of struggle against the iron lung? of the attempt to touch an unreachable world?)—perhaps even a renunciation of life altogether. The song is organized around an arch of shifting pitch levels, as the voices gradually rise to a climax (at 1:35), then fall back to their starting places.

It is organized also by a technique we have heard often since the Renaissance: imitative polyphony. Listen for this especially in the half-step motives at the beginning and end, which wind together like the clawed tree roots and branches alluded to in the poem, or at the repeated word *magnolia* starting at 1:01.

Song 4   Here images from *The Bell Jar* eerily summon up Plath's own suicidal thoughts, only to turn to the life force of a beating heart. We can hear this song as a free **A B A′** form, with the **A** section formed of harsh, impassioned panting. The longer, fully sung **B** section (starting at 0:19) rises steadily to an ecstatic, almost unbearable climax on "I am I am I am"; along the way, the panting from **A**, now sung, returns. An abrupt collapse (at 1:25) ushers in **A′**, made up of fading, panting repetitions of "I am" in heartbeat-like rhythms. Song 4 seems to affirm that the renunciation of life, desire, and self hinted at in Song 3 does not come without struggle.

LISTEN

Kaija Saariaho, *From the Grammar of Dreams*

6   3

23-25   33-35

23
33
SONG 1

Soprano 1   ("Paralytic," stanzas 1–4)

It happens. Will it go on? —
My mind a rock,
No fingers to grip, no tongue,
My god the iron lung
   That loves me, pumps
My two
Dust bags in and out,
Will not
   Let me relapse
While the day outside glides by like ticker tape.
The night brings violets,
Tapestries of eyes,
   Lights,
The soft anonymous
Talkers: "You all right?"
The starched, inaccessible breast.

Soprano 2   (from *The Bell Jar*; sung simultaneously with soprano 1)
A bad dream.
I remembered everything.

24
34
SONG 3

Sopranos 1 and 2   ("Paralytic," stanza 8—the last stanza)
The claw
Of the magnolia,
Drunk on its own scents,
Asks nothing of life.

25
35
SONG 4

Soprano 1   (*The Bell Jar*)
I thought I would swim out

until I was too tired to swim back.
As I paddled on, my heartbeat
boomed like a dull motor in my ears.
I am I am I am

Soprano 2   (*The Bell Jar*)
I took a deep breath and listened
   to the old brag of my heart.
I am I am I am

Minimalism

One of the most interesting new musical styles to develop in the last thirty years is called **minimalism.** A sharp reaction to the complexities of modernist composition, minimalist music uses very simple melodies, motives, and harmonies repeated many, many times. Terry Riley's *In C*, mentioned on page 370, is an ancestor of minimalism (some say, the first great example of it).

Minimalism has proved to be an unusually successful style for American opera: a scene from *Nixon in China* (1987) by John Adams.

This style has worked wonders for American opera, which has become the success story of modern music since *Einstein on the Beach* (1976) by a leading minimalist composer, Philip Glass (b. 1937). Later works by Glass, *Satyagraha* and *Akhnaten,* and *Nixon in China* and *The Death of Klinghoffer* by John Adams (b. 1947) have been performed again and again in this country and abroad, all of them in spectacular productions.

STEVE REICH (b. 1936)
Tehillim (1981)

Steve Reich, a philosophy major at Cornell, studied music subsequently and has become the acknowledged old master of the minimalist style. A keyboardist, he has performed his work with his own special group—a procedure that a number of other contemporary composers follow, including Philip Glass. Reich has written operas—*The Cave* (1998) and *Three Tales* (2002)—with his wife, video artist Beryl Korot.

Steve Reich

Tehillim (tehéelim) is the Hebrew word for "psalms," and in Reich's composition, verses from several biblical psalms are sung by a women's choir accompanied by a small instrumental group. There are four sections, running into one another. The first two are fast, the third slow, and the climactic fourth section is fast again, so the piece amounts to a sort of minimalist "symphony of psalms."

The text for the last movement comes from Psalm 150, "Praise ye the Lord," the last in the Book of Psalms. And the very last *word* in this psalm, "hallelujah," has echoed down through the ages at the heart of worship. The word is the same in Hebrew, Latin, English, and German (see pages 66, 95, 158, and 161).

Section 4 (Psalm 150: "Haleluhu")   To begin, the full text of "Haleluhu" is sung to a sprightly melody backed by an insistent beat on tambourines. The text, with its reiterations of "haleluhu" and "haleluyah," seems perfectly suited to Reich's repetitious musical technique.

1 Haleluhu betof umachol,   a Praise the Lord with tambourines and dancing,
  Haleluhu beminim ve-ugav;   praise him with flute and strings;
2 Haleluhu betzil-tzilay shamah, b praise him with the clash of cymbals,
  Haleluhu betzil-tzilay teruah;   praise him with triumphant cymbals;
3 Kol hanshamah tehalail Yah, Haleluyah.   c let everything that has breath praise the Lord!
                                               Hallelujah.

  Kol hanshamah tehalail Yah, Haleluyah. c′ *Let everything that has breath praise the Lord!*
                                               Hallelujah.

Each syllable gets a single note, and these notes are arranged in lively irregular rhythms—we show the climactic last phrases, c and c′:

The melody falls into an **a b c c′** form, though this is not easy to hear, since there is so much repetition of tiny melodic cells within the phrases. The phrases shown above are built entirely out of the steps D–E (or E–D) and G–A. Repetitions *within* the melody, combined with the many repetitions *of* the melody, give this music its feeling of incantation, both static and ecstatic, always changing yet always the same.

Behind the singing, a few chords are played by the orchestral strings and then sustained—a solemn counterpoint to the sprightly melody. These strange,

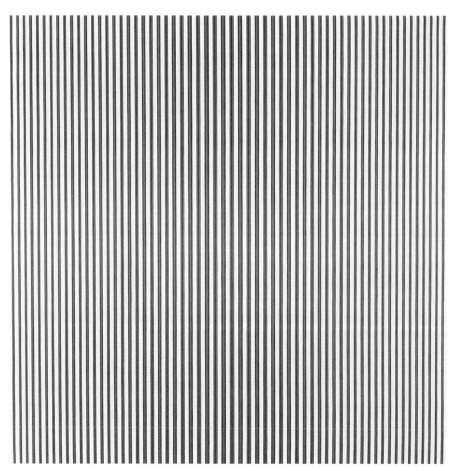

Minimalism in music and art: *Chant II* by Bridget Riley (b. 1931).

LISTENING CHART 29

Reich, *Tehillim*, fourth section

6 min., 44 sec.

26	0:00	Transition from part 3—accelerates to a new steady beat	
	0:14	**Theme: a b c c′:**	Two sopranos in harmony with irregularly placed chords accompanying the singing
27	0:43	**Variation 1**	Two-part canon **a b c c′**
:28	1:11	**Variation 2**	Four-part canon—**a** repeated many times
:11	1:54		After a brief punctuation, **b** (starts with voices alone)
:36	2:19		After a brief punctuation, **c** (starts with voices alone)
28	2:54	**Variation 3**	Two voices with clarinets, drums
:47	3:41	**Instrumental interlude**	Background chords continue
29	4:17	**Variation 4**	
:55	5:12		Climactic high note
30	5:28	**Coda**	on the word "Hallelujah" only; electric organ, bells
:13	6:41		Abrupt stop

a

Haleluhu betof . . .

b

Haleluhu betzil . . .

c

Kol hanshamah . . .

irregularly placed chords continue through nearly the whole of the movement, including the orchestral interlude.

Section 4 of *Tehillim* is a type of free variation movement: The instrumentation changes with each variation. After the theme has been sung by two sopranos in harmony, they sing it in variation 1 as a round, one starting several beats after the other. The constant melodic intertwining adds new energy and charm. In variation 2, the longest and most complicated variation, four sopranos sing the melody as a four-part round—and what is more, each phrase is sung several times before the next is heard. In variation 3, the melody is slowed down and altered so as to include several exhilarating high notes for the soprano. Step by step, the psalm singing grows more intense.

After an orchestral interlude, the chords in the stringed instruments grow more intense too. Variation 4 follows, with the melody varied even further, but something like the original "Hallelujah" melody is heard again at the end of **c**, with the highest soprano note yet.

In an enthusiastic *coda,* extra instruments pile in—a vibraphone, two organs, and bells. United in their joyous ritual, the voices cry out "Hallelujah" again and again. The piece ends—after a particularly emphatic "Hallelujah"—without the feeling of finality we would expect from a traditional cadence. After all the mounting excitement, the music simply *ceases,* as though someone has switched off the current.

Web: *Research and test your understanding of late twentieth-century music at* <bedfordstmartins.com/listen>.

Music in America: Jazz and Beyond

As we have observed a number of times in this book, in the nineteenth century a rift opened up between popular music and the music we now call "classical." Nowhere has this rift been more apparent than in the United States of America, the most populist of all nations. And nowhere else have such strenuous efforts been made to close the rift. We can see this if we think back to the various American composers discussed in the last few chapters, from the unlikely modernist Charles Ives, who quoted marches, ragtime, and hymns in his symphonic music, to the minimalist Steve Reich, American pioneer in a worldwide movement. It is not accidental that we have seen more than one of these composers working with popular as well as "classical" music sources—and that in this chapter we shall see more.

"Popular" and "classical" are fuzzy terms; think of the *popularity* of the Three Tenors, singing opera excerpts in stadiums around the world; think how broad the application of *classical* and the related *classic* can be, from the "classical antiquity" of Greece and Rome to "classic rock." For music in America, the terms "cultivated" and "vernacular" have proven to be more illuminating. To "cultivate" means to nurture, as microorganisms are cultivated in a petri dish in a laboratory, or orchids in a greenhouse. "Vernacular," on the other hand, refers to one's native language, as opposed to some other that may be in use, such as the Latin used, long after people stopped speaking it every day, in the church, universities, and law courts of the Middle Ages. **Cultivated music,** then, is music that has been brought to this country and consciously developed, fostered at concerts, and taught in conservatories. **Vernacular music** is music we sing and hear as naturally as we speak our native argot.

There is a bitter twist to this terminology as applied to American music. The word *vernacular* comes from the Latin word *vernaculus,* which is itself derived from *verna*: and "verna" means a family slave. The heritage of African American music was and is central to the story of American music.

1 Early American Music: An Overview

Long before European settlers and African slaves arrived here, Native Americans had their own musical styles. (We touched on one of these in discussing sacred chant; see page 72.) As Native Americans were pushed farther and farther west, however, their music played little role in the development of European American and African American music.

The history of music among the early European settlers and their descendants is not a rich one. The Puritans disapproved of music; they thought it was frivolous, except for its supporting role in religion. In Puritan church services, rhyming versions of the psalms were sung like hymns, but when the words of the psalms were printed in the *Bay Psalm Book* of 1640—the first book ever printed in North America—the music was not included, because just a few tunes, known to everyone, were used for all 150 psalms. In succeeding years, much of the energy of early American musicians was devoted to the composition of new psalm and hymn tunes, and to the teaching and improvement of church singing.

William Billings (1746–1800) of Boston is often mentioned as our first composer. He wrote hymns and **fuguing tunes,** which are simple anthems based on hymns, with a little counterpoint. (An anthem is a choral piece in the vernacular for use in Protestant services.) When sung with spirit, fuguing tunes sound enthusiastic, rough, and gutsy.

Billings's more secular-minded contemporaries enjoyed the Classical music of the era. Benjamin Franklin, who tried his hand at most everything, also tried composing. But without well-established musical institutions, there was not much support for native composers outside the church. The problem in those years is hardly that of distinguishing between cultivated and vernacular music. The problem is finding written music to listen to and talk about at all.

"Cultivated" music in America: a scene from Philadelphia society of the 1890s, *The Concert Singer,* by Thomas Eakins.

A concert at New York's Castle Garden in 1850, in a print issued by Currier & Ives. Their
hand-colored lithographs are famous for vividly illustrating nineteenth-century America.

The "Cultivated" Tradition

After the United States won its independence, things changed. As cities grew,
first on the East coast and then progressively to the West, more and more concerts appeared, and with them inveterate concertgoers. One such was a New
York lawyer and civic leader named George Templeton Strong, who left a four-
and-a-half-million-word diary discussing (among other things) all the symphonies, oratorios, and organ music he heard, in unending enthusiastic detail.*
By the mid-1800s, all our major cities had their concert halls and opera organizations and amateur choral societies. The 1860s saw the foundation of our
first conservatories of music, in Boston, Cincinnati, and elsewhere.

Americans eagerly bought tickets to hear traveling celebrities from Europe,
and skilled native composers and performers began to appear. The first American
musicians to gain worldwide reputations were the immigrant German composer Anthony Philip Heinrich (1781–1861), a quirky early Romantic, and the
Louisiana piano virtuoso Louis Moreau Gottschalk (1829–1869).

On the whole, however, Americans were content to look to Italy for opera
and to Germany for instrumental music. That the cultivated tradition in American music was essentially German in orientation is not surprising. Ever since the
time of Mozart and Beethoven, German music had achieved wonders and had
earned enormous prestige all over Europe. The mid-nineteenth-century immi-

- *Vivaldi's concertos in parts*
- *Bach's songs 2nd collection*
- *Handel's Coronation anthems*
- *Heck's art of playing the harpsichord*
- *Hayden's [sic] cantatas. . .*

In 1783 Thomas Jefferson's
music library contained these
and a hundred other items.

*Bits of Strong's diary are cited on pages 228 and 230.

gration from Germany brought us many musicians who labored long and hard for the cause of music in this country. We can hardly blame them for their German bias.

There were significant native composers at the end of the nineteenth century: John Knowles Paine, Arthur Foote, and Henry Chadwick of the so-called Boston School, and Edward MacDowell of New York. They wrote symphonies, piano "miniatures," and so on, in a competent but conservative German Romantic style. Time has not been kind to their work, despite recent efforts to revive it.

The music of Amy Beach (1867–1944), in particular, has stirred interest in recent years. Active as both a composer and a pianist, she made her debut with the Boston Symphony Orchestra at the age of seventeen. "Mrs. H. H. A. Beach" (as she always signed her works) contributed to many traditional genres, such as the piano concerto, the piano quintet, and the symphony. Her *Gaelic* Symphony of 1896 was the first symphonic work ever composed by an American woman.

The emergence of Charles Ives in the midst of this conservative tradition seems like a miracle of music history (see page 348). Yet Ives profited more than he sometimes cared to admit from the grounding in European concert music he received from his German-trained professor, Horatio Parker.

Louis Moreau Gottschalk

Music in the Vernacular

We might well count the psalms and hymns mentioned above as vernacular music, for in colonial days everybody who could carry a tune sang them at church and in the home, and later they were widely sung at revival meetings and the like. Nineteenth-century America was also rich in secular popular

Hymn singing at home in Revolutionary times, an engraving by Paul Revere (Psalm 23, "The Lord is my shepherd").

music. Our two most famous composers wrote timeless tunes and ever-popular marches, respectively: Stephen Collins Foster (1826–1864) and John Philip Sousa (1854–1932).

Foster, it is sad to say, led a dispiriting life. Even in those days, song writing was closely tied to the music business; Foster was dependent on Christie's Minstrels, the leading traveling theater troupe of the time. They had exclusive rights to his songs and helped popularize them—indeed, some of them soon achieved the status of folk songs. But Foster had a hard time making ends meet. His marriage broke up. He turned to drink and died at the age of thirty-eight.

John Philip Sousa, son of Spanish and German immigrant parents, was a Marine Corps bandmaster who later formed a wildly successful touring band of his own. Every American knows his masterpiece *The Stars and Stripes Forever* (even if they don't all know its name). Leonard Bernstein once said that his greatest regret as a musician was that he hadn't composed that march.

African American Music

Foster excelled in sentimental ballads, such as "Jeanie with the Light Brown Hair" and "Beautiful Dreamer." But his most notable songs have to do with the black slaves of his time. There are sentimental "plantation songs" such as "Swanee River" ("The Old Folks at Home") and "Old Black Joe," and comic minstrel songs such as "Oh, Susanna!" and "Camptown Races." The **minstrel show**, performed by white actors in blackface, was very popular at mid-century; it consisted of comedy routines, "Ethiopian" songs, dances, and solos on the banjo (an instrument with African roots). Though today this kind of entertainment strikes us as an ugly parody of black speech and character, it was also an acknowledgment of the vitality of the slaves' music. From at least the time of Foster, African American music has had a profound effect on the music of America at large.

What was the slaves' music like? This is hard to say, for there were no devoted folk-song collectors to write it down, as in Europe (Bártok is a case in point; see page 356). Nonetheless, by studying somewhat later black American music and comparing it with today's African music, scholars have been able to show how much the slaves preserved of their native musical cultures.

For example, a musical procedure known as **call and response** is common in West Africa. Phrases sung by a leader—a soloist—are answered or echoed again and again by a chorus. This procedure is preserved in black American church music, when the congregation answers the preacher's "call," as well as in spirituals, work songs, and "field hollers," by which the slaves tried to lighten their labors. It is also an important feature in blues and in jazz, as we shall see.

Spiritual is a term for a religious folk song that came into being outside an established church (white or black). Moving "Negro spirituals," such as "Nobody Knows the Trouble I've Seen," "Go Down, Moses," and others, were the first black American music to gain the admiration of the white world. After Emancipation, black colleges formed touring choirs. To be sure, spirituals in their concert versions were considerably removed from folk music.

The music of African Americans got a powerful boost from the first major European composer to spend time in America, Antonín Dvořák. This highly respected Bohemian musician, head of New York's National Conservatory of Music (ancestor of the Juilliard School) in the 1890s, announced his special admiration for spirituals, advised his American colleagues to make use of them in their concert music, and showed the way himself. He incorporated the essence

Original illustration accompanying a song by Stephen Foster (1862).

The singing was accompanied by a certain ecstasy of motion, clapping of hands, tossing of heads, which would continue without cessation for about half an hour. One would lead off in a kind of recitative style, others joining in the chorus.

A former slave recalls call-and-response singing, 1881

Negro spirituals were first popularized after the Civil War by groups like the Fisk Singers. In 1871, this group of former slaves toured to raise funds for Fisk, one of the earliest African American colleges.

of spirituals so skillfully in his ever-popular *New World* Symphony that one of his own tunes was later adapted to made-up "folk song" words, "Goin' Home." This is the first of several examples we shall see of the conscious effort to narrow the gap between America's vernacular and cultivated styles.

Go-in' home, . . .

2 Jazz: The First Fifty Years

But if Dvořák and his contemporaries could have been whisked for a moment into the twenty-first century, they would have been astonished to see and hear what actually happened. With little help from the cultivated tradition, a strictly vernacular type of music emerged from African American communities. It was called—at first contemptuously—**jazz.** From the most modest beginnings, this music developed prodigiously. It produced a whole series of new musical styles, performers of the greatest artistry, and composers of genius.

Jazz developed into America's most distinctive—many would say greatest—contribution to the arts worldwide. And if our time-travelers were to find it hard to believe their ears, there would be something else to amaze them. All this music was actually preserved—preserved on acetate discs by means of a revolutionary new technology, sound recording.

Jazz is a performance style that grew up among black musicians around 1910 and has since gone through a series of extraordinary developments. Its first key feature is *improvisation.* When jazz musicians play a song, they do not play it the way they hear it or see it on paper; they always improvise *around* a song. They add ornaments and sometimes also short interludes, called **breaks;** in effect, they are always playing variations on whatever tunes they are working with.

The second key feature of jazz is a special rhythmic style involving highly developed *syncopation* (see below). Notice that jazz is not so much a kind of music—the music it is based on usually consists of popular songs, blues, or abstract chord-series called "changes"—but a special, highly charged way of performing that music.

Jazz Syncopation

Syncopation occurs when some of the accents in music are moved away from the main beats, the beats that are normally accented (see page 13). For example, in **2/2** meter, instead of the normal ONE *two* ONE *two*, the accent can be displaced from beat 1 to beat 2—*one* TWO *one* TWO. This is called a "back beat" in jazz parlance.

Some syncopation occurs in all Western music. In jazz, there is much more of it. Syncopation becomes a regular principle, so much so that we can speak of at least two rhythmic "levels" in a jazz piece. One rhythmic level is a simple one—the **rhythm section** of percussion (drums, cymbals), piano, string bass, and sometimes other instruments, emphasizes the meter forcefully, and continuously. A second, more complex rhythmic level is produced by the melody instruments—trumpet, clarinet, trombone, piano, and the saxophones that were so brilliantly developed in jazz. They play a constantly syncopating music that always cuts across the rhythm section.

In addition, jazz developed syncopation of a more subtle kind, sometimes called **beat syncopation.** Derived from African drumming (see page 398), this technique can also be traced in earlier black American music. In beat syncopation, accents are moved *just a fraction of a beat* ahead of the metrical points. When this happens in just the right way, the music is said to "swing."

The Blues

The **blues** is a special category of black folk song whose subject is loneliness, trouble, and depression of every shade. Indeed, the blues is more than song, more than music: It is an essential expression of the African American experience. Though gloom and dejection are at the heart of the blues, not infrequently blues lyrics also convey humor, banter, and especially hope and resilience.

Emerging around 1900, the blues was a major influence on early jazz—and has remained a major force in American music ever since.

A blues melody consists typically of stanzas made up of three four-measure phrases ("twelve-bar blues"), repeated again and again as the blues singer develops a thought by improvising more stanzas. The stanzas are just two lines long, with the first line of words repeated and with the ends of the lines rhyming. Each line is sung to one of the three phrases of the twelve-bar pattern. Here are stanzas 1 and 4 of *"If You Ever Been Down" Blues:*

> STANZA 1   *a*   If you ever been down, you know just how I feel,
> *a*   *If you ever been down, you know just how I feel,*
> *b*   Like a tramp on the railroad ain't got a decent meal.
>
> STANZA 4   *a*   Yes, one thing, papa, I've decided to do,
> *a*   *Oh pretty daddy, I've decided to do,*
> *b*   I'm going to find another papa, then I can't use you.

I'd like to think that when I sing a song, I can let you know all about the heartbreak, struggle, lies, and kicks in the ass I've gotten over the years for being black and everything else, without actually saying a word about it.

Blues, gospel, and soul singer Ray Charles, 1970

Ragtime: Scott Joplin (1868–1917)
5

Ragtime, a precursor of jazz, was a style of piano playing developed by black musicians playing in bars, dives, and brothels. The music resembled march music, but while the left hand played strictly on the beat, the right hand syncopated the rhythm in a crisp, cheerful way. "To rag" meant to play in a syncopated style; "ragging" evolved into jazz syncopation.

In the early 1900s, when phonographs were still new and most music in the home was played on the piano, ragtime became enormously popular throughout America by means of sheet music and piano rolls for mechanical ("player") pianos. The term ragtime could also be applied to nonpiano music: witness the famous song *Alexander's Ragtime Band* of 1911 by Irving Berlin.

Scott Joplin was the leading rag composer. Frustratingly little is known about his early life. The son of an ex-slave, he grew up in Texarkana and worked as a pianist and band musician in many midwestern towns. "Maple Leaf Rag," named after the Maple Leaf Club in Sedalia, Missouri, where Joplin played, was published in 1899. It quickly sold a million copies. You can hear this famous rag on your Study Guide CD-ROM; see also page 15.

Joplin followed "Maple Leaf" with "The Entertainer" and many other rags. They stand out for an elegance that might not have been expected in this simple and com-

mercial genre. In *Solace: A Mexican Serenade* Joplin mixed ragtime with Latin American dance styles in a work of nostalgic sophistication. He even published a small treatise on the playing of ragtime, warning those who would race through his pieces: "Never play ragtime fast at any time." And to those who saw ragtime as a style too lowbrow for their tastes, he wrote: "Syncopations are no indication of light or trashy music, and to shy (i.e., throw) bricks at 'hateful ragtime' no longer passes for musical culture."

Joplin's evident desire to break into cultivated musical circles was not realized. After he moved to New York in 1907 he gradually faded from the limelight. He wrote two operas, the second of which, *Treemonisha*, received a single unstaged, unsuccessful performance in 1915. His death in 1917 was noted by few.

There was a strong new surge of interest in ragtime in the 1960s. At last, in 1972, *Treemonisha* was fully staged and recorded. In 1975 Joplin was posthumously awarded the Pulitzer Prize in composition.

Composed blues—for example, W. C. Handy's famous *St. Louis Blues*—can be more complicated than this one, but the *a a b* poetic scheme is basic for the blues.

Blues melodies (and especially the bass lines under blues melodies) provided jazz musicians with powerfully emotional patterns for improvisation. But more than that, blues also provided jazz with a sonorous model. Jazz instrumental playing has an astonishing vocal quality, as though in imitation of the blues. The trumpet, saxophone, and trombone sound infinitely more flexible and "human" played in jazz style than when played in military band or symphonic style. Jazz instruments seem to have absorbed the vibrant accents of black singing. (This is another feature that jazz passed on to rock, where the electric guitar is the instrument that powerfully imitates the voice.)

SIPPIE WALLACE
"If You Ever Been Down" Blues (1927) (Composed by G. W. Thomas)

Here is an example of unvarnished blues singing, by one of the legendary woman blues singers who dominated the earliest recordings. Sippie Wallace is not as renowned as Mamie Smith, Ma Rainey, or the great Bessie Smith, but she poured her heart out with the best of them in response to the eternal themes of the blues:

> STANZA 2   I'm a real good woman but my man don't treat me right,
> He takes all my money and stays out all night.

31   36

LISTEN

Thomas, *"If You Ever Been Down" Blues*

0:10   **Stanza 1**
0:45   **Stanza 2**
1:19   **Trumpet**
1:51   **Stanza 3**
2:24   **Stanza 4**

STANZA 3   I'm down today but I won't be down always,
             'Cause the sun's going to shine in my back door some day.

Perhaps the essential sound of jazz is Louis Armstrong improvising the breaks in the blues sung by [famous blues-singer] Bessie Smith. . . . In the break we have the origin of the instrument imitating the voice, the very soil in which jazz grows.

Composer Leonard Bernstein, 1955

Wallace accompanies herself on the piano. The recording adds two jazz musicians, but she would have sung just about the same way if she had been performing alone. One of the musicians is the outstanding genius of early jazz, Louis Armstrong.

After a brief instrumental introduction, Wallace sings two blues stanzas from the piano bench. The instruments play short breaks in between her lines—the trumpet (Armstrong) in stanza 1, the clarinet (the little-known Artie Starks) in stanza 2. Sympathetic respondents to her "call," they deepen the melancholy of her song and nuance it:

If you ev-er been down   you   know __ just how I   feel _____   If   you   ev-er . . .

Then Armstrong plays a solo section—an entire twelve-bar blues stanza. He does not play the blues melody note by note, but improvises around the melody and its bass. Armstrong has a wonderful way of speeding up the dragging blues rhythm, and his rich, almost vocal tone quality echoes and complements the singer's bleak sound. The clarinet joins him; this is a simple example of improvised jazz polyphony.

Wallace, too, joins in quietly during this instrumental chorus; she too, no doubt, was singing on impulse. She then sings two more stanzas, with instrumental breaks as before.

It's necessary to listen to this recording in a different spirit from that in which we approach the other recordings of Western music accompanying this book. The scratchy sound on these old discs cannot be helped by digital remastering, and the music itself is not "composed," of course. It lies somewhere in between true folk music and jazz, a fascinating juxtaposition of the direct, powerful simplicity of Sippie Wallace and the artistry of Armstrong. With a little imagination, one can virtually hear history happening in this recording: Jazz is evolving from the blues.

Sippie Wallace (1898–1986)—her nickname is said to derive from a childhood lisp—was equally known for gospel music and for the blues. And indeed **gospel** music—ecstatic choral singing associated with black American church services—grew up at the same time as ragtime and the blues. Wallace was also a pianist and songwriter, who usually sang her own compositions, and published a good many of them. Her long performing career began at little churches in Houston and ended with a concert at Lincoln Center, the sprawling New York music facility that houses the New York Philharmonic Orchestra and the Metropolitan Opera.

New Orleans Jazz

Early jazz was local entertainment for black audiences, an informal, low-budget, and even a somewhat casual art. Small bands, usually of six to eight players, typically featured three melody instruments to do the "swinging"—trumpet, clarinet, and trombone. The rhythm section could include piano, banjo, string bass, or even tuba, along with drums and other percussion.

Sippie Wallace

Louis Armstrong (1901–1971)

Louis Armstrong was born into abject poverty in New Orleans. He learned to play the cornet in the Colored Waifs' Home, where he had been placed as a juvenile delinquent. Determined to become a musician, Armstrong played in seedy clubs and on riverboats, which were floating dance halls that traveled from town to town on the Mississippi every summer. Riverboats became a cradle of early jazz, importing it up the river from New Orleans to Kansas City and other centers.

Soon Armstrong was playing in the pioneering jazz bands led by King Oliver (see page 394) and Fletcher Henderson. He rapidly emerged as a more exciting artist than any of his colleagues. His sophisticated, flowing rhythms, his imaginative "breaks" and variations, and the power and beauty of his trumpet tone—all these were unique at the time. A famous series of records he made in the 1920s, playing with small New Orleans–style bands, drew jazz to the serious attention of musicians all over the world.

In the 1930s the popularity of jazz led to a great deal of commercialization, and to the cheapening and stereotyping that always seem to result from this process. Armstrong went right along, while often contributing moments of breathtaking beauty to records that were "listenable virtually only when Louis is playing," according to one jazz critic of the time. Armstrong became a nationally loved star, familiar from his appearances in nearly twenty movies. The State Department sponsored him on so many international tours that people called him "Ambassador Satch" ("Satchmo," his nickname, was derived from "satchel-mouth").

However, the more successful Armstrong became in the world of popular music, the more he drifted away from true jazz, to the distress of jazz enthusiasts. His last hit record was *Hello, Dolly!*, the title song of a 1964 Broadway musical; in this number he sang (with his famous raspy delivery) more than he played the trumpet.

Encore: Listen to *West Side Blues, Heebie Jeebies, Hotter Than That, St. Louis Blues* (with Bessie Smith).

Early jazz players developed the art of collective improvisation, or "jamming." They learned to improvise simultaneously, each developing the special resources of his instrument—bright melodic spurts for the trumpet, fast running passages from low register to high for the clarinet, forceful slides for the trombone. They also acquired a sort of sixth sense for fitting in with the other improvisers. The nonimitative polyphony produced in this way is the hallmark of early jazz.

The first important center of jazz was New Orleans, home of the greatest early jazzman, Louis Armstrong, who played cornet and trumpet. Armstrong and his colleagues developed wonderfully imaginative and individual performance styles; aficionados can recognize any player after hearing just a few measures of a jazz record. With players of this quality, it is not surprising that solo sections soon became a regular feature in early jazz, along with collective improvisation.

Recording technology was already crucial in the dissemination of jazz. As popular records in those days were all just three minutes long, the jazz that has survived from that era is all slimmed down into three-minute segments. (If not for this, Sippie Wallace and Louis Armstrong would have given us many more blues stanzas.) Originally issued on labels that appealed to black audiences—

Jazz in the early 1920s: Louis Armstrong (center) in his first important band, Joe ("King") Oliver's Creole Jazz Band. The pianist, Lil Hardin—also a bandleader and songwriter—later married Armstrong and is credited with directing his early career.

coldly categorized as "race records" by the music business—Armstrong's discs of the late 1920s and 1930s not only attracted white listeners, but also excited the admiration of a new breed of jazz musicologists and critics.

Swing

Around 1930, jazz gained significantly in popularity, thanks in part to Armstrong's recordings. With popularity came changes, not all of them to the good. Jazz now had to reach bigger audiences in ballrooms and roadhouses. This meant **big bands,** with ten to twenty-five players—and such large numbers required carefully written out arrangements of the songs played. Improvisation, which was really the rationale behind jazz, was necessarily limited under these conditions.

However, big-band jazz—called <u>swing</u>—compensated for some of its lost spontaneity by variety of tone color and instrumental effects. A novel style of band orchestration was developed, based on the contrast between brass (trumpets and trombones) and "reed" (mainly saxophone) groups. Soloists cut in and out of the full-band sounds. Jazz "arrangers," who arranged current songs for the bands, treated this style with the greatest technical ingenuity and verve; they deserve the name of composers. Sometimes they contrived to allow for some improvisation within their arrangements.

Swing in the late 1930s: one of the most famous of the "big bands" (Glenn Miller)—brass to the left, reeds to the right. Miller's sideman Bobby Hackett (cornet) was one of many white musicians inspired by Louis Armstrong.

With popularity, too, came white musicians and managers, who moved in on what had previously been a relatively small black operation. Not only were black jazzmen marginalized in the mass market, but their art was watered down to suit the growing audience. The big swing bands that were commercial successes were white, and their leaders—Benny Goodman, Glenn Miller, Artie Shaw— were household names in the 1930s and 1940s. But the best of the big bands were black: those led by Count Basie (1904–1984), Jimmie Lunceford (1902–1947), Chick Webb (1909–1939), and Duke Ellington.

DUKE ELLINGTON (1899–1974)
Conga Brava (1940)

32   37

The tune used in *Conga Brava* was written by Ellington together with his Puerto Rican sideman Juan Tizol. (A conga is a dance of Afro-Cuban origin, named after the *conga* drum.) In it, the characteristic beat of Latin American music is appropriated by jazz—a mild tit-for-tat on behalf of a musical style that had given up much more to the nonblack world.

Only the beginning of this unusual tune—the **a a** section of the **a a b** form— has a Latin beat. Played by trombonist Tizol, the first **a** is presented with a minimal and mysterious accompaniment; but after this ends with a fancy

Duke Ellington (1899–1974)

Edward Kennedy Ellington was born in Washington, D.C., son of a butler who occasionally worked at the White House. The young Ellington considered a career as an artist, but he started playing the piano in jazz bands—ragtime was a major influence—and soon organized his own. He learned arranging too, and became an almost unique phenomenon: a major bandleader who was also its composer and its arranger.

He was called "Duke" because of a certain aristocratic bearing—and he was fastidious about his music, too. Ellington held fast to his own high standards of innovation and stylishness. And although his band never "went commercial," it did as well as any black band could in the 1930s and 1940s. "Duke Ellington and His Famous Orchestra" were renowned as the backup to sumptuous revues put on at the Cotton Club, an upscale Harlem night spot that catered to white audiences. Their recordings from around 1930 to 1940 constitute Ellington's major legacy.

After World War II, Ellington went his own imperturbable way, keeping his big band at a time when such organizations were regarded as jazz dinosaurs. He had experimented with long, symphonic-style jazz compositions as a young man, and now wrote more of these, as well as movie scores, a ballet, and an opera. The Ellington band, which had toured Europe twice in the 1930s, now toured all over the world, including the Soviet Union.

Ellington was finally recognized for what he was, just about America's most eminent composer, and he received the Presidential Medal of Freedom and other tributes. His last creative phase found him writing lengthy religious pieces, called *Sacred Concerts*, for the Ellington band with a Swedish soprano, Alice Babs, who was not really a jazz singer at all.

Ellington's *Sacred Concerts* would have been impossible without Babs—but the same is true of his earlier, better-known music and the musicians of his early bands. These individual soloists, or *sidemen*, as they are called—among them Barney Bigard (clarinet), Cootie Williams (trumpet), Johnny Hodges (alto saxophone), and Juan Tizol, who is featured on valve trombone in *Conga Brava* (below)—were vital to Ellington's art in a way singers or instrumentalists very rarely are in classical music. He molded his music so closely to their sometimes eccentric styles of playing that we cannot conceive of his music without them.

Ellington's sidemen can be regarded as co-composers of his music—or, better, as its *material*, like the songs and the blues that were transformed by Ellington's magic.

Chief Works: Very many songs—one estimate is 2,000—and jazz arrangements ▪ Large-scale jazz compositions, including *Creole Fantasy* and *Black, Brown, and Beige* ▪ Musical comedies, ballets, an incomplete opera *(Boola)* and other stage music ▪ Five film scores; *Sacred Concerts*

Encore: Listen to *Mood Indigo, Harlem Airshaft, Saddest Tale, Concerto for Cootie, Ko-ko, Don't Get Around Much Anymore, Sophisticated Lady.*

---

clarinet break, the second **a** includes brilliant interjections from the muted brass (an Ellington specialty). From now on things change rapidly. The brass choir plays **b**, with a speedy low clarinet cutting in. The rhythm section switches from a Latin beat to a typical jazz back-beat duple meter. The music begins to swing hard, as the trumpets remove their mutes.

The second appearance of the tune is a dazzling free improvisation by tenor sax player Ben Webster. He sounds genuinely spontaneous; he probably never again improvised around this melody in just this way. After he has gone through **a** and **a**, the muted brass come in again with a lively variation of **b**.

Webster has strayed far from the tune, so it is good to hear the third appearance of the tune in its original form (more or less), now on the reed choir (saxophones). This time the brilliant interpolations are by sideman Rex Stewart on trumpet. And this time, after a single **a**, there comes an extraordinary brass-choir version of **b**, with wildly syncopated rhythms. The coordination of the brass instruments is breathtaking, and the sheer verve of their variation makes this the high point of the composition.

LISTEN

Ellington, *Conga Brava*

0:03	a a	Trombone
0:45	b	Brass and alto sax
0:59	a a	Sax
1:39	b	Muted brass
1:46	a	Reed Choir (with trumpet)
2:07	b′	Brass Choir
2:32	a	Trombone

My band is my instrument.

Duke Ellington

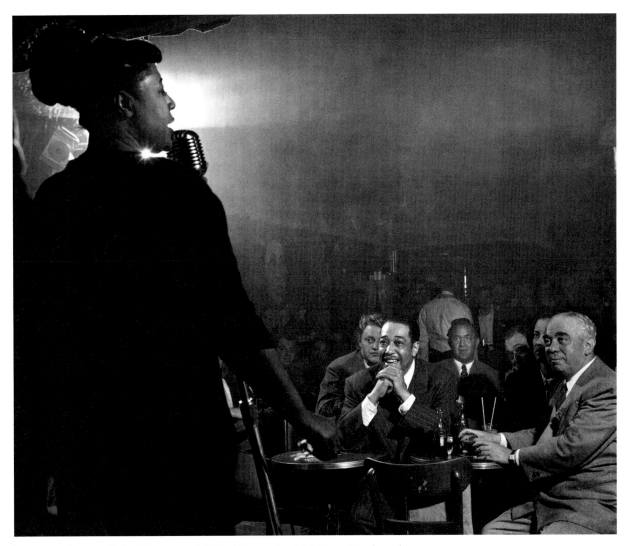

Jazzmen as listeners: Duke Ellington and (behind him to the right) Benny Goodman listen to Ella Fitzgerald, one of the greatest vocalists of the jazz era. You can hear her sing "Who Cares?" on the Study Guide CD-ROM.

7

At the piano, Duke gives a quiet signal for this brass episode before it starts; he also plays a single, hardly audible note in the middle of the episode, as though to remind us who is in charge. The piece ends as it started, with the tune played by Tizol, but it fades halfway through.

How strange to be back to the rather mournful and still conga melody, with its Latin beat! The listener to *Conga Brava* can end up feeling a bit mystified. All that exhilarating jazz activity that blew up so suddenly and has now been cut off—was it some kind of dream? Only a master of musical form like Ellington could make you think of such questions, make you feel that way about a piece of music.

GLOBAL PERSPECTIVES   6

African Drumming

38   41

We said before that the syncopated rhythms of ragtime, blues, and jazz derived from traditional African music, particularly drumming. We don't know enough about African or African American music in the nineteenth century to detail this connection in all its stages, but we can surmise that the rhythmic complexities of modern jazz and today's African drumming are connected in a history that reaches back centuries.

Listen now to our recording of a drum ensemble from Benin, a small West African nation situated be-tween Ghana and Nigeria. This music is used in the worship of ancestral spirits among the Yoruba people—one of a wide variety of religious and nonreligious uses of drumming in the region.

Syncopation and Polyrhythms

The rhythms of this music cannot be said to *swing* precisely in the manner of jazz, but they show a complexity and vitality related to jazz rhythms and not found in the European classical music tradition through the nineteenth century.

These rhythms are related to what we have termed "beat syncopation" in jazz (see page 390). A single drum lays down a basic, fast, four-plus-four pulse;

A drumming club in Ghana

each group of four feels like a beat, and two groups of four take about a second. (This quick pulse is heard all the way through the recording, except for three brief moments: This drummer speeds up momentarily at 1:09, 1:46, and 2:33, with stunning, energizing effect, fitting six strokes into the space usually taken up by four.)

Against the main drum's consistent pulse, the other drums play a variety of different rhythms. Sometimes they underscore the main drum's even pulse, or even duplicate it. Often, however, they play off it with more complicated and varied rhythms, including extensive syncopation within the groups of four (or beats), and occasionally they boldly contradict it.

Such overlapping of varied patterns with the main pulse is essential in West African drumming. Since several rhythmic formulas can be heard at once, it is sometimes called *polyrhythm*. From its polyrhythms the musical whole gains an extraordinary richness of rhythmic profile. And from the syncopations within the beat it derives its irresistible vitality (irresistible also to the ancestral spirits invoked).

A Closer Look

For those who wish to study this recording more closely, here are a few clear polyrhythmic interactions to listen for:

⁊ One drummer aligns a regular syncopated formula against the main pulse, in this manner:

Listen for this four times in the recording, at 0:23–0:29, 0:50–0:53, 1:23–1:28, and 2:13–2:19.

⁊ Another drummer plays an even 3 + 3 pulse against the main 4 + 4, seeming to contradict its duple meter with a triple orientation. This occurs prominently twice, at 0:41–0:44 and again at 2:22–2:26.

⁊ One drummer in particular departs freely from the main pulse all the way through this recording. He is the soloist, so to speak, improvising against the more regular and predictable playing of his ensemble-mates. His drum is recognizable by its wooden, clickety-clack timbre and by the fact that it plays two distinct pitches (the higher pitch is more wooden-sounding than the lower).

One good way to listen for his distinctive, irregular syncopations is to clap along with the main pulse as you listen, once every four strokes. You will be clapping about twice a second. Then compare the regularity of your own clapping with the seemingly free fantasy of the clickety-clack drum.

3 Later Jazz

After World War II the popularity of the big bands collapsed suddenly. They were too expensive to run; furthermore, styles in entertainment had changed, and the smooth, high-powered band sound struck people as cold and slick. The mass market turned to rock'n'roll, itself the outcome of a vital new genre of African American music, rhythm and blues (see page 411). Even during the war, this collapse had been forecast by a revolutionary new movement within jazz called *bebop*.

Bebop

During the early 1940s, young black jazz musicians found it harder to get work than white players in big bands. When they did get jobs, the setup discouraged free improvisation, the life and soul of jazz; the big bands seemed to have co-opted and distorted a style grown out of black experience. These musicians got together in small groups after work for jam sessions at clubs in Harlem. There they developed a new style that would later be called **bebop.** Contrasting sharply with the big bands, the typical bebop combo (combination) was just trumpet and saxophone, with a rhythm section including piano.

Bebop was a determined return to improvisation, then—but improvisation of a new technical virtuosity. "That horn ain't supposed to sound that fast," an elder musician is said to have complained to bebop saxophonist Charlie Parker. In addition to unprecedented velocity, Parker and leading bebop trumpeter Dizzy Gillespie (1917–1993) cultivated hard, percussive sounds and sharp, snap rhythms (one derivation of the term "bebop").

Equally radical was the treatment of harmony in bebop. New Orleans jazz used simple, in fact naïve, harmonies. The swing arrangers used much more sophisticated ones. Bebop musicians took these complex harmonies and improvised around them in a more and more "far out" fashion. In long stretches of their playing, even the tonality of the music was obscured. Bebop melodies grew truly fantastic; the chord "changes" became harder and harder to follow.

Playing bop is like playing Scrabble with all the vowels missing.

Duke Ellington, 1954

CHARLIE PARKER (1920–1955) and MILES DAVIS (1926–1991)
Out of Nowhere (1948)

33   38

The life of Charlie ("Bird") Parker, bebop's greatest genius, reads like a modern-day version of a persistent Romantic myth—the myth of the artist who is driven by the demon of his creativity, finding fulfillment only in his art. Parker was on drugs from the age of fifteen, and in later years could not control his immoderate drinking and eating. A legend in his own lifetime, Parker died at the age of thirty-four after a suicide attempt and a period of hospitalization in a California mental institution.

Out of Nowhere is one of the many popular songs of the 1930s that were used as the basis for jazz, swing, and bebop singles. Our version of the number was recorded live in a New York nightclub, so it can give us an exact idea of what an improvised bebop number actually sounded like. Notice the informal opening—no arranged introduction as in Ellington's *Conga Brava,* or even in the Wallace-Armstrong blues number. Parker plays the attractive song fairly "straight" to begin with, but he inserts a sudden skittering passage just before the **A′** section (the song is in **A A′** form). This is a preview of things to come.

LISTEN

Parker, *Out of Nowhere*

0:00 **Tune**
0:51 **Trumpet**
1:36 **Sax**
2:26 **Piano**
2:49 **Tune**

The trumpet solo by Miles Davis has the characteristic tense, bright bebop sound, some very rapid passage work, and one or two piercing high notes. Then Parker's improvisation shows his impressive powers of melodic development. He works mainly with the opening motive of three eighth notes in the original song:

He had already expanded these three notes to many more, much shorter and faster ones, in his original presentation of the tune. Now he builds a whole series of phrases of different lengths, all starting with fast, increasingly elaborate runs derived from this basic rhythmic idea.

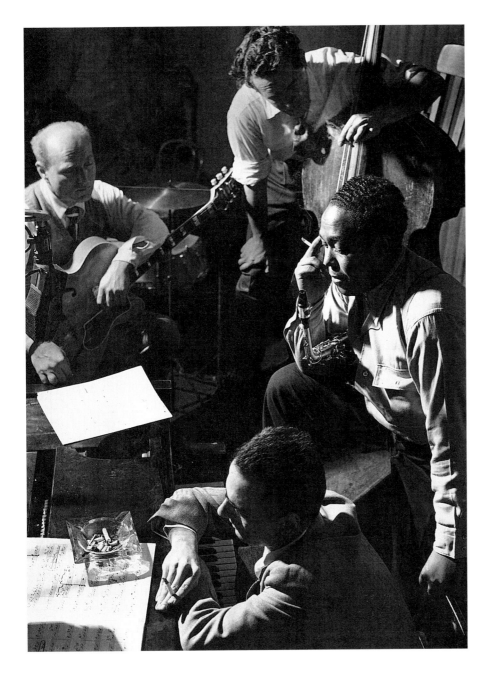

In a recording studio, Charlie Parker listens to a playback as the other musicians wait for his reaction. Will he approve this "take" of the number they are recording, or will they have to do another?

The irregular, almost discontinuous-sounding rests between Parker's phrases have their own special fascination. You may recognize an Irish jig, named "The Kerry Dancers," which seems to have popped into Parker's head right in the middle of the solo, as the outgrowth of a short melody figure he had come to. He plays the jig at a dizzying rate for just a moment, before inventing something else; fantastically, it fits right in.

At the end of his solo the nightclub audience applauds, and the pianist plays his own improvised solo on the tune's **A** section. The number ends with the **A′** section of *Out of Nowhere* played once again quite simply, except for new trumpet breaks and a new, comical ending.

Jazz after Bebop

Melody, harmony, and tonality—these were the very elements in music that had been "emancipated" by Schoenberg, Stravinsky, and other avant-gardists in the early 1900s. With the bebop movement, the avant-garde finally came to jazz.

Many new jazz styles followed after the bebop emancipation, from the 1950s to the present day. Jazz aficionados distinguish between cool jazz, free jazz, modal jazz, Afro-Cuban jazz, electric jazz, and even avant-garde jazz. Among the leaders in this diverse, exciting music were pianist Thelonious Monk (1917–1982), trumpeter Miles Davis (1926–1991), keyboardist Sun Ra (1928–1994), and saxophonists John Coltrane (1926–1967) and Ornette Coleman (b. 1930). They were the first to improvise really freely—that is, without a song or blues or any pre-existing chord changes as a basis.

The synthesizer has changed everything, whether purist musicians like it or not. It's here to stay and you can either be in it or out of it. I choose to be in it because the world has always been about change.

From Miles Davis's autobiography, 1989

MILES DAVIS (1926–1991)
Bitches Brew (1969)

34   39

Trumpeter Miles Davis, one of the most innovative figures in the whole history of jazz, started out playing with Charlie Parker and other bebop musicians, but soon realized that his own aptitude (or at least one of his main aptitudes) was for a more relaxed and tuneful kind of melody. Davis's style went through many stages—from bebop to cool jazz to modal jazz and beyond—as he worked in various groups with a veritable who's-who of modern jazz artists.

Bitches Brew, one of his biggest hits, was also one of his most original. A conscious (and controversial) attempt to blend jazz with rock, the album used a rhythm section with electric guitar, bass, and two electric keyboards in addition to regular jazz drums, acoustic bass, and augmented percussion. Instead of the traditional chord changes of jazz, this group produced repetitive, rocklike rhythms of the greatest variety and, often, delicacy. This backdrop provides an unlikely but also unforgettable setting for Davis's haunting improvisations.

Our selection covers a solo from the title track of *Bitches Brew.* Before Davis begins, the electric piano and guitar pick out rhythmic patterns against a quiet jazz drum background; mostly the electric guitar has isolated single notes and the electric piano has syncopated chords. As the piano and guitar die down, new fascinating rhythms are heard in the bass.

The trumpet solo starts with short patterns of relatively long notes, a Davis signature. The mood is meditative, almost melancholy: an evocation of the blues. A rocklike ostinato is heard in the bass. Soon Davis is employing more elaborate patterns—a string of repeated notes, scalelike passages up and

LISTEN

Davis, *Bitches Brew* (part)

0:00 **Backdrop**
0:42 **Dies down**
1:04 **Trumpet solo**
2:56 **Ostinato**
3:39 **Climax**

Miles Davis

Cuban pianist Gonzalo Rubalcaba, leading light of a new jazz generation.

down—but the effect is, in its own way, as repetitive as the backdrop. Then he explodes into a series of little snaps: a recollection of bebop. As the backdrop drives harder and harder, we realize that Davis has now arrived at a wild, free ostinato in the high register. The solo sinks down again after a climactic high trumpet squeal, another Davis hallmark.

With jazz-rock or *fusion*, Davis and others reached out for vernacular roots in American music. Still, jazz in its modern stage is usually complex and often difficult to follow. Formerly America's dominant form of truly popular music, today this music can really only be described as "popular" with loyal fans who crowd to jazz festivals from Newport, Rhode Island, to Monterey, California. These fans view with mixed emotions efforts by Washington's Smithsonian Institution and New York's Lincoln Center to cultivate jazz in a classical-concert format, led especially by the latest great jazz trumpet virtuoso, Wynton Marsalis (b. 1961). The life and soul of jazz is its spontaneity. Will spontaneity survive institutionalization?

Jazz continues to flower cumulatively, taking on and transforming the new without ever abandoning the old. It is a fugue with a life of its own, endlessly recapitulating.

Time magazine, 1976

4 The Influence of Jazz and Blues

How was jazz first received in this country's "cultivated" musical circles? Many longtime symphony and opera subscribers certainly hated it. They considered its saxophones and muted trumpets vulgar, its rhythms dangerously sexual and likely to corrupt their children. This reaction was strongly tinged with racism.

On the other hand, jazz was from the first an inspiration as well as a delight for less hidebound musicians, music students, and young composers.

The 1920s era was a confident one, and composers coming of age at that time promised a bright new day for American music. A vital, fresh musical idiom had emerged—the decade from 1920 to 1930 called itself the Jazz Age—and the idea of working jazz into concert music was both natural and exciting.

Jazz in the Concert Hall

We have already heard one example of this trend in Maurice Ravel's blues-influenced Piano Concerto in G (see page 355). Ravel heard the new African American styles when they took Paris by storm in the 1920s, making that city the first jazz center outside the United States.

In America, the composer who most successfully carried off the fusion of jazz with concert-hall music was George Gershwin (1898–1937). Born in New York, Gershwin received a sketchy musical education. He quit school at sixteen to work as a song plugger, or music publisher's agent, playing through the newest sheet music hits for potential customers and promoting them to singers and bandleaders. Soon he was writing his own songs, and he went on to compose some of the finest tunes of the 1920s—"Lady be Good," "Embraceable You," "The Man I Love," and dozens of others. He was an accomplished and original jazz pianist.

Harboring an ambition to enter the world of cultivated music, Gershwin electrified musical America with his *Rhapsody in Blue* of 1924. Billed as "An Experiment in Modern Music," this fourteen-minute work for piano and orchestra was first performed by Paul Whiteman's Orchestra, a sleek forerunner of the 1930s big bands. This music is not true jazz, but is Gershwin's translation of jazz into his own individual idiom, halfway between jazz and the concert hall's concerto.

After *Rhapsody in Blue,* Gershwin wrote more works importing jazz and blues styles into concert-hall genres: *An American in Paris,* a symphonic poem for orchestra; a piano concerto; and an opera, *Porgy and Bess*—works that have remained widely popular, known and loved by millions of Americans. Gershwin had thrown a bridge across the canyon between vernacular and cultivated music. Of course, the existence of bridges doesn't mean that the rift has gone away.

> Oh sweet and lovely
> Lady be good,
> Oh lady be good
>   To me.
> I'm just a lonely
> Babe in the wood,
> Oh lady be good
>   To me . . .
>
> *Gershwin song lyric*

GEORGE GERSHWIN
Prelude No. 1 (1926)

Gershwin's Prelude No. 1 for piano is the first in a set of three he published in 1927. In its dimensions it looks back to Romantic piano miniatures (see page 246); its title recalls collections of such works by Chopin and Debussy that Gershwin knew well. Indeed, Gershwin originally intended a set of twenty-four preludes, just the number Chopin had published. He had the idea of calling this set *The Melting Pot,* a reference to the various cultivated and vernacular styles he would bring together in it.

Prelude No. 1 recalls Romantic miniatures also in its simple **A B A′** form. **A** and **A′** each consist of little more than a statement of the main melody of the piece:

35   40

LISTEN

Gershwin, Prelude No. 1

0:00 **A**
0:07 Left-hand syncopations begin
0:22 **B**
0:54 Beginning of **A**: buildup
1:04 **A′**

B is a longer section. It changes key frequently, employing many sequences, and is dominated by a melody that begins with repeated notes, a favorite gesture of Gershwin in his piano music.

What gives this music its distinctive appeal, however—and what makes it sound nothing like Chopin—are the elements it borrows from jazz and blues. Both the little half-step slide up that begins the main theme and the unexpected note that ends its second bar are borrowed from the so-called *blues scale*—a scale characteristic of blues singing but not of the European classical tradition. Such "blue notes" come back again and again in the melodies of the piece.

Even more distinctive is the jazzy syncopation that marks the left-hand part. Listen to the accompaniment at the beginning, before the main melody joins it, counting two fairly slow beats per measure. The beginning of each measure—the downbeat—is clearly marked by a thudding low note. The *second* beat, however, is not struck, but instead undercut by a syncopated chord that anticipates it by a fraction. Syncopated patterns like this one continue throughout the piece, playing off against the melodies to give the piece its rhythmic verve.

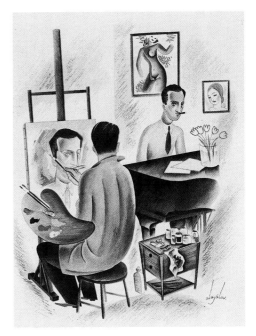

Constantin Alajálov, who left unforgettable pictures of the Jazz Age, sketched himself painting George Gershwin in 1932.

The American Musical

Throughout the ages and throughout the world, the theater has always provided fertile soil for the growth of popular music. America, once the Puritan spirit had subsided somewhat, proved no exception. One of the main sources of modern American popular music can be located in the thriving New York theatrical scene in the decades around 1900. Then, as now, the New York City theater district was located at, and known as, Broadway.

Broadway was first of all home of **operetta**, a very popular European genre of light opera in the nineteenth and early twentieth centuries. Operettas employ spoken dialogue (rather than recitative) between the musical numbers—light, attractive tunes and plenty of dances. Their plots are amusing, farfetched, and frothy. Typically they are set in some mythical eastern European country, where amorous, fun-loving aristocrats rub shoulders with merry, contented peasants.

Among the best European composers of operettas were Johann Strauss Jr., the "Waltz King" (*Die Fledermaus*—"The Bat": 1874), and Arthur Sullivan (*The Mikado, HMS Pinafore,* and others—these are called "Gilbert and Sullivan" operettas as a tribute to the very witty librettist, W. S. Gilbert). The most important American composer in this tradition was Victor Herbert (1859–1924). Born in Ireland and educated in Germany, Herbert produced more than forty operettas from the 1890s on; chiefly remembered today is *Babes in Toyland* (1903).

Musical Comedy and Popular Song

It was around 1910 that the American popular theater picked up its characteristic accent. It was a musical accent, and it came from jazz. Although Broadway did not employ actual jazz, it swiftly appropriated and assimilated jazz syncopation and swing. As projected by white theater bands and carried over into popular songs, this jazz accent contributed more than anything else to the appeal of a new kind of musical show.

A vaudeville team of the 1890s, the Southern Four.

Theatergoers had also begun to demand stories that were American and up to date, and so the writers of the song lyrics learned to make up smart, catchy verses full of American locutions. To distinguish them from operettas—with their Old World ambience, aristocrats, waltzes, and students' drinking songs—these new shows were called **musical comedies,** or **musicals.**

The rise of the musical in the 1920s and thirties was closely tied to the great outpouring of popular songs in this era. It was truly a golden age for song. Not all of them were written for musicals, of course (Ellington, for example, wrote many songs that had no link to the theater). But the theater provided songwriters with an extra fee and gave songs invaluable exposure, magnified after 1926 by "talking pictures." Theater songs were popularized by the very successful movie musicals of the 1930s, as well as by radio and 78-rpm recordings.

The two principal composers of early American musical comedy were also composers of many favorite old tunes: Jerome Kern (1885–1945) and George Gershwin. Kern's masterpiece, *Show Boat* (1927), has returned to the stage again and again, and Gershwin's *Porgy and Bess* (1935), which is more like a jazz opera than a musical, occupies a solid place in the operatic repertory.

Gershwin's actual musicals are seldom heard because most of the plots now seem so silly—but there are exceptions, notably *Of Thee I Sing* (1931), a hilarious spoof of the presidential election process. There is a song from this show on our Study Guide CD-ROM.

Irving just loves hits. He has no sophistication about it— he just loves hits.

Said of Irving Berlin (1888–1990), author of "Alexander's Ragtime Band," "Always," "Easter Parade," and "White Christmas," among other hits

7

The Musical after 1940

Show Boat and *Of Thee I Sing* both look forward to the new dramatic sophistication of the musical in the postwar era. From the 1940s on, the plots of musicals were worked out with more care. Instead of the plot being a mere pretext for songs and dances in the manner of a revue, musical numbers grew logically out of a plot that had interest in its own right.

Richard Rodgers (1902–1979) and his lyricist Oscar Hammerstein (1895–1960) dominated this period. Their works such as *Oklahoma!* (1943) and *The King and I* (1951) ran for thousands of performances on Broadway. They still define the golden age of the musical—perhaps especially because they offered a sentimental and innocent vision of the world as America in the postwar era wished to see it.

Other musicals tackled more challenging subjects—psychoanalysis, trade unionism, gang warfare—but these rarely rivaled the megahits of Rodgers and Hammerstein. One exception to this rule is *West Side Story*, with music by the classical composer and symphony conductor Leonard Bernstein. Here we see the cultivated tradition reaching out to the vernacular—but in a genre defined by the vernacular.

LEONARD BERNSTEIN (1918–1990)
West Side Story (1957)

Leonard Bernstein was one of the most brilliant and versatile musicians ever to come out of America, the consummate crossover artist before the term was invented. Composer of classical symphonies and hit musicals, internationally acclaimed conductor, pianist, author, and mastermind of wonderful shows in the early days of television, he won Grammys, Emmys, and a Tony.

West Side Story (1957) boasts three exceptional features—its moving story, its sophisticated score, and its superb dances, created by the great American choreographer Jerome Robbins. The musical, by turns funny, smart, tender, and enormously dynamic, gave us song classics such as "Maria" and "Tonight." Our recording of *West Side Story* is from the soundtrack to the 1961 movie version of the show.

The great thing about conducting is that you don't smoke and you breathe in great gobs of oxygen.

Chain-smoker Leonard Bernstein

Background   Shakespeare's play *Romeo and Juliet* tells of young lovers frustrated and driven to their deaths by a meaningless feud between their families, the Montagues and the Capulets of Verona. *West Side Story* transplants this plot to a turf war between teenage gangs on the West Side of Manhattan. In Shakespeare, the feud is a legacy from the older generation, but in *West Side Story* the bitter enmity is the kids' own, though it has ethnic overtones. The Jets are whites, the Sharks Puerto Ricans.

Bernardo, leader of the Sharks, is livid when he learns that his sister Maria is in love with Jet Tony. As in Shakespeare, one Jet (Capulet) and one Shark (Montague) die tragically on stage, in a street fight. Tony is shot in revenge, and Maria is left distraught.

Some of the transpositions into the modern world are ingenious. Shakespeare's famous soliloquy "Romeo, Romeo, wherefore art thou Romeo?" shows the lovestruck Juliet fondly repeating her lover's name; Tony cries "Maria" over and over again in his famous song of that title. (An aria in an opera or a song in a musical is, in fact, often equivalent to a soliloquy in a play.) And whereas Shakespeare's young lovers fall in love at a Capulet masked ball, which Romeo has crashed, Bernstein's are smitten at a gym dance organized by a clueless teacher who hopes to make peace between the gangs.

Cha-cha   This is the music danced to by the Puerto Rican girls—the Sharks' girlfriends—at the gym where Tony and Maria first meet. The cha-cha, a Cuban dance, was new to the United States when *West Side Story* was written.

West Side Story: trouble at
the gym

The charm of the fragile cha-cha melody owes a good deal to Bernstein's skillful accompaniment. Melody and accompaniment seem nervously aware of each other, but they keep slipping out of sync:

Meeting Scene   Tony and Maria catch sight of one another. The cha-cha may be continuing, but they don't hear it, so neither do we. Or at most they hear fragments of the cha-cha slowed down and made unexpectedly tender, as background for their voice-over.

And when Tony gets to sing the big romantic number, "Maria," the music is yet another transformation of the cha-cha melody, now sounding rich and enthusiastic. Thematic transformation technique, which Bernstein knew from Liszt and other Romantic composers, allowed him to show Tony's love emerging and blossoming out of that one heart-stopping moment in the gym.

"Cool"   A little later in the action, the Jet leader, Riff, tries to persuade his troops to stay calm in the face of Shark provocations. The main production number of Act I, it consists of an introduction, again with voice-over; a short song by Riff; a dazzling dance; and then Riff's song again.

The song's introduction uses the motive of the cha-cha melody—the same motive that turns into "Maria"—in a highly charged, syncopated form:

LISTEN

Bernstein, "Cool"

0:14 **Riff:** "Cool"
1:13 **Fugue** begins
2:40 Fugue breaks down
3:10 Band version of "Cool"
3:39 **Jets:** "Cool"
4:08 **Countersubject**

Ma‑ri‑a! _ I've just met a

girl named Ma‑ri‑a! _

37

Boy,   boy   crazy boy, __   Get cool, boy! _   Got a   rocket   in your   pocket   Keep coolly cool, __ boy!

After the introduction, Riff sings two stanzas of his song, in 1950s "hip" street language. There is a steady jazz percussion accompaniment.

The dance that follows, subtitled "Fugue," is accompanied throughout by the soft jazz drum beat. First played by muted trumpet, the fugue subject consists of four slow notes, with an ominous snap at the end of the last of them. Soon another theme—the fugue countersubject (see page 140)—comes in, played by flute and vibraphone, featured instruments of 1950s "cool jazz." The two themes combine in counterpoint, along with fragments of the introduction, getting louder and more intricate as the dance proceeds. Bernstein must have thought that fugue, about the most "controlled" of musical forms, would depict perfectly the Jets' effort to stay cool.

But things appear to get out of hand toward the end of the dance. The music stomps angrily and breaks into electrifying improvised drum solos. The Jets yell various words taken from the song, and the song's melody returns, orchestrated in the exuberant, brash style of a big swing band. While the brasses blare away on the tune, breaks (see page 390) are played by the reeds at the end of each line.

To conclude, the Jets sing parts of "Cool" quietly, prior to its atmospheric conclusion. The vibraphone recollects the fugue countersubject.

Stephen Sondheim (b. 1930), who wrote the lyrics for *West Side Story,* was himself an aspiring composer. He has gone on to write words and music for a string of successful musicals with an intellectual bent: *A Little Night Music* (1972), *Sweeney Todd* (1979), and *Into the Woods* (1987). *Sweeney Todd* in particular pushed at the border between musical and opera, as Gershwin had done forty years earlier in *Porgy and Bess.*

Meanwhile the musical in the 1960s began to acknowledge the rock revolution: *Hair* (Galt MacDermott, 1967) has been described as a "plotless American tribal love-rock musical." It was as much celebrated in its time for its onstage nudity as for any noteworthy rock music. In spite of its recent revival and such follow-ups as *Rent* (Jonathan Larson, 1997), true rock musicals have never ruled Broadway. Instead it has in recent years been home to anodyne foreign musicals, especially by the English composer Sir Andrew Lloyd Webber: *Cats* (1981), *The Phantom of the Opera* (1986), and others.

Just at this moment, however, the musical in an old-fashioned guise was revitalized from an unexpected quarter. In a series of Disney full-length animated films, including *Beauty and the Beast, The Little Mermaid,* and *The Lion King,* the musical was transplanted from stage to film. Of course musicals had been filmed before—think of *The Sound of Music, My Fair Lady,* or *The Music Man.* But these Disney musicals were created expressly to be animated. In a predictable twist, one of them, *The Lion King,* has now made its way back to live action as a Broadway hit.

Today the tradition of the musical thrives in many forms. On Broadway it can go so far as to erase the distinction between vernacular and cultivated

Boy, boy, crazy boy,
Get cool, boy!
Got a rocket
In your pocket,
Keep coolly cool, boy!
Don't get hot
'Cause, man, you got
Some high times ahead.
Take it slow,
And, Daddy-o,
You can live it up
    and die in bed!

MUTED BRASS

traditions, as in the 2002 production in full of Puccini's opera *La Bohème*, sung in Italian. Elsewhere it ranges from the Hollywood film *Moulin Rouge*, set in a Paris music hall from the 1800s, to the annual student revivals of Broadway hits of the past in thousands of high schools and summer camps across the country.

5 Rock: The First Fifty Years

Throughout the jazz age in the first half of the twentieth century, another, re- lated type of vernacular music poured forth from American composers: popular songs. We have seen the beginnings of this tradition in the nineteenth century in the works of Stephen Foster (see page 388), and we have also discussed one of the best popular songwriters of the 1920s and 1930s, George Gershwin (page 404).

One thing that often happened to the best-known songs—"standards" when they became popular enough to be hummed by everyone "in the know"—was that they served as a platform for jazz improvisors. The example of Charlie Parker's *Out of Nowhere* (page 404) shows that standards could sometimes support even the most progressive jazz styles. To *become* a stan- dard, however, such songs needed to catch on with the public through versions by the best-loved singers of the day. Vocalists like Bing Crosby and Frank Sinatra sang the sentimental, jazzy tunes to dance-hall audiences, to the ever- growing radio audience, in the movies, and—most importantly by the end of the 1940s—on records.

After World War II, the popularity of such songs began to be rivaled by another set of styles, less tame, louder, and with a driving beat that made the subtleties of jazz syncopation plainer and cruder—all in all, more brash and youthful. By the middle of the 1950s the new style took a name that captured this compelling rhythm: *rock'n'roll*. (Later, in the 1960s, the name of choice became **rock**.) Teenagers went wild. Their parents, reacting much as parents had thirty years earlier in the face of jazz, bemoaned the demise of civil cul- ture and decent society.

Nevertheless, rock endured and evolved—indeed, it positively burgeoned. Its explosive development from 1955 to 1970 and its reinvention in the fol- lowing decades have put rock on a historical par with jazz. If jazz can claim to be America's most distinctive contribution to world art from the first half of the twentieth century, rock can make similar claims for the last fifty years. Today the development of global pop, discussed in Global Perspectives 7 (page 418), depends on various styles of American-derived rock more than on any other musical idiom.

Early Rock'n'Roll

The origins and subsequent history of rock and related popular styles conform to a pattern in American vernacular music we have seen as early as the minstrel show and then in 1930s swing: the mixing of African American and white Amer- ican styles. Sometimes in rock history this mix was a relatively balanced meet- ing of differing styles; at other times it looks more like the appropriation of African American idioms by white musicians. In either case it shows that the history of pop music, like so many other American histories, unfolded against the backdrop of white/black race relations.

With his sultry voice and sexual stage presence, Elvis Presley had a gripping effect on audiences of the 1950s.

The very earliest rock'n'roll shows this pattern, emerging after World War II from the blending of *hillbilly* or *country* music with **rhythm and blues**. Country music was a white rural style derived from southern and southwestern folk song and emphasizing acoustic guitar, fiddle, and voice. Rhythm and blues was a black urban updating of earlier blues, marked by more pronounced, driving rhythms and electric guitar accompaniment. Together they created the first rock'n'roll style, *rockabilly*.

The first superstar of rock'n'roll, Elvis Presley, continued the trend. His amazing string of hits in the late 1950s ("Heartbreak Hotel," "Love Me Tender," and many others) combined a lyrical style derived from white popular singers with the strong beat and passionate, throaty vocal delivery of rockabilly. Many of these hits (for example, "Hound Dog") were Elvis's versions of songs originally recorded by black artists—"covers," as we now call them.

Millions in white America loved Elvis's music while millions more found it threatening. Across the late 1950s a string of both white (Jerry Lee Lewis, Buddy Holly) and black musicians (Fats Domino, Little Richard, Chuck Berry) followed him up the charts—and soon it was "Rock around the Clock," as Bill Haley had declared in his 1955 hit. Radio stations and record companies alike realized there was a lasting market for the new sound.

So did Elvis's manager, Colonel Tom Parker, who shrewdly calculated the sales potential of Elvis's crossover style and advanced his stardom by securing him TV appearances and signing him to movie contracts. Parker made Elvis the first great example of manipulative rock marketing. He would not be the last.

The 1960s: Rock Comes of Age

The blending of black and white styles that resulted in early rock'n'roll lasted into the 1960s and has reappeared in various forms down to this day. At the same time, the early and mid 1960s witnessed the emergence of new styles, many of them clearly black or white in their origin and target audience. There was an explosion of new sounds, distinct from one another and gaining the allegiance of different groups of fans.

Motown, Soul, and Funk   As the civil rights movement of the 1950s evolved into the Black Power movement of the late 1960s, a succession of important black styles asserted their independence from white rock. These grew out of several sources: the remnants of black rhythm and blues in the late 1950s, most notably represented by singer-pianist Ray Charles, urban doo-wop groups that spawned such hit-makers as the Drifters ("Under the Boardwalk"), and "girl groups" such as the Shirelles ("Will You Love Me Tomorrow?").

The first in this line was the *Motown* style, created by the part-time songwriter and record producer Berry Gordy Jr. of Detroit—"Motorcity" or "Motown." Gordy was the most important black entrepreneur in early rock history. The groups he sponsored, among them the Supremes ("Where Did Our Love Go?") and the Temptations ("My Girl"), evolved polished, lyrical styles and performances featuring dance steps and sequins.

A more visceral style that emerged around the same time was *soul*. Soul derived especially from southern gospel singing combined with the rhythm and blues of Ray Charles. Its leading lights were the powerful Aretha Franklin ("Respect") and James Brown, self-styled as "the hardest working man in show business"—and certainly one of the hardest singing ("I Got You (I Feel Good)"). Its most haunting vocal presence was Otis Redding, whose only number-one hit, "(Sittin' On) The Dock of the Bay," is doubly haunting since it was recorded just days before he died in a 1967 plane crash.

By the end of the 1960s, soul was evolving into *funk,* a style in which the large bands with wind instruments typical of soul gave way to a sparer, hip sound (fuzztone bass guitar ostinatos, syncopated guitar scratching). One of the early groups pointing in this direction was the Bay Area–based Sly and the Family Stone ("Thank You (Falettinme Be Mice Elf Agin)"). A decade later, in the hands of George Clinton and his band Funkadelic, funk was the source early DJs sampled to accompany the first rappers.

The British Invasion

On February 7, 1964, the Beatles landed in New York for their first American tour. The resulting Beatlemania changed the face of rock'n'roll, and in a certain sense it has never ended. More than thirty years after their disbanding, the Beatles remain one of the highest-grossing entertainment institutions in the world.

Dozens of other British rock bands followed in the wake of the Beatles' arrival, some good, some not. The best of them, cast from the first as a kind of evil-twin mirroring of the Beatles, was the Rolling Stones. What British groups had in common at the start was their emulation of American rhythm and blues and the styles of black American rockers like Chuck Berry and Little Richard. One of the most influential of these British rockers, Eric Clapton, has ranged widely in the early history of the blues for his inspiration.

The difference between the Beatles and the Rolling Stones was not merely the good/bad contrast of their carefully groomed market images. It was musical as well. The Stones, despite nods in other directions, specialized in a blues-oriented, hard-rocking style led by Mick Jagger's manic vocal presence, heard in such hits as "Satisfaction" and "Honky Tonk Woman." The Beatles, in contrast, seemed to blossom in all musical directions—reflecting the differing musical interests of John Lennon, Paul McCartney, and George Harrison that would tear the group apart by 1970. From covers of Chuck Berry ("Roll Over, Beethoven") and sneakily insightful pop/rock numbers ("She Loves You," "Help!"), they moved on to countless other approaches: lyrical

January 1969: The Beatles in their final concert, an impromptu affair on the roof of the Apple Records building. From left: Ringo, Paul, John, and George.

ballads ("Yesterday," "Blackbird"), hymnlike anthems ("Hey Jude," "Let It Be"), visionary and psychedelic rock ("A Day in the Life," "Strawberry Fields"), and irresistible pop songs harkening back to the 1930s ("When I'm Sixty-Four," "Maxwell's Silver Hammer"—surely the sweetest tune imaginable about a serial killer). And they easily returned, led by Lennon, to straight-ahead, blues-derived rock ("Revolution").

American Counteroffensives

The irony of the British groups' interest in American rhythm and blues is that their massive popularity chased dozens of American groups, black and white, off the charts and out of business. About the only American music that swam well during the highest tide of the British invasion was the surfing sound out of southern California, typified by the Beach Boys ("I Get Around," "Good Vibrations").

Meanwhile another movement looking back to the hillbilly side of rock's ancestry was gaining steam. *Folk rock* was led by Bob Dylan, whose evocative, often socially conscious lyrics ("Blowin' in the Wind," "The Times They Are A-Changin'") rivaled his music in importance. Dylan's resuscitation of white country and folk styles, building on "folkies" such as Woody Guthrie and Pete Seeger, had long-lasting consequences. The most important of these was creating a place, at the edge of the rock tradition, for the singer-songwriter using acoustic accompaniment. Dylan and the folkies inspired musicians as different

Like many singer-songwriters, Tori Amos has adopted a confessional style in her lyrics; her personal revelations have captivated audiences as much as her passionate stage presence and strong piano playing.

as Paul Simon, originally part of the folk-rock duo Simon and Garfunkel; the straight-ahead rocker Bruce Springsteen; and the unpredictable, versatile Elvis Costello. Women musicians in particular have found the singer-songwriter niche congenial. Their line extends from Joan Baez and Joni Mitchell in the 1960s down to Tori Amos, k.d. lang, and Alanis Morissette today.

In the late 1960s a broad, mainly white, stratum of American youth, espousing free love, free drugs, and ever-louder opposition to the U.S. war in Vietnam, embraced new styles. From San Francisco, a center of this counterculture, came *acid rock*, named after LSD, known as "acid." In the hands of groups like the Grateful Dead, the style involved long, jazzlike improvisations on electric guitar alongside hallucinatory images in the words; the Dead was the first great "jam band."

Other guitar virtuosos embraced the new, improvisational style and linked it back to rhythm and blues guitar playing. The most famous of them were Jimi Hendrix, a rare black musician in the midst of psychedelic acid rock ("Purple Haze"), and the Latin-influenced Carlos Santana ("Black Magic Woman"). This powerful new guitar style would find its way into groups on both sides of the Atlantic; the best were the Who (creators of the "rock opera" *Tommy*), Cream (led by Clapton; "Sunshine of Your Love"), and Led Zeppelin ("Whole Lotta Love"). The guitar work of such groups formed the roots of *heavy metal*.

After the 1960s

By 1970, many of the trends that evolved over the following decades were in place. Self-conscious *art rock* (for example, Pink Floyd's album *Dark Side of the Moon*), singer-songwriter rock, heavy metal, and funk can all be seen, retrospectively, as outgrowths of music at the end of the 1960s.

The decade of the 1970s was perhaps most influential, however, in its consolidation of the global *business* of rock. Tendencies begun in the 1960s came to exert ever greater control over the music people heard: high-tech mass-marketing, aggressive promotion of "superstars" (the word itself came into common usage at this time, alongside "supertanker" and "superpower"), and play-listed, market-researched, repetitive radio stations. In 1981 a powerful new outlet emerged to promote a small and carefully selected sample of rock music: MTV began broadcasting nonstop on cable.

In the wake of the 1970s it is wise to remember that even the music that seems to rage loudest "against the machine" is usually brought to you by a multinational communications conglomerate.

Trends since 1980: Punk, Rap, and Post-Rock

Despite—or perhaps on account of—this commercialization, rock has survived. Indeed the last twenty-five years or so have brought something of a rejuvenation. Three trends can be summarized here:

🎵   The youthful disaffection that set in by the end of the 1960s, as the idealistic counterculture began to sense its impotence, hardened in the next decade. Its most influential expression was the nihilistic alienation of *punk rock*. In New York City and Britain, groups like the Patti Smith Group ("Gloria"), the Ramones ("Blitzkrieg Bop"), and the Sex Pistols ("Anarchy in the UK") reacted against the commercial flashiness of much rock with what we might call an anti-aesthetic: All expression was possible, including no expression. All musical

The Jimi Hendrix Experience, on the cover of their first album, dressed in their Carnaby Street best.

Kurt Cobain

expertise was acceptable, including none. (Some of the punks knew that in this move they were following the lead of arch-modernists like John Cage; see page 376.)

The punk approach gave strong impetus to a kind of populist movement in rock, encouraging the formation of countless "garage bands" and today's *indie rock*, distributed on small, independent labels. Some punk singers also pioneered an alienated, flat vocal delivery that contrasts both with the impassioned singing of earlier rock and with the streetwise cool of rap. In these features punk looked forward to the unpolished, moving, but somehow distant style of *grunge rock*, led by Kurt Cobain (until his death in 1994) and his band Nirvana ("Lithium," "Smells Like Teen Spirit").

First emerging about the same time as punk, *hip-hop* or **rap** has compiled a quarter-century history as a primary black rhetorical and musical mode. Early on, its influence was transmitted, with stunning postmodern quickness, around the globe. Rap is now a strong undercurrent sweeping through world pop-music traditions. Its influence is heard in the vocal delivery of countless rock groups.

The early 1990s marked rap's moment of highest notoriety in the American mass media. One strain of rap—the violent, misogynist variety known as *gangsta rap*—figured centrally in the public debate, which was marked not only by some justifiable distaste at the vision of these rappers but also by unmistakable racist undertones. However, the debate tended to miss two important points: First, while rap originated as a pointed expression of black urban concerns, it was marketed successfully to affluent whites, especially suburban teens. Second, the clamor against gangsta rap ignored the wider expressive terrains that rap as a whole had traveled. Already in 1980 rap was broad enough to embrace the hip-hop dance numbers of the Sugarhill Gang ("Rapper's Delight") and the trenchant social commentary of Grandmaster Flash ("The

Message"). By the 1990s, rap could range from the black empowerment messages of Public Enemy ("Don't Believe the Hype") through sensuous love lyrics and tongue-twisting word games to Queen Latifah's assertions of women's dignity and strength ("Latifah's Had It Up 2 Here"). And the 2000s would bring Eminem, the first white superstar of rap.

Around 1990 a new, experimental rock movement began to take shape; soon it was dubbed *post-rock*. Early post-rock groups (for example, Slint: "Good Morning Captain") emerged from the indie rock movement. They typically employed rock instrumentation and technology in a style that features hypnotically repeated gestures (especially bass ostinatos), juxtaposition of contrasting plateaus of sound, slow transitions and buildups, free improvisation, and emphasis of instruments rather than voice. (When a voice is present, it often doesn't so much *sing* as recite fragments of poetry in front of the instrumental backdrop.) This thumbnail sketch alone is enough to reveal post-rock's relation to two other musical movements we have encountered: minimalism (page 380) and avant-garde jazz (page 402).

And, just as jazz and classical music purists questioned those styles, some listen to post-rock and wonder, "But is it rock'n'roll?" The question grows more pressing still in the presence of recent post-rock groups (for instance, Godspeed You Black Emperor!; "Storm") that have featured acoustic rather than electrified instruments and even avoided the foremost trait of rock: a strong beat.

Questions of style, it seems to us, are not a matter of pre-set categories but of fluid affiliations, changing always as new music develops. Rock will accommodate post-rock, just as jazz accommodated fusion and classical concert music accepted minimalism, but it will be transformed in the process. In fact, the transformation is already under way. One of the most widely noticed rock bands of the late 1990s, Britain's Radiohead, began around 2000 to expand its earlier, song-oriented style with traits of post-rock ("Pyramid Song").

Web: *Research and test your understanding of jazz and popular American music at* <bedfordstmartins.com/listen>.

At a rave, dancing to *techno*, one of several varieties of electronic dance music that emerged in the 1980s.

GLOBAL PERSPECTIVES 7

Global Music

We have seen in Global Perspectives 2 (page 90) that European efforts to colonize foreign lands never resulted in the simple substitution of European cultures for native ones, but rather in new, complex mixed cultures. Such is the way of all meetings of distinct cultures and distinct musics. An Andean chorus singing Catholic Church polyphony to Quechua words and accompanying itself on Inca flutes and drums is the perfect example of such mixture.

But a funny thing happened to mixed musical cultures on their way through the twentieth century: recorded sound. Around the globe, the impact on music of technologies that store and play back sound has been nothing short of revolutionary. Combined with radio and TV broadcasts, and indeed with the modern ease of travel and commerce, it has given musicians and listeners from all parts of the world access to a much wider variety of music than ever before. Nothing in the whole history of culture, probably, has ever traveled more widely and easily than certain kinds of music do today.

Complexities of Globalism

Two opposing tendencies have arisen from this situation. The first works toward the worldwide *homogenization* of musics. Huge stretches of the sonic landscape are now inhabited by styles that are similar in certain basic features: electrified instruments, especially guitars; strong percussive presence; extensive syncopation; and relatively brief song-form presentation.

These features spread out from the American and especially African American pop-music revolution that occurred in the decades after World War II. Since the 1960s the dispersion of styles such as rhythm and blues, rock, soul, and rap has been powerful. Musical currents have, to be sure, flowed in both directions. *Reggae,* to take one example, was formed in the 1960s from a merger of native Jamaican styles with American rhythm and blues and soul, but by the late 1970s it had crossed back over to exert a great influence on American rock. The global dispersion has been enabled by a recording industry that has grown increasingly

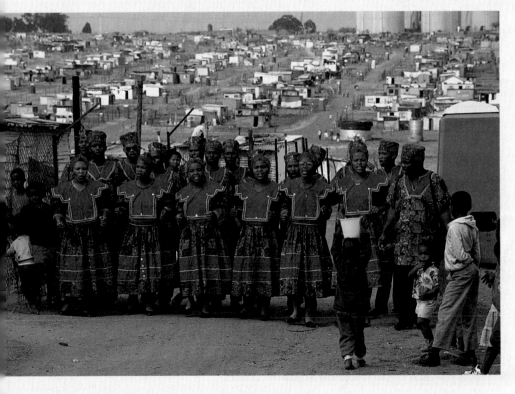

A choir—not for isicathamiya, given the many women participating—rehearses in South Africa. The beauty of the singers' costumes contrasts with the stark landscape of Soweto Township behind them.

Isicathamiya praktisa: a rehearsal at the Beatrice St. YMCA, Durban, South Africa, 1996.

rich, increasingly multinational, and increasingly influential in determining our musical tastes. It is enough to make one observer of these developments speak—with some worry—of a "universal pop aesthetic."

There is another tendency, however, opposing this move toward sameness, a move to *localize* music making. People are never willing simply to take on foreign things without in some way making them their own. Even as musicians around the world have felt the influence of American pop styles, they have combined these styles in their local musics to forge new, distinct styles. (Reggae is one example of this process.)

Pop music is now, in some general way, recognizable worldwide. We know it when we hear it, and we easily distinguish it from traditional folk musics like Andean panpipe groups or Appalachian fiddling and traditional elite musics like Japanese gagaku or European classical music. Nevertheless, what we recognize as pop music comes in an immense variety of distinct idioms derived from specific interactions of global and local tendencies.

South African Choral Song: Isicathamiya

SOUTH AFRICA

A South African musical tradition with a difficult name, *isicathamiya* (ees-ee-caht-ah-mée-ah), provides an example reaching back many decades of this diversity-within-sameness. It has become familiar to listeners worldwide through the recordings of the singing group Ladysmith Black Mambazo, famous from their participation in Paul Simon's album *Graceland* of 1986. Isicathamiya is an all-male, *a cappella* song style that arose among an impoverished class of black, mostly Zulu-speaking migrant laborers. A chief diversion in the laborers' camps were Saturday-night contests among singing groups, and for the musical styles the performers looked back to earlier, complex international roots.

Standing behind isicathamiya are traditions of choral polyphony native to the Zulus and other groups of the region. In the nineteenth century, these traditions seem to have merged readily with the four-part harmony of Christian hymn-singing brought to the area by European and American missionaries. Then another ingredient was added to the mix: American vaudeville or minstrel shows, with their syncopated, ragtime songs (see page 391 and the picture on page 406). An enormously influential African American minstrel—not a white minstrel in blackface—named Orpheus McAdoo toured South Africa extensively in the 1890s, to the great acclaim of black audiences.

By the 1930s, these musical influences were put together by the first recording stars of the local Zulu singing scene, Solomon Linda and the Evening Birds. Their greatest hit, "Mbube" or "Lion," known to most of us today as "The Lion Sleeps Tonight," was originally recorded around 1939. Then it was re-recorded by pop singers and became a top-40 hit in the 1960s. You likely know it in a more recent version from Disney's animated film *The Lion King.*

So when, not so many years back, you watched a McDonald's commercial on TV featuring this song and Disney's animation, you were participating in a rich musical and cultural convergence utterly dependent on recording and broadcast technology. You heard a song first recorded in Africa a half-century ago, remade by one multinational corporation (Disney) and exploited to sell the products of another (McDonald's), that traces its musical origins to native African choral polyphony, European hymn-singing, and ragtime styles created largely by African Americans. The modern global village may be a small place, but it is immensely complex.

"Anoku Gonda"

Solomon Linda's song "Anoku Gonda" ("You Must Understand This"), from the same period as "Mbube," combines two distinct styles that are still heard today in isicathamiya. The first is a richly-harmonized, homophonic style that recites the text freely and shows no clear or consistent sense of meter—*choral declamation,* we can call it. We hear two phrases of choral declamation, each stated and repeated in the pattern **a a b b a a**. Notable here, and frequent in isicathamiya, is the slide in all voices from high to lower pitches.

Then, after about a minute, the music takes on a clear meter. This is the second style common in isicatha-miya. It is still organized in repeating phrases, but now the texture departs from the simple homophony of the recitational opening section. It uses call-and-response techniques (see page 388), pitting Linda against the rest of the group at first; later the basses in the chorus sing against the group as a whole. The call-and-response phrases alternate with a falling cadential phrase sung by the whole chorus.

LISTEN	
"Anoku Gonda"	39

0:00	Unmetered choral declamation
0:00	a
0:13	a
0:25	b
0:30	b
0:35	a
0:47	a
0:57	Metrical call and response: Solomon Linda against the full chorus
1:26	Metrical call and response: Basses against the full chorus

6 Conclusion

Just a few words in conclusion: not so much as a conclusion to this chapter, but rather to our total effort in this book as a whole.

We might recall what was said at the end of the introductory unit, on page 51. Our basic goal has been to learn how to listen better, in order to understand and appreciate music—music of the European art tradition, mostly, but also other musics, other musical traditions. Some musical terminology has been introduced that should help clarify listening, and a somewhat rapid trip has been conducted through the history of Western music from Hildegard of Bingen to Kaija Saariaho, by way of Bach, Mozart, Beethoven, Wagner, Stravinsky, and Ellington. There have been side trips beyond Europe, gaining us perspectives on music around the globe. The most important thing we've done, by far, is *listen*: listen with some care to numerous individual pieces of music. Not all, but many of them are famous works that listeners have found rewarding over a period, in most cases, of many generations.

Rewarding is a pale, neutral term that will cover beautiful, fascinating, profound, exciting, comforting, and any other adjective that may correspond to something deep in your personal experience. Feelings of this kind about music tend to last a long time. If you have come to appreciate and love some of the music this book has introduced you to, it may be forever. Consider yourself ahead.

[Music] takes us out of the actual and whispers to us dim secrets that startle our wonder as to who we are, and for what, whence and whereto.

Ralph Waldo Emerson, 1838

Appendix
Further Listening, Suggested Readings, and Recommended Web Sites

This appendix directs you to music that the authors of Listen *believe is especially attractive for further listening, and to books and Web sites that will give you further information about that music. It's probably unnecessary to note that this is a personal list, and that other musicians would undoubtedly come up with different entries.*

Further Listening

Symphonies, operas, and other "standard" items, recorded by many different artists, will be available at any college record library or can be purchased. For help in choosing among the various recordings, most record stores have the latest copies of the *Penguin Guide to Classical CDs* or the *Gramophone Classical Good CD Guide* on hand for customers to consult. Buy budget labels—Naxos is a good one—when available.

With more specialized music, however, including early music and non-Western music, particular recommended items may not be so easy to find.

The booklets included with CDs vary greatly in quality, but they will almost always be of some value as listening supplements. With vocal music, always follow along with the (translated) texts.

Early Music

Medieval The group that sings the plainchant "Vere dignum" on CD 1, Ensemble Organum, directed by Marcel Pérès, has issued many fascinating discs combining Gregorian chant and various kinds of organum. (Ask the clerk in the record store.) Other excellent groups for medieval music are Anonymous Four and Gothic Voices. The latter have issued several discs of music by Hildegard of Bingen.

Renaissance Look for CDs of Masses by Renaissance composers that are recorded along with the plainchants sung in the actual Mass service. One such is *Palestrina: Missa Viri Galilaei*, recorded by Philippe Herreweghe (Harmonia Mundi); there are also a number of such recordings of the beautiful Masses of William Byrd. English groups often record miscellaneous collections of music from Elizabethan times, bringing together favorite madrigals, songs, and instrumental music.

Early Baroque There are numerous recordings of Monteverdi's madrigals—very impressive works, but it is especially important to follow along closely with the words. Look in particular for the "Lament of the Nymph." If you want to explore another Monteverdi opera, listen to his *Orfeo* (Orpheus); the recording of John Eliot Gardiner is first-rate. Listen to the whole of Purcell's *Dido and Aeneas*, which is about fifty-five minutes long.

Global Perspectives

In this area, you need to beware of commercialized recordings that can be very far from the actual music itself. The place to start is with the recordings from which the *Listen* selections have been taken. They are worth a search in your college music library. Here they are, along with a few additional suggestions:

GP 1: *The Music of Islam*, vol. 10 (Celestial Harmonies 13150-2); *Hawaiian Drum Dance Chants: Sounds of Power in Time* (Smithsonian Folkways 40015); *Navajo Songs from Canyon de Chelly* (New World 804062)

GP 2: *Spain in the New World* (Koch 3-7451 2 H1); also, for music of seventeenth-century Mexico, listen to *Missa Mexicana* by The Harp Consort (Harmonia Mundi 907293).

GP 3: *Sudan: Music of the Blue Nile Province* (Auvidis D8073); *Mbuti Pygmies of the Ituri Rainforest* (Smithsonian Folkways 40401); for more pygmy polyphony, *Africa: The Ba-Benzélé Pygmies* (Rounder 5107)

GP 4: *Gagaku: The Imperial Court Music of Japan* (Lyrichord 7126); *Music of Bali: Gamelan Semar Pegulingan* (Lyrichord 7408); *Anthology of Indian Classical Music* (Auvidis D8270). For more gamelan music, try *Yogyakarta: Gamelan of the Kraton*

(Celestial Harmonies 7869); for more gagaku, *Gagaku: Court Music of Japan* (JVC 5354-2).

GP 5: Our kabuki performance is not available on CD; listen instead to *Japan: Kabuki and Other Traditional Music* (Nonesuch 9 72084-2); for our Beijing opera excerpt, *China: The Peking Opera* (Playasound 65197).

GP 6: *Yoruba Drums from Benin, West Africa* (Smithsonian Folkways 40440); for a different, wonderful African tradition, *Zimbabwe: The Soul of Mbira* (Nonesuch 9 72054-2).

GP 7: *Mbube Roots: Zulu Choral Music from South Africa, 1930s–1960s* (Rounder 5025); many recordings of Ladysmith Black Mambazo are also available.

Finally, two fascinating samplers of music from around the world: *Voices of Forgotten Worlds* (Ellipsis Arts 3252) and *The Secret Museum of Mankind: Ethnic Music Classics, 1925–1948* (Yazoo 7004-6, 7010, 7014)

Jazz

The famous, truly classic jazz anthology, available in every library, is the *Smithsonian Collection of Classic Jazz*. Its five CDs present expertly chosen numbers by Armstrong, Ellington, Parker, Davis, and many other jazz greats. A fine two-CD anthology is *Visions of Jazz*, selected by leading jazz critic Gary Giddens (Capitol). Many Ellington collections are available; any one will be an ear-opener.

Listen to these other artists, not featured in this book: Count Basie, Bix Beiderbecke, Ornette Coleman, John Coltrane, Ella Fitzgerald, Dizzy Gillespie, Billie Holliday, Wynton Marsalis, Thelonious Monk, Art Tatum, Lester Young, and blues singers Robert Johnson and Bessie Smith.

Major European Composers

The main works of the major composers are listed in the *Listen* biography boxes. Needless to say, we recommend them all, especially those marked in the boxes for "Encores." Here are further recommendations for selected composers:

Bach: If you like Bach, you must get to know all six *Brandenburg* Concertos (we recommend the recording by Jordi Savall).

Berg: There is a very good video of *Wozzeck* available (Kultur).

Berlioz: Listen to the whole hour-long *Fantastic* Symphony, watching page 266 for transformations of the *idée fixe*.

Brahms: Work your way into the symphonies by first hearing the shorter movements: the second movement in Symphony Nos. 1 and 2 and the third movement in Nos. 3 and 4.

Copland: The video of *Appalachian Spring* (DVD, Kultur), which presents Martha Graham's choreography, brings a whole new dimension to Copland's music.

Handel: Many selections from Handel operas are available. You can choose almost at random (we recommend recordings by Nicholas McGegan).

Mendelssohn: Listen to the *Midsummer Night's Dream* music; *Hebrides* Overture; *Italian* Symphony.

Mozart: After the Symphony in G Minor, you might go to the two very different masterpieces written with it in 1788: No. 39 in E-flat and No. 41 (*Jupiter*). View the *Don Giovanni* DVD from La Scala Opera House in Milan (Image).

Puccini: The Metropolitan Opera DVD of *La Bohème* is the perfect introduction to Puccini—indeed, to opera altogether (Pioneer).

Strauss: Listen to his symphonic poems *Don Juan* and *Till Eulenspiegel's Merry Pranks* and to his Four Last Songs.

Verdi: Watch the Metropolitan Opera DVD of *Aida*, starring Placido Domingo (DGG).

Vivaldi: A must-hear recording of *The Four Seasons* is by Fabio Biondi and L'Europa Galante (Opus 111).

Suggested Readings

The New Grove Dictionary of Music and Musicians (2nd edition, 23 volumes) is a superb reference tool, though probably more detailed than most readers will require. There are also specialized *Grove* dictionaries, in two to four volumes, devoted to American music, jazz, opera, and musical instruments. For world music, the standard reference is the illustrated *Garland Encyclopedia of World Music* (10 volumes). The standard single-volume reference works are *The Harvard Dictionary of Music* for all material except biographies, and *Baker's Biographical Dictionary of Musicians* for biographies.

Outstanding program notes by Michael Steinberg on the classical masterpieces are assembled in two books, covering symphonies and concertos. For operas, consult the two-volume *International Dictionary of Opera*. Single-volume collections of notes covering orchestral repertory are Jonathan D. Kramer, *Listen to the Music*, and D. Kern Holoman, *Evenings with the Orchestra* (Holoman has also authored a useful guide, *Writing about Music*).

Strange as it may seem, there is no good one-volume history of Western music available—none, at least, of a reasonable length (*The Concise Oxford History of Music* by Gerald Abraham runs to 968 pages). A detailed but very interesting series, *Music and Society* (8 volumes), investigates the relationship of music to society in various locations and historical periods. A book that concentrates on musical style is *A History of Musical Style* by Richard Crocker. An excellent anthology of historical readings, *Music in the Western World*, has been assembled by Piero Weiss and Richard Taruskin. Highly regarded texts on world music are Bruno Nettl, *Excursions in World Music*, and Jeff Titon, *Worlds of Music*.

For works on composers, there is quite a jump from the three or four densely packed pages in *Baker* to the thirty or forty equally packed pages in *Grove*. Check "Musical Lives" under serials on your computerized library catalogue for biographies that are concise and up-to-date. There are beautifully illustrated biographies by Christopher Hogwood on Handel and H. C. Robbins Landon on Beethoven and Mozart.

You might prefer to consult "documentary biographies," which reprint letters, notices, and all sorts of other contemporary documentation of the lives of early composers. Nobody reads these books from cover to cover, but they are fascinating to browse in: *The Bach Reader*, *The Schubert Reader*, *Mozart: A Documentary Biography*. *The Diary of Cosima Wagner* also makes for an astonishing browse.

Finally, a scattering of favorites with *Listen*'s authors: Hector Berlioz, *Memoirs*; Robert Craft, *Conversations with Igor Stravinsky*; Thomas Kelly, *First Nights*; Greil Marcus, *Mystery Train* (rock'n'roll); Susan McClary, *Conventional Wisdom*; Leonard Meyer, *Emotion and Meaning in Music* (musical aesthetics); Richard Powers, *The Time of Our Singing* (a novel set in the Civil Rights era); Paul Robinson, *Opera and Ideas*; John Rockwell, *All-American Music*; George Bernard Shaw, *The Perfect Wagnerite*;

Tim Taylor, *Global Pop*; Donald Francis Tovey, *Essays in Musical Analysis* (a program note collection, old but good).

Recommended Web Sites

The following sites will provide the start of an excellent Web library of reference materials relating to genres and composers we have discussed in *Listen*. Many more reference materials and additional Web site links can be found on the *Listen* Web site at <bedfordstmartins.com/listen>.

General Reference Web Sites for Classical and Popular Music

The Classical Music Pages
http://w3.rz-berlin.mpg.de/cmp/classmus.html
Designed by an orchestra conductor and Web wizard as a resource for "everyone from 'beginners' to the musical professional," this well-organized site provides information extracted from the *Grove Concise Dictionary of Music* on a wide variety of topics including musical periods, genres, composers, and basic theory. It also features excellent articles on select topics and a concise "History of Music" by musicologist James Zychowicz.

Women Composers
http://www.kapralova.org/DATABASE.htm
This database provides links to information on numerous women composers of various styles and genres. (The Kapralova Society)

Women in Music: Historical Women Composers
http://music.acu.edu/www/iawm/historical/historical.html
Part of the International Alliance for Women in Music web ring, this site provides links to online materials about individual women composers, special articles, historical surveys, collections, and databases. (IAWM)

Carolina Classical Connection: An Index of Classical Music Web Sites
http://classicalmus.hispeed.com/links.html
A substantial collection of links to information on composers, historical periods, instruments, genres, opera, and much more. (Charles K. Moss)

Ethnomusicology Resources on the Web
http://echarry.web.wesleyan.edu/ethno.html
Substantial database of links, the main categories cover African music and drumming, Indonesian music, Caribbean and Latin American music, South Asian music, music of Australia and Oceania, East Asian music, West Asian music, European music, and American music. (Eric Charry)

All-Music Guide
http://www.allmediaguide.com/
Enormous collection of information covering popular musical styles and artists. Features include "music maps" that trace the development of musical styles, articles, biographies, a glossary, and record reviews; also includes an "All-Classical" guide. (AEC One Stop Group, Inc.)

OperaGlass
http://opera.stanford.edu/main.html
Enormous "opera information server" with pages on opera libretti, source texts, performance histories, synopses, discographies, composers, librettists, companies, people, and more.

Unit I Web Sites

Solomon's Glossary of Technical Musical Terms
http://music.theory.home.att.net/glossary.htm
Supplementary glossary of terms. (Larry J. Solomon)

Teoría: Online Music Theory Reference
http://www.teoria.com/reference/index.htm
Basic guide to scales, intervals, and chords with audio examples. (José Rodriguez Alvira)

Unit II Web Sites

Medieval and Renaissance Music: Early Music Resources on the Web
http://www.angelfire.com/mi/spanogle/emusic.html
Directory of Internet resources. (Sharon Spanogle)

Selected Early Music Links
http://www.vanderbilt.edu/htdocs/Blair/Courses/MUSL242/earlymus.htm
Link directory. (Dr. Cynthia Cyrus, Blair School of Music, Vanderbilt University)

Welcome to the Wonderful World of Baroque Music
http://www.baroquemusic.org/
Educational page with "over two hours" of audio files, a portrait gallery, information on specific composers, and much more. (Michael Sartorius)

Chapter 5

Hildegard von Bingen: Symphony of the Harmony of Heaven
http://historymedren.about.com/gi/dynamic/offsite.htm?site=http://www.uni%2Dmainz.de/%7Ehorst/hildegard/music/music.html
Information on Hildegard of Bingen's music, including definitions of musical terms and genres, and a select discography. An icon of Hildegard hyperlinks you to the Hildegard.org page with historical and modern images of the town of Bingen on the Rhine. (Nancy Fiero)

International Machaut Society: Machaut on the Web
http://www.vanderbilt.edu/~cyrus/machaut/imslinks.htm
This helpful directory of links provides access to a variety of Machaut-related pages, including sound clips.

Troubadours, Trouvères and Minnesingers
http://www.hoasm.org/IIA/IIATroubadours.html
Overview with information on numerous songwriters of these traditions. (Chris Whent)

Chapter 6

Giovanni Pierluigi da Palestrina
http://www.npr.org/programs/specials/milestones/motm.palestrina.html
Installment of NPR's *Milestones of the Millennium* lecture series focusing on the composer, featuring Professor Tom Kelly. (National Public Radio, Washington, D.C.)

Nymphes des bois: Introduction to the music of Josquin Desprez
http://perso.wanadoo.fr/josquin.desprez/Ecouter_e.htm
MIDI transcriptions of several compositions. (Arnaud Saint-Antonin)

Chapter 7

Claudio Monteverdi

http://www.npr.org/programs/specials/milestones/990519.motm
.monteverdi.html

Installment of NPR's *Milestones of the Millennium* lecture series focusing on the composer, featuring Jan Swafford. (National Public Radio, Washington, D.C.)

Purcell Page

http://www.geocities.com/Vienna/Strasse/9570/purcell/index
.html

Documents and letter, lyrics to select pieces, list of works taken from the Zimmermann catalogue, a chronology of the events in the life of Purcell and in contemporary England, and images. (Alexandre H. Hohmann)

Unit III Web Sites

Eighteenth-Century Resources: Music

http://newark.rutgers.edu/~jlynch/18th/music.html

This directory of links to online resources specifically on music is part of a larger index of links on eighteenth-century topics. (Jack Lynch, Department of English, Rutgers University)

See also under Unit II, **Welcome to the Wonderful World of Baroque Music.**

Chapters 9 and 10

J. S. Bach Home Page

http://www.jsbach.org/

Rich compendium of information on Bach's life and works. Biographical essay, index of works, picture gallery, bibliography, recording recommendations and reviews, plus a large annotated directory of Bach links. (Jan Hanford/Jan Kloster)

GFHandel.org

http://www.gfhandel.org

Handy, well-maintained compilation of Handel resources, including detailed time lines, a list of works, anecdotes, a compositional catalog, interviews, an essay on and libretto for *Messiah,* a potpourri of images taken from trading cards, medallions, portraits and other interesting historical sources, recording and release information, news about concerts, festivals, radio/TV events, conferences and workshops, a list of musicological resources (bibliographies, current research), and directory links. (Additional content owner/manager: Brad Leissa/David Vickers)

Antonio Vivaldi Homepage

http://www.antonio-vivaldi.org/

Biography and time line, directory of links, song texts, recording recommendations, and reviews.

Chapters 12 and 13

Franz Joseph Haydn

http://home.wxs.nl/~cmr/haydn/

Features of this site include a biography that may be browsed by period or keyword, a select discography, a catalog of works, a links page, and a list of recommended books.

The Mozart Project

http://www.mozartproject.org

This top-notch reference site contains an in-depth biography of Wolfgang Amadeus Mozart's early years (to 1765) and annotated timelines for the rest of his life; brief biographical overviews of Mozart's father, mother, and sister; a Mozart-Weber family tree; Köchel listings of all Mozart's compositions (arranged by date and by genre category); selected essays by Mozart scholars, and more. (Steve Boerner)

Unit IV Web Sites

Nineteenth-Century Music: The Romantic Era

http://www.emory.edu/MUSIC/ARNOLD/HOMEPAGE.HTM

A variety of materials and information on Romanticism and Romantic composers, including chronologies of the eighteenth and nineteenth centuries. (Ben Arnold)

Chapter 14

Ludwig van Beethoven: The Magnificent Master

http://raptusassociation.org/index.html

Impressive collection of resources on Beethoven and related topics. Offers a detailed biography, index of works, essays, and reviews. The numerous "creation histories" of specific pieces are very well done, using citations from musicologists, critics, and performers. There is also a section on "Musicians on music and Beethoven" and "Beethoven and other great minds." (Additional content owner/manager: Ingrid Schwaegermann/Raptus Association for Music Appreciation)

Chapter 15

Romantic Links, Electronic Texts and Home Pages

http://www.english.upenn.edu/~mgamer/Romantic/

Categorized index of links to resources on Romanticism and related topics. (Dr. Michael Gamer, Department of English, University of Pennsylvania)

Chapter 16

The Magic of Berlioz

http://www.ozemail.com.au/~phillijr/Berlioz.html

Informative and enthusiastic introduction to Berlioz that provides detailed biographical information, essays on topics such as "Berlioz and Wagner," and a directory of related links. (Phillip Rutherford)

The Official Chopin Homepage

http://www.chopin.pl/spis_tresci/index_en.html

Compiled by the Frederick Chopin Society in Warsaw, the original version of this site is in Polish, but the Society has conveniently provided an excellent version in English. There are biographical essays, a time line of major life events and works, overview essays on Chopin's compositional output and the stylistic change in his music, an alphabetical works list, information on relevant organizations and competitions, and an essay on the "Chopin tradition." Numerous pages are in the process of being added to this ambitious project, so viewers should check back often. (Frederick Chopin Society in Warsaw)

Franz Liszt: 1811–1886

http://www.emory.edu/MUSIC/ARNOLD/liszt_content.html

This page provides general information on the composer's life and the characteristics of his music. Also contains several images, including photos of Liszt's tomb. (Ben Arnold)

Clara Wieck Schumann
http://www.geneva.edu/~dksmith/clara/schumann.html
Created in celebration of the hundredth anniversary of Clara Schumann's death, this site continues to offer up-to-date information and resources. Includes an "exhaustive" discography, a list of works, an image gallery, lyric translations of all of Clara Schumann's lieder, a list of films on her life, program notes, release notices and reviews, select bibliographies, and a directory of links.

Robert Schumann: Then, Now, and Always
http://www.geocities.com/Athens/Rhodes/9533/
Chronology of Robert Schumann's life, a list of works, trivia and quotations, book recommendations, and an article by Roland Barthes called "Loving Schumann."

The Schubert Institute-UK
http://myweb.tiscali.co.uk/franzschubert/intro/index.html
This site brings together knowledgeable biographical information (timelines, a biography from 1886, quotations, information on Schubert friends, the Schubert family tree), work lists, assorted articles, and a bibliography.

Chapter 17

Verdiana! Giuseppe Verdi
http://www.r-ds.com/verdiana.htm
Superb collection of materials on this opera composer, including a biographical time line with links to other relevant pages on the site, annotated work lists, information on the making of select operas, images, a bibliography, an overview of Verdi's librettists, and a tribute to Verdi's wife, soprano Giuseppina Strepponi, "the great woman behind the great man." (Anne Lawson)

Richard Wagner Web Site
http://home.no.net/wagner/
An eclectic site that includes such features as a "comparative chronology" (with Wagner events listed alongside other important contemporary happenings), an introduction to the Wagnerian technique of *leitmotifs* (with sound samples), an interactive map, Wagner quotes, and an essay on "The *Star Wars* series and Wagner's *Ring*." (Kristian Evensen)

Chapter 18

Gustav Mahler: 1860–1911
http://www.netaxs.com/~jgreshes/mahler/
This site claims nearly three hundred pages of materials on Mahler and his works, including a full-length illustrated biography. Also contains articles, a time line, a list of works, CD release information and reviews, and a budget guide to recordings. (Jason Greshes)

The Composers of Bohemia
http://members.aol.com/abelard2/bohemia.htm
Short essay on the musical achievements of Bedřich Smetana, Antonín Dvořák, and Leos Janáček. (The Davidsbündler)

Johannes Brahms WebSource
http://www.johannesbrahms.org/
Directory of links to online biographies, works lists, festivals and special events, societies, a museum, scholars, an excellent image gallery, and other resources. (Mary I. Ingraham)

Unit V Web Sites

Twentieth century music
http://bubl.ac.uk/link/t/twentiethcenturymusic.htm
Catalogue of Internet resources on a variety of twentieth-century music subjects. (BUBL Information Service)

Chapter 19

Dr. Christopher Witcombe: Modernism
http://witcombe.sbc.edu/modernism/
Extensive essay with graphics covering modernist art, modernism and politics, and modernism and post-modernism. (Department of Art History, Sweet Briar College)

Modernism
http://www.artsmia.org/modernism/
Photo gallery and commentary on many of the main modernist arts movements, such as British and American Arts and Crafts, European and American Art Nouveau, Bauhaus, and European and American Art Deco. (The Minneapolis Institute of Arts)

Chapter 20

Claude Debussy and Impressionism
http://classicalmus.hispeed.com/articles/debussy.html
Intelligent, multimedia overview of Debussy's life and musical style, with real-audio files and images. (Charles K. Moss)

Alban Berg: Resources for All
http://www.geocities.com/al6an6erg/albanberg.html
This impressive fan page and home of the "Strictly Borderless Alban Berg Society" offers biographical information, notes on select pieces, and a forum for discussion. (Erik "Richard" Andersen)

The Charles Ives Society
http://www.charlesives.org/
This well-organized, first-rate resource contains a brief, scholarly biography, a catalogue of Ives's published music, a photo gallery, a performance calendar, and a link to Yale University's descriptive catalogue of the works.

Arnold Schoenberg Center
http://www.schoenberg.at/default_e.htm
The English-language version of the Center's excellent site offers a detailed timeline of Schoenberg's life, thematic and chronological catalogues of his works, readable photographs of many of Schoenberg's writings, a bibliography and discography, information on the composer as a teacher, release information, and a categorized directory of links. Also contains an essay by Hermann Danuser entitled "Arnold Schoenberg: Portrait of a Century," a substantial photo album, and a fascinating virtual gallery of Schoenberg's own paintings and drawings. (Arnold Schoenberg Center)

Second Viennese School
http://astro.ocis.temple.edu/~kreinber/PowerPoint_Lectures/second_viennese_files/frame.htm
Slide-show overview of the musical school identified with Arnold Schoenberg and his students, Alban Berg and Anton

Webern. (Dr. Steven Kreinberg, Esther Boyer College of Music, Temple University)

Chapter 21

Copland House
http://www.coplandhouse.org/
The homepage of the Copland House, which has become "a focal point for the continuation and enhancement of his life-long advocacy of American music," this site offers information on the composer's life and works and a bibliography. (Copland House)

Chapter 22

The Official George Crumb Home Page
http://www.georgecrumb.net/
This introduction to the composer of *Black Angels* provides a thumbnail biography, an index of works with detailed information on each piece, an extensive bibliography including lectures, Web sites, dissertations, and a discography. The site also contains a fascinating essay by Crumb himself, "Music: Does It Have a Future?" (Robert Starobin)

Edgard Varèse: Father of Electronic Music
http://csunix1.lvc.edu/~snyder/em/varese.html
Essay on Varèse's influence in the area of electronic music with images and recommended listening. (Jeff Snyder)

John Cage Online
http://home.flash.net/~jronsen/cagelinks.html#interviews
Directory of links to articles, interviews, writings, paintings and visual art by Cage, sound files, discographies and filmographies, lists of works, photos, online videos, and other resources. (Josh Ronsen)

Kaija Saariaho
http://www.saariaho.org/
Biographical information, indexes of works, a discography, and a directory of links to other related sites.

Steve Reich
http://www.stevereich.com/
The official site for this innovative composer offers a biography, news, discography, a few multimedia resources, articles and interviews, a schedule of concerts, and information on new pieces.

Chapter 23

The BigBands Database Plus
http://www.nfo.net
Archive of overviews and essays on jazz and big bands in America, Canada, Britain, and Europe. Offers concise histories of jazz, Dixieland, and swing, a glossary of terms, an explanation of the etymology of *jazz*, and an index of links. (Murray Pfeffer)

What is Jazz?
http://www.town.hall.org/Archives/radio/Kennedy/Taylor/
This site contains audio files of four extensive lectures on jazz delivered by noted jazz pianist, historian, and educator Dr. Billy Taylor for the ArtsEdge program at the John F. Kennedy Center for the Performing Arts. Also offers information in the form of commentary or an audio extract from the lectures related to particular jazz artists, styles, and geographical areas. (The Internet Multicasting Service)

Louis "Satchmo" Armstrong
http://www.redhotjazz.com/louie.html
Part of the Red Hot Jazz Archive—devoted to jazz history before 1930—this page combines biographical information and real-audio samples for an extensive multimedia introduction to Armstrong. Also includes discographies for Armstrong and the many ensembles with which he played. (Scott Alexander)

Bernstein's Studio
http://www.leonardbernstein.com/
This charmingly designed site offers an intimate glimpse into Leonard Bernstein's creative world through a rich compilation of commentary, letters, audio and video files, photographs, interviews, articles, original scripts, working notes, news items, and reviews. (Leonard Bernstein.com, Inc./Primate, LLC)

The Official Miles Davis Web Site
http://www.milesdavis.com/
An excellent resource on this "trumpeter, composer, bandleader, and artist," the site provides a biography, audio and video files, a discography, images of Davis's original artworks, and related links. (Miles Davis Properties, LLC and The Estate of Miles Davis)

The Duke Ellington Society
http://museum.media.org/duke/
Dedicated to promoting appreciation of Ellington's musical creations, the homepage of this association offers an entertaining and informative collection of essays and commentary. The "Sing a Song" section also features real-audio samples of famous vocal interpreters of Ellington's art. Also features a tribute to Billy Strayhorn, Ellington's long-time collaborator and friend. (Media.org)

George and Ira Gershwin: The Official Web Site
http://www.gershwin.com/
A snazzy multimedia presentation on these brothers and creative partners, combining an historical overview and time lines, information on select films and shows featuring Gershwin music and/or lyrics, concert schedules, news items, and recommendations for further reading and listening. The real hit of this site, however, is the "jukebox" with audio clips featuring outstanding Gershwin interpreters. (Gershwin Enterprises)

Scott Joplin International Ragtime Foundation, Inc.
http://www.scottjoplin.org/
Contains an excellent biographical essay by Joplin scholar Edward A. Berlin, an online ragtime catalog, and a directory of related links.

Charlie "Yardbird" Parker: Jazz Original
http://www.cmgww.com/music/parker/
Full-service official site of this celebrated saxophonist with many multimedia features. (Estate of Charlie Parker/CMG Worldwide)

Classic Motown
http://www.motown.com/classicmotown/
Engaging multimedia tour of the history of Motown Records. Visitors navigate the timeline to the diverse resources (biography, discography, audio-video gallery, and news) on famous Motown artists from the 1960s to the 1980s. This attractive site also has a "jukebox" full of audio clips, which you can search by artist or year.

The Red Hot Jazz Archive
http://www.redhotjazz.com/
This top-notch site offers a wealth of information on jazz music and artists before 1930. Includes numerous audio files and images. (Scott Alexander)

Elvis Presley: Elvis.com
http://www.elvis.com/
The official site of "The King" presents biographical information, a list of gold and platinum records, billboard chart statistics, a filmography (including TV appearances), Elvis quotes, related writings, links to family and friends, and fan goodies. (EPE, Inc.)

The Beatles
http://www.thebeatles.com/
The deceptively simple layout of this site hides a wealth of rare audio and video clips, photos, and other resources on some of the Beatles's most popular songs. (Beatles.com)

Global Perspectives

Global Perspectives 1

Islamic Art, Music, and Architecture around the World
http://www.uga.edu/islam/IsArt.html
The music section of this site connects to a broad array of materials, including scholarly articles, multimedia presentations with audio/video files, and descriptive commentary. The homepage offers information on other Islamic topics and issues. (Dr. Alan Godlas, University of Georgia, Islamic Studies)

The Hawaiian Home Page
http://www.geocities.com/~olelo/home.html
An extraordinary resource on Hawai'ian culture, this site has an impressive directory of links on Hawai'ian music, including artists, history, lyrics, mp3 clips, and Hawai'ian radio stations, many with live stream via the Internet.

Gathering of Nations Web Site
http://www.gatheringofnations.com/
The home site of this organization, which promotes Native American culture and tradition. Features include "all-Native-music" internet radio, audio clips from powwows and other events, photographs and pictures, and artwork.

Navajo Sites
http://unr.edu/homepage/daved/natlinks.html
Directory of links to Navajo and Native American resources. (Dave DuBois)

Global Perspectives 2

Mission Music
http://www.californiamissions.com/music/index.html
Part of an extensive "California Missions" Web tour, this section contains an essay by musicologist William Summers on the history of mission music and real-audio files of music primarily from the Renaissance period that blends European and indigenous traditions.

What is Andean Music?
http://otto.cmr.fsu.edu/~cma/andes.htm
This site features an essay by CMA director and ethnomusicologist Dale A. Olsen on the music and common instruments of the central Andes and includes photographs. (Center for Music in the Americas, Florida State University)

Aztec Music
http://history.smsu.edu/jchuchiak/HST%20350—Theme%203—Aztec_music.htm
Small collection of images of Aztec instruments and sound clips.

(Dr. John F. Chuchiak IV, Department of History, Southwest Missouri State University)

Global Perspectives 3

African Music
http://www.africana.com/Articles/tt_422.htm
Article presenting the history of African music, common characteristics and regional styles, African music in society, popular music, and influence of African music on music from other parts of the world.

The Mbuti of Zaire
http://www.ucc.uconn.edu/~epsadm03/mbuti.html
This brief essay on the pygmy population of the Ituri Forest in northern Zaire addresses the influence of the physical environment on their way of life, describes the traditional Molimo ritual, and discusses the effects of historical events (colonialism, war) on the Mbuti people. (Cathy Suroviak)

Pygmies of the Congo
http://www.cwu.edu/~yaegerl/pygmypage.htm
Brief essay on the pygmy population of Central Africa with a bibliography. (Lewis Yaeger)

Global Perspectives 4

Some Thoughts on the Origins of Gagaku
http://aris.ss.uci.edu/rgarfias/gagaku/gagaku.html
Created by ethnomusicologist Robert Garfias, this site offers an engaging introduction to gagaku and related topics with concise essays, colorful images, and real-audio samples.

Indonesian Music: Gamelan
http://indonesia.elga.net.id/music.html#GAMELAN
Directory of links to online information on the gamelan. (Budi Rahardjo)

Sify Carnatic Music
http://www.carnaticmusic.com/main.asp
The first Web resource to visit for in-depth information on Carnatic music, including its history, instruments, and raga and tala types. Also provides an impressive audio gallery. (Sify.com)

Fundamentals of Rag
http://www.chandrakantha.com/articles/indian_music/raga.html
This specialist-authored site offers an excellent introduction to raga, with a glossary of terms, images of instruments, audio files, and a list of recommended books and CDs. (David and Chandrakantha Courtney)

Global Perspectives 5

Kabuki for Everyone
http://www.fix.co.jp/kabuki/kabuki.html
This attractive, multimedia introduction to kabuki theater features essays on kabuki history, an online video theater, sound samples, information on and images of kabuki makeup, and links to related sites. (Matthew Johnson)

Kabuki Page
http://www.aichi-gakuin.ac.jp/~jeffreyb/kabuki.html
With sample stories of kabuki productions at the Misonoza in Nagoya, Japan, this site also provides a time line of four hundred years of kabuki theater, historic images, and links to other resources. (Jeff Blair)

The Development of Beijing Opera during
the Cultural Revolution
http://home.earthlink.net/~athenart/opera/bodevelop.html
This noteworthy site contains an extensive essay on the development of Beijing opera during the Cultural Revolution, an impressive gallery of images of performers and instruments, and a small directory of links to resources on China and Chinese music. (Wendy A. Levine)

Global Perspectives 6

C.K. Ladzekpo: African Music and Drumming
http://www.cnmat.berkeley.edu/~ladzekpo/
An attractive collection of graphics, audio files, and video clips on African drums and drumming and African ethnic groups, particularly Ewe culture. (University of California, Berkeley, Music Department)

Yoruba Bata in Nigeria
http://www.batadrums.com/background/yoruba.htm
Handy assortment of resources on Yoruba culture and the bata drumming of Nigeria and Benin, including field-recording audio files. (BataDrums.Com)

Global Perspectives 7

African Voices: Traditional Culture
http://www.africanvoices.co.za/culture/culture
.htm#Isicathamiya
Information on the Xhosa and Zulu people and isicathamiya.

Glossary of Musical Terms

The italicized words refer to other definitions in the glossary, which you can look up if necessary. The page numbers refer to fuller explanations in the text.

A cappella (ah kah-pél-la): Choral music for voices alone, without instruments *(79)*

Accelerando (a-chel-er-áhn-do): Getting faster *(14)*

Accent: The stressing of a note—for example, by playing it somewhat louder than the surrounding notes *(11)*

Accidentals: In musical notation, signs indicating that a note is to be played *sharp, flat,* or *natural*

Accompanied recitative: See *recitative (152)*

Adagio: Slow tempo *(14)*

Alap: In Indian music, a slow movement without meter that introduces the performance of a *rag (219)*

Alba: *Troubadour* song about a knight leaving his lady at dawn *(62)*

Allegro; allegretto: Fast; moderately fast *(14)*

Allemande: A Baroque dance in moderate *duple meter (143)*

Alto, contralto: The low female voice

Andante: A fairly slow tempo, but not too slow *(14)*

Andantino: A little faster than *andante (14)*

Antiphon: A genre of plainchant usually showing a simple melodic style with very few melismas *(60)*

Aria: A vocal number for solo singer and orchestra, generally in an opera, cantata, or oratorio *(99, 152)*

Arioso: A singing style between *recitative* and *aria (100)*

Ars antiqua, ars nova: Contemporary terms for the "old technique" of 13th-century *organum* and the new *polyphonic* music of the 14th century *(67)*

A tempo: At the original tempo *(14)*

Atonality: The absence of any feeling of *tonality (327)*

Avant-garde: In the most advanced style *(314)*

Azan: An Islamic call to worship, issued five times daily by a muezzin *(71)*

Bar: Same as *measure (11)*

Baritone: A type of adult male voice similar to the *bass,* but a little higher

Bar line: In musical notation, a vertical line through the staffs to mark the measure *(11)*

Bass (not spelled "BASE"): (1) The low adult male voice; (2) the lowest vocal or instrumental line in a piece of music

Basso continuo: See *continuo (96)*

Basso ostinato: An *ostinato* in the bass *(96, 132)*

Beam: In musical notation, the heavy stroke connecting eighth notes (two beams connect sixteenth notes, etc.) *(20)*

Beat: The regular pulse underlying most music; the lowest unit of *meter (10)*

Beat syncopation: In jazz, the fractional shifting of accents away from the beats *(390)*

Bebop: A jazz style of the 1940s *(400)*

Bel canto: A style of singing that brings out the sensuous beauty of the voice *(272)*

Bel canto opera: Term for early Romantic opera, which featured *bel canto* singing *(272)*

Big bands: The big jazz bands (10 to 20 players) of the 1930s and 1940s *(394)*

Binary form: A musical form having two different sections; **AB** form *(144)*

Biwa: A Japanese four-stringed lute; heard in *gagaku (213)*

Blue note: A note deliberately sung or played slightly off pitch, as in the *blues (19)*

Blues: A type of African American *vernacular music,* used in jazz, rhythm and blues, rock, and other styles of popular music *(390)*

Bourrée: A Baroque dance in fast *duple meter (143)*

Break: In jazz, a brief solo improvisation between song phrases *(390)*

Bridge: In *sonata form,* the section of music that comes between the first theme and the second group and makes the *modulation;* also called "transition" *(180)*

Bunraku (bóon-ráh-koo): Japanese tradition of puppet theater *(308)*

Cadence: The notes or chords (or the whole short passage) ending a section of music with a feeling of conclusiveness. The term *cadence* can be applied to phrases, sections of works, or complete works or movements *(25)*.

Cadence theme: In *sonata form*, the final conclusive theme in the *exposition (180)*

Cadenza: An improvised passage for the soloist in a concerto, or sometimes in other works. Concerto cadenzas usually come near the ends of movements *(137, 201)*.

Cakewalk: Around 1900, a dance of African American origin associated with *ragtime (327, 350)*

Call and response: In African and early African American music, a style in which a phrase by a leading singer or soloist is answered by a larger group or chorus, and the process is repeated again and again *(388)*

Canon: Strict *imitative polyphony*, with the same melody appearing in each voice, at staggered intervals

Cantata: A composition in several movements for solo voice(s), instruments, and perhaps also chorus. Depending on the text, cantatas are categorized as secular or *church cantatas (159)*.

Canzona: A lively, fugue-like composition, one of several sixteenth- and seventeenth-century genres of instrumental music *(105)*

Chaconne (cha-kón): Similar to *passacaglia (132)*

Chamber music: Music played by small groups, such as a string quartet or a piano trio *(205)*

Chance music: A type of contemporary music in which certain elements, such as the order of the notes or their pitches, are not specified by the composer but are left to chance *(370)*

Chanson (shahn-sohn): French for song; a genre of French secular vocal music *(77)*

Chant: A way of reciting words to music, generally in *monophony* and generally for liturgical purposes, as in *Gregorian chant (57, 70)*

Character piece: A short Romantic piano piece that portrays a particular mood *(259)*

Choir: (1) A group of singers singing together, with more than one person singing each voice part; (2) a section of the orchestra comprising instruments of a certain type, such as the string, woodwind, or brass choir

Choral declamation: Chordal recitation by a chorus with free, speech-like rhythms *(420)*

Chorale (co-ráhl): German for hymn; also used for a four-part *harmonization* of a Lutheran hymn, such as Bach composed in his Cantata No. 4 and other works *(160)*

Chorale prelude: An organ composition based on a *chorale* tune *(162)*

Chord: A grouping of pitches played and heard simultaneously *(27)*

Chromaticism: A musical style employing all or many of the twelve notes of the *chromatic scale* much of the time *(107, 244)*

Chromatic scale: The set of twelve pitches represented by all the white and black notes on the piano, within one *octave (17)*

Church cantata: A *cantata* with religious words *(159)*

Clef: In musical notation, a sign at the beginning of the *staff* indicating the pitches of the lines and spaces. The main clefs are the treble (or G) clef, 𝄞; and the bass (or F) clef, 𝄢 *(21)*.

Climax: The high point of a melody or of a section of music *(25)*

Closing theme: Same as *cadence theme (180)*

Coda: The concluding section of a piece or a movement, after the main elements of the form have been presented. Codas are common in *sonata form (181)*.

Coloratura: An ornate style of singing, with many notes for each syllable of the text *(150)*

Compound meter: A meter in which the main beats are subdivided into three, e.g. **6/8**—*one* two three *four* five six *(11)*

Con brio: Brilliantly, with spirit

Concerto, solo concerto: A large composition for orchestra and solo instrument *(129)*

Concerto grosso: The main early Baroque type of concerto, for a group of solo instruments and a small orchestra *(129)*

Concert overture: An early 19th-century genre resembling an opera overture—but without any following opera *(264)*

Con moto: Moving, with motion

Consonance: Intervals or chords that sound relatively stable and free of tension; as opposed to *dissonance (27)*

Continuo (basso continuo): (1) A set of chords continuously underlying the melody in a piece of Baroque music; (2) the instrument(s) playing the continuo, usually cello plus harpsichord or organ *(96, 124)*

Contralto, alto: The low female voice

Counterpoint, contrapuntal: (1) *Polyphony*; strictly speaking, the technique of writing *polyphonic* music; (2) the term *a counterpoint* is used for a melodic line that forms polyphony when played along with other lines; (3) *in counterpoint* means "forming polyphony" *(29)*.

Countersubject: In a *fugue*, a subsidiary melodic line that appears regularly in *counterpoint* with the *subject (140)*

Courante (koor-ahnt): A Baroque dance in moderately slow *triple meter (143)*

Crescendo (kreh-shén-do): Getting louder *(8)*

Cultivated music: In America, genres and styles of music that were brought from Europe and subsequently nurtured here through formal training and education *(384)*

Da capo: Literally, "from the beginning"; a direction to the performer to repeat music from the beginning of the piece up to a later point *(152)*

Da capo aria: An aria in **ABA** form, i.e., one in which the **A** section is sung *da capo* at the end *(152)*

Dance suite: See *suite (104, 143)*

Declamation: The way words are set to music, in terms of rhythm, accent, etc. *(82)*

Decrescendo (dáy-kreh-shén-do): Getting softer *(8)*

Development: (1) The process of expanding themes and short motives into larger sections of music; (2) the second section of a *sonata-form* movement, which features the development process *(180)*

Diatonic scale: The set of seven pitches represented by the white notes of the piano, within one *octave (16)*

Dies irae: "Day of wrath": a section of the *Requiem Mass (268)*

Diminuendo: Getting softer *(8)*

Dissonance: Intervals or chords that sound relatively tense and unstable; in opposition to *consonance (27)*

Divertimento: An 18th-century genre of light instrumental music, designed for entertainment *(167)*

Dotted note: In musical notation, a note followed by a dot has its normal duration increased by a half *(20)*.

Dotted rhythm: A rhythm of long, dotted notes alternating with short ones *(20)*

Double-exposition form: A type of *sonata form* developed for use in concertos *(201)*

Downbeat: A strong or accented *beat*

Duet, duo: A composition for two singers or instrumentalists *(210)*

Duple meter: A meter consisting of one accented beat alternating with one unaccented beat: *one* two *one* two *(11–12)*

Duration: The length of time that a sound is heard *(9)*

Dynamics: The volume of sound, the loudness or softness of a musical passage *(7)*

Eighth note: A note one-eighth the length of a whole note *(20)*

Electronic music: Music in which some or all of the sounds are produced by electronic generators or other apparatus *(367)*

Ensemble: A musical number in an opera, cantata, or oratorio that is sung by two or more people *(207)*

Episode: In a *fugue*, a passage that does not contain any complete appearances of the fugue *subject (140)*

Erhu (áhr-hoo): A Chinese low-pitched fiddle; heard in Beijing opera *(311)*

Espressivo: Expressively

Estampie (ess-tom-pée): An instrumental dance of the Middle Ages *(64)*

Ethnomusicology: The scholarly study of music and society, usually oriented toward music outside the European classical tradition *(360)*

Étude (áy-tewd): A piece of music designed to aid technical study of a particular instrument *(259)*

Exposition: (1) The first section of a *fugue (139)*; (2) the first section of a *sonata-form* movement *(179)*

Expressionism: An early 20th-century movement in art, music, and literature in Germany and Austria *(323)*

Fermata: A hold of indefinite length on a note; the sign for such a hold in musical notation *(14)*

Festive orchestra: A brilliant-sounding Baroque orchestra with drums, trumpets, and/or French horns, used for gala occasions *(115, 123)*

Figured bass: A system of notating the *continuo* chords in Baroque music, by means of figures; sometimes also used to mean continuo *(125)*

Finale (fih-náh-lay): The last movement of a work, or the *ensemble* that concludes an act of an *opera buffa* or other opera

First theme: In *sonata form*, a *motive* or tune (or a series of them) in the *tonic* key that opens the *exposition* section *(180)*

Flag: In musical notation, a "pennant" attached to a note indicating that the length is halved (two flags indicate that it is quartered, etc.) *(20)*

Flat: In musical notation, a sign (♭) indicating that the note to which it is attached is to be played a *semitone* lower. A double flat (♭♭) is sometimes used to indicate that a note is played two semitones lower *(17)*.

Form: The "shape" of a piece of music *(46)*

Forte (fór-teh); **fortissimo:** Loud; very loud (*f; ff*) *(7)*

Fragmentation: The technique of reducing a theme to fragmentary *motives (228)*

French overture: A Baroque type of overture to an opera, oratorio, or suite *(144)*

Frequency: Scientific term for the rate of sound vibration, measured in cycles per second *(6)*

Fugue (fewg): A composition written systematically in *imitative polyphony*, usually with a single main theme, the fugue *subject (105, 139)*

Fuguing tune: A simple anthem based on a hymn, with a little *counterpoint (385)*

Functional harmony, functional tonality: From the Baroque period on, the system whereby all chords have a specific interrelation and function in relation to the *tonic (96)*

Gagaku (gáh-gáh-koo): A group of Japanese orchestral styles, named by the Chinese characters meaning "elegant music," which were performed in traditional court ceremonies and rituals; includes togaku (tó-gáh-koo) and komagaku (ko-má-gáh-koo) *(212)*

Gakuso: A Japanese zither with thirteen strings; heard in *gagaku (213)*

Galliard: A Renaissance court dance in *triple meter (88)*

Gamelan: A traditional Indonesian orchestra consisting of gongs, *metallophones*, and other instruments *(214)*

Gapped chorale: A setting of a *chorale* melody in which the tune is presented in phrases with "gaps" between them, during which other music continues in other voices or instruments *(160)*

Gat: In Indian music, a moderate or fast movement with clear meter in the performance of a *rag (219)*

Gavotte: A Baroque dance in *duple meter (143)*

Genre (jáhn-ruh): A general category of music determined partly by the number and kind of instruments or voices involved, and partly by its form, style, or purpose. "Opera," "symphonic poem," and "sonata" are examples of genres *(50, 264)*.

Gesamtkunstwerk (geh-záhmt-kuhnst-vairk): "Total work of art"—Wagner's term for his music dramas *(279)*

Gigue (zheeg), **jig:** A Baroque dance in a lively *compound meter (143)*

Glissando: Sliding from one note to another on an instrument such as a trombone or violin *(336)*

Gospel, gospel music: Genre of African American choral church music, associated with the *blues (392)*

Grave (grahv): Slow; the characteristic tempo of the first section of a *French overture* (14)

Gregorian chant: The type of *chant* used in the early Roman Catholic Church (57)

Ground bass: An *ostinato* in the bass (96, 132)

Half note: A note half the length of a whole note (20)

Half step: The *interval* between any two successive notes of the *chromatic scale;* also called a *semitone* (18)

Harmonize: To provide each note of a melody with a chord (27)

Harmony, harmonic: Having to do with chords, or the "vertical" aspect of musical texture (27). The term *harmonic* is sometimes used to mean *homophonic.*

Heterophony: *Monophonic* texture in which subtly different versions of a single melody are presented simultaneously (28)

Hichiriki (hée-chee-ree-kée): A Japanese double-reed wind instrument; heard in *gagaku* (212)

Hocket: The alternation of very short melodic phrases, or single notes, between two or more voices (69)

Homophony, homophonic: A musical texture that involves only one melody of real interest, combined with chords or other subsidiary sounds (28)

Hymn: A simple religious song in several stanzas, for congregational singing in church (75)

Idée fixe (ee-day feex): A fixed idea, an obsession; the term used by Berlioz for a recurring theme used in all the movements of one of his program symphonies (265)

Imitation, imitative polyphony, imitative counterpoint: A *polyphonic* musical texture in which the various melodic lines use approximately the same themes; as opposed to *non-imitative counterpoint* (29). See also *point of imitation.*

Impressionism: A French artistic movement of the late 19th and early 20th centuries (319)

Interval: The difference or distance between two pitches, measured by the number of *diatonic scale* notes between them (15)

Introduction: An introductory passage: the "slow introduction" before the *exposition* in a symphony, etc.; in an opera, the first number after the overture

Inversion: Reading or playing a melody or a *twelve-tone series* upside down, i.e., playing all its upward intervals downward and vice versa (140, 326)

Isicathamiya (ees-ee-caht-ah-mée-ah): An *a cappella* song style that is part of the South African choral song tradition (419)

Isorhythm: In 14th-century music, the technique of repeating the identical rhythm for each section of a composition, while the pitches are altered (68)

Jangar: A type of lyre played to accompany singing in the Sudan (108)

Jazz: A major African American performance style that has influenced all 20th-century popular music (389)

Jing (cheeng): A male role in *jingju,* or Beijing opera, enacting a warrior, a bandit, or a god (310)

Jinghu (chéeng-hoo): A Chinese high-pitched, two-string fiddle; heard in Beijing opera (311)

Jingju (chéeng-chu): The most famous variety of Chinese musical drama; meaning "theater of the capital," it is known in English as Beijing (or Peking) opera (310)

Jongleur (jawn-gler): A medieval secular musician (56)

Kabuki (kah-bóo-kee): A Japanese tradition of musical drama involving singing actors, chorus, and orchestra (309)

Kakko: A Japanese two-headed barrel drum; heard in *gagaku* (213)

Key: One of the twelve positions for the *major-* and *minor-mode* scales made possible by using all the notes of the *chromatic scale* (32)

Key signature: Sharps or flats placed at the beginning of the staffs to indicate the *key,* and applied throughout an entire piece, in every measure and in every octave (22)

K numbers: The numbers assigned to works by Mozart in the Köchel catalog; used instead of *opus* numbers to catalog Mozart's works (182)

Largo; larghetto: Very slow; somewhat less slow than largo (14)

Ledger lines: In music notation, short lines above or below the staff to allow for pitches that go higher or lower (21)

Legato (leh-gáh-toe): Playing in a smooth, connected manner; as opposed to *staccato* (21)

Leitmotiv (líte-moh-teef): "Leading motive" in Wagner's operas (281)

Lento: Very slow (14)

Libretto: The complete book of words for an opera, oratorio, cantata, etc. (151)

Lied (leed; pl. *Lieder*): German for "song"; also a special genre of Romantic songs with piano (249)

Line: Used as a term to mean a melody, or melodic line (24)

Madrigal: The main secular vocal genre of the Renaissance (85)

Major mode: One of the modes of the *diatonic scale,* oriented around C as the *tonic;* characterized by the interval between the first and third notes containing 4 *semitones,* as opposed to 3 in the *minor mode* (32)

Mass: The main Roman Catholic service; or the music written for it. The musical Mass consists of five large sections: Kyrie, Gloria, Credo, Sanctus, and Agnus Dei (77).

Mazurka: A Polish dance in lively *triple meter* (247)

Measure (bar): In music, the unit of *meter,* consisting of a principal strong beat and one or more weaker ones (11)

Medieval modes: See *mode* (58)

Mele pule (mél-eh póol-eh): Hawai'ian prayer song (71)

Melisma: In vocal music, a passage of many notes sung to a single syllable (66)

Melody: The aspect of music having to do with the succession of pitches; also applied ("a melody") to any particular succession of pitches (24)

Meno: Less (as in *meno forte*, less loud) *(7)*

Metallophone: An instrument like a xylophone, but with keys of metal, not wood *(215)*

Meter: A background of stressed and unstressed beats in a simple, regular, repeating pattern *(11)*

Metronome mark: A notation of tempo, indicating the number of beats per minute as ticked out by a metronome, the mechanical or electrical device that ticks out beats at all practicable tempos *(14)*

Mezzo (mét-so): Italian for half, halfway, medium (as in *mezzo forte* or *mezzo piano—mf, mp*) *(7)*

Mezzo-soprano: "Halfway to soprano": a type of female voice between *contralto* and *soprano*

Miniature: A term for a short, evocative composition for piano or for piano and voice, composed in the Romantic period *(246)*

Minimalism: A late 20th-century style involving many repetitions of simple musical fragments *(380)*

Minnesingers: Poet-composers of the Middle Ages in Germany *(62)*

Minor mode: One of the modes of the *diatonic scale*, oriented around A as the *tonic*; characterized by the interval between the first and third notes containing 3 *semitones*, as opposed to 4 in the *major mode* *(32)*

Minstrel show: A type of variety show popular in 19th-century America, performed in blackface *(388)*

Minuet: A popular 17th- and 18th-century dance in moderate *triple meter*; also a movement in a sonata, symphony, etc., based on this dance *(143, 191)*

Mode, modality: In music since the Renaissance, one of the two types of *tonality: major mode* or *minor mode*; also, in earlier times, one of several orientations of the *diatonic scale* with D, E, F, and G as tonics *(31)*

Moderato: Moderate tempo *(14)*

Modulation: Changing key within a piece *(32)*

Molto allegro: Faster than *allegro* *(14)*

Monophony: A musical texture involving a single melodic line, as in *Gregorian chant*; as opposed to *polyphony* *(28)*

Motet: (Usually) a sacred vocal composition *(67, 85)*. Early motets were based on fragments of Gregorian chant.

Motive: A short fragment of melody or rhythm used in constructing a long section of music *(26)*

Movement: A self-contained section of a larger piece, such as a symphony or concerto grosso *(129)*

Musical comedy, musical: American development of *operetta*, involving American subjects and music influenced by jazz or rock *(406)*

Music drama: Wagner's name for his distinctive type of opera *(279)*

Musicology: The scholarly study of music history and literature

Music video: Video "dramatization" of a popular song, rock number, or rap number

Musique concrète (moo-zeek kohn-krét): Music composed with natural sounds recorded electronically *(368, 375)*

Mute: A device put on or in an instrument to muffle the tone

Nagauta (náh-gáhoo-ta): A genre of music involved in Japanese *kabuki* theater; translated as "long song," it is used especially to accompany dance *(309)*

Nationalism: A 19th-century movement promoting music built on national folk songs and dances, or associated with national subjects *(294)*

Natural: In musical notation, a sign (♮) indicating that a sharp or flat previously attached to a note is to be removed *(22)*

Neoclassicism: (1) An 18th-century movement in the arts returning to Greek and Roman models *(169)*; (2) a 20th-century movement involving a return to the style and form of older music, particularly 18th-century music *(336)*

Nocturne: "Night piece": title for Romantic "miniature" compositions for piano, etc. *(261)*

Noh: A Japanese tradition of musical drama, often based on Zen Buddhist philosophy, which includes singing, highly stylized and symbolic movement, and instrumental accompaniment by percussion and flute *(308)*

Non-imitative polyphony, counterpoint: A *polyphonic* musical texture in which the melodic lines are essentially different from one another; as opposed to *imitation* *(29)*

Non troppo: Not too much (as in *allegro non troppo*, not too fast)

Note: (1) A sound of a certain definite pitch and duration; (2) the written sign for such a sound in musical notation; (3) a key pressed with the finger on a piano or organ

Octatonic scale: An eight-note scale (used by Stravinsky and others) consisting of half and whole steps in alternation *(327)*

Octave: The *interval* between a pair of "duplicating" notes, eight notes apart in the *diatonic scale* *(15)*

Office services, Divine Office: The eight daily services, other than the Mass, specified by the Roman Catholic Church *(57)*

Opera: Drama presented in music, with the characters singing instead of speaking *(97, 149)*

Opera buffa (bóo-fa): Italian comic opera *(207)*

Opera seria: A term for the serious, heroic opera of the Baroque period in Italy *(150, 207)*

Operetta: A 19th-century type of light (often comic) opera, employing spoken dialogue in between musical numbers *(405)*

Opus: "Work"; opus numbers provide a means of cataloging a composer's compositions *(130)*.

Oratorio: Long semidramatic piece on a religious subject for soloists, chorus, and orchestra *(155)*

Orchestra: A large group of instruments playing together *(43)*; at different periods of Western music *(123, 173, 244)*; see *festive orchestra, gamelan, gagaku*

Orchestra exposition: In Classical concerto form, the first of two *expositions*, played by the orchestra without the soloist *(201)*

Orchestration: The technique of writing for various instruments to produce an effective total orchestral sound

Organ chorale: See *chorale prelude* *(162)*

Organum: The earliest genre of medieval *polyphonic* music *(65)*

Ornament, ornamentation: Addition of fast notes and vocal effects (such as *trills*) to a melody, making it more florid and expressive. Ornamentation is typically improvised in the music of all cultures, and in Western music is often written out *(123)*.

Ostinato: A motive, phrase, or theme repeated over and over again *(96, 108, 132, 335)*

Overtone: In acoustics, a secondary vibration in a sound-producing body, which contributes to the tone color; also called *partial (9)*

Overture: An orchestral piece at the start of an opera, oratorio, etc. (but see *concert overture*) *(144)*

Paraphrase: The modification and decoration of *plainchant* melodies in early Renaissance music *(74)*

Part: Used as a term for (1) a section of a piece; (2) one of the *voices* in contrapuntal music; (3) the written music for a single player in an orchestra, band, etc. (as opposed to the *score*)

Partial: Scientific term for an *overtone (9)*

Passacaglia (pas-sa-cáhl-ya): A set of variations on a short theme in the bass *(106, 132)*

Passion: A long, oratorio-like composition telling the story of Jesus' last days, according to one of the New Testament gospels

Pavane (pa-váhn): A slow, 16th-century court dance in *duple meter (88)*

Pedal board: That keyboard of an organ which is played with the feet *(45)*

Pentatonic scale: A five-note *scale* (familiar from folk music) playable on the black notes of a keyboard *(327)*

Phrase: A section of a melody or a tune *(25)*

Piano; pianissimo: Soft; very soft *(p; pp) (7)*

Piano trio: An instrumental group usually consisting of violin, cello, and piano; or a piece composed for this group; or the three players themselves

Pitch: The quality of "highness" or "lowness" of sound; also applied ("a pitch") to any particular pitch level, such as middle C *(7)*

Più: More (as in *più forte*, louder) *(7)*

Pizzicato (pit-tzih-cáh-toe): Playing a stringed instrument that is normally bowed by plucking the strings with the finger *(36)*

Plainchant, plainsong: Unaccompanied, *monophonic* music, without fixed rhythm or meter, such as *Gregorian chant (57)*

Poco: Somewhat (as in *poco adagio* or *poco forte*, somewhat slow, somewhat loud)

Point of imitation: A short passage of *imitative polyphony* based on a single theme, or on two used together *(80)*

Polonaise: A Polish court dance in a moderate *triple meter (261)*

Polyphony, polyphonic: Musical texture in which two or more melodic lines are played or sung simultaneously; as opposed to *homophony* or *monophony (28)*

Prelude: An introductory piece, leading to another, such as a fugue or an opera (however, Chopin's Preludes were not intended to lead to anything else)

Premiere: The first performance ever of a piece of music, opera, etc.

Presto; prestissimo: Very fast; very fast indeed *(14)*

Program music: A piece of instrumental music associated with a story or other extramusical idea *(245)*

Program symphony: A symphony with a program, as by Berlioz *(265)*

Quarter note: A note one-quarter the length of a whole note *(20)*

Quarter-tone scale: A 24-note scale, used in the 20th century, consisting of all the *semitones* of the *chromatic scale* and all quarter tones in between the semitones *(327)*

Quartet: A piece for four singers or players; often used to mean *string quartet*

Quintet: A piece for five singers or players

Qur'anic recitation: An Islamic tradition in which the revelations of the prophet Muhammad gathered in the Qur'an (or Koran) are chanted in Arabic *(70)*

Rag: In Indian music, a set of pitches, gestures, patterns of ornamentation, and other guidelines for producing melody *(218)*

Ragtime: A style of American popular music around 1900, usually for piano, which led to *jazz (391)*

Range: Used in music to mean "pitch range," i.e., the total span from the lowest to the highest pitch in a piece, a part, or a passage

Rap: Genre of African American popular music of the 1980s and '90s, featuring rapid recitation in rhyme *(416)*

Recapitulation: The third section of a *sonata-form* movement *(181)*

Recitative (reh-sih-ta-téev): A half-singing, half-reciting style of presenting words in opera, cantata, oratorio, etc., following speech accents and speech rhythms closely. Secco recitative is accompanied only by *continuo;* accompanied recitative is accompanied by orchestra *(98, 151, 152)*

Reciting tone: Especially in *chant*, the single note used for musical "recitation," with brief melodic formulas for beginning and ending *(59, 71)*

Reed: In certain wind instruments (oboe, clarinet), a small vibrating element made of cane or metal *(38)*

Registration: In organ music, the choice of stops with which to play a passage

Requiem Mass, Requiem: The special *Mass* celebrated when someone dies

Resolve: To proceed from *dissonant* harmony to *consonance (27)*

Rest: A momentary silence in music; in musical notation, a sign indicating momentary silence *(20)*

Retransition: In *sonata form*, the passage leading from the end of the *development* section into the beginning of the *recapitulation (181)*

Retrograde: Reading or playing a melody or twelve-tone *series* backwards *(326)*

Rhythm: The aspect of music having to do with the duration of the notes in time; also applied ("a rhythm") to any particular durational pattern *(9, 10)*

Rhythm and blues: Genre of African American music of the early 1950s, forerunner of *rock (411)*

Rhythm section: In jazz, the instrumental group used to emphasize and invigorate the meter (drums, bass, and piano) *(390)*

Ritardando: Slowing down *(14)*

Ritenuto: Held back in tempo

Ritornello: The orchestral material at the beginning of a concerto grosso, etc., which always returns later in the piece *(129)*

Ritornello form: A Baroque musical form based on recurrences of a *ritornello (129)*

Rock: The dominant popular-music style of the late 20th century *(410)*

Rondo: A musical form consisting of one main theme or tune alternating with other themes or sections (**ABACA, ABACABA,** etc.) *(194)*

Round: A simple type of sung *canon*, with all voices entering on the same note after the same time interval *(29)*

Row: Same as *series (326)*

Rubato: "Robbed" time; the free treatment of meter in performance *(242)*

Ryuteki (ree-óo-tay-kée): A Japanese side-blown flute; heard in *gagaku (213)*

Sampling: Especially in rap, the extraction, repetition, and manipulation of short excerpts from other popular songs, etc. *(368)*

Sarabande: A Baroque dance in slow *triple meter*, with a secondary accent on the second beat *(143)*

Scale: A selection of ordered pitches that provides the pitch material for music *(14)*

Scherzo (scáir-tzo): A form developed by Beethoven from the *minuet* to use for movements in larger compositions; later sometimes used alone, as by Chopin *(227)*

Score: The full musical notation for a piece involving several or many performers *(22)*

Secco recitative: See *recitative (152)*

Second group: In *sonata form*, the group of themes following the *bridge*, in the second key *(180)*

Second theme: In *sonata form*, one theme that is the most prominent among the second group of themes in the *exposition (180)*

Semitone: Same as *half step (18)*

Sequence: (1) In a melody, a series of fragments identical except for their placement at successively higher or lower pitch levels *(25)*; (2) in the Middle Ages, a type of *plainchant* in which successive phrases of text receive nearly identical melodic treatment *(61)*

Serialism, serial: The technique of composing with a *series*, generally a twelve-tone series *(317, 326)*

Series: A fixed arrangement of pitches (or rhythms) held to throughout a serial composition *(326)*

Sforzando: An especially strong accent; the mark indicating this in musical notation (*sf* or >) *(11)*

Shamisen (shah-mée-sen): A Japanese three-stringed lute; used as accompaniment in *kabuki (309)*

Sharp: In musical notation, a sign (♯) indicating that the note it precedes is to be played a *semitone* higher. A double sharp (✕) is occasionally used to indicate that a note is played two semitones higher *(17)*

Sho: A Japanese mouth reed-organ with seventeen pipes; heard in *gagaku (213)*

Siciliana: A Baroque dance type in *compound meter (143)*

Simple meter: A meter in which the main beats are not subdivided, or are subdivided into two, e.g., **2/4, 3/4, 4/4** *(11)*

Sixteenth note: A note one-sixteenth the length of a whole note *(20)*

Slur: In musical notation, a curved line over several notes, indicating that they are to be played smoothly, or *legato (21)*

Solo exposition: In Classical concerto form, the second of two *expositions*, played by the soloist and the orchestra *(201)*

Sonata: A chamber-music piece in several movements, typically for three main instruments plus *continuo* in the Baroque period, and for only one or two instruments since then *(197)*

Sonata form (sonata-allegro form): A form developed by the Classical composers and used in almost all the first movements of their symphonies, sonatas, etc. *(179)*

Song cycle: A group of songs connected by a general idea or story, and sometimes also by musical unifying devices *(253)*

Sonority: A general term for sound quality, either of a momentary chord, or of a whole piece or style *(74)*

Soprano: The high female (or boy's) voice

Spiritual: Religious folk song, usually among African Americans (called "Negro spiritual" in the 19th century) *(388)*

Sprechstimme: A vocal style developed by Schoenberg, in between singing and speaking *(340)*

Staccato: Played in a detached manner; as opposed to *legato (21)*

Staff (or stave): In musical notation, the group of five horizontal lines on which music is written *(21)*

Stanza: In songs or ballads, one of several similar poetic units, which are usually sung to the same tune; also called verse

Stop: An organ stop is a single set of pipes, covering the entire pitch range in a particular tone color *(45)*

Stretto: In a *fugue*, overlapping entrances of the fugue *subject* in several voices simultaneously *(140)*

String quartet: An instrumental group consisting of two violins, viola, and cello; or a piece composed for this group; or the four players themselves *(204)*

Strophic form, strophic song: A song in several *stanzas*, with the same music sung for each stanza; as opposed to *through-composed song (251)*

Structure: A term often used to mean *form*

Style: The combination of qualities that make a period of art, a composer, a group of works, or an individual work distinctive *(50)*

Subito: Suddenly (as in *subito forte* or *subito piano*, suddenly loud, suddenly soft) *(7)*

Subject: The term for the principal theme of a *fugue (139)*

Subject entries: In a *fugue*, appearances of the entire fugue *subject* after the opening *exposition (140)*

Suite: A piece consisting of a series of dances *(104, 143)*

Swing: A type of big-band jazz of the late 1930s and 1940s *(394)*

Symbolism: A late 19th-century movement in the arts that emphasized suggestion rather than precise reference *(319)*

Symphonic poem: A piece of orchestral *program music* in one long movement *(290)*

Symphony: A large orchestral piece in several movements *(178)*

Syncopation: The accenting of certain beats of the meter that are ordinarily unaccented *(13)*

Synthesizer: An electronic apparatus that generates sounds for electronic music *(45, 368)*

Tempo: The speed of music, i.e., the rate at which the accented and unaccented beats of the meter follow one another *(14)*

Tenor: The high adult male voice

Ternary form: A three-part musical form in which the last section repeats the first: **ABA** form *(192)*

Texture: The blend of the various sounds and melodic lines occurring simultaneously in a piece of music *(28)*

Thematic transformation: A variation-like procedure applied to short themes in the various sections of Romantic *symphonic poems* and other works *(248)*

Theme: The basic subject matter of a piece of music. A theme can be a phrase, a short *motive,* a full tune, etc. *(26)*.

Theme and variations: A form consisting of a tune (the theme) plus a number of variations on it *(187)*

Through-composed *(durchkomponiert)* **song:** A song with new music for each stanza of the poem; as opposed to *strophic song (251)*

Tie: In musical notation, a curved line joining two notes of the same pitch into a continuous sound *(20)*

Timbre (tám-bruh): Another term for *tone color (8)*

Time signature: In musical notation, the numbers on the staff at the beginning of a piece that indicate the meter *(21)*

Toccata: Especially in Baroque music, a written-out composition in improvisational style, generally for organ or harpsichord *(105)*

Tonality, tonal: The feeling of centrality of one note (and its chord) to a passage of music; as opposed to *atonality (31)*

Tone: A sound of a certain definite pitch and duration; same as *note*

Tone color: The sonorous quality of a particular instrument, voice, or combination of instruments or voices *(8)*

Tone poem: Same as *symphonic poem (290)*

Tonic (noun): In *tonal* music, the central-sounding note *(31)*

Transition: A passage whose function is to connect one section of a piece with another; see *bridge*

Transpose: To move a whole piece, or a section of a piece, or a *twelve-tone series,* from one pitch level to another *(326)*

Trill: Two adjacent notes played very rapidly in alternation

Trio: (1) A piece for three instruments or singers; (2) the second or B section of a *minuet* movement, *scherzo,* etc. *(144, 191)*

Trio sonata: A Baroque sonata for three main instruments plus the *continuo* chord instrument

Triple meter: Meter consisting of one accented beat alternating with two unaccented beats: *one* two three *one* two three *(12)*

Triplet: A group of three notes performed in the time normally taken by two *(21)*

Troubadours, trouvères: Aristocratic poet-musicians of the Middle Ages *(62)*

Tsuridaiko (tzóo-ree-díe-koh): A large Japanese barrel drum; heard in *gagaku (213)*

Tune: A simple, easily singable melody that is coherent and complete *(24)*

Twelve-tone series (or row): An ordering of all twelve notes of the *chromatic scale,* used in composing *serial* music *(326)*

Twelve-tone system: Method of composition devised by Arnold Schoenberg in which the twelve pitches of the octave are ordered and strictly manipulated *(326)*

Upbeat: A weak or unaccented beat leading to a *downbeat*

Variation form: A form in which a single melodic unit is repeated with harmonic, rhythmic, dynamic, or timbral changes *(105, 132)*

Vernacular music: Music that was developed in America outside the European concert music tradition *(384)*

Vivace, vivo: Lively *(14)*

Vocables: Sung syllables which have no precise meaning, e.g. "tra-la-la" *(72)*

Voice: (1) Throat sound; (2) a contrapuntal line—whether sung or played by instruments—in a *polyphonic* piece such as a *fugue*

Walking bass: A bass line consisting of steady equal note values, usually eighths or quarters *(121, 147)*

Waltz: A 19th-century dance in *triple meter*

Whole note: The longest note in normal use, and the basis of the duration of shorter notes (half notes, quarter notes, etc.) *(20)*

Whole step, whole tone: The interval equal to two half steps (semitones) *(18)*

Whole-tone scale: A scale, used sometimes by Debussy, comprising only six notes to the octave, each a whole tone apart (i.e., two semitones) *(327)*

Word painting: Musical illustration of the meaning of a word or a short verbal phrase *(82)*

Yueqin (yuéh-chin): A Chinese lute; heard in Beijing opera *(311)*

Music and Literary Credits

6, 10, 24, 46 Aaron Copland, brief excerpts from *What to Listen for in Music* by Aaron Copland. Copyright © 1939 by Aaron Copland. Reprinted by permission of the Aaron Copland Fund for Music, Inc., copyright owner.

26 "Who Cares?" by George Gershwin and Ira Gershwin. © 1931 (Renewed) WB Music Corp. All rights reserved. Used by permission of Warner Bros. Publications U.S. Inc., Miami, FL 33014.

33 "Happy Birthday to You," by Mildred J. Hill and Patty S. Hill © 1935 (Renewed) Summy-Birchard Music, a Division of Summy-Birchard Inc. All rights reserved. Used by permission of Warner Bros. Publications U.S. Inc., Miami, FL 33014.

321 Arnold Schoenberg. Excerpts from Piano Concerto. Used by permission of Belmont Music Publishers, Pacific Palisades, CA 90272.

334–35, 337 Igor Stravinsky. Excerpts from "The Adoration of the Earth." From *The Rite of Spring*. Copyright © 1912, 1921 by Hawkes & Son (London) Ltd. Copyright Renewed. Reprinted by permission.

341 Arnold Schoenberg. Excerpt from *Pierre lunaire*. Used by permission of Belmont Music Publishers, Pacific Palisades, CA 90272.

343–44 Alban Berg. Excerpts from *Wozzeck*. © 1931 by Universal Edition A.G. Vienna. © Renewed. All Rights Reserved. Used by permission of European American Music Distributors Corporation, sole U.S. and Canadian agent for Universal Edition A.G. Vienna.

350 Charles Ives. Excerpts from "The Rockstrewn Hills Join in the People's Outdoor Meeting," from Second Orchestral Set, No. 2. Copyright © 1971, 1978 by Peer International Corporation. Used by permission.

355–56 Maurice Ravel. Excerpts from Piano Concerto in G (1931). Courtesy Durand Music Publishing (France).

359–61 Béla Bartók. Excerpts from Music for Strings, Percussion, and Celesta from String Quartet No. 2. © 1920 by Universal Edition A.G. Vienna. © Renewed. All Rights Reserved. Used by permission of European American Music Distributors Corporation, sole U.S. and Canadian agent for Universal A.G. Vienna.

364 Aaron Copland. Excerpt from *Appalachian Spring*. Copyright © 1945 by The Aaron Copland Fund for Music, Inc. Copyright Renewed. Boosey & Hawkes, Inc., Sole Publisher and Licensee. Used by permission.

370 Anton Webern. Excerpt from Five Orchestral Pieces, Opus 10, No. 4. Copyright © 1923 by Universal Edition A.G. Vienna. © Renewed. All Rights Reserved. Used by permission of European American Music Distributors Corporation, sole U.S. and Canadian agent for Universal Edition A.G. Vienna.

370 Terry Riley. Excerpt from *In C*. © 1964 Terry Riley. Reprinted by permission of Celestial Harmonies, Tucson, AZ.

376 John Cage. *Aria*. Copyright © 1960 by C.F. Peters Corporation. On Behalf of Henmar Press, Inc. Used by permission. All rights reserved.

378 George Crumb. Excerpts from *Black Angels*. © 1971 by C.F. Peters Corporation. Used by permission. All rights reserved.

380 Sylvia Plath. Excerpts from "Paralytic" from *The Collected Poems of Sylvia Plath* by Sylvia Plath. Copyright © 1963 by Ted Hughes. Excerpts from *The Bell Jar* by Sylvia Plath. Copyright © 1971 by Harper & Row, Publishers, Inc. Reprinted by permission of HarperCollins Publishers Inc. and Faber & Faber Ltd.

382–83 Steve Reich. Excerpts from *Tehillim*. Copyright © 1981 by Hendon Music, Inc., a Boosey & Hawkes Company. Revised edition Copyright © 1994 by Hendon Music, Inc. Reprinted by permission.

401 Johnny Green and Edward Heyman. Excerpt from *Out of Nowhere*. Copyright © 1931 by Famous Music Corporation. Copyright renewed 1958 and assigned to Famous Music Corporation. Reprinted by permission.

404 Prelude No. 1, by George Gershwin. © 1927 (Renewed) WB Music Corp. All rights reserved. Used by permission of Warner Bros. Publications U.S. Inc., Miami, FL 33014.

408–09 "Maria," "Cool" from *West Side Story*, music by Leonard Bernstein, lyrics by Stephen Sondheim. Copyright © 1956, 1957 (renewed) by Leonard Bernstein and Stephen Sondheim. Boosey & Hawkes, Inc., Publisher. "Cha-cha" from *West Side Story*. Copyright © 1956, 1957, 1958, 1959 by Amberson Holdings LLC and Stephen Sondheim. Copyright Renewed. Leonard Bernstein Music Publishing company LLC, Publisher, Boosey & Hawkes, Inc., Sole Agent. Reprinted by permission.

Illustration Credits

xiii Henry VIII psalter (c. 1540), British Library, London, UK/Bridgeman Art Library

xiv Adolph von Menzel, *The Flute Concert*, 1850/52. Stattliche Museen zu Berlin—Preussischer Kulturbesitz—Nationalgalerie

xxviii Bob Krist/CORBIS

3 Copyright The Pierpont Morgan Library/Art Resource, NY

7 *top*: Richard Megna/Fundamental Photographs; *bottom*: Copyright British Museum

9 © Jack Vartoogian

11 Carol Simowitz

14 Musée de la Musique—Cité de la Musique, Paris, France/Bridgeman Art Library

16 Bill Stanton/Image State

19 Josef Albers Museum, Bottrop

25 Bettmann/CORBIS

27 George Pickow/Photo Media

30 Private Collection, Switzerland

33 Scala/Art Resource, NY

36 *left*: © Steve J. Sherman; *right*: Boltin Picture Library

37 *top*: © Ebet Roberts; *bottom left*: © Jack Vartoogian; *bottom right*: Lebrecht Music Collection

38 *both*: © Steve J. Sherman

39 Carol Simowitz

40 Lebrecht Music Collection

41 *top*: Carol Simowitz; *bottom*: Bob Daemmrich/The Image Works

42 © Steve J. Sherman

43 Square piano by Nunn and Clark, New York, 1853. The Metropolitan Museum of Art, Gift of George Lowther, 1906. (06.1312) Photograph © 1977 The Metropolitan Museum of Art

44 *top*: Boltin Picture Library; *bottom*: Lawrence Migdale/Photo Researchers

45 Caravaggio, *Young Man Playing a Lute*, Hermitage, St. Petersburg, Russia/Bridgeman Art Library

47 Kunsthistorisches Museum, Vienna

48 Paul Steel/CORBIS Stock Market

51 Joseph Sohm, ChromoSohm, Inc./CORBIS

55 Institut Amatller d'Art Hispànic

56 Institut Amatller d'Art Hispànic

57 Lambeth Palace Library, London, UK/Bridgeman Art Library

59 Institut Amatller d'Art Hispànic

61 Wisse der Wege, Scivias. Otto Müller Verlag, Salzburg, 8. Aufl. 1987. Photo Courtesy Abtei Sankt Hildegard

63 *left*: Grosse Heidelberger Liederhandschrift (Codex Manesse), fol. 399r. Universitätsbibliothek, Heidelberg; *right*: Bibliothèque Nationale de France, Paris

65 *tiles*: Institut Amatller d'Art Hispànic; *bottom*: Culver Pictures

66 Robert Harding Picture Library

70 Christine Osborne/CORBIS

71 William Waterfall/Pacific Stock

72 Gunter Marx/CORBIS

73 *both*: Scala/Art Resource, NY

75 Wallraf-Richartz Museum, Cologne. Photo: Rheinisches Bildarchiv, Cologne

76 Bibliothèque Nationale de France, Paris/Giraudon-Bridgeman Art Library

77 University of California at Berkeley Music Library

78 Francis G. Mayer/CORBIS

79 *top*: Bettmann/CORBIS; *bottom*: Austrian National Library, Vienna

83 Bayerische Staatsbibliothek, Munich

84 Bettmann/CORBIS

86 Berkeley Castle, Gloucestershire, UK/Bridgeman Art Library

89 Copyright British Library

90 Centre Nationale de la Recherche Scientifique

91 Museo de Arte Religioso, Cuzco, Peru

93 Canaletto, *The Rialto Bridge*. Photo: Scala/Art Resource, NY

97 Museum für Kunst und Gewerbe, Hamburg

98 *both*: Bibliothèque Nationale de France, Paris

100 *left*: Conservatory of St. Peter, Naples, Italy/Giraudon-Bridgeman Art Library; *right*: Bettmann/ CORBIS

102 By courtesy of the National Portrait Gallery, London

105 Scala/Art Resource, NY

107 David Lees/CORBIS

108 H. Rogers/TRIP

109 Giacomo Pirozzi/Panos Pictures

113 *top*: Pierre Patel, *Carriages Arriving at Versailles*, 1688. Photo: Giraudon/Art Resource, NY; *bottom*: Scala/Art Resource, NY

114 G.G. Bibiena, stage set for Metastasio's *Didone Abbandonata*. Photo: Blauel/Artothek

115 Giovanni Battista Tiepolo, Painted Ceiling, Residenz, Würzburg. Photo: Scala/Art Resource, NY

116 National Gallery of Scotland, Edinburgh/Bridgeman Art Library

117 Scala/Art Resource, NY

118 *top*: Giraudon/Art Resource, NY; *center, bottom*: from LeBrun's Conférence sur l'Expression, 1698

120 Oliviero, Performance at Teatro Reggio, Turin. Photo: Scala/Art Resource, NY

122 Munari, *Still Life with Instruments* (detail). Photo: Scala/Art Resource, NY

124 Agence France Presse

126 © Steve J. Sherman

128 *both*: Boltin Picture Library

130 Bettmann/CORBIS

132 Bettmann/CORBIS

133 Gaspar Netscher, *The Viola da Gamba Lesson*. Photo: Giraudon/Art Resource, NY

137 Private Collection

138 *top*: Bettmann/CORBIS; *bottom*: University of California at Berkeley Music Library

141 University of California at Berkeley Music Library

144 Scala/Art Resource, NY

145 Thomas Rowlandson, *Old Vauxhall Gardens*. Victoria & Albert Museum, London

146 Private Collection

150 Sächsische Landesbibliothek—Staats- und Universitätsbibliothek Dresden/Abteilung Deutsche Fotothek

151 School of Pietro Longhi, *Opera Seria*. Photo: Scala/Art Resource, NY

152 Royal College of Music, London, UK/Bridgeman Art Library

154 Carol Rosegg

155 Bettmann/CORBIS

157 *both*: Mary Evans Picture Library

159 Private Collection

161 Herbert Kratz, gouache, 1885. Photo: AKG London/Photo Researchers

163 Lüneburg Marketing GmbH

165 Archivo Iconografico, S.A./CORBIS

166 *top*: H.H. Arnason, by permission of the Comédie Française; *bottom*: Guildhall Library, Corporation of London, UK/Bridgeman Art Library

167 *top*: faïence plaque, *The Magic Flute*, Museum of Fine Arts Lille. Photo: Giraudon/Art Resource, NY; *bottom*: Jean-Antoine Houdon, bust of Thomas Jefferson, 1789, marble, Museum of Fine Arts, Boston, George Nixon Black Fund. Photograph © 2003 Museum of Fine Arts, Boston

168 *top*: Jean-Antoine Houdon, bust of Rousseau (detail). Photo H.H. Arnason, Collection of Edmond Courty; *bottom*: Bettmann/CORBIS

169 *top*: Peter Jacob Horemans, *Court Musicians with Stringed Instruments*. Photo: Blauel/Artothek; *bottom*: Jean-Antoine Houdon, statue of Gluck (detail), Stiftung Weimarer Klassik, Goethe-Nationalmuseum

170 Bettmann/CORBIS

172 Johann Zoffany (1733–1810), *George, 3rd Earl Cowper, with the Family of Charles Gore*, c. 1775 (oil on canvas). Yale Center for British Art, Paul Mellon Collection/Bridgeman Art Library

176 Scala/Art Resource, NY

177 Jean-Antoine Houdon, bust of Mme. Houdon, Louvre. Photo: Giraudon/Art Resource, NY

180 Spinet, probably by Thomas Hitchcock, English, 1742, Fenton House, Hampstead, London/Bridgeman Art Library

183 *top*: Historisches Museum der Stadt Wien, Vienna, Austria/Bridgeman Art Library; *bottom*: Mozart Museum, Salzburg, Austria/Bridgeman Art Library

184 *top*: Ali Meyer/CORBIS; *bottom*: University of California at Berkeley Music Library

186 *top left*: Jasper Johns, Painted Bronze, 1960. Reproduced Courtesy of Universal Limited Art Editions; *top right, bottom left and right*: Monotypes #7, #16, #4 from *Jasper Johns* by Judith Goldman. Reproduced Courtesy of Universal Limited Art Editions

188 Pesci, *Esterháza Castle*, Orszagos Müemleki Felügveloség. Photo: Gabor Barca

190 *top*: John Hoppner, *Franz Joseph Haydn* (detail), 1791. The Royal Collection, copyright 2003 Her Majesty Queen Elizabeth II; *bottom*: The Metropolitan Museum of Art, The Crosby Brown Collection of Musical Instruments (89.4.1235)

192 Lebrecht Music Collection/AL

194 Bettmann/CORBIS

198 *left*: Marie-Louise-Elizabeth Vigée-LeBrun, *The Duchess of Polignac*, 1783. Waddesdon Manor, The Rothschild Collection (The National Trust); *right*: Charles Bird King, *Mrs. John Quincy Adams*, ca. 1824. Oil on canvas, 130.8 x 100.6 cm. Adams-Clement Collection, gift of Mary Louisa Adams Clement in memory of her mother, Louisa Catherine Adams Clement. Smithsonian American Art Museum, Washington, DC/Art Resource, NY

200 Mozart Museum/Archive

203 University of California at Berkeley Music Collection

205 *top*: Bettmann/CORBIS; *bottom*: © Steve J. Sherman

206 *top*: © Jack Vartoogian; *bottom*: Courtesy Holland Festival

208 *top*: University of California at Berkeley Music Library; *bottom*: Culver Pictures

209 University of California at Berkeley Music Library

210 Bettmann/CORBIS

211 Winnie Klotz/ Metropolitan Opera

212 © Jack Vartoogian

213 © Jack Vartoogian

214 © Jack Vartoogian

215 William Waterfall/Pacific Stock

216 © Jack Vartoogian

217 Roman Sorimar/CORBIS

218 © Dugowson/STM Concept/CORBIS Sygma

224 Hulton-Deutsch Collection/CORBIS

225 Jacques-Louis David, *The Coronation of Napoleon* (detail), Louvre. Photo: Giraudon/Art Resource, NY

226 Library of Congress

227 Bettmann/CORBIS

230 Beethoven-Archiv, Bonn, H.A. Bodmer Collection

232 *Beethoven Nearing the End* by Batt (plate 18, *The Oxford Companion to Music*, copyright Mrs. W.A. Barrett) is reproduced by kind permission of the copyright owner.

236 Bettmann/CORBIS

237 Private Collection/Archives Charmet/Bridgeman Art Library

238 Henry Fuseli, *The Nightmare*, 1771. Founders Society Purchase with funds from Mr. and Mrs. Bert L. Smokler and Mr. and Mrs. Lawrence H. Fleischman. Photograph © 1995 The Detroit Institute of Arts

239 J.M.W. Turner, *The Fighting Téméraire*, © National Gallery Collection. By kind permission of the Trustees of the National Gallery, London/CORBIS

240 *left*: Caspar David Friedrich, *Mountainous Landscape*, c. 1812, Kunsthistorisches Museum, Vienna. Photo: Erich Lessing/Art Resource, NY; *right*: John Martin, *The Bard*, c. 1817, oil on canvas, 50 x 40", Yale Center for British Art, Paul Mellon Collection/ Bridgeman Art Library

241 *left*: Hulton Archive/Getty Images; *right*; Carnegie Hall Archives

244 The Metropolitan Museum of Art. The Crosby Brown Collection of Musical Instruments, 1889 (89.4.1851)

245 Bettmann/CORBIS

246 Wilhelm von Lindenschmidt the Younger, *The Music Makers*, 1856. Neue Pinakothek, Munich. Photo: Blauel/Artothek

247 Bettmann/CORBIS

250 Max Klinger, *Beethoven*, bronze, marble, ivory, etc. Museum der Bildenden Künste, Leipzig/Maximilian Speck von Sternberg Stiftung

251 Kunsthistorisches Museum, Vienna, Austria/Bridgeman Art Library

252 *top*: Private Collection; *bottom*: Historisches Museum der Stadt Wien, Vienna, Austria/Bridgeman Art Library

256 Bettmann/CORBIS

257 Robert-Schumann-Haus, Zwickau

258 Archiv/Photo Researchers

261 Bettmann/CORBIS

262 Ludwig von Hofmann, *Notturno*, Neue Pinakothek, Munich. Photo: Blauel/Artothek

263 *top left*: © Steve J. Sherman; *top right, bottom*: Mary Evans Picture Library

265 *both*: Bettmann/CORBIS

267 Francisco Goya, *Witches' Sabbath* (detail). Photo: Scala/ Art Resource, NY

268 Bettmann/CORBIS

271 Deutsches Theatermuseum, Munich. Photo: Klaus Broszat

368 Pablo Picasso, *The Pianist,* Cannes, 1957. Museo Picasso, Barcelona, Spain/Index/Bridgeman Art Library © 2000 Estate of Pablo Picasso/Artists Rights Society (ARS), New York

369 *top*: Bill Stanton/Image State; *bottom*: © Steve J. Sherman

372 Mark Rothko, *Violet, Black, Orange, Yellow on White and Red,* oil on canvas, 81½ x 66". The Solomon R. Guggenheim Museum, Gift of Elaine and Werner Dannheisser and the Dannheisser Foundation. Photo: David Heald, The Solomon R. Guggenheim Foundation

373 University of Louisville, Courtesy Mrs. Doris Keyes. Photo: Anderson/Schott Archive

374 Bettmann/CORBIS

375 Lucien Hervé, Paris. Research Library, Getty Research Institute, Los Angeles (2002.R.41)

376 *top*: © Jack Vartoogian

377 G. D. Hackett/Getty Images

379 Maarit Kyotohärju/FIMIC

381 *top*: Martha Swope © Time Inc.; *bottom*: © Jack Vartoogian

382 Private Collection

385 Thomas Eakins, *The Concert Singer*, 1892 (detail), The Philadelphia Museum of Art, Given by Mrs. Thomas Eakins and Miss Mary Adeline Williams

386 Nathaniel Currier, *First Appearance of Jenny Lind in America: At Castle Garden*, September 11, 1850, lithograph. Clarence J. Davies Collection, Museum of the City of New York

387 *both*: Bettmann/CORBIS

389 Culver Pictures

391 Bettmann/CORBIS

392 © Syndey Byrd

393 Bettmann/CORBIS

394 Culver Pictures

395 Underwood & Underwood/CORBIS

396 Institute of Jazz Studies, Rutgers

397 © Herman Leonard

398 Jak Kilby, Arena/Stage Image

401 © Herman Leonard

403 *left*: © Amalie R. Rothschild; *right*: David Redfern/Retna

405 Private Collection

406 Culver Pictures

407 Barton Silverman/NYT Pictures

408 Martha Swope © Time Inc.

411 Getty Images

413 © Apple Corps, Camera Press/Retna

414 Matthew Mendelsohn/CORBIS

415 Courtesy Reprise Records

416 S.I.N./CORBIS

417 Gianni Muratore, Camera Press Digital/Retna

418 Louise Gubb/The Image Works

419 Carol Muller

421 Guy Marche/Image State

Index

Listen's Study Guide CD-ROM, a Multimedia Companion

The Study Guide CD-ROM, included with each copy of *Listen*, provides the **interactive Listening Charts** designed to work with the 6-CD and 3-CD sets purchased separately. In addition, it enhances the listening experience with twelve key recordings that coordinate with six **focused listening exercises** in Unit I on music fundamentals. The CD-ROM concludes with a thirteenth recording, Benjamin Britten's *Young Person's Guide to the Orchestra*.

User Guidelines

To use this CD-ROM, simply insert the disk into your CD-ROM drive and select the "Setup" file located on the disk. Then follow the directions offered. For more assistance, select the "ReadMe" file located on the disk. You may also insert this disk into your CD player to listen to the thirteen recordings. For technical assistance, please contact our technical support team at 1-800-936-6899 or <techsupport@bfwpub.com>.

Minimum System Requirements

PC: Windows 95/98/NT4/2000/ME/XP—Intel Pentium processor or equivalent—32 MB of installed RAM—Color monitor: at least 800 x 600 with support for 16-bit color—Keyboard—Mouse—Quad-speed (4x) or faster CD-ROM drive—Browser software: Netscape 4.0 or later/Internet Explorer 4.0 or later/AOL 4.0 or later.

Macintosh: OS 8.1 or higher/PowerPC processor—32 MB of installed RAM—Color monitor: at least 800 x 600 monitor with support for 16-bit color—Keyboard—Mouse—Quad-speed (4x) or faster CD-ROM drive—Browser software: Netscape 4.0 or later/Internet Explorer 4.5 or later/AOL 4.0 or later.

The track numbers for each recording are as follows:

1–3 Berlioz, *Fantastic* Symphony, IV, March to the Scaffold

4 Schubert, from Symphony No. 8 ("Unfinished"), I

5 Joplin, "Maple Leaf Rag"

6 Rachmaninov, from *Rhapsody on a Theme by Paganini*

7 Gershwin, "Who Cares?"

8 Beethoven, "Joy Theme" from Symphony No. 9, IV

9 Stravinsky, from *Symphony of Psalms*, II

10 Schubert, Moment Musical No. 3

11 Beethoven, from Piano Concerto No. 5 ("Emperor"), III

12 Mahler, from Symphony No. 1, III

13 Chaikovsky, from *The Nutcracker Suite:* Dance of the Sugar-Plum Fairy

14–16 Beethoven, Symphony No. 5, III

17–22 Britten, *The Young Person's Guide to the Orchestra*

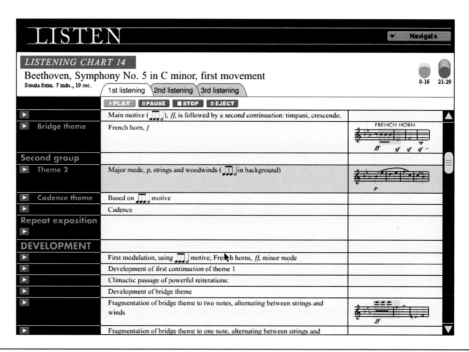